INTRODUCTION TO THE
OLD TESTAMENT

INTRODUCTION
TO THE
OLD TESTAMENT

*with a comprehensive review of
Old Testament studies
and a special supplement on the Apocrypha*

by

R. K. HARRISON

*Professor of Old Testament
Wycliffe College, University of Toronto*

WILLIAM B. EERDMANS PUBLISHING COMPANY
GRAND RAPIDS, MICHIGAN

To My Parents

PREFACE

The present work is an attempt to evaluate the contents of the Old Testament and Apocrypha against the vast background of knowledge that is now available for students of ancient Near Eastern life and culture. The more detailed introduction to the books of the Old Testament is prefaced by seven sections dealing with important areas of Old Testament study; although this procedure results in some repetition throughout the book, it is hoped that it will serve the interests of the beginning student in furnishing a resume of the history of thought in each particular branch of study. The section dealing with the Apocrypha was added at the request of the publishers. Its presence should not be taken to imply that its contents are to be regarded as of equal inspiration or authority with the Old Testament.

Considerable emphasis has been placed upon methodology in an endeavor to permit the Hebrew Scriptures to speak for themselves against their ancient Near Eastern background. Much of what has passed for critical study in this field has in fact consisted largely of the application of *a priori* literary-critical theories, often in apparent isolation from methodological approaches involving archaeology, comparative religion, sociology, history, linguistics, and aspects of the biological and physical sciences. All of these have a part to play in the proper understanding of the Scriptural record, and must now take their place beside literary and textual criticism as valid means to this end. The methodology adopted in this book is inductive, and the writer has been at considerable pains in resisting temptations to "burke any issue," to borrow the quaint Victorian phrase favored occasionally by H. H. Rowley.[1] The conclusions that appear in the book are tentative and amenable to modification in the light of whatever relevant factual information may emerge in the future.

I wish to acknowledge my indebtedness for permission to quote from copyright works to the following: to Dr. G. E. Wright for allowing the use of material contained in various numbers of *The Biblical Archaeologist*; to the University of Chicago Press for permission to reprint sections from

---

[1] H. H. Rowley, *BJRL*, XXXVII (1955), p. 550 n. 3, *et al.*

A. Heidel, *The Gilgamesh Epic and Old Testament Parallels* (1949 edition), D. D. Luckenbill, *Ancient Records of Assyria and Babylonia* (2 volumes, 1926); to Y. Kaufmann, *The Religion of Israel,* translated by Moshe Greenberg (1960); to the American Philosophical Society for their kindness in allowing the use of copyright material in S. N. Kramer, *Sumerian Mythology* (1947 edition), originally published in 1944 in Volume 21 of the Society's *Memoirs,* and to Dr. Kramer himself for his generous consent; and to Princeton University Press for permitting quotations from J. Finegan, *Light From the Ancient Past* (1946), and J. B. Pritchard (ed.), *Ancient Near Eastern Texts Relating to the Old Testament* (1950).

I would like to take this opportunity of thanking those who have been of particular assistance and encouragement in the preparation of this book, including Principal Leslie Hunt of Wycliffe College, and my past and present colleagues, Professors T. W. Harpur, J. Jocz, T. R. Millman, W. Prior, R. F. Stackhouse, and the Rev. Dr. R. A. Ward. I want also to express my gratitude to Mr. J. Freeman of Montreal for his interest in my work; to Mrs. G. G. Simms for typing out portions of the manuscript; to Dr. S. J. Mikolaski for a critical reading of Part Seven; to Mrs. H. Bohne, librarian of Wycliffe College, for her generous help with source materials, and to the Rev. Norman Green, Field Secretary of Wycliffe College for his diligence in correcting the proofs. Finally my thanks are due to the editorial and production staffs of the Wm. B. Eerdmans Publishing Company for their painstaking attention and unfailing courtesy in the making of this book.

—R. K. HARRISON

Wycliffe College,
University of Toronto.

CONTENTS

CONTENTS

ABBREVIATIONS

AASOR	*The Annual of the American Schools of Oriental Research*
AAT	L.E.T. André, *Les Apocryphes de l'Ancien Testament* (1903)
AJ	Flavius Josephus, *The Antiquities of the Jews* (1829 edition)
AJA	*American Journal of Archaeology*
AJSL	*American Journal of Semitic Languages and Literatures*
ANE	J.B. Pritchard (ed.), *The Ancient Near East* (1958)
ANET	J.B. Pritchard (ed.), *Ancient Near Eastern Texts Relating to the Old Testament* (1950)
AP	W.F. Albright, *The Archaeology of Palestine* (1949)
APOT	R. H. Charles (ed.), *The Apocrypha and Pseudepigrapha of the Old Testament* (1913), 2 vols.
ARAB	D.D. Luckenbill, *Ancient Records of Assyria and Babylonia* (1926), 2 vols.
ARE	J.H. Breasted, *Ancient Records of Egypt* (1906-07), 5 vols.
ARI	W.F. Albright, *Archaeology and the Religion of Israel* (1955)
BA	*The Biblical Archaeologist*
BACP	Y. Kaufmann, *The Biblical Account of the Conquest of Palestine* (1953)
BANE	G.E. Wright (ed.), *The Bible and the Ancient Near East* (1961)
BASOR	*Bulletin of the American Schools of Oriental Research*
BCIA	L.H. Brockington, *A Critical Introduction to the Apocrypha* (1961)
BCNE	H. Frankfort, *The Birth of Civilisation in the Near East* (1956)
BHI	J. Bright, *A History of Israel* (1959)
BJRL	*Bulletin of the John Rylands Library*
BPAE	W.F. Albright, *The Biblical Period from Abraham to Ezra* (1963)
BZAW	*Beihefte zur Zeitschrift für die Alttestamentliche Wissenschaft*
CAEM	A.L. Perkins, *The Comparative Archaeology of Early Mesopotamia* (1949)
CBQ	*Catholic Biblical Quarterly*
DILOT	S.R. Driver, *An Introduction to the Literature of the Old Testament* (1912 edition)
DJD	D. Barthélemy and J.T. Milik, *Discoveries in the Judean Desert I. Qumran, Cave I* (1955); II Murabba' at (1961)
DOTT	D. Winton Thomas (ed.), *Documents from Old Testament Times* (1958)
EB	*Encyclopedia Biblica* (1899), 4 vols.
EQ	*The Evangelical Quarterly*
ERE	J. Hastings (ed.), *Encyclopaedia of Religion and Ethics* (1911-22), 12 vols.

ET   *The Expository Times*
ETOT   O. Eissfeldt, *The Old Testament, An Introduction* (1965)
FSAC   W.F. Albright, *From the Stone Age to Christianity* (1957 edition)
GBB   C.H. Gordon, *Before the Bible* (1962)
GI   M. Noth, *Geschichte Israels* (1950)
HDB   J. Hastings (ed.), *Dictionary of the Bible* (1911), 5 vols.
HNTT   R.H. Pfeiffer, *A History of New Testament Times* (1949)
HUCA   *Hebrew Union College Annual*
IAAM   H.A. Frankfort, *et al.*, *The Intellectual Adventure of Ancient Man* (1948)
IB   *The Interpreter's Bible* (1952-7), 12 vols.
IBOT   W.O.E. Oesterley and T.H. Robinson, *An Introduction to the Books of the Old Testament* (1934)
ICC   *International Critical Commentary*
IDB   *The Interpreter's Dictionary of the Bible* (1962), 4 vols.
IHANE   R.C. Dentan (ed.), *The Idea of History in the Ancient Near East* (1955)
IOTT   C.H. Gordon, *Introduction to Old Testament Times* (1953)
ISBE   *The International Standard Bible Encyclopedia* (1915), 5 vols.
JAOS   *Journal of the American Oriental Society*
JBL   *Journal of Biblical Literature*
JCS   *Journal of Cuneiform Studies*
JE   *The Jewish Encyclopedia* (1901-1905), 12 vols.
JEA   *Journal of Egyptian Archaeology*
JJS   *Journal of Jewish Studies*
JNES   *Journal of Near Eastern Studies*
JPOS   *Journal of the Palestine Oriental Society*
JQR   *Jewish Quarterly Review*
JRAS   *Journal of the Royal Asiatic Society*
JTS   *Journal of Theological Studies*
KRI   Y. Kaufmann, *The Religion of Israel,* translated by Moshe Greenberg (1960)
LAP   J. Finegan, *Light from the Ancient Past* (1946 edition)
MNHK   E.R. Thiele, *The Mysterious Numbers of the Hebrew Kings* (1965 ed.)
MTA   B. Metzger, *An Introduction to the Apocrypha* (1957)
NBD   *The New Bible Dictionary*
OLZ   *Orientalistische Literaturzeitung*
OTFD   A. Weiser, *The Old Testament: Its Formation and Development* (1961)
OTMS   H.H. Rowley (ed.), *The Old Testament and Modern Study* (1951)
PEF   *Palestine Exploration Fund*
PEQ   *Palestine Exploration Quarterly*
PG   *Patrologia Graeca* (ed. Migne)
PIOT   R.H. Pfeiffer, *Introduction to the Old Testament* (1941)
PJB   *Palästinajahrbuch*
PL   *Patrologia Latina* (ed. Migne)
PTR   *Princeton Theological Review*
RA   *Revue d'assyriologie et d'archéologie orientale*

ABBREVIATIONS

RB	*Revue Biblique*
RDM	H.H. Rowley, *Darius the Mede and the Four World Empires of the Book of Daniel* (1935)
RHPR	*Revue d'histoire et de philosophie religieuses*
RSL	H.H. Rowley, *The Servant of the Lord and Other Essays on the Old Testament* (1952)
SRA	*Syria, Revue d'Art orientale et d'archéologie*
TAL	C.C. Torrey, *The Apocryphal Literature: A Brief Introduction* (1945)
TH	O.R. Gurney, *The Hittites* (1952)
UC	C.L. Woolley, *Ur of the Chaldees* (1950 edition)
UL	C.H. Gordon, *Ugaritic Literature* (1949)
UP	M. Noth, *Überlieferungsgeschichte des Pentateuchs* (1948)
VDJD	G. Vermès, *Discovery in the Judean Desert* (1956)
VT	*Vetus Testamentum*
WBA	G.E. Wright, *Biblical Archaeology* (1957)
WHAB	G.E. Wright and F.V. Filson, *Westminster Historical Atlas to the Bible* (1953 edition)
WJ	Flavius Josephus, *Wars of the Jews* (1829 edition)
WMTS	M. Burrows, *What Mean These Stones?* (1941)
YIOT	E.J. Young, *Introduction to the Old Testament* (1960 edition repr. 1963)
ZA	*Zeitschrift für Assyriologie und verwandte Gebiete*
ZAW	*Zeitschrift für die alttestamentliche Wissenschaft*
ZDMG	*Zeitschrift der Deutschen Morgenländischen Gesellschaft*

CDC	*Cairo Damascene Covenanters*
1QIsa[a]	St. Mark's Monastery Isaiah Scroll
1QIsa[b]	Hebrew University's Isaiah Scroll
1Q, etc.	The first, etc., Qumran Cave
1QH	The Qumran Hymn Scroll
1QM	The Qumran Military Scroll
1QpHab	The Qumran Habakkuk Commentary
1QS	*The Community Rule* or *Manual of Discipline*
AV	Authorized (King James) Version (1611)
RV	Revised Version (1881)
RSV	Revised Standard Version (1952)
LXX	Septuagint Greek version

AT	*Altes Testament*
ch.	chapter
d.	died
ed.	edition, edited by
E. tr.	English translation (by)
MT	Massoretic text
n.	note
n.d.	no date
pl.	plate

N.F.	*Neue Folge*
NT	New Testament, *Neues Testament*
O.S.	Old series
OT	Old Testament
rev.	revision, revised (by)
tr.	translated (by)
V.F.	*Vierte Folge*

Part One

THE DEVELOPMENT OF OLD
TESTAMENT STUDY

I. THE BACKGROUND—THROUGH THE EIGHTEENTH CENTURY

A. EARLY AND MEDIEVAL CRITICISM

The present survey of the growth and development of Old Testament study can well commence with the observation that, even before the Jews adopted an official formulation of their canon of sacred writings, the Christian Church had accepted the three traditional divisions of the Law, Prophecy, and Writings as constituting Scripture. Although many of the early Christians used the LXX version in preference to the Hebrew, they nevertheless maintained an unswerving stand that these writings possessed an authority of such degree as to be compatible only with divine inspiration and authorship.[1] As such the Scriptures demanded implicit belief and obedience on the part of all those who accepted and venerated them. The teachings of the various Old Testament books were regarded as basically identical in nature, the result of this conclusion being that the principal task concerning the understanding of this teaching was thought to be the presentation of Biblical doctrines in systematic form.

This situation did not last for any length of time, however, for even in the first century of the Christian era there were those who perverted the teachings of Scripture,[2] thereby calling into question the genuineness and authority of the sources. With the rise of Gnosticism in the second century of our era the Church witnessed the first onslaught of destructive criticism, and this, interestingly enough, was directed against the Old Testament. Epiphanius recorded that a certain Simon (whether or not the Simon Magus of Acts 8:10 is unknown) denied the divine source and inspiration of the Law and the Prophets.[3] In the *Clementine Homilies* Simon is cited as having criticized certain anthropomorphic passages in

---

[1] Cf. *Westminster Confession of Faith*, I:4. Article VI of the *Book of Common Prayer* (1662) was concerned primarily with the sufficiency of the Holy Scriptures for salvation, as was the fifth of the Forty-Two Articles of 1553. Cf. W. H. Griffith Thomas, *The Principles of Theology* (1930), pp. 104ff.

[2] I Tim. 1:19f., 2 Tim. 2:17f. Cf. *The Acts of Paul and Thecla*, XIV, in M. R. James, *The Apocryphal NT* (1924), p. 275.

[3] *PG*, XLI, Col. 292.

the Old Testament.[4] The Ophites, who were the precursors of the Gnostics, scorned the God of the Old Testament as wicked and ignorant,[5] while the Cainites held that their progenitor Cain had been sacrificed in order to appease the wrath of the Demiurge.[6] Among the Gnostics of Syria, the Antiochan Satornilus, who was contemporary with Ignatius (d. *ca.* A.D. 110), taught that certain of the prophecies were of Satanic origin, while others had come from the lips of angels who, according to Gnostic thought, had created the world.[7] Even Tatian, who is renowned for his compilation of extracts from the Gospels in the form of a single narrative (the *Diatessaron,* or *Harmony of the Gospels—ca.* A.D. 174), held that the Old Testament was the product of an inferior deity.[8]

From Alexandria, which had become a remarkable center of Greek culture and philosophy, the activities of Valentinus led an assault upon the text of the Old Testament. This prominent Gnostic leader, who subsequently propagated his doctrines in Rome, rejected certain parts of the Torah and the Prophets as unauthentic, and altered other portions of the Hebrew text with a view to improving it. To Valentinus was attributed the involved Gnostic theory of the aeon-origin of the universe, which he substituted for the creative activity of the Old Testament deity.[9] Another form of Pentateuchal criticism was furnished by a certain Ptolemy of Italian origin, who taught between A.D. 145 and 180. His arguments, preserved in a letter found among the writings of Epiphanius,[10] raised the basic question as to the origin of the Torah. Ptolemy concluded that the five books attributed to Moses could not possibly have come from one author, but that they were compiled by Moses from sources emanating from God, from Moses himself, and from the Elders.

More serious than the foregoing attacks upon the witness of the Early Church to the authority and authenticity of the Scriptures, however, were the speculations and teachings of the prominent second-century heretic Marcion, the son of a Christian bishop. Arriving in Rome about A.D. 138, he studied under a Gnostic teacher and ultimately developed a complicated intellectual system based upon the concepts of his philosophical dualism. He was the first of many subsequent critics of Biblical writings to apply canons of a subjective nature in the prosecution of his activities. He adopted a literalistic interpretation of the text, and arrived at the conclusion that God was weak, unjust, lacking in prescience, and

---

[4] *PG,* II, Col. 436.
[5] *PG,* VII, Cols. 675ff., XLI, Cols. 641ff.
[6] *PG,* XLI, Col. 656.
[7] *PG,* VII, Cols. 675ff.
[8] *PG,* VI, Col. 848, XLI, Cols. 831ff.
[9] *PG,* VII, Col. 523.
[10] *PG,* XLI, Cols. 557ff.

essentially fickle.[11] Consequently he ejected the Old Testament completely from his canon of Scripture, which in the end consisted mainly of
Pauline material along with an expurgated edition of the Gospel of
Luke.[12] His criticisms of the Old Testament cannot be regarded as
scientific in any sense of that term, since they were dictated by purely
subjective philosophical considerations, but they are of importance in
any study of the growth of Biblical criticism generally.

The Nazarites, a Jewish-Christian sect, also denied the Mosaic authorship of the Pentateuch,[13] and according to Epiphanius[14] the Ebionites
rejected certain parts of the Torah and in addition manifested a complete disregard for the writings of the prophets. The *Clementine Homilies*,[15] which, though later than the second century in their extant
form, were actually the product of the Judaic-Gnostic school, applied
subjective and rationalistic principles in their attempts to cast doubt
upon the authenticity of certain events mentioned in the Old Testament.
Passages which presented obvious difficulties were alleged to have been
interpolated by the Devil, and only those parts of Scripture were accepted as genuine which were thought to be in accord with the tenets of
this school relating to the creation of the world and men.

The first definite and reasoned attack upon Christianity's claim to be an
exclusive and universal religion came from Celsus, a man about whom
very little is known. His treatise, *The True Word*, was written about A.D.
180, and it is due largely to the labors of Origen, who refuted the work
systematically in his great apologetic document *Contra Celsum*,[16] written about A.D. 249, that scholars have been able to reconstruct his
arguments to any significant extent. Although Celsus did not reject the
Mosaic authorship of the Pentateuch, he showed only a slight acquaintance with Old Testament history and religion in general. Consequently
he disparaged the Jews and ridiculed a great many of their institutions.
His entire approach was derogatory, and to him belongs the dubious
distinction of assembling most of the arguments which have been
levelled against Christianity and the Bible by subsequent generations of
rationalists, atheists, and agnostics. In the third century after Christ the
mystical philosophy known as Neoplatonism arose to challenge the
Christian faith. Porphyry, one of its chief exponents, published an attack
on historic Christianity entitled *Against the Christians,* a treatise even

[11] *PL*, II, Cols. 263ff.
[12] For the Marcionite Prologues to the Pauline epistles see D. de Bruyne, *Revue
Benedictine*, XXIV (1907), pp. 1ff.; P. Corssen, *Zeitschrift für die neutestamentliche
Wissenschaft*, X (1909), pp. 37ff.
[13] *PG*, XLI, Col. 257, XCIV, Cols. 688f.
[14] *PG*, XLI, Col. 436.
[15] Cf. A. Neander, *Die pseudoclementinischen Homilien* (1818); the 1953 edition
of the *Homilies* by A. R. M. Dressel was reproduced in *PG*, II.
[16] Cf. *PG*, XI, Cols. 315ff.; H. Chadwick, *Origen: Contra Celsum* (1953), pp. 3ff.

more damaging in its effects than that of Celsus. Porphyry was the first
to argue that Daniel was not the work of the prophet to whom tradition
had attributed it but was in fact composed in the time of Antiochus IV
Epiphanes (175-163 B.C.). He based his conclusions on the premise that
Daniel could not have predicted the future in such minute detail, and
that therefore the later chapters of the book must have been roughly
contemporary with the events described. It is not easy to determine
whether Porphyry denied the Mosaic authorship of the Pentateuch or
not,[17] but at all events he appeared to accept the historical existence of
Moses.

Criticism of the Biblical text of Daniel is also found in the third-century writings of Julius Africanus (*ca.* A.D. 225), who in his *Epistola ad
Originem* argued that Susanna could not have formed part of the
Hebrew-Aramaic composition attributed to Daniel, since it was originally
written in Greek.[18] Certain statements of Jerome (d. A.D. 420) have
sometimes been interpreted as implying that Ezra re-edited the Pentateuch,[19] but there seems little doubt that he accepted the orthodox
attribution of the Pentateuch to Moses,[20] although he does record that
Deuteronomy had been found in the Temple during the reign of
Josiah.[21]

A rudimentary form of literary criticism was applied by Theodore of
Mopsuestia (*ca.* A.D. 400) to certain books of the Old Testament. He
was the first to assign the authorship of certain of the Psalms to the Jews
of the Maccabean period. He also rejected the titles of the Psalms, and
maintained that they were added during the days of Hezekiah and
Zerubbabel. He criticized the book of Job by alleging that the author was
not of Hebrew stock,[22] and refused to espouse an allegorical view of the
Song of Songs, holding that it was meant to be interpreted literally as an
erotic composition.[23]

Questions concerning the text and canon of the Scriptures that had
arisen sporadically in the Early Church were dealt with by Cassiodorus
(d. A.D. 562) in a work entitled *De Institutione Divinarum Scrip-
turarum.* Although the book was intended to be a compendium of
theology, it included several sections on the copying of manuscripts and
the general methods to be adopted in a study of the text, as well as a
survey of matters relating more particularly to the canon. As such the
work constituted a valuable contribution to the beginnings of Biblical

[17] Cf. R. M. Grant, *The Journal of Religion,* XXV (1945), pp. 183ff.
[18] *PG,* XI, Cols. 11f.
[19] Cf. *PL,* XXIII, Col. 199.
[20] *PL,* XXIII, Col. 226.
[21] *PL,* XXV, Col. 17; cf. XXIII, Col. 227.
[22] *PG,* LXVI, Col. 698.
[23] *PG,* LXVI, Col. 699.

criticism as applied specifically to the text of the Hebrew Bible, a discipline which in a later age came to be known as "lower criticism."

Individual authors in subsequent centuries raised certain problems presented by the Old Testament narratives. In the process they contrived to challenge to a greater or lesser degree the traditions of orthodox Christianity about questions of authorship and date of particular books. A number of the difficulties raised in connection with the Pentateuch by some who had already abandoned the Christian faith were collected by Anastasius, a patriarch of Antioch, towards the end of the seventh century in his *Guide*.[24] A similar though more polemical approach was adopted by the ninth-century Jewish rationalist Hiwi al Balkhi, who listed numerous alleged contradictions in the Old Testament.[25]

The tenth and eleventh centuries witnessed a number of critical attacks in Spain upon various parts of the Hebrew Scriptures, one of which was made by Ibn Hazam of Córdova about A.D. 994. He discovered what he considered serious errors in the chronology of the Old Testament, and claimed that much of the Pentateuch was actually the work of Ezra.[26] The motivation for his attack upon the integrity of the Hebrew Scriptures was not impartial, however, for he was concerned to defend the claims of Islam, which for him constituted the true faith. A decade later another writer, Ibn Yashush (*ca.* 1000), maintained that there were a number of post-Mosaic sections in the Pentateuch, but his arguments generally exhibit a good deal of confusion. His opinions were denounced by the celebrated Spanish exegete Ibn Ezra (1092-1167), who himself maintained the existence of several late insertions in the Pentateuch while at the same time regarding these to be compatible with Mosaic authorship. Ibn Ezra was one of the first Biblical scholars to suggest that the last twenty-six chapters of the book of Isaiah might be considerably later than the eighth century B.C., and written by someone other than Isaiah ben Amoz. In the twelfth century the book of Daniel was subjected to further criticism by Hugo of St. Victor, who gave impetus to the view that the latter chapters of that prophecy could only be interpreted in the light of events that transpired within the Maccabean period.[27]

B. THE REFORMATION

While the foregoing inquiries represented the beginnings of a movement towards a more critical examination of the Old Testament writings, they were by no means systematized in nature. Their concern was with a comparatively small number of books in the canon. Nor can it be said

---

[24] *PG*, LXXXIX, Cols. 284f.

[25] J. Rosenthal, *JQR*, XXXVIII (1947-48), pp. 317ff., 419ff., XXXIX (1948-49), pp. 79ff.

[26] Cf. A. Guillaume, *Prophecy and Divination* (1938), pp. 415ff.

[27] *PL*, CLXXV, Cols. 9ff.

that the Reformation introduced Biblical criticism as such, even though individual Reformers sometimes adopted a standpoint towards certain books in the canon which was not in complete harmony with earlier ecclesiastical traditions. For the most part Martin Luther (1483-1546) confined his critical observations to books in the New Testament canon. Using a primarily theological criterion, Luther excluded four compositions generally considered canonical (Hebrews, James, Jude, and Revelation). According to Luther's standards, writings purporting to be Scriptural stood or fell according to the extent to which they promoted Christ.[28] For obvious reasons this standard could not be applied directly to the Old Testament without some difficulty, and it was largely because of this that Luther never undertook a revision of the Old Testament canon, although he consistently emphasized that the Old Testament itself claimed its fullest meaning in proportion to the extent to which it pointed to the gospel of Christ.[29]

While Calvin (1509-1564) did not go quite as far as Luther in expurgating the New Testament canon, he displayed considerably more interest than the latter in the composition of certain Old Testament books. His studies led him to the conclusion that Joshua and Samuel were not the authors of the books attributed to them, though he was unable to arrive at any firm conclusions as to the actual authors of these writings. Of all the Old Testament books that he expounded in his *Commentaries*, the Song of Songs was the only one he neglected almost completely. He adhered to a high view of the inspiration of Scripture,[30] maintaining the essential spiritual unity of the Old and New Testaments.[31]

An attack upon the Mosaic authorship of the Pentateuch was made by Andreas Rudolf Bodenstein (1480-1541), a contemporary and rival of Martin Luther.[32] Arguing from the fact that Moses could not possibly have written the account of his own death, he proceeded to reject the Mosaic authorship of the entire Pentateuch, since it seemed to him to be composed in the same general style as the obituary passage.

Zwingli (1484-1531) agreed with Calvin in asserting the divine origin of Scripture.[33] But, as an adherent of a rather more radical philosophical rationalism than either Luther or Calvin—an attitude which brought him into conflict with the former—he concentrated upon the practical application of the ethic of Jesus to the social and theological problems of the day, and did not apply his range of talents to a minute exegetical survey of Scripture as Luther and Calvin did. The importance of the Reforma-

---

[28] Luther affirmed that Christ was the *punctus mathematicus sacrae Scripturae, Werke* (Weimar ed., 1892), II, p. 439.

[29] *Ibid.*, V, pp. 47ff.

[30] Cf. *Institutes of the Christian Religion*, I, 7, 5.

[31] *Ibid.*, II, 11, 1.

[32] Cf. C. F. Jaeger, *Andreas Bodenstein von Karlstadt* (1856).

[33] *Werke* (ed. M. Schuler and J. Schulthess, 1828-42), III, pp. 156ff.

tion for Biblical criticism lay not so much in a concern for the historical or literary processes involved in the formulation of the Biblical canon as in a continued insistence upon the primacy of the simple grammatical meaning of the text in its own right, independent of any interpretation by ecclesiastical authority.

C. THE SIXTEENTH AND SEVENTEENTH CENTURIES

A more developed critical approach to the Old Testament appeared in the writings of several men who were not professional theologians. One of these was a Roman Catholic lawyer named Andreas Masius (d. 1573), who in a commentary on Joshua supported the earlier view that Ezra and his associates had added certain sections to the Pentateuch, although he did not deny the essential Mosaic authorship of the composition as a whole.[34] Another celebrated lawyer, Hugo Grotius (1583-1645), wrote a series of *Annotationes* on the books of the Bible, of which the sections dealing with the Old Testament were published only a year before he died. Like some earlier critics he dealt principally with the rather more peripheral works in the Old Testament canon, such as Canticles and Ecclesiastes, and adopted a fairly independent standpoint on some of the books he considered. He accepted the Solomonic authorship of the Song of Songs, although he apparently did not subscribe to the allegorical interpretation which saw in it an expression of the relationship between Christ and His Church. He regarded Ecclesiastes as a collection of human opinions on the subject of happiness by someone other than Solomon, backing up his view of a post-Solomonic period of origin by an appeal to the vocabulary of Aramaic portions of the Old Testament, which, he claimed, had the greatest affinity with the text of the Song of Songs. Grotius also assigned the book of Job to a date not earlier than the exile, and in addition he expressed doubts as to the historicity of Esther. His commentaries were of importance in that they espoused the principles adopted by the Reformers in their endeavor to interpret Scripture solely by the application of grammatical rules independently of *a priori* dogmatic assumptions.[35]

A further attempt in the sixteenth century to investigate the questions involving the authorship and date of Old Testament writings was made by the Deistic philosopher Thomas Hobbes (1588-1679). While his examination of Scripture constituted the basis of his search for a source of ultimate authority for the State, the principles which he utilized represented an advance on the approach which had been adopted by Grotius. Using internal evidence as a criterion for determining questions of authorship and date, he concluded that Moses long antedated the Pentateuch in its written form, although he did not deny the Mosaic

---

[34] *Josuae Imperatoris Historia* (1574).

[35] Cf. his remarks on the authority of the Old Testament writings, *De Veritatione Religionis Christianae* (1627), III, sect. 16.

authorship of those sections which were specifically attributed to him.[36] In the main, however, he did not regard the titles of books as a reliable indication of authorship, holding that Joshua and Judges were compiled long after the events which they described. The books of Samuel, Kings, and Chronicles were to him as obviously post-exilic as the writings of Ezra and Nehemiah.

Hobbes, like some of his successors in the field, professed a complete inability to assign a date to the book of Job, and regarded it less as history than as a "Treatise concerning a question in ancient time much disputed, *why wicked men have often prospered in this world, and good men have been afflicted.*" Proverbs, Ecclesiastes, and the Song of Songs were regarded as Solomonic, with the exception of the inscriptions of the latter two. Concerning the book of Jonah, Hobbes remarked:

> ...the Book of Jonas is not properly a Register of his Prophecy...but a History or Narration of his frowardnesse and disputing God's commandments, so that there is small probability he should be the Author, seeing he is the subject of it.

The Jewish philosopher Benedict Spinoza (1632-1677) continued the tendencies of Hobbes, whose work he doubtless knew and utilized, in his *Tractatus Theologico-Politicus,* published anonymously in 1670. Starting from the premise that no speculative or scientific investigation ought to be regarded as putting religion in jeopardy, Spinoza applied such procedural canons as to make his treatise the first significant contribution to the modern discipline of Biblical criticism. His rules for the interpretation of Scripture involved a consideration of the life, character, and aims of each author of the various books as a means of determining the purpose, occasion, and date of writing.[37] Following Ibn Ezra to some extent, Spinoza rejected the Mosaic authorship of the Pentateuch, and appeared to think that all the books from Genesis through 2 Kings were the work of Ezra.[38] He agreed with Ibn Ezra that Job was probably the product of a Gentile author who wrote in a language other than Hebrew, and he assigned dates in the Maccabean period to Daniel, Ezra, Nehemiah, Esther, and Chronicles.

The critical tendencies evident in the writings of Hobbes and Spinoza also appear in the work of a professional theologian named Richard Simon (1638-1712), a Roman Catholic priest who for a number of years was professor of philosophy at Juilly. Lacking the restraints of the Protestant Reformers, whose dictum "*Scriptura sola*" precluded their criticism of such a pre-eminent authority, Simon approached the problem of Biblical criticism from the Romanist standpoint, which maintained that Scripture was merely one source of authority, along with tradition, papal

---

[36] *Leviathan,* III, ch. 33.
[37] *Tractatus Theologico-Politicus,* ch. VII.
[38] *Ibid.,* ch. VIII and following.

pronouncements, and conciliar decrees. Unfortunately this uninhibited approach was not matched by an equal degree of responsibility, for in his *Histoire critique du Vieux Testament* (1678), Simon allowed himself to make some very injudicious statements, including one to the effect that the Christian faith could have sustained itself by tradition alone, without any Scriptural corpus in evidence. Simon abandoned the kind of textual criticism which had been adopted by earlier medieval writers as a methodological procedure, and resorted to the use of literary criticism proper. On the basis of his studies he concluded that the Pentateuch in its extant form could not possibly be the work of Moses, and he declared that the historical books were the result of a long process of compilation and redaction of annals and chronicles by a guild of "public scribes."

Not only did Simon provoke the antagonism of Protestant writers by his sharp attacks upon their principles, but he also aroused vigorous opposition among Roman Catholics, and within a few months after publication his book was ordered to be destroyed. Of those who replied to Simon, the Arminian professor Le Clerc was the most prominent because of his protests that the views of Protestant writers had been accorded unfair treatment. While Le Clerc challenged the theories of Simon regarding the composition of the historical books, his own views, expressed in his *Sentiments de quelques Théologiens de hollande sur l'Histoire Critique du Vieux Testament par R. Simon* (1685), tended to date bo'h the Pentateuch and the historical books of the Old Testament even later than the period assigned to them by Simon himself.

During the seventeenth century a number of introductions to the Bible were written. One of these, published in 1636 by Michael Walther, and entitled *Officina Biblica Noviter Adaperta*, was notable for the manner in which it distinguished between the problems of a general introduction to the Bible and the special consideration that the individual books themselves required. This work was followed by several others that dealt with the canon and text of the Old Testament, including an important treatise by John Leusden entitled *Philologus Hebraeus*, published in 1657, and the celebrated Polyglot Bible of 1657, edited by Bishop Walton of Chester.

D. Source Criticism and Eighteenth-Century Enlightenment

In 1689, an orthodox theologian named Campegius Vitringa suggested in his *Observationes Sacrae* that Moses had had access to ancient sources from the patriarchal period, and that these, along with other information, formed the basis of the Pentateuch. This early attempt at source-criticism was subsequently developed by Jean Astruc (1684-1766), who studied medicine and ultimately taught as a professor in several French universities. Some thirteen years before his death he published anonymously a treatise on the book of Genesis, an event that marked the

11

beginnings of Pentateuchal source-criticism proper.[39] He argued that the material upon which Moses drew had been transmitted over several centuries either orally or in written form, and was of the opinion that the latter type was predominant. Thus Moses compiled Genesis by dividing up these ancient memoirs and reassembling them so as to furnish a continuous narrative.

To substantiate his conclusions Astruc pointed out that Genesis contained duplicate narratives of such events as creation and the Flood, and that God was referred to by the names *Elohim* and *Jehovah*[40] both in Genesis and also in the early chapters of Exodus. By adopting the divine names as a criterion for source-analysis, Astruc was following in the tradition of Witter, who had been the first to suggest that they could be employed for that purpose.[41] Finally he concluded that the compiler had confused the chronological picture of Genesis so that certain events were narrated out of their proper order.

Astruc then went on to claim that this confusion could be resolved by a simple analysis and reconstruction of the Hebrew text, and as a preliminary step towards this goal he isolated all the passages in which God was designated as *Elohim* and placed them in one column (A) of his reorganized text. This he regarded as the original documentary source for the material which it contained, and despite the purely subjective nature of this conclusion he proceeded on this basis to reduce all those passages which spoke of God as *Jehovah* to the content of another underlying document, which he placed in a parallel column (B). Between these he inserted column C, comprising repetitions, chapters 23 and 24 of Genesis, and perhaps chapter 34, and column D, comprising non-Israelite material from various sources, which he divided into nine subsections,[42] some of which he regarded as interpolations.

This kind of analysis seemed to him to answer all the problems posed by the state of the text, and as a result of his researches Astruc felt confident that Moses had actually compiled Genesis on the basis of these four columns, which later copyists had edited and rearranged. He did not merely affirm the substantial Mosaic authorship of the Pentateuch, but he actually went to considerable lengths to defend it.[43] However, the thesis had some disadvantages, for as Young has pointed out,[44] Astruc

---

[39] *Conjectures sur les mémoires originaux dont il paraît que Moyse s'est servi pour composer le Livre de la Genèse. Avec des Remarques qui appuient ou qui éclaircissent ces Conjectures* (1753).

[40] The latter is a genuine hybrid form of the tetragrammaton יהוה, and not a "mistaken medieval form," as K. Grobel (*IDB*, I, p. 410) has suggested.

[41] H. B. Witter, *Jura Israelitarum in Palaestina* (1711).

[42] E, Gen. 14; F, Gen. 19:29ff.; G, Gen. 22:20-24; H, Gen. 25:12-29; I, Gen. 34; J, Gen. 26:34ff.; K, Gen. 28:6-10; L, Gen. 36:20-31; M, Gen. 39.

[43] Cf. A. Lods, *RHPR*, IV (1924), pp. 109ff., 201ff.

[44] *YIOT*, pp. 118ff.

realized that the divine names were inadequate criteria for a satisfactory analysis of Genesis into its underlying sources, and that they needed to be supplemented by other elements if the process was to be carried out to a proper conclusion. The question could not be settled merely by adducing the presence of subsidiary documents in the extant corpus, for it was found necessary to invoke the existence of textual interpolations so as to reinforce the testimony of the other criteria. This facile, though somewhat arbitrary, analysis of the text into alleged underlying documents misled Astruc and subsequent critics into thinking that the delineation of such material was a comparatively easy task, a notion which later events were to dispel.

The critical methods of Simon were revived some seventy years after the *Histoire Critique* was written, when J. S. Semler (1725-1791), a Protestant professor at Halle, translated the work into German. A moderate Rationalist, Semler adopted the critical procedures outlined by Simon but contrived to produce results which proved to be largely negative in character. Somewhat of a reaction to Semler's methodology appeared in the writings of the poet J. G. von Herder (1744-1803), who in 1783 published his celebrated work on Hebrew poetry entitled *Vom Geist der hebräischen Poesie*. Herder was attracted to the monism of Spinoza insofar as it presented God as an object of satisfaction alike for the feelings and the intellect, and he endeavored to convey this sentiment as he discerned that it was expressed spiritually in the literary structure of Hebrew verse. Despite his attempts to stress the aesthetic and moral elements inherent in Old Testament poetry, however, Herder's theological conclusions were largely speculative in nature, although his critical tendencies were of a unifying and constructive, rather than of an analytical, order. He was one of the first Old Testament scholars to base his observations concerning Scripture upon an acquaintance with the larger background of ancient Near Eastern culture. Further interest in Hebrew poetry was made evident during this same period by the work of Bishop Robert Lowth, who made a pioneer study of the parallelisms and other features of Hebrew poetic structure, and published his findings in a work entitled *De Sacra Poesi Hebraeorum* (1753).

The Age of Enlightenment was characterized by the enthroning of human reason, accompanied by a revolt against external authority. One offshoot of this situation was the claim that the Old Testament ought to be subject to the same principles of careful scrutiny as those applied to secular writings generally. Even more important than this was the feeling that such an investigation should be able to be pursued independently of ecclesiastical authority, religious dogmas, or church traditions of any sort. This attitude crystallized largely as the result of the work of J. G. Eichhorn (1752-1827), a rather conservative Rationalist who had fallen somewhat under the influence of Herder. In the end his activities proved to be directed principally against the rationalists and humanists of his own day, and he set himself to the task of winning back the educated classes to religion.

Eichhorn commenced the long series of modern introductions to the Old Testament writings with his three-volume *Einleitung in das Alte Testament* (1780-1783), a work which earned him the title of "father of Old Testament criticism."[45] Although Eichhorn professed to be affected profoundly by the literary grandeur of the Hebrew Scriptures, he reacted against the position of the Reformers and orthodox theology generally regarding the inspiration and authority of Scripture in his conclusion that the Old Testament displayed more of the character of Hebrew national literature than what might be expected to constitute Holy Scripture as such. Eichhorn extended the criteria postulated by Astruc for documentary analysis of the Pentateuch by suggesting that the means for differentiating between the underlying sources should include diversities of literary style and consideration of words or phrases peculiar to one or the other of the documents previously isolated. However, apart from this his opinions largely corresponded with those traditionally held concerning the nature and content of the Old Testament.

In 1792 a Scottish Roman Catholic theologian named Geddes published a translation of the Pentateuch and the book of Joshua; he followed this in 1800 with a work entitled *Critical Remarks.* In these two compositions Geddes assigned the Pentateuch to the Solomonic period and assumed that it had been compiled by a single redactor or editor from a mass of fragments, some of which antedated Moses. He accepted Astruc's contention that the incidence of the divine names could be employed as a criterion for purposes of discerning two series of fragmentary sources, but rejected the actual delineation of Elohistic and Jehovistic documents which Astruc and Eichhorn had recognized. He anticipated later critical writers by claiming that the book of Joshua belonged properly with the Pentateuch to compose a Hexateuch, and maintained that the same redactor was responsible for the compilation and editing of these six books. Official conservative Romanism was naturally distressed by these rationalistic observations, and Geddes was subjected to stern rebukes by the ecclesiastical authorities.

The fragmentary hypothesis which Geddes had postulated was developed by J. S. Vater, who in his *Commentar über den Pentateuch,* published in 1805, postulated the existence of as many as forty separate fragmentary sources underlying the Pentateuchal writings. He thought that some of these may have antedated Moses, while others obviously belonged to his general era. However, Vater assigned the Pentateuch

---

[45] Cf. T. K. Cheyne, *Founders of OT Criticism* (1893), pp. 13ff., 21ff.

in its final form to the period of the exile. His analysis embraced the entire Pentateuch, unlike those of his predecessors who had for the most part restricted themselves to Genesis.

The rationalistic tendencies of Geddes found another adherent in the person of W. M. L. De Wette, who supported to some extent the fragmentary theory of Pentateuchal origins in his *Beiträge zur Einleitung in das Alte Testament*, published in 1807. He parted company with previous critics in affirming that the earliest portions of the Pentateuch could only be dated from the period of David, and maintained that the different books were compiled by separate redactors who drew upon independent fragmentary sources. De Wette was the first to identify the original legal nucleus of Deuteronomy with the Book of the Law discovered during the reign of King Josiah,[46] an opinion that was to exercise a good deal of influence in subsequent discussions of that subject. De Wette felt that the literary phenomena of Genesis could be explained more readily by recourse to the documentary theory espoused by Astruc and Eichhorn than to its fragmentary counterpart as maintained by Geddes. Accordingly he postulated the existence of an Elohistic type of document as source material for Genesis and the first six chapters of Exodus. Reflecting some of the opinions of Herder, he maintained that much of Genesis was in the nature of epic poetry, a view which was not wholly lacking in support at a later period.[47]

Vater and De Wette were vigorously opposed by a number of scholars who felt convinced of the essential Mosaic authorship of the Pentateuch.[48] What is probably the most devastating attack upon the fragment theory was made by H. Ewald, who in his commentary on Genesis presented strong arguments for the underlying unity of the book on philological and other grounds.[49] While he did not adhere to the traditional view that Moses was the author of Genesis, he assigned the composition of the book to a comparatively early period. Ewald was undoubtedly more constructive in his approach to the literary problems of the Pentateuch than many of his predecessors, and in line with this tendency he proposed a supplementary theory which in nature reflected to some extent the views of De Wette on the composition of Genesis. Ewald maintained that an Elohistic source underlay the composition of the Pentateuch and Joshua, and that it had been supplemented by the addition of older sections such as the Decalogue. At a later time a

[46] In his doctoral thesis, *Dissertatio qua Deuteronomium a prioribus Pentateuchi libris diversum alius cuiusdam recentioris auctoris opus esse demonstratur* (1805), subsequently reprinted in his *Opuscula* (1833).

[47] Cf. O. Pfleiderer, *The Development of Theology in Germany since Kant* (1890), pp. 97ff.

[48] Cf. *YIOT*, pp. 123f.

[49] H. Ewald, *Die Komposition der Genesis kritisch untersucht* (1823).

compilation of sources of a Jehovistic character arose, from which portions were placed in the basic Elohistic document.

Whereas the majority of scholars had maintained that the "Foundation Document" or *Grundschrift* was early, Wilhelm Vatke in his book entitled *Die biblische Theologie wissenschaftlich dargestellt* (1835) followed the trend set by De Wette and roundly declared that a great many sections of the *Grundschrift* could be dated as late as the exile, so that in fact the source was of late rather than of early origin. He anticipated later writers by stating that the Torah was the product of the Hebrew state rather than the basis upon which it was founded, and he went so far as to reconstruct the history of the Israelites on what amounted to an evolutionary pattern.[50]

The supplementary theory postulated by Ewald received some backing from De Wette, who from 1840 adhered to the view that the Elohistic document had been augmented by means of extracts from the Jehovistic document, which, with the Deuteronomic source, made for a threefold redaction of the Hexateuch. In 1843 J. J. Stähelin suggested in his *Kritische Untersuchungen über den Pentateuch* that the early monarchy saw the redaction of the Hexateuch, and that Samuel may have been the responsible agent. He affirmed that the Elohistic source was the most comprehensive of its kind in the Pentateuch, including as it did the bulk of Exodus, Leviticus, and Numbers, and maintained that because of its archaic form it was certainly the earliest of the Pentateuchal sources.

The final form of the supplement theory found expression in the work of J. C. F. Tuch, who in his *Kommentar über die Genesis* (1838), maintained that the Pentateuch was undergirded by two documentary sources which could be distinguished quite readily by their use of the two divine names. The Elohistic document was the basic Pentateuchal source, and was dignified by the name of *Grundschrift*. This was augmented by extracts from the Jehovistic material, which Tuch dated in the Solomonic era. Even this formulation, which seemed to many contemporary scholars to meet the situation quite adequately, came under heavy criticism. J. H. Kurtz in his *Die Einheit der Genesis*, which was published in 1846, raised the question as to why the Elohistic passages, which according to the theory had been written considerably prior to the time when the Jehovistic *Ergänzer* or "supplementer" commenced his scribal activities, presupposed or in other ways referred to the contents of the Jehovistic portions. Although Kurtz subsequently abandoned his position, an answer to this enigmatic situation was never forthcoming from other supporters of the supplement hypothesis.

A further blow at Tuch's view was struck by Ewald, who modified his earlier position to the point of asserting in his *Geschichte des Volkes*

[50] Cf. Pfleiderer, *op. cit.*, pp. 252ff.

Israel (1843) that there were certain sections of the Pentateuch which did not belong either to the Elohistic, Jehovistic, or Deuteronomic documents. He claimed that these additional sources included a *Book of Covenants*, dating perhaps from the Judges period, a *Book of Origins*, compiled during the Solomonic era, and the work of three narrators, all of whom were prominent in the compilation of the Hexateuch about 500 B.C.

This "crystallization hypothesis," as it is sometimes called, was modified by Hermann Hupfeld, who in his investigation of the sources of Genesis[51] argued that the *Grundschrift* regarded by earlier critics as a unity was in fact the product of two writers, both of whom had employed *Elohim* as the name of God. He further maintained that the second scribe was closer in linguistic peculiarities and style to the Jehovistic author than to the first Elohistic scribe (*die Urschrift*), who distinctly manifested priestly tendencies. There were now four principal sources to be borne in mind in all considerations relating to the compilation of the Pentateuch or Hexateuch: these consisted of a Jehovistic (J) document, an Elohistic (E) compilation, a Priestly (P) source (formerly considered to be part of the "Foundation Document"), and the book of Deuteronomy (D). This theory was formulated as a means of dispensing with the problems raised by the supplement hypothesis, and its appeal depended to a considerable extent upon the successful functioning of a redactor or editor who had been responsible for reducing the four originally separate sources to their present combined form, a process in which a good deal of imagination was required on his part. The anonymous redactor proved to be a very useful ground of appeal when textual obscurities, chronological and topographical difficulties, or other problematical issues of a like nature threatened to make havoc of the theory. In point of fact, many later scholars followed Hupfeld in allotting to the redactor or his colleagues a good deal of responsibility for what they regarded as errors, conflations, confusions, and the like.

While the various theories relating to the origin and composition of the Hexateuch were being promulgated with some degree of consistency, they were being attacked continually by more orthodox scholars on a variety of grounds. One of the most important opponents of the various documentary hypotheses was E. W. Hengstenberg (1802-1869), a brilliant classical student who subsequently specialized in Old Testament studies at Berlin.[52] He quickly acquired a reputation in scholarly circles for disliking every form of rationalism, and throughout his lifetime he was a consistent challenger of Biblical liberalism. His enormous literary output,

[51] *Die Quellen der Genesis und die Art ihrer Zusammensetzung von neuen untersucht* (1853).
[52] Cf. F. Lichtenberger, *A History of German Theology in the Nineteenth Century* (1889), pp. 212ff.

some of which was translated into English, included his *Beiträge zur Einleitung in das Alte Testament* (1831-1839), *Die Bücher Mosis und Ägypten* (1841), and *Commentar über die Psalmen* (1842-1847). Others who followed the general tradition of Hengstenberg included M. Drechsler, H. Ch. Havernick, and C. F. Keil. The last collaborated with F. Delitzsch to produce a series of conservative commentaries on the various Old Testament books.

II. THE GRAF-WELLHAUSEN HYPOTHESIS

A. GRAF AND WELLHAUSEN

The decade following the division of the "Foundation Document" by Hupfeld saw a significant return to the position of Vatke, as a result of the work of K. H. Graf.[1] Like Vatke Graf tried to show that the *Grundschrift* was one of the latest rather than the earliest of the proposed documentary sources of the Pentateuch.[2] This view was based substantially upon the opinions of his teacher, Eduard Reuss, who in the summer of 1834 had suggested to his students at the University of Strasbourg that the Elohistic source was not the earliest but the latest of the documents which were thought to underlie the Pentateuch. Graf took up this theory, and maintained that the priestly interests of the "Foundation Document" indicated a date of composition subsequent to the contents of the book of Deuteronomy. As a result he assigned the document to the post-exilic period and associated it with the promulgation of the Law in the time of Ezra. However, he held that Leviticus 18–26, the so-called "Holiness Code," belonged properly to the period of Ezekiel.

With regard to the rest of the Pentateuch Graf adhered to the supplement theory, asserting that the Jehovistic additions were subject to redaction by the editor of Deuteronomy. The criteria upon which Graf based his late dating of the Priestly document were purely subjective in nature, and although his conclusions were challenged on this and other grounds he still clung to his contention that the basic Pentateuchal document was late rather than early. One result of this scholarly activity was to introduce a further branch of criticism to the study of the Old Testament. By attempting to assign dates to the proposed documents, the various writers transcended the bounds of literary criticism as such and moved into the area of historical criticism.

---

[1] It has been thought possible by some that the objections raised to Vatke's late date for the "Foundation Document" and his subsequent reconstruction of Israelite history were in fact a reaction against the obvious Hegelian tendencies of Graf.

[2] Graf, *Die geschichtlichen Bücher des AT: Zwei historisch-kritische Untersuchungen* (1865).

Basic to this approach was a comparison of the date furnished by the literary sources themselves with the events of history as recorded by the Old Testament historical and prophetic writings in an attempt to determine the authenticity and age of the material under study. Unfortunately this useful branch of criticism was dominated almost from the very beginning by the wholly fallacious assumption that, because the more significant regulations were either ignored entirely or at best rather neglected for prolonged periods in the early history of the Israelite nation, they could not possibly have been promulgated in the time of Moses or even in the early monarchy. Such a standpoint was adopted by De Wette,[3] Vatke, and later writers. The fallacy of this position has only been exposed within comparatively recent years with the realization that the peoples of the ancient Near East habitually lived for long periods according to inherited customs and traditions, many of which were frequently quite independent of legal promulgations.[4]

During the general period in which Graf was writing, a further contribution to the study of the problem was made by John William Colenso (1814-1883), who when Bishop of Natal undertook a critical examination of the Hexateuch in a series of seven treatises published between 1862 and 1879 under the general title, *The Pentateuch and the Book of Joshua Critically Examined.* Like Graf he concluded that the principal documentary source claimed by earlier scholars was late in nature, and that it contained purported historical material that was in actual fact anything but historical. He held that the minute ecclesiastical organization depicted in Leviticus and Numbers could only be the work of writers who belonged to a much later age than the Mosaic period, and in accordance with this general tendency he assigned Deuteronomy to a time subsequent to the settlement of the Hebrew tribes in Canaan. He inferred that the Book of the Law discovered during the reign of Josiah was Deuteronomy itself, and concluded that Chronicles had been compiled with the deliberate intention of exalting the priests and Levites.

Colenso's views stirred up a storm of controversy, and for this achievement as well as for other reasons he was deposed from his See and prohibited from preaching in England. However, his opinions had attracted the attention of the Dutch scholar Abraham Kuenen, who came to the conclusion that the prophetic material of Genesis, Exodus, and Numbers was considerably older than the *Grundschrift.* In *De Godsdienst van Israël,* published in 1870, Kuenen lent strength to the theories of Graf in suggesting that the Jehovistic source was basic to the Pentateuch and that it had been supplemented by extracts from an Elohistic document, by the addition of Deuteronomy, which was dated in the period of Josiah, by the legislative material emerging from the exilic era,

---

[3] Developed in his *Beiträge zur Einleitung in das AT* (1806-1807).
[4] Cf. *IOTT*, pp. 238ff.

including the "Law of Holiness," and by the incorporation of the Priestly document, which was assigned to the time of Ezra. Thus the former order of composition in terms of a P E J D arrangement was replaced by a projected J E D P scheme of compilation.

This basic theory was given its classic expression in the work of Julius Wellhausen (1844-1918), who studied theology under Ewald at the University of Göttingen. A man of wide spiritual vision, Wellhausen possessed a brilliant and penetrating mind, the quality of which is perhaps seen most clearly in his work on the text of the books of Samuel,[5] a study that surpassed all others on the subject until the discovery of the Qumran scrolls. Wellhausen followed Vatke in adopting the evolutionary concepts characteristic of the philosophy of Hegel, and was also influenced to some extent by the views of Herder on the Old Testament.[6] He lived in an age when the intellectual climate was dominated by theories of evolution, and, as Hahn has remarked,[7] he occupied a position in the field of Old Testament criticism analogous to that of Darwin in the area of biological science.

Wellhausen at once acknowledged his indebtedness to Graf.[8] By applying the developmental approach of Vatke, a thoroughgoing Hegelian, to the study of Hebrew religious institutions and combining it with the successive arrangement of ritual laws made by Graf, Wellhausen attempted to prove that the connection between the succession of the legal codes and the progressive development of religious practices among the Israelites could only be compatible with a late date for the Priestly document. Wellhausen apparently did not subject the theories of Graf to searching criticism, but developed them to what he deemed to be their logical conclusion. In consequence he regarded the Pentateuch as essentially of composite origin, consisting of a Jehovistic source (J), dated in the ninth century B.C.; an independent Elohistic document (E), coming from the eighth century B.C.; the basic content of the book of Deuteronomy (D), which was assigned to the time of King Josiah (640/39-609 B.C.); and a Priestly source (P), from about the fifth century B.C. According to the process outlined in his book entitled *Die Komposition des Hexateuchs*, published in 1877, the Jehovistic author compiled a narrative document from the sources J and E, and this was supplemented by the addition of Deuteronomy in the time of Josiah. Leviticus 17–26 was added to the Priestly document somewhat after the time of Ezekiel, while the remainder of the priestly material in the Elohistic source was compiled by Ezra. At a subsequent period the

---

[5] *Der Text der Bücher Samuelis untersucht* (1871).

[6] Cf. H. J. Kraus, *Geschichte der historisch-kritischen Erforschung des AT* (1956), p. 248.

[7] *OT in Modern Research* (1954), p. 11.

[8] *Geschichte Israels*, I (1878), pp. 3ff.

entire corpus was revised and edited to form the extant Pentateuch, perhaps by about 200 B.C.

Wellhausen then applied his conclusion that the Mosaic legislation was the basic law code of post-exilic Judaism rather than the starting-point for the development of Israelite religious institutions to a reconstruction of Hebrew religion. Rejecting current theological interpretations in favor of Hegelian principles of causation and evolution, he envisioned the early religious activity of Israel in terms of primitive impulses of an animistic character; consequently, he dismissed as unhistorical the sources which described patriarchal religion as monotheistic in nature. This completely arbitrary action was followed by the affirmation that the history of Hebrew religion could only commence with the beginnings of the peoples themselves. While there is a sense in which the latter is obviously true, Wellhausen failed to see that the religion of the settlement and the earlier Wilderness period had its antecedents in the Hebrew patriarchs; as a result, he asserted that the Israelites emerged on the historical scene as a people no earlier than the time of Moses.[9]

For Wellhausen the adaptation of the Israelites to Canaanite patterns of worship subsequent to the settlement of the tribes in Palestine was a step towards the emergence of a monotheistic faith, and this largely resulted from the activity of the prophets. Wellhausen maintained that prior to the reforms of Josiah there had been no central sanctuary, with the result that sacrifices were offered at various places in Canaan. Ultimately the prophetic teachings concerning monotheism led to the centralization of cultic worship in Jerusalem, an event which provided the impetus for that kind of ritual activity which in the post-exilic period culminated in the formulation of the Priestly Code.[10]

Although Wellhausen had added little or nothing that was specifically new to the critical conclusions of Graf, his method brought to a climax the investigations of earlier liberal scholars and served to show the fundamental difference between the nineteenth-century *Zeitgeist* and the theological exegesis of an earlier age. Wellhausen had contrived to reduce the elements of law, covenant, religion, and history to one comprehensive and controlled scheme, consisting of three major periods of Hebrew historical development in which simple forms evolved into progressively differentiated aspects. His scheme bore all the marks of Hegelian evolutionism, and by its very simplicity and comprehensiveness it commended itself to an age which was endeavoring to resolve the many into the one by means of a single interpretative principle.

So completely did the scheme which Wellhausen elaborated meet the needs of his day that it gained wide acceptance within a very short period of time. In Holland, the views of Wellhausen were disseminated

[9] Wellhausen, *Prolegomena zur Geschichte Israels* (1883), pp. 363ff.
[10] Wellhausen, *Israelitische und jüdische Geschichte* (1897), pp. 110ff.

enthusiastically by Kuenen;[11] in France the aged Reuss propounded with renewed vigor the theories which he had advanced in 1834 when he affirmed that the basic Elohistic document was in fact the latest of all those thought to underlie the Pentateuch.[12]

However, other equally notable scholars were far from being convinced of the merits of many aspects of the evolutionary position that had been set out so plausibly by Wellhausen. Eduard Riehm attacked the view that the Priestly Code was the latest part of the Pentateuch, observing that the Deuteronomic legislation presupposed acquaintance with it.[13] Dillmann placed the Priestly Code considerably prior to Deuteronomy in terms of development, and assigned the bulk of the Holiness Code, to which he accorded the designation S(inai), to an even earlier date.[14] Baudissin placed the Law of Holiness in the pre-Deuteronomic period,[15] while Kittel held that the Priestly literature had existed for a prolonged time as a document of ecclesiastical law, available only to the priests at first but subsequently made public by force of circumstances.[16]

Whereas Dillmann, Kittel, and Baudissin tended towards a mediating view of the Priestly material, Franz Delitzsch openly attacked the entire Wellhausenian scheme in his commentary on Genesis.[17] He held that all sections of the Pentateuch specifically attributed to Moses in the text were in fact from his hand, while other portions of his legal enactments were given their final form by priestly circles during the settlement period. Delitzsch was attracted to the possibility that Joshua was compiled by the author of Deuteronomy from Jehovistic and Elohistic models from details of ecclesiastical arrangement and organization he argued for a pre-exilic date for much of the Priestly writings,[18] and stoutly defended the genuineness of the Decalogue,[19] which even Smend had originally attributed to Moses.[20]

A different form of attack upon the views of Wellhausen came in 1893, when A. Klostermann rejected the developmental hypothesis and replaced it with his own version of the crystallization theory of Ewald and Knobel. In his work on the Pentateuch he postulated the existence of an original Mosaic nucleus of law which, because of its liturgical use, was expanded by priestly editors. Although he adhered to the ideas of a

---

[11] *Historisch-Critisch Onderzoek naar het Ontstaan en de Verzameling van de Boeken des Ouden Verbonds* (3 vols., 1885-1893).

[12] *L'Histoire Sainte et la Loi* (1879).

[13] *Einleitung in das AT* (1889), I, p. 218.

[14] *Numeri, Deuteronomium und Josua* (1886), pp. 605, 644ff., 660.

[15] *HDB*, IV, p. 88.

[16] *Geschichte der Hebräer* (1888), I, pp. 100ff.

[17] *Neuer Kommentar über die Genesis* (1887), E. tr. 1888.

[18] *Zeitschrift für kirchliche Wissenschaft und kirchliches Leben* (1880), p. 268.

[19] *Ibid.* (1882), pp. 281ff.

[20] *Theologische Studien und Kritiken*, XLIX (1876), p. 643.

Jehovistic and an Elohistic recension, he held that these were united at a comparatively early period,[21] making for a definite pre-exilic origin for the Priestly sources. Like many other scholars he held that Deuteronomy had been added to the Pentateuchal corpus in the time of Josiah of Judah.

B. WELLHAUSEN AND HIS FOLLOWERS

Despite the weighty criticisms levelled against it, the Graf-Wellhausen hypothesis became very appealing to the younger scholars of the day, since it seemed to furnish the answer to their critical needs with simplicity and conviction. From rather humble textual beginnings the theory had grown through the work of successive thinkers to the point where, under Wellhausen, it had become a precision instrument for examining the rationale of Hebrew history against a background of Hegelian evolutionism. Having developed critical methodology to this point, Wellhausen devoted his time to grappling with the literary analysis of the Gospels, relinquishing the application of his methods to other aspects of Old Testament study to his followers. The challenge was taken up with enthusiasm by such able investigators as Smend, Kautzsch, Stade, Budde, Cornill, and others of like caliber, and within a very short time the volume of literary output based on the Graf-Wellhausen methodology had assumed enormous proportions, virtually stifling other opposing views through sheer bulk. In common with other disciplines of the age, the literary-critical method of Old Testament study claimed the title "scientific," and from this it was only a short step to its being regarded by the followers of Wellhausen as the new orthodoxy.

There can be little doubt that when Wellhausen promulgated his theory of Pentateuchal origins he was endeavoring to develop an instrument for the deeper understanding of Scripture. To him and to his supporters the scholarly activities in which they were engaged were far superior methodologically to the older canons of theological exegesis, which left a great many questions unanswered. More particularly, the humanistic approach of the Enlightenment had liberated Scripture from the confines of Roman Catholic and Lutheran "fundamentalism," and had made the Old Testament in particular a legitimate object of intellectual inquiry. Wellhausen approached his task with a lucid mind and a sympathetic understanding, and his writings conveyed clearly the appreciation he had for the significance of the religious phenomena in the lives of the Hebrew people. Had he continued to apply his principles to parts of the Old Testament other than the Hexateuch, the results of his study might well have been very different from what actually obtained.

---

[21] *Der Pentateuch* (1893), p. 185.

What Wellhausen did not appreciate, however, in handing over his methodology to his disciples, was that the *Zeitgeist* was characterized by profound emotional overtones, so that the critical discipline which he had evolved quickly degenerated in nature to the point where it became the unwitting vehicle for the expression of specific weaknesses implicit in the German national character. In the end it failed to develop into a reliable and objective scientific approach to literary study. It is merely a matter of observation that the writings of contemporary German scholars manifested an egotistical inability to appreciate any standpoint other than the one to which they themselves subscribed, and this tendency was compounded by clearly defined trends towards intellectual aggression and domination, a self-assured ideological superiority, and a general consciousness of the monopoly of truth.

The followers of Wellhausen accepted his intellectual leadership uncritically, as Wellhausen himself confessed to having done with respect to the opinions of Graf concerning the late dating of the Law. The single-minded devotion to detail of these men, combined with their general lack of respect for the opinions of those scholars who were in a minority position, soon rewarded their diligence and application by making Wellhausen's scheme the dominant ideology in the field of Old Testament studies. Ultimately this attitude produced such self-assured results of criticism as the divided authorship of Isaiah and the assigning of the book of Daniel to a Maccabean date.

Influenced in part by considerations of academic patronage, the enthusiasm of the more junior European scholars for the critical methodology resulted in a thoroughgoing application of the Graf-Wellhausen analytical and developmental schemes to nearly every book in the Old Testament canon. All too frequently the basic subjectivity of the method encouraged a wide diversity of opinion upon matters of specific detail, such as the exact delineation of the various proposed documentary sources of the Pentateuch. In certain areas of study its application produced some lamentable extremes of literary analysis against which a subsequent generation was to react. But for the younger scholars, devotion to the literary-critical method brought with it a feeling that it could be developed still further and made more efficient as a result. Accordingly they devoted themselves increasingly to the more technical requirements of analyzing the scope and formation of the documents adduced by earlier scholars, with the result that successive students broke down the basic sources thought to underlie the Pentateuch into even smaller components than Wellhausen himself had done.

So vigorous was this tendency that scholars in Europe became preoccupied to an ever greater extent with the task of isolating and subdividing such elemental categories, and not infrequently they found themselves caught up in involved and ponderous arguments relating to the provenance of isolated verses or sentences. Whereas Wellhausen had

25

endeavored to maintain a view of the panorama of Hebrew history in his delineation of supposed documentary sources, his followers manifested an increasing concern for the analysis of "documents" as an end in itself, thus contributing materially to the general sterility of their results.

Even Wellhausen himself, it is reported, became more and more anxious as time went on about the usage to which his methodology was being put and the results which were being obtained,[22] but by that time the movement had gained momentum and reached a stage where it was largely out of control. Before his death in 1918 Wellhausen conceded that the rationalism which he had embraced so avidly in earlier years had made havoc of his own faith in the authority and authenticity of the Old Testament.

Up to this point liberal criticism had emerged as a threefold discipline for the examination of the Hebrew Scriptures. Its aims were the reconstruction of the original text with the greatest degree of accuracy, so as to determine the manner and date of writing of the various books, the establishment of the nature of their underlying sources as far as possible, and the attempt to arrive at some decision relating to questions of authorship of the various compositions in the canon.

The earliest phase of this activity, which in fact antedated the rise of literary criticism, was marked by the growth of textual criticism, the objective of which was to discover to the fullest degree possible the original wording of the documents under study. This constituted an extremely important branch of study, partly because the basic reliability of the Hebrew text was the foundation upon which all other areas of criticism erected their superstructures, and partly because transcriptional errors were considerably more frequent in the days when all manuscripts were copied out by hand than they were after the invention of printing when the manuscript as such was replaced by a book. Since no autograph manuscript of any Old Testament composition has survived, it was rightly deemed important for the Hebrew text to represent as accurate a copy of the original as was possible under the circumstances.

The second branch of criticism was the purely literary kind, which had been given the designation of "higher" by Eichhorn in the preface to the second edition of his *Einleitung* (1787), in order to distinguish it from "lower" or textual criticism. Literary-critical activities included an examination of the sources considered to underlie a particular book or document, as well as some pronouncement on matters relating to the authorship and date of the material. Higher criticism was also concerned to classify literature according to type, with the aim of isolating legal enactments, biographical sections, poetry, prophetic oracles and the like.

---

[22] See P. J. Wiseman, *New Discoveries in Babylonia about Genesis* (1958), pp. 121f.

The final branch of criticism was due in no small measure to the work of Wellhausen, who by relating literary criticism to the exigencies of his evolutionary view of Old Testament history laid considerable stress upon the necessity for developing historical criticism as a means of determining the historicity and credibility of the events under consideration.

Within a decade of the publication by Wellhausen of the *Prolegomena* in 1883, a large number of histories of Israel, surveys of Old Testament religion, commentaries on various canonical books, and introductions to the Old Testament as a whole appeared under the names of distinguished scholars, the vast majority of whom employed the literary-critical methods made popular by Wellhausen. A high standard of historical and critical investigation was fostered by the appearance of two German commentaries on the Old Testament books, the fifteen-volume *Handkommentar zum Alten Testament* (1892-1903) and the twenty-volume *Kurzer Handkommentar zum Alten Testament* (1897-1904).

A similar series, *The International Critical Commentary on the Holy Scriptures*, made an appearance at approximately the same time in England and the United States under the editorial auspices of S. R. Driver, A. Plummer, and C. A. Briggs. Although the Old Testament section was planned to consist of twenty-six volumes, it was never in fact completed.

C. THE SPREAD OF WELLHAUSEN'S METHOD TO ENGLAND AND AMERICA

While their New Testament counterparts were busily employed in refuting the theories of the Tübingen school, British Old Testament scholars were avidly embracing the views of Wellhausen and his followers in Europe. Chiefly responsible for this trend were A. B. Davidson and W. Robertson Smith. The latter in particular accorded unquestioned orthodoxy to the writings of Wellhausen. Whereas Davidson was primarily a teacher,[23] Robertson Smith was a man of considerable literary ability who wrote extensively in support of the growing literary-critical movement. In 1875 he contributed an important article to the *Encyclopaedia Britannica* which, along with other material, resulted in his trial for heresy and ultimate expulsion from the Free Church College of Aberdeen in 1881. In the same year he published his lectures on *The Old Testament in the Jewish Church*, and in the following year he issued *The Prophets of Israel*. In 1885 he published a monograph dealing with *Kinship and Marriage in Early Arabia*, and four years later his book entitled *The Religion of the Semites* appeared, quickly becoming a classic of the day. Less influential were the writings of T. K. Cheyne, who contributed commentaries on *Micah* (1882) and *Hosea* (1884) to

[23] Cf. H. W. Robinson, *ET*, XLI (1929-1930), pp. 247f.

the Cambridge Bible series, as well as publishing books dealing with the Psalms and the Wisdom Literature.[24] Unfortunately Cheyne fell victim to the practice of excessive textual emendation—a procedure necessary in order to fit certain awkward portions of the Hebrew text into the Wellhausenian evolutionary scheme—and much of what he contributed to the *Encyclopaedia Biblica,* of which he was an editor, must be assessed in the light of this fact.

But by far the most influential figure in the dissemination of Biblical criticism in England was S. R. Driver of Oxford. He succeeded to the Regius Professorship of Hebrew on the death of E. B. Pusey in 1882, supplanting A. H. Sayce, whose election to the chair was vetoed by Gladstone on the ground that Sayce was one of the leading exponents of German criticism at Oxford, and therefore an "unsafe" candidate for the chair.[25] Ironically enough, while Sayce subsequently turned to archaeological investigation and ultimately became a distinguished champion of orthodox belief, it was Driver who made one of the most important contributions to the promulgation of Old Testament criticism in the English language.

Driver had already established his reputation as a scholar with the publication in 1874 of his *Hebrew Tenses,* and after this he set about modifying the extremes of German critical ideology in order to accommodate it to the less radical tastes of the British. The result was his *Introduction to the Literature of the Old Testament,* published in 1891. Although this work was simply no match for the flowing prose and lucid artistry of many of the contemporary German writings, it made up in diligence what it lacked in imagination and originality. Driver's *Introduction* was by far the most influential of his numerous writings;[26] and it served an important function in establishing a pattern of critical orthodoxy which became normative for British scholars. A close if unofficial surveillance was imposed upon potential candidates for positions in the Old Testament field in British universities, and only those who displayed proper respect for the canons of critical orthodoxy were appointed to academic posts. Consequently scholars of a more conservative bent were relegated to comparative obscurity in theological colleges of various denominations and other independent institutions of learning. The bulk of the literary material which emerged from this general

---

[24] *The Book of Psalms* (1888), *The Origin of the Psalter* (1891), *Job and Solomon* (1887).

[25] Cf. D. E. Hart-Davies, *Biblical History in the Light of Archaeological Discovery since A.D. 1900* (1935), pp. 1ff.

[26] Including his *Notes on the Hebrew Text of the Books of Samuel* (1890), in which he leaned heavily on the work of Wellhausen, and commentaries on *Deuteronomy* (*ICC* series, 1895), *Daniel* (Cambridge Bible, 1900), *Genesis* (Westminster Commentaries series, 1904), and *Exodus* (Cambridge Bible, 1911).

period consisted of uncritical expositions of German liberal criticism based upon the mediating pattern established by S. R. Driver, with only slight variations on the fundamental theme being countenanced. Such were characteristics of the books by J. E. Carpenter, H. E. Ryle, A. F. Kirkpatrick, W. H. Bennett, J. Strachan, A. T. Chapman, and A. B. Davidson.[27]

Although the tide of literary criticism was running high at the end of the nineteenth century, its onslaught by no means went unchallenged. In 1885 E. C. Bissell attacked the basic presuppositions of the Wellhausenian hypothesis,[28] while in the following year Geerhardus Vos castigated the current scheme of literary analysis, rejected the late date assigned the Priestly material, and claimed substantial Mosaic authorship for the Pentateuch.[29] From a more theological standpoint James Orr made an important criticism of the Wellhausenian hypothesis and censured severely the contemporary efforts at the critical reconstruction of Old Testament history.[30] Orr not only pointed out the essential weaknesses of the application of the analytical method by the more extreme members of the Wellhausen school, but he showed that the method itself was characterized by fundamentally inadequate postulates in a number of important areas. In his refutation of the analytical approach and his defense of orthodox conservatism Orr was not, as Hahn implies,[31] unable to understand the significance of historical research. It is of some interest to note that his penetrating criticisms were never accorded the dignity of an answer, much less an attempt at refutation, by those whose views he challenged. A similar situation obtained in the case of Baxter, who also subjected the methodology of Wellhausen to a searching criticism in the light of Hebrew religious institutions, rejecting the late date accorded to the Priestly sections by critical scholars.[32]

In the meantime the distinguished scholar A. H. Sayce was bringing the developing science of modern archaeology to bear upon some of the more pressing problems of the Old Testament. As a result of his studies he abandoned his earlier support for the German liberal position and became an influential advocate of more traditional views. Outstanding among his many writings were The "Higher Criticism" and the Verdict of

---

[27] Carpenter, *The Composition of the Hexateuch* (1902); *The Hexateuch* (with G. Harford-Battersby, 2 vols., 1900), *The Pentateuch* (1900). Ryle, *The Canon of the OT* (1892). Kirkpatrick, *The Divine Library of the OT* (1896), *The Book of Psalms* (1902). Bennett, *A Primer of the Bible* (1897), *The Book of Joshua* (1899). Strachan in *ERE*, IV, pp. 314ff. Chapman, *Introduction to the Pentateuch* (1911). Davidson in the Cambridge Bible commentaries on *Job* (1884), *Ezekiel* (1892), and *Nahum, Habakkuk and Zephaniah* (1896).

[28] *The Pentateuch: Its Origin and Structure* (1885).

[29] *The Mosaic Origin of the Pentateuchal Codes* (1886).

[30] *The Problem of the OT* (1906).

[31] *OT in Modern Research*, p. 23.

[32] *Sanctuary and Sacrifice: A Reply to Wellhausen* (1895).

the Monuments (1894), *Early Israel and the Surrounding Nations* (1899), and *Monument Facts and Higher Critical Fancies* (1904).

Other attacks by conservative writers were directed at the criteria used by critical scholars in their documentary analyses and reconstructions. One such investigation by Dahse examined the criterion of the divine names and showed that it was impossible to maintain that the names of Jacob and Israel were indications of the existence of different literary sources.[33] In a study of the occurrence of the divine names in the LXX Dahse pointed out significant variations from the usage in the Hebrew text, and argued from such inconsistencies to the comparative unsuitability of the divine names as a criterion for documentary analysis. He also emphasized that the cultural and religious conditions depicted in the Old Testament narratives reflected a far more advanced degree of maturity than Wellhausen and his followers were prepared to concede,[34] a position which was to be reinforced by Mesopotamian archaeology some forty years later.

Although Dahse adhered to the view that the literary form of the legal material contained in the Pentateuch was comparatively late, he maintained that the ritual practices which it reflected were considerably older than the form of the laws themselves, since they depicted theological concepts which belonged to an early age.[35] In general he rejected the idea that the beginnings of institutions necessarily had to be simple in form, and with this he jettisoned the evolutionary interpretation of Hebrew religious institutions that was propounded by Wellhausen. But Dahse's appeal to the comparatively advanced nature of other ancient Near Eastern religious and cultural forms, although supported by the archaeological discoveries of the day, fell on deaf ears; for the liberal critics were preoccupied with the analysis of purely internal evidence as supplied by the Hebrew text, and had neither the time nor the taste for archaeology.

In 1912 the English lawyer H. M. Wiener wrote in opposition to the critical scheme of Old Testament study.[36] Like Dahse, Wiener attacked the criterion of the divine names, pointing out the variation of usage between the Massoretic text and the LXX. He maintained the substantial Mosaic authorship of the Pentateuch, although he recognized the existence of certain post-Mosaic sections. In 1908 B. D. Eerdmans commenced a series of studies, subsequently published under the title of *Alttestamentliche Studien I-IV* (1908-14), in which he also rejected the theory that the divine names could be employed as valid criteria for the

[33] J. Dahse, *Archiv für Religionswissenschaft*, VI (1903), pp. 305ff. Cf. also his *Textkritische Materialen zur Hexateuchfrage* (1912).

[34] *Alttestamentliche Studien, II: Die Vorgeschichte Israels* (1909), pp. 38ff., *III: Das Buch Exodus* (1910), p. 126.

[35] *Ibid. IV: Das Buch Leviticus* (1912), pp. 143f.

[36] *Pentateuchal Studies* (1912); cf. *ibid., Essays on Pentateuchal Criticism* (1909).

purpose of distinguishing underlying documents. He held that the material as a whole belonged to four different stages of development, of which the earliest was polytheistic and the latest monotheistic. In the post-exilic period the accumulated body of written tradition was re-edited from a monotheistic standpoint and augmented by means of other material to become the extant Pentateuch. At a later period Eerdmans attempted to modify the Wellhausenian reconstruction of Hebrew religious history in his *Godsdienst van Israël*, published in 1930,[37] but his views met with little enthusiasm.

The spread of German critical methods in Old Testament study to the United States occurred at approximately the same time as their acceptance by British scholars. In the forefront of those who acclaimed the new methodology were Francis Brown and C. A. Briggs, who introduced it to Union Theological Seminary in New York City. Both men were eminent Hebrew scholars who cooperated with S. R. Driver in producing the *Hebrew Lexicon of the Old Testament* in 1906, a volume which was based upon the work of the renowned Semitic philologist Gesenius. The early writings of Briggs[38] were not particularly distinguished by their critical acumen as compared with similar European compositions, although in 1893, when he published *The Higher Criticism of the Hexateuch*, he had absorbed the general principles of higher criticism. Like some of his predecessors in the field he had a feeling for the beauty and poetry of the Hebrew Psalter, and in 1886 he contributed a series of articles dealing with the form and structure of Hebrew poetry to the third volume of *Hebraica*, a technical journal founded in 1884 by W. R. Harper, then the President of the University of Chicago. Subsequently this journal became *The American Journal of Semitic Languages and Literatures*. These studies constituted a preparatory step towards the production of his *magnum opus*, the two-volume work, *A Critical and Exegetical Commentary on the Psalms*, which appeared in 1906-07. His *General Introduction to the Study of the Old Testament* was published in 1899.

As was the case with Robertson Smith, Briggs became heavily involved in controversy as a result of his views relating to the Graf-Wellhausen hypothesis; and in 1892 he was tried for heresy by the presbytery of New York. He was subsequently acquitted, but when an appeal was launched before the General Assembly he was suspended from office in 1893. Seven years later he was ordained to the priesthood in the Episcopal Church, where he ministered until his death in 1913.

The critical views prevalent in Europe were also reflected in the commentary *The Genesis of Genesis* (1892) by B. W. Bacon,[39] and in

---

[37] E. tr. rev., *The Religion of Israel* (1947).
[38] *Biblical Study* (1884), *Messianic Prophecy* (1886).   See E. G. Kraeling, *The OT Since the Reformation* (1955), p. 294 n. 13.
[39] See also his *The Triple Tradition of Exodus* (1894).

contributions to the *International Critical Commentary* series by G. F. Moore, H. P. Smith, C. H. Toy, W. R. Harper, G. A. Barton, and L. B. Paton.[40] Among others W. H. Green of Princeton Theological Seminary challenged the opinions of Harper, as a result of which a debate appeared in the fifth volume of *Hebraica* (1888) on the entire scope of the Pentateuchal problem. The discussion attained a high standard of literary and academic achievement, and the charitable tone which prevailed throughout was in marked contrast to the acrimony which existed elsewhere. Green was a competent Hebrew scholar who had already issued a reply to the opinions of Bishop Colenso,[41] and had challenged the views espoused in Kuenen's critical study of the Hexateuch[42] in his *Moses and the Prophets* (1883). Green subsequently issued two important works on the Pentateuch in one year,[43] both of which furnished eloquent testimony to the erudition of the author and constituted fundamental challenges to the entire methodological system of Wellhausen and his followers.

[40] Moore, *A Critical and Exegetical Commentary on the Book of Judges* (1895); Smith, *Samuel* (1899); Toy, *Proverbs* (1899); Harper, *Amos and Hosea* (1905); Barton, *Ecclesiastes* (1908); Paton, *Esther* (1906).

[41] *The Pentateuch Vindicated from the Aspersions of Bishop Colenso* (1863).

[42] *Historisch-Critisch Onderzoek naar het Ontstaan en de Verzameling van de Boeken des Ouden Verbonds, I-III* (1885-1893); E. tr. of sect. I, *The Hexateuch* (1886).

[43] *The Unity of the Book of Genesis* and *The Higher Criticism of the Pentateuch* (1895).

III. REACTIONS TO THE GRAF-WELLHAUSEN HYPOTHESIS

A. Philology, Archaeology, and Anthropology

While the limitations of literary criticism were already painfully apparent as a result of the unfortunate excesses of certain European scholars, new sources of knowledge were becoming available for the study of the Old Testament which were themselves demanding a modification of the extreme attitudes reflected by many adherents of the critical position. The decipherment of Mesopotamian cuneiform and Egyptian hieroglyphic scripts made available for purposes of comparative study an enormous number of sources having an important bearing on all periods of Old Testament history. As a result it was becoming increasingly possible to study Hebrew life generally in terms of the larger ancient Near Eastern environment. With the development of archaeology as a scientific discipline a more assured basis was furnished for philology and comparative linguistics as a whole. Important contributions to the study of Semitic languages had already been made by H. F. W. Gesenius, the father of modern Hebrew lexicography, by E. Renan, Friedrich Delitzsch, A. H. Sayce, W. Wright, H. Zimmern, T. Nöldeke, and E. König.[1] These studies were to be enriched and extended by the labors of subsequent generations of scholars.

Most significant of all, however, was the realization that while Semitic philology was a well-grounded subject in its own right, it had an invaluable part to play in constituting one aspect of legitimate critical inquiry for the elucidation of some of the mysteries of the ancient Near Eastern

---

[1] Gesenius, *Hebräisches und Chaldäisches Handwörterbuch* (1812). Renan, *Histoire générale des langues semitiques* (1863). Delitzsch, *Prolegomena eines neuen Hebräisch-Aramäischen Wörterbuchs zum AT* (1886); *Assyrisches Wörterbuch zur gesampten bisher veröffentlichen Keilschriftliteratur* (1887-1890); *Assyrische Grammatik* (1889). Sayce, *Assyrian Grammar for Comparative Purposes* (1872); *Principles of Comparative Philology* (1874); *Introduction to the Science of Language* (1879). Wright, *Lectures on the Comparative Grammar of the Semitic Languages* (1890). Zimmern, *Vergleichende Grammatik der semitischen Sprachen* (1898). Nöldeke, *Die Semitischen Sprachen* (1899). König, *Historisch-Kritisches Lehrgebäude der Hebräischen Sprache* (1881); *Hebräisch und Semitisch* (1901).

environment that various Old Testament books reflect. Since that time comparative linguistics has become an essential adjunct to any serious study of the Old Testament, and has contributed enormously to the modern understanding of traditions, allusions, and practices, which by their very nature were entirely unfamiliar to the occidental mind. With the enrichment of Hebrew philology there came also a more scientific approach to the study of the Hebrew text, making it possible for scholars to come closer to the original autographs and thereby clarifying some of the problems which had arisen during the processes of textual transmission.

Other methods of study relating to the Hebrew Scriptures, which were different from those normally envisaged by philology and archaeology, were also being investigated at this period. It is to the credit of Robertson Smith that attention was first focused on a specifically anthropological approach to the study of Hebrew religion. Although in his *Lectures on the Religion of the Semites* he examined the earliest forms of Hebrew beliefs and rituals from the standpoint, common among anthropologists of his day, that the more developed forms of a religion could best be understood by a detailed study of the primitive or rudimentary phases from which it had evolved, he ultimately parted company with some of the views of Wellhausen by maintaining the cohesiveness and compulsion of social rather than purely personal customs and convictions. Through the study of such ritual institutions as sacrifice Smith endeavored to grapple with the nature of primitive religious belief among the Semites, and concluded that the ideas of atonement and communion were basic concepts of primitive Semitic religion.[2]

A more diversified approach to this same subject was reflected in the writings of Sir James G. Frazer. For many years Frazer collected material relating to the fundamental thought-forms and activities of savage and primitive peoples for the successive editions of his work *The Golden Bough*.[3] In the field of Old Testament studies Frazer attempted to find in the narratives traces of survivals of the most primitive stage of Hebrew religious beliefs,[4] but while the method of analogy and comparison which he utilized frequently did much to illumine the meaning of an obscure passage, he was unable to present his data in the coherent and logical manner characteristic of the work of Robertson Smith. Frazer unfortunately had little or no concept of the religious growth of the Hebrews, so that for the Biblical scholar his attempts to recover the most

[2] *The Religion of the Semites*, pp. 251ff., 312ff.

[3] *The Golden Bough: A Study in Magic and Religion* (1890 ed.), 2 vols., (1900 ed.), 3 vols., (1910-1915 ed.), 12 vols. A one-volume abridgement was published in 1922.

[4] *Folk-lore in the OT: Studies in Comparative Religion* (3 vols., 1918).

primitive aspects of belief or ritual procedure were at best somewhat unfruitful, if only because they appeared to be out of proportion in terms of the total picture.

B. FORM-CRITICISM—GUNKEL AND HIS FOLLOWERS

Although these approaches were valuable in attempting to rectify and give proper dimensions to an imbalanced literary criticism, they had less effect upon the excesses of the Graf-Wellhausen school than did the rise of form-criticism. With an increasing number of objections to the results obtained by the exercise of literary criticism, and with decided uncertainty in many quarters about the validity of the proposed solutions, it became clear that a new approach to the problem was a matter of some urgency. Utilizing the conclusions which had emerged from the comparative study of religions, and relating them to the literary products of the Hebrew people, a group of German scholars associated with Hermann Gunkel began an attempt to trace the basic religious ideas of the Hebrews as enshrined in the Massoretic text back to their original oral form. Gunkel laid considerable emphasis upon the importance of the life-situation or *Sitz im Leben des Volkes* as a means of understanding the various extant literary forms, which he subjected to a careful though generally sympathetic criticism.

Gunkel also took pains to compare the religious *motifs* of the Hebrews with the mythological and cultic forms of Mesopotamian, Egyptian, and Hittite religion, so as to determine, if possible, the extent to which the Hebrews had been influenced by the cultures of the ancient Near East. Since Gunkel considered the literature of a people to be in fact the tangible expression of their spiritual history, he deemed it of great importance to be able to penetrate the extant literary form and recover the ultimate sources in terms of oral tradition. In his work on Genesis,[5] which formed an introduction to his larger commentary in the *Handkommentar zum Alten Testament*, he advanced the view that the narratives of Genesis had originally been transmitted orally in the form of independent sagas, which subsequently had become associated with some particular person. The art of the storyteller was later reduced to a literary form of considerable aesthetic value prior to the prophetic period, and collections of these sagas formed the basis of the Jehovistic and Elohistic documents which were ultimately united in their extant form in the Pentateuch.

Gunkel emphasized that his method of literary appreciation was a means of grasping the religious values of the Old Testament, which had been largely obscured as a result of the critical activities of the Graf-

[5] *Die Sagen der Genesis* (1901).

Wellhausen school.[6] However, he also made it clear that the sagas of Genesis were for him basically folklore, like that of any other ancient people, and not necessarily the embodiment of historical fact as such. He deemed his task to be that of uncovering the original oral form of these sagas through an examination of the various types of literary composition in the Hebrew Scriptures in terms of his particular methodology. Though Gunkel claimed allegiance to the Wellhausenian hypothesis his work represented a fundamental criticism of it, since his assertion that the documents were collections of sagas rather than the writings of individual authors had elements in common with the fragmentary hypothesis advocated by Geddes and Vater. Furthermore, Gunkel argued for the antiquity of the original form of the sagas, as opposed to the late dating assigned by the members of the Graf-Wellhausen school.

Reflecting the influence of Herder, Gunkel applied his methodology to the Hebrew Psalms in a series of writings which surveyed the peculiarities of linguistic expression found in the Psalter and estimated the place occupied by these compositions in the stream of Israelite literary history.[7] On the assumption that certain conventions of form had become traditional over many centuries of usage, Gunkel assigned a long history to Hebrew poetry, suggesting that, as with the Genesis sagas, the Psalms had originally existed in an oral form that attained an apogee in the pre-exilic period. Although he had some difficulty tracing the growth of many of his principal literary types (*Gattungen*), owing to the traditional fashion of associating certain forms of composition with specific categories of subject-matter, he was able to find sufficient indications of growth with regard to poetic forms to produce a fruitful classification of the literature as a whole.

Gunkel maintained that the majority of the post-exilic psalms had been composed in virtually their extant form, but he also recognized that many of them contained elements of much older literary compositions. This was a considerable advance upon earlier critical tendencies,[8] which had in general regarded the individual psalms as late rather than early in point of time. Gunkel, however, did not question the assumption commonly espoused by liberal scholars that the Psalter as a unit had been compiled at a late date.

This method of classification by literary types in relation to a characteristic cultural setting has contributed more to the understanding of the Psalter than any other facet of literary-critical activity. The rigorous insistence upon relating Hebrew poetry to the larger background of

---

[6] *Deutsche Rundschau*, CLXI (1914), pp. 215ff.; see also his *What Remains of the OT? and Other Essays* (1928), pp. 13ff.

[7] *Ausgewählte Psalmen* (1904); *Die Psalmen* in *Handkommentar zum AT* (ed. Nowack, 1926), II, vol. 2; *Einleitung in die Psalmen: Die Gattungen der religiösen Lyrik Israels* (1928-1933), parts I, II.

[8] Cf. Gunkel, *Einleitung in die Psalmen*, pp. 514ff.

ancient Near Eastern literary products resulted in some penetrating liturgical and exegetical insights, and indicated that further information about the origins of Hebrew psalmody would most probably be derived through the comparative study of religion. This situation was made even more clear with the discovery of the poetic material from Ras Shamra (Ugarit) in 1929, some three years before Gunkel died. These tablets, however, required some modification of the *Sitz im Leben des Volkcs* approach which Gunkel had adopted, since they indicated that Hebrew poetry did not depend so much upon analogous forms in Egyptian and Babylonian religious texts as upon the literature of Ugarit, which contained a vast number of stylistic forms, phrases, and grammatical expressions in common with the Hebrew.

Another challenge to the Graf-Wellhausen hypothesis resulted from the work of Sievers, who applied the principles underlying his studies on Hebrew poetic meters to the Pentateuch.[9] Sievers intended to demonstrate the validity of the documentary analysis by this means, but in point of fact he returned, like Gunkel, to the fragmentary hypothesis of Geddes and Vater by subdividing the documents of J, E, and P into five, three, and six different sources respectively. As G. Ch. Aalders has pointed out, if Sievers had investigated the meter of the book of Genesis without recourse to the principles of the Graf-Wellhausen school, he would almost certainly have arrived at an entirely different conclusion, positing one principal source supplemented by means of six secondary ones.[10]

The techniques that Gunkel applied to the sagas of Genesis and the contents of the Psalter were employed by his followers to investigate other areas of the Old Testament. Outstanding in this regard was the work of Hugo Gressmann, whose major concern was with the historical writings. Starting from the saga-concept of Gunkel, he postulated the theory that the narrative qualities of the extant historical literature could be related directly to the form of the narrative art as it existed during the oral stage of the source material. From this he was led to the study of the individual narratives in terms of literary types, which in his view was more important than an analysis of the manner in which a book was thought to have been compiled from documentary sources. His study of the historical writings[11] attracted the attention of other scholars. A fragmentation of the historical books resulted from the work of Wiese on Judges[12] and from the studies of Caspari[13] and Rost[14] dealing with the books of Samuel. All of these labored diligently in an attempt to identify the separate sources original to these compositions, from which they be-

---

[9] *Metrische Studien I-III* (1901-1907).
[10] *A Short Introduction to the Pentateuch* (1949), pp. 19f.
[11] *Die älteste Geschichtsschreibung und Prophetie Israels* (1910).
[12] *Zur Literaturkritik des Buches der Richter* (1926).
[13] *Die Samuelbücher* in *Kommentar zum AT* (ed. E. Sellin, 1926), vol. VII.
[14] *Die Überlieferung von der Thronnachfolge Davids* (1926).

lieved the extant documents had been formulated. While the application of form-critical principles was not intended in the first instance as a substitute for the Graf-Wellhausen hypothesis, its growth represented a decided reaction against an excessive preoccupation with the minutiae of literary analysis, and made abundantly clear the importance of certain considerations which fell outside the narrow concern of the Graf-Wellhausen scheme proper.

Although the methods employed by Gunkel and his followers represent a valuable contribution to the problem of determining how the various Old Testament books assumed their present form, there can be little doubt that Gunkel laid a disproportionate amount of emphasis upon what he considered to be the general usage in the matter of ancient literary styles. In this connection it ought to be noticed that the Psalms in particular frequently exhibit a considerable degree of independence from stylized literary conventions in the essentially personal nature of their approach to the problems of the spiritual life. Although it is true that certain literary sources are referred to in the historical writings, which may be taken as being representative of the underlying source material, there is little actual evidence for the contention of critical scholars that these existed for long periods in saga form, or that they were placed in juxtaposition mechanically to constitute a description of a particular period in the life of the nation. Indeed, certain histories, notably Chronicles, show marked indications of the personality of the compiler, who selected his material according to certain predetermined principles in order to present his readers with a particular metaphysical interpretation of the historical process.

C. EARLY TWENTIETH-CENTURY ATTACKS

The period of pure literary criticism as such may be said to have been concluded with two impressive works, Steuernagel's *Lehrbuch der Einleitung in das Alt Testament* (1912), which furnished a comprehensive and sympathetic consideration of the Graf-Wellhausen analytical scheme, and Sellin's *Einleitung in das Alte Testament* (1910), which argued convincingly against it at many points, including the question of the late dating assigned to Hexateuch sources, while at the same time accepting in general outline the developmental hypothesis.

Events took yet another turn just prior to World War I when Rudolph Smend published his work on the Hexateuch.[15] Although he professed adherence to the Graf-Wellhausen analytical patterns, he actually substituted a major modification of the original scheme in developing a theory advanced in 1885 by Charles Bruston. Smend maintained that there were two Jehovistic authors—whom he designated J[1] and J[2]—whose work

---

[15] *Die Erzählung des Hexateuchs auf ihre Quellen untersucht* (1912); cf. *ZAW*, XXXIX (1921), pp. 181ff.

was to be found throughout the entire Hexateuch. Whereas he regarded Deuteronomy and the Priestly material as exhibiting numerous additions, he denied that the Elohistic source had been supplemented in any way, and drew attention to the powerful literary execution of the document as a whole, a characteristic which he also attributed to the Jehovistic source.[16]

The suggestion of two Jehovistic authors was adopted by Eichrodt,[17] who undertook an analysis of the patriarchal narratives in order to establish this hypothesis. While his interests were of a primarily theological nature, he was at some pains to demonstrate the fact of growth and development, not merely in the historic beliefs of the Hebrews but also in the manner in which those beliefs had been transmitted and had assumed their definitive form. The theories of Smend and Eichrodt were given their fullest development in the work of Otto Eissfeldt, who in 1922 expounded what in fact was a five-document theory of Hexateuchal origins.[18] He followed the twofold division of the Jehovistic source suggested by Smend, but maintained that J^1 was the older of the two, and constituted a secular collection or "laity-source" (*Laienquelle*) which had originated during the semi-nomadic phase of Israelite history. Such material typified the Rechabite ideal, was uniformly hostile to Canaanite culture and religion, and constituted the polar extremity of the sacerdotal Priestly material. In his analysis Eissfeldt neglected Leviticus and the bulk of Deuteronomy almost entirely, preferring to base his contentions, like Eichrodt, upon the early chapters of Genesis. Such an approach to the problem reflected what has been described as an "atomizing of sources," a tendency which was fostered to some extent by the growth of form-criticism itself.

Persistent attacks upon the Graf-Wellhausen theory had been made from 1899 on by Wilhelm Möller, a scholarly pastor who had once been an ardent supporter of the documentary theory. His most important work, *Wieder den Bann der Quellenscheidung* (1912), subjected the critical hypothesis to a searching examination.[19] In repudiating its general approach to Pentateuchal problems, and arguing both for the unity and the Mosaic authorship of the Pentateuch, Möller explained the two divine names as being in fact indicative of two different functions. Thus *Elohim* was employed when the reference was to the activity of God in nature, whereas the tetragrammaton *YHWH* was used specifically of the God of revelation. Two years later Edward König criticized the Graf-Wellhausen scheme of literary analysis in a book[20] that also took Dahse

[16] *Die Erzählung des Hexateuchs auf ihre Quellen untersucht*, pp. 345ff.
[17] *Die Quellen der Genesis* (1918).
[18] *Hexateuch-Synopse* (1922).
[19] See also his *Are the Critics Right?* (1903).
[20] *Die Moderne Pentateuchkritik und ihre neueste Bekämpfung* (1914).

to task for his efforts to show how unreliable the divine names were as criteria for purposes of documentary analysis by comparing their incidence in the Massoretic text and in the LXX.

Although continental European scholars such as Kittel[21] and Gressmann[22] made it clear shortly after the end of World War I that the minutiae of literary-critical research had reached the limits of their usefulness, many British and American scholars continued to follow the patterns laid down by the Graf-Wellhausen school. British liberal scholarship, having erected its superstructure upon the foundation laid by S. R. Driver, was represented by the work of such men as G. B. Gray, J. Skinner, C. F. Burney, A. S. Peake, A. R. S. Kennedy, and G. A. Smith.[23] In the United States the leading advocates of the critical position included P. Haupt, who illustrated the principles of Biblical criticism by means of a gaily colored Polychrome Bible, J. A. Bewer, H. Preserved Smith, who subsequently became embroiled in controversy concerning his critical views, G. F. Moore, C. H. Toy, and C. C. Torrey.[24]

These and other scholars of like persuasion produced their major works in a period when the results of the literary-critical movement appeared to be solidly established for all time. In consequence, certain of the writings which emerged after World War I manifested a degree of arrogance and patronage towards those who adhered to different opinions, an unfortunate reflection on one of the less praiseworthy attributes of the Anglo-Saxon character. English liberal scholars were

---

[21] ZAW, XXXIX (1921), pp. 84ff.

[22] ZAW, XLII (1924), p. 8.

[23] Gray, *Hebrew Proper Names* (1896); in the *International Critical Commentary* series, *Numbers* (1903), *Isaiah, Chapters 1-27* (1912), and *Job* (with S. R. Driver, 1921). Skinner, *Isaiah I-XXXIX, XL-XLVI* in the Cambridge Bible series (1896-98); *A Critical and Exegetical Commentary on the Book of Genesis* (*ICC*, 1910); *I and II Kings* in the Century Bible series (n.d.); *Prophecy and Religion* (1922). Burney, *Notes on the Hebrew Text of the Books of Kings* (1903); *Israel's Hope of Immortality* (1909); *The Book of Judges* (1918). Peake, *The Problem of Suffering in the OT* (1904); *Job* and *Jeremiah* in the Century Bible series (1904-1911); *A Commentary on the Bible* (1919). Kennedy, *I and II Samuel* in the Century Bible series (n.d.); *The Book of Ruth* (1928). Smith, *Isaiah I-XXXIX, XL-XLVI* in *The Expositor's Bible* (n.d.); *The Book of the Twelve Prophets* (2 vols., 1896); *Deuteronomy* in the Cambridge Bible series (1918); *The Book of Isaiah* (2 vols., 1927).

[24] Haupt, *The Sacred Books of the OT* (1893); *The Book of Nahum* (1907). Bewer, in the *International Critical Commentary* series, *Obadiah and Joel* (1911), *Jonah* (1912); *The Literature of the OT* (1922). Smith, *Inspiration and Inerrancy* (1893); in the *ICC* series, *The Books of Samuel* (1899); *OT History* (1903); *The Religion of Israel: An Historical Study* (1914); for the reply to his critics see his *The Heretic's Defence: A Footnote to History* (1926). Moore, *Judges* (*ICC* series, 1895); *The Literature of the OT* (1928). Toy, *Judaism and Christianity* (1890); *Proverbs* (*ICC* series, 1899). Torrey, *The Composition and Historical Value of Ezra-Nehemiah* (1896); *Ezra Studies* (1910); *The Second Isaiah* (1928).

accustomed to adopt an attitude of condescension towards the views of more conservative writers if they did not ignore their work altogether, and the general impression which one derives from perusing the literature of the period is that of a completely unwarranted confidence in the evolutionary *Zeitgeist* and an uncritical acceptance of the hypotheses advanced by European scholars of the liberal variety.

In the United States there was a stronger and more vociferous group of conservative writers, and these men attacked the liberal position with great vigor and considerable learning, if not always with quite that degree of courtesy which the situation seemed to require. From this onslaught there emerged a continuing debate between what were rather derisively styled as "fundamentalists" and the exponents of the modern liberal approach to the understanding of Scripture. One of the most learned advocates of scholarly conservatism in the United States was Robert Dick Wilson, whose linguistic talents reputedly made him familiar with some forty-five languages and dialects. His *Studies in Daniel* made an attempt to maintain the traditional view of the authorship and date. Although he concentrated his work on Daniel, he wrote a great number of technical articles dealing with the problems of higher criticism generally, in which he frequently challenged the methods employed by the liberal school. The results of his studies were published in 1929[25] and formed an important contribution to the discussion of critical problems.

Despite the optimistic pronouncements of the advocates of literary-critical method, the results obtained by this approach were by no means as assured as many liked to think, and continued criticisms of the Graf-Wellhausen scheme were being made by European scholars as well as English-speaking conservative writers. What was tantamount to a denial that the Priestly Code ever existed as a literary corpus was made by Max Löhr in 1924. Although he recognized the existence of priestly interests in certain portions of the Pentateuchal writings, he advanced the view that Ezra had formulated the Torah from small groups of laws and narratives rather than from extended documentary sources.[26]

Still another attack upon the critical theories regarding the compilation of the Pentateuch was made by Volz, who questioned the unity of Priestly sources in Genesis and who joined with Rudolph in an examination of that book in order to determine the nature of the documentary substructure. They rejected the four-document hypothesis in favor of giving priority to the Jehovistic narrator, and on the basis of independent study they concluded that he had compiled his collection of ancient Hebrew traditions against a background of deep religious insight at some

---

[25] *A Scientific Investigation of the OT* (1929), rev. E. J. Young (1959).
[26] *Untersuchungen zum Hexateuchproblem, I: Der Priesterkodex in der Genesis,* BZAW, XXXVIII (1924).

time in the Solomonic era, welding his sources into one consecutive narrative. As far as Volz and Rudolph were concerned the Elohistic material had never enjoyed an independent existence as a document, and they maintained that those sections of Genesis which were usually assigned to Elohistic sources were either original portions of the Jehovistic narrative or the work of redactors who may have functioned during the time of King Josiah.[27]

This theory failed to gain wide acceptance among scholars. One of the most important reasons for this was that the authors had confined their work to Genesis, with Volz investigating chapters 15–36 and Rudolph studying the Joseph narratives. Feeling that the phenomena of Genesis alone were inadequate as a foundation for a theory involving the reconstruction of the Pentateuch as a whole, Rudolph subsequently extended the theory which he and Volz had adopted so that it embraced the remainder of the Hexateuch.[28] Unfortunately his analysis of the situation was gravely weakened by the fact that he almost completely neglected the corpus of legal material in the Pentateuch in favor of dealing with the narrative sections of the Hexateuch. In his work he again gave prominence to the Jehovistic narrator, and ascribed to his activity those passages and narratives which other scholars had attributed to Elohistic sources. Unlike Volz, however, he did not deny the existence of the Priestly Code, nor did he reject the basic premises of the Graf-Wellhausen analytical scheme.

A further important assault upon the unity of the proposed Genesis Priestly material resulted from the incisive observations of von Rad in 1934.[29] This eminent scholar sought to demonstrate that the P document actually consisted of two independent, although parallel, sources standing in juxtaposition. In his subsequent work, *Das formgeschichtliche Problem des Hexateuchs* (1938), he attempted to show the manner in which the Jehovistic author had unified the previously existing Hebrew literary sources and had given them the perspective of the traditions associated with the Exodus and Sinai on the one hand, and with the narratives of the patriarchal period on the other. The Jehovistic author, according to von Rad, augmented and organized this material in such a manner that the outworking of the divine purpose in history was clearly evident. Von Rad was careful to stress that, in his view, this concept was a marked feature of Israelite corporate existence from its earliest stages, and not a comparatively late development for which post-exilic priestly circles were responsible.

---

[27] Volz and Rudolph, *Der Elohist als Erzähler, ein Irrweg der Pentateuchkritik?*, *BZAW*, LXIII (1933), pp. 13ff. For a criticism of their views see *UP*, pp. 23f., and the review by R. E. Wolfe, *JBL*, LX (1941), pp. 417ff.

[28] W. Rudolph, *Der "Elohist" von Exodus bis Josua*, BZAW, LXVIII (1938).

[29] *Die Priesterschrift im Hexateuch* (1934).

D. THE PLACE OF DEUTERONOMY

Perhaps the most damaging assault of all on the Graf-Wellhausen hypothesis was the criticism levelled against the place accorded to Deuteronomy in the evolutionary scheme. For several decades scholars had become accustomed to think in terms of the religious reformation of King Josiah, about 630 B.C., and to insist that the basis of the revival was the centralization of worship in Jerusalem. On such a premise scholars had ventured to attempt something approaching an absolute dating of the various elements making up the Pentateuch,[30] but the hazards attached to this procedure became evident through the work of J. B. Griffiths.[31] A former adherent of the Graf-Wellhausen position, he argued from archaeological and philological considerations that Deuteronomy could not possibly have originated in the days of Josiah. To substantiate this contention he pointed out that scarcely more than three of the twenty-five laws that critical scholars regarded as being peculiar to the Deuteronomic legislation could have had any real significance for the circumstances obtaining in the days of Josiah, and even these three could have originated at an earlier period of Israelite history.

In 1919 Kegel examined the implications of the reformation under Josiah in a work that repudiated the theory that the "Book of the Law" was a recent composition that was being foisted upon the people of Judah by priestly interests, and argued convincingly for its antiquity and the general correctness of the historical narrative describing the event.[32] He also took issue with the critical contention that the purpose of the reformation was to restrict sacrificial worship to the central shrine in Jerusalem, and maintained instead that its primary aim was to remove alien religious practices from the cult itself, with other considerations assuming a secondary place. He insisted further that the newly discovered book must have consisted of the entire Torah rather than the book of Deuteronomy alone, positing an early date for the Law in its complete written form. That the document provoking the reforms of Josiah was in fact the whole Torah seems unlikely, however, as Gordon has indicated,[33] and in all probability comprised only one comparatively small portion of the Law.

In 1920, Kennett assigned a later dating to Deuteronomy than was commonly accepted by liberal scholars of the period, regarding it as a distinct product of the exilic age.[34] According to this view it was compiled by priestly circles in Palestine, and reflected Levitical interests predominantly. However, Kennett failed to account satisfactorily for the

---

[30] E.g. *IBOT*, pp. 57ff.

[31] *The Problem of Deuteronomy* (1911).

[32] *Die Kultus-Reformation des Josia* (1919).

[33] *IOTT*, p. 238.

[34] *Deuteronomy and the Decalogue* (1920); cf. his *OT Essays* (1928).

presence of such influential priestly groups in the ravaged land of Judah during the exilic period, and this unfortunate deficiency must be regarded as a serious flaw in his arguments. Despite this obvious weakness his theory attracted the attention of Hölscher, who in 1922 affirmed his belief that the Deuteronomic legislation could not possibly have originated until after the return from exile, thereby assigning Deuteronomy to a rather later period than Kennett had done.[35]

Hölscher questioned the common identification of the Priestly writings with the law code of Ezra, and completely opposed the views of the Graf-Wellhausen school by regarding Deuteronomy as fundamentally priestly rather than prophetic in character. He urged that the provisions of Deuteronomy were completely unsuited to a theory that placed their origin in the days of Josiah, and concluded that the idealistic nature of the legislation pointed to a time when the Judaean kingdom no longer existed and the people were in subservience to foreign domination. The vigor with which Hölscher proclaimed his convictions was not meant to be anti-critical in intention, but rather to serve as an improvement upon the speculations of the Graf-Wellhausen school. This laudable objective had a somewhat different effect, however, since any attempt to enhance a situation which had already reached the peak of its development was bound to constitute a criticism of it in one manner or another.

An opposite tendency regarding the dating of Deuteronomy became apparent the following year, when Oestreicher denied any connection between Deuteronomy and the reformation of Josiah.[36] He followed Kegel in the assumption that the purpose of the religious revival was the purification of the cultus rather than its centralization at any one shrine, and he emphasized that the reforming activities of Josiah applied to all the shrines in the kingdom of Judah. The result of his speculations was that he dated Deuteronomy well in advance of the age of Josiah. Such an attempt to overthrow the Wellhausenian position by striking what has been spoken of as its "Achilles heel" received powerful support from Staerk. The latter had already subjected Deuteronomy to a more minute analysis than had been customary among the adherents of the Graf-Wellhausen methodology, and had discovered traces of older legislation along with clear indications of editorial activity in successive periods.[37] In 1924 he openly disavowed any connection between Deuteronomy and the legal enactments that promoted the centralization of worship associated with the reforms of Josiah.[38] Like Oestreicher he assigned

---

[35] *Geschichte der israelitischen und jüdischen Religion* (1922), pp. 130ff., also, ZAW, XL (1922), pp. 161ff.

[36] *Das Deuteronomische Grundgesetz* (1923).

[37] *Das Deuteronomium: sein Inhalt und sein literarische Form* (1894). Similar conclusions were reached by J. Hempel, *Die Schichten des Deuteronomiums* (1914).

[38] Staerk, *Das Problem des Deuteronomiums* (1924).

Deuteronomy to a period long prior to the age of Josiah, and in this he was followed by Adam Welch, who advanced cogent arguments for a comparatively early date for the book of Deuteronomy, assigning it to the period of Samuel.[39]

Welch maintained that Deuteronomy consisted of many ancient legal principles which had circulated in the northern kingdom, and had originated as a result of prophetic censures of Baal worship. He insisted that the main point at issue in the book was not the conflict between one shrine and many shrines, but between the depraved Baal religion and the ancestral faith of the Israelites. The Mosaic authorship of Deuteronomy was again urged by Möller, who attempted to demonstrate the way in which Deuteronomy contained allusions to and implied the existence of the remainder of the Pentateuch.[40]

An important contribution to the study of the Deuteronomic problem was made by Edward Robertson, who in a series of studies undertaken between 1936 and 1949[41] maintained that Deuteronomy had been compiled by Samuel from the religious traditions associated with the local shrines prior to the Kingdom period. He emphasized the importance of the Samaritan sources for an understanding of the religious situation existing in Canaan before the time of King David,[42] and in this he was followed by Brinker,[43] who held that Samuel compiled Deuteronomy for the twelve tribes, as contrasted with the Priestly material of the Pentateuch, which he deemed to have originated in religious circles at Gibeon. The essential Mosaicity of Deuteronomy was also supported by an eminent Jewish scholar, J. H. Hertz, who reflected the traditions of Hoffmann[44] and Jacob[45] in his conservative commentary on the Pentateuch,[46] which gained wide scholarly acclaim.

G. von Rad also allied with those who repudiated the idea that Deuteronomy furnished the moral and legal impetus for the reforms of Josiah in a work published in 1947.[47] Using the principles of form-

---

[39] *The Code of Deuteronomy: A New Theory of Its Origin* (1924); see also his *Deuteronomy: The Framework to the Code* (1932) and in ZAW, XLIII (1925), pp. 250ff.

[40] W. Möller, *Rückbeziehungen des 5. Buches Mosis auf die vier ersten Bücher* (1925).

[41] *BJRL*, XX (1936), pp. 134ff., XXV (1941), pp. 182ff., XXVI (1942), pp. 369ff., XXVII (1943), pp. 359ff., XXX (1946), pp. 91ff., XXXIII (1949), pp. 19ff. These were subsequently published under the title *The OT Problem with Two Other Essays* (1950).

[42] *The OT Problem*, pp. 163ff.

[43] *The Influence of Sanctuaries in Early Israel* (1946).

[44] *Die wichtigsten Instanzen gegen die Graf-Wellhausensche Hypothese* (1916).

[45] *Quellenscheidung und Exegese im Pentateuch* (1916).

[46] J. H. Hertz, *The Pentateuch and Haftorahs* (5 vols., 1936; one-volume edition, 1937).

[47] *Deuteronomium Studien* (1947), E. tr., *Studies in Deuteronomy* (1953).

criticism with which he had previously investigated the composition of the Hexateuch, he emphasized that the tradition associated with the giving of the Law on Mount Sinai had been fostered at the religious center of Shechem.[48] It was against this kind of background that Deuteronomy was composed by a group of priests who were anxious to restore and maintain the traditions associated with the cultic center of the Israelite amphictyony.

Despite the diverse nature of the attacks made upon the Graf-Wellhausen theory and the manner in which they were presented,[49] the majority of liberal scholars remained unshaken in their adherence to the principles espoused by the literary-critical school.[50] In his presidential address to the Society for Old Testament Study[51] in 1924, A. S. Peake expressed himself as convinced that the main lines of the critical hypothesis were unassailable.[52] Recognizing that there were still scholars who were discovering new "documents" or sub-documents in various parts of the Pentateuch,[53] and the historical writings,[54] Peake was confident of the essential reasonableness of the moderate critical position.

E. The Liturgical Tradition—Mowinckel and His Followers

Peake apparently did not fully appreciate the significance of the researches being undertaken by those scholars who were following the methods laid down by Gunkel[55] and Gressmann in an attempt to trace the development of the units of tradition in a wider area than that of the Pentateuchal writings as such, and to reconstruct the original form of that tradition insofar as it was possible. Prominent in the search for cultic connections in relationship to Hebrew poetry was Sigmund Mowinckel, a brilliant Old Testament scholar, who in a series of studies on the Psalms[56] analyzed and discussed the various literary types before

---

[48] *Das formgeschichtliche Problem des Hexateuchs* (1938).

[49] Cf. J. E. McFadyen in *The People and the Book* (ed. A. S. Peake, 1925), pp. 183, 218f.

[50] E.g. D. C. Simpson, *Pentateuchal Criticism* (1914), rev. ed., 1924; G. B. Gray, *A Critical Introduction to the OT* (1913).

[51] For a survey of the history of this group see H. W. Robinson (ed.), *Record and Revelation* (1938), pp. 499ff.; G. H. Davies, *The Society for OT Study: A Short History, 1917-1950* (n.d.).

[52] *BJRL*, XII (1928), pp. 72f.

[53] E.g. J. Morgenstern, *HUCA*, IV (1926-1927), pp. 1ff.; R. H. Pfeiffer, ZAW, XLVIII (1930), pp. 66ff.; *PIOT*, pp. 159ff.

[54] O. Eissfeldt, *Die Quellen des Richterbuches* (1925); *Die Komposition der Samuelisbücher* (1931); cf. his *Einleitung in das AT* (1934), p. 306; *ETOT*, pp. 281ff.

[55] *Schöpfung und Chaos in Urzeit und Endzeit* (1895); *Genesis in Handkommentar zum AT* (ed. W. Nowack, 1901).

[56] *Psalmenstudien I-VI* (1921-1924).

attempting to interpret them in terms of pre-exilic sanctuary rituals and the like.

Whereas Gunkel had placed considerable stress upon the individual nature of Hebrew religious compositions, Mowinckel related them more consistently to the operation of social forces. He argued that, in ancient Israel, God was enthroned as universal king in a ritual which formed a prominent part of the autumn New Year festival. For him this was the cultic significance of the "enthronement psalms" or *Thronbesteigungs-lieder* (Pss. 47, 93, 97–99, 106:10ff.) that Gunkel had isolated, for which there was already a well-attested prototype from the Babylonian New Year festival.

Mowinckel assigned a date in the early monarchy for the origin of this festival in Israel,[57] but subsequently withdrew it.[58] He also identified an oracular type of Psalm (e.g. Pss. 60:6ff., 75, 82), which he held to have constituted the divine answers to the intercessions of the worshippers as pronounced by the cult-prophets attached to the various sanctuaries.[59] The weakness of his analysis seems to lie in his assumption that each class of Psalm was used for only one ritual occasion in the cults, an idea that led to the extremely questionable conclusion that every Psalm that spoke of God as creator or king was *ipso facto* to be relegated to the New Year enthronement-festival concept, and not to wider or more general circumstances.[60] His association of the prophets with the cultic shrines, however, was an advance upon earlier views,[61] which had generally stressed the denunciation of cult-worship by the prophets.

There seems little doubt on reflection that Mowinckel had been influenced by the opinions of Hugo Winckler, Alfred Jeremias, and Friedrich Delitzsch in his conjectures about the extent to which Israelite cultic worship reflected the Babylonian New Year festival customs. Winckler had suggested that Hebrew thought generally contained little that could be regarded as unique, and that in fact the Israelites were merely participating in a cultural situation common to all the nations of the ancient Near East.[62] Delitzsch developed the "pan-Babylonian" concepts of Winckler and precipitated a storm of controversy with his suggestion that anything of significance in the Old Testament was based upon earlier Babylonian ideas and practices.[63] Despite the attempts of

[57] *Ibid.*, II (1922), p. 204; cf. H. J. Kraus, *Worship in Israel* (1966), pp. 8f.
[58] *ZAW*, XLVIII (1930), p. 267.
[59] *Psalmenstudien III* (1923), pp. 20ff.
[60] Cf. Gunkel's criticisms, *Einleitung in die Psalmen* (1928-1933), pp. 100ff.
[61] E.g. J. Skinner, *Prophecy and Religion: Studies in the Life of Jeremiah* (1922), pp. 53ff.
[62] *Der alte Orient* (1901), III, pp. 2f.; *Geschichte Israels* (1900), II.
[63] *Babel und Bibel* (1902); cf. W. L. Wardle, *Israel and Babylon* (1925), pp. 301ff.

Jeremias to sustain the theory,[64] it lost favor when archaeologists and students of comparative religion demonstrated the extent to which Egyptian influence was evident in the life and thought of the ancient Hebrews.[65] With the work of Gunkel a more sober and balanced perspective replaced the sweeping generalizations of Winckler and his followers, and the "pan-Babylonian" movement faded into obscurity.

Following Mowinckel, numerous scholars sought to discover the liturgical usage of ancient traditions in other areas of the Old Testament. Thus P. Humbert postulated the theory that the first chapter of Genesis and Psalm 104 were recited ceremonially at an Israelite New Year festival, in accord with a similar Babylonian custom in which the creation epic was read aloud as part of the festive ritual.[66] In a comparable manner J. Pedersen ignored the classical analysis of the early chapters of Exodus for the purposes of his investigation, and treated that material as a literary unit which he thought was used as a cult-legend in the Passover celebrations.[67] So obsessed did some scholars become with the *Sitz im Leben des Volkes* concept that they even assigned an attested liturgical function to the documentary sources that had resulted from the critical studies of the Wellhausenian school, regardless of the fact that the material thus extracted from the Massoretic text furnished not the slightest hint of such a usage.[68]

A final application of the methodology pioneered by Gunkel was to the Pentateuch itself. The various laws enshrined in the Torah were subjected to attempts at classification by Jepsen[69] and Jirku,[70] who, working independently, followed the same general pattern of separating those laws that had demonstrable affinity with other ancient Near Eastern legislation from those that, because of their unique features, could be regarded as specifically Israelite in origin. This distinction was followed by Albrecht Alt, who in a treatise on the origins of Israelite law described the first of these categories as "casuistic" and the second

---

[64] *Das AT im Lichte des alten Orients* (1904), E. tr., *The OT in the Light of the Ancient East* (2 vols., 1911); *Handbuch der altorientalischen Geisteskultur* (1913).

[65] E.g. L. W. King, *A History of Babylon* (1915), pp. 291ff.; G. Foucart, *Histoire des religions et méthode comparative* (1912), pp. 305ff.; J. H. Breasted, *A History of Egypt* (1905), pp. 371ff., *The Dawn of Conscience* (1933), pp. 368, 384.

[66] Humbert, *RHPR*, XV (1935), pp. 1ff.

[67] Pedersen, *ZAW*, LII (1934), pp. 161ff.

[68] E.g. E. Sellin, *Einleitung in das AT* (1929 ed.), pp. 60f.; P. Humbert, *RHPR*, XII (1932), pp. 1ff. and *Problèmes du livre d'Habacuc* (1944); A. Haldar, *Studies in the Book of Nahum* (1947); I. Engnell, *BJRL*, XXXI (1948), pp. 54ff. and *The Call of Isaiah: An Exegetical and Comparative Study* (1949); A. Bentzen, *JBL*, LXVII (1948), pp. 37ff.; C. Lindhagen, *The Servant Motif in the OT* (1950); J. Lindblom, *The Servant Songs in Deutero-Isaiah* (1951).

[69] *Untersuchungen zum Bundesbuch* (1927).

[70] *Das weltliche Recht im AT* (1927).

as "apodictic."[71] The casuistic or case-law type is the dominant form of law known from the ancient Near East, as illustrated by the Hittite code, which emanates from the middle of the second millennium B.C. in Asia Minor, the Code of Hammurabi, which dates from seventeenth-century B. C. Babylonia, and some other older legislation from Mesopotamia. Because of its consonance with the Babylonian *Sitz im Leben des Volkes*, the "casuistic" group of Israelite enactments was alleged to be the earlier of the two groups isolated. On the other hand, the apodictic or categorical laws emanated from accredited priestly sources, and in consequence it seemed to Alt that they had originally constituted solemn prescriptions uttered in the course of priestly legislative functioning. Their life-situation was therefore religious, as opposed to the secular court-origin of the casuistic legislation.

Mowinckel had already anticipated the observations of Volz with regard to the Elohistic source. The former thought of the growth of that document in terms of an oral process extending over several centuries in the life of the southern kingdom.[72] As far as the promulgation of legalistic material was concerned, Mowinckel suggested that certain groups of legal-ceremonial prescriptions had been recited as a preliminary to ritual observances at the shrines. Allowing for procedural variations, he held that probably more than one decalogue had been in existence, and that, if this had actually been the case, the content might well have exhibited a certain degree of variation in different parts of the country.[73]

In separating the smaller units of Hebrew law from the Priestly Code, Eissfeldt had concluded that they represented the literary product of earlier legislative activity at the local shrines. He also felt that they reached back even further to the stage when they were transmitted simply in the form of oral tradition.[74] Noth developed this general concept to indicate the manner in which Israelite law was thought to have grown through the legislative activities of the priests at the sanctuaries or at the city gates, and related the entire creative process to the Hebrew cultural situation.[75] In a somewhat similar manner Begrich saw the development of the Torah in terms of a process of oral transmission, during which the legal traditions of the Israelite priests were handed down over a period of many generations and enlarged in matters of

---

[71] *Die Ursprünge des israelitischen Rechts* (1934), pp. 12ff.; cf. W. F. Albright, *JBL*, LV (1936), pp. 164ff.

[72] *ZAW*, XLVIII (1930), pp. 233ff.

[73] Cf. Mowinckel, *Le décalogue* (1927), pp. 154ff., also in *ZAW*, LV (1937), pp. 218ff.

[74] *Einleitung in das AT* (1934 ed.), pp. 26ff.; *ETOT*, pp. 212ff.

[75] *Die Gesetze im Pentateuch* (1940); also Köhler, *ZAW*, XXXIV (1914), p. 146.

detail to suit the needs of a developing social and religious economy.[76]

F. HISTORICAL ANTHROPOLOGY

At the beginning of the twentieth century the researches of Tylor,[77] Robertson Smith, and Frazer were modified by an approach that placed less emphasis upon individual primitive psychology and devoted increasing attention to the place that the forces of society as a whole occupied in the formulation of religious beliefs and customs. Wilhelm Wundt was the first to stress the importance of group-experience as a formative influence in the growth of primitive psychology.[78] His theories were developed by Durkheim[79] and his followers, who associated such concepts as *mana*[80] with the dynamics of group life. Lévy-Bruhl pointed to the essential unity of those forces upon which the individual drew for his magical rites, and which at the same time furnished the basis for collective religious functioning, by showing that, for primitive man, causation resulted from the activity of invisible animistic forces which were deemed to be at work in the natural environment.[81]

Praiseworthy as all these theories were, they suffered from the basic defect of the nineteenth-century *Zeitgeist*, namely the endeavor on the part of scholars to explain the incidence of all phenomena in terms of one relatively uncomplicated single feature, process, or principle. In the biological sphere the concepts of organic evolution as expounded by Darwin and Wallace were held to constitute the key to terrestrial and human origins alike, while in the burgeoning realm of psychological study the dominant principle of human motivation was held by Freud to be intimately related to primitive sexual urges buried deep in the unconscious mind. As far as Old Testament studies were concerned, the one basic principle upon which an understanding of the origins of Israelite literature depended had been expounded at length by Graf and

[76] In *Werden und Wesen des AT* (ed. P. Volz, 1936), pp. 63ff. On oral transmission cf. *FSAC*, pp. 64ff., S. Gandz, *Osiris* (1939), VII, pp. 415ff.

[77] *Researches into the Early History of Mankind and the Development of Civilisation* (1865), *Primitive Culture: Researches into the Development of Mythology, Philosophy, Religion, Language, Art and Custom* (1871), and *Anthropology* (1881).

[78] *Völkerspsychologie* (2 vols, 1900-1909).

[79] *Les formes élémentaires de la vie religieuse* (1912), E. tr. J. W. Swain, *The Elementary Forms of the Religious Life* (1915).

[80] R. H. Codrington, *The Melanesians: Studies in Their Anthropology and Folklore* (1891).

[81] Cf. Lévy-Bruhl, *Les fonctions mentales dans les sociétés inférieures* (1910), E. tr. *How Natives Think* (1926); *L'âme primitive* (1923), E. tr. *The Soul of the Primitive* (1928); *La mentalité primitive* (1922), E. tr. *Primitive Mentality* (1923). In *Les Carnets de Lucien Lévy-Bruhl* (1949), published after his death, Lévy-Bruhl abandoned the principal lines of the argument he had expressed in *Les fonctions mentales dans les sociétés inférieures*.

Wellhausen; in the field of anthropology the unifying factor which was popularly alleged to underlie all primitive religious activity was being interpreted by scholars in terms of concepts such as *mana,* magic, tabu, and the like.

The error of this type of approach became evident—to students of anthropology at least—when it was discovered that, as research progressed, it was increasingly impossible to relate the phenomena of primitive life to one comprehensive principle of interpretation. An attempt to remedy the deficiencies of theoretical anthropology was made by Franz Boas,[82] who rejected the idea of primitive culture as a general condition characteristic of all mankind in favor of an approach which studied patterns of culture in specific geographic areas and related them to corresponding cultural phenomena in neighboring localities.

The application of historical method in anthropology to the problems of early Semitic religion was undertaken by S. A. Cook in a series of studies prefacing the third edition of *Lectures on the Religion of the Semites,* by Robertson Smith. Recognizing the close interrelationship that Smith had pointed out between secular and sacred in primitive life, Cook saw that such situations were typified by a remarkable degree of complexity. For him, therefore, the problem did not consist so much of postulating some sort of evolutionary process from comparatively simple to more highly differentiated forms as of making some attempt to assess the significance of individual cultural patterns as they were related to the larger environment of society.[83]

A development of this concept occurred in the work of the so-called "myth and ritual" school under the leadership of the British scholar S. H. Hooke, who has been called the "high priest" of cultic patternism. Basing their conclusions on the theory that there had been a diffusion of one cultural pattern of ritual mythology throughout the religions of the ancient Near East, Hooke and his followers applied the form-critical techniques employed by Mowinckel in an attempt to show that a recognizable set of rituals and myths had been the common property of the various ancient Near Eastern cultures.[84] Although these scholars did not go to the extremes of the "pan-Babylonian" school, they stressed that all mythical conceptions had their origin in cultic rites, and that Hebrew myths and rituals, particularly those connected with sacral kingship and

---

[82] *The Mind of Primitive Man* (1911), *Anthropology and Modern Life* (1932), and in *American Anthropologist,* XXII (1920), pp. 311ff.; cf. A. Goldenweiser, *Early Civilisation* (1922).

[83] Cf. S. A. Cook (ed.), *Lectures on the Religion of the Semites* (1927 ed.), pp. xlvi, 590ff.; his articles in *Cambridge Ancient History* (1923), I, pp. 182ff., and in *The People and the Book* (ed. A. S. Peake, 1925), pp. 42ff.

[84] Hooke (ed.), *Myth and Ritual: Essays on the Myth and Ritual of the Hebrews in Relation to the Cultic Pattern of the Ancient East* (1933), *The Labyrinth: Further Studies in the Relation Between Myth and Ritual in the Ancient World* (1935).

the so-called "enthronement festival," were intimately connected with similar concepts in the thought of other Near Eastern peoples, particularly those of Babylonia.

Hooke endeavored to establish a parallel between the Hebrew pre-exilic Feast of Asiph, or Ingathering, and the Babylonian *akîtu* or New Year festival.[85] The latter consisted of a dramatic re-enactment of the role which the king played in community life as the "divine figure," and the ritual patterns involved a representation of the death and resurrection of the god, the deification of the king, the recitation of the creation myth,[86] a ritual battle between the deity and his enemies in which the god emerged victorious, a sacred marriage, a triumphal procession in which the king acted as a substitute for the personage of the deity, and an emphasis upon the importance of the royal personage for communal well-being.[87]

There is evidence for the belief that Babylonian myths were used in conjunction with accredited Mesopotamian rituals of a religious nature, as King showed,[88] but there is almost no ground at all for attempting to discern elements of the Babylonian *akîtu* rituals either in the pre-exilic Feast of Ingathering or in its post-exilic counterpart, the three festivals of Tishri, as Snaith has remarked.[89] Thus, in the end the findings of Hooke are just as subjective and just as inadequately grounded as those of Mowinckel.

However, the hypothesis that a pattern of myth and ritual was associated with regnal functions was explored by several other scholars. Following Mowinckel, the general position of the king in relation to the New Year rituals in Jerusalem was examined by Morgenstern,[90] who concluded that the king served as chief priest of the nation. This process was taken a step further by A. R. Johnson,[91] who claimed that there were distinct points of contact between the Israelite New Year festival and the Babylonian *akîtu* ceremonies, particularly with regard to the person and function of the king in Israel, whom he alleged to have been regarded as the responsible agent for communal prosperity and the symbol of national virility for the ensuing year. Again, this theory was

[85] For a description of this ceremony see S. A. Pallis, *The Babylonian Akitu Festival* (1926), pp. 250ff.; cf. H. Zimmern, *Das Babylonische Neujahrsfest* (1926).

[86] Cf. Hooke, *The Origins of Early Semitic Ritual* (1938), pp. 16ff.

[87] Cf. Hooke in *Journal of the Manchester Egyptian and Oriental Society*, XIII (1927), pp. 29ff.

[88] *The Legends of Babylon and Egypt in Relation to Hebrew Tradition* (1918), pp. 50f.

[89] In H. W. Robinson (ed.), *Record and Revelation*, p. 260.

[90] In *AJSL*, LV (1938), pp. 1ff., 183ff., 360ff.

[91] A. R. Johnson in *The Labyrinth* (ed. S. H. Hooke), pp. 71ff.; cf. Johnson's article in *ET*, LXII (1950-1951), pp. 36ff.

based upon pure conjecture, and could not be substantiated at any point by concrete evidence from the Old Testament.

Hooke subsequently modified his views on cultic patternism in a series of essays published in 1956, in which he conceded a certain nucleus of law and custom as uniquely Mosaic, while at the same time viewing the bulk of Israelite worship and cultic forms in the light of Egyptian and Babylonian ritual and liturgical patterns.[92] In the meantime Cook had put the comparative method of anthropological study to better use by endeavoring to show that, though many concepts in the Old Testament narratives could be paralleled by similar ideas in other ancient Near Eastern religions, they may well have undergone a process of transformation and change during the early period of Hebrew history to the point where, in their final form, they had acquired a uniquely Israelite character.[93]

A further attempt by Mowinckel to throw light upon the religious development of ancient Israel utilized the approach of earlier anthropologists in speculating upon the place of magic in religious activity. He argued for the influence of pagan magical concepts in Hebrew cultic life by interpreting the term "evil" in certain psalms of petition as a reference to the practice of magic. Similarly he held that the rituals of blessing and cursing found in the Psalter and elsewhere presupposed the activity of magical practitioners. However, as Gunkel pointed out,[94] Mowinckel was wrong in assuming that magical rites and customs had survived for a longer period than that generally indicated by the historical records of the Hebrew people. Hempel[95] adhered to the view that although some of the formulas of malediction and benediction may have been motivated by considerations of magic in the distant past, their presence in the religious activities of the Hebrew monarchy suggested that they had become orthodox in nature, and that their religious content was genuine.

G. Old Testament Sociology

Whereas the comparative study of Near Eastern religions and the growth of form criticism had been largely concerned with the cultural roots of characteristic Hebrew religious concepts and with attempts to relate particular cultic manifestations to the life-situations of social groups, there was no branch of study readily established which would consider the sociological background of Hebrew culture as a uniquely religious manifestation. Although one or two authors had written on the

---

[92] Hooke, *The Siege Perilous: Essays in Biblical Anthropology and Kindred Subjects* (1956), pp. 173ff.

[93] Cook, *The OT: A Reinterpretation* (1936), pp. 88ff.

[94] *Einleitung in die Psalmen* (1928), pp. 196ff.

[95] In *ZDMG*, LXXIX (1925), pp. 20ff.

general subject of social customs among the ancient Israelites,[96] little attempt had been made to relate questions of social organization to the growth of Hebrew religion. The first serious efforts expended in this direction were the sociological studies of Max Weber,[97] who employed the results of the Graf-Wellhausen school to interpret the economic situation obtaining at an early period of Hebrew history. Weber stressed the significance of the Covenant as an important agent for insuring political and social solidarity in the pre-monarchical period and was the first scholar to speak of the leadership which obtained during the Judges era as "charismatic" in nature.[98] He also held to the view that the great majority of the prophetic protests about social conditions were the result of popular accommodation to the existing social, rather than religious, configurations of the native Canaanites.[99] In general he sought to show that new perspectives on Hebrew history could be obtained by envisaging the development of national life against a background of tensions furnished by the interaction of urban Canaanite organization within the radically different sociological pattern of family and tribe exhibited by the Israelites.

This theme was expounded by Adolphe Lods,[100] and to a lesser extent also by Causse,[101] both of whom emphasized the part that the prophets played in an attempt to restore the "nomadic ideal" in preference to the urban civilization of Canaan. But they also made it clear that the prophets were more than potential social reformers; they proclaimed high standards of personal morality and made the ethical concept of righteousness a consideration of paramount importance. Although this exposition of the religio-historical situation suffers from the assumption of the Graf-Wellhausen school that the prophets—particularly those of the eighth century B.C.—were the first to formulate a doctrine of ethical monotheism, its general approach was of great value in that it drew attention to the importance of yet another aspect of the *Sitz im Leben des Volkes.*

[96] E.g. J. Fenton, *Early Hebrew Life: A Study in Sociology* (1880) and P. J. Baldensperger, *The Immovable East. Studies of the People and Customs of Palestine* (1913).

[97] Especially his *Gesammelte Aufsätze zur Religionssoziologie* (3 vols., 1920-1921), E. tr. T. Parsons, *The Protestant Ethic and the Spirit of Capitalism* (1936).

[98] Cf. Weber, *Grundriss der Sozialökonomik* (1922), III, pp. 140ff. He was followed in this by A. Alt, *Die Staatenbildung der Israeliten in Palästina* (1930), pp. 7ff., 16ff.

[99] Weber, *Gesammelte Aufsätze*, III, pp. 120ff., 290ff.

[100] *Israël des origines au milieu du VIIIe siècle* (1930), E. tr. S. H. Hooke, *Israel from its Beginnings to the Middle of the Eighth Century* (1932); *Les prophètes d'Israël et les débuts du judaisme* (1935), E. tr. Hooke, *The Prophets of Israel* (1937).

[101] *Du groupe ethnique à la communauté religieuse* (1937).

The most prominent scholar in the United States to give consideration to questions of Old Testament sociology was Louis Wallis, an erudite thinker who owed much of his inspiration to the work of Weber. Over a period of thirty years he published several works dealing with the process by which Hebrew religion was thought to have originated and developed.[102] Like others of his generation Wallis tended to look for a single interpretative principle that could be applied readily to the phenomena of the historical situation in order to resolve them into some sort of consistent pattern. In consequence he inclined to the view that the kind of ethical monotheism that the eighth- and seventh-century B.C. prophets proclaimed was the result of the clash between the economic ideals of settled Canaanite society and the more austere morality of the Hebrew Wilderness code.

In adopting this position Wallis overlooked the fact that Israel's violation of the fundamental provisions of the Sinai Covenant was the real issue at stake in the minds of the prophets, and that questions dealing with social inequality and injustice were merely secondary manifestations of the larger issue. Like others of his day, Wallis erred in failing to take account of the growing body of extra-Biblical evidence, which in his case threw direct light upon the religious and social forms of ancient Canaan.[103] His position with regard to the nature of the local Baals was essentially that of the Wellhausen school, a position that has had to be revised drastically as a result of the archaeological discoveries at Ras Shamra (Ugarit).[104] Perhaps the greatest deficiency in the approach adopted by Wallis was that its author, like so many of his contemporaries, failed to accommodate his own speculations to the evidence furnished by the discoveries of archaeologists.

This deficiency was remedied to a considerable extent by the researches of Graham,[105] although he too was hampered by an uncritical acceptance of the theory that monotheism was the end-result of a slow process of growth from rudimentary theological principles. He rejected Wallis' suggestion that monotheism had emerged from something like a "class struggle" between the sedentary Canaanites and the semi-nomadic Israelites, preferring to consider instead the possibility of a genetic relationship between the Hebrew faith and the Ras Shamra cultus. He thought of the work of the prophets as a regenerating activity, bringing new life to the cultural and religious patterns of Palestine, which had begun to disintegrate somewhat prior to the founding of the monarchy. The new social ideal of such prophetic functioning primarily stressed personal

---

[102] A *Sociological Study of the Bible* (1912), *God and the Social Process* (1935), *The Bible Is Human* (1942).

[103] Cf. H. G. May in *Journal of Bible and Religion*, XII (1944), pp. 98ff.

[104] Cf. W. F. Albright in *Religion in Life*, XXI, No. 4 (1952), pp. 544f.

[105] In *Journal of Religion*, XIV (1934), pp. 306ff., also his *The Prophets and Israel's Culture* (1934).

values, according to Graham, and demanded an opportunity for the development of the individual human spirit.[106] As a sociological appraisal of the contribution of the prophets to their own life and times, his researches exhibited remarkable deficiencies, the chief of which was his inability to recognize that the prophets of Israel were not so much social reformers as evangelists, calling men to a new way of life based upon repentance and faith rather than on the amelioration of social evils.

A more successful interpretation of the prophetic situation was furnished by S. W. Baron, who stressed the essentially "chosen" nature of the Israelites as an important element in the unfolding of the divine plan for human history.[107] The destiny of the Hebrew people was to be a "light to the nations," and this was firmly grounded upon an historical monotheism whose original formulation constituted part of the work of Moses. The prophets uttered their oracles in order to call the people back to an observance of their commitments under the Covenant relationship. In process of this they elaborated upon the monotheistic theme found in the Torah. Prominent in their teaching was the assertion that, if the ethical ideals of Sinai were taken to heart, the issues of social justice, which were intimately bound up with the concept of the Covenant, would manifest themselves in the normal behavior of the people.

From a different sociological standpoint the present writer attempted an inquiry as to the extent to which, if at all, the influence of the ancient Egyptian matriarchate could be traced in the social configurations of the early monarchy.[108] The *Sitz im Leben des Volkes* approach virtually demanded an explanation different from those normally tendered for certain facets of the relationships existing between David and Saul, and for such events as the violation of Tamar by her half-brother Amnon (2 Sam. 13:2ff.). Accordingly it was felt that the best way of accounting for these and other apparently peculiar forms of social behavior was to postulate the influence in southern Palestine of a traditional Egyptian sociological phenomenon in which all real property and inheritance generally descended through the female of the line rather than through the male.[109]

Definite traces of matriarchal patterns appear during the period of the early monarchy, but a fuller demonstration is hampered by lack of

[106] Graham, *The Prophets and Israel's Culture*, pp. 86ff.

[107] *A Social and Religious History of the Jews* (3 vols., 1937; rev. ed., 2 vols., 1952).

[108] R. K. Harrison, *EQ*, XXIX (1957), pp. 29ff. and *A History of OT Times* (1957), pp. 143f., 150ff.

[109] For the concept of *Mutterrecht* in Egypt see A. Erman and H. Ranke, *Ägypten und Ägyptisches Leben im Altertums* (1923), pp. 175ff.; J. Černý and T. E. Peet, *JEA*, XIII (1927), pp. 30ff.; J. Černý, *Bulletin de l'Institut Français d'Archéologie Orientale*, XXXVII (1937-1938), pp. 41ff.; A. Gardiner, *JEA*, XXVI (1940), pp. 23ff.; J. Černý, *JEA*, XL (1954), pp. 23ff.

evidence in certain important areas. Thus it is impossible to be sure that the person named Ahinoam, who was married to David (1 Sam. 25:43), was identical with Ahinoam daughter of Ahimaaz and wife of Saul, which is important for the theory of matriarchal descent and the consequent inheritance by David of the Israelite throne. Again, there is some doubt as to the identity of Maachah, daughter of Absalom, who in 2 Samuel 14:27 is called Tamar and in 2 Chronicles 11:21 was known as Maachah, the favored spouse of Rehoboam.[110] However, if the ancient Egyptian matriarchate did in fact exert some influence in Canaan during the immediate premonarchic period, its recognition would help to clarify some of the issues involved in regal succession during the early monarchy.

The social organization of the early settlement period was examined in the light of form-critical procedures by Albrecht Alt and Martin Noth in studies that have exerted considerable influence in the world of Old Testament scholarship. The wide difference in political structure and social configuration between the Palestinian peoples and those of Transjordan in the eleventh century B.C. was pointed out by Alt,[111] who contrasted the various social forms with what he called the "charismatic" leadership in Israel during the period of the Judges,[112] which for him constituted the basic political organizational form among the early Israelites. Alt also held that the apodictic legislation of the Torah, with its reflection of a monotheism characterized by an advanced ethical content, was specifically Israelite in nature, and maintained that much of it could be assigned with confidence to Moses. He further stated that the sociological phenomenon of the "Judges" was in all probability the channel through which such casuistic legal material as that found in the Book of the Covenant (Exod. 21–23) penetrated to Israel.[113] Alt appears to have followed Max Weber in regarding the leadership which obtained during the era of the Judges as "charismatic." In this and other areas he was evidently attempting to relate Israelite institutions to the traditions of the Heroic Age, but he missed the essential point, common to the Mycenaean age and the Judges period, that the Judges were not inspired leaders produced from the proletariat by some kind of divine afflatus, but were in fact accredited members of the aristocracy, from whom leadership invariably came.[114]

Alt and his followers also stressed the comparatively uncomplicated social and political status of early Israel in their studies relating to the organizational system of the tribes. They pointed out that the nation con-

---

[110] Cf. 1 Kgs. 15:10; *AJ*, VII, 8, 5; VII, 10, 3.

[111] *Die Staatenbildung der Israeliten in Palästina*, pp. 31ff.

[112] *Ibid.*, pp. 16ff.

[113] Alt, *Die Ursprunge des israelitischen Rechts* (1934), pp. 31ff.

[114] Cf. *GBB*, pp. 295ff., also Gordon in *Biblical and Other Studies* (ed. A. Altmann, 1963), p. 12.

sisted of several tribes or "clan-groups," traditionally twelve in number, which were bound together by the religious provisions of the Covenant relationship and were associated with a central sanctuary at Shiloh. Alt thought of this tribal organization in terms of an amphictyony, following the social structures of certain Aegean people; and Noth elaborated upon this general theme.

Making the Covenant ideal the basis for this kind of social formulation in Israel, Noth argued from what he regarded as the original form of the sources to the conclusion that the tradition of the "twelve" tribes had begun in the period of charismatic rule,[115] and that it constituted an enumeration of an early Hebrew amphictyonic association.[116] In this area of investigation Noth supported the general historical process entertained by Caspari,[117] who had maintained that the Covenant concept took its rise from a religious league that was in existence prior to the settlement of Israel in Canaan, while at the same time he made it fundamental to the organization of the amphictyony.[118] These conclusions are open to serious criticism on historical and other grounds, and fail to take sufficient cognizance of the great antiquity of the covenant-form in the Near East. Despite this, however, the work of Alt and Noth proved to be of value in bringing some semblance of order to bear upon the decidedly confused picture that had emerged of the Judges period as the result of critical studies. For liberal scholars in particular the studies of Alt and Noth succeeded in showing the manner in which form criticism had availed to throw light upon the origin and meaning of important areas in the historical tradition of the Hebrew people, which had previously been rejected by advocates of the Graf-Wellhausen hypothesis as unhistorical and untrustworthy as sources for purposes of reconstructing historical sequences.[119]

H. OLD TESTAMENT ARCHAEOLOGY

The discovery of numerous literary artifacts in Mesopotamia, Palestine, Egypt, and elsewhere in the Near East during the middle and latter portion of the nineteenth century had demonstrated beyond question the immense antiquity of writing, and had also furnished material which supplemented and corroborated the historical data of the Old Testament

---

[115] For the dating of the city-lists in Joshua 15 to the period of Josiah see Alt, *Kleine Schriften zur Geschichte des Volkes Israel* (1953), II, pp. 276ff.

[116] Noth, *Das System der zwölf Stämme Israels* (1930), pp. 39ff.

[117] *Die Gottesgemeinde von Sinai und das nachmalige Volk Israel* (1922), pp. 15ff., 137f.

[118] Cf. M. Noth, *Zeitschrift für die Deutschen Palästina-Vereins*, LVIII (1935), pp. 185ff.

[119] For a critical evaluation of the school of Alt and Noth see J. Bright, *Early Israel in Recent History Writing* (1956), pp. 79ff. For a criticism of the conclusions regarding the border-lists of the tribes see S. Mowinckel, *Zur Frage nach dokumentarischen Quellen in Josua 13-19* (1946).

in certain significant areas. Some of the material made reference to events that were not recorded in the Massoretic text, such as the fact that Ahab was an important military leader in the battle of Qarqar (853 B.C.), and that Jehu had paid tribute to Shalmaneser III rather than oppose him. The dramatic discoveries of Layard at Nineveh[120] had excited wide interest in the nature of Mesopotamian antiquities, and this was sustained by the researches of Sir Henry Rawlinson and J. E. Taylor, who visited Ur and other Babylonian sites from 1849 on.

A decade earlier Rawlinson had translated some two hundred lines of the bilingual inscription of Darius the Great at Behistun, which he had copied at considerable risk to his life when he served as British Representative at Baghdad. When the syllabic nature of cuneiform was recognized by Edward Hincks in 1847, it was merely a question of time before the true values of a great many combinations of wedges were known. The translation of cuneiform took a dramatic step forward with the work of George Smith, an engraver employed by the British Museum, who in the course of his duties recognized and deciphered the celebrated Babylonian Deluge tablets, publishing his results in 1872. From that time on the study of cuneiform was assigned a degree of importance only accorded previously to the language of ancient Egypt, and it remained for the philologists to exploit the situation as fully as possible.

Despite the establishment of the Palestine Exploration Fund in 1865, and the spectacular discovery by Clermont-Ganneau of the famous Moabite Stone,[121] the unearthing of significant archaeological material from Palestinian sources lagged far behind similar activity in other areas of the Near East. A discouragement to Biblical scholars was the fact that the Graf-Wellhausen school mostly ignored the possible effect which extra-Biblical sources might have as a control over the more extravagant use of purely theoretical speculations, an attitude that was still maintained when Winckler[122] so dramatically disproved the contentions of liberal scholars concerning the place which the Hittites occupied in ancient Near Eastern history.[123] What was perhaps even more calamitous was the tendency of European scholars generally to describe such archaeological artifacts from Palestine of which they took cognizance as though they were merely "antiquities."[124]

---

[120] *Nineveh and Its Remains* (2 vols., 1849).

[121] C. S. Clermont-Ganneau, *La Stèle de Mésa* (1887).

[122] *Sonderabzug aus der Orientalistischen Litteratur Zeitung*, Dec. 15, 1906; *Mitteilungen der Deutschen Orientgesellschaft*, XXXV (1907), pp. 1ff.; Winckler and Puchstein, *Smithsonian Report for 1908*, pp. 677ff.

[123] It was left for S. R. Driver (*Modern Research as Illustrating the Bible* [1909]) to correct this tendency.

[124] E.g. W. Nowack, *Lehrbuch der hebräischen Archäologie* (2 vols., 1894); I. Benzinger, *Hebräische Archäologie* (1894; rev. ed., 1927).

Palestinian archaeology as such finally came into its own after World War I with the carefully disciplined pragmatic approach of the American excavators. Chief among these towered the figure of W. F. Albright, the foremost Biblical archaeologist of the century, a man who combined prodigious mental capacities with unusual linguistic talents, reputedly being familiar with over twenty-five languages and dialects. As one of his students, John Bright, has remarked, Albright's innumerable contributions to linguistic science, Biblical archaeology, and the entire field of ancient oriental history have enabled him to exercise an influence over Old Testament studies in particular of a more abiding nature than that of probably any other single scholar in the twentieth century.[125]

Albright first went to Palestine in 1919 as a Fellow of the American Schools of Oriental Research. He quickly surpassed his teachers, who included W. J. Phythian-Adams, H. Vincent, and C. S. Fisher. With his emphasis upon careful ceramic study he ushered in a new era of archaeological activity in Palestine, and it was as a result of his unremitting labors that Palestinian archaeology finally attained its majority between 1920 and 1940.[126] In particular, the general pattern of life in the Middle Bronze Age is now well attested, due in no small measure to the efforts of Albright, as is also the broad outline of Biblical chronology. Since Albright is, as one of his pupils has described him, conservative but critically informed,[127] he was able to attract the more conservative students as well as those who, although liberal by training, were aware of the inadequacies of the Graf-Wellhausen categories of method and interpretation, and who wished to pursue a more independent approach to the problems of the Old Testament text. A major effect of the work of Albright has been that all books written before 1940 about the themes of Old Testament history and archaeology must be regarded as obsolete.

Shortly after World War I Kittel[128] and Gressmann[129] suggested that the future course of Old Testament studies would be marked by an increasing use of new material, including the utilizing of archaeology as a method of external control, as well as a study of ancient Near Eastern culture as a whole with a view to determining the true theological outlook of the Old Testament writers. These predictions were borne out to a very large extent by subsequent events, due again in no small measure to the work of Albright and his pupils. Archaeological activity has now furnished a vast amount of material which enables a reasonably precise picture of life in the lands of the Bible to be drawn as far back as

---

[125] *BANE*, p. 13. A biographical sketch appears in *History, Archaeology and Christian Humanism* (1964), pp. 301ff. A bibliography of Albright's works from 1911 through May 1958 is assembled as Appendix II of *BANE*, pp. 363ff.

[126] *BANE*, pp. 73f.

[127] D. N. Freedman, in *BANE*, p. 203.

[128] *ZAW*, XXXIX (1921), pp. 84ff.

[129] *ZAW*, XLII (1924), pp. 1ff.

the Neolithic period, and perhaps even beyond. Comparative studies have resulted in a substantial correlation of Palestinian culture with its counterparts in Egypt, Asia Minor, the Aegean, and Mesopotamia. In consequence the background against which the events narrated in the Old Testament took place has been widened immeasurably since the days of Wellhausen, so that it is now possible to reconstruct entire periods of Old Testament history in a manner unknown to earlier generations of scholars.

Despite the overwhelming nature of much of the evidence, however, there are still some who prefer subjective speculations to control by extraneous factors such as archaeology. Chief among these are the followers of Albrecht Alt, who in particular exercise a studied disregard for the evidence presented by archaeological excavations in relationship to whole periods of time, such as, for example, the Middle Bronze Age (ca. 2100-1550 B.C.), except on those rather rare occasions when some especial facet of the discipline happens to suit their purposes. Such an attitude overlooks the important fact that the present age is no longer one of the "grand design," in which facts must be made to conform to an *a priori* theory of one kind or another, or else be disregarded completely if they prove to be embarrassing to the theoretician.[130]

One of the most important benefits of archaeological studies is that they have given the *Sitz im Leben des Volkes* approach a dimension which could scarcely have been imagined in the days of Gunkel. The evaluation of the many cultural facets evident in the pattern of ancient Near Eastern life will undoubtedly contribute much additional information as linguistic, historical, religious, and other studies progress, and no approach to the problems of the Old Testament can be regarded as legitimate or valid unless it is firmly based upon an appreciation of the contribution which archaeology has to make. It should be observed, however, that the basic function of this latter discipline is to illumine the general background of Old Testament events, and not to "prove" the truth of particular happenings as such. The integrity of Biblical scholarship is now generally such that, given the basic facts, the "truth" can usually be relied upon to follow without undue difficulty. Although there will always be the tendency in some quarters to restrict the study of archaeology to a technical examination of artifacts and stratigraphic levels, there can be little doubt that such major discoveries as those at Mari, Nuzu, Ugarit, and Qumran will emphasize the necessity for comprehensiveness in study rather than the more restricted approach of much earlier writing in the Old Testament field.

[130] Cf. M. Noth, *PJB*, XXXIV (1938), pp. 7ff.; *GI*, pp. 70f.

IV. OLD TESTAMENT SCHOLARSHIP
SINCE WORLD WAR I

A. The 1930s

The rise of particularized methods of Biblical study did not deter independent criticism of the classical scheme of Pentateuchal analysis. In 1931 Wilhelm Möller followed his earlier defense of the Mosaic authorship of the Pentateuch with a spirited challenge to the methodology and general conclusions of the critical school.[1] Umberto Cassuto was another vigorous opponent of the adherents of documentary analysis, and in 1934 he published his criticisms in a work which set out to examine the various problems raised by Genesis.[2] Cassuto argued for the organic unity of this composition, and maintained that it had been written in the later years of King David by a person of some genius who had compiled patriarchal and other earlier narratives to form a homogeneous account of Hebrew beginnings.

Two decades earlier Kyle had applied certain facets of archaeological discovery to the problem of the Pentateuch in an attempt to determine the authorship of the various books. In a work published in 1919 he argued against the documentary analysis by urging that the consistent use of Egyptian words throughout the various alleged documents indicated their essential unity of authorship.[3] A year later he followed up this argument in a further work, in which he again argued that the Egyptian influence evident in the Pentateuchal writings pointed to the Mosaic authorship of the corpus. He took decided issue with the "pan-Babylonian" school in repudiating the suggestion that the Mosaic sacrificial system had either Babylonian or Egyptian origins, and concluded that the Pentateuchal records ought to be read as they stood. He accounted for certain peculiarities adduced by critical scholars on the ground that differences could be attributed to the varieties of the laws

---

[1] *Die Einheit und Echtheit der fünf Bücher Mosis* (1931). A similar position was adopted by D. B. Macdonald, *The Hebrew Literary Genius* (1933).

[2] U. Cassuto, *La Questione della Genesi* (1934), *The Documentary Hypothesis*, E. tr. Israel Abrahams (1962). Cf. B. Jacob, *Das Erste Buch der Thora* (1934).

[3] *Moses and the Monuments: Light from Archaeology on Pentateuchal Times* (1920), pp. 41ff.

and the usages for which they were intended, and relegated the legal material of the Pentateuch generally to Moses as the responsible author.[4]

A further criticism of Wellhausenism, based upon archaeological evidence, was made by A. S. Yahuda. Following the example of Naville, he began to investigate the data of the Pentateuch in the light of the knowledge furnished by archaeological activity in Egypt. A skilled linguist, Yahuda published in 1929 the results of a decade of research dealing with the influence of the Egyptian language upon the Hebrew of the Pentateuch.[5] His minute and detailed studies, which throw considerable light upon the meaning of obscure phrases in the Joseph narratives, led him to conclude that the literary origin presupposed a cultural milieu in which Hebrews and Egyptians were living together. Yahuda adduced this as a decisive argument for the compilation of the Pentateuch in the days of Moses, or at the latest in the immediate post-Mosaic period. While many of his arguments were based upon solid philological foundations, some of his conclusions went beyond the available evidence, for example, his claim that the Babylonian Deluge story contained distinctive Egyptian elements, which was also the case for the Tower of Babel narrative. Despite this and other similar matters, however, Yahuda made it clear that the influence of Egypt upon the Old Testament narratives was far from negligible, a conclusion that was reinforced by subsequent archaeological discoveries.

On different grounds considerable disfavor was expressed with the Graf-Wellhausen theory by the brilliant Orientalist T. J. Meek, who, in the preface of his *Hebrew Origins*, written in 1936, spoke disparagingly of the analytical theory. In the preface to the second edition, published in 1950, Meek explained that while he did not repudiate it entirely, he took the view that it was far too artificial in nature, a conclusion which had been arrived at by many other critics of the scheme. Meek maintained the existence of a cycle of tradition in the southern kingdom which could approximate to J, and an equivalent cycle for the northern kingdom which was then absorbed into J. However, he expressed uncertainty as to whether the J cycle was ever reduced to written form, and repudiated any attempt to separate the northern from the southern cycle. On this basis Meek preferred to think in terms of a "stratum" hypothesis rather than of a purely documentary one. His views appear to have been of a mediating order, and attracted little attention in the scholarly world.

An important step towards an understanding of the manner in which Genesis was compiled in the light of the ancient Babylonian "life-

---

[4] *The Problem of the Pentateuch: A New Solution by Archaeological Methods* (1920), p. 284.

[5] *Die Sprache des Pentateuch in ihren Bezeihungen zum Aegyptischen*, I (1929), E. tr. *The Language of the Pentateuch in its Relation to the Egyptian* (1931). Cf. his *The Accuracy of the Bible* (1934).

situation" was made in 1936 by P. J. Wiseman. A British air-commodore of decidedly antiquarian bent, Wiseman examined the literary forms of ancient Babylonian tablets with a view to solving the literary problem of the origin of Genesis. From the existence of colophons, catch-lines, scribal dating, and other devices of antiquity familiar to the Assyriologist, Wiseman argued towards the presence of similar phenomena in the bulk of Genesis. He interpreted the enigmatic phrase "these are the generations of" as in fact constituting a colophon in the text, and pointing to the preceding verses as a complete unit which in cuneiform would have constituted a tablet.[6] He further adduced the presence in the early Genesis narratives of such Babylonian literary mechanisms as scribal attempts at dating, the linking of passages in series, specific titles of sections, and the use of catch-lines.

Wiseman's theory postulated documentary sources for Genesis, although of a completely different nature from those suggested by the adherents of the Graf-Wellhausen school. He stressed the strictly Mesopotamian nature of much of the source-material which he had uncovered, and suggested that it had been combined with the Joseph narratives to form the book of Genesis, presumably under the direct influence of Moses. His approach had the distinct advantage of relating the ancient Mesopotamian sources underlying Genesis to an authentic Mesopotamian life-situation, unlike the attempts of the Graf-Wellhausen school, and showed that the methods of writing and compilation employed in Genesis were in essential harmony with the processes current among the scribes of ancient Babylonia.

From a study of Greek literature F. Dornseiff launched an attack in 1934 upon the validity of using the divine names in the Pentateuch as a criterion for purposes of literary analysis. Referring to the Iliad of Homer, he remarked that the name "Alexandros" was frequently found in association with "Paris," which on the basis of the literary analysis adopted by the Graf-Wellhausen school could serve as a valid criterion for dividing the Iliad up into "Alexandrosist" and "Parisist" sources. He also compared the legal sections interpolated into the historical narratives of the Pentateuch with similar occurrences in ancient Classical literature, notably the *Opera et Dies* of Hesiod. Ridiculing the "paste-and-scissors" method for the compilation of such a majestic work as the Iliad, he also rejected it as a valid method for the literary formulation of the extant Pentateuch. What was perhaps most remarkable of all about his study was that these pronouncements were published in a journal that had been founded by the distinguished advanced critic, Bernhard Stade.[7]

---

[6] *New Discoveries in Babylonia About Genesis* (1936), pp. 45ff.; cf. *GBB*, p. 282.

[7] F. Dornseiff, ZAW, LII (1934), pp. 57ff., LIII (1935), p. 154, LV (1937), pp. 127ff., LVI (1938), pp. 64ff.

On the basis of early excavations at Ras Shamra, the deficiencies inherent in the conclusions of the Graf-Wellhausen school were pointed out by the scholarly conservator of the Paris Louvre, René Dussaud. Remarking on the tremendous importance that the discoveries at the site of ancient Ugarit had for an understanding of Phoenician-Canaanite culture, Dussaud maintained that, in the light of the new evidence, the Graf-Wellhausen hypothesis had assigned too late a date to the alleged sources, and had also greatly underestimated the value of Israelite tradition itself. He concluded his criticisms of the classical analytical scheme by stating that it would need to be subjected to a total revision as a result of the discoveries at Ras Shamra,[8] an opinion which has been amply substantiated since that time. Small wonder, therefore, that J. Coppens could declare that, even for the faithful, the magnificent critical edifice was palpably rocking on its foundations.[9]

In 1930 Mowinckel anticipated somewhat the later conclusions of Volz and Rudolph by maintaining that the Elohistic source belonged properly to Judah rather than to Israel, and that it had existed over several centuries as an oral process rather than as a written tradition in the best sense of that term.[10] He also stated that the Elohistic material did not contain any traditions that were independent of the Jehovistic document; rather, it invariably harked back to the parallel Jehovistic forms in its narration of early traditions. However, by 1937 Mowinckel had taken a different view of the situation, assigning the Flood sections of Genesis to the Elohistic source and the non-Flood material to the Jehovistic author.[11]

Abandonment of the traditional Wellhausenian position was announced in 1931 by Pedersen,[12] who repudiated the Hegelian overtones of the analytical scheme and pointed to the problems involved in the minute delineation of supposed literary sources and the precisions of dating which accompanied the process. Although he granted that certain collections of material could possibly be designated by the sigla J, E, D, and P, these were parallel and variegated sources that could not by their very nature be organized within the framework of some a priori evolutionary scheme. Pedersen continued his attack upon the current form of the Pentateuchal theory some three years later in an article that firmly rejected the Wellhausenian analysis of Exodus 1–15, and examined the Passover material in general against the background of cultic history

[8] Dussaud, *Les Découvertes de Ras Shamra (Ugarit) et L'Ancien Testament* (1937), pp. 110ff.
[9] *L'Histoire Critique de l'Ancien Testament* (1938), p. 87.
[10] *ZAW*, XLVIII (1930), pp. 233ff.
[11] Mowinckel, *The Two Sources of the Predeuteronomic Primeval History (JE) in Gen. i-xi* (1937).
[12] *ZAW*, XLIX (1931), pp. 161ff.

rather than the principles of literary analysis.[13] Pedersen held that this cult-legend appeared in its earliest form shortly after the Israelite settlement in Canaan, although its extant structure may have been post-exilic.[14]

B. THE UPPSALA SCHOOL

What many scholars consider to be the most devastating attacks by far upon classical Pentateuchal literary criticism have been made by the so-called "Uppsala School" of Sweden. While certain aspects of the work of these Scandinavian scholars have affinity with the British "Myth and Ritual" school (somewhat to the embarrassment of the latter, it is said) and with the concepts of kingship[15] and cultic prophecy advocated by Mowinckel, it cannot be denied that the emphasis of the Uppsala school upon the importance of oral tradition ultimately reaches back to Gunkel. An enthusiastic advocate of the place which oral transmission held in the general growth of the Old Testament corpus was H. S. Nyberg,[16] who claimed that the Graf-Wellhausen theory of origins did despite both to the native Hebrew intuition and to the techniques of those who preserved and circulated the sagas of early Israel. Furthermore, Nyberg and his followers urged that adhering to a belief in the existence of documentary sources as such militated against the reliability and significance of oral tradition. This latter was held to have been preserved by circles or centers of tradition over prolonged periods of time, and remained substantially in this form until after the exile.

This general standpoint was applied to the composition of the prophetical writings by Birkeland,[17] who maintained that the literary fixity of the prophetical compositions was a comparatively late individual phenomenon which represented the literal form of an already crystallized oral tradition. According to his theories, each prophet was surrounded by followers who, after his death, transmitted his utterances orally and reworked them in the light of the traditions that had grown up around the individual concerned. For Birkeland, therefore, it was virtually impossible to be sure that any particular verse contained the *ipsissima verba* of any given prophet,[18] so that final pronouncements on such

---

[13] ZAW, LII (1934), pp. 161ff.; cf. his *Israel: Its Life and Culture* (1940 ed.), III-IV, pp. 726ff.

[14] For a criticism of the general position of Pedersen see C. R. North, *OTMS*, p. 77.

[15] Cf. I. Engnell, *Studies in Divine Kingship in the Ancient Near East* (1943).

[16] ZAW, LII (1934), pp. 241ff.; see also his *Studien zum Hoseabuche: zugleich ein Beitrag zur Klärung des Problems der alttestamentlichen Textkritik* (1935).

[17] *Zum hebräischen Traditionswesen: die Komposition der prophetischen Bücher des AT* (1938).

[18] Cf. I. Engnell, *Svensk Exegetisk Arsbök* (1947), XII, pp. 94ff., and *The Call of Isaiah* (1949), pp. 54ff.

matters could only be made on a traditio-historical, rather than on a literary-critical basis.[19]

Another prominent scholar who followed the lead of Nyberg was Engnell, who went further than either Volz or Pedersen had done in repudiating both the Wellhausenian evolutionary view of Israelite religion and the documentary hypothesis of Pentateuchal origins itself. Nyberg agreed with Noth in separating the Deuteronomy-Kings corpus from that of Genesis-Numbers, styling the former "P-work" and the latter "D-work." These sigla did not indicate documents in the classical analytical sense, but rather symbolized the circles of tradition which transmitted this material until it ultimately assumed its extant form. Basic to an understanding of this process was a recognition of the role that oral tradition exercised in antiquity.

In this connection Engnell maintained that oral tradition and written fixity were complementary forms of the same general process, which dispensed with anonymous redactors in favor of circles and schools of tradition.[20] He rejected the Graf-Wellhausen scheme of analysis categorically as an anachronistic European interpretation, and repudiated the idea that there ever existed the kind of parallel sources of narrative in the Pentateuch that were fundamental to the speculations of the Wellhausenist school. Engnell followed Dahse and Dornseiff in attacking the criterion of the divine names, and argued from a comparison of the Massoretic text with the LXX that the variation in usage of the divine names in the former was largely due to later processes of unification.[21] Generally he emphasized the reliability of the Massoretic text.

Engnell followed Pedersen in proclaiming that the "Passover-legend" of Exodus 1–15 was the central passage of a Priestly complex which seemed to him to be roughly equivalent to the Priestly source of the Graf-Wellhausen school. This "P-work" enshrined the traditions of the southern kingdom and rested for the most part upon oral tradition, with the possibility that certain sections—notably the legal enactments—had assumed an early written character but were also preserved concurrently in the form of oral statements. The final structure of this tradition was assigned to the period of Ezra and Nehemiah. In much the same way the legal sections of Deuteronomy were assumed to have been in writing at a comparatively early period, and to have mirrored the customs of the northern kingdom more consistently than the "P-work," although by the time the book had assumed its final form in the days of Ezra and

---

[19] For a criticism of this proposed methodological change see J. van der Ploeg, *RB*, LIV (1947), pp. 5ff.

[20] Engnell, *Gamla Testamentet: En traditionshistorisk inledning* (1945), I, pp. 8ff.

[21] *Ibid.*, pp. 191ff. For a demonstration that the Hebrew text is superior to the LXX see J. Skinner, *The Divine Names in Genesis* (1914).

67

Nehemiah it had begun to exhibit noticeable overtones of the theological standpoint current in Judaea.

The general position established by Nyberg and Engnell was adopted by a number of Scandinavian scholars and applied to various aspects of prophecy,[22] Israelite religion,[23] the Wisdom Literature,[24] and general problems of Old Testament introduction.[25] The approach of the Uppsala scholars and their followers has brought a new outlook to bear upon Pentateuchal studies in particular, but it has come in for a certain amount of criticism.[26] Many of those who stand outside this group have felt that the Uppsala writers have fallen into the same trap as the adherents of the Graf-Wellhausen theory by pushing their method beyond its logical limits. While their emphasis upon oral tradition is of great importance in focusing attention upon one of the ways in which material was transmitted in the ancient Near East, it appears to have been emphasized to the virtual exclusion of writing, which also occupied a prominent position in the preservation and transmission of ancient religious materials in Mesopotamia, Egypt, and elsewhere in the Near East. Engnell in particular appears, as Bright has pointed out,[27] to have substituted one form of source-criticism for another of the same general kind, which can hardly be construed as a telling criticism of the classical documentary hypothesis if imitation is to be considered as the sincerest form of flattery. Quite aside from this, however, is the fact that the Scandinavian scholars appear to have entirely misunderstood the function of oral tradition in the Near East, which was used predominantly for spatial and contemporary dissemination of material, and only incidentally for purposes of transmission over a period of time, since it was the general practice to commit anything of importance to written

[22] E.g. J. Lindblom, *Profetismen i Israel* (1934); S. Mowinckel, *JBL*, LIII (1934), pp. 199ff., *Acta Orientalia*, XIII (1935), pp. 264ff., XIV (1936), p. 319, *JBL*, LVI (1937), pp. 261ff., *Prophecy and Tradition* (1946); A. Haldar, *Associations of Cult Prophets Among the Ancient Semites* (1945), *Studies in the Book of Nahum* (1947); A. S. Kapelrud, *Joel Studies* (1948); G. Widengren, *Literary and Psychological Aspects of the Hebrew Prophets* (1948); C. Lindhagen, *The Servant Motif in the OT: A Preliminary Study to the 'Ebed-Yahweh Problem in Deutero-Isaiah* (1950).

[23] J. Lindblom, *Israels religion i gammaltestamentlig tid* (1936); cf. his *Den gammaltestamentliga religionens egenart* (1935).

[24] J. Lindblom, *Boken om Job och hans lidande* (1940); G. Widengren, *The Accadian and Hebrew Psalms of Lamentation as Religious Documents* (1937); H. Ringgren, *Word and Wisdom: Studies in the Hypostatization of Divine Qualities and Function in the Ancient Near East* (1947).

[25] A. Bentzen, *Indledning til det Gamle Testamente* (1941), E. tr. rev. as *Introduction to the OT* (2 vols., 1948-1949); G. Oestborn, *Tōrā in the OT. A Semantic Study* (1945) and *Cult and Canon: A Study in the Canonization of the OT* (1951).

[26] Cf. C. R. North, *OTMS*, pp. 77ff.

[27] *BANE*, p. 22.

form shortly after the events concerned had transpired. While written and oral forms of the same material doubtless co-existed for lengthy periods, the latter was never meant to supplant the former or to serve as its antecedent.

C. BRITAIN AND THE UNITED STATES—1930-1950

Except for occasional minor variations upon the main critical theme, British scholars in the decade prior to World War II continued to follow the pattern set by S. R. Driver, nervously depending on one another and on their German mentors. The writings of W. O. E. Oesterley and T. H. Robinson, A. S. Peake, S. A. Cook, W. J. Phythian-Adams, H. W. Robinson, and H. H. Rowley are typical of this period.[28] As events turned out, Rowley was to become the most distinguished Old Testament scholar of the post-war era in Great Britain. A man of profound erudition and wide sympathies, he established a tradition of accuracy and detail in scholarly studies that could well be emulated, not merely by his compatriots in the field of Old Testament writing, but also by other contributors to the general area of the humanities. Along with S. H. Hooke, Rowley was one of the most independent thinkers of his generation, and was largely responsible for an increased emphasis in Britain upon the unity of the Biblical writings.[29]

Contemporary liberal scholarship in the United States was strongly influenced by the writings of C. A. Briggs, C. C. Torrey, J. A. Bewer, A. T. Olmstead, J. M. Powis Smith, and R. H. Pfeiffer.[30] The critical extremes of their speculations were subjected to the moderating influences of the Albright school and others similarly engaged in archaeological activity. This situation was quite different from the one in Britain and Europe, where only a very few scholars in the Old Testament field were at all versed in the disciplines of archaeology, and where, in consequence, there was much more opportunity for men to become susceptible to the vagaries of subjective literary criticism.

[28] Representative works are: Oesterley and Robinson, *Hebrew Religion, Its Origin and Development* (1930), *A History of Israel* (2 vols., 1932), *An Introduction to the Books of the OT* (1934). Peake, *The Servant of Yahweh and Other Lectures* (1931). Cook, *The OT: A Reinterpretation* (1936). Phythian-Adams, *The Call of Israel* (1934). Robinson, *The OT: Its Making and Meaning* (1937), *The History of Israel: Its Facts and Factors* (1938). Rowley, *Darius the Mede and the Four World Empires of Daniel* (1935).

[29] Cf. Rowley, *The Relevance of the Bible* (1941), *The Unity of the Bible* (1953).

[30] American writings include: Briggs, *The Higher Criticism of the Hexateuch* (1897). Torrey, *The Composition and Historical Value of Ezra-Nehemiah* (1896), *Ezra Studies* (1910), *The Second Isaiah* (1928), *Pseudo-Ezekiel and the Original Prophecy* (1930). Bewer, *The Literature of the OT* (1912). Olmstead, *History of Assyria* (1923), *History of Palestine and Syria* (1931), *History of the Persian Empire* (1948). Powis Smith, *The Origin and History of Hebrew Law* (1931). Pfeiffer, *Introduction to the OT* (1941).

The period of World War II imposed severe restrictions upon scholarly activity, although some studies managed to appear in print, particularly in the United States and in a few neutral countries. A few German scholars continued to espouse the classical form of Wellhausenism,[31] studiously ignoring the works of Scandinavian and other writers, and found a degree of fellow-feeling in British circles.[32] Other scholars, however, notably Artur Weiser,[33] were careful to point out the hindrances that political circumstances had imposed upon their contact with scholars of other countries. Despite this unfortunate situation, the post-war German literature in the Old Testament field soon began to show the influence of Scandinavian scholarship. Thus, while von Rad[34] still employed the sigla J, E, D, and P, the age that he assigned to the traditions had a very different relationship to their final written form from that envisaged by the school of Wellhausen. Martin Noth made a concession to the emphasis upon oral tradition by regarding the documents as the crystallization of generations of oral transmission, but apart from this he proceeded along the classical lines of literary criticism, except perhaps for his assertion that the "deuteronomic" history commenced with the book of Deuteronomy and carried on until the exilic period.[35]

The post-war era also witnessed a revival of the attack upon the Graf-Wellhausen position from a variety of sources. In 1943 Oswald Allis urged the acceptance of the substantial Mosaic authorship of the Pentateuch in a careful examination of the issues connected with the traditional liberal position.[36] E. J. Young published his conservative *An Introduction to the Old Testament* in 1949, which subjected scholarly thought in the field to searching scrutiny.[37] F. V. Winnett also made a careful examination of the traditions underlying the Pentateuch, and concluded that Exodus and Numbers drew upon a continuous Mosaic tradition which took its rise in the northern kingdom.[38] When Samaria fell to the Assyrians in 722 B.C., this tradition was transferred to the southern kingdom, where it survived in priestly circles and was revised in accordance with the prevailing national ethos. In the seventh century B.C. the Mosaic tradition was drastically reshaped, according to Winnett, and issued in the form of Deuteronomy. The post-exilic priestly

---

[31] E.g. G. Hölscher, *Die Anfänge der Hebräischen Geschichtsschreibung* (1942); cf. his *Geschichtsschreibung in Israel. Untersuchungen zum Jahvisten und Elohisten* (1952).

[32] E.g. C. A. Simpson, *The Early Traditions of Israel: A Critical Analysis of the Pre-Deuteronomic Narrative of the Hexateuch* (1948).

[33] In the Foreword to the second edition (1949) of *Einleitung in das AT.*

[34] *Deuteronomium-Studien* (1948 ed.), *Das erste Buch Mose, Genesis Kapitel 1-12, 9* (1949).

[35] In his *Überlieferungsgeschichte des Pentateuch* (1948).

[36] *The Five Books of Moses* (1943).

[37] Revised edition, 1960.

[38] *The Mosaic Tradition* (1949).

circles in Jerusalem (P) attempted to harmonize the original Mosaic tradition with its Deuteronomic form, but without success.

Winnett cautioned against the application of the sigla J and E to his Mosaic tradition, although on balance he expressed a preference for J, on the understanding that it be clearly recognized as a product of the northern kingdom, where the national traditions of the Israelites took shape. He interpreted the problems of the Pentateuch historically rather than textually, seeing the key to the situation in an awareness of the fact that the extant form of the tradition reflected the claim of the Jerusalem sanctuary and its priestly officiants to primacy over the "Samaritan" or northern priesthood, a claim that was without foundation. Although this theory did not gain wide acceptance, it is important for the emphasis laid upon the place of the Samaritans in the formulation of the Pentateuchal canon, a matter that had been largely ignored by the Graf-Wellhausen school.

A series of studies made by the Roman Catholic scholar A. van Hoonacker, in which he contrived to accept both the documentary analysis and the Mosaic authorship of the Pentateuch, appeared in 1949.[39] This series was edited by J. Coppens, who himself argued subsequently for the strong impress of the Mosaic character upon the material of the Pentateuch.[40] The Roman Catholic scholar J. Steinmann went considerably further in ascribing to Moses a major part in the assembling and formulation of the religious and historical traditions which underlay the Pentateuch.[41] Additional attempts to reverse the tendencies of classical Wellhausenism by maintaining the literary homogeneity and Mosaic authorship of the Pentateuch were made by Helling[42] and Levy,[43] who adduced fresh arguments in support of their positions.

In 1955 W. J. Martin argued on stylistic and philological grounds for the general Mosaicity of the Pentateuch and attacked one of the basic presuppositions for composite authorship by postulating the presence of an elliptical interrogative in the passage in Exodus 6:3 involving the divine names. Martin pointed to the characteristics that indicated the homogeneous nature of Genesis, and urged the adoption of a methodology based upon a more objective approach to Old Testament problems than had been the case with the activities of the Graf-Wellhausen school.[44] In 1957 G. T. Manley undertook a study of Deuteronomy, in

[39] J. Coppens (ed.), *De Compositione Literaria et de Origine Mosaica Hexateuchi. Disquisitio Historico-Critica* (1949).

[40] *Chronique d'Ancien Testament, Le Problème de l'Hexateuque* (1953); cf. Coppens' article in *Nouvelle revue théologique*, LXV (1938), p. 513: E. tr. in chap. 1 of E. A. Ryan and E. W. Tribbe, *The OT and the Critics* (1942), pp. 11ff.

[41] *Les plus anciennes Traditions du Pentateuque* (1954).

[42] *Die Frühgeschichte des israelitischen Volkes* (1947).

[43] *The Growth of the Pentateuch* (1955).

[44] *Stylistic Criteria and the Analysis of the Pentateuch* (1955), pp. 5ff.

71

which he rejected the contention of the Uppsala school and its supporters that Deuteronomy shared a common authorship with the Joshua-
Kings literary corpus.[45] In disavowing any connection between the
reforms of Josiah and the origin of Deuteronomy, he held that the author
of the book was someone other than Moses, who related those things that
he had heard and received from others for the benefit of the Israelite
nation. Arguing from the fact that the topographical and geographical
data bore every indication of originality, he thought that the book might
have been written in the time of Eli.

In the second edition of his *Einleitung*,[46] Artur Weiser moved some
little distance away from the theories of Pentateuchal origins associated
with Noth and von Rad. While crediting the supplementary hypothesis
of Volz and Rudolph, the fragmentary theory of Gunkel, and the more
classical documentary concepts of Smend and Eissfeldt with some measure of truth, Weiser acknowledged that each view of the situation had
its own particular limitations. He protested against the atomizing process
that so frequently resulted from literary-critical study by indicating the
impossibility of analyzing literary sources to the last detail, and by showing that the completed Pentateuch consisted of considerably more than
the sum of its respective parts. Weiser related the origin of the literature
to the life-situation of the cult, and recognized that oral tradition may
well have co-existed over long periods with written sources. He inclined
to the belief that the authors of the various sources were in fact individuals, and not circles or schools of tradition as Gunkel had suggested. Because the Pentateuch partook of a quasi-sacramental nature, originating,
as he maintained, in the cult-festivals, the questions of provenance constituted something more than literary-historical problems in the generally accepted sense of that term.

The influence of Mowinckel and Hooke was apparent in the work of
A. R. Johnson, who attempted to demonstrate the functional equality of
priest and prophet in the sanctuary rituals.[47] In Johnson's view the
prophet was the responsible agent for the pronouncing of oracles as well
as for the exercise of his own particular prophetic gifts, which would
include divination and prayer. From the existence of prophetic guilds in
the pre-exilic period Johnson argued that the groups of prophets at
Jerusalem became the guilds of singers mentioned in Priestly writings
and in Chronicles. Unfortunately his treatment of the latter topic suffers
from an inadequate appreciation of the cultural conditions which existed
in pre-exilic Canaan. As Albright has shown,[48] the tradition that em-

---

[45] *The Book of the Law* (1957).
[46] Published in 1948; rev. E. tr. by D. M. Barton, *The OT: Its Formation and
Development* (1961).
[47] *The Cultic Prophet in Ancient Israel* (1944).
[48] *ARI*, pp. 125ff.

phasized the place of music and psalmody in the early days of the Hebrew monarchy has been amply verified by archaeological discoveries.

From these it would appear that the Canaanites had a class of temple personnel, referred to in cuneiform sources as "sarim,"[49] and in the time of David the Hebrew singers were organized in terms of a guild, following Ugaritic patterns. This persisted independently of prophetic activity as such until long after the exile; in consequence, it is not easy to see exactly how the Jerusalem prophetic cults postulated by Johnson could be transformed into singers and musicians. In general the author appeared to convey the impression that the prophets were little more than cultic functionaries, and this is certainly not the view presented by the Old Testament narratives.

D. OLD TESTAMENT SCHOLARSHIP SINCE 1950

The immediate post-war period in Britain witnessed the major contributions of H. H. Rowley,[50] while in the United States the members of the Albright school were resuming their literary productions, along with other scholars whose work had been interrupted by the war. One notable feature of the American scene has been the extent to which Jewish authorities have contributed consistently to Old Testament study, as represented in the writings of T. H. Gaster, H. M. Orlinsky, H. L. Ginsberg, L. Finkelstein, Nelson Glueck, and numerous other scholars.[51]

The impetus given to Roman Catholic Biblical scholarship by the papal encyclical *Divino Afflante Spiritu*, issued in 1943, resulted in increased attention being given to the influence of liberal Protestant Biblical criticism upon the traditional forms of Roman Catholic thought, as well as the extent to which archaeological discoveries had a bearing upon the dogma of the Roman Catholic Church. While some scholars of Roman Catholic persuasion adhered to the traditional position of their church in

---

[49] Cf. C. H. Gordon, *Ugaritic Handbook* (1955), p. 272, No. 1934, cf. No. 1991.

[50] Including *The Rediscovery of the OT* (1944), *The Missionary Message of the OT* (1945), *The Authority of the Bible* (1949), *From Joseph to Joshua: Biblical Traditions in the Light of Archaeology* (1950), *The Growth of the OT* (1950), *The Teach-Yourself Bible Atlas* (1960).

[51] Represented by: Gaster, *Thespis: Ritual, Myth, and Drama in the Ancient Near East* (1950); he also edited *The New Golden Bough* (1959). Orlinsky, *The Septuagint: The Oldest Translation of the Bible* (1949), *Ancient Israel* (1954). Ginsberg, *Ugaritic Texts* (1936), *The Legend of King Keret* (1946), *Studies in Koheleth* (1950). Finkelstein, *The Jews: Their History, Culture and Religion* (1949). Glueck, *The Other Side of the Jordan* (1940), *The River Jordan, Being an Illustrated Account of the Earth's Most Storied River* (1946), *Rivers in the Desert* (1949).

matters of literary criticism,[52] others tacitly adopted theories which were being discarded increasingly by Protestant and Jewish scholars, making for a considerable increase of tension within the dogmatic confines of the Roman ecclesiastical corpus.[53]

A new era of Biblical scholarship was ushered in with the accidental discovery of a manuscript deposit in a cave at the northern end of the Dead Sea. Millar Burrows, an eminent American scholar who had earlier published an important work on Biblical archaeology,[54] was responsible with J. C. Trever for the earliest stages of identification and publication of one section of the Qumran scrolls. When the nature of the discovery was communicated to the world of scholarship, it was immediately recognized as being of the highest importance for Biblical studies. A veritable flood of learned treatises arose in the field, in which contributions by younger English-speaking scholars were a welcome and conspicuous feature. The priceless value of the Qumran Biblical manuscripts for the textual critic became apparent immediately when it was certain that they represented a genuine pre-Christian tradition which in itself had advanced the textual evidence for the Hebrew Old Testament by at least a millennium. Decades of study in this general field had accustomed scholars to the idea of a prolonged interval of time between the period when the latest Hebrew writings were compiled and the date of the extant manuscripts, but with the discovery of the Qumran Biblical scrolls this gap was bridged to an undreamed-of extent.

When Professor E. L. Sukenik reported that none of the scrolls that had come into his possession needed to be dated later than A. D. 70, a furious discussion arose among scholars, who were frankly skeptical of the genuineness and proposed date of the manuscript material, remembering previous hoaxes in the Biblical field. However, the authenticity of the scrolls was placed beyond reasonable doubt when a party of competent archaeologists rediscovered and excavated the cave where the manuscripts had been deposited originally. Since that time a number of manuscript caches have been discovered, revealing a wide range of Biblical and non-Biblical literature associated with a religious community that had occupied the Khirbet Qumran area intermittently from about 150 B.C. to the fall of Jerusalem in A.D. 70. The classification and publication of the many manuscript fragments by an international team of experts commenced a few years after the initial discoveries, and the

[52] E.g. C. Schedl, *Geschichte des AT* (4 vols., 1956); F. Michaeli, *Le livre de la Genèse (Chapitres 1 à 11)* (1957); B. Mariani, *Introductio in libros Veteris Testamenti* (1958); P. O'Connell, *Science of Today and the Problems of Genesis* (1959).

[53] For a study of the Roman Catholic Biblical movement see J. Levie, *The Bible, Word of God in Words of Men* (1962), pp. 40ff., 191ff.

[54] *What Mean These Stones?* (1941).

speed of modern methods of communication enabled the scholarly world to have access to photographic reproductions of numerous manuscripts and fragments within a comparatively short interval of time.

Of the many appraisals that have been made of the Qumran scrolls and their importance for Biblical studies, few have failed to stress their revolutionary effect upon all future approaches to traditional problems. The first decade of study was sufficient to reveal the manner in which the scrolls upheld the general trustworthiness of the Massoretic text, and to throw some light upon the processes which underlay its transmission through the centuries. Scholars of many countries have participated in Qumran studies of various kinds. This has resulted in a staggering output of literature on the subject, which shows no sign of abating at the time of writing. It is safe to say that very few books in the future that deal with the manifold problems of the Old Testament can expect to be immune to the influence of the Qumran scrolls. A brief survey of the manuscripts themselves and the importance of Qumran studies generally for the Old Testament will be undertaken subsequently in the present work.

Of the books published in the second half of the twentieth century that were not immediately concerned with the Dead Sea Scrolls, several ought to be noticed if only for the effect that they have had upon the course of Biblical studies. Of particular importance was the monumental synthesis of Old Testament religious history published in Hebrew by Yehezkel Kaufmann, which was translated and abridged in a one-volume edition by Moshe Greenberg.[55] While Kaufmann generally accepted the conclusions of the Graf-Wellhausen school regarding the isolation of the Pentateuchal sources J, E. D, and P, his views on other matters were in diametrical opposition to those of classic European Biblical criticism. His revolutionary study of the history of Israelite religion was based upon the premise that, although rooted in the advanced cultures of the ancient Near East, the religion of the Hebrews was absolutely different from anything else that was known to the nations of antiquity.

Kaufmann postulated the existence of a monotheistic world-view among the Hebrews from a very early stage, and rejected uncompromisingly the Wellhausenian theory of an evolutionary unfolding faith from primitive beginnings to its culmination in the ethical monotheism of the major prophets. Instead, he maintained that the monotheistic *Weltanschauung* was fundamental to the Hebrew concept of a national culture, and underlay every aspect of it from its very beginning. Although his work was marked by certain Wellhausenian overtones, it had the effect of making a significant break with earlier critical views on the origin and

---

[55] Kaufmann, תולדות האמונה הישראלית: מימי קדם עד סוף בית שני (8 vols., 1937-1956), E. tr. *The Religion of Israel: From Its Beginnings to the Babylonian Exile* (1960).

development of Israelite religion,[56] and laid a foundation for a fresh approach to this extremely important area of Old Testament study.

Many of the vexing problems associated with the chronology of the Hebrew monarchy were afforded a radical solution by E. R. Thiele in 1954.[57] His purpose was to determine the exact methods by which the scribes of antiquity compiled their chronologies, and he commenced his task by assuming that the Massoretic text was basically reliable and correct in its extant form. As a result he was able to trace the presence of accession-year and nonaccession-year methods of scribal computation in the books of Kings and Chronicles, and to relate them successfully both internally and also to certain fixed points in ancient Near Eastern chronology. His procedures, which succeeded where all earlier attempts had failed, claimed the advantage of being firmly grounded upon a methodology appropriate to oriental categories of thinking, a state of affairs which was conspicuously different from that which had obtained in the great bulk of previous attempts to resolve the chronological problems of the Hebrew monarchy.

A new emphasis upon the basic unity of the Hebrew faith found expression prior to World War II in the work of W. Eichrodt,[58] who departed to a considerable extent from the customary method of historical presentation of data and related the various elements of the ancient Israelite faith to one central idea, namely that of the Covenant at Sinai.[59] A similar approach was also adopted by Sellin,[60] who selected as central ideas the basic doctrines of God, man, and salvation, on the ground that they furnished a wider foundation than the Covenant for purposes of demonstrating the unity of Biblical teaching. Sellin interpreted the theology of Israel in a Christocentric manner, an approach that was developed at greater length by Vischer, who in a two-volume work[61] endeavored to present a theological system so formulated as to comprise universally valid eternal truth. A major work written by the Roman Catholic scholar P. Van Imschoot[62] reflected the influence of Köhler and Eichrodt in certain particulars, although it adopted a more

[56] As those expressed, for example, by Oesterley and Robinson in *Hebrew Religion*.

[57] *The Mysterious Numbers of the Hebrew Kings: A Reconstruction of the Chronology of the Kingdoms of Israel and Judah* (1954, rev. ed., 1965).

[58] *Theologie des AT* (3 vols., 1933-1939), E. tr. J. Baker, *Theology of the OT* (vol. 1, 1961).

[59] Cf. L. Köhler, *Theologie des AT* (1935), E. tr. A. S. Todd, *OT Theology* (1957); C. Alves, *The Covenant* (1957); R. de Vaux, *Ancient Israel: Its Life and Institutions* (1962); J. B. Payne, *The Theology of the Older Testament* (1962).

[60] *Alttestamentliche Theologie auf religionsgeschichtlicher Grundlage* (2 vols., 1933).

[61] *Das Christuszeugnis des AT* (2 vols., 1934, 1942), E. tr. *The Witness of the OT to Christ* (vol. 1, 1949).

[62] *Théologie de l'Ancien Testament* (2 vols., 1954, 1956).

dogmatic approach to Old Testament theology, and did not attempt to demonstrate the unity of Hebrew faith in terms of a central idea such as the Covenant. Other authors who dealt with various aspects of Old Testament theology at a slightly later period included N. H. Snaith, Wheeler Robinson, Millar Burrows, Th. C. Vriezen, O. J. Baab, W. A. L. Elmslie, A. R. Johnson, H. H. Rowley, R. C. Dentan, and G. E. Wright.[63]

An English translation of E. Jacob's *Théologie de l'Ancien Testament* (1955) appeared in 1958. In 1957 the first volume of an Old Testament theology by von Rad was published.[64] The English version of an important theological contribution by Mowinckel, originally entitled *Han som kommer*, was issued in 1956,[65] and was notable in that it represented a modification by the author of many of his earlier views on such matters as the Servant of the Lord. In this book Mowinckel also took the stand that the Christian Church was completely justified in finding in the person and work of Jesus Christ the true fulfilment of the Servant prophesies of Isaiah.[66] G. A. Knight attempted a Christian interpretation of Old Testament theological concepts,[67] while J. Jocz stressed the importance of the election of Israel and the place of the nation in the divinely revealed plan of salvation.[68]

The vast increase of archaeological knowledge resulted, among other things, in a renewed interest in the production of numerous treatises on the geography of the Holy Land,[69] thereby bringing older treatments of

---

[63] Snaith, *The Distinctive Ideas of the OT* (1944). Robinson, *Inspiration and Revelation in the OT* (1946). Burrows, *An Outline of Biblical Theology* (1946). Vriezen, *Hoofdlijnen der Theologie van het Oude Testament* (1949), E. tr. *An Outline of OT Theology* (1958). Baab, *The Theology of the OT* (1949). Elmslie, *How Came Our Faith: A Study of the Religion of Israel and its Significance for the Modern World* (1949). Johnson, *The One and the Many in the Israelite Concept of God* (1942), *The Vitality of the Individual in the Thought of Ancient Israel* (1949). Rowley, *The Biblical Doctrine of Election* (1950). Dentan, *Preface to OT Theology* (1950, rev. ed., 1963). Wright, *The God Who Acts: Biblical Theology as Recital* (1952).

[64] *Theologie des AT, I* (1957), E. tr. D. M. G. Stalker, *OT Theology I: The Theology of Israel's Historical Traditions* (1962); II (1965).

[65] E. tr. G. W. Anderson, *He That Cometh* (1956).

[66] Cf. C. R. North, *The Suffering Servant in Deutero-Isaiah* (1948), p. 218.

[67] *A Biblical Approach to the Doctrine of the Trinity* (1957), *A Christian Theology of the OT* (1959), *Law and Grace* (1962).

[68] J. Jocz, *A Theology of Election: Israel and the Church* (1958), *The Spiritual History of Israel* (1961).

[69] E.g. G. E. Wright and F. V. Filson, *Westminster Historical Atlas to the Bible* (1945); L. H. Grollenberg, *Atlas of the Bible* (1956); E. G. Kraeling, *Bible Atlas* (1956); D. Baly, *The Geography of the Bible* (1957); M. du Buit, *Géographie de la Terre Sainte* (2 vols., 1958); H. H. Rowley, *The Teach-Yourself Bible Atlas* (1960); M. A. Beek, *Atlas of Mesopotamia* (1962); C. F. Pfeiffer, *Baker's Bible Atlas* (1962).

the subject[70] abreast of modern knowledge. Other publications dealt with the artistic productions of the ancient Near East,[71] and with the everyday life of the Old Testament world.[72] The works of S. Moscati[73] and C. H. Gordon[74] have thrown a great deal of light upon many facets of ancient Near Eastern culture, while Old Testament scholarship in general has owed a long-standing debt to the editorial labors of individuals such as F. Pohl (*Orientalia* and *Analecta Orientalia*), F. F. Bruce (*The Palestine Exploration Quarterly* and *The Evangelical Quarterly*), G. E. Wright and F. M. Cross (*The Biblical Archaeologist*), de Boer (*Oudtestamentische Studiën*), T. Fish (*The Journal of the Manchester University Egyptian and Oriental Society*), C. J. Bleeker (*Numen*), and many other distinguished scholars who have served in similar capacities.

The English-speaking world has derived particularly great benefit from a profusion of Bible dictionaries, encyclopedias, and commentaries, replacing the older works such as those edited by Hastings[75] and Orr,[76] and reflecting many of the advances in knowledge that are the property of the mid-twentieth century.[77] Besides producing similar

[70] E.g. T. H. Horne, *A Summary of Biblical Geography and Antiquities* (1856); G. A. Smith, *The Historical Geography of the Holy Land* (1894); J. B. Calkin, *Historical Geography of Bible Lands* (1904); F.-M. Abel, *Géographie de la Palestine* (1933).

[71] E.g. H. Frankfort, *The Art and Architecture of the Ancient Orient* (1954); J. B. Pritchard, *The Ancient Near East in Pictures Relating to the OT* (1954); A. Malroux and G. Salles (eds.), *The Arts of Mankind: Sumer* (A. Parrot, 1960), *Nineveh and Babylon* (Parrot, 1961), *Iran, Parthians and Sassanians* (R. Ghirshman, 1962).

[72] E.g. M. S. and J. L. Miller, *Encyclopedia of Bible Life* (1944); E. W. Heaton, *Everyday Life in OT Times* (1956); P. R. Ackroyd, *The People of the OT;* W. Corswant, *A Dictionary of Life in Bible Times* (1960 ed.); R. de Vaux, *Ancient Israel: Its Life and Institutions* (1962).

[73] *Storia e Civilta dei Semiti* (1949), E. tr. *Ancient Semitic Civilisations* (1957); *L'epigrafia ebraica antica 1935-1950* (1951); *L'oriente Antico* (1952); *Oriente in nuovo luce* (1954); *Il Profito dell' Oriente Mediterraneo* (1956), E. tr. *The Face of the Ancient Orient* (1960); *Il predecessori d'Israele* (1956).

[74] C. H. Gordon, *Ugaritic Handbook* (1947), *Ugaritic Literature: A Comprehensive Translation of Poetic and Prose Texts* (1949), *Introduction to OT Times* (1952), *Adventures in the Nearest East* (1957), *The World of the OT: An Introduction to OT Times* (1958), *Before the Bible* (1962).

[75] J. Hastings (ed.), *Dictionary of the Bible* (5 vols., 1911).

[76] J. Orr (ed.), *The International Standard Bible Encyclopedia* (5 vols., 1915).

[77] E.g. M. S. and J. L. Miller, *Harper's Bible Dictionary* (1952); G. A. Buttrick *et al.* (eds.), *The Interpreter's Bible* (12 vols., 1952-1957); G. A. Buttrick *et al.* (eds.), *The Interpreter's Dictionary of the Bible* (4 vols., 1962); J. D. Douglas *et al.* (eds.), *The New Bible Dictionary* (1963); M. Black and H. H. Rowley (eds.), *Peake's Commentary on the Bible* (1962); M. C. Tenney (ed.), *The Zondervan Pictorial Bible Dictionary* (1963); J. Marsh *et al.* (eds.), *The Torch Bible Commentaries* (1949ff.); E. J. Young (ed.), *The New International Commentary on the OT* (1965ff.); W. F. Albright and D. N. Freedman (eds.), *The Anchor Bible* (1964ff.).

works in their own language, German scholars have lent their efforts to a series in English under the editorship of G. E. Wright and others, entitled *The Old Testament Library*,[78] which includes compositions other than purely Biblical commentaries,[79] and in point of fact has drawn heavily upon the noted German series *Das Alt Testament Deutsch*. Notable translations of the Bible embodying new archaeological and theological knowledge have also been conspicuous in the literature of the mid-twentieth century.[80] Yet another outstanding achievement was the publication of a new edition of the Massoretic text by the British and Foreign Bible Society.[81]

One of the most important repudiations of the Graf-Wellhausen theory was made by C. H. Gordon in an article in *Christianity Today*.[82] Gordon, a veteran Near Eastern archaeologist and a brilliant linguistic scholar, stated the reasons which led to his change of outlook from an earlier liberal position,[83] and drew upon parallels in ancient Near Eastern literature to show the complete inadequacy of using the divine names in the Pentateuch as a criterion for documentary analysis. In particular he warned, as others had done, against employing a critical methodology which was out of harmony with the observed facts of the ancient Near Eastern *Sitz im Leben*, and which could only result in the conclusion that little or nothing in the Old Testament was authentic. This extremely important criticism of the Graf-Wellhausen analytical method, reflecting as it does a vast knowledge of oriental life and customs, will of necessity have to be taken into account by all serious students of the Old Testament.

In 1962 Gordon published a valuable contribution to the study of the background common to the Greek and Hebrew civilizations in which he demonstrated that, so far from being totally different from one another, they were actually parallel structures erected upon the same east-Mediterranean cultural foundations.[84] Gordon was concerned not so much with the Hellenistic age, when the union of Greece with other areas of the Near East was an accomplished fact that is now recognized on all sides, but with the "Heroic Age" of Greece and Israel. The period under consideration extended from the beginning of the Egyptian Amarna Age (fifteenth century B.C.) to the tenth century B.C. By reference to

---

[78] E.g. G. von Rad, *Das erste Buch Mose, Genesis* (1956), E. tr. J. H. Marks, *Genesis* (1961); M. Noth, *Das zweite Buch Mose, Exodus* (1959), E. tr. J. S. Bowden, *Exodus* (1962)

[79] E.g. W. Eichrodt, *Theologie des AT, I* (1959), E. tr. J. Baker, *Theology of the OT, I* (1960).

[80] E.g. *The Revised Standard Version* (1952), *The Bible*, published by the Jewish Publication Society of America (vol. 1, 1963).

[81] Ed. N. H. Snaith (1958).

[82] *Christianity Today*, IV, No. 4 (1959), pp. 131ff.

[83] Already apparent in *UL*, pp. 7f.

[84] *Before the Bible* (1962).

numerous similarities and differences Gordon furnished a convincing account of the extent to which Greek and Hebrew texts alike reflected authentic traditions of the Heroic Age of the eastern Mediterranean during the last half of the second millennium B.C.

Although W. F. Albright attempted to disparage to some extent the conclusions that Gordon arrived at,[85] the latter was equally emphatic as to the validity and importance of his work for Homeric and Old Testament studies alike;[86] and for anyone who is well grounded in both disciplines the facts of the matter are quite evidently on the side of Gordon. Particularly valuable for the whole question of Pentateuchal origins is his insistence upon a maximum of written sources underlying the narratives, as opposed to the general emphasis of liberal orthodoxy, which adheres to the concept of a prolonged period of oral transmission before the written material assumed its final form. This conclusion led Gordon to a rejection of the notion that the Pentateuch was the "work of an editor who pasted together various documents," and an espousal of the view that it was instead the epic of nationhood.[87]

E. THE CURRENT STATUS OF OLD TESTAMENT SCHOLARSHIP

It is a commonplace for those who comment upon the situation in the area of critical analysis from the mid-twentieth century to state that it is far more difficult to assess than was the case with that same movement fifty years earlier.[88] The faith of a great many in the philosophical rationale of critical orthodoxy has undergone a severe testing, as indicated by the comments of Bright in 1960:

> ... after two total wars and countless other unmentionable horrors, few are left today who would find a melioristic evolution a sufficient explanation of human history—and, by the same token, of Israel's history.[89]

He further pointed out that scholars have recognized increasingly the impossibility of arranging documents in neat chronological progression, or of adducing such documents to support an equally concise picture of the evolution of Israelite religion.[90] Yet he also made it clear that the documentary hypothesis was not the express prerogative of the Graf-Wellhausen school, and that it rises or falls independently of that body of opinion to a large extent. In noting that many scholars still adhered to the classical formulation of documents, thus substantiating to a large extent the predictions of Peake[91] that a "central position" on the matter

[85] *Christianity Today*, VII, No. 8 (1963), p. 359.
[86] *Ibid.*, VII, No. 12, p. 580; cf. *IOTT*, pp. 89ff., *HUCA*, XXVI (1953), pp. 84ff.
[87] *GBB*, p. 284.
[88] E.g. G. W. Anderson, *A Critical Introduction to the OT* (1959), p. v.
[89] *BANE*, p. 16.
[90] *Ibid.*, p. 18.
[91] *BJRL*, XII (1928), pp. 28f.

would be adopted, Bright was faced with the same problematical situation as that which confronted Kaufmann under similar circumstances.

The latter wrote:

> Wellhausen's arguments complemented each other nicely, and offered what seemed to be a solid foundation upon which to build the house of biblical criticism. Since then, however, both the evidence and the arguments supporting the structure have been called into question and, to some extent, even rejected. Yet biblical scholarship, while admitting that the grounds have crumbled away, nevertheless continues to adhere to the conclusions. The critique of Wellhausen's theory which began some forty years ago has not been consistently carried through to its end. Equally unable to accept the theory in its classical formulation and to return to the precritical views of tradition, biblical scholarship has entered upon a period of search for new foundations.[92]

Many professional students of the Old Testament, including some scholars of the highest intellectual caliber, have come to the conclusion that it is becoming increasingly impossible to ignore or dismiss the results of honest scholarship and research any longer. Accordingly they have begun to devote themselves to the task of ascertaining as far as is possible the actual facts of the ancient Near Eastern cultural situation, and against such a background are making a strenuous attempt to interpret the literary and other phenomena of the Old Testament.

In this endeavor the initiative appears to the present writer to rest quite clearly with American scholarship, and not least with the members of the Albright school and the followers of C. H. Gordon. The creative period of critical study in Germany has long since terminated, and the naturalism and nihilism of scholars such as Noth militate against any realistic progress towards a more assured methodology. Indeed, if such an emphasis is permitted to continue its influence over German thought, it appears difficult to avoid the conclusion that the products of German Old Testament scholarship will become increasingly of merely antiquarian value and interest, representing the product of an academic backwater far removed from the main stream of thought in the area of Old Testament studies.

The work of Gunkel, along with the insights of the Scandinavian scholars, points towards more fruitful results than could otherwise be expected, although even here a careful rein needs to be kept upon the purely speculative element, the exercise of which has been so conspicuous in European scholarship generally. British writers, who had followed faithfully the mediating views of S. R. Driver, found themselves in the pre-Qumran period the victims of what in economic circles would be known as the law of diminishing returns, and apart from the work of S. H. Hooke and H. H. Rowley were only rescued from this perilous condi-

[92] *KRI*, p. 1.

tion to some limited extent by the activities of the few younger scholars who participated actively in the investigation of the Qumran material.[93]

It seems abundantly clear that all future scholarship must adopt a much more critical attitude towards its theoretical presuppositions, particularly in the light of the increasingly large corpus of information which is now available on almost every aspect of life in the ancient Near East. As wide an acquaintance as possible with the assured facts of the situation would seem to the writer to be a far more desirable prerequisite for scholarship than an indoctrination with *a priori* critical speculations, many of which have been advanced with enthusiasm but never demonstrated conclusively.

If, with C. H. Gordon, one is prepared to go where the facts lead regardless of the consequences this may have for a pietistic approach to past scholarship, one will still encounter difficult problems, but at the very least one will confront them in the assurance that the methodological approach which one has adopted is grounded securely in proper inductive procedures of reasoning, and is not an arbitrary instrument for subjective exercise. This is not an easy path for scholars to follow, however, as Gordon has pointed out,[94] particularly for those who have been trained exclusively in the methods of literary analysis as expounded by the Graf-Wellhausen school. Yet it is just a matter of observed fact that the old foundations have proved grossly inadequate to the situation demanded by the exercise of critical faculties, and, until they are replaced, the superstructure, erected with such enthusiasm by so many diverse hands over a prolonged period, is in incessant danger of collapse, as indicated by the widely divergent state of mid-twentieth-century opinion on the whole question of literary-critical findings.

In the end, therefore, it is a matter of method, and in the view of the present writer it is only when criticism is properly established upon an assured basis of ancient Near Eastern life rather than upon occidental philosophical or methodological speculations that Old Testament scholarship can expect to reflect something of the vitality, dignity, and spiritual richness of the law, prophecy, and the sacred writings.

[93] Especially J. M. Allegro, *The Dead Sea Scrolls* (1956), *The Treasure of the Copper Scroll* (1960), and P. Wernberg-Møller, *The Manual of Discipline* 1957).

[94] *Christianity Today*, IV, No. 4 (1959), p. 134.

Part Two

OLD TESTAMENT ARCHAEOLOGY

I. HISTORICAL SURVEY OF SCIENTIFIC ARCHAEOLOGY

As a scientific discipline, archaeology, which endeavors to evaluate the significance of the material remains of past human activity, is a comparatively new facet of the long interest in and exploration of the lands of the Near East. In this connection, as Albright has pointed out,[1] Palestine has long held a unique position among the countries that are of significance for the Bible student. Not merely did it serve as the place where Judaism and Christianity were nurtured, but for many centuries during the Christian era it was the undisputed geographical locale of Islam.

A. Prescientific Archaeology

1. Pilgrimages. Almost from the earliest days of Christianity it was customary for the devout to make pilgrimages to the Holy Land,[2] possibly in imitation of similar journeys made to Mount Sinai in the Old Testament period. Even though the Crusades halted this expression of interest in sacred sites for some time, it was subsequently permitted to continue, since, among other reasons, the Moslem inhabitants of Palestine found it to be a profitable source of income. Most medieval accounts of journeys to the Holy Land and neighboring countries followed the basic pattern common to travel diaries, whether ancient or modern. It was not until the sixteenth century that the first systematic observations relating to the natural history of Palestine in general, and to its flora in particular, were recorded by Leonhard Rauwolf.[3]

Certain notations concerning archaeological data were preserved in the writings of Pietro della Valle, who travelled in the Near East at the beginning of the seventeenth century,[4] but it was in 1743 that the first systematic plans of sacred locations and copies of inscriptions were published by Bishop Pococke, describing what he had encountered

---

[1] *AP*, p. 23.

[2] For one such account *ca.* A.D. 333, see the Bordeaux Pilgrim's *Itinerary from Bordeaux to Jerusalem*, tr. A. Stewart, *Palestine Pilgrims' Text Society* (1887).

[3] Leonhard Rauwolf, *Aigentliche beschreibung der raiss . . . inn die Morgenländer* (1583).

[4] The first portion of the *Travels*, describing his adventures in Palestine and Turkey, was published in 1650, two years before his death.

during his tour of Palestine and the East.[5] The records of previous pilgrimages were largely superseded, however, by the activities of the Dutch scholar Reland, who collected a great deal of archaeological and topographical information from a wide variety of sources, and in attempting to systematize it furnished the first critical examination of the study of Palestinian antiquities.[6]

2. *Napoleon in Egypt.* Prior to 1798 Near Eastern archaeology had been loosely associated with the pillaging of tombs and with the uncritical admiration of sites that tradition had connected with some of the major events or personalities of the Judaeo-Christian continuum.

That year Napoleon invaded Egypt, including in his entourage about a hundred scholars and artists, who gazed with unconcealed admiration and amazement upon the antiquities of Egyptian culture. Modern archaeology may be said to have its beginnings in the manner in which the Napoleonic scholars and artists copied out hieroglyphic inscriptions, made numerous water-color illustrations, and wrote systematic descriptions of the sites and monuments that they encountered.[7] Some scholars in the post-Napoleonic era published independent works dealing with Egyptian archaeology,[8] so that by the middle of the nineteenth century there was a vast fund of available literary material relating to the antiquities of Egypt.

3. *Surface explorations.* Modern surface exploration of Palestine as such commenced in 1805 with the activities of Seetzen, who travelled extensively in Transjordan and discovered the sites of 'Amman and Gerasa.[9] Nearly twenty-five years later the erudite American scholar Edward Robinson journeyed across Palestine with his companion and student Eli Smith, studying the general topography of the country and identifying many Biblical sites in Judah. Their discoveries included the line of the Third or Agrippan Wall of Jerusalem, the validity of which was subsequently disputed by most of the experts, and which has only been vindicated within recent years.[10]

Widespread interest in the archaeological potential of Mesopotamia was aroused at the beginning of the nineteenth century when C. J. Rich, the resident of the East India Company at Baghdad, explored neighbor-

---

[5] *A Description of the East and Some Other Countries* (2 vols., 1743-1745).

[6] *Palaestina ex monumentis veteribus illustrata* (1714).

[7] *Description de l'Égypte ou Recueil des observations et des recherches qui ont été faites en Égypte pendant l'expédition de l'armée française, publié par les ordres de sa majesté l'Empereur Napoléon le Grand* (21 vols., 1809-1828).

[8] E.g. J. F. Champollion, *Monuments de l' Égypte et de la Nubie* (4 vols., 1835-1845); K. R. Lepsius, *Denkmäler aus Ägypten und Äthiopen* (12 vols., 1849-1856); A. Mariette, *Voyage dans la Haute-Égypte* (2nd ed., 2 vols., 1893).

[9] *Reisen* (Kruse ed., 4 vols., 1854).

[10] E. L. Sukenik and L. A. Mayer, *The Third Wall of Jerusalem* (1930); cf. BASOR, No. 83 (1941), pp. 5ff., No. 89 (1943), pp. 18ff.

ing mounds and recovered numerous cuneiform inscriptions. When the French consular agent at Mosul, Paul Émile Botta, discovered the ruined remains of a palace belonging to Sargon II at Khorsabad (Dur-Sharrukin) in 1843,[11] the resulting wave of enthusiasm for Mesopotamian antiquities saw A. H. Layard commence excavations at Nimrod (Calah) and Nineveh from 1845. Almost immediately the palace of Ashurnasirpal II was uncovered, and the following year excavations there yielded the valuable Black Obelisk of Shalmaneser III,[12] an ancient monument which recorded that Jehu of Israel had been made tributary to the Assyrians. In 1847, while digging at Kuyunjik (Nineveh), Layard uncovered the great palace of Sennacherib, which was almost completely excavated during a second expedition from 1849 to 1851.[13]

As a result of these discoveries, interest in Near Eastern archaeology took a practical turn with the establishment of the Palestine Exploration Fund in 1865. Two years later the PEF sent Charles Warren to Jerusalem as its first representative to conduct excavations there. Although Warren's work was marred by the use of unreliable chronological methods, his ordnance survey of the city and its environs has remained the basis for all subsequent work at the site.[14]

At this time the brilliant French scholar Clermont-Ganneau served with the French Consulate in Palestine, and within a very few years he distinguished himself by announcing the discovery of the celebrated Moabite Stone.[15] This black basalt *stele*, which told of the extent to which Omri (*ca.* 885-873 B.C.) had gained control of northern Moab, had been discovered initially by a German missionary named Klein when visiting ancient Dibon in Moab. The *stele* was sent to the Louvre in Paris in 1870. Under C. R. Conder and H. H. Kitchener a careful survey of western Palestine was made from 1872 to 1877, and this material is still of considerable value to the archaeologist and topographer.[16]

One of the most urgent tasks confronting Egyptian archaeologists was accomplished by the indefatigable labors of J. H. Breasted (1865-1935), who set himself the objective of copying and translating as many inscrip-

[11] Subsequently explored intensively by the Oriental Institute of the University of Chicago. Cf. G. Loud, *Khorsabad I, Excavations in the Palace and at a City Gate* (1936), Oriental Institute Publications XXXVIII; G. Loud and C. B. Altman, *Khorsabad II, The Citadel and the Town* (1938), Oriental Institute Publications XL.

[12] A. H. Layard, *Nineveh and Its Remains* (1849), I, p. 282; cf. C. J. Gadd, *The Stones of Assyria* (1936), p. 48.

[13] Layard, *The Monuments of Nineveh* (1853), *A Second Series of the Monuments of Nineveh* (1853), *Discoveries Among the Ruins of Nineveh and Babylon* (1875).

[14] Cf. C. Warren and C. R. Conder, *The Survey of Western Palestine*, PEF *Memoirs*, "Jerusalem" Volume (1884). For an account of Warren's work see R. A. S. Macalister, *A Century of Excavation in Palestine* (1925), pp. 32ff.

[15] C. S. Clermont-Ganneau, *La Stèle de Mésa* (1887).

[16] Conder and Kitchener, *Map of Western Palestine in 26 Sheets*, PEF (1880).

tions as could be found in Egyptian temples and other monuments. This gigantic task took well over a decade, and involved a good deal of arduous travel.[17] When complete, the material that Breasted had collected furnished scholars and students with an authoritative compilation of historical sources extending from the First Dynasty of Egypt to the time of the Persian conquest.[18]

B. Scientific Archaeology Since Flinders Petrie

1. The spread and development of archaeological techniques. The scientific development of Palestinian archaeology began to make vast strides with the work of the scholarly Flinders Petrie. While excavating the mound of Tell el-Hesi in southwestern Palestine, during the last decade of the nineteenth century, Petrie became aware of the fact that each particular occupational level had its own distinctive pottery, which could be differentiated by means of expert examination from that of earlier and later periods. When he correlated pottery fragments with similar ceramic styles of known date from Egyptian and other deposits, he was able to introduce the principle of ceramic dating-sequences for estimating the age of archaeological strata. Although doubt was cast upon the validity of his dating-criterion at that particular time, it has been amply vindicated by subsequent research and now occupies an extremely important place in all archaeological activity.

Of the many skilled archaeologists who followed Flinders Petrie, mention should be made of the brilliant German scholar Ernst Sellin, who excavated Taanach from 1901 to 1904,[19] and who was associated with Watzinger in an attempt to uncover the secrets of Jericho (Tell es-Sultan) from 1907 to 1909.[20] R. A. S. Macalister investigated several mounds situated in the Judaean Shephelah from 1898 with A. C. Dickie and F. J. Bliss;[21] from 1902 to 1909 he was responsible for the excavations at Gezer (Tell Jezer).[22] G. A. Reisner supervised the first American excavations in Palestine at Samaria between 1908 and 1910 with C. S. Fisher and D. G. Lyon.[23] Reisner's major contribution to the science of archaeology was his introduction of an excavating technique that included the formulation of an elaborate analysis of stratigraphic material, comprehensive recording of all artifacts and other relevant data,

[17] See C. Breasted, *Pioneer to the Past* (1943), pp. 78f.

[18] Compiled in his *Ancient Records of Egypt* (5 vols., 1906-1907).

[19] Sellin, *Tell Ta'annek* (1904).

[20] Sellin and Watzinger, *Jericho* (1913).

[21] Macalister, *A Century of Excavation in Palestine*, pp. 47ff.

[22] Macalister, *The Excavation of Gezer* (3 vols., 1912); cf. his *Bible Side-Lights from the Mound of Gezer* (1906).

[23] Reisner, Fisher, and Lyon, *Harvard Excavations at Samaria, 1908-1910* (2 vols., 1924).

careful study of the architectural features of buildings, and an emphasis upon accurate surveying of sites to be excavated.

Meanwhile excavations in Mesopotamia were proceeding apace. From 1899 onwards the *Deutsche Orientgesellschaft* under the direction of R. Koldewey began to uncover the remains of Babylon as it existed in the days of Nebuchadnezzar II.[24] Elaborate fortifications, magnificent temples, carefully planned streets, and waterways gradually emerged from the vast complex of ruins, testifying to the highly developed standard of life in ancient Babylon. Still more important was the discovery of the foundation of Babylonian culture as a result of the work of H. R. Hall and C. L. Woolley at Tell el-Obeid from 1923 on,[25] and the excavations of Chiera and Starr at Nuzu beginning in 1925.[26] The latter was enlarged by the activities of the *Musée du Louvre* working from 1933 under André Parrot at Tell Harari, the site of the ancient city of Mari,[27] where a culture very similar to that at Nuzu flourished during the third millennium B.C.

The spectacular recovery of the ancient Hittite civilization of Asia Minor was another remarkable result of the archaeological activity that flourished at the beginning of the twentieth century. Until that time it had only been possible to hint at the nature and extent of the Hittite empire by studying a few scattered monuments.[28] In 1906 Hugo Winckler began excavating the site of Boghazköy,[29] the ancient Hittite capital, and uncovered a large number of cuneiform clay tablets written in several different tongues. When deciphered some of these revealed at once the splendor and advanced culture of the ancient Hittite empire.[30]

In Palestine, the British mandate established after World War I was favorable to a policy of systematic excavation of sites in the Holy Land. A Department of Antiquities was set up, and was headed by John Gar-

[24] Koldewey, *Das Ischar-Tor in Babylon* (1918), *Das wieder erstehende Babylon* (1925).

[25] Hall and Woolley, *Ur Excavations I, Al-'Ubaid* (1927); C. L. Woolley, *Ur of the Chaldees* (1929).

[26] R. F. S. Starr, *Nuzi, Report on the Excavations at Yorgan Tepa near Kirkuk, Iraq, Conducted by Harvard University in Conjunction with the American Schools of Oriental Research and the University Museum of Philadelphia, 1927-1931* (2 vols., 1937-39).

[27] For the early reports see A. Parrot, SRA, XVI (1935), pp. 1ff., 117ff., XVII (1936), pp. 1ff., XVIII (1937), pp. 54ff., XIX (1938), pp. 1ff., XX (1939), pp. 1ff.

[28] E.g. the works of W. Wright, *The Empire of the Hittites* (1884); A. H. Sayce, *The Hittites, The Story of a Forgotten Empire* (5th ed., 1910).

[29] Winckler, *Sonderabzug aus der Orientalistischen Litteratur-Zeitung*, Dec. 15, 1906, *Mitteilungen der Deutschen Orientgesellschaft*, XXXV (1907), pp. 1ff.; ∴. Winckler and O. Puchstein, *Excavations at Boghaz-keui in the Summer of 1907* (Smithsonian Report for 1908), pp. 677ff.

[30] For the philological observations of a leading scholar who assisted in the decipherment of the tablets see F. Hrozný, *Die Sprache der Hethiter* (1917).

stang of the University of Liverpool. During the following fifteen years work was undertaken at a number of important Palestinian sites, including Beth-shan (Tell el-Husi) from 1921 until 1933.[31] In 1922 W. F. Albright commenced work at ancient Gibeah (Tell el-Ful), and uncovered the fortress of King Saul.[32] The largest excavation ever undertaken in Palestine began in 1925 at Megiddo (Tell el-Mutesellim) under C. S. Fisher, P. L. O. Guy and G. Loud, continuing until 1939[33] the work that had been initiated by Schumacher and the *Deutsche Orientgesellschaft* in 1903.

In 1929 a discovery of very great significance was made by the French archaeologist C. F. A. Schaeffer at Ras Shamra, the ancient Ugarit, where a rich tomb had been found by accident the previous year. The result of this was the recovery of remains of a highly developed civilization that had flourished in Canaan in the Egyptian Amarna period (fifteenth to fourteenth centuries B.C.), and which claimed close affinities with the culture of the Biblical Hebrews.[34] Without any question the discovery of the remains of ancient Ugaritic society represents one of the major achievements of twentieth-century archaeological activity.

From 1929 to 1936 John Garstang conducted a series of excavations at Jericho continuing the work first begun by Sellin. During these campaigns a number of the stratigraphic problems that the *Deutsche Orientgesellschaft* had confronted were resolved and the tremendous antiquity

[31] Cf. A. Rowe, *The Topography and History of Beth-Shan* (1930); G. M. FitzGerald, *Beth-Shan Excavations 1921-23* (1931); A. Rowe, *Beth-Shan, Four Canaanite Temples* (1940); W. F. Albright, *BASOR*, No. 6 (1926), pp. 51ff.; G. E. Wright, *AJA*, XLV (1941), pp. 483ff.; C. C. McCown, *The Ladder of Progress in Palestine* (1943), pp. 151ff.

[32] Cf. Albright, *BASOR*, No. 4 (1924), pp. 51ff.

[33] Cf. G. Schumacher and C. Steuernagel, *Tell el-Mutesellim, I, Fundbericht* (1908); G. Watzinger, *II, Die Funde* (1929); R. S. Lamon and C. S. Shipton, *Megiddo I: Seasons of 1925-34* (1939); G. Loud, *Megiddo II: Seasons of 1935-1939* (1948); H. G. May, *Material Remains of the Megiddo Cult* (1935); R. S. Lamon, *The Megiddo Water System* (1935); P. L. O. Guy and R. M. Engberg, *Megiddo Tombs* (1938); G. Loud, *The Megiddo Ivories* (1939); W. F. Albright, *AJA*, LIII (1949), pp. 213ff.; G. E. Wright, *JAOS*, LXX (1950), pp. 56ff., *BA*, XIII, No. 2 (1950), pp. 28ff.; Y. Yadin, *BA*, XXIII, No. 2 (1960), pp. 62ff.; A. Goetze and S. Levy, *'Atiqot* (1959), II, pp. 121ff.

[34] For the excavation reports up to World War II see C. F. A. Schaeffer, *SRA*, X (1929), pp. 285ff., XII (1931), pp. 1ff., XIII (1932), pp. 1ff., XIV (1933), pp. 93ff., XV (1934), pp. 105ff., XVI (1935), pp. 141ff., XVII (1936), pp. 105ff., XVIII (1937), pp. 125ff., XIX (1938), pp. 193ff., XX (1939), pp. 277ff. For some subsequent studies see R. de Langhe, *Les Textes de Ras Shamra-Ugarit et leurs Rapports avec le Milieu biblique de l'Ancien Testament* (1945), I-II; C. H. Gordon, *Ugaritic Literature* (1949); G. R. Driver, *Canaanite Myths and Legends* (1956); C. F. A. Schaeffer, *Ugaritica* (1956), III; C. Virolleaud, *Le Palais Royal d'Ugarit* (1957), II.

of human occupation of the site was definitely established.[35] Problems raised by the work of Reisner at Samaria (Sebastiyeh) were cleared up by the excavations of Crowfoot, Kenyon, and Sukenik from 1931 to 1935.[36] In 1934 W. F. Albright and J. L. Kelso commenced work on the mound at Bethel.[37] Meanwhile Nelson Glueck had already begun an extensive archaeological survey in Transjordan, during which he located hundreds of sites and established the date of their occupational periods through the study of surface ostraca. In 1937 Glueck cleared a Nabataean shrine at Khirbet et-Tannur, and in the same year he began a series of campaigns which resulted in the discovery of a copper refinery at Ezion-geber (Tell el-Kheleifeh) dating from the Solomonic era.[38]

The Arab-Israeli conflict which followed World War II made the excavation of certain archaeological sites an extremely difficult matter. Despite this, work has been carried on at Beth-yerah (Khirbet Kerak) under B. Mazar, M. Avi-Yonah, Y. Yadin, and others since 1944, at Tirzah (Tell el-Far'ah) in a spasmodic fashion since 1946 under R. de Vaux, and also at other sites.

The spectacular discovery of the Dead Sea Scrolls in 1947, which has been described as one of the most sensational in the entire history of archaeological investigation, prompted a flurry of activity from 1948 in the Khirbet Qumran, Wadi Murabba'at, and Khirbet Mird areas under the direction of R. de Vaux, G. L. Harding, W. L. Reed, and others. Work was resumed at the site of Jericho in 1952 under Kathleen M. Kenyon,[39] one result of which was to assign an occupational history to Jericho reaching back to the seventh millennium B.C. The excavation of the large mound of ancient Hazor (Tell el-Qedah) was begun in 1954 by Y. Yadin,[40] while in 1956 digging was resumed at Shechem (Balatah) by G. E. Wright. As political conditions become increasingly favorable there will be many more opportunities for the excavation of

[35] J. Garstang, *Annals of Archaeology and Anthropology, University of Liverpool* XIX (1932), pp. 3ff., XX (1933), pp. 3ff., XXI (1934), pp. 99ff., XXII (1935), pp. 143ff., XXIII (1936), pp. 67ff.; J. and J. B. E. Garstang, *The Story of Jericho* (1948).

[36] J. W. Crowfoot, K. M. Kenyon, and E. L. Sukenik, *The Buildings at Samaria* (1942).

[37] Albright, *BASOR*, No. 56 (1934), pp. 2ff., No. 74 (1939), pp. 15ff.

[38] For his reassessment see N. Glueck, *BA*, XXVIII, No. 3 (1965), pp. 70ff.

[39] For the earlier reports see *PEQ*, LXXXIV (1952), pp. 62ff., LXXXV (1953), pp. 81ff., LXXXVI (1954), pp. 45ff., LXXXVII (1955), pp. 106ff., LXXXVIII (1956), pp. 67ff., LXXXIX (1957), pp. 101ff.; K. M. Kenyon, *Digging Up Jericho* (1957); also her articles in *BA*, XVI, No. 3 (1953), pp. 46ff., XVII, No. 4 (1954), pp. 98ff., and the volume *Jericho I* (1960).

[40] For preliminary reports see *Israel Exploration Journal*, VI (1956), pp. 120ff., VII (1957), pp. 118ff., VIII (1958), pp. 1ff., IX (1959), pp. 74ff.; *BA*, XXI, No. 2 (1958), pp. 30ff., XXII, No. 1 (1959), pp. 2ff.; Yadin, *Hazor I* (1958), II (1960); cf. A. Malamat, *JBL*, LXXIX (1960), pp. 12ff.

Biblical sites, thereby adding significantly to the already impressive accumulation of archaeological data.

2. *Radiocarbon dating.* Modern nuclear physics made an extremely important contribution to scientific archaeology subsequent to World War II through the development of the carbon-14 system of dating artifacts. This process is based upon the recognition of the fact that every living organism contains a proportion of radioactive carbon. The ordinary carbon present in living creatures is stable, and has an atomic weight of 12. Radioactive carbon, formed in the upper atmosphere through the bombardment of nitrogen-14 atoms by cosmic rays, is unstable in nature and has an atomic weight of 14. It has been discovered that, in practice, oxygen combines with the heavy carbon-14 atom to produce a variety of carbon dioxide, which is then ingested by all living things in a constant proportion of approximately one-trillionth of a gram of carbon-14 to one gram of carbon-12.

When the life of the particular organism terminates, the absorption ceases, and its radioactive carbon content begins to deteriorate at a regular rate in much the same way as radium gradually degenerates to become lead. Since carbon-14, like radium, exhibits a progressive rate of deterioration, the time when the assimilation of the unstable radioactive element ceased can be estimated with a reasonable degree of accuracy by measuring the amount of carbon-14 which remains in the specimen. The half-life of a carbon-14 atom has been estimated to be 5500 years; and in order to compute the age of organic remains it is necessary to reduce the material to carbon by burning, after which the carbon-14 content of the residue is measured by means of a highly sensitive radiation-counter. The first of these machines was developed by Professor W. F. Libby of the University of Chicago, and there are now many others in use in different parts of the world.[41]

As with so many other scientific procedures there is a certain margin of experimental error, sometimes in excess of five per cent. As newer and more sensitive radiation-counters are developed the range of measurement can be expected to be increased considerably, and to be accompanied by a reduction in the margin of error. Tests carried out to date have shown that certain types of organic material lend themselves more readily to carbon-14 dating than others. The carbon-14 technique is also extremely valuable for dating bones which contain a measurable amount of collagen. Sometimes radically wrong readings are furnished when disinterred remains have been allowed to become contaminated by such sources as the radioactive fallout from nuclear explosions, a fact

---

[41] Cf. W. F. Libby, *Radiocarbon Dating* (1954); K. Rankana, *Isotope Geology* (1954). For a survey of the various scientific methods which aid in archaeological evaluation see L. Bieck, *Archaeology and the Microscope* (1962), D. R. Brothwell and E. S. Higgs (eds.), *Science in Archaeology* (1962), pp. 21ff.

which demonstrates the desirability of independent dating-control on the basis of ceramic and stratigraphic techniques.

C. THE FUNCTION OF ARCHAEOLOGY

One of the principal functions of archaeological activity is to awaken a sense of the vitality of the Hebrew past in the student of Old Testament life and times. This is of great importance for the simple, though frequently unappreciated, reason that the essential message of the Old Testament cannot be fully comprehended without a knowledge of the cultural, religious, historical, and social background of the people to whom the revelation of God was given. Archaeological investigation has brought to light many new facets of Israelite life that had been lost with the passing of the ages and has helped to set Hebrew culture in proper perspective in relation to the trends and currents of ancient Near Eastern life generally. Many details of Hebrew history and religion have been confirmed by the spade of the excavator; yet, the main function of Biblical archaeology is to expose the human environment and furnish a properly accredited background to the study of the ancient Hebrews. It should never be expected to demonstrate the veracity of the spiritual truths implicit in the Old Testament, since archaeology is essentially a human activity and cannot therefore as such confirm theology or open the realm of faith.[42]

Bearing these considerations in mind, however, it can be said at once that the results of archaeological discovery have contributed enormously to the understanding of Biblical history and culture and have gone far towards confirming the veracity of the Old Testament writers. New light has been thrown upon pressing problems of chronology; forgotten languages have been discovered and made intelligible once more, obscure events and ideas have been clarified, and curious social customs set against their correct historical and sociological background. The selective nature of many of the Old Testament records is clearly such that certain occurrences that did not serve the predominantly religious purposes of the various authors to any significant extent were either omitted completely or only mentioned briefly in passing. Recent archaeological discoveries have enabled some of these omissions to be rectified in the interests of a continuous historical picture, while at other points they have furnished much new information on subjects which constituted matters of understatement in the Old Testament.

The character of modern archaeology is such that it can be said to constitute the *sine qua non* of any realistic understanding of ancient man and his world, a fact which is of particular importance for ancient Near Eastern and Biblical studies generally. Unfortunately, however, as with all observed "scientific facts," archaeological data can be sifted and

[42] G. W. Van Beek, *IDB*, I, p. 205.

blended to conform to all kinds of preconceived schemes, and not least in the realms of Old Testament history and religion. Against this tendency is the growing realization among scholars that the results of lower criticism and the evidence from excavated sites generally reinforce one another. When a *schema* for the historical development of the Hebrews is formulated on such a basis, it is seen to be considerably closer to the historical orthodox position than any other, including the conjurations of those who postulated the documentary and fragmentary theories of Pentateuchal origins.

The positive values which have accrued for students of the Old Testament as the outcome of archaeological activity in the late nineteenth and the twentieth centuries have included, among others, the confirmation of the Biblical narrative at most points, and this, as R. A. Bowman has remarked,[43] has led to a new respect for the Biblical tradition and a more conservative conception of Biblical history. In this same connection an even more forthright statement, which was subsequently quoted widely, was made by the eminent Biblical archaeologist Nelson Glueck. In a *New York Times* review of *The Bible as History* by Werner Keller, Glueck stated that he had spent many years in Biblical archaeology, and in association with his colleagues had made discoveries confirming in outline or in detail historical statements in the Bible. He was consequently prepared to go on record as stating that no archaeological discovery has ever been made that contradicts or controverts historical statements in Scripture.

Not long after the present writer had published his popularly written *A History of Old Testament Times*, in 1957, a reviewer remarked that the book had been compiled in such a way as to suggest that the Old Testament, as traditionally interpreted, was confirmed by every new archaeological find.[44] Quite aside from the fact that the purpose of the work was to show the extent to which the Biblical self-estimate had been vindicated and supported by the discoveries of the Near Eastern archaeologists, the writer has yet to become acquainted with any single archaeological find which by itself or in conjunction with others specifically and categorically disproves the testimony of the Old Testament to itself in any single area of history or religion, or discredits its basic trustworthiness in the manner in which liberal scholars have been endeavoring to do for many years.

This is not to say, of course, that each newly excavated archaeological site has thrown immediate and convincing floods of light upon one or another of the numerous problems presented to the western mind by the Old Testament narratives. All too often the testimony of artifacts proves to be ambiguous, due to a wide variety of conditions in which the purely

---

[43] In *The Study of the Bible Today and Tomorrow* (ed. H. R. Willoughby, 1947), p. 30.

[44] L. H. Brockington, *JTS*, IX (1958), p. 416.

human element is not infrequently dominant. But when taken as part of a vast cultural complex, such discoveries enrich and enlarge contemporary knowledge of the manifold facets of ancient Near Eastern life, and supply precisely the kind of information that will enable the Old Testament narratives to be interpreted authoritatively against their social, historical, and cultural background.

It is not the purpose of the present review to adduce every possible scrap of evidence in favor of the veracity of the Old Testament narratives and to ignore the problems presented by certain of the excavated sites. At the same time the writer has been at some pains to portray the positive results of archaeological activity as they relate to the Hebrew Scriptures, rather than ignoring them so as to concentrate upon the difficulties raised, an approach that is the favored methodological procedure in certain scholarly circles.

II. THE ARCHAEOLOGY OF EARLY MESOPOTAMIA

On the basis of what is now known one can formulate a remarkably detailed picture of life in ancient Mesopotamia, particularly as it affected the origins of the Hebrew peoples. Archaeological activity in the land of the Tigris and Euphrates has now demonstrated conclusively that culture originated in that general geographical area rather than in Egypt, as was thought during the middle of the nineteenth century. Some of the earliest inhabited sites of Mesopotamia represented by present-day mounds,[1] belong to the Neolithic period (*ca.* 6000-4500 B.C.) of northern Mesopotamia. These include the mound at Nineveh and the *tell* at Tepe Gawra, twelve miles northeast of Nineveh. Professor M. E. L. Mallowan took soundings of the mound at Nineveh in 1931, and at a depth of about ninety feet he uncovered the remains of prehistoric villages. Decayed wood and ashes were mingled with pieces of crude pottery marked by notches and other rough decorative attempts.[2]

The first traces of Chalcolithic (*ca.* 4500-3000 B.C.) culture were unearthed at Tell Halaf in northern Mesopotamia by Baron von Oppenheim just before World War I.[3] Remains such as these are styled Halafian, in conformity with the practice of designating the different cultural stages in terms of the sites where they were originally discovered. The most important feature of the excavations at Tell Halaf was the delicate painted pottery which was unearthed from the lowest levels of the mound. One vase was decorated with the picture of a wheeled vehicle, perhaps a wagon or a chariot, and this represents the earliest known drawing of a spoked wheel. Most experts agree that the design, texture, and temperature-control exhibited by Halafian pottery were unsurpassed in the ancient world.[4]

---

[1] *Tell* (pl. *tulul*), an ancient Babylonian term surviving in modern Arabic. References to both ruined and inhabited mounds occur in Josh. 8:28 and 11:13.

[2] M. E. L. Mallowan, *Annals of Archaeology and Anthropology, University of Liverpool*, XX (1933), pp. 127ff., *Proceedings of the First International Congress of Prehistoric and Protohistoric Sciences*, 1932 (1934), pp. 165ff. M. von Oppenheim, *Der Tel Halaf, eine neue Kultur im ältesten Mesopotamien* (1931).

[3] *CAEM*, pp. 16ff.

[4] *FSAC*, p. 90; *LAP*, p. 15 and pl. 1.

The work of C. L. Woolley and H. R. Hall at Tell el-Obeid enabled them to date the earliest Obeid levels about 4000 B.C.[5] A later Obeid stratum (XIII) at Tepe Gawra[6] revealed the existence of three large shrines whose construction was characterized by a series of recessed vertical niches in the walls, an architectural technique that made possible the construction of the Egyptian pyramids many centuries later.[7]

Excavations by Jordan at Uruk[8] brought to light the next cultural phase, known as the Uruk period. The site yielded black, grey, and red ceramic ware that had been made on a potter's wheel. An important discovery was that of the remains of the first Babylonian *ziggurat*,[9] which was about forty-five yards square. Another building at the site was decorated by means of patterned mosaics of flattened clay cones executed in three colors and reminiscent of Obeid patterns.[10] The earliest-known cylinder seal was found at Uruk; this device replaced the decorative button-like stamp seal that was used for identifying property in the earlier Obeid period. The stone cylinder seal was engraved in relief in such a manner that when it was rolled on soft clay surfaces it left a distinctive impression, which in later times was often a matter of some artistic achievement. Uruk culture also produced a rough pictographic script written on clay tablets, which was the precursor of Babylonian cuneiform. The Uruk texts were inscribed in perpendicular columns from left to right, and employed a sexagesimal system of computation that was subsequently enlarged by the Sumerians.[11]

The beginning of the third millennium B. C. at Jemdet Nasr[12] in central Mesopotamia saw the development of an increasingly complex urban life, in which bronze first came into use and the scope of agriculture was extended by the cultivation of wheat, barley, grapes, olives, onions, beans, and other vegetables.[13] Although the cultural expansion of southern Mesopotamia had been hindered initially through the difficulties encountered in attempts to drain the rich alluvial mud of the Tigris-Euphrates delta, the efforts expended in this direction were finally so successful that by the beginning of the third millennium B. C. a range

[5] Hall and Woolley, *Ur Excavations I, Al 'Ubaid* (1927).

[6] E. A. Speiser, *BASOR*, No. 65 (1937), p. 8, No. 66 (1937), pp. 3ff.; *CAEM*, pp. 44ff., 162ff.

[7] *BCNE*, pp. 126ff.

[8] The "Erech" of Gen. 10:10. Cf. J. Jordan, *Uruk-Warka nach den Ausgrabungen durch die Deutsche Orient-gesellschaft* (1920); *CAEM*, pp. 97ff.

[9] An artificial mound on which a shrine was erected. The term was often used to include the structure also. Cf. *CAEM*, pp. 110ff.

[10] *BCNE*, p. 55.

[11] A. Falkenstein, *Archaische Texts aus Uruk* (1940), pp. 49, 61; *FSAC*, p. 146.

[12] *CAEM*, pp. 106f., 143ff.

[13] *FSAC*, p. 145.

of crops and vegetables as varied as those of northern Mesopotamia was being grown in the southern part of the country also.

About 4000 B.C. a people of superior intellectual caliber, known as Sumerians after their central area Sumer, occupied the marshy regions of the Tigris-Euphrates delta. Although their place of origin is far from certain, they may have come from the Caucasus, or perhaps from the mountainous regions east of Mesopotamia. They were a swarthy, non-Semitic group, and were characterized by a high degree of cultural attainment and considerable organizational ability. Their advanced religious concepts prompted them to draw up a list of deities and develop theological principles that dominated the religious life of Mesopotamia for many centuries.[14] Remains of articles found in temple storerooms[15] have pointed to the activities of craftsmen who initiated and developed commercial dealings with India, Asia Minor, and Syria in such articles as toilet sets, gold and silver jewelry, decorated pottery, and agricultural implements including plows.

Mesopotamia had always been subject to devastating inundations, and a flood or series of floods was a firmly established part of the early dynastic traditions of Sumeria. Several versions of a flood-narrative were extant in the third millennium B. C., some of which spoke of Shuruppak as the site of the deluge. One fragmentary clay tablet found at Nippur preserved the tradition of that time with an account of the way in which the gods first created mankind and then regretted their having done so, and decided upon the destruction of the human race. The fourth column of the tablet recorded how Enki, the powerful water-deity, revealed the plan of devastation to Ziusudra, the pious king-priest who is the Sumerian counterpart of the Biblical Noah.

The fifth column described the way in which Ziusudra survived the tremendous flood:

> All the windstorms, exceedingly powerful, attacked as one...
> After, for seven days and seven nights,
> The deluge had raged in the land,
> And the huge boat had been tossed about on the great waters...
> Ziusudra opened *a window* of the huge boat....
> Before Utu prostrated himself.
> The king kills an ox, slaughters a sheep...[16]

Late Jemdet Nasr levels at Shuruppak[17] revealed the existence of a large alluvial deposit, while the excavations of Langdon at Kish[18] uncovered a similar stratum measuring some eighteen inches in depth. Lang-

---

[14] S. N. Kramer, *IDB*, IV, pp. 460f.

[15] *BCNE*, p. 67.

[16] S. N. Kramer, *Sumerian Mythology* (1944), pp. 97f.

[17] E. F. Smith, *The Museum Journal*, XXII (1931), pp. 200f.

[18] L. C. Watelin and S. Langdon, *Excavations at Kish IV, 1925-30* (1934), pp. 40ff.; *LAP*, pl. 8.

don described the latter in terms of the flood of Noah,[19] a distinction that was also claimed by Woolley for an eight-foot middle-Obeid alluvial deposit at Ur.[20] What was unfortunate about this situation was that the alluvial levels at Ur and Kish were not contemporary, and that similar deposits at Lagash, Kish, Uruk, and Shuruppak did not correspond with the dating of the Ur stratum. Matters were further complicated when Watelin excavated Kish and uncovered several more alluvial layers, two of which were separated by a nineteen-foot level of debris.[21] When Woolley carried out work on the mound known as Tell el-Obeid, four miles distant from ancient Ur, he failed to find any traces whatever of water-laid strata.

This attempt at correlation furnishes some idea of the difficulties involved in the interpretation of archaeological material, and has even led some scholars to state that the excavations in Mesopotamia have failed to uncover any traces of the Noachian deluge.[22] What is immediately clear is that it is far from easy to associate any one of these deposits at all closely with the flood described in the book of Genesis. Yet it is still a fact that Mesopotamia suffered from cataclysmic inundations at different periods in antiquity. Since the depth of the alluvial levels varied from site to site, it is reasonable to conclude from the available evidence that the deluge recorded in Genesis constituted one such flood of major proportions that occurred in a comparatively localized area.[23] As far as later Semitic tradition was concerned, the inundation was important because it involved the ancestors of the Biblical patriarchs, and unlike other ancient Mesopotamian floods it had a basis in morality.

The excavations of Watelin at Kish uncovered cylinder impressions of Gilgamesh, the legendary hero of Babylonian epic poetry, at levels which were beneath the ones identified by Langdon with the deluge of Genesis.[24] From this it would appear that the Babylonian account of the flood was already known at Kish, which is striking testimony to the antiquity of the tradition. In the light of the evidence available to date it is impossible to state with any degree of certainty either the origin of the Babylonian and Hebrew accounts of the flood or the extent of their interrelationship.[25] From a purely archaeological standpoint the most

[19] *JRAS* (1930), p. 603.
[20] *UC*, pp. 21ff.; C. L. Woolley, *The Antiquaries Journal*, X (1930), pp. 329ff.
[21] L. C. Watelin, *Kish IV* (1934), pp. 42ff.
[22] E.g. J. Bright, *BA*, V, No. 4 (1942), p. 58.
[23] J. C. Whitcomb and H. M. Morris, *The Genesis Flood* (1961), expounded the view that the Genesis deluge was a universal aqueous catastrophe, and rejected the uniformitarian theories of geology.
[24] L. C. Watelin, *Kish IV*, pp. 40ff.
[25] In *WBA*, p. 119, the tradition underlying the Flood story is assigned to the end of the Stone Age (*ca.* 4000 B.C.).

that can be said at the time of writing is that the Genesis deluge cannot be associated with any one particular archaeological level.[26]

Similar problems are immediately encountered when attempts are made to recover and identify the ark used by Noah to escape from the worst effects of the Flood. The mountains of Ararat, the traditional resting-place of the ark, can quite possibly be identified with the *Urartu* of Assyrian inscriptions, corresponding to the neighborhood of Lake Van in modern Armenia. However, the other attempts to locate the Biblical Ararat have witnessed archaeological activity in Iranian and Russian territory, as well as that of Turkey. Periodic endeavors have been made to recover pieces of the "original ark,"[27] and even though radiocarbon dating has established the antiquity of some of the fragments brought back from possible locations by travellers and explorers, it is completely illogical to try to identify such pieces with Noah's ark. There is very little likelihood that the ark has survived in any form to the present day, and even if traces of an ancient vessel[28] were recovered from a probable site, there would be no means of knowing with certainty whether or not the fragments were in fact part of the original ark.

The excavations of Woolley at Ur have furnished graphic proof of the advanced nature of the First Dynasty culture. A burial area outside the walls of the primitive city yielded a variety of funerary objects including cups, weapons, tools, and jewelry.[29] The celebrated "royal tombs" of Ur were unearthed at a lower level, and were found to consist of an upper and lower vault constructed from blocks of imported limestone. The body which was entombed in the upper vault was identified from a lapis lazuli cylinder as that of Queen Pu-abi, while an accompanying cylinder seal designated the occupant of the lower tomb as A-bar-gi.

Adjacent burial pits contained the remains of male and female attendants, along with a variety of funerary objects including some beautifully inlaid harps and two statues of goats standing erect before a bush.[30]

---

[26] Among those connecting the Ur alluvial stratum with the Genesis flood are H. Peake, *The Flood: New Light on an Old Story* (1930), p. 114; C. Marston, *The Bible Is True* (1934), pp. 67ff.; S. Caiger, *OT and Modern Discovery* (1938), p. 34; F. Kenyon, *The Bible and Archaeology* (1940), p. 140; A. R. Short, *Modern Discovery and the Bible* (1942), p. 98; A. Rehwinkel, *The Flood* (1951), pp. 47ff., 174ff.; E. F. Kevan, *New Bible Commentary* (1953), p. 84; W. Keller, *The Bible as History* (1956), pp. 48ff. Those rejecting this association include R. L. Harris, *The Bible Today*, XXXVII, No. 9 (1943), pp. 575ff.; B. C. Nelson, *Before Abraham* (1948), p. 108; F. R. Steele, *Eternity*, III (1952), p. 44; M. F. Unger, *Archaeology and the OT* (1954), p. 47; WBA, p. 119; J. C. Whitcomb and H. M. Morris, *The Genesis Flood*, pp. 110ff.

[27] Described by A. Parrot, *The Flood and Noah's Ark* (1955), pp. 63ff.

[28] Ancient Mesopotamian craft are figured in *ibid.*, pls. 6 and 7.

[29] UC, pp. 74ff. For the suggestion that Ur of the Chaldees was in the region of Harran, as maintained by some nineteenth-century authors, see GBB, pp. 287f.

[30] UC, pl. 5 (a), 6.

The high degree of contemporary artistic skill was made clear by the recovery of the magnificent golden helmet of Ur, found in the grave of "Meskalam-dug, Hero of the Good Land." It was fashioned from solid gold in the form of a wig, with the locks of hair hammered in relief and engraved in a delicate symmetrical form.[31] From another stone vault came the celebrated "Standard of Ur," a mosaic panel of shell and lapis lazuli depicting the themes of war and peace, and perhaps constituting a banner or standard which was carried in procession on ceremonial occasions.[32]

During the fourth millennium B.C. some Semitic tribes settled in the northern part of the plain of Shinar and began to establish trading relationships with the Sumerians. About 2400 B.C. they became a powerful nation under the vigorous leadership of Sargon of Agade, and were known from that time as Akkadians. Sargon defeated Lugalzaggesi of Sumeria about 2355 B.C., occupied the territory thus gained, and assimilated the bulk of Sumerian culture into his own dynasty. For a short time there was a dramatic revival of the classic Sumerian culture as expressed in the Third Dynasty of Ur (ca. 2113-1991 B.C.), during which Ur-Nammu, "king of Sumer and Akkad" erected the massive ziggurat at Ur which was excavated by Woolley in 1922.[33] A fragmentary stele of the king recovered from the site depicted him as a workman carrying compasses, a pick, and a trowel,[34] while a flying angel gave divine sanction to the work being undertaken.[35] The Third Dynasty terminated in devastation at the hands of Elamite raiders from the north, and for a time Mesopotamia reverted to the ancient city-state system. But under Hammurabi (ca. 1728-1686 B.C.), the last king of the First Babylonian Dynasty, the dominance of Babylon was clearly established.

Hammurabi was an outstanding military and political figure, who exerted great cohesive force upon the society of his day. He was responsible, among other things, for the earliest known attempts at town-planning,[36] as well as for the celebrated collection of legal decisions which has become known as the Code of Hammurabi. This landmark of Mesopotamian jurisprudence was first uncovered by J. de Morgan at Susa in 1901 in the form of a black diorite stele,[37] having been carried there from its original site by marauding Elamites about 1200 B.C. The stele

---

[31] UC, pp. 59f.; C. L. Woolley, The Sumerians (1928), pl. 9.
[32] C. L. Woolley, The Sumerians, pp. 50ff. and pl. 14.
[33] UC, pp. 89ff.; Ur Excavations: V, The Ziggurat and Its Surrounding (1939).
[34] LAP, pl. 20.
[35] UC, pl. 10 (a); cf. C. L. Woolley, The Development of Sumerian Art (1935), p. 112.
[36] Cf. A. Parrot, Babylon and the OT (1958), pp. 68ff.
[37] LAP, pp. 48ff. and pl. 22.

was a copy of the original, and on examination was found to contain fifty-one columns of cuneiform.

Hammurabi's Code was based upon earlier legal material from Sumeria that had been adapted to the needs of Babylonian society. A prologue recorded the divine commission that had prompted the work, and this was followed by nearly three hundred prose sections[38] dealing with a wide variety of commercial, moral, social, and domestic matters. Society at that period was divided into three classes, comprising the *awilum* or patrician, the *mushkenum* or free artisan, and the *wardum* or chattel-slave classes. When legal satisfaction of any sort was required, the principle of retaliation in kind (*lex talionis*) was applied in terms of these divisions. The Code makes it clear that a great many kinds of medical and surgical procedures were in common use, and that there were serious attempts made to regulate the activities of the medical practitioners by the prescribing of fee-scales and the enacting of severe punishments in instances of proven malpractice. The construction of houses and public buildings, tax-collection, animal husbandry, river navigation, and many other topics were the subject of legislation in the Code, furnishing an indication of the highly complex nature of contemporary political and social life. Scholars have frequently drawn instructive parallels between the Code of Hammurabi and the Mosaic legislation.[39] In the matter of adultery the Code (Section 129) and the Torah (Lev. 20:10; Deut. 22:22) prescribed capital punishment for both offenders. In Exodus 21:16, as in the Code (Section 14), the kidnapping and selling of a person was punishable by death. Again, the principle of retaliation as enunciated in Exodus 21:23ff., and Deuteronomy 19:21 was identical with that underlying many parts of the Code of Hammurabi (e.g. Sections 197, 210, 230). It is interesting to note that the Mosaic legislation differed from the legal provisions of Hammurabi (Section 142) in refusing to allow women equal rights of divorce with men. While there is a complete absence of a reliance upon magic in the Code of Hammurabi, it is not especially notable for its emphasis upon ethical and spiritual principles, and in general it can be said that the legislation placed a decidedly inferior valuation upon human life than did the Mosaic enactments.

During the days of Hammurabi the Babylonian scribes expanded and rewrote Sumerian literary originals to produce the celebrated creation epic known from its opening words as *Enuma elish* or "When from above. . . ." The finished form of this composition ran to about one thou-

---

[38] *ANET*, pp. 164ff.; *ANE*, pp. 138ff.

[39] E.g. S. A. Cook, *The Laws of Moses and the Code of Hammurabi* (1903); W. W. Davies, *The Codes of Hammurabi and Moses* (1905); W. Eilers, *Die Gesetzesstele Chammurabis* (1932); F. M. Böhl, *King Hammurabi of Babylon in the Setting of His Time* (1940); J. Rapaport, *PEQ*, LXXIV (1941), pp. 158ff.; W. J. Martin in *DOTT*, pp. 27ff.

sand lines of cuneiform written on seven tablets linked in series, and contained many of the familiar religious traditions of Mesopotamia.[40] The sixth tablet described the creation of mankind from the blood of a mythical deity named Kingu, while the concluding tablet established Marduk firmly as the accredited leader of the entire Babylonian pantheon.

Another well-known composition which emerged from the First Babylonian Dynasty was the Epic of Gilgamesh,[41] which, like *Enuma elish*, was first recovered from the ruined palace library of Ashurbanipal (669-627 B.C.) at Nineveh. The Epic described the exploits of the legendary Sumerian king of Uruk early in the third millennium B.C., who became engaged in a search for the "plant of life." The eleventh tablet in the series preserved the Babylonian account of the Deluge, in which Utnapishtim, keeper of the "plant of life," warned Gilgamesh that the gods planned to engulf Shuruppak by means of a devastating flood. Utnapishtim[42] was ordered to construct an ark, and shortly after it was finished a terrible tempest arose:

> Six days and (six) nights
> the wind blew, the downpour, the tempest (and) the flood,
> When the seventh day arrived . . .
> The sea grew quiet, the storm abated, the flood ceased.
> I opened a window and light fell upon my face. . .
> On Mount Nisir the ship landed. . . .[43]

In the days of Rim-Sin of Larsa, an older contemporary of Hammurabi, a group of people arose in Mesopotamia who were referred to frequently in tablets and inscriptions by means of the ideogram SA.GAZ, and elsewhere as Habiru or Hapiri.[44] They were of obscure origin, and did not appear to have had any established role in the society of the day, since they occurred in the cuneiform texts as mercenary soldiers, government employees, musicians, captives, landless troops, domestic servants, and the like.[45] Albright has maintained that there is some philological connection between the Habiru, whom he thinks were more properly designated 'Apiru, and the 'Ibhrîm or Biblical Hebrews.[46] While there

[40] A. Heidel, *The Babylonian Genesis* (1951 ed.), pp. 8ff.

[41] A. Heidel, *The Gilgamesh Epic and OT Parallels* (1949).

[42] The Semitic Babylonian form of the name *Ziusudra* (Sumerian).

[43] A. Heidel, *The Gilgamesh Epic*, pp. 85f.

[44] The latter may be equivalent to the 'Aperu or 'Apiru of Egyptian inscriptions such as the *stele* of Sethi I (*ca.* 1319-1300 B.C.). Cf. W. F. Albright, *AASOR*, VI (1926), pp. 35f.; A. Rowe, *The Topography and History of Beth-Shan* (1936), pp. 29f.

[45] For a survey of the problems connected with the origin of the Habiru see M. Greenberg, *The Hab/piru* (1955), pp. 3ff.; M. G. Kline, *Westminster Theological Journal*, XX (1957), pp. 46ff.

[46] *FSAC*, p. 240; *BPAE*, pp. 5, 11.

are still some unsolved problems connected with this matter, there seems little valid reason for rejecting the theory that the Hebrews may have been a small ethnic component of the larger Habiru group. At all events, the varied nature of the social units which existed in the second millennium of Mesopotamian history certainly leaves room for such a possibility.

III. THE ARCHAEOLOGICAL BACKGROUND OF THE OLD TESTAMENT

A. PATRIARCHAL HISTORY

With the fall of the Third Dynasty of Ur, a Semitic group known as the Amorites (Amurru) took advantage of the struggle for power between Babylon and Larsa to establish their capital at Mari (Tell Hariri). Under Shamshi-Adad I (*ca.* 1748-1716 B.C.) they became the dominant military force in the northern part of the country subsequently known as Assyria, and by the eighteenth century B.C. they were so powerful that they virtually monopolized the important public offices in Mesopotamia. The nature of the culture at Mari was brought to light by the excavations of Parrot in 1933,[1] who identified the *tell* by means of a statue from the temple of Ishtar which bore the inscription: "Lamgi-Mari, king of Mari, high-priest of Enlil, dedicated his statue to Ishtar."[2] The excavation of the royal palace at Mari in 1935 furnished convincing proof that Mari had kept abreast of the cultural developments of the day. The palace buildings numbered nearly three hundred, spread over an area of 150 acres.[3] Some of the original bathrooms were found to contain twin terra-cotta baths, beside which were simple covered toilets.[4] Parrot and his colleagues were amazed to discover that the pottery conduits which drained the palace roof were still in working order some three-and-a-half millennia after their installation.[5]

Tablets recovered from the palace archives included correspondence between Zimri-Lim, the last ruler of Mari, and Hammurabi, showing that the military attachés of the former relayed regular intelligence reports to Mari from the court of Hammurabi. One such record spoke of a Mari

[1] For the early reports see *SRA*, XVI (1935), pp. 1ff., 117ff., XVII (1936), pp. 1ff., XVIII (1937), pp. 54ff.
[2] G. E. Mendenhall, *BA*, XI, No. 1 (1948), p. 5.
[3] In contrast Jericho was probably not more than 8 acres at this time. Cf. *WBA*, pp. 36f., pl. 11.
[4] Mendenhall, *BA*, *loc. cit.*, pp. 8f., pl. 5.
[5] A. Parrot, *Mari, une ville perdue* (1935), p. 161.

diplomat as saying: "Whenever Hammurabi is occupied with any affair he writes to me, and I go to him wherever he may be. Whatever the affair may be, he tells it to me."[6]

This phase of Amorite history has important bearings upon the origins and traditions of the Biblical patriarchs. In the Balikh valley south of Haran (spelled Harran in the cuneiform texts), the names of certain patriarchal personages were commemorated in the designations of sites such as Serug, Peleg, and Terah.[7] In the Mari texts Nahor occurred as Nakhur, and was referred to as the home of some of the Habiru. By the beginning of the second millennium B.C. the names Abraham, Isaac, Jacob, Laban, and Joseph were in common usage. Abraham appeared in syllabic form as *A-ba-ra-ma*, *A-ba-am-ra-ma*, and *A-ba-am-ra-am*, while Jacob, written as *Ya-'qub-el*, was found as a Palestinian place name by 1740 B.C.[8] The name of Jacob in the form *Ya-ah-qu-ub-il* occurred on tablets from Tell Chagar Bazar in northern Mesopotamia about 1725 B.C.

In second-millennium B.C. texts of Mari an aggressive group of nomads known as the Banu-Yamina were mentioned periodically. These "sons of the right (south)," along with another nomadic group, the Khanu, proved to be very troublesome for the rulers of Mari, and in the end Zimri-Lim managed to slay one of the chiefs of the Banu-Yamina. Some scholars have connected this group with the Benjamites (Gen. 49:29, cf. Judg. 20:16, 1 Chron. 12:2), though this cannot be definitely established as yet. The Mari term *dawidum*, translated "chieftain," was held by some early interpreters of the texts probably to have constituted the original form of the name David, but subsequent studies have raised objections to this suggestion,[9] and it now appears probable that the word may instead mean "defeat."

The excavations of Chiera, Starr, and others at Nuzu (Yorgan Tepe) and adjacent mounds near Kirkuk in Iraq from 1925 have proved to be of great importance also for an understanding of the patriarchal era. During work at the site of Nuzu some twenty thousand clay tablets, written in a Babylonian dialect with a cuneiform script, were unearthed from the family archives of several villas, and are of significance because on being translated they were found to have preserved a remarkable record of the social and legal structure of the fifteenth-century B.C. Hurrians, who at that time were in control of Nuzu. Although this is somewhat later than the period of the Biblical patriarchs, there is evidence that many of the customs mentioned in the texts had been observed for some centuries previously, and that the Hurrians had been a

[6] Mendenhall, *BA, loc. cit.*, p. 13.
[7] *FSAC*, pp. 236f.; Albright in *JBL*, XLIII (1924), pp. 385ff.; *BPAE*, p. 2; Mendenhall, *BA, loc. cit.*, pp. 15f.
[8] *FSAC*, pp. 237f.; *WBA*, p. 42.
[9] Cf. Mendenhall, *BA, loc. cit.*, p. 17; H. Tadmor, *JNES*, XVII (1958), p. 130; J. J. Stamm, *VT*, suppl. VII (1960), pp. 165ff.

virile part of the population of northern Mesopotamia and Syria from the eighteenth century B.C. Consequently, the tablets throw an interesting light upon the life and times of Abraham, Isaac, and Jacob, setting them accurately against the cultural background of second-millennium B.C. Assyrian society.[10]

The bulk of the cuneiform material excavated concerned family or private life, and some of the texts mentioned the Habiru's contracting for domestic service in wealthy households. One legal document told of the nefarious activities of the mayor, Kush-shiharbe (*ca.* 1500 B. C.), who was immoral in his private life and corrupt in his attitude towards civic administration. Ultimately the citizens of Nuzu had him arrested and brought to trial, and his misdemeanors were suitably punished.[11] By far the most prominent social institution in ancient Nuzu was the practice of adoption. Contemporary law prohibited the sale of land, probably because it was believed to be held in trust from the gods who were venerated as its sole owners. In consequence adoption was employed as a convenient device for transferring real property from one person to another. The usual procedure consisted in an individual's being "adopted" by one or more families, to whom he usually gave a "filial gift" for the privilege of acquiring title to the lands which he would inherit on the death of the adopting parents.

Not all adoptions were of this kind, however, for it was not uncommon for childless couples to adopt a particular person as a means of perpetuating their estate and family name. Even slaves were adopted for this purpose from time to time, as the Nuzu texts clearly indicate. The obligations associated with adoption entailed the performance of normal filial duties as well as the fulfilment of mourning rites on the death of the parents. The majority of contracts associated with adoption at Nuzu contained a proviso that if a natural son was born to the parents after adoption, their own offspring should have the precedence as the legal heir, and to him should go the terra-cotta household gods (the *teraphim* mentioned in Gen. 31:19).

There can be no doubt that Nuzu society laid great stress upon procreation rather than companionship as the primary purpose of marriage. In consequence, a married woman who proved to be unable to bear children for one reason or another was in an extremely invidious position. The normal marriage contract often made provision for such a contingency by requiring a childless wife to supply her husband with a

---

[10] E. Chiera, *Publications of Baghdad School I-III* (1927-1931); E. R. Lachemann *et al., Excavations at Nuzi I-IV* (1929-1955); C. H. Gordon, *The Living Past* (1941), pp. 156ff.; *IOTT*, pp. 100ff. For some roughly contemporary north-Syrian texts see D. J. Wiseman, *The Alalakh Tablets* (1953); cf. C. L. Woolley, *A Forgotten Empire* (1953), pp. 51ff.

[11] R. H. Pfeiffer and E. A. Speiser, *AASOR*, XVI (1936), pp. 59ff.

concubine by whom he could obtain an heir. One such clause from a Nuzu marriage contract read as follows:

> If Gilimninu (the bride) will not bear children, Gilimninu shall take a woman of N/Lullu-land (whence the choicest slaves were obtained) as a wife for Shennima (the bridegroom).[12]

While certain privileges were thus conferred upon a concubine, the position of the wife in the household was normally protected to the point where the concubine was recognized as being of inferior status in the domestic economy. The rights of the concubine were also safeguarded by an important provision of Nuzu law which made it mandatory for the concubine and her offspring to remain within the family circle. As a consequence of this enactment, any attempt to expel a concubine and her children was regarded in a most serious light. Once again, however, if the legal wife subsequently bore a son to her husband, the child obtained the precedence as the heir to the family fortunes, a situation similar to that at Alalakh (Tell el-'Atshana) in northern Syria at about the same period.

Contemporary Nuzu society permitted a certain degree of latitude to be exercised in connection with the birthright, one of the most treasured possessions of the ancient Semites.[13] Thus it was legitimate for the birthright to be exchanged for something else, or negotiated in any other fashion warranted by the prevailing circumstances. One Nuzu tablet recorded the transfer of inheritance rights to an adopted brother, while another contained the agreement by which a man named Tupkitilla sold his birthright:

> On the day they divide the grove . . . Tupkitilla shall give it to Kurpazah as his inheritance share. And Kurpazah has taken three sheep to Tupkitilla in exchange for his inheritance share.[14]

Against this background of information it is immediately apparent that the patriarchal narratives of Genesis reflect the cultural and social trends of Nuzu society with a remarkable degree of fidelity. It now seems most probable that Terah and his family migrated from the region of Ur during the early part of the nineteenth century B.C., when northern Mesopotamia was largely under Amorite control. The proposals regarding the adoption of Eliezer as the heir-presumptive of Abraham (Gen. 15:2ff.) reflect contemporary practices in Nuzu very closely, as

---

[12] C. H. Gordon, *BA*, III, No. 1 (1940), p. 3.

[13] From 2 Kgs. 2:9 it appears that possession of the birthright carried with it a double portion of the inherited estate, along with other responsibilities (cf. Deut. 21:15ff., 2 Chron. 21:1ff.). This custom obtained both in Mesopotamia and at Alalakh.

[14] Gordon, *BA, loc. cit.*, p. 5.

contrasted with the implications of the divine assurance that Eliezer would in fact not be the true heir of Abraham in the last analysis.[15]

The way in which the childless wife Sarah gave her Egyptian slave Hagar to her husband Abraham as a concubine (Gen. 16:2; see also Gen. 30:3) in order to provide him with an heir (Ishmael) was in full accord with the prevailing local customs in northern Mesopotamia. When Sarah subsequently bore Isaac, the natural son was entitled by law to the rights of primogeniture. As far as Sarah was concerned, the continuing presence of Hagar and Ishmael in the confines of the household constituted a threat to the position of Isaac, who may have been of delicate physical constitution as a child. The apprehension that Abraham felt when Sarah expressed her determination to expel Hagar and Ishmael (Gen. 21:11) was prompted as much by the knowledge that such action was in direct contravention of Nuzu law and social custom as by purely humanitarian considerations. However, it is important in this connection to notice that Sarah's action could have been defended according to the ancient Sumerian code of Lipit-Ishtar (ca. 1850 B.C.),[16] one of the sources underlying the legislation of Hammurabi, which stated that the freedom received by the dispossessed slave was to be considered adequate compensation for the act of expulsion. This piece of legal sophistry was particularly ironic in a patriarchal society, where for a woman membership in a household was essential to her very existence.

The transfer of the birthright from Esau to Jacob (Gen. 25:31), a story which has always sounded a little bizarre to occidental ears, is now seen to mirror contemporary Nuzu social practices, which frequently condoned similar equally uneven transactions. At present it is not possible to say whether the birthright was ever sold to a complete stranger, since all extant transactions deal only with negotiations between members of the same family. Since the birthright was so intimately connected with private family affairs in a patriarchal society, it seems improbable that it would be an element in transactions between strangers, whatever conditions of duress might have prompted such a sale or disposition.

The nature of the relationship between Jacob and Laban has come into decidedly clearer focus as a result of the archaeological discoveries at Nuzu. The adoption of Jacob that Laban entertained apparently took place at a time when Laban had no sons of his own; and, as was usual in those days, he gave his daughters to Jacob for wives when certain stipulated conditions had been met. These included a clause that Jacob would forfeit his inheritance rights if he entered into marriage with other

---

[15] *Ibid.*, p. 2. Cf. Albright, *The Archaeology of Palestine and the Bible* (1935 ed.), pp. 137ff.

[16] *ANET*, pp. 159f.

women. A tablet from Nuzu which contained similar provisions read as follows:

> The adoption tablet of Nashwi, son of Arshenni. He adopted Wullu, son of Puhishenni. . . . When Nashwi dies, Wullu shall be heir. Should Nashwi beget a son (the latter) shall divide equally with Wullu but (only) Nashwi's son shall take Nashwi's gods. But if there be no son of Nashwi's, then Wullu shall take Nashwi's gods. And (Nashwi) has given his daughter Nuhuya as wife to Wullu. And if Wullu takes another wife he forfeits Nashwi's land and buildings. . . .[17]

The manner in which Laban asserted his rights as a patriarch (Gen. 31–43) shows clearly that he regarded Jacob as his legally adopted son, not merely as a son-in-law. Within the next two decades it would appear that natural sons were born to Laban (Gen. 31:41), an event that disqualified under Nuzu law the adopted son from receiving and exercising the coveted rights of primogeniture. An attempt to remedy the imbalance may perhaps be seen in the action of Rachel in stealing and hiding the household gods (Gen. 31:19). Such images were normally the property of the natural rather than the adopted son, and their possession could be adduced in support of any claim Jacob might have cared to press to the inheritance of Laban.

From a strictly legal standpoint, Jacob and his family would be judged guilty by contemporary Nuzu society for leaving the household of Laban without first securing permission and a formal patriarchal blessing. Yet it is clear from the narratives that there was also fault on the side of Laban, for his daughters complained that he had treated them as "foreign women" (Gen. 31:15), thereby relegating them to the position normally occupied by household slaves at that period. The entire incident reflects the embarrassment of both parties, and the solution arrived at is eloquent testimony to the ability of oriental peoples to extricate themselves with dignity from an involved and delicate situation.

One feature of Nuzu society noticeable from the texts is the way in which impending death furnished the patriarchal figure with the supreme opportunity for bestowing his blessings, a practice also recorded in the book of Genesis (Gen. 27:27ff., 49:3ff.). Since at that time it was not the custom for written dispositions of property to be made, the deathbed pronouncements recorded in the Nuzu tablets constituted in effect the last will and testament of the dying man, and as such were regarded as legally binding upon all concerned and irrevocable in nature (cf. Gen. 27:33). That these testaments were apt to take strange courses in antiquity, as indeed in more recent times, is illustrated by a particular tablet

---

[17] Gordon, *BA, loc. cit.*, p. 5.

in which the moribund man "willed" a certain woman as wife to his unmarried son:

> My father, Huya, was sick and lying in bed, and my father seized my hand and spoke thus to me: "My other older sons have taken wives, but thou hast not taken a wife, and I give Zululishtar to thee as wife."[18]

In a subsequent court action the son succeeded in maintaining his right to marry this woman, even though it is highly probable that neither party had been consulted prior to the declaration of patriarchal intention.

During the Mari Age it was customary for the Amorites to ratify covenants or treaties by the sacrifice of an ass. This *khayaram katalum*, as the texts phrased it, was regarded as an essential element in concluding all agreements, whether they were of a business or commercial nature between individuals, or of a more international stature affecting the well-being of different peoples. One of the tablets has preserved a diplomatic communication from a government official to Zimri-Lim (*ca.* 1730-1700 B.C.) of Mari:

> I sent that message to Bina-Ishtar (and) Bina-Ishtar replied as follows: "I have killed the ass with Qarni-Lim and thus I spoke to Qarni-Lim under the oath of the gods: 'If you despise [?] Zimri-Lim and his armies, I will turn to the side of your adversary.' "[19]

A survival of this practice is to be seen in the habits of the semi-sedentary stockbreeders of patriarchal and later times, and it is particularly evident among the descendants of Shechem, who claimed the title "Bene Hamor" or "sons of the ass,"[20] and offered spiritual allegiance to the Canaanite deity Baal-berith or "Lord of the Covenant."

As a result of the recovery of certain Hittite legal texts from Boghazköy, the purchase of the Cave of Machpelah by Abraham (Gen. 23:3ff.) comes into considerably clearer perspective.[21] Ephron the Hittite wished to dispose of the property for an apparently exorbitant price, an offer that Abraham seemed reluctant to entertain. Under ancient Hittite law the one who purchased the entire property of the vendor assumed at the time of transfer certain legal obligations to render feudal services, the nature and extent of which are at present obscure. If, however, only a portion of the property was purchased, these duties were not mandatory. As a result, Abraham expressed interest in only a part of the total estate with a view to avoiding any attendant legal

---

[18] *Ibid.*, p. 8.

[19] G. E. Mendenhall, *BA*, XI, No. 1 (1948), p. 18, XVII, No. 3 (1954), pp. 52f.; M. Noth, *Gesammelte Studien zum AT* (1957), pp. 142ff.

[20] Cf. Josh. 24:32; Judg. 9:4. For other aspects of covenant-making at Mari which illustrate Old Testament practices see M. Noth, *Mélanges Isidore Lévy* (1958), pp. 433ff.

[21] Cf. *GBB*, pp. 29f.

obligations (Gen. 23:9). Ephron declined to accede to this suggestion; for reasons which are not stated in the Genesis narrative he found it to his advantage to dispose of the entire property. Ultimately Abraham agreed to the stated terms, and in accordance with the custom of the day the sale was conducted in public with the purchase price being measured in weighed amounts of silver.[22] The mention of trees in the narrative reflects the Hittite practice of listing the exact number of trees growing on each piece of property sold.[23]

From this brief survey of archaeological material from the second millennium B.C. of Assyrian culture, it will be clear that the patriarchal narratives are set firmly against a contemporary social and cultural background. To talk of Abraham and the Hebrew patriarchs generally as real personages who enjoyed an independent existence is not to beg the entire question as to whether Abraham and the Biblical tradition concerning him is historical, as Jacobsen would imply.[24] Rather, as W. F. Albright has remarked:

> Abraham, Isaac, and Jacob no longer seem isolated figures, much less reflections of later Israelite history; they now appear as true children of their age, bearing the same names, moving about over the same territory, visiting the same towns (especially Harran and Nahor), practising the same customs as their contemporaries.[25]

From an Egyptian tomb at Beni-Hasan has come some indication of the way in which the Semites of the time of Abraham must have dressed. A relief dated about 1900 B. C. depicted a group of semi-nomadic Semites on a visit to Egypt,[26] and showed, among other things, that the men wore beards while the women kept their flowing hair in position by means of clips or bands. Their clothes were multi-colored, and whereas the men wore short skirts and sandals, the women were attired in long dresses which they fastened at the shoulder with a clasp.[27]

The work of Nelson Glueck in the Hashemite Kingdom of Jordan[28] has made it clear that at this time (ca. 2000-1700 B.C.) the sites of Dothan, Gerar, Shechem, and Bethel were all inhabited, lending substance to the Genesis tradition that associated the patriarchs with the densely wooded hill country of Palestine (cf. Gen. 13:18; 26:23; 28:10; 33:18; 35:1; 37:17). The political atmosphere of the day is conveyed quite aptly by the story

---

[22] *IOTT*, p. 111.

[23] Gen. 23:17. M. R. Lehmann, *BASOR*, No. 129 (1953), pp. 15ff. Cf. J. C. L. Gibson, *JNES*, XX (1961), pp. 224ff.

[24] *IDB*, IV, p. 738.

[25] Quoted by G. F. Owen, *Archaeology and the Bible* (1961), p. 120.

[26] *WHAB*, p. 23.

[27] *WBA*, p. 46.

[28] N. Glueck, *The Other Side of the Jordan* (1940), pp. 114ff., *BA*, XVIII, No. 1 (1955), pp. 2ff.; *WMTS*, p. 71.

of Sinuhe, a prominent state official in Egypt who lived in the twentieth century B.C. at a time when southern Syria and Palestine were organized in terms of city-states. The political upheaval which had taken place on the death of the Egyptian pharaoh Amenemhet I made it desirable for Sinuhe to seek asylum in Palestine. His *Tale*[29] described the dangers attached to his crossing of the heavily guarded border and the hardships that he experienced en route to Kedem, where he fell in with an Amorite chieftain of the same kind as Abraham, Laban, and Jacob.

Sinuhe gained the confidence of the Amorites to the point where he ultimately commanded one of their tribes in a series of raids. His account of Amorite life closely resembles that experienced by the patriarchs, while his description of the highlands of Palestine is distinctly reminiscent of Deuteronomy 8:8.

> There were figs in it, and vines,
> More plentiful than water was its wine,
> Copious was its honey, plenteous its oil;
> All fruits were upon its trees.
> Barley was there, and spelt,
> Without end all cattle....[30]

B. THE EXODUS

1. Israel's sojourn in Egypt. The political and social problems of the Egyptian Middle Kingdom period (*ca.* 2000-1776 B.C.) were compounded by an increase in trading relations with the Semitic nomads of Canaan and Arabia, and by the appearance upon the horizon of the Hyksos, a people of mixed Semitic-Asiatic descent.[31] By introducing the horse-drawn iron-fitted chariot and the compound Asiatic bow as military weapons, the Hyksos swept unconquered into the Nile delta about 1715 B.C., and by about 1680 B.C. they had subjugated the people of the Two Lands, a state of affairs that lasted for almost a century-and-a-half.

If elements of the Habiru were involved in some manner with the Hyksos ("chiefs of foreign lands") invasion of Egypt, it would be comparatively easy to understand why the descendants of Jacob were able to thrive in a land which was normally hostile, or at best only tolerant, towards strangers and immigrants. Such a connection between the Avar-

---

[29] *ANET*, pp. 18ff.
[30] *ARE*, I, Sect. 496. Cf. *ANET*, pp. 19f.; *LAP*, p. 82.
[31] For a discussion of Hyksos origins see H. Stock, *Studien zur Geschichte und Archäologie der 13. bis 17. Dynaste Ägyptens* (1942), pp. 19ff.; R. M. Engberg, *The Hyksos Reconsidered* (1939), pp. 4ff.; T. Säve-Söderberg, *JEA*, XXXVII (1951), pp. 53ff.; *FSAC*, pp. 202ff.; W. F. Albright, *Tell Beit Mirsim II*, pp. 27ff. For a description of contemporary weapons see Y. Yadin, *The Art of Warfare in Biblical Lands* (1963), I, pp. 77ff.

is era of Hyksos rule and the patriarchal migration around 1700 B.C. would also throw light on the reference to Joseph's buying up the land for Pharaoh (Gen. 47:13), a procedure that reflected the social disruption in Palestine under Hyksos rule and which resulted in a form of feudalism.[32]

Against such a background it would not be unwarranted to expect considerable local color in the sagas of Joseph. The phrase "overseer over his house" (Gen. 39:4) is a translation of a title used of officers in the houses of Egyptian nobility; the designations "over my house" and "father to Pharaoh . . . lord of all his house . . . ruler throughout all the land of Egypt"(Gen. 41:40; 45:8) correspond exactly to the office of vizier or prime minister of Egypt.[33] One post not mentioned in the Old Testament is that of "Superintendent of the Granaries," an office of considerable importance in a country such as Egypt, where so much depended upon the proper storage and distribution of the grain. Since Joseph exercised these functions, he probably assumed the title also.[34] The suggestion that the office which Joseph held was a high one created especially in a time of emergency does not take adequate cognizance of the fact that Joseph was already very prominent politically before the catastrophes overtook Egypt.

The procedure by which the vizier was invested with a golden chain of office has been illustrated by a mural from the reign of Seti I (ca. 1308-1290 B.C.).[35] Riding in chariots was reserved for important state personages, to whom ordinary individuals were required to pay proper respect as the chariots passed. The incidence of periodic famines has been commemorated in inscriptions on tomb walls, as for example at Beni-Hasan (ca. 1980 B.C.),[36] and El Kab.[37] The familiar Egyptian "Tale of the Two Brothers,"[38] narrating the attempted seduction of a virtuous man, Bata, by the wife of his older brother, has points of contact with the account of Joseph and the wife of Potiphar (Gen. 39:7ff.), although in other respects it is quite different. In the "Tale," which was invariably related in ancient Egypt for entertainment rather than for moral instruction, the amorous wife made some suggestive remarks to the unfortunate Bata, and then she

> . . .stood up and took hold of him. . .then the lad (became) like a leopard with (great) rage at the wicked suggestion which she had made to him, and she

[32] Cf. Steindorff and Seele, *When Egypt Ruled the East* (1942), p. 88.

[33] *WBA*, p. 53.

[34] K. A. Kitchen, *Tyndale House Bulletin*, No. 2 (1957), pp. 4ff.; cf. W. A. Ward, *Journal of Semitic Studies*, V (1960), pp. 144ff.; J. Vergote, *Joseph en Égypte* (1959), pp. 32ff.

[35] J. A. Thompson, *Archaeology and the OT* (1959), pp. 37f.

[36] Cf. S. L. Caiger, *Bible and Spade* (1936), p. 61.

[37] Cf. R. K. Harrison, *Archaeology of the OT* (1962), p. 38.

[38] *ANE*, p. 12.

was very, very frightened. Then he argued with her, saying, "See here—you are like a mother to me, and your husband is like a father to me...What is this great crime which you have said to me? Don't say it to me again!"[39]

That this general theme was not unknown in other parts of the ancient world is evident from the presence of the Bellerophon story in the eastern Mediterranean texts of the Amarna-Mycenaean age, a narrative describing an adulterous wife who attempts to seduce a virtuous youth and maligns him when she is unsuccessful in her scheme.

Deliverance from Hyksos rule came for the Egyptians about 1560 B.C. When the hated invaders had finally been expelled, all possible traces of Hyksos domination, including public buildings, inscriptions, and the like, were eradicated.[40] During the Nineteenth Dynasty the pharaoh Rameses II moved his capital from Thebes to Tanis (Avaris), and enlarged the city that had been reconstructed by Seti I. Excavations at the site by Montet recovered *stelae* and other artifacts bearing the name of Rameses and his successors.[41] Since contemporary Egyptian texts mentioned that some 'Apiru were employed to drag the huge stones used in temple construction at sites that probably included Pithom and Rameses, it may well be that the narrative in Exodus 1 points to this period of reconstruction under Rameses II. Pithom has been identified with Tell el-Retabeh, and excavations there have uncovered some of the massive brick structures dating from the time of Rameses II in the Nineteenth Dynasty. Since no traces of construction or expansion in the preceding dynasty were evident at the site, it would appear that the Exodus tradition of bondage refers to the forced labor on constructional projects in the days of Rameses II. To this evidence may be added the fact that for two centuries (ca. 1300-1100 B.C.) Tanis was known as *Per Re'emasese* or "House of Rameses."[42] In sum this would appear to point to a thirteenth-century B.C. date for the Exodus.

With the discovery of the site of Rameses, the route followed by the withdrawing Israelites on their way to Sinai can be established with reasonable accuracy.[43] Clearly it was important for them to journey southeast to Succoth in order to avoid the heavily fortified frontier post of Zilu, which guarded the "Way of the Land of the Philistines." Thus they could not possibly have taken the northern route out of Egypt, as older scholars mistakenly supposed.[44] It is almost certain that the Israel-

[39] *ANET*, p. 24.
[40] Cf. *ARE*, II, sect. 303.
[41] P. Montet, *Les Nouvelles fouilles de Tanis* (1929-1933).
[42] *WBA*, p. 59.
[43] For a tentative map of the route see *WHAB*, p. 41.
[44] Cf. M. K. Schleiden, *Die Landenge von Sues* (1959); H. K. Brugsch, *L'Exode et les Monuments Égyptiens* (1875); C. S. Jarvis, *Yesterday and Today in Sinai* (1931). A. Gardiner, *JEA*, XIX (1933), pp. 127f., withdrew his earlier objections to the substantial historicity of the Exodus account.

ites crossed over a vast papyrus marsh, the Yam Suph or "Reed Sea,"[45] situated between the Bitter Lakes and the town of Zilu (Thiel), on their way to the Sinai peninsula, where sites such as Elim (Wadi Gharandel), Dophkah (Serabit el-Khadem), and Rephidim have been identified with reasonable certainty. More or less restricted to travel by asses, the wandering Israelites were compelled to keep fairly close to the oases and grazing lands to the southwest of the Dead Sea. This may well explain why the thirty-seven years of wilderness wanderings prior to the entrance into Canaan were actually spent in the region of Kadesh ('Ain Qudeirat—'Ain Qudeis) (Deut. 1:46).

2. *Canaan prior to the conquest.* The study of the history and religion of the Canaanites before the arrival of the Israelites has been considerably enlightened by the recovery of two second-millennium B.C. cultures. The activities of Winckler at Boghazköy (Khattusas) in east-central Asia Minor brought to light the majesty of the ancient Hittites, who made up the first Indo-European migration from the Caucasus region to reach the inland areas of Cappadocia.[46] They intermingled with the native Khatti, whose territory they conquered, and established a number of city-states beginning about 1850 B.C., while the ancient Assyrians were gaining the ascendancy in Mesopotamia. The Old Empire period lasted from about 1800 B.C. to approximately 1600 B.C., at which time internal strife seriously weakened the Hittite nation and led to a revival of Hurrian influence in the old Mitanni kingdom of northern Mesopotamia. The New Empire period began under the leadership of Suppiluliuma (*ca.* 1375-1340 B.C.), and was characterized by friendly relations with Egypt. Of the thousands of clay tablets written in several different languages—including Nesian and some dialects of Luvian—that were recovered from Boghazköy, one diplomatic text contained a greeting from Suppiluliuma to Amenhotep III (Huria) of Egypt as follows:

> Thus hath Suppiluliuma the great king, king of Hatti-land, to Huria, king of Egypt, my brother, spoken: "I am well. With thee may it be well...just as thy father and I mutually requested presents, so wilt also thou and I now be mutually good friends. . . ."[47]

By the time Hattusilis III (*ca.* 1275-1250 B.C.) came to the throne, Hittite power had been weakened by intrigue in neighboring confederate states. The Hittite empire finally crumbled under a series of powerful attacks by the "Sea Peoples" from the Aegean, and about 1200 B.C. the Hittites vanished from the historical scene.

---

[45] Cf. G. E. Wright, *IDB*, II, pp. 197ff.

[46] Cf. H. Winckler, *Sonderabzug aus der Orientalistischen Litteratur-Zeitung*, Dec. 15, 1906; *Mitteilungen der Deutschen Orientgesellschaft*, XXXV (1907), pp. 1ff.; H. Winckler and O. Puchstein, *Smithsonian Report for 1908*, pp. 677ff.; A. Götze, *Hethiter, Churriter und Assyrer* (1936), p. 27.

[47] *LAP*, p. 167; J. A. Knudtzon, *Die El-Amarna Tafeln* (1901-1905), I, No. 41.

Cuneiform texts from Boghazköy have demonstrated conclusively the cultural virility of these people, who were once relegated by liberal critics to an insignificant place in ancient Near Eastern history.[48] It is now known that the Hittites were in possession of advanced technological processes for smelting iron for all commercial purposes. They were renowned horsemen, and were the first to manufacture chariots with iron fittings and use them as weapons of war.[49] From the extant Royal Addresses it is evident that the ancient Hittites valued the arts of peace also, for the texts indicate that they had already enjoyed a prolonged tradition of settled court life.[50] The form that their society ultimately adopted seems to have been that of an exclusive caste superimposed upon the indigenous Anatolian Khatti. At an earlier time it had consisted of numerous separate townships governed by bodies of elders.[51]

Legal tablets from Khattusas showed that the Hittites thought in terms of the same general concepts of justice as the ancient Babylonians. Their legal corpus was based on several earlier collections, some of which may indicate stages in the development of a Code.[52] The inviolability of oaths, covenants, and treaties was consistently emphasized, as in other ancient Near Eastern systems of jurisprudence; but in contrast to the codes of Hammurabi and Moses the principle of retaliation was subordinate to that of restitution. One additional feature of Hittite legislative and social enlightenment can be seen in the marked degree of respect accorded to women.[53]

An advanced degree of syncretism characterized Hittite religion, whose pantheon included Sumerian, Akkadian, Egyptian, and native Khatti deities. Unlike their Babylonian counterparts the Hittite shrines were constructed in such a manner as to allow only a select few to observe the rituals of the holy place or *cella*.[54] The temple priests appear to have been occupied predominantly with ritual ministrations to the weather-deity of Hatti, who was known as "King of Heaven, Lord of the Land of Hatti." The cuneiform texts contained occasional references to human sacrifices, but for the most part the offices of the priests were directed towards the propagation of a nature-worship, which included spring rites for the quickening of the earth. Extant tablets indicate very little connection, if any, between the Hittite royal festival and the ceremonies that marked the commencement of the Babylonian New Year.[55]

[48] So, e.g. H. Ewald, *The History of Israel* (1883 ed.), I, pp. 233f., 235.
[49] *TH*, pp. 104f.
[50] *Ibid.*, p. 67.
[51] *Ibid.*, pp. 68f.
[52] *Ibid.*, p. 88.
[53] For Hittite legal texts see F. Hrozný, *Code hittite provenant de l'Asie Mineure* (1922); J. M. P. Smith, *The Origin and History of Hebrew Law* (1931), pp. 246ff.; E. Neufeld, *The Hittite Laws* (1951); *ANET*, pp. 188ff.
[54] *TH*, p. 145, pl. 9.
[55] *Ibid.*, pp. 152ff.

The second of these cultures that flourished in the second millennium B.C. was that of the Canaanites, a culture that was considerably more advanced than its counterpart in Israel during the period following the death of Joshua. The Canaanites made widespread use of Hittite technological developments in the field of iron manufacture, and shared with the Philistines the bulk of the export trade in the metal to Egypt. The actual recovery of ancient Canaanite culture was the result of an accidental discovery at Ras Shamra (Ugarit) in 1928. The site was excavated by Schaeffer the following year, and was found to date from the Neolithic period. Known as Ugarit in the Egyptian Amarna Age, its culture became dominant in Canaan during the fourteenth century B.C., after which it declined under Hittite and Egyptian influence. The tablets that were unearthed had been written in a Hurrian dialect and in an unfamiliar northwest Semitic language, transcribed in an alphabetic rather than a syllabic script, and were closely akin to Phoenician and Biblical Hebrew.[56]

Whereas the ancient Egyptians had employed a combination of syllabic writing (in which each sign represents a syllable) and logographic writing (in which each sign stands for a word) to produce the complicated hieroglyphic script, the Canaanites were the first to utilize the principle of alphabetism in cuneiform, thereby making a break with the syllabics of the Mesopotamians. The alphabet in consonantal form was subsequently transmitted through the Hebrews and the Phoenicians to the Greeks, who modified it, introduced diphthongs, and gave the language its classical form. At a later period the alphabet was modified still further by the Romans. Ancient Ugaritic culture is thus very important in the history of the development of pure alphabetism.[57]

The literature of Ugarit was predominantly mythological, consisting of legends and epic cycles, but the prose texts reflected the highly organized nature of Ugaritic society in describing land-ownership, civic affairs, administration, taxation, diplomatic matters, veterinary medicine, and many other topics.[58] What is of particular significance in these compositions, as far as the student of Scripture is concerned, is their exhibition of grammatical and literary forms that also occur in various parts of the Hebrew Bible, notably the Psalter. This discovery has already done much to clear up the alleged textual anomalies in the Psalms and other poetical writings, indicating that many forms that were previously

[56] Cf. C. H. Gordon, *Orientalia*, XIX (1950), pp. 374ff.; E. A. Speiser, *BASOR*, No. 121 (1951), pp. 17ff.; J. Friedrich, *Scientia*, LXXIV (1949), pp. 220ff.; W. F. Albright, *BASOR*, No. 150 (1958), pp. 36ff.; *FSAC*, p. 39; C. F. Pfeiffer, *Ras Shamra and the Bible* (1962), pp. 15, 25ff.; *BANE*, p. 58.

[57] Cf. *IOTT*, p. 81; D. Diringer, *The Story of the Aleph Beth* (1960), pp. 32ff.; C. H. Gordon, *Ugarit and Minoan Crete* (1965), p. 15.

[58] *ANET*, pp. 129ff.; *ANE*, pp. 92ff.; C. H. Gordon, *Ugaritic Handbook*, pp. 129ff.; *UL*, pp. 11ff.

thought to be corrupt are in fact peculiarities of Canaanite linguistic and grammatical structure whose significance had been forgotten with the passing of the generations and ages. Literary parallelism was a conspicuous feature of Ugaritic poetry, as seen in the citation:

> Lo thine enemies, O Baal,
> Lo thine enemies wilt thou smite.
> Lo thou wilt vanquish thy foes.[59]

which closely resembles the form of Psalm 92:9:

> For behold thine enemies, O Lord,
> For behold thine enemies shall perish.
> All the workers of iniquity shall be scattered.

Further parallels to Hebrew thought can be seen in the description of Baal as the "Rider of the Clouds" (cf. Pss. 68:4; 104:3), who was enthroned in the heavens (cf. Pss. 2:4; 103:19) and hurled down lightnings and thunderbolts (cf. Pss. 18:13; 77:18; 144:6).[60] The references of the Psalmist (Ps. 74:13f.) to "dragons" and "leviathan" may be somewhat reminiscent of the legend cycle of Baal and Anat, in which the marine monster Tannin was invoked for magical purposes.[61] But in this connection there are other considerations which have to be borne in mind, and these will be discussed elsewhere in the present work.

Ugaritic cult-worship as revealed by the cuneiform texts has done much to illumine the Old Testament references to Canaanite religion. The depraved nature of the pagan deities Anat and Astarte is evident in all phases of the poetic cycles from Ugarit. Both these mythical personages were styled "the great goddesses which conceive but do not bear," and the seduction of Anat by Baal was a popular element of contemporary mythology. In one text Anat was depicted as a butcher, slaying young and old alike in a frantic effort of destruction.[62] Asherah, the "creatress of the Gods," was commonly represented to be a nude prostitute called "Holiness," as was also the case in Egyptian cult-worship.[63] There was a recognized homosexual guild (Cinaedus) in the Canaanite temples, and ritual prostitution of both sexes was a commonplace occurrence.

Worship seems for the most part to have been carried out at the altars located on or near the summits of hills. To these "high places" the

---

[59] *UL*, p. 15; cf. H. L. Ginsberg, *Orientalia*, V (1936), p. 171; W. F. Albright, *Religion in Life*, XXI, No. 4 (1952), pp. 542ff.

[60] Cf. A. S. Kapelrud, *The Ras Shamra Discoveries and the OT* (1965), pp. 30ff.; W. F. Albright, *CBQ*, VII (1945), pp. 5ff.; T. H. Gaster, *Thespis* (1949 ed.), pp. 115ff.; W. F. Albright, *Religion in Life*, XXI, No. 4 (1952), pp. 542f.

[61] *UL*, p. 49.

[62] *UL*, pp. 17f.; cf. *ARI*, pp. 77, 88; *BPAE*, pp. 16f.

[63] W. F. Albright in *The Jews, Their History, Culture and Religion* (ed. L. Finkelstein, 1949), I, p. 10; *BPAE*, pp. 16f.

worshippers brought their offerings of cereals or meat, and the ritual in which they engaged normally included prayer and the presentation of offerings. A sacrificial feast of some kind seems also to have been a general part of the ceremony. The texts indicate that Canaanite sacrificial ritual was more diversified than was the case among the Israelites.[64] The Old Testament narratives speak of specific cult-objects, including the *asherah* and the sacred pillar or *maççebah* as being associated with sanctuary-worship in Canaan. The Ugaritic texts leave no doubt as to the gross sensuality and immorality of the Canaanite cultic rites, and it is sobering to realize that its barbarity and license had a widespread appeal to the contemporary Near Eastern nations.

3. *The conquest of Canaan.* Just before the death of Moses the Israelites crossed into Transjordan, preparatory to an attack on Jericho, a former Hyksos fortress that guarded access to Canaan proper. During the Middle Bronze Age (*ca.* 2100-1500 B.C.) the Hyksos had enlarged Jericho and strengthened its defenses by the addition of a huge embankment. About 1550 B.C. they retreated to Jericho after being expelled from Egypt, but they were unable to make a firm stand against Egypt's armies and lost their fortress by fire. Shortly after this period Jericho was apparently rebuilt on a smaller scale, and fortified by means of a double wall of mud brick, the inner structure following the general lines of the Early Bronze Age wall.

Garstang designated this as "City D," which he held to have been destroyed about 1400 B.C. under the leadership of Joshua.[65] However, the work of Kathleen Kenyon at the site has necessitated some revision of this estimate. She found very few if any purely demonstrable traces of the Joshua period in the mound, and no remains whatever of Late Bronze Age walls. Indeed, the structures which Garstang had ascribed to "City D" were actually found to date from the third millennium B.C., and evidently constituted part of a defensive system erected during that period.[66] As a result, it is at present extremely difficult to make any reliable pronouncement upon the nature and extent of Jericho in the time of Joshua. However, it is certainly in the realm of possibility that the military forces of the Eighteenth Dynasty of Egypt had reduced the once-powerful Hyksos fortress to little more than an outpost after 1600 B.C., although it was still imposing due to its strategic location.[67]

The general picture presented by archaeological excavation at the site is one of thorough desolation at Late Bronze Age levels, so that if these were exposed at the time of Joshua, the following five centuries, during which the site lay uninhabited (1 Kgs. 16:34), would furnish ample

---

[64] *ARI*, p. 92.

[65] J. and J. B. E. Garstang, *The Story of Jericho*, pp. 135ff.

[66] Cf. K. M. Kenyon, *BA*, XVI, No. 3 (1953), pp. 46ff., XVII, No. 4 (1954), pp. 98ff.; also her *Digging Up Jericho*, pp. 170ff., 259ff.

[67] Cf. *WBA*, p. 79; K. A. Kitchen, *NBD*, pp. 612f.

opportunity for the forces of erosion to obliterate traces of Late Bronze Age strata. It is apparent from other areas of the mound that this may well have been the case, for Jericho's Middle Bronze Age levels were considerably denuded by erosion. Whatever sections of the site were not occupied by the Iron Age settlement of Ahab and subsequent periods have been exposed to erosive forces down to the present day. Thus it can be said that archaeological evidence from Jericho relating to a thirteenth-century B.C. date for the conquest is inconclusive, and it is not too much to suppose that this situation may be one result of the conquest itself.

Excavations at the sites of Ai, Bethel, Lachish, and Debir have furnished important evidence for their destruction in the thirteenth century B.C., and of these only the first presents any real difficulties in the matter of interpretation. Madame Marquet-Krause undertook work at Ai (et-Tell, some thirteen miles northwest of Jericho) in 1933, and showed that the site had been one of the major fortresses in Canaan between 3200 and 2400 B.C. It was destroyed shortly after this time, apparently by Amorite raiders, and seems to have remained uninhabited except for a small village settlement about 1100 B.C.[68] Ai was thus already in ruins at the time when the invading Israelites under Joshua conquered the land, and it may be that its name, which means "ruin," was given to it at that period.

The mention of Ai in the narrative dealing with the conquest of Bethel (Josh. 8:1ff.),[69] a mile-and-a-half distant, probably arose because the *tell* served as an advanced observation and strongpoint for the defenders of Bethel, and not, as Noth suggested,[70] because the entire narrative of the destruction of Ai constituted an aetiological legend introduced in order to account for the significance of the Hebrew term. There can be no doubt that the Biblical description of that aspect of the campaign involving Ai and the surrounding territory intended to convey the impression that the inhabitants of the locality made a firm defensive stand at Ai, and that the invaders subsequently destroyed the site as a means of forestalling any subsequent offensive action by the military forces of Ai and Bethel. This fact, combined with the strategic role which Ai had played prior to 2300 B.C., should constitute sufficient evidence for the existence of this important site, and furnish proper justification for the action taken by the conquering Israelites.

The Biblical account of the battle for Ai and its environs appears to envisage it as an inhabited—or at the very least occupied—site having

---

[68] *AJA*, LX (1936), p. 158; J. A. Callaway, *RB*, LXXII (1965), pp. 409ff.

[69] Cf. *BPAE*, pp. 29f.

[70] M. Noth, *PJB*, XXXIV (1938), pp. 7ff. Albright, *BASOR*, No. 74 (1939), pp. 15ff., suggested that the ruins of Ai had been associated by a subsequent generation with the destruction of Bethel.

its own ruler. This man, however, was most probably not so much a petty king as a military commander-in-chief whose troops were firmly entrenched in a defensive strongpoint—either of a temporary or a permanent nature—where the Israelites encountered initial resistance. Even when the text is taken as it stands, the narrative exhibits clear military purpose and plan on the part of Joshua, as will be made evident in a subsequent chapter. From an archaeological point of view, as observed above, no completely satisfactory explanation of the situation has been offered to date. It may be that Late Bronze Age levels at the site have been obliterated, as at Jericho, or even that the identification of Ai with et-Tell is incorrect. Certainly more work will need to be undertaken at Ai before the archaeological picture can be regarded as completely clarified.

Excavations at Bethel under W. F. Albright in 1934 revealed that the city had enjoyed considerable prosperity during the Middle and Late Bronze Ages. It was destroyed by a tremendous conflagration during the thirteenth century B.C., as indicated by the huge quantities of charred debris, burnt brick, and ashes that were unearthed at lower Late Bronze Age levels.[71]

Excavations by J. L. Starkey at Lachish,[72] which commenced in 1933, showed that the city had been one of great importance from the beginning of the Middle Bronze Age, and that at the time of Joshua it had attained the status of a Canaanite royal city, controlled by an Amorite governor. The reconstruction of a fragmentary bowl recovered from the site pointed to a thirteenth-century B.C. date for the destruction of the city. The pieces of pottery were inscribed with a notation, possibly made by an Egyptian tax collector, in which the fourth year of a certain pharaoh was mentioned. Despite the absence of a specific name, the script is clearly contemporary with Meneptah (ca. 1224 B.C.); and, since the bowl was broken when the city fell, it would appear that Lachish was destroyed between 1220 and 1200 B.C.[73]

The third stage of the Israelite occupation of Canaan was marked by the destruction of Hazor in Galilee. Garstang made a few soundings at the site (Tell el-Qedah) in 1926, but apart from his work it was nearly thirty years before anything was known from an archaeological standpoint about the Galilee campaign of Joshua. The huge rectangular plateau just to the north of the *tell* proper had been identified by Garstang as an enclosure for Hyksos chariotry, partly because he had been impressed with the huge earthen defensive rampart that stood some fifty feet in height. From 1954 on an expedition from the Hebrew University of Jerusalem under Yigael Yadin began to excavate the mound thoroughly,

---

[71] Albright, *BASOR*, No. 56 (1934), pp. 2ff.; *AASOR*, Vol. 39 (1968).
[72] Finally identified with Tell ed-Duweir by Albright, *ZAW*, XLVII (1929), p. 3.
[73] Albright, *BASOR*, No. 68 (1937), pp. 23f., No. 74 (1939), pp. 20ff.

and it was not long before something of the extent of ancient Hazor began to be apparent.[74]

The site was first settled about 4000 B.C. The rampart surrounding the enclosure was found to be of Hyksos origin, as Garstang had surmised, but the discovery of a cemetery from the Middle and Late Bronze Ages indicated that the last occupation of the site was in the thirteenth century B.C., and not about 1400 B.C., as Garstang had suggested.[75] Thus it would appear that the Biblical tradition, which relates a rather rapid occupation of Canaan under Joshua, as distinct from a systematic reduction of each strongpoint in the way of the advance, is substantially correct when correlated with the evidence of destruction revealed by the Late Bronze Age levels of various Palestinian sites mentioned in the early chapters of Joshua.

C. THE ISRAELITE KINGDOM

1. United. The political, social, and religious background of the early monarchy has been illuminated to a considerable extent as the result of archaeological excavations at sites associated with the activities of Saul, David, and Solomon. At Gezer, tenth-century B.C. levels yielded the celebrated "calendar," a small tablet of limestone that described the various months of the year and the particular type of agricultural work undertaken at that time:

> His two months are (olive) harvest; his two months are grain-planting; his two months are late planting; his month is hoeing up of flax; his month is barley-harvest; his month is harvest and festivity; his two months are vine-tending; his month is summer fruit.[76]

The excavations of Albright at Gibeah (Tell el-Ful) brought to light a fortress which most probably served as the headquarters of Saul when he was engaged in conflict with the Philistines. The defensive walls reflected Hittite designs, and were similar in character to those of Shechem, Beth-shemesh, and Tell Beit Mirsim in the eleventh to tenth centuries B.C.[77] The remains of pottery vessels and a plow at Gibeah pointed to continuous agricultural activity in the area, and an iron plow-point in the *tell* was hailed as the earliest datable iron implement found to date in the uplands of Palestine.[78] Albright assigned it to about 1010

---

[74] Y. Yadin, *BA*, XIX, No. 1 (1956), pp. 2ff., XX, No. 2 (1957), pp. 34ff.; Yadin *et al., Hazor I* (1958), pp. 5ff., *II* (1960). Cf. A. Malamat, *JBL*, LXXIX (1960), pp. 12ff.

[75] *Joshua-Judges* (1931), p. 383.

[76] Albright, *BASOR*, No. 92 (1943), pp. 16ff.; *ANET*, p. 320; *DOTT*, pp. 201ff.

[77] Cf. *WMTS*, pp. 141f.

[78] Cf. Albright, *AASOR*, IV (1924), pp. 51f., *BASOR*, No. 52 (1933), pp. 6ff., *AP*, pp. 120ff.; L. A. Sinclair, *BA*, XXVII, No. 2 (1964), pp. 52ff.

B.C., and its presence at Gibeah is an important comment on the monopoly which the Philistines had come to exercise over the manufacture and distribution of iron from about 1100 B.C.

The choice of Jerusalem as a capital for the Davidic kingdom was necessitated as much by political reasons as by geographical considerations. This Jebusite stronghold, built on a site that had been occupied as early as 3000 B.C., had never been conquered by Joshua and his followers, and the native defenders considered it to be impregnable. The city itself was erected upon a limestone promontory known as Ophel, where massive walls, bastions, and gates which go back to Jebusite origins have been discovered.[79] Complications arising from deficient water-supplies had been met in antiquity by means of tunnels similar to those excavated beneath Gezer, Megiddo, and Gibeon, which may have antedated the period of King David by as much as a millennium.[80] One such structure designed to bring water from the spring of Gihon in the Kidron valley southeast of Ophel consisted of a long aqueduct which emptied into the "old pool" just outside the city walls.

To enter Jerusalem by means of such an underground water system would have been a strenuous undertaking by any standards. An alternative access route has been furnished by Albright, who suggested that the word çinnôr, which is commonly translated "gutter" or "water-shaft," is in fact a Canaanite term meaning "hook."[81] Thus the reference would imply that David and his followers gained access to the fortress by means of grappling-hooks thrown over the parapets of the walls, and not by a penetration of the underground water-shafts.

Biblical traditions concerning the Solomonic period have been widely confirmed by archaeological discoveries in Palestine and elsewhere. Solomon revised the Egyptian bureaucratic patterns which his father David had adopted,[82] and divided the country into twelve areas for purposes of administration.[83] Taking advantage of Phoenician maritime skills and experience, Solomon built a large fleet of merchant ships for trade with southwest Arabia and Ethiopia. He also accumulated a number of ore-carrying or "Tarshish" ships in order to transport smelted

---

[79] Cf. G. A. Smith, *Jerusalem, I* (1907), pp. 152ff.; H. Vincent, *Jérusalem Antique* (1917), pp. 187ff.; G. Dalman, *Jerusalem und sein Gelände* (1930), pp. 123ff.; J. Simons, *Jerusalem in the OT* (1952), pp. 64ff. For a survey of the Jerusalem excavations see K. M. Kenyon, *BA*, XXVII, No. 2 (1964), pp. 34ff.

[80] Cf. R. A. S. Macalister, *The Excavation of Gezer* (1912), I, pp. 256ff.; R. S. Lamon, *The Megiddo Water System* (1935).

[81] In *OT Commentary* (ed. H. C. Alleman and E. E. Flack, 1954), p. 149. Cf. H. Vincent, *Jérusalem Antique*, pp. 146ff., also in *RB*, XXXIII (1924), pp. 357ff.; J. Simons, *Jerusalem in the OT*, pp. 168ff.

[82] Cf. J. Begrich, *ZAW*, LVIII (1940-1941), pp. 1ff.

[83] Cf. W. F. Albright, *JPOS*, V (1925), p. 17.

metal from mining areas in the western Mediterranean that had been developed by the Phoenicians.[84]

In the Wadi Arabah Nelson Glueck uncovered the first copper refinery ever found in the Near East. Built for Solomon in the tenth century B.C. by Phoenician workmen who were experienced in the construction of copper furnaces and the refining of ore, it was located at Ezion-geber (Tell el-Kheleifeh) between the hill-country of Sinai and the land of Edom. Its location was ideal, for, standing squarely as it did in the path of the north winds that howled down the Arabah rift-valley, it caught their full force and directed them to the furnace areas where the copper and iron ores were refined. The building in which the latter activity took place presented a blank surface to the prevailing north winds, and the only apertures in its structure were two parallel rows of holes linked by means of air-ducts to form flues. The ore was placed in crucibles above a wood or brush fire, and the air from the flues was then directed on the blaze to produce heat intense enough to smelt the ore. Imports of raw or partly refined material from Sardinia or Spain were augmented by plentiful deposits of copper and iron (cf. Deut. 8:9) in the soft sandstone of this inhospitable region.[85] The presence of numerous slag-heaps adjacent to the buildings indicates that the ore underwent preliminary processing at the site before being transported elsewhere. Adjoining the slag-heaps Glueck discovered the ruins of foundry rooms and the living-quarters of the miners themselves, many of whom were probably slaves. The development of the mining and smelting industry of the Arabah was as important economically in the early monarchy as it was technologically, since it furnished King Solomon with the principal export of his day and added to his immense wealth. As a result he was able to enter into commercial dealings with the Arabian monarchs, including the celebrated Queen of Sheba (Saba), whose position as head of a tribal confederacy in southern Arabia has been largely vindicated from cuneiform sources.

Traces of the ambitious building projects of Solomon have been unearthed at Megiddo and Gezer.[86] At the former site tenth-century B.C. levels yielded the remains of a palace fortified by means of massive walls and defensive towers. A stable compound was unearthed to the southeast of the *tell*, revealing the presence of hitching-posts which also helped to support the roof. Standing beside the posts on the cobblestone

---

[84] For the name "Tarshish" see F. Thieberger, *King Solomon* (1947), p. 206; cf. Albright, *BASOR*, No. 83 (1941), pp. 14ff., *BPAE*, p. 54.

[85] Glueck, *The Other Side of the Jordan*, pp. 50ff.; *BASOR*, No. 90 (1943), pp. 13f. For his revised views cf. *BA*, XXVIII, No. 3 (1965), pp. 70ff.

[86] G. E. Wright, *BA*, XXI, No. 4 (1958), pp. 103f.; Yadin, *Israel Exploration Journal*, VIII (1958), pp. 80ff.; *BA*, XXXIII, No. 3 (1970), pp. 65ff.

floor were several stone mangers.[87] From an examination of the masonry elements of the walls it is clear that earlier Phoenician constructional techniques were amply represented, appearing again in a similar form at Gezer, Lachish, and Ezion-geber.[88]

The rebuilding of the Millo and the extension of the mound of Ophel were part of the spectacular constructional activity which culminated in the erection of the royal palace and the Temple at Jerusalem. Although few actual remains of the Solomonic period are extant in Jerusalem, it is obvious from the style and structure of contemporary buildings that the Temple was a characteristically Phoenician edifice. Examples of a proto-Aeolic pilaster capitol have been recovered from eleventh-century B.C. strata at Samaria and Shechem, as well as from eleventh- and eighth-century B.C. levels at Megiddo. The lilies and palmettes that were used to decorate the temple were familiar *motifs* in Syro-Phoenicia, and cherubim were commonly found in the iconography of western Asia between 1800 and 600 B.C.[89]

2. Divided. The prosperity that was a feature of the kingdom of Israel under Omri (885/4-874/3 B.C.) saw the fortification of the capital city Samaria (modern Sebastiyeh) against possible Syrian attack. The Harvard expedition, which commenced work at the site in 1908 and continued there for two years,[90] was joined by teams from the Hebrew University and the British School of Archaeology in Jerusalem between 1931 and 1935. Of the sixteen levels of occupation at the site, seven have been assigned to the Israelites. Periods I and II, extending over the approximately twenty-eight years of Kings Omri and Ahab, were found to exhibit a high degree of constructional activity. A great many ivory inlays, the earliest of which belonged to the period of Omri, were recovered.[91] They consisted mainly of small panels in relief, and had as their subjects a variety of animals, plants, and winged human figures, reflecting both Egyptian and Phoenician cultural interests. The discovery of the Moabite Stone in 1866, which had been erected by King Mesha of Dibon about 840 B.C., revealed something of the vigor that characterized the rule of Omri. From the inscription it is evident that the latter

[87] *WBA*, pl. 85. J. W. Crowfoot, *PEQ*, LXXIII (1940), pp. 143ff., dated the stables in the time of Ahab, whereas Albright, *AJA*, CLIV (1940), pp. 546ff., assigned Stratum IV to the Solomonic period. Yadin, *BA*, XXIII, No. 2 (1960), pp. 62ff., postulated a date in the period of Ahab, with traces from the Solomonic era.

[88] *AP*, pp. 125ff.

[89] *ARI*, p. 216 n. 65.

[90] G. A. Reisner, C. S. Fisher, and D. G. Lyon, *Harvard Excavations at Samaria 1908-1910* (2 vols., 1924).

[91] J. W. and G. M. Crowfoot, *Early Ivories from Samaria* (1938); J. W. Crowfoot et al., *The Objects from Samaria* (1957).

had gained control of northern Moab and was exacting heavy tribute from that land:

> I am Mesha, son of Chemosh. . .king of Moab, the Dibonite. . .Omri, king of Israel. . .oppressed Moab many days because Chemosh was angry with his land. And his son succeeded him, and he also said, "I will oppress Moab. . . ."[92]

Artifacts relating to the period of Shalmaneser III (*ca.* 859-824 B.C.) have furnished independent confirmation of events that took place in the period of Ahab and Jehu. The Monolith Inscription of Shalmaneser gave an account of the battle at Qarqar on the Orontes in 853 B.C., a military engagement not mentioned in the Old Testament. In the text of this inscription, "Ahab the Israelite" was credited by Shalmaneser with the most powerful military elements in the coalition of Israelite and Syrian rulers.[93] The Black Obelisk of Shalmaneser, found by Layard in 1846, recorded the subjugation of Jehu and the amount of tribute which he paid to the Assyrians:

> Tribute of Jehu, son of Omri. Silver, gold, a golden bowl, a golden beaker, golden goblets, pitchers of gold, staves for the hand of the king, javelins, I received from him. . . .[94]

From the time of Jeroboam of Israel (782/1-753 B.C.) came a jasper seal belonging to "Shema, servant of Jeroboam," which was found at Megiddo by Schumacher in 1904.[95] The celebrated Samaritan (or Samarian) ostraca, recovered by the Harvard expedition in 1910, are also dated within this period.[96] These consist of administrative documents recording shipments of wine and oil to Samaria, and throw interesting light upon the social conditions of the age, which came under such intense prophetic censure (Am. 6:6).[97] One such ostracon read:[98]

> In the tenth year. To Shamariah from Beeryam, a jar of old wine.
>
> | | |
> |---|---|
> | Raga, son of Elisha | 2 |
> | Uzzah . . . | 1 |
> | Eliba | 1 |
> | Baala, son of Elisha | 1 |
> | Jedayah | 1 |

[92] *HDB*, III, p. 407; *LAP*, p. 157 and pl. 67; *ANET*, pp. 320f.

[93] *ARAB*, I, sect. 611.

[94] *LAP*, p. 173 and pl. 73; *ANET*, p. 281.

[95] *WBA*, p. 110 (a). S. Yeivin, *JNES*, XIX (1960), pp. 205ff., prefers to assign the seal to the time of Jeroboam I.

[96] Cf. J. W. Jack, *Samaria in Ahab's Time* (1929), pp. 37ff.; *ANET*, p. 321; *DOTT*, pp. 204ff.

[97] Cf. B. Maisler, *JPOS*, XXI (1948), pp. 117ff.

[98] Cf. *WBA*, p. 158.

The Assyrian annals of Tiglathpileser III record the nature of the tribute that Menahem of Israel (1 Kgs. 15:19ff.) paid about 740 B.C.:

> As for Menahem, terror overwhelmed him . . . he fled and submitted to me . . . silver, colored woollen garments, linen garments . . . I received as his tribute. . . .[99]

Around 727 B.C. Shalmaneser V, the successor of Tiglathpileser III, besieged Samaria when Hoshea of Israel (732/1-723/2 B.C.) sought to make an alliance with Egypt and refused to pay tribute to Assyria. Before Samaria fell in 722 B.C. Shalmaneser was succeeded by Sargon II (*ca.* 722-705 B.C.), who reduced Samaria and carried the Israelite tribes into captivity. The Khorsabad Annals furnished this account of the end of the northern kingdom:

> I besieged and captured Samaria, carrying off 27,290 of the people who dwelt therein. Fifty chariots I gathered from among them . . .[100]

Twenty years later Hezekiah of Judah was faced with a military threat from the Assyrians when Sennacherib invaded Palestine, isolated Tyre, and reduced Joppa, Ekron, and a number of other cities in the Philistine plain. An Egyptian relief force was heavily defeated at Lachish in 701 B.C., and Hezekiah decided to become tributary to Sennacherib in order to gain a brief respite while Jerusalem was made ready for a siege. The principal problem confronting the inhabitants of the capital city was that of the water supply. In order to improve on the earlier Jebusite attempts, Hezekiah had his engineers excavate a tunnel to bring the waters of Gihon into the old city proper. The conduit (2 Kgs. 20:20, 2 Chron. 32:30) that was planned was dug by means of simple hand tools through nearly six hundred yards of solid rock; and terminated just inside the southeastern corner of the city where the pool subsequently known as Siloam was situated. The record of this amazing feat of engineering was preserved for posterity in an inscription on the right-hand wall of the tunnel, some twenty feet from the Siloam entrance. Written in eighth-century B.C. script it reads:

> Now this is the story of the boring through; while the excavators were still lifting up their picks, each towards his fellow, and while there were yet three cubits to excavate, there was heard the voice of one calling to another, for there was a crevice in the rock on the right hand. And on the day they completed the boring-through, the stone-cutters struck pick against pick, one against the other; and the waters flowed from the spring to the pool, a distance of 100 cubits. And a hundred cubits was the height of the rock above the heads of the stone-cutters.[101]

[99] *ARAB*, I, sect. 816.
[100] *ARAB*, II, sect. 55; *ANET*, pp. 284f.
[101] G. A. Barton, *Archaeology and the Bible* (1946 ed.), p. 475. Cf. *LAP*, p. 160; *DOTT*, pp. 209ff.

Sennacherib appears to have been sufficiently gratified by his exploits at Lachish to have had a carved stone panel placed in his palace at Nineveh in order to commemorate the event. It depicted him seated in triumph upon his throne, receiving the spoils of victory,[102] and conveyed no hint whatever as to any catastrophe which his forces might have encountered during the Palestinian campaign, namely the destruction of 185,000 Assyrian troops.

The discovery of a number of inscribed ostraca at Lachish by J. L. Starkey from 1935 has provided dramatic illustration of Jeremiah's portrayal of the last days of Judah.[103] The potsherds were recovered in two groups from the mound at Tell ed-Duweir, the first fifteen in 1935 in the ruins of a small guard-room located just outside the city gate and the remaining three in the same general area three years later. The bulk of the ostraca can be dated from the autumn of 589 B.C., since they belong to the layer of ash representing the final overthrow of Lachish by Nebuchadnezzar. Although the sherds are in a bad state of preservation, with only about one third of the text being reasonably intelligible, they are of great importance philologically, quite apart from their significance for the age of Jeremiah. They consisted for the most part of dispatches written from a military outpost north of Lachish by a person named Hoshaiah to another individual, Joash, who may have been a staff officer at Lachish.

Ostracon III mentions a certain "prophet":

> . . . And it hath been reported to thy servant, saying, "The commander of the host, Coniah, son of Elnathan, hath come down in order to go into Egypt; and unto Hodaviah, son of Ahijah, and his men hath he sent to obtain . . . from him." And as for the letter of Tobiah, servant of the king, which came to Shallum, son of Jaddua through the prophet, saying, "Beware!" thy servant hath sent it to my lord.[104]

Considerable discussion has centered upon the identity of the "prophet," some scholars claiming that an unknown prophet was being referred to, others that the allusion was to Jeremiah himself. Torczyner favors an identification with Uriah of Kiriath-jearim (Jer. 26:20ff.), whose treasonous acts resulted in his extradition from Egypt and execution in

---

[102] A. H. Layard, *Discoveries Among the Ruins of Nineveh and Babylon* (1875), pp. 126ff.; *WBA*, pl. 117.

[103] Cf. H. Torczyner, *Lachish I, The Lachish Letters* (1938), *BASOR*, No. 70 (1938), pp. 11ff., No. 73 (1939), pp. 16ff., No. 80 (1940), pp. 11ff., No. 82 (1941), p. 24. On the excavations see also O. Tufnell, *Lachish II, The Fosse Temple* (1940), *Lachish III, The Iron Age* (1953), *Lachish IV, The Bronze Age* (1958), *PEQ*, XCI (1959), pp. 90ff.; R. D. Barnett, *Israel Exploration Journal*, VIII (1958), pp. 161ff.

[104] *ANET*, p. 322; *DOTT*, pp. 214f.

Jerusalem.[105] Ostracon VI contains the complaint of a patriotic official alleging that the *sarim* (royal personages or notables) were "weakening the hands" of the people by issuing demoralizing communications.[106] Ironically enough, it was this very accusation that had been levelled against Jeremiah during the days of Zedekiah (Jer. 38:4).

3. *Exiled.* As a result of the discovery in 1956 by D. J. Wiseman of four additional tablets of the Babylonian Chronicle in the archives of the British Museum, it is now possible to fix the precise date for Jerusalem's fall to the Babylonians with reference to an extra-Biblical source. The Babylonian texts make it clear that the city fell on the second of Adar (March 15-16), 597 B.C., and in addition they record that the Egyptians suffered a shattering defeat at Carchemish in 605 B.C., thus enabling the Babylonians to occupy "the whole area of Hatti."[107] A previously unrecorded engagement between the Babylonians and the Egyptians occurred in 601 B.C., in which both sides suffered heavy losses and Nebuchadnezzar was compelled to withdraw to Babylon for one year in order to obtain new equipment for his forces. The following twelve months were spent in exploratory attacks in Syria prior to the campaign against Judah which resulted in the fall of Jerusalem in 597 B.C. The evidence furnished by the Babylonian Chronicle thus confirms the Biblical tradition that Jerusalem collapsed under the Babylonian onslaughts of 597 and 587 B.C.

Conclusive evidence for the presence of Jewish captives in Babylonia has been provided by discoveries near the Ishtar Gate of Ancient Babylon, where several tablets were found that listed the rations of grain and oil allotted to captives in Babylon between 595 and 570 B.C.[108] The list of royal princes included "Yaukin, king of the land of Yahud,"[109] which substantiated the statement in 2 Kings 25:27 that Jehoiakin was a recipient of Babylonian royal bounty. Three stamped jar-handles from Debir and Beth-shemesh[110] bore the words "belonging to Eliakim, steward of Yaukin,"[111] implying that a crown steward was in charge of the royal property between 598 and 587 B.C. A seal impression recovered from

---

[105] For the unknown prophet identification, see C. H. Gordon, *The Living Past* (1941), p. 189; for Jeremiah, J. W. Jack, *PEQ*, LXX (1938), pp. 165ff.; also H. Torczyner, *The Lachish Letters*, p. 62. Other discussions are found in D. W. Thomas, "The Prophet" in the Lachish Ostraca (1946), pp. 7ff.; J. Hempel and L. Rost (eds.), *Von Ugarit nach Qumran* (1958), pp. 244ff.

[106] *ANET*, p. 322.

[107] D. J. Wiseman, *Chronicles of Chaldean Kings (626-556 B.C.) in the British Museum* (1956), pp. 32ff.

[108] R. Koldewey, *Das Wieder Erstehende Babylon* (1925), pp. 90ff. Cf. E. F. Weidner, *Mélanges Syriens offerts à M. René Dussaud* (1939), II, pp. 923ff.

[109] W. F. Albright, *BA*, V, No. 4 (1942), pp. 49f.

[110] *DOTT*, p. 224.

[111] *WBA*, pl. 125; D. J. Wiseman in C. F. H. Henry (ed.), *Revelation and the Bible* (1958), p. 313.

Lachish in 1935 carried the inscription, "to Gedaliah who is over the household," the owner of the seal being without doubt the governor of Judah appointed by Nebuchadnezzar (2 Kgs. 25:23).[112] On the reverse side the impression showed traces of the papyrus document to which it had been originally attached, and which had long since perished. The title "who is over the house" was invariably borne by the chief administrative official next in rank to the king. That the family of Gedaliah had been civil servants for some generations is evident from the fact that both his father and grandfather had occupied important offices in the state.

Archaeological discoveries of the twentieth century have furnished striking confirmation of many previously disputed aspects of the book of Ezra. C. C. Torrey and others maintained that the language of the book was late, and dated it from the third century B.C., after the time of Alexander the Great.[113] This position was seriously weakened with the discovery in 1903 of the celebrated Elephantine papyri at a military colony on an island near Aswan in Upper Egypt.[114] These documents were Aramaic letters written by the Jews of Elephantine between 500 and 400 B.C., when the colony was known as Yeb. Although it was of a military nature, the island's occupants derived a livelihood from trading, stone-quarrying, customs duties, and other administrative functions, in addition to furnishing a garrison. The papyri included legal contracts, deeds, official documents, agreements, diplomatic texts, and private letters. One papyrus was found to be a copy of a letter dispatched by the priests of the Jewish temple at Elephantine to Bagoas, the governor of Judah, complaining that anti-Semitic activity on the part of the Egyptians in 410 B.C. had resulted in the temple's being destroyed, and requesting financial aid in rebuilding it.

Estate transactions were prominently represented in the papyri, which showed that both men and women could engage in business on equal terms. One text contained the names of individuals who had donated gifts to the temple at Yeb, many of whom were women. All business dealings reflected in the contracts and agreements were drawn up in an accredited legal manner and attested by witnesses. They were then sealed and identified as to general content by means of a notation on the outside of the papyrus, following the traditional Babylonian method still in use later in the Persian empire. Quite apart from the way in which the papyri indicate the extent to which Aramaic had become the general

---

[112] *WBA*, pl. 128.

[113] Torrey, *The Composition and Historical Value of Ezra-Nehemiah* (1896); *Ezra Studies* (1910).

[114] E. Sachau, *Aramaeische Papyrus und Ostraka aus einer juedischen Militaer-Kolonie zu Elephantine* (2 vols., 1911); A. Ungnad, *Aramäische Papyrus aus Elephantine* (1911); A. Cowley, *Aramaic Papyri of the Fifth Century B. C.* (1923). A subsequent group, discovered in 1947 in the archives of the Brooklyn Museum, were published by E. G. Kraeling, *The Brooklyn Museum Aramaic Papyri* (1953). Cf. *ANET*, pp. 222f., 491ff.; *ANE*, pp. 278ff.; *DOTT*, pp. 256ff.

language of trade and diplomacy in the Persian period, the texts are important for demonstrating the historicity of Ezra, because they show conclusively that the Aramaic used in that book was characteristic of the fifth century B.C.

The authenticity of the royal decrees in Ezra 1:2ff. and 6:3ff. has also been vindicated by modern archaeological discoveries, against the assertions of older historians who argued that there was no evidence that Cyrus ever made such a decree as recorded there. Others who also denied their authenticity adopted a less radical position by conceding that there may have been some underlying historicity for the material.[115] It is now apparent by comparison with other ancient Near Eastern royal decrees from the Persian period (ca. 539-331 B.C.) that both documents are substantially accurate and authentic.[116] The first was a typical royal proclamation drawn up for utterance in the language of the people who were being addressed, whereas the second was a *dikrona* or official memorandum recording a decision to be implemented by the administrative official concerned. The memorandum was filed in the archives with other government documents once appropriate action had been taken on its contents, and in this connection it is important to note that, according to the Ezra narratives, the decree was discovered in the repository at Ecbatana (Achmetha), where Cyrus is known to have stayed in his first regnal year (538 B.C.).

Some sidelights on the book of Esther have emerged from excavations at Susa from 1851 under Williams and Loftus.[117] A trilingual inscription recovered from the throne room of the palace on the north side of the mound recounts the way in which Artaxerxes II had restored the building during his reign:

> Says Artaxerxes, the great king, the king of kings...the son of king Darius, the son of king Darius Hystaspes: My ancestor Darius built this *apadana* (throne room of the palace) in former times. In the time of Artaxerxes, my grandfather, it was burnt by fire. I have restored it....[118]

Further work at the site by Marcel Dieulafoy from 1884 showed that in the Persian period the city had covered nearly five thousand acres, and

[115] Some of the historians denying that Cyrus made the decree were B. Stade, *Geschichte des Volkes Israel* (1888), II, pp. 122n., 159n.; C. C. Torrey, *The Composition and Historical Value of Ezra-Nehemiah*, pp. 7ff., 55ff.; G. Hölscher in *Die Heilige Schrift des AT* (ed. Kautzsch and Bertholet, 1923), II, pp. 494f.; L. E. Browne, *Early Judaism* (1929), pp. 36ff., 44f. The more moderate group is represented by J. Wellhausen, *Nachrichten von der Gesellschaft der Wissenschaften zu Göttingen* (1895), pp. 169, 175f.

[116] Cf. E. Bickermann, *JBL*, LXV (1946), pp. 244ff.; Albright, *Alexander Marx Jubilee Volume* (1950), pp. 61ff.

[117] W. K. Loftus, *Travels and Researches in Chaldea and Susiana; With an Account of Excavations at Warka, the "Erech" of Nimrod, and Shush, "Shushan the Palace" of Esther, in 1849-1852* (1857).

[118] I. Price, *The Monuments and the OT* (1925), p. 403.

was divided into four separate areas—the citadel mound, the royal city ("Shushan the Palace"), the residential and business area ("the city Shushan"), and the district of the plain to the west of the river.[119] The palace fortress covered 123 acres, and consisted of the Throne Room or *apadana,* the "House of the King," and the "House of the Women," along with numerous courts, stairways, arches, and terraces. Among the debris removed from the adjacent "King's Gate" Dieulafoy discovered a quadrangular prism on which were engraved the numbers 1, 2, 5, and 6. This "die" (or *pur,* as it was known in its contemporary Assyrian designation) thus explains how Haman was able to "cast lots" for establishing a date on which the Jews would be destroyed, for the Persian method of throwing dice was equivalent to the Jewish custom of "casting the lot."

Additional information relating to fourth-century B.C. Samaria was unexpectedly furnished by the discovery in 1962 of some papyrus documents, consisting of fragments and strips of papyri and several relatively well-preserved rolls.[120] These comprise legal and administrative documents, in which familiar Biblical names such as Sanballat and Nehemiah occur. Neither of these two individuals was the Biblical personage of that specific name, but the fragments have made it possible to reconstruct with a fair degree of certainty the sequence of the governors of Samaria.[121] Even more important, however, is the significance of this material for palaeographical science. As far as the chronology of the third-century B.C. Biblical manuscripts from Qumran is concerned, it is already evident that the dates proposed by Cross for the Exodus manuscript from 4Q (*ca.* 250 B.C.) and the archaic fragment of Samuel (*ca.* 225 B.C.)[122] are definitely minimal, and may need to be revised upwards.

The fourth century B.C. has very few other dated Jewish documents, and material from Babylonia or Egypt that would throw light on the fortunes of the Jewish colonies in those countries is also virtually nonexistent. In Palestine, the rise of Arab power in the fifth century B.C. compelled the Edomites to migrate to Judaea, where they became known as Idumeans. They in turn were replaced by the Nabataeans, another Arab group who established a capital at Petra and carved temples and dwellings out of the soft red sandstone of the valley. Strategic areas of their frontier were protected by a series of fortresses, and their distinctive culture has finally become known through the excavation of Nabataean sites.[123]

[119] M. Dieulafoy, *L'acropole de Suse* (4 vols., 1890-1892).

[120] F. M. Cross, *BA,* XXVI, No. 4 (1963), pp. 110ff.

[121] *Ibid.,* p. 120.

[122] *BANE,* pp. 140ff.

[123] N. Glueck, *The Other Side of the Jordan,* pp. 158ff.; J. Starcky, *BA,* XVIII, No. 4 (1955), pp. 84ff.; W. H. Morton, *BA,* XIX, No. 2 (1956), pp. 26ff.; S. Moscati, *The Semites in Ancient History* (1959), pp. 117ff.; S. Cohen, *IDB,* III, pp. 491ff.

IV. THE DEAD SEA SCROLLS

Perhaps the most famous archaeological discovery of all times was the finding of the Dead Sea Scrolls in the Judaean wilderness in the late 1940s. The result of this discovery has been a vast increase of evidence bearing on Biblical studies. No attempt to sketch briefly their nature and significance could properly begin without a passing reference to the remarkable circumstances attending the discovery of the first Qumran cave.[1] Unfortunately, as Cross has remarked, these circumstances have been obscured by time and by the incidence of legendary accretions.[2] The general consensus of opinion, however, has it that the contents of the first Qumran cave (1Q) were discovered accidentally by two Ta'amireh tribesmen who were tending a mixed flock of sheep and goats in the Wadi Qumran area.[3] The elongated jars that the tribesmen found contained decaying rolls of leather instead of the expected coinage and other negotiable treasure, and it was some time, according to informed opinion, before the rolls came into the hands of a dealer in antiquities whose home was in Bethlehem.

During this interval a number of clandestine explorations of caves had apparently been taking place, so that by about 1948 there were two distinct collections of manuscripts from the Qumran area in existence. One of these passed into the hands of the Syrian Metropolitan of Jerusalem, Mar Athanasius Samuel, and included a complete copy of the book of Isaiah, a commentary on the book of Habakkuk, a document dealing with the rules of a religious community, another scroll that could not be unrolled at the time, and a few fragments of manuscripts. The other collection was brought to the attention of the late E. L. Sukenik of

---

[1] For a survey of the Wadi Qumran and related discoveries see R. K. Harrison, *The Dead Sea Scrolls* (1961). For English translations of the scrolls see T. H. Gaster, *The Dead Sea Scriptures in English Translation* (1956); G. Vermès, *The Dead Sea Scrolls in English* (1962). For a pointed Hebrew version see *Megilloth Midhbar Yehudhah* (ed. A. M. Habermann, 1959). For an early bibliography see W. S. LaSor, *Bibliography of the Dead Sea Scrolls, 1948-57* (1958).

[2] *The Ancient Library of Qumran and Modern Biblical Studies* (1958), p. 5.

[3] Cf. *DJD*, I, pp. 1ff.; G. L. Harding, *PEQ*, LXXXI (1949), pp. 112ff.; W. H. Brownlee, *JNES*, XVI (1957), pp. 236ff.

the Hebrew University of Jerusalem by the dealer in Bethlehem, and steps were taken to acquire the documents for the Hebrew University. This group of scrolls included an imperfect copy of Isaiah, a war document, and a hymnary in several sections.

In 1948 the Syrian Metropolitan allowed the manuscripts in his possession to be taken to the American Schools of Oriental Research in Jerusalem, where J. C. Trever and W. H. Brownlee studied and photographed the material. Their convictions regarding the antiquity of the material were confirmed by W. F. Albright, who after examining a print of part of the Isaiah scroll unhesitatingly declared it to be the "greatest manuscript discovery of modern times." Millar Burrows, who was Director of the American School in Jerusalem in 1948, concurred in this judgment, and on April 11 of that year he made the first announcement of the discovery.[4] Two weeks later Sukenik announced that the Hebrew University also possessed a collection of ancient scrolls of tremendous antiquity.[5]

This state of affairs put G. L. Harding, who was at that time in charge of antiquities in Transjordan and Arab Palestine, in an extremely delicate position, partly because the artifacts had been removed in contravention of Jordanian nationalization legislation, and partly because the problem of rediscovering and excavating the site under properly controlled conditions was now immeasurably more difficult. Meanwhile the scrolls which had been acquired by the Syrian Metropolitan were smuggled to the United States, and were subsequently published by the American Schools of Oriental Research.[6] After indirect negotiations these scrolls were finally purchased for the Hebrew University of Jerusalem in the summer of 1954 for an amount of money in the neighborhood of $250,000.

Due to the strenuous activities of Harding and R. de Vaux, the original Qumran cave was rediscovered in 1949, and despite the fact that they had obviously been preceded by illicit investigators, the archaeologists were able to recover some six hundred fragments of leather and papyrus. Spurred on by the hope of financial gain, the Arabs discovered other caves in 1951 to the southwest of the original Qumran location in what was known as the Wadi Murabba'at area. Material from this site

[4] Cf. G. E. Wright, *BA*, XI, No. 2 (1948), pp. 21ff.; W. F. Albright, *BASOR*, No. 110 (1948), pp. 2f.

[5] Cf. the extracts from his diary in E. L. Sukenik and N. Avigad (eds.), *'Oṣar hammegilloth haggenuzoth* (1954), p. 20.

[6] M. Burrows (ed.), *The Dead Sea Scrolls of St. Mark's Monastery* (1950-1951), Vol. I, *The Isaiah Manuscript and the Habakkuk Commentary;* Vol. II, fasc. 2, *Plates and Transcription of the Manual of Discipline.* The remaining scroll was unrolled six years later by J. Biberkraut, and proved to be an Aramaic version of parts of Genesis. It was published in 1956 by N. Avigad and Y. Yadin under the title, *A Genesis Apocryphon.*

included inscribed potsherds, fabric, Greek and Hebrew papyri, along with some documents written by Simon Bar-Kokhba to a certain Joshua ben Galgola. Subsequent discoveries at Qumran and Khirbet Mird brought the number of caves containing artifacts to eleven. In order to simplify identification and reference, the various sites are described in terms of the order of discovery in each particular location. Thus 1Q refers to the first Qumran cave, 2Mu to the second Murabba'at cave, and so on.

Explorations in 1951 on a shelf of rock near the Wadi Qumran uncovered the remains of a community building complete with copious reservoirs fashioned in the rock. As digging progressed it became apparent that the site had been occupied by a religious community from about 110 B.C. to 31 B.C., after which an earthquake (mentioned by Josephus, *AJ*, XV, 5, 2) damaged the building. Occupation was resumed at the beginning of the Christian era and lasted until A.D. 68, when the Romans took over the entire area. During the Second Jewish Revolt (A.D. 132-135) the area was used as a base by the Jewish guerrilla fighters, but at a later time the site became derelict.

The community settlement included the principal building, some 120 feet square, which was situated to the north of the main refectory. An adjoining kitchen was unearthed, and revealed the remains of hundreds of pottery vessels. Other rooms included assembly halls and the community *scriptorium*, which contained writing tables, ink-wells, and benches in fragmentary condition.[7] The recovery of an intact jar that was identical in shape to the remains of those recovered from the first Qumran cave established a decisive link between the scrolls and the people who had lived in the settlement. The site also contained facilities for smelting ore and baking earthenware vessels, indicating that the community was self-supporting. A number of cisterns had been dug into the rocks, and some of them were approached by means of steps, which might indicate that they had been used for baptismal rites or formal lustrations. A cache of coins found in 1955 furnished an almost continuous occupational history of the site from about 140 B.C. to the time of the Second Jewish Revolt against Imperial Rome.[8] A burial ground adjacent to the *khirbeh* showed that members of both sexes had enjoyed membership in the religious community.[9] The austerity of the sect was reflected by the simplicity of the graves and the absence of funerary ornamentation, although these conditions could have resulted from other factors.[10]

---

[7] J. M. Allegro, *The Dead Sea Scrolls* (1956), pp. 88f. and pls. 32-35.

[8] R. de Vaux, *RB*, LXI (1954), pp. 230f. For a plan of the community complex after excavation see *RB*, LXIII (1956), pl. 3; *The National Geographic Magazine*, CXIV, No. 6 (1958), pp. 790f.

[9] *VDJD*, p. 17.

[10] R. de Vaux, *RB*, LX (1953), p. 103.

The scope of the manuscript discoveries affords some indication of the literary interests and religious activities of the Qumran sect. In addition to the Sukenik Isaiah scroll (1QIsaᵇ),[11] the War document (1QM), the Thanksgiving Hymns (1QH), the Community Rule (1QS), the Saint Mark's Monastery large Isaiah scroll (1QIsaᵃ), and the Commentary on Habakkuk (1QpHab), the community possessed a significant number of extra-canonical writings as well as specifically apocryphal and pseudepigraphal works. The Pentateuch, the Psalms, the prophetic writings, and the book of Daniel were popular with the sectaries, and most of these works have survived in several copies or manuscript portions.

One of the more spectacular finds at Qumran came from 3Q in 1952. It consisted of two oxidized rolls of beaten copper that had been preserved almost by accident when the entrance of the cave, near which they had been placed, had collapsed in antiquity. Some delay occurred while experts in the United States and Britain determined the best method for opening the tightly rolled, eroded copper. Ultimately the two rolls were cut into strips at the Manchester College of Technology in 1956, with an ultimate textual loss of less than five per cent.[12] The two sections of scroll, translated by Allegro, were found to contain directions concerning the locations of treasure hoards, which unfortunately cannot be identified.[13] K. G. Kuhn, who had surmised correctly what the contents of the copper scroll would be before it was unrolled, has suggested that the scrolls may contain a record of the treasures in the Herodian Temple, which was destroyed in A.D. 70.[14]

The excellent state of preservation of the large Isaiah manuscript (1QIsaᵃ) is eloquent testimony to the care taken in sealing up the scroll against the time when it could be used once more by the sectaries. The technique of jar-storage most probably originated in ancient Egypt, but it was popular throughout the Near East for many centuries as a convenient means of preserving valuables or documents that were intended for posterity.[15] The Sukenik Isaiah manuscript (1QIsaᵇ) had not been fortunate enough to enjoy such a good state of preservation, for when found it was coated with a sticky layer of decayed leather which naturally presented formidable problems for those attempting to restore the text. The manuscripts were written in columnar form in non-metallic ink, and the letters were suspended for the most part from faintly ruled lines.[16] The fact that so many thousands of fragments were

11 For an explanation of the designations used to refer to the scrolls see R. K. Harrison, *The Dead Sea Scrolls*, p. 29.

12 J. M. Allegro, *The Dead Sea Scrolls*, pp. 181ff.

13 J. M. Allegro, *The Treasure of the Copper Scroll* (1960), pp. 33ff.

14 *Theologische Literaturzeitung* (1956), cols. 541ff.

15 Cf. Jer. 32:14; *The Assumption of Moses*, I, 18; J. M. Allegro, *The Dead Sea Scrolls*, pp. 78f.

16 *DJD*, I, p. 39. Cf. S. A. Birnbaum, *VT*, I (1951), pp. 97f.

discovered or eventually acquired through purchase from Arab sources has created an enormous amount of work for the international committee engaged in restoring, editing, and publishing the Qumran texts. Though this task is proceeding with regularity, it will be many years before the work will be completely satisfactory.

The world of Hebrew scholarship received with decidedly mixed reactions the news that the manuscripts in the possession of Professor Sukenik were to be dated not later than A.D. 70. Some were frankly skeptical that the latest Hebrew manuscripts at that time (from the eighth and ninth centuries A.D.) could have been antedated by almost a millennium as the result of a single discovery. Others were suspicious of fraud or forgery, remembering that eminent scholars had been thus victimized in previous generations. At once an acrimonious debate concerning the authenticity and dating of the scrolls sprang up among several eminent scholars who, unfortunately, had not had the opportunity of first-hand acquaintance with the discoveries. In England the early date assigned on palaeographic and other grounds by Albright, Burrows, Sukenik, and Trever was challenged by G. R. Driver, who in turn was immediately taken to task by S. A. Birnbaum, an eminent British palaeographer. In the United States, the chief protagonist was Solomon Zeitlin, the distinguished co-editor of the *Jewish Quarterly Review*, who promptly denounced the manuscripts as forgeries, envisaged the entire proceedings in terms of a gigantic hoax, and assigned a medieval date to the extant documents.[17]

Admittedly the whole situation was unfortunate at the time, since it was complicated by the lack of proper corroborating evidence from Qumran, but this situation has now been remedied by further discoveries. As a result there is substantial scholarly agreement that the scrolls emerged from a period beginning about 250 B.C. and ending

---

[17] Driver's views are found in *The Times* of August 23, 30, and September 22, 1949 (cf. R. Eisler's *Times* article of September 8, 1949), and in *The Hebrew Scrolls from the Neighbourhood of Jericho and the Dead Sea* (1951), pp. 30ff. For Birnbaum's views see BASOR, No. 113 (1949), pp. 33ff., No. 115 (1949), pp. 20ff.; *PEQ*, LXXXI (1949), pp. 140ff.; *JBL*, LXVIII (1949), pp. 161ff. Since then Driver has reduced his original dating by several centuries, now holding them to be approximately contemporary with the New Testament writings (*The Judaean Scrolls* [1963]). Zeitlin has written in *JQR*, XXXIX (1948-49), pp. 171ff., 235ff., 337ff., XL (1949-50), pp. 57ff., 291ff., 373ff., XLI (1950-51), pp. 1ff., 71ff., 247ff., XLII (1951-52), pp. 133ff., XLIII (1952-53), pp. 72ff., 140ff., XLIV (1953-54), pp. 85ff., XLV (1954-55), pp. 1ff., 83ff., 174ff., XLVI (1955-56), pp. 1ff., 116ff., XLVII (1956-57), pp. 745ff., XLVIII (1957-58), pp. 71ff., 243ff., XLIX (1958-59), pp. 1ff., 221ff., LI (1960-61), pp. 156ff., 265ff. Persistent rumors that Dr. Zeitlin has abandoned his militant position on the dating of the scrolls are unfounded: in private correspondence with the author he has reaffirmed his stand that the documents are medieval in date, and that they have no value for either the Old or New Testament.

just before the fall of Jerusalem in A.D. 70. Burrows dated the earliest Qumran fragments to about the third century B.C., a decision which may now need to be revised upwards, and assigned 1QIsa[a] and 1QS to about 100 B.C. He held that 1QpHab was written in the last quarter of the first century B.C.,[18] and that 1QH, 1QM, and 1QIsa[b], along with the *Genesis Apocryphon*, were written in the first half of the first century B.C. Carbon-14 dating furnished a range of 168 B.C. to A.D. 233.[19] Generally this has confirmed the dates arrived at by Albright,[20] Birnbaum,[21] and Sukenik[22] on other grounds.

To a considerable extent the nature of the community (*yaḥad*) which had apparently deposited the manuscripts in the Qumran caves was evident from the contents of the scrolls themselves, particularly from 1QS, the document that enshrined the rules of the brotherhood. It is apparent that the sect consisted of a group of priests and laymen living a communal life of strict dedication to God. Specific requirements had to be met by those desiring to participate in the way of life followed by the sectaries (1QS, I:1-15), and all members of the community were required to renew their pledge of obedience to the discipline of the fellowship at an annual ceremony (1QS, II:19-25). Under the leadership of elders and priests the sectaries engaged in constant Biblical study and in a sacramental type of worship (1QS, V:1-IX:26), the aim of which was to foster the growth of personal holiness, justice, equity, and mercy that was in accord with the nature of God as manifested in the ancient Hebrew Scriptures (cf. 1QS, V:3f.).

The sectaries laid great emphasis upon the study of the Law, and their documentary legacy makes it clear that they regarded themselves as the remnant of the true Israel, awaiting patiently the establishing of divine rule upon earth. As Brownlee has commented, the brotherhood had its birth in Biblical interpretation, because God had revealed the mysteries of prophecy to the Righteous Teacher (1QpHab, VII:3ff.).[23] This individual had founded the Qumran brotherhood, and the members felt that their eternal destiny was inextricably bound up with fidelity to his person and precepts (1QpHab, VIII:1ff.), for his very presence and activity implied the near approach of the Messiah. But apparently he was killed by the Wicked Priest (1QpHab, XI:4f.), the leader of his spiritual enemies, who in turn was overtaken by divine retribution.

The Habakkuk Commentary compiled by the sect spoke cryptically of the Kittim as its temporal enemies, under whom the Righteous Teacher

[18] For a date *ca.* 64 B.C., see *VDJD*, p. 84.

[19] M. Burrows, *BASOR*, No. 122 (1951), pp. 4ff., No. 123 (1951), pp. 24ff.; cf. O. R. Sellers, *BA*, XIV, No. 1 (1951), p. 29.

[20] *BASOR*, No. 118 (1950), p. 6.

[21] *BASOR*, No. 115 (1949), p. 22.

[22] *Megilloth Genuzoth*, I, pp. 14f.

[23] W. H. Brownlee, *BA*, XIV, No. 3 (1951), pp. 54f.

may have been put to death. The Qumran covenanters envisaged them as agents of divine anger in the last days of the age. As such they were proud and ferocious, the unconquerable scourge of nations and kingdoms, who made a practice of venerating their standards and other weapons of war. Considerable speculative effort has been expended in an attempt to determine the identity of the Kittim. In late Jewish authors the name was used cryptically of any victorious power, and in consequence scholars have identified them variously with the forces of Antiochus IV Epiphanes,[24] the Seleucid[25] or Roman[26] armies in the time of Alexander Jannaeus (103-76 B.C.), the military power of the Roman period proper,[27] some aggressive group in the period of the First Jewish War (A.D. 66-70),[28] or the Crusaders of the medieval period.[29]

A reference in the Habakkuk Commentary to the Kittim sacrificing to their weapons (1QpHab, VI:4f.) might perhaps be an allusion to the Romans, who venerated their "eagles" in sacrificial rites.[30] If this identification is correct, the Commentary may have had in mind the period which ended with the capture of Jerusalem under Pompey in 63 B.C. There are several unsolved problems associated with the identity of the individuals and groups mentioned in the Habakkuk Commentary, and final judgment will have to be deferred until more conclusive evidence is forthcoming.

From 4Q came a mutilated manuscript which assisted considerably in

[24] So B. Reicke, *Studia Theologica*, II, fasc. I (1949), pp. 45ff., later he abandoned this position in *Handskrifterna Fran Qumran* (1952); G. Lambert, *Nouvelle Revue Théologique*, LXXIV (1952), pp. 259ff.; H. H. Rowley, *The Zadokite Fragments and the Dead Sea Scrolls* (1952), pp. 62ff.; A. Michel, *Le Maître de Justice après les documents de la Mer Morte* (1954), pp. 232ff.

[25] Those maintaining this view included R. de Vaux, *RB*, LVII (1950), pp. 428f., LVIII (1951), pp. 442f.; M. Delcor, *Les Manuscrits de la Mer Morte: Essai sur le Midrash d'Habacuc* (1951), pp. 56ff., see also his article in *Revue de l'Histoire des Religions*, CXLII (1952), pp. 129ff.

[26] Cf. J. van der Ploeg, *Bibliotheca Orientalis*, VIII (1951), pp. 9f.; M. H. Segal, *JBL*, LXX (1951), pp. 131ff.; W. H. Brownlee, *BA*, XIV, No. 3 (1951), p. 63; D. Barthélemy, *RB*, LIX (1952), pp. 207ff.

[27] Cf. A. Dupont-Sommer, *Revue de l'Histoire des Religions*, CXXXVII (1950), pp. 129ff. *Aperçus préliminaires sur les manuscrits de la Mer Morte* (1950), p. 40; R. Goosens, *La Nouvelle Clio*, I-II (1940-50), pp. 336ff., 634ff., III-IV (1951-52), pp. 137ff.; K. Elliger, *Studien zum Habakuk-Kommentar vom Toten Meer* (1953), pp. 226ff.; F. F. Bruce, *Second Thoughts on the Dead Sea Scrolls* (1961), pp. 71ff.

[28] So J. Teicher, *JJS*, II (1951), pp. 67ff., III (1952), pp. 53ff.; R. Tournay, *RB*, LVI (1949), pp. 204ff.; G. Vermès, *Ephemerides Theologicae Lovanienses*, XXVII (1951), pp. 70ff.; compare his *Cahiers Sioniens* (1953), pp. 3ff.

[29] Cf. P. R. Weis, *JQR*, XLI (1950-51), pp. 125ff.; S. Zeitlin, *JQR*, XLI (1950-51), pp. 251ff.

[30] H. H. Rowley, *PEQ*, LXXXVIII (1956), pp. 102ff.; R. Goosens, *La Nouvelle Clio*, III-IV (1951-52), pp. 137ff.; *WJ*, VI,6,1.

attempts to identify the Qumran sect itself. This fragment was found to have affinity with an ancient Jewish work dated between the tenth and twelfth centuries A.D., which had first been discovered in 1896 in the *genizah* or storage room of a Cairo synagogue. Published in 1910,[31] this Zadokite composition, commonly styled the *Cairo Damascene Covenanters* (CDC), narrated the fortunes of certain dispossessed Jerusalem priests who had migrated to Damascus during a reform movement in Judaism and had established a monastic sect under the leadership of a "Righteous Teacher." The fragments from 4Q contained parts of CDC. These were supplemented by some other manuscript pieces from 6Q. On the basis of this and additional evidence many scholars have identified the sect of CDC with the Qumran fellowship, and have placed the Damascus migration just prior to the first century B.C.[32]

The Qumran sectaries have also been closely associated with the Essenes, about whom much was written at the beginning of the Christian era. Pliny described one such settlement near the Dead Sea in his *Natural History* (V, 15); Philo commented on their devotional procedures and general manner of life.[33] Josephus[34] and Hippolytus[35] also wrote descriptions of varying length on Essene customs. From these accounts it would appear that the Essenes pursued a communal existence in isolated places, working on the land and exercising themselves in devotions that included synagogue worship, private study, and prayer. They abstained from marriage on the ground that wives were a hindrance to the pursuit of their spiritual ideals. One Essene sect, however, condoned marriage, not for the sake of pleasure or companionship, but as a means of insuring the perpetuation of the community. Under normal conditions membership in Essene groups could be entered into by those who approached the sect with a view to voluntary renunciation of secular life. The Essenes seem to have been pacifist by nature, and did not indulge in animal sacrifice.

[31] S. Schechter (ed. and transl.), *Documents of Jewish Sectaries* (2 vols., 1910), Vol. I, *Fragments of a Zadokite Work*. Cf. APOT, II, pp. 785ff.; S. Zeitlin, *The Zadokite Fragments* (JQR Monograph Series No. 1, 1952); C. Rabin, *The Zadokite Documents* (1954).

[32] Cf. H. H. Rowley, *The Zadokite Fragments and the Dead Sea Scrolls*, p. 3. Scholars who interpreted "Damascus" literally included M. H. Segal, JBL, LXX (1951), pp. 131ff.; J. T. Milik, *Ten Years of Discovery in the Wilderness of Judaea* (1959), pp. 90f.; cf. R. de Vaux, RB, LXI (1954), pp. 235f.; C. T. Fritsch, JBL, LXXIV (1955), pp. 173ff. T. H. Gaster, *The Dead Sea Scriptures in English Translation*, pp. 4, 101 n. 23, thinks the term symbolical, while F. M. Cross, *The Ancient Library of Qumran and Modern Biblical Studies*, p. 82, holds it to be a "prophetic name" for the Qumran desert.

[33] *Quod Omnis Probus Sit Liber*, written ca. A.D. 10; *Hypothetica*, XI.

[34] WJ, II, 8, 2; AJ, XVIII, 1, 5.

[35] *The Refutation of All Heresies*, IX, 13ff., in *The Ante-Nicene Fathers* (1886), V, pp. 134f.

Most scholars have followed Milik in identifying the Qumran sect with one or more of the contemporary Essene groups. While there are obvious points of similarity, there are equally important differences between the two religious bodies. The Essenes were mostly celibates, unlike the Qumran sectaries who admitted women into their fellowship and appear to have had married residents at the community site. Whereas the Essenes tended to spiritualize the sacrificial system, the Damascus group certainly indulged in animal sacrifices (CDC, XIII:27, XIV:2), and the absence of specific instructions in 1QS could be taken as implying that sacrifices were to be carried out in accordance with the normal provisions of the Torah. Whatever interpretation may ultimately be placed upon the Qumran Military Scroll, there can be no doubt whatever that the Qumran sectaries were far from being pacifist by nature or inclination. Again, whereas some of the Essenes not infrequently worked in neighboring villages, the Qumran brotherhood isolated itself from all contact with the outside world. In view of these objections alone it should be clear that the brotherhood at Qumran can only be designated as Essene in the most general sense.[36]

Another cave group known as the Magharians is mentioned in the writings of the tenth-century Jewish sectary Kirkisani, who placed it chronologically somewhat after the Sadducees but prior to the Christian era.[37] This sect is also mentioned by two Moslem writers, Al Biruni (973-1048) and Shahrastani (1071-1153), the latter placing its origin in the first century B.C. The fact that the Qumran covenanters flourished about this time and that they hid their sacred writings in a cave might perhaps indicate some connection between them and the Magharians. The discovery of a rock-dwelling containing books near Jericho about A.D. 800 was mentioned in a Syriac letter from the Nestorian Patriarch of Seleucia, Timotheus I (A.D. 726-819) to Sergius, the Metropolitan of Elam.[38] The cave in question could perhaps have been 1Q, and if this were to be the case it would seem that the cave-sectaries of Kirkisani were identical with the Qumran society. It must be said, however, that actual proof of a connection between the two groups is lacking at the time of writing.[39]

The Therapeutae, who flourished in Egypt about 200 B.C., also bore a superficial resemblance to the fellowship at Qumran. Philo described the Therapeutae as recluses who devoted their efforts to prayer, meditation,

---

[36] Cf. C. T. Fritsch, *The Qumran Community* (1956), p. 110; W. H. Brownlee, *The Dead Sea Manual of Discipline* (*BASOR*, suppl. stud. X-XII, 1951), p. 4; R. Marcus, *JBL*, LXXIII (1954), p. 161; C. Rabin, *Qumran Studies* (*Scripta Judaica*, II, 1957), pp. 59f., 69f.

[37] Cf. L. Nemoy, *HUCA*, VII (1929-30), pp. 363f.

[38] G. R. Driver, *The Hebrew Scrolls from the Neighbourhood of Jericho and the Dead Sea*, pp. 25f.

[39] H. H. Rowley, *The Zadokite Fragments and the Dead Sea Scrolls*, pp. 24f.; L. Nemoy, *JQR*, XLII (1951-1952), p. 127.

and the study of their sectarian documents, only assembling for community worship of a quasi-sacramental nature on the sabbath day or on specifically designated holy seasons. This group admitted women to their fellowship, and wrote commentaries and poetry, much in the manner of the Qumran sectaries, as an essential part of their devotional exercises.[40]

The flood of literature that has emerged following the discovery of the Dead Sea Scrolls is eloquent testimony to the importance which scholars have attached to this remarkable phase of archaeological activity. No work dealing with the Bible generally can now be regarded with any seriousness if it fails to take into account the significance of the Qumran discoveries for its own particular area of study. The vast and highly diversified nature of the subject as reflected by the enormous current bibliography presents its own special problems, but despite this there can be absolutely no doubt whatever as to the revolutionary nature of its impact upon the discipline of theology in general and upon Biblical studies in particular. Although no final pronouncements on many of the problems that have arisen may be possible at the present stage of knowledge, it is already abundantly clear that a great deal of what was formerly accepted as fact will stand in need of radical revision, as will become evident in subsequent chapters of the present work. Again, much that was known in earlier days has been amply confirmed, thus furnishing a more secure basis for future advances in the field of Biblical scholarship.

[40] *De Vita Contemplativa* (Loeb Classical Library Translation), IX, pp. 113ff.

Part Three

ANCIENT NEAR EASTERN CHRONOLOGY

I. CHRONOLOGY FROM ADAM TO ABRAHAM

A. GENEALOGIES AND KING-LISTS

Despite the enormous amount of information available for the modern scholar as the result of historical and archaeological research, formidable difficulties are involved in any attempt to draw up an internally coherent scheme of chronology for any one of the various cultures that flourished in the ancient Near East. There is still an insufficiency of primary source materials for such a task, and the situation is further complicated because some of the necessary information already available is amenable to different interpretations. In the past no comprehensive system of Near Eastern or specifically Biblical chronology has proved entirely satisfactory in matters of detail: frequently it has happened that adjustments to the scheme of dating have been required because of new archaeological or other discoveries, and an already precarious balance has been upset.

Extra-Biblical sources are naturally of very great importance when they furnish fixed dates, and it is often in the light of such material that schemes of Biblical dating have to be modified. Where events in Biblical and extra-Biblical sources can be synchronized to a very narrow range, it is possible to utilize the results in order to establish a framework around which a specific chronology can be built. Fixed points of this nature have been formulated for Babylonian and Assyrian chronology on the one hand, and for Egyptian dating-sequences on the other. Against such vertical patterns it has been possible to establish horizontal synchronisms for certain of the other Near Eastern nations of antiquity, including Israel, so as to form a reasonably assured grid upon which the chronologies of these peoples can be imposed.[1] It must be stressed, however, that the chronologies of Babylonia and Egypt are themselves by no means completely assured in matters of detail, so that certain aspects of the larger picture will need to be modified for some time to come in the light of an expanding knowledge of ancient Near Eastern life and times.

[1] D. N. Freedman, *BANE*, p. 203.

What is probably the earliest, and undoubtedly the most celebrated, attempt at a chronological system in the English-speaking world was furnished by Archbishop James Usher (or Ussher) in the seventeenth century.[2] Taking the genealogies of the Bible as descriptive of strict lineal succession in the sense in which a modern genealogy would be understood, Usher reckoned backwards, computing the dates of the era of the patriarchs on the basis of the figures mentioned in the Massoretic text of Genesis (5:3ff., 7:11ff., 10:1ff., 11:10ff.), concluding that the world was created in 4004 B.C. This chronology, based upon a wealth of archiepiscopal erudition, was accepted without much question at the time, and on the authority of some unknown individual it was incorporated into the margins of reference editions of the Authorized Version of the Bible, which had been published in 1611. While it still continues to occupy this position to the present in some editions of the King James Version, it has no warrant for being there other than tradition.

The system devised by Usher depended inferentially upon the supposition that the Old Testament genealogies did not omit any names, and that the periods of time mentioned in the text were consecutive, assumptions that have been proved to be entirely gratuitous. A careful comparison of the genealogies contained in 1 Chronicles with their counterparts in the historical books will be sufficient to show that on occasions names have been omitted in certain lists. For example, the LXX has retained *Kainan* in Genesis 11:13, whereas the Massoretic text omits it. The situation is further complicated when one realizes that the figures given for the ages of many of the individuals mentioned in the Massoretic text do not agree with the corresponding records in other versions such as the LXX and the Samaritan Pentateuch. Several examples will be sufficient to illustrate this tendency. The age of the patriarch Adam at the birth of Seth was given as 130 years by the Massoretic text and the Samaritan Pentateuch, but this figure was enlarged by a century in the LXX. Kenan was said by the Massoretic text and the Samaritan Pentateuch to have been 70 years of age at the birth of his successor Mahalalel, whereas the LXX again extended this statement by 100 years. However, the LXX agreed with the Massoretic text in stating that Jared was 162 years old when his son was born, compared to the 62 years reported by the Samaritan Pentateuch. In contrast, all three versions agreed in assigning ages of 50 and 100 years respectively to Noah and Shem at the birth of their successors. For the remainder of the lines of these patriarchal figures there is a tendency on the part of the LXX to shorten the period, whereas the Samaritan Pentateuch exhibits close agreement with

---

[2] J. Usher, *Annales Veteris et Novi Testamenti* (1650-1654); cf. *MNHK*, pp. 228ff., 252f.

the Massoretic text in all cases except those of Jared, Methuselah,[3] and Lamech.

A careful examination of the list of ante- and post-diluvian patriarchs in Genesis indicates that the compilation exhibits a conventional and schematic structure which contains two units of ten names each (if Kainan is included from the LXX). This pattern is similar to the genealogy in Matthew 1, where the generations extending from Abraham to Jesus were reduced to three basic units of fourteen names each. Oriental chronological computation is discussed in Part 5, pp. 295ff.

A comparison of the Massoretic text with the LXX and the Samaritan Pentateuch leaves little doubt that the Hebrew text is the original, constituting the foundation upon which the other versions have built. Presumably in an attempt to introduce some sort of chronological balance into the lives of the earlier patriarchs, the LXX added 100 years to the respective ages of these individuals at the time when their successors were born. For the latter part of their lives the LXX subtracted proportionate periods so as to bring the total life-span of each patriarch into general accord with the figures furnished by the Massoretic text. The Samaritan Pentateuch, on the other hand, tended to shorten the lives of the antediluvian figures and lengthen those of the post-diluvians. According to the chronology of the LXX, Methuselah survived the Flood by some 14 years, whereas the Massoretic text dated his demise in the year in which the Flood occurred (Gen. 7:23). The Samaritan Pentateuch appears to have indicated the commencement of a new era in human affairs with the activities of Noah and his sons by implying that Jared, Methuselah, and Lamech all died in the year of the Flood, presumably as a result of the cataclysm. The low figures furnished by the Massoretic text for the chronology between Arpachshad and Nahor would seem to account for the rather unusual fact that all the patriarchs from Noah to Terah were alive when Abraham was born. The texts of the LXX and the Samaritan Pentateuch, on the other hand, record that all the ancestors of Abraham had died well in advance of his journey to Canaan at the age of 75.

Both the LXX and the Samaritan Pentateuch avoid the sharp decline in the ages of the post-diluvians at the birth of their successors by adopting the device of adding a century to most of the figures contained in the Massoretic text. By this means their records achieve something like parity with the dates assigned in the Hebrew Scriptures for the ante-

---

[3] Though this name and the מתושאל of Gen. 4:18 were both rendered Μαθουσάλα by the LXX, there is no reason to assume that the two names represent the same person.

diluvian patriarchs generally. Table 1 will assist in illustrating some of the matters raised in the foregoing discussion.

TABLE 1: EARLY PATRIARCHAL GENEALOGIES

Name	Age at birth of successor			Balance of life			Total years		
	MT	LXX	Sam. P.	MT	LXX	Sam. P.	MT	LXX	Sam. P.
Adam	130	230	130	800	700	800	930	930	930
Seth	105	205	105	807	707	807	912	912	912
Enosh	90	190	90	815	715	815	905	905	905
Kenan	70	170	70	840	740	840	910	910	910
Mahalalel	65	165	65	830	730	830	895	895	895
Jared	162	162	62	800	800	785	962	962	847
Enoch	65	165	65	300	200	300	365	365	365
Methuselah	187	167	67	782	802	653	868	969	720
Lamech	182	188	53	595	565	600	777	753	653
Noah	500	500	500	450	450	450	950	950	950
Shem	100	100	100	500	500	500			600
Arpachshad	35	135	135	403	430	303			438
Kainan		130			330				
Shelah	30	130	130	403	330	303			433
Eber	34	134	134	430	370	270			404
Peleg	30	130	130	209	209	109			239
Reu	32	132	132	207	207	107			239
Serug	30	130	130	200	200	100			230
Nahor	29	79	79	119	129	69			148
Terah	70	70	70				205	205	145

As de Vries has pointed out, the enormously long ages assigned to the Genesis antediluvians finds a striking analogy in the extended lives of the Sumerian kings prior to the great flood of the late Jemdet Nasr period at Shuruppak.[4] This list of kings, known as the Weld-Blundell prism,[5] was apparently completed during the prosperous Third Dynasty of Ur, and furnished the names of eight kings in chronological succession.

[4] S. J. de Vries, *IDB*, I, pp. 581f.
[5] Published by S. Langdon, *Oxford Editions of Cuneiform Texts* (1923), II. For a critical edition of the king-list using subsequently discovered sources see T. Jacobsen, *The Sumerian King List* (1939), *Assyriological Studies XI, Oriental Institute*; cf. *ANET*, pp. 265f.; C. L. Woolley, *The Sumerians*, p. 21.

TABLE 2: EARLY SUMERIAN KING-LIST

City	Ruler	Regnal years
	Alulim	28,800
Eridu	Alalgar	36,000
	Enmenlu-Anna	43,200
Badtibira	Enmengal-Anna	28,800
	Dumuzi	36,000
Larak	Ensipazi-Anna	28,800
Sippar	Enmendur-Anna	21,000
Shuruppak	Ubar-Tutu	18,600

Total 241,200

Whatever the epic or schematic principles underlying such a composition, it is evident that they are not wholly consistent internally, since the earliest kings are ascribed reigns of the most exaggerated length. This king-list appeared in a later form in writings of Berossus, a priest of Marduk in Babylon under Antiochus I (281-261 B.C.). He extended the list to include two other royal personages, and nearly doubled the sum of their individual reigns (Table 3).

TABLE 3: REVISED SUMERIAN KING-LIST (Berossus)

Ruler	Regnal years
Alorus	36,000
Alaparos	10,800
Amelon	46,800
Ammenon	43,200
Megalaros	64,800
Daos (Daonos)	36,000
Euedorachos	64,800
Amempsinos	36,000
Otiartes	28,800
Xisouthros	64,800

Total 432,000

Xisouthros was the ruler when the great flood descended, according to Berossus. The names are obviously Greek in form, and it may be that some confusion has resulted, with Amelon and Ammenon perhaps being corrupt forms of the cognomen Enmenlu-Anna. What is more probable, however, is that there is some connection between the tradition which underlay the record of Berossus concerning the ten antediluvian kings and that which recorded the existence of ten patriarchs from Adam to Moses.[6] Both forms appear to be schematic, and related to definite chronological sequences whose significance or importance may have been interpreted numerically. To what extent the two sources refer to the same area of Mesopotamia and the same general period, however, is difficult to determine.

It would seem evident that while the numbers assigned to the ages of the patriarchs in Genesis had real meaning for those who were responsible for their preservation in the first instance, they cannot be employed in a purely literal sense as a means of computing the length of the various generations mentioned in the text. Nor is it satisfactory to assume that the various names are those of dynasties or peoples, rather than of individuals, since certain of the narratives regard those mentioned as individual personages and narrate their exploits in the form of a summary. Unfortunately there is as yet no absolute date for an event in the secular history of Babylonia to which the doings of these patriarchal figures can be related for purposes of chronological control. The best that can be done under such circumstances is to assign the historical background of the narratives in question to one or other of the cultural periods established as a result of archaeological discoveries in Mesopotamia.

B. CULTURAL PERIODS OF EARLY MESOPOTAMIA

In any attempt to establish a sequence of Old Testament chronology it must always be remembered that the Bible was not designed primarily as a textbook of history or culture; hence, it can hardly be expected to present a carefully formulated and internally consistent pattern of chronological sequences as understood by the occidental mind. In some of the earlier sources from Mesopotamia it is apparent that dates, numbers, and the general computation of time follow certain symbolic configurations whose ratio and overall significance were evidently quite clear to the ancient writers employing them, but whose meaning is completely unknown to the modern western mind. There are still other occasions when the Biblical writers employed dates and numbers as a means of illustrating profound spiritual concepts that they were endeavoring to promote, for example, in connection with the triumphant Exodus of Israel from Egypt. Again, although there are some demonstrable omissions and conflations present in Old Testament sequences of chronology, there are also a great many accurately dated events as well as clear indications of order and arrangement in the succession of individuals,

[6] G. A. Barton, *Archaeology and the Bible* (1937), p. 320.

state officials, and the like, making for a high degree of reliability once the basic pattern of computation is understood.

One unfortunate difficulty which stands in the way of attempts to establish an assured sequence of chronology for the Old Testament is the fact that the various books and sources were not dated in terms of one particular era, as can be done with events which occur in the Christian age, for example. The point of departure for a given historical period in early Mesopotamian life is quite different in many respects from its equivalent at a much later date in the history of that area. Again, the system of chronological computation in Judah during the days of Jeremiah differed in certain important respects from that which was employed by contemporary Babylonian scribes. A good many of the dates and allusions to time-sequences in the Old Testament are of a comparative nature, being frequently related to the reign of a particular king (e.g. 2 Kgs. 15:32) or to some unusual physical phenomenon such as an earthquake (Am. 1:1, Zech. 14:5). Only occasionally did the writers refer to an event like the Exodus, which for them marked the commencement of a new era alike of faith and history (Judg. 11:16, 26, 1 Kgs. 6:1).

As a result of discoveries that archaeologists have made at various sites, it is now possible to envisage the earliest inhabitants of the Near East in terms of Stone Age settlements. In Mesopotamia, the body of a Stone Age baby estimated to have died 75,000 years ago was discovered in the Shanidar Cave, located some 50 miles northeast of Mosul. The skeletons found in the caves of Mount Carmel and elsewhere in the neighborhood of Galilee are of great importance because they indicate the way in which anthropological considerations can contribute materially to the formulation of chronological sequences in critical areas. The deposits were dated in the general period known as Levalloiso-Mousterian, between 150,000 and 120,000 years ago.[7] Upon examination they proved to constitute the remains of a Paleolithic group in which the characteristics of neanthropic man (*Homo sapiens*) and paleoanthropic man (*Homo neanderthalensis*) were so intermingled as to represent a hybrid race.[8] As Albright has pointed out, these discoveries would seem to indicate that *Homo sapiens* entered Europe from the southwest, driving Neanderthal man before him and subsequently interbreeding freely with the various Neanderthaloid types then in existence.[9]

---

[7] D. A. E. Garrod and D. M. A. Bate, *The Stone Age of Mount Carmel: Excavations at the Wady el-Mughara* (1937), I; T. D. McCown and Sir Arthur Keith, *The Stone Age of Mount Carmel: The Fossil Human Remains from the Levalloiso-Mousterian* (1939), II.

[8] G. H. R. von Koenigswald, *Meeting Prehistoric Man* (1956), pp. 71, 206. Cf. Sir Arthur Keith, *New Discoveries Relating to the Antiquity of Man* (1931), pp. 173ff.; J. P. Hyatt, *The Journal of Bible and Religion*, XII (1944), pp. 232ff.

[9] *AP*, pp. 56f.

The characteristic Mesolithic period of Palestine was represented by deposits dated about 8000 B.C., and styled Natufian by Dorothy Garrod. From skeletons recovered from various sites in Palestine, as well as from a slightly later period at Helwan in Egypt, it is apparent that the Natufians had certain points in common with the predynastic Egyptians. They were slender in build and were little more than five feet in height. Natufians are usually credited with introducing agricultural activity to the Near East. The discovery of a wide range of flint artifacts has indicated that they obtained some of their food through the cultivation of crops such as millet, which was harvested by means of flint sickles and subsequently ground to a rough consistency in stone mortars. Although these enterprising peoples belonged technically to a pre-pottery phase, they displayed artistic skill in the carving of small images and the fashioning of animal bones to form beads, pins, pendants, and other ornaments. The position of the skeletons indicated that the Natufians generally buried their dead in the contracted manner of predynastic peoples of Egypt, with the arms folded across the chest and the knees drawn up under the chin.[10] It was during this general period that the dog is thought to have been domesticated.

Neolithic culture was characterized in Palestine by successive early occupations of Jericho, one of the most ancient inhabited sites in the entire Near East. The excavations of Kathleen Kanyon have confirmed Garstang's findings of a definite pre-pottery phase in the cultural history of Jericho during which characteristic flint artifacts were made. This was followed, prior to 5000 B.C., by a period in which the manufacture of pottery was a pronounced feature of cultural activity, along with an established flint industry.[11] In the pre-pottery period Neolithic man began to live in villages composed of primitive dwellings clustered around a central shrine. The best representative of this phase in Palestine is found at Jericho, where the houses and shrines were made from small, rounded mud bricks or beaten earth. The shrine was designed in such a manner that it had an outer and an inner chamber of considerable size, and normally contained animal figurines and cult-objects of a sexual nature.[12]

In northern Mesopotamia the village-settlements unearthed at Nineveh, at Tepe Gawra some twelve miles to the northeast, and at Tell Hassuna, a few miles south of modern Mosul, are the best representatives of Neolithic culture discovered to date, and they exhibit the characteristic prehistoric forms. The lowest levels at Tepe Gawra revealed the existence of a delicate decorated ceramic ware, some of which was found in

[10] *AP*, pp. 59ff.

[11] Kenyon, *Digging Up Jericho* (1957), pp. 51ff.

[12] *AP*, pp. 62f. For a survey of the archaeological chronology of Palestine from the Neolithic to the Middle Bronze Age see W. F. Albright in *Relative Chronologies in Old World Archaeology* (ed. R. W. Erich, 1954), pp. 28ff.

association with Neolithic skeletons.[13] This culture of northern Mesopotamia and the Assyrian uplands probably antedates the fifth millennium
B.C., thus making the construction of houses and the invention of pottery matters of great antiquity. In Syria this variety of primitive village-
culture is found in the lowest levels at Tell ej-Judeideh in the plain of
Antioch.[14] In Palestine it is represented at Jericho.[15] In Egypt the
Neolithic settlers seem to have been active somewhat before 5000 B.C.,
as indicated by the remains of occupational levels at Deir Tasa,
Merimdeh, Beni-Salameh, and in the Fayyum.[16]

The Chalcolithic or "copper-stone" period (ca. 4500-3000 B.C.), which
succeeded the Neolithic, saw the flowering of the first major culture of
antiquity. Its best representative site is Tell Halaf, but similar deposits
have been found at Carchemish, over 100 miles west of Tell Halaf, at
Tell Chagar Bazar, some 50 miles east of Tell Halaf, at Tepe Gawra, and
in other areas.[17] To the same period belongs the Badarian culture of
ancient Egypt, where serious attempts were made to cultivate grain and
to bring certain animals under domestication. There are some indications
that the Badarian economy was influenced to a certain extent by the
trade-relations they had with other peoples. One example of this tendency may be seen in the fact that the Badarians used eye-paint made from
powdered green malachite, a substance which in all probability had
been imported from the Sinai peninsula. The Badarians were also
familiar to some extent with the malleable properties of copper, although
it is doubtful that they actually understood the principles underlying the
fusion of metals. Excavation of their burial-sites has shown that they
interred their dead in a sleeping position, and that they deposited food
offerings and other objects in the graves.[18]

---

[13] E. A. Speiser, *Asia*, XXXVIII (1938), p. 543, *BASOR*, No. 66 (1937), p. 18,
No. 70 (1938), pp. 6f.

[14] R. J. Braidwood, *Mounds in the Plain of Antioch, An Archaeological Survey*
(1937), pp. 6f.; C. W. McEwan, *AJA*, XLI (1937), pp. 10f.

[15] G. E. Wright, *The Pottery of Palestine from the Earliest Times to the End of
the Early Bronze Age* (1937), pp. 7ff., 107.

[16] For Deir Tasa, see G. Brunton, *Antiquity, A Quarterly Review of Archaeology*,
III (1929), pp. 456ff.; for Merimdeh, Beni-Salameh, V. G. Childe, *New Light on the
Most Ancient East* (1935), pp. 58ff., H. Ranke, *JAOS*, LIX, No. 4 (1939), suppl. p.
8; for the Fayyum, G. Caton-Thompson and E. W. Gardner, *The Desert Fayyum* (2
vols., 1934), H. J. Kantor in *Relative Chronologies in Old World Archaeology*, p. 3;
Kantor dated the Fayyum culture around 4250 B.C.

[17] Cf. M. von Oppenheim, *Der Tell Halaf, eine neue Kultur im ältesten Mesopotamien* (1931); M. E. L. Mallowan and J. C. Rose, *Prehistoric Assyria, The Excavations at Tell Arpachiyah, 1933* (1935), pp. 17ff., 104f.

[18] G. Brunton and G. Caton-Thompson, *The Badarian Civilisation* (1928), pp.
20ff.

The successors to the Badarians were Amrateans of Upper Egypt, with whom commenced the real beginnings of the predynastic period (ca. 4500-2900 B.C.). An essentially sedentary people, they are thought to have been the first to attempt the systematic cultivation of the fertile Nile valley. In the Nagada I phase of Upper Egyptian culture they expanded along the entire length of the Nile River. From excavations at Amratean sites it is evident that these early peoples engaged in the weaving of flax and the manufacture of a wide range of small copper tools and implements. Representations of animals and men on pottery objects interred with the dead may perhaps reflect the beginnings of magic in primitive Egyptian life.[19]

Under the Gerzeans, who succeeded the Amrateans, there came an expansion of trade with Mesopotamia and India. Cast metal implements unearthed at Gerzean sites show that they had mastered the art of casting tools and weapons. At this period totemistic symbols were becoming increasingly associated with the villages and towns, and the place of magic was further indicated by distinct evidences of ritual procedure at the time of interment. The rich were buried in graves that had been lined with mud bricks, and at one site walls were found decorated with a mural painting.[20]

The corresponding Palestinian culture was named Ghassulian, after the site where it was first discovered. Excavations at Teleilat Ghassul, just north of the Dead Sea in the vicinity of Jericho, uncovered traces of painted pottery at Chalcolithic levels. The houses from this period were of mud brick construction, and their plastered walls were adorned with well-executed mural paintings.[21]

In Mesopotamia, the most clearly defined culture of the prehistoric period was that uncovered at al 'Ubaid, four miles northwest of Ur. This phase, which is also represented at a number of other ancient Mesopotamian sites, including Erech (Uruk), Ur, and Eridu, can be dated approximately 4000 B.C. Whereas domestic architecture as such exhibited little if any significant advance upon its counterpart in the Halafian period, the 'Ubaid phase is notable for the construction of three shrines found at Tepe Gawra whose architectural features dominated the style of Mesopotamian temples for many centuries. While 'Ubaid culture generally tended towards preserving the self-sufficiency of the Neolithic economy,[22] the presence in contemporary deposits of beads made from amazonite and lapis lazuli points to contact with central Asia and India,

[19] V. G. Childe, *New Light on the Most Ancient East*, pp. 69ff.
[20] J. E. Quibell, *Hierakonpolis*, II (1902), pp. 20f.
[21] A. Mallon, R. Koeppel, and R. Neuville, *Teleilat Ghassul I, Compte rendu des fouilles de l'Institut Biblique Pontifical, 1929-1932* (1934); N. Glueck, *BASOR*, No. 97 (1945), pp. 10f.
[22] V. G. Childe, *What Happened in History* (1942), p. 74.

where such stones were in use as ornaments at that time.[23] The pottery of the al 'Ubaid culture reflects the influence of the Persian highlands, and its appearance can be taken as marking the first attempts at colonizing the southern area of Mesopotamia.[24]

The Uruk phase, which is usually dated towards the end of the fourth millennium B.C., saw the emergence of a new people who exhibited distinctive elements of civilization as prominent marks of their culture. These included engraved cylinder seals, temples constructed of stone rather than of sun-dried mud bricks, sculpture in the round, and writing on clay.[25] The Uruk period was continued in central Mesopotamia towards the end of the fourth millennium B. C. at the site of Jemdet Nasr.[26] Bronze implements discovered there indicated that the Chalcolithic period proper in Mesopotamia was terminating, and that it was being replaced by the Bronze Age. Sculpture in stone was a marked feature of the Jemdet Nasr phase, and the recovery of clay tablets inscribed with a semi-pictographic form of writing made it clear that significant advances upon the achievements of the Uruk period had been made in this area of cultural activity. Such ancient sites as Kish and Shuruppak were most probably founded at this time. The Jemdet Nasr era is so close to recorded history and to the king-lists of Mesopotamia that it can be assigned approximately to a date of 3000 B.C. Some scholars have divided up the chronological sequence in greater detail, designating the latter part of the Uruk phase as Protoliterate A-B or Early Protoliterate, and the early Jemdet Nasr period as Protoliterate C-D or Late Protoliterate, but the basic dating is not seriously affected by such classifications.[27]

The Uruk culture contained numerous elements that foreshadowed in many respects the achievements of the first historical civilized community in southern Mesopotamia. This latter was known as Sumeria, the home of a vigorous people who entered the marshy delta region about 4000 B.C. Between this time and the beginning of the Early Dynastic period, about 2800 B.C., the Sumerians attained to cultural supremacy, and laid the foundations of social organization and behavior in such a manner as to exert a lasting influence over all subsequent Mesopotamian civilizations. The Early Dynastic period came to an end with the rise of the First Dynasty of Ur, during which four kings reigned for a total period of 177 years, according to the king-list. A small limestone tablet

---

[23] E. Mackay, *The Indus Civilisation* (1935), pp. 170, 191ff.

[24] S. Piggott, *Prehistoric India* (1952), p. 55.

[25] *LAP*, pp. 19ff.

[26] E. Mackay and S. Langdon, *Report on Excavations at Jemdet Nasr, Iraq* (1931).

[27] E.g. A. L. Perkins, *CAEM*, pp. 97ff. A. Parrot, *Archéologie mésopotomienne*, II (1953), pp. 272ff., prefers to use the term "Predynastic," whereas A. Moortgat, *Die Entstehung der sumerischen Hochkultur* (1945), pp. 59ff., employed "Early Historic" for the Protoliterate period, commencing about 3300 B.C.

unearthed by Woolley at Tell el-Obeid dated *ca.* 2700 B.C. proved to be contemporary with the First Dynasty of Ur. It read:

> A-Anne-pada, king of Ur, son of Mes-Anne-pada, king of Ur, has built this for his Lady Nin-kharsag.[28]

This discovery proved to be extremely important for the chronology of this period, for it confirmed the claim of the Sumerian king-list that Mes-Anne-pada was the monarch who had founded the First Dynasty.[29] Equally significant was the light that it shed upon the unusually long reign of 80 years attributed to him, by showing that in all probability his son and successor, whose name was very similar, had somehow been dropped from the king-list and that his reign had been added to that of Mes-Anne-pada, making a total of 80 years. The revised king-list would thus read as in Table 4.

TABLE 4: REVISED SUMERIAN KING-LIST

Ruler	Regnal Years
Mes-Anne-pada⎫ A-Anne-pada ⎬	80
Meskiag-Nanna	36
Elulu	25
Balulu	36

Total 177

In ancient Egypt, the expansion of community life during the Gerzean period proved to be one of the most important factors contributing to the development of the predynastic era. Towards the end of this phase, about 2900 B.C., two powerful states known as Upper and Lower Egypt came into being. Their unification under Menes of Thinis is generally taken to be the beginning of the Egyptian Protodynastic period (*ca.* 2900-2760 B.C.). The foundations of the Old Kingdom era were laid by the pharaohs of the First and Second Dynasties in the twenty-ninth to the twenty-seventh centuries B.C., and with the rise of the Third Dynasty, *ca.* 2700 B.C., there emerged the Old Kingdom period proper.[30] The Old

---

[28] *UC*, pp. 72f.

[29] Woolley dated the First Dynasty "Royal Cemetery" at Ur *ca.* 3500-3200 B.C. (*Ur Excavations II, The Royal Cemetery* [1934], p. 223), but this has been criticized for being too high by V. Müller, *JAOS*, LV (1935), pp. 206ff., and H. Frankfort, *JRAS* (1937), pp. 332ff. W. F. Albright has suggested a date of *ca.* 2500 B. C., *BASOR*, No. 88 (1942), p. 32, *AJA*, XLVII (1943), p. 492.

[30] Cf. Albright, *BASOR*, No. 119 (1950), p. 29.

Kingdom lasted for about 500 years, and was the classical period of Egyptian culture. During this time the pyramids were built, the religion of the country assumed its normative character, and the impact of Egyptian life upon the outside world was enhanced by expanding trade relations with the Orient. The glory of the Old Kingdom period waned about 2200 B.C. at the end of the Sixth Dynasty, and from the Seventh to the Eleventh Dynasties (ca. 2200-1989 B.C.) a succession of weak pharaohs proved unable to maintain a vigorous central government. This phase, generally known as the First Intermediate period, ended with the beginning of the Twelfth Dynasty under Amenemhet I, ca. 1989 B.C.

During the twenty-fourth century B.C., the inhabitants of Mesopotamia witnessed the rise to power of Sargon of Agade, who established the Old Akkadian period (ca. 2360-2180 B.C.) with the defeat of Lugalzaggesi of Sumeria and the incorporation of his territory into a Semitic realm. Under Naram-Sin, grandson of Sargon, this empire extended from central Persia to the Mediterranean, and when it was at its height it fell into the hands of the Gutians of Caucasia, ca. 2180 B.C. A revival of Sumerian culture at Lagash, about 2070 B.C., coincided with a decline in Gutian influence, and upon their downfall the magnificent Third Dynasty of Ur, marking the Neo-Sumerian period (ca. 2113-1991 B.C.), arose. Its founder Ur-Nammu was remarkable for his encouragement of literary activity during this period, and in particular for his law code, which is one of the oldest known from Mesopotamia.[31] This cultural revival also flourished at Lagash under the *ensi* Gudea, a viceroy associated with one of the kings of the Third Dynasty.[32] Although the revival continued under Dungi (Shulgi), Bur-Sin, and their successors, the end of Sumerian culture was close at hand, and its demise occurred with the period of the Elamite and Amorite invasions (ca. 1960-1830 B.C.), during which Ur was sacked[33] and Mesopotamia saw the beginnings of the Old Babylonian period (ca. 1830-1550 B.C.).

The most important single individual of this era, a man whose dates have been revised by scholars from time to time, was Hammurabi, the last great ruler of the First Dynasty. Attempts to identify him on the basis of information contained in Genesis 14 resulted in the association of him with Amraphel, king of Shinar, by many nineteenth-century scholars.[34] C. P. Tiele and W. H. Kosters rejected this identification, and F. Hommel held that Amraphel was the father of Hammurabi.[35] At the

---

[31] S. N. Kramer, *Orientalia*, XXIII (1954), pp. 40ff. and *From the Tablets of Sumer* (1956), pp. 47ff.

[32] *ARI*, p. 224.

[33] Cf. S. N. Kramer, *Lamentation Over the Destruction of Ur* (1940), *Assyriological Studies XII, Oriental Institute*, p. 57.

[34] E.g. T. K. Cheyne, *EB*, I, col. 159, who dated him ca. 2250 B.C.

[35] Tiele and Kosters, *EB*, I, col. 733; Hommel, *Geschichte Babyloniens und Assyriens* (1885), pp. 123ff.

same time some scholars were identifying Arioch of Ellasar (Gen. 14:1, 9) with Rim-Sin of Larsa, or with Warad-Sin (Eri-Aku), a king of Larsa dated by Rogers about 2172-2160 B.C.[36] On the basis of the Babylonian king-lists Rogers assigned a date of 2130-2087 B.C. to the reign of Hammurabi,[37] and a date of 2160-2099 B.C. to his contemporary Rim-Sin of Larsa. It is worthy of note that the name Arriwuk occurred in some tablets from Mari as the designation of the fifth son of Zimri-Lim of Mari, ca. 1750 B.C., and perhaps constitutes a parallel form of the Old Testament "Arioch."[38]

In the light of the discoveries at Mari, a date of 2150 B.C. for Hammurabi appears too high. Some of the diplomatic correspondence from the Mari palace archives consisted of messages that passed between Hammurabi and Zimri-Lim, the last king of Mari, who appears to have come to power after Shamshi-Adad I of Assyria (ca. 1748-1716 B.C.) had sent his son Yasmah-Adad to govern Mari on a temporary basis.[39] The Mari documents spoke of Shamshi-Adad I as an Amorite contemporary of Hammurabi, which brings him into the latter part of the Mari Age. On the basis of this important evidence it is now possible to date Hammurabi about 1728-1686 B.C. with reasonable confidence.[40] At present it is extremely difficult to arrive with any degree of certainty at the identity of King Amraphel of Shinar, but it is now evident that he was not the same person as Hammurabi of Babylon.[41]

The beginning of the Middle Bronze Age (ca. 2100-1550 B.C.) saw the rise of another important group, the Hittites, who can be fitted reasonably well into the chronological sequences so far established. A little after 2000 B.C. several groups of Indo-European origin began to move along the northern portion of the Fertile Crescent towards Asia Minor. They mingled freely with the earlier native population of Anatolia who spoke a non-Indo-European language known as Hattic or Proto-Hittite, and in succeeding centuries they built up an empire which covered vast tracts of territory in Anatolia and Syria.

[36] Cf. T. G. Pinches, HDB, I, p. 148. This identification was rejected by L. W. King, The Letters and Inscriptions of Hammurabi (1898-1900), I, pp. xxv, xxvi, xlix. For the dating of Warad-Sin, see Rogers, History of Babylonia and Assyria (1915), II, p. 84.

[37] Ibid., I, p. 516. On the basis of the Nabonidus Inscription he dated Hammurabi ca. 2075 B.C. (ibid., pp. 492f.).

[38] Cf. M. Noth, VT, I (1951), pp. 136ff.

[39] A. Poebel, who published the Khorsabad List of Assyrian kings recovered from the palace of Sargon II, dated Shamshi-Adad I from 1726-1694 B.C., JNES, I (1942), pp. 247ff., 460ff., II (1943), pp. 56ff.

[40] W. F. Albright, BASOR, No. 88 (1942), pp. 28ff., AJA, XLVII (1943), p. 492; BHI, p. 52.

[41] W. F. Albright, JPOS, VI (1926), p. 179. Cf. his articles in Journal of the Society for Oriental Research, X (1926), p. 232 and in JPOS, I (1921), p. 71; also E. A. Speiser, AASOR, XIII (1933), p. 45n.; R. de Vaux, ZAW, LVI (1938), p. 231 and RB, LV (1948), p. 331.

In Genesis 10:15 the offspring of the eponymous progenitor Heth were included in the list of nations of which the population of Canaan was composed. How far these people were connected with the Anatolian Hatti or the later Indo-European invaders is difficult to determine.[42] Part of the confusion has arisen from the fact that the movement of the Indo-European groups into Anatolia was only one part of a great migratory upsurge at the beginning of the second millennium B.C., a later phase of which witnessed the entrance of the Hebrew patriarchs into Palestine.

Another aspect of this movement of peoples was the migration of the Hurrians from an Indo-European source into Upper Mesopotamia, coinciding roughly with the invasion of Anatolia by the peoples who were subsequently known as the Hittites. However, these non-Semitic Hurrians (or Horites, as they are called in Genesis 14:6 and elsewhere) spread westward and penetrated into central Canaan[43] where they were well established in the patriarchal age.[44] Their greatest accomplishment in the political realm was the establishing of the Mitanni empire, whose capital was situated in the Middle Euphrates valley. During the second millennium B.C. the Mitanni dominated the region later known as Assyria, and in the Amarna period they held the balance of power between the Hittites, the Assyrians, and the Egyptians. Thereafter the influence of the Mitanni declined, and they succumbed to the Hittites about 1370 B.C. at the height of the New Empire period and were subsequently absorbed into the Hittite domain.[45]

The history of the Hittites as a military and political force falls into two major divisions. The Old Empire period began with the regime of Pitkhanas, king of Kussar, about 1800 B.C., although later Hittite rulers preferred to trace their ancestry back to the ancient King Labarnas.[46] Under Tudhaliyas I (ca. 1740-1710 B.C.) and his successors the Old Empire flourished for about a century and a half. The strength of earlier days diminished, however, under Mursilis I (ca. 1620 B.C.), due primarily to internal strife.

The New Empire period began with the reign of Tudhaliyas II (ca. 1460-1440 B.C.), but it was only under the influence of Suppiluliuma (ca. 1375-1340 B.C.) that Hittite power became a major factor once again in the Near East. A century later, further internal dissension combined with the invasions of the Aegean "Sea Peoples" to bring about the downfall of the Hittite empire about 1200 B.C., probably during the reign of Suppiluliuma II.

The foregoing synchronisms have been arrived at largely as the result

[42] Cf. E. O. Forrer, *PEQ*, LXVIII (1936), pp. 190ff., LXIX (1937), pp. 100ff.

[43] Cf. E. A. Speiser, *AASOR*, XIII (1933), pp. 13ff., *JAOS*, LXVIII (1948), pp. 1ff.; B. Landsberger, *JCS*, LVIII (1954), p. 59.

[44] E. A. Speiser, *IDB*, II, pp. 665f.

[45] F. F. Bruce, *The Hittites and the OT* (1948), pp. 17f.

[46] *TH*, pp. 19f.

of comparative study of archaeological, linguistic and anthropological data. While there may well be modifications in certain matters of detail as more information concerning the Hittites becomes available to scholars, the general outlines of Hittite history appear reasonably assured.

An analysis of the conclusions arrived at in the foregoing discussion can now be presented for convenience in Table 5.

TABLE 5: EARLY CHRONOLOGY

Approx. Date B.C.	Mesopotamia	Palestine	Syria-Asia Minor	Egypt
Before 100,000	Shanidar Cave baby	Palean- thropus pales- tinensis.		
Before 8000	Paleolithic period (Old Stone Age)			
8000-6000	Mesolithic period (Middle Stone Age) Natufian			
6000-4500	Neolithic period (New Stone Age)			
	Tepe Gawra Nineveh Tell Hass- una	Jericho (pre-pottery and pottery Neolithic)		
4500-3000	Chalcolithic period			
4500-2900				Predynastic
	Tell Halaf Tell el- Obeid Uruk	Jericho III Ghassulian		Fayyum A Deir Tasa Badari Amratean Gerzean
3300-2800	Proto- literate phase Jemdet Nasr			
3200-2000	Early Bronze Age			
2900-2700				Protodynastic period
2800-2360	Early dy- nastic period		Ancient Hatti	
2700-2200				Old Kingdom
2360-2180	Old Akkadian period			
2200-1989				First Interme- diate period
2180-2070	Gutian phase			
2060-1950	Neo-Sumerian revival Ur III			
2100-1550	Middle Bronze Age			
2000-1780		Seminomadic incursions		Middle Kingdom

Approx. Date B.C.	Mesopotamia	Palestine	Syria-Asia Minor	Egypt
1960-1830	Elamite-Amorite invasions	Patriarchs		
1830-1530	Old Babylonian period			
1800-1600			Hittite Old Empire	
1780-1570				Second Intermediate period
1728-1686	Hammurabi			
1570-1150				New Kingdom
1500-1200	Late Bronze Age			
1460-1200			Hittite New Empire	

The traditions of Genesis, which associated the ancestors of the later Israelites with the nomadic and semi-sedentary peoples who traversed the Fertile Crescent towards the end of the second millennium B.C. and the early centuries of the first millennium B.C., have been strikingly confirmed by linguistic and other data uncovered by archaeological excavations in Mesopotamia. This activity has also made it possible with a high degree of confidence to assign the patriarchal narratives of Genesis to the Middle Bronze Age (ca. 2100-1550 B.C.) for their origin and formulation. As a result, scholars are now able to relate the patriarchal tradition of a migration from Harran to a roughly contemporary eruption of Amorite military and cultural activity in the civilized areas of northern Mesopotamia. Such widely divergent sources as the texts from Mari and Nuzu, and Middle Kingdom Egyptian writings such as the Execration Texts and the Tale of Sinuhe can be adduced in order to illuminate the social and political conditions then prevailing in Palestine.

Despite this encouraging situation, however, it has proved impossible in the light of presently available evidence to assign precise dates to the individual Hebrew patriarchs, or to associate them with any detailed chronological scheme amenable to control by means of extra-Biblical sources. While the literary form of certain portions of the Biblical material presents difficulties, it is not necessary to suppose, with Freedman,[47] that its completed form was the culmination of a long process of oral transmission, since it is highly probable from the literary structure of the elements which constitute the narratives themselves that the material was committed to writing not long after the activities of the individuals named.

[47] BANE, p. 204.

II. THE CHRONOLOGY OF ISRAEL'S EARLY HISTORY

A. THE PATRIARCHS—GENESIS 14

The nature of the genealogical scheme associated with the patriarchs in Genesis 14 has raised important problems of Old Testament chronology. As has been observed above, the association of Amraphel, king of Shinar (Gen. 14:1), with Hammurabi of Babylon led scholars in the first two decades of the twentieth century to assign Hammurabi to a period as early as 2123-2081 B.C.[1] In 1928 S. H. Langdon and J. K. Fotheringham placed the reign of Hammurabi ca. 2067-2025 B.C.[2] and gave impetus to a movement that resulted in a progressively later dating for the period of Hammurabi. Thureau-Dangin reduced the dating by more than half a century to ca. 2003-1961 B.C;[3] Pirot brought it still lower to ca. 1947-1905 B.C.[4] Evidence from Mari led to the general conclusion that the earlier dates were much too high,[5] and when Thureau-Dangin published evidence in 1937 that Shamshi-Adad I was contemporary with the earlier portion of the reign of Hammurabi, Albright suggested a date for the accession of the latter at ca. 1870 B.C, which in turn was criticized by Parrot as being too low.[6]

Two years later, however, Albright again revised his conclusions on the basis of new evidence from Mari published by Sidney Smith and reduced his earlier date by some 70 years, assigning Hammurabi to ca.

---

[1] Supported by W. F. Albright, *RA*, XVIII (1921), p. 94; S. A. Cook, *Cambridge Ancient History* (1924), I, p. 154; L. W. King, *A History of Babylon from the Foundation of the Monarchy to the Persian Conquest* (1919), pp. 106ff.

[2] Langdon and Fotheringham, *The Venus Tablets of Ammizaduga* (1928), pp. 66f. They were supported by D. Sidersky in A. Wertheimer, J. de Somogyi, and S. Löwinger (eds.), *Dissertationes in honorem Dr. Eduardi Mahler* (1937), pp. 253ff. and A. G. Shortt, *Journal of the British Astronomical Association*, LVII (1947), p. 208.

[3] *RA*, *Y*XIV (1927), pp. 181ff.

[4] L. Pirot, *Supplément au Dictionnaire de la Bible* (1928), I, cols. 7ff.

[5] Cf. G. Contenau, *Manuel d'Archéologie orientale*, IV (1947), pp. 1804ff.

[6] F. Thureau-Dangin, *RA*, XXXIV (1937), pp. 135ff.; cf. C. F. Jean, *RA*, XXXV (1938), pp. 107ff. W. F. Albright, *BASOR*, No. 69 (1938), pp. 18f. A. Parrot, *SRA*, XIX (1938), p. 184.

1800-1760 B.C.[7] The same year Smith reduced his date even further to *ca.* 1792-1750 B.C., a conclusion that Ungnad had arrived at quite independently at the same time.[8] With Poebel's publication of the Khorsabad king-list in 1942 and the dating of Shamshi-Adad I to 1726-1694 B.C., Albright reduced his own dating still further to 1728-1686 B.C.[9] This accorded generally with the conclusions of Neugebauer, who had argued that the Venus astronomical observations required the date of 1792-1750 B.C. or 64 years earlier or later for Hammurabi's reign.[10] A date of 64 years later (1728-1686 B.C.) corresponds to that arrived at by Albright; and this general consensus was further reinforced by the independent investigations of Cornelius, who employed the materials preserved by Berossus to date Hammurabi *ca.* 1728-1686 B.C.[11] Two years later Cornelius raised his dating by one year.[12]

This system, which places the First Dynasty of Babylon *ca.* 1830-1530 B.C., as opposed to other higher dates, is now known as the "low" chronology, and its sequences have been adopted by many scholars. Because of the extremely technical and complex questions involved, it is not surprising that other authorities have disagreed with the conclusions arrived at by Albright and Cornelius. Sidney Smith rejects the "low" chronology, preferring instead to adhere to his own system of dating.[13] Mallowan, arguing from the stratigraphic evidence of Cretan archaeological discoveries, feels that reducing the accession date of Hammurabi to 1728 B.C. raises other chronological difficulties.[14] These might even affect the chronologies of several nations of antiquity, a fact that Gurney recognized in following the dating of Smith rather than that of Albright in establishing the sequences of Hittite chronology.[15]

---

[7] S. Smith, *The Antiquaries Journal,* XIX (1939), pp. 45ff. W. F. Albright, *BASOR,* No. 77 (1940), pp. 25f.

[8] S. Smith, *Alalakh and Chronology* (1940), pp. 10ff. Smith's dating was adopted by M. Noth, *Zeitschrift des deutschen Palästina-Vereins,* LXV (1942), p. 15. Ungnad dated Hammurabi *ca.* 1791-1748 B.C. Cf. his articles in *Mitteilungen der altorientalischen Gesellschaft,* XIII, No. 13 (1940), p. 17, and *Orientalia,* XIII (1944), pp. 83ff. In *Archiv für Orientforschung,* XIII (1940), pp. 145f., Ungnad had assigned a somewhat earlier date to Hammurabi (*ca.* 1801-1759 B.C.). D. Sidersky independently dated the Babylonian ruler *ca.* 1848-1803 B.C. Cf. *RA,* XXXVII (1940), pp. 45ff.

[9] A. Poebel, *JNES,* I (1942), pp. 247ff., 460ff., II (1943), pp. 238, 357ff. W. F. Albright, *BASOR,* No. 88 (1942), pp. 28ff.

[10] *JAOS,* LXI (1941), p. 59.

[11] Cornelius, *Klio,* XXXV (1942), p. 7.

[12] *Forschungen und Fortschritte,* XX (1944), p. 75.

[13] *AJA,* XLIX (1945), pp. 18ff. Albright attempted to justify his position against Smith's arguments in *BASOR,* No. 99 (1945), p. 10 n.; see also *Bibliotheca Orientalis,* V (1948), p. 126.

[14] *Iraq,* IX (1947), pp. 4n., 86n.

[15] *TH,* p. 217.

As a result there is a wide divergence of scholarly opinion regarding the date that is to be assigned to the First Dynasty of Babylon.[16] At one extreme is a date *ca.* 1900 B.C., proposed by Landsberger,[17] which appears prohibitively high. A somewhat lower sequence proposed by Goetze, Sidersky, and Thureau-Dangin would date the First Babylonian Dynasty about 1848-1806 B.C.[18] A "middle" chronology would place it *ca.* 1792-1750 B.C.[19] The "low" dating of Cornelius and Albright was supported by Bright,[20] Van der Waerden, and initially by Rowton, as has been observed above. An "ultra-low" sequence of dating, which places the First Babylonian Dynasty about 1704-1662 B.C., was advocated by Böhl and followed by Schubert and Weidner.[21]

[16] With respect to the dating of Hammurabi, the position of Albright and Cornelius was followed by de Vaux, *RB*, LIII (1945), p. 335, Rowton, *Iraq*, VIII (1946), pp. 94ff., O'Callaghan, *Aram Naharaim, A Contribution to the History of Upper Mesopotamia in the Second Millennium B.C.* (1948), pp. 6ff., and others. C. F. A. Schaeffer, who had suggested an eighteenth- or seventeenth-century date, *Ugaritica* (1939), p. 18n., later inclined towards a date between 1800 and 1700 B.C., in *SRA*, XXV (1946-1948), p. 187. E. Cavaignac, while allowing for a date of 1728 B.C. as a possible alternative, placed the date for the beginning of Hammurabi's reign at 1720 B.C., *RA*, XL (1945-1946), p. 22. R. Weill disputed the results of Cornelius in *Chronique d'Egypte*, XLI (1946), p. 42; F. M. Th. Böhl expressed some hesitation, preferring to state only that the greater part of the reign of Hammurabi ought to be dated subsequent to 1700 B.C., *Mededeelingen der Koninklijke Nederlandsche Akademie van Wetenschappen, Afd. Letterkunde*, IX, No. 10 (1946), pp. 341ff. and *Bibliotheca Orientalis*, I (1944), pp. 57ff. Mediating positions between Smith and Albright were adopted by Van der Meer (*ca.* 1778-1736 B.C.), *Jaarbericht Ex Oriente Lux*, IX (1944), pp. 143f., and Kramer, who stated that his date of 1750 B.C. for the beginning of Hammurabi's reign was merely a compromise that might well need adjustment, *AJA*, LII (1948), p. 163n. Subsequently, Van der Meer proposed an even later date for Hammurabi, *ca.* 1712-1670 B.C., with an addition of up to twenty years, *The Chronology of Ancient Western Asia and Egypt* (1947), pp. 13, 22. B. L. Van der Waerden assigned greater mathematical probability to the dates offered by Cornelius and Albright than to those of Smith and Ungnad, *Jaarbericht Ex Oriente Lux*, X (1945-1948), pp. 414ff. In 1958 Rowton, who had earlier preferred the lower dates, *JNES*, X (1951), pp. 184ff., revised his position and advocated the higher dating of Smith, *JNES*, XVII (1958), pp. 97ff.

[17] *JCS*, VIII (1954), pp. 31ff., 47ff., 106ff.

[18] Goetze, *BASOR*, No. 122 (1951), pp. 18ff., No. 127 (1952), pp. 21ff., No. 146 (1957), pp. 20ff.; Sidersky, *RA*, XXXVII (1940), pp. 45ff.; Thureau-Dangin, *Mémoires de l'Académie des Inscriptions et Belles Lettres*, XLIII, pt. 2 (1942), pp. 229ff.

[19] Supported by Albright, *BASOR*, No. 77 (1940), pp. 20ff., Rowton, *JNES*, XVII (1958), pp. 97ff., Smith, *Alalakh and Chronology* (1940), *AJA*, XLIX (1945), pp. 1ff., and Ungnad, *Mitteilungen der altorientalischen Gesellschaft*. XIII, No. 3 (1940), p. 17.

[20] *BHI*, p. 42.

[21] K. Schubert, *Wiener Zeitschrift für die Kunde des Morgenlandes*, LI (1948-1952), pp. 21ff. E. Weidner, *Archiv für Orientforschung*, XV (1945-1951), pp. 85ff.

In the light of these considerations the majority of scholars have favored a date for the patriarchal age at a later rather than an earlier period of the Middle Bronze Age, placing the origin of the traditions in the seventeenth and sixteenth centuries B.C. rather than in the twentieth and nineteenth centuries. The enigmatic character of Genesis 14 presents one of the chief obstacles to a fuller understanding of the archaeological sequences, and this difficulty can only be removed by additional informative excavations in Mesopotamia, preferably at sites hitherto unexplored. Some scholars have employed the genealogical records associated with the patriarchs in attempting a reasonably assured dating of the events of the patriarchal age. Preferring to regard the chronology of this period as clear and unambiguous, they have dated the patriarchs in the Late Bronze Age, and have based their estimates upon certain references (Exod. 6:16, 18, 20; cf. Gen. 46:26) which would imply that the sojourn in Egypt only lasted for two or three generations at the most. Thus Gordon, arguing from the fact that Egypt was known as the "land of Rameses" (Gen. 47:11) when Jacob went there as an old man, concluded that this event took place during the Amarna period.[22] Since Moses was apparently a grandson of Kohath, son of Levi, who accompanied Jacob into Egypt, he could well have been born before Joseph died, thus spanning the gap between the entrance of Israel into Egypt and the birth of Moses by a single lifetime.

Bowman and Rowley have also dated the patriarchal era in the Late Bronze Age, making the Amarna period the background for the narratives of Joseph rather than the Hyksos setting that the majority of scholars have assumed to have been the case.[23] Part of the difficulty which these scholars are attempting to face consists in the prolonged interval of time between the patriarchs themselves and those who made up the generation of the Exodus, about which the Bible records little or nothing. While genealogies have always constituted an important means of reckoning for oriental peoples, they should not be employed in this instance to the exclusion of the Biblical figures with which they come into conflict. According to Genesis 15:13, the offspring of Abraham were to be afflicted in a foreign land for 400 years, while Exodus 12:40, 41 recorded the stay of the Hebrews in Egypt as 430 years. The LXX of the latter passage allotted a 430-year period to cover the sojourn of the patriarchs in Palestine as well. For this last period Genesis (12:4; 21:5; 25:26; 47:9) allotted a span of 215 years, thus reducing proportionately

---

[22] *IOTT*, pp. 75, 102ff.; *JNES*, XIII (1954), pp. 56ff.

[23] R. A. Bowman, *JNES*, VII (1948), pp. 68f. Rowley, *From Joseph to Joshua* (1950), pp. 109ff., *RSL*, pp. 273f., 290. Other scholars who assign the entry into Egypt to the Amarna Age include W. C. Wood, *JBL*, XXXV (1916), pp. 166f., C. F. Burney, *Israel's Settlement in Canaan* (1918), pp. 87ff., R. Kittel, *Geschichte des Volkes Israel* (1923), I, p. 336, and T. J. Meek, *Hebrew Origins* (1960 ed.), pp. 18f.

the amount of time spent in Egypt. The Hebrew text of Exodus 12:40 is preferable to the LXX reading, since the following verse clearly indicates that the "selfsame day" constituted the 430th anniversary of the time when Jacob and his family first entered Egypt, thus assuring a lengthy stay in that land.

The principal difficulty that besets the approach of Rowley and Gordon is the assumption, based on the genealogical tables, that there were only three generations between the patriarchal period and the time of the Exodus. This supposition may well be entirely gratuitous since there are reasons for believing that the genealogical record of Exodus 6:16ff., which, of course, can hardly cover 430 years if taken strictly at face value, has been drawn up in terms of the operation of specific principles of selectivity, a procedure commonly adopted by oriental peoples. It is curious that Rowley, who has inveighed so frequently against those who are inclined to accept Biblical statements literally, should be scornful of those who posit the existence of gaps in the chronology of this passage, and should attempt to maintain a closed genealogy.[24] It is merely a matter of record that Egyptian king-lists pass over centuries at a time without formal indication or explanation of the fact. Again, other ancient Near Eastern regnal lists occasionally omit the names of particular individuals, as for example in the case of King Halparutas II of Gurgum in southeastern Asia Minor, who in his genealogy named his father and great-grandfather, but omitted the name of his grandfather, who is listed in the more complete genealogy of Halparutas III.[25]

B. THE SOJOURN IN EGYPT

These considerations are of considerable importance when attempts are made to interpret the chronological scheme of Exodus. Although Moses is regarded as the son of Amram and Jochebed, it is almost certain that the term "son" should in this instance be regarded as the equivalent of "descendant." That Moses was their offspring, though rather considerably removed, seems indicated by the fact that the parents of Moses were not named in the detailed account of his infancy, and also that Amram and his three brothers had several descendants within a year of the Exodus itself (Num. 3:27f.). Although Moses appeared in the fourth generation from Jacob, through Levi, Kohath, and Amram (Exod. 6:20; 1 Chron. 6:1ff.), Bezaleel his contemporary was in the seventh generation from Jacob, through Judah, Perez, Hezron, Caleb, Hur, and Uri (1 Chron. 2:18ff.). His younger contemporary Joshua appeared in the twelfth generation from Jacob, through Joseph, Ephraim, Beriah, Rephah, Resheph, Telah, Tahan, Laadan, Ammihud, Elishama,

---

[24] *From Joseph to Joshua*, pp. 72f., 78.
[25] The kings of Malatya frequently omitted the father, naming only the grandfather; cf. T. C. Mitchell, *NBD*, p. 457.

and Nun (1 Chron. 7:23ff.). These comparisons would seem to indicate that the genealogy of Moses has been abbreviated.

Furthermore, the sons of Kohath gave rise to the clans of the Amramites and the others mentioned in Numbers 3:27, who numbered 8,600 males within a year of the Exodus. This would be a rather improbable situation, to say the least, unless Amram and his brothers had lived considerably prior to the time of Moses.[26] From this it seems legitimate to assume that the genealogical tables upon which Gordon and Rowley have based their arguments did not in fact preserve detailed and complete information with regard to ancestry prior to the conquest period. It is well known that early genealogies frequently pass directly from the name of the father to that of the clan.[27] Thus, in effect the Exodus reference states that Moses was the descendant of Amram of the clan of Kohath, of the tribe of Levi; hence it preserves only the general designation of clan and tribe.[28]

If the tradition of a prolonged Israelite stay in Egypt, perhaps based upon the Avaris era, has some validity in fact, it still presents certain difficulties when attempts are made to assign a date to Abraham, the ancestor of the later Hebrew peoples. Like Hammurabi, with whom he was once regarded as contemporary, Abraham has sometimes been assigned to the latter part of the twentieth century B.C.[29] Others have maintained a seventeenth-century B.C. date for Abraham.[30] Albright at first followed Kraeling's seventeenth-century dating; then he assigned Abraham to the period between 1800 and 1600 B.C.; and subsequently to a date not earlier than the nineteenth century B.C. In 1942 he returned to a seventeenth-century B.C. date for the patriarchs, but seven years later he dated the migration from Ur to Harran in the twentieth and nineteenth centuries B.C.[31]

There is at present no conclusive evidence that can be adduced for an accurate dating of Abraham or his immediate descendants; the best that can be done is to assign them to the Middle Bronze Age without further

---

[26] Cf. H. S. Gehman, *The Westminster Dictionary of the Bible* (1944), p. 153; K. A. Kitchen and T. C. Mitchell, *NBD*, p. 214.

[27] Cf. *WBA*, p. 50 n. 5.

[28] D. N. Freedman, *BANE*, p. 206.

[29] Among scholars holding this view are P. E. Dhorme, *RB*, XL (1931), pp. 506ff., G. E. Wright, *BASOR*, No. 71 (1938), p. 34, and Millar Burrows, *WMTS*, p. 71.

[30] These include E. G. H. Kraeling, *Aram and Israel* (1918), p. 32, A. Jirku, *ZAW*, XXXIX (1921), pp. 152ff., 313f., and *Geschichte des Volkes Israel* (1931), pp. 61ff., and F. M. Th. Böhl, *ZAW*, XLII (1924), pp. 148ff. Earlier (*ZAW*, XXXVI [1916], pp. 65ff.), Böhl had placed Abraham much later, *ca.* 1250 B.C. At first W. F. Albright followed Kraeling's dating, *AJSL*, XL (1923-1924), pp. 125ff., *BASOR*, No. 14 (1924), p. 7, *AASOR*, VI (1926), p. 62.

[31] *JPOS*, VI (1927), p. 227, *The Archaeology of Palestine and the Bible* (1932), p. 137, *BASOR*, No. 88 (1942), p. 35, *AP*, p. 83, *FSAC*, p. 200, *BPAE*, p. 2.

specification, so as to maintain a reasonable degree of flexibility in the chronology. Placing the patriarchal migrations and the patriarchs themselves later than the sixteenth century B.C. appears unsatisfactory from an historical point of view.

The narratives and their peculiar nomenclature are closely paralleled by the texts of the early second millennium B.C. The stories of Laban and Jacob are in harmony with the political and social conditions in Upper Mesopotamia both before and after the eighteenth century B.C., when the population of that area was predominantly Amorite. At a later period the region had succumbed to the Mitanni, while Palestine and portions of Syria were firmly established as Egyptian spheres of influence. Subsequently the decline of the Mitanni left Upper Mesopotamia torn between the political ambitions of the Hittites and the increasing power of resurgent Assyria.

Again, the Palestinian setting of the patriarchal narratives is strictly that of the Middle Bronze Age, and not of the later Egyptian Empire period. As Bright has pointed out, the patriarchs wandered in the central mountainous area, in the south, and in Transjordan, meeting no city-kings except those of the Jordanian plain (Gen. 14:1ff.), Melchizedek, king of Jerusalem (Gen. 14:18), and the ruler of Gerar on the coastal plain (Gen. 20:2ff; 26:1ff.). This description is in full accord with the sparsely settled nature of Middle Bronze Age Palestine.[32] Shechem (Gen. 33:18ff.; 34:2ff.) appeared to be in the hands of a tribal confederacy during the patriarchal period, while Hebron, founded "seven years before Zoan in Egypt" (Num. 13:22) was at that time known by its original name of Kiriath-arba (Gen. 23:2; 35:27; the reference in Gen. 13:18 is an explanatory gloss). Since Tanis-Avaris-Zoan was rebuilt by the Hyksos prior to 1700 B.C., the patriarchs would have to be dated even earlier than that time. It is interesting to note that the patriarchal figures never encountered any Egyptians in Palestine, which is consistent with the political situation during the Middle Kingdom period of Egyptian history, and also with the subsequent Hyksos era, when Egyptian control of southern Canaan was non-existent, but out of harmony with the conditions of the turbulent Amarna Age as reflected in the Tell el-Amarna tablets, when local rulers, aided by elements of the Habiru, were engaged in self-aggrandizement or in the complete repudiation of Egyptian overlordship.

Although it is impossible to say with complete confidence precisely when Jacob and his family migrated to Egypt, the general conditions reflected in the Biblical narratives would favor an entry during the Hyksos regime. Although Semites had access to Egypt during all periods of Egyptian history, the eclipse of a strongly nationalistic rule by the alien Hyksos would seem to furnish the most appropriate conditions for

[32] *BHI*, p. 70.

the rise to power of a talented Semite such as Joseph. Against this conclusion must be set the fact that, since the Biblical sources apparently do not present a uniform view of the length of time during which Jacob and his descendants stayed in Egypt, it is obviously impossible to reckon backwards from a presumed date of the Exodus in order to arrive at a suitable time for the arrival of Joseph in Egypt. Furthermore, though it may be attractive to suppose that the pharaoh under whom Joseph rose to prominence was of Hyksos origin, and the ruler who did not recognize his work or reputation was of native Egyptian ancestry, there is to date absolutely no proof for such a position. As is so frequently the case with historical descriptions of aspects of other cultures in widely differing ages, it is highly probable that the comparatively uncomplicated narratives that deal with the Egyptian sojourn of Israel actually conceal a much more involved and complex state of affairs than might appear from a casual reading of the material. Despite all of this, however, it seems best on the evidence available to relate the work of Joseph to the general period of Hyksos rule in Egypt.[33] The political and social conditions reflected in the Genesis narratives suit the Hyksos regime admirably, as Kitchen has shown,[34] whereas they do not by any means conform as closely to the conditions obtaining during the Late Bronze Age.

At this juncture it may be advantageous to devote a little closer attention to the chronology of ancient Egypt in order to supplement what has been said previously on this subject. Although Egyptian chronology, like its Babylonian counterpart, has been revised from time to time, the general picture appears rather more stable than that of early Mesopotamian history. Despite the fact that scholars have been unable to agree upon a precise chronology for Egypt prior to the Saitic revival (663-525 B.C.), the area of disagreement on dates within the Old Testament period is not particularly wide, and can frequently be reduced to the extent of a single generation. This situation is due partly to the fact that the Egyptians preserved their king-lists and annals, thus furnishing valuable source material for chronological study.[35] Another factor is the literary activities of Manetho, an Egyptian priest who lived in the third century B.C. On the basis of various available sources Manetho compiled a history of Egypt in which he listed the pharaohs by dynasties, at first thirty and subsequently thirty-one, a classification that has proved so convenient that it has been retained to the present.

[33] In this connection it is interesting to note that Archbishop Usher should have assigned a date of 1728 B.C. for the arrival of Joseph in Egypt, *Annales Veteris Testamenti*, pp. 1f., 6, 14; cf. *WMTS*, p. 72, *BHI*, p. 74.

[34] *NBD*, pp. 342, 657ff.

[35] Herodotus (II, 77) comments that "the Egyptians. . .are the most careful of all men to preserve the memory of the past, and none. . .have so many chronicles."

171

Unfortunately comparatively little has survived from his work, and even those portions of king-lists and other citations which are extant have obviously suffered in process of transmission.[36]

The rulers of the first two dynasties were listed on small ivory tablets, whereas the annals of the first six dynasties were recorded at somewhat greater length in antiquity on the celebrated Palermo Stone, dated about 2400 B.C.[37] This source gives the names of nine rulers in Lower Egypt, probably supplemented by others on a lost portion of the stone, which doubtless contained a list of Upper Egyptian rulers also. The First and Second Dynasties are usually assigned by scholars to the Protodynastic period, about 2900-2760 B.C.,[38]the dates furnished by older chronologies being generally too high.[39]

The position adopted here is that of the "low" chronology, so called from the dates assigned to the early dynasties of Egypt in terms of synchronisms and agreements with a comparably low dating for the First Dynasty of Babylon. The Old Kingdom period, embracing the Third to the Sixth Dynasties, has been dated *ca.* 2700-2200 B.C., though the chronological studies of Scharff and Moortgat have reduced this date by a period of fifty or more years. The Seventh to Eleventh Dynasties have been assigned to the period *ca.* 2200-1989 B.C., with some slight variations connected with the beginning of the succeeding Middle Kingdom period.[40]

The dating of the Twelfth Dynasty was placed by Scharff and Moortgat at 1991-1778 B.C.; Edgerton dated it 1989-1776 B.C. R. A. Parker and W. F. Albright varied slightly from the latter estimate, assigning it to a

---

[36] Cf. W. G. Waddell, *Manetho* (1940), H. W. Helck, *Untersuchungen zu Manetho und den Ägyptischen Königslisten* (1956), pp. 10ff.

[37] *LAP*, pl. 27.

[38] Cf. A. Scharff and A. Moortgat, *Ägypten und Vorderasien im Altertum* (1950), pp. 25ff.; H. Stock, *Studia Aegyptiaca II* (*Analecta Orientalia* 31, 1949); W. F. Albright, *BASOR*, No. 119 (1950), p. 29; P. van der Meer, *Orientalia Neerlandica* (1948), pp. 23ff.

[39] J. H. Breasted, *The Conquest of Civilisation* (1938), pp. 64f., dated the union of the Two Lands which commenced the First Dynasty *ca.* 3400 B.C. Cf. his *The Dawn of Conscience* (1934), p. 10. This constituted a significant reduction of the estimate of Champollion (5867 B.C.) and Petrie (4777 B.C.). J. A. Wilson, *The Culture of Ancient Egypt* (1956), p. 43, dated the beginning of the First Dynasty *ca.* 3100 B.C., and in *IDB*, II, p. 44, *ca.* 3000 B.C.

[40] A. Scharff and A. Moortgat dated the Eleventh Dynasty *ca.* 2052-1991 B.C.; H. Stock, *BASOR*, No. 119 (1950), p. 29, placed it *ca.* 2040-1991 B.C. Cf. H. E. Winlock, *JNES*, II (1943), pp. 249ff., W. C. Hayes, *The Sceptre of Egypt, Part I* (1953), pp. 34ff. For the dating of the early Egyptian Dynasties see also É. Drioton and J. Vandier, *Les peuples de l'Orient Méditerranéen, II: L'Égypte* (1952).

date of 1991-1786 B.C.[41] The Second Intermediate period, embracing the Thirteenth to the Seventeenth Dynasties, can be placed in the period from *ca.* 1776 B.C. to 1570 B.C.[42] The brief revival of Egyptian power under Neferhotep I (*ca.* 1740-1729 B.C.), who attempted to restore Egyptian control of Byblos and dispossess the occupying Amorite forces, may perhaps furnish a valuable synchronism between Egypt and Mesopotamia. This will be particularly the case if the Amorite ruler, known in the Egyptian texts as Enten (Antina), is to be identified with Yantin-ammu, whose name occurs in tablets recovered from Mari.[43]

The New Kingdom period, consisting of the Eighteenth to Twentieth Dynasties, was instituted by Khamosis (*ca.* 1580 B.C.) and continued with the rule of Amosis (*ca.* 1570-1546 B.C.), flourishing after the expulsion of the Hyksos.[44] The chronology of the Eighteenth Dynasty usually follows that drawn up by Borchardt, revised by Rowton and Albright, which assigns a date of *ca.* 1570-1310 B.C. for that period.[45] There is some variation of opinion about the dates of certain pharaohs within the New Kingdom period, for example that of Thutmosis III (*ca.* 1490-1435 B.C.).[46] Dating of the Nineteenth Dynasty (*ca.* 1310-1200 B.C.) also allows some diversity of opinion, but the differences here are minor.[47]

Egyptian historical sources from the New Kingdom period include numerous contemporary inscriptions of pharaohs, often containing the dates of regnal years, as well as similar inscriptions of their officials. The latter not infrequently included genealogical tables in their records, a practice which seems to date back at least to the twentieth century B.C. The earliest extant representative of this genealogical tradition is that of Ukhhotep, count of the fourteenth Upper Egyptian nome in the reign of the pharaoh Amenemhat II, *ca.* 1925 B.C., roughly contemporary with

[41] W. F. Edgerton, *JNES*, I (1942), pp. 307ff. Cf. L. H. Wood, *BASOR*, No. 99 (1945), pp. 5ff. R. A. Parker, *The Calendars of Ancient Egypt* (*Studies in Ancient Oriental Civilisation*, No. 26, 1950), pp. 63ff. Cf. his article in *Encyclopedia Americana* (1962), X, pp. 14b ff. W. F. Albright, *BASOR*, No. 127 (1952), pp. 27ff. For a general survey of this period see H. E. Winlock, *The Rise and Fall of the Middle Kingdom in Thebes* (1947).

[42] Cf. W. F. Albright, *JPOS*, XVI (1935), pp. 222ff.

[43] W. F. Albright, *BASOR*, No. 99 (1945), pp. 9ff.

[44] For the chronology of the reign of Amosis I see W. F. Albright, *BASOR*, No. 68 (1937), p. 22 n. 2.

[45] L. Borchardt, *Die Mittel zur zeitlichen Festlegung von Punkten der ägyptischen Geschichte und ihre Anwendung* (1935), pp. 87ff. M. B. Rowton, *BASOR*, No. 126 (1952), p. 22. W. F. Albright, *BASOR*, No. 118 (1950), p. 19. Cf. *BASOR*, No. 88 (1942), p. 32 and W. F. Edgerton, *AJSL*, LIII (1936-1937), pp. 188ff. For a popular survey of the New Kingdom period see G. Steindorff and K. C. Seele, *When Egypt Ruled the East* (1957 ed.).

[46] Cf. R. A. Parker, *JNES*, XVI (1957), pp. 39ff.

[47] Cf. M. B. Rowton, *JEA*, XXXIV (1948), pp. 57ff., A. Malamat, *JNES*, XIII (1954), pp. 233f., and W. F. Albright, *AJA*, LIV (1950), p. 170.

the period suggested by many scholars for Abraham. From the tomb-chapel of Ukhhotep was recovered a complete list of his forbears and predecessors in office, along with the names of their wives. The record, which appears to be in chronological order, dates back to about 2500 B.C., and extended over a period of some 600 years.[48] The genuineness of the document is attested by the differing styles of the names recorded.

Perhaps the most remarkable of the king-lists from the New Kingdom period is the celebrated Turin papyrus, which catalogued the names of almost all the rulers of Egypt from the earliest times down to what is probably the period of Rameses II (*ca.* 1290-1224 B.C.). Another, though rather restricted measure of chronological control, is to be found in the mention of lunar dates and the rising of Sirius (Sothis), the Dog-Star, in Egyptian texts of the Middle and New Kingdom periods.[49] There are also definite links with other elements of ancient Near Eastern chronology, particularly regarding synchronisms with kings of western Asia, which are extremely valuable in arriving at approximate dates for both individuals and eras.[50]

C. The Date of the Exodus

At the beginning of the twentieth century the majority of scholars of all schools dated the Exodus towards the end of the thirteenth century B.C., although some rejected the Biblical evidence in favor of a twofold entrance to Palestine at widely separated times.[51] Thus Albright identified the tribe of Joseph with the Habiru, and maintained that they were in Palestine about 1400 B.C., while other tribes, particularly the descendants of Judah, left Egypt under the leadership of Moses early in the reign of Rameses II.[52] Meek conflicted completely with Biblical tradition in taking the view that Joshua long antedated Moses.[53] He associated the attack on the central uplands under Joshua with the encroachments of the Habiru during the Amarna period, and placed the settle-

[48] A. M. Blackman, *Rock Tombs of Meir, III* (1915), pp. 16ff., and pls. 10, 11, 29, 33:1, 35:1, 36:1, 37:1, 2; L. Borchardt. *Die Mittel zur zeitlichen Festlegung von Punkten der ägyptischen Geschichte und ihre Anwendung,* pp. 112ff.

[49] Cf. R. A. Parker, *JNES,* XVI (1957), pp. 39ff.; J. A. Wilson, *The Culture of Ancient Egypt,* p. 61.

[50] Cf. P. van der Meer, *The Chronology of Ancient Western Asia and Egypt* (*Documenta et Monumenta Orientis Antiqui,* II, 1947); R. B. Rowton, *Iraq,* VIII (1946), pp. 94ff.; H. J. Kantor in R. W. Erich (ed.), *Relative Chronologies in Old World Archaeology,* pp. 7ff.; A. Scharff and A. Moortgat, *Ägypten und Vorderasien im Altertum,* pp. 35ff.

[51] Cf. A. H. Sayce, *The Early History of the Hebrews* (1897), pp. 158ff.; E. L. Curtis, *HDB,* I, p. 398.

[52] W. F. Albright, *BASOR,* No. 58 (1935), pp. 10ff. He was followed by Burrows, *WMTS,* p. 79, Wright, *WHAB,* pp. 39f., and Finegan, *LAP,* pp. 105ff.

[53] T. J. Meek, *Hebrew Origins,* pp. 21ff. Cf. *BASOR,* No. 61 (1936), pp. 17ff.; cf. G. A. Danell, *Studies in the Name Israel in the OT* (1946), p. 44n.

ment of Judah later than the occupation of the central highlands. The tribes led by Moses subsequently entered Canaan from the south about 1200 B.C., making for an interval of at least a century between Moses and Joshua.[54] Such a view is adequately refuted by the fact that, although the Biblical narratives can perhaps be made to support a twofold entry into Canaan—even though it is made clear that the initial attack in the south was abortive in nature—there is absolutely no textual evidence whatever for a twofold Exodus, a point that even Albright conceded.[55]

The beginning of the twentieth century also witnessed a significant change of opinion in favor of a fifteenth-century B.C. date for the Exodus.[56] This was reinforced by the discoveries of Garstang at Jericho, particularly by his statement that the city had fallen prior to 1400 B.C., which appeared to confirm the chronological statement of 1 Kings 6:1, and place the Exodus in the middle of the fifteenth century B.C.[57] This dating-sequence was accepted immediately by many scholars, some of them regarding it enthusiastically as a signal vindication of the general accuracy of the Biblical narratives.[58] Even though T. H. Robinson claimed confidently that, with a very few exceptions, Old Testament scholars had abandoned the Nineteenth Dynasty date, the facts proved to be otherwise.[59]

The question cannot be settled simply by an appeal to the book of Kings in the light of an arbitrary dating for the fall of Jericho. More recent excavations have cast considerable doubt upon the methods and conclusions of Garstang at Jericho, and the entire question of the date when Jericho fell has been shown to be in fact far from settled. Even Garstang modified his original date to one occurring between 1400 B.C. and the accession of Akhenaton (ca. 1370-1353 B.C.), which Albright subsequently lowered to between 1360 and 1320 B.C., and later to about 1300 B.C., finally concluding that the Exodus occurred in the latter part

[54] For a criticism of this view see H. H. Rowley, From Joseph to Joshua, pp. 141ff.

[55] JBL, XXXVII (1918), pp. 138ff.

[56] E.g. J. Orr, The Problem of the OT (1909), pp. 422ff.; T. E. Peet, Egypt and the OT (1922), p. 121; J. W. Jack, The Date of the Exodus (1925).

[57] Garstang, Joshua-Judges (1931), p. 146.

[58] T. H. Robinson, History of Israel (1931), I, p. 80; A. S. Yahuda, The Accuracy of the Bible (1934), pp. 116ff.; L. Dennefeld, Histoire d'Israël (1935), pp. 64ff.; S. L. Caiger, Bible and Spade (1936), pp. 68ff.

[59] Robinson, ET, XLVII (1934-1935), p. 54. Scholars holding to the Nineteenth Dynasty date included Jirku, Geschichte des Volkes Israel, pp. 67ff., Vincent, RB, XLI (1932), pp. 264ff. and XLIV (1935), pp. 583ff., Barton, Archaeology and the Bible (1933), pp. 41f., Albright, BASOR, No. 58 (1935), pp. 10ff., Lavergne, Chronologie Biblique (1937), p. 48, Noth, Die Welt des AT (1940), p. 173, Burrows, WMTS, p. 79, Gordon, The Living Past (1941), pp. 36f., Finegan, LAP, pp. 105ff., and others.

of the fourteenth century or the early years of the thirteenth century B.C.[60]

The diversity of opinion on this matter is further illustrated by Vincent, who proposed a date of between 1250 and 1200 B.C. for the fall of Jericho.[61] Although Schaeffer and de Vaux tended to agree with Vincent, this date has been rejected by Wright as being too low.[62] Bearing in mind the conclusions of Kathleen Kenyon that it is at present impossible to state with certainty the date when Jericho fell,[63] it would seem from the available evidence that a date in the middle of the thirteenth century B.C. is required for the crossing of the Jordan.[64]

This conclusion is supported by the evidence of the Meneptah *stele*, the nature of which demands the presence of Israel in Canaan about 1200 B.C. Furthermore, as Glueck has shown, the detour that the Israelites were compelled to make around Edom and Moab (Num. 20:14ff.; 21:4ff.) would, if the narratives are to be regarded as historical, rule out a date prior to the thirteenth century B.C. for the Exodus, since these two kingdoms had not been established before that time.[65] The general testimony of archaeology, although rather ambiguous in certain areas, seems to point to a date in the latter part of the thirteenth century B.C. for the destruction of sites such as Debir, Lachish, and Eglon, if the latter probably can be identified with Tell el-Hesi. The date of the fall of Lachish was assigned to a period not later than 1260 B.C. by Starkey, and to about 1231 B.C. by Albright, who subsequently reduced his date to *ca.* 1221 B.C., whereas Noth and Vincent inclined to a somewhat earlier time.[66]

---

[60] Garstang's original date is given in *Palestine Exploration Fund Quarterly Statement* (1930), p. 132; his revised suggestion *ibid.* (1936), p. 170. Cf. Albright, BASOR, No. 58 (1935), p. 13, No. 74 (1939), p. 20; AP, pp. 108f.; AJA, XXXIX (1935), p. 40; BPAE, pp. 14ff.

[61] L.-H. Vincent, RB, XXXIX (1930), pp. 403ff., XLI (1932), pp. 264ff., XLIV (1935), pp. 583ff., XLVIII (1939), p. 580.

[62] C. F. A. Schaeffer, *Stratigraphie Comparée et Chronologie de l'Asie Occidentale [IIIe et IIe millenaires]* (1948), pp. 129ff., held that City D was destroyed by fire at the end of the thirteenth century B.C. Cf. R. de Vaux, ZAW, LVI (1938), p. 237; G. E. Wright, BASOR, No. 86 (1942), p. 33; J. Bright, BHI, pp. 112f.

[63] K. M. Kenyon, BA, XVII, No. 4 (1954), pp. 98ff., and her *Digging Up Jericho* (1957), pp. 262f.

[64] Cf. W. F. Albright in H. C. Alleman and E. E. Flack (eds.), *OT Commentary* (1948), p. 141.

[65] Glueck, BASOR, No. 55 (1934), pp. 3ff., No. 86 (1942), pp. 14ff., No. 90 (1943), pp. 2ff.; BA, X, No. 4 (1947), pp. 77ff.

[66] J. L. Starkey, *Palestine Exploration Fund Quarterly Statement* (1934), p. 174. Starkey modified his conclusion three years later, favoring then a period towards the end of the Nineteenth Dynasty, *ibid.* (1937), p. 239. For the date of 1231 B.C. see Albright, BASOR, No. 68 (1937), p. 24, No. 74 (1939), p. 21; cf. AJA, XXXIX (1935), pp. 139ff. For the date of 1221 B.C., Albright, FSAC, p. 255; cf. G. E. Wright, JNES, V (1946), p. 111. For earlier dating, Noth, PJB, XXXIV (1938), p. 16, Vincent, RB, XLVIII (1939), p. 419n.

Certain problems have been posed by the narratives concerning the destruction of Bethel and Ai, the former, according to Albright, being overthrown in the first half of the thirteenth century B.C. or possibly a little earlier.[67] A similar date for the destruction of Ai-Bethel was accepted in a guarded fashion by Burrows and Wright, both of whom expressed uncertainty as to the nature of Ai in the time of Joshua.[68] Ai, which is usually, though not uniformly,[69] identified with et-Tell near Bethel, is supposed to have been in ruins from *ca.* 2000 to *ca.* 1200 B.C.[70] This has led some scholars to declare that the account of its capture was fictitious,[71] while others assumed that the narrative of an earlier destruction of the site had been transferred to the time of Joshua.[72] Still others have suggested that the confusion arose through associating Ai with the neighboring site of Bethel,[73] or that Ai may have been a temporary fortified outpost of Bethel during the days of Joshua.[74]

Excavations at Hazor by Yigael Yadin have shown that the last Canaanite city to be erected on the site was destroyed in the thirteenth century B.C., which is in conformity with the narratives of Joshua 11:10ff.[75] The general date to be assigned to the conquest of Canaan will naturally vary somewhat, according to whether the Exodus is dated in the first or second half of the thirteenth century B.C. If the Biblical tradition is to be regarded as substantially accurate, the beginning of the conquest can be dated about 1235 B.C., or slightly later,[76] on the assumption that the Exodus occurred in the thirteenth rather than the fifteenth century B.C.

D. THE JUDGES

The chronological tradition of the period of the Judges presents some difficulties. Over against the larger schematic pattern which established

---

[67] *BASOR*, No. 57 (1935), p. 30, No. 58 (1935), p. 13; cf. No. 74 (1939), p. 17.

[68] *WMTS*, p. 76; *WHAB*, pp. 39f.

[69] F. G. Kenyon, *The Bible and Archaeology* (1940), p. 190; J. Simons, *Jaarbericht Ex Oriente Lux*, VI (1939), p. 156, IX (1944), pp. 157ff.

[70] Cf. J. Marquet-Krause, *SRA*, XVI (1935), pp. 325ff.; L.-H. Vincent, *RB*, XLVI (1937), pp. 231ff. Cf. *BASOR*, No. 56 (1934), pp. 2ff.

[71] Such a view is held by R. Dussaud, *SRA*, XVI (1935), p. 351, W. J. Phythian-Adams, *Palestine Exploration Fund Quarterly Statement* (1936), pp. 141ff., A. Alt, *Werden und Wesen des AT* (1936), pp. 20ff.

[72] E.g. W. F. Albright, *BASOR*, No. 74 (1939), p. 17, M. Noth, *PJB*, XXXI (1935), pp. 7ff., XXXIV (1938), p. 14n.

[73] W. F. Albright, *BASOR*, No. 56 (1934), p. 11; *WHAB*, p. 40; *WMTS*, p. 76.

[74] L.-H. Vincent, *RB*, XLVI (1937), pp. 258ff.

[75] Y. Yadin, *BA*, XIX, No. 1 (1956), pp. 2ff., XX, No. 2 (1957), pp. 34ff., XXI, No. 2 (1958), pp. 30ff., XXII, No. 1 (1959), pp. 2ff.; Y. Yadin *et al.*, *Hazor I, An Account of the First Season of Excavations, 1955* (1958); *II*, (1960).

[76] *FSAC*, pp. 278f.; *WBA*, pp. 69ff.

a period of 480 years, or 12 forty-year generations, between the time of the Exodus and the construction of the Solomonic Temple is a series of smaller computations throughout the Judges and the two books of Samuel, in which periods of 20, 40, and 80 years were allotted to various judges and oppressors of the Israelites. In the light of the statistics preserved in the book of Judges, the total for the period of charismatic rule in Israel is 410 years, as shown by Table 6:[77]

TABLE 6: THE JUDGES

Judge or Deliverer	Oppressor	Scripture reference, Judges	Duration
	Cushan-Rishathaim	3:8	8
Othniel		3:11	40
	Eglon	3:14	18
Ehud		3:30	80
	Jabin	4:3	20
Deborah and Barak		5:31	40
	Midianites	6:1	7
Gideon		8:28	40
Abimelech		9:22	3
Tola		10:2	23
Jair		10:3	22
	Ammonites	10:8	18
Jephthah		12:7	6
Ibzan		12:9	7
Elon		12:11	10
Abdon		12:14	8
	Philistines	13:1	40
Samson		15:20; 16:31	20

When this figure of 410 years is added to a forty-year period for the Wilderness wanderings (a tradition which, as Freedman has pointed out, must contain a chronological factor[78]), and is supplemented by an indeterminate period for Joshua and the Elders (Judg. 2:7), a forty-year interval for the ministry of Eli (1 Sam. 4:18), a period in excess of twenty years for the charismatic leadership of Samuel (1 Sam. 7:2, 15), another interval of indeterminate length for the rule of Saul (1 Sam. 13:1),[79] a period of forty years during which David reigned (1 Kgs. 2:11), and four years at the beginning of the Solomonic regime until the Temple was constructed, the result is a total considerably in excess of 554 years.

[77] After H. H. Rowley, *From Joseph to Joshua*, p. 87.
[78] *BANE*, p. 266 n. 14. Cf. A. E. Cundall, *Judges* (1968), pp. 28ff.
[79] Cf. Acts 13:21. See S. R. Driver, *Notes on the Hebrew Text of the Books of Samuel* (1913), p. 97, for discussion of this passage.

However, there is no *a priori* reason why the compiler of Judges should have felt it desirable to make his computations agree with the figure represented by 1 Kings 6:1. Nor is it necessary to suppose that the reference in Kings is not original, and is less preferable than the lower LXX reading, a position which was adopted by Wellhausen,[80] since the figure is clearly schematic. The continuity of this pattern is evident in the fact that Kings gives an additional period of the same length for the total reigns of the kings of Judah from the fourth year of Solomon to 597 B.C., with the addition of a half-century to cover the time from the destruction of the Temple to its reconstruction after the Exile.[81] As J. W. Jack has pointed out, this can hardly be accidental, and the contrived nature of the chronological scheme may in fact indicate that the reference itself is a post-exilic insertion.[82] On the other hand, Rowley has dismissed arguments against the originality of the reference in 1 Kings, and has shown that attention is not focused upon the second period of 480 years in the way in which it is on the earlier one.[83]

For those who accept a fifteenth-century B.C. date for the Exodus, the chronology of the Judges period need not be subjected to the same degree of compression as for those who posit an extent of some 200 years (*ca.* 1200-1000 B.C.) between Joshua and David. On the basis of an early date for the Exodus it would be possible to assign Joshua and the Elders to a period about 1407-1383 B.C., and to place the Judges in succession with the exception of Samson, so that they would then be dated according to Table 7.

TABLE 7: THE JUDGES

Judge	*ca. B.C.*
Othniel	1376-1336
Ehud	1320-1240
Deborah and	
Barak	1240-1200
Gideon	1197-1157
Abimelech	1157-1154
Tola	1154-1131
Jair	1131-1109
Jephthah	1089-1083
Ibzan	1083-1076
Elon	1076-1066
Abdon	1066-1058
Samson	1071-1051

[80] *Die Composition des Hexateuchs und der historischen Bücher des AT* (1899), pp. 264f.

[81] C. F. Burney, *Notes on the Hebrew Text of the Book of Kings* (1903), pp. 59f.

[82] *The Date of the Exodus* (1925), p. 204.

[83] *From Joseph to Joshua*, p. 90.

Such a system of dating fails to take account of the possibility that, whether the Judges were tribal heroes or national leaders, it is quite possible that their careers were sometimes contemporaneous and not generally in continuous succession, as a casual perusal of the narratives in Judges might seem to imply.

In all questions of chronology it is important to remember that oriental modes of reckoning are reflected by the Hebrew text. In general, ancient scribes did not draw up synchronistic lists in the modern fashion, but instead recorded each series of rulers and reigns separately. If synchronisms were desired for any particular purpose they were normally supplied from sources different from the king-lists or historical narratives, which had been compiled with other intentions in view. The lack of cross-references between those Judges who may have been contemporaries can be paralleled closely by a similar state of affairs in Sumerian, Old Babylonian, and ancient Egyptian history, indicating that special methods of compilation and computation were evidently employed in drawing up Judges, in which the forty-year pattern was a prominent element.[84]

Although the problems of chronology cannot be solved completely without more detailed information, a recognition of the customs of the ancient scribes, taken together with the archaeological findings that require an interval of some 230 years between Joshua and David, should go far towards resolving most of the difficulties arising from a strictly literal interpretation of the figures in Judges. There is thus no need to invoke a chronological scheme that rests upon the succession of High Priests, as Wellhausen did, or an elaborate pattern that arbitrarily ignores certain aspects of the Biblical dating and reduces awkward chronological sequences, as suggested by Garstang.[85]

[84] D. N. Freedman, *BANE*, pp. 207f.; K. A. Kitchen and T. C. Mitchell, *NBD*, p. 216.

[85] J. Wellhausen, *Prolegomena to the History of Israel* (1885), p. 230. Cf. A. Gampert, *Revue de théologie et de philosophie*, V (1917), p. 246. J. Garstang, *Joshua-Judges*, pp. 55ff.

III. OLD TESTAMENT HISTORY—
THE MONARCHY AND AFTER

A. Kings of Israel and Judah

The chronology of the period of the Israelite monarchy, especially the divided kingdom, deals with much more exact numbers than that of an earlier period. These figures are based on official records that are catalogued in a manner more amenable to the western mind. The historical sources for the rise and development of the monarchy[1] are of very great value; many of them are contemporaneous, or nearly so, with the events described.[2] The chronological pattern of these narratives probably has more in common with the synchronistic chronicles of Babylon than with the king-lists of Egypt.[3] The recorded figures exhibit some variation, due partly to attempts at synchronistic dating with foreign monarchs as well as with events in Israel and Judah. A further problem resides in the calendrical basis for the figures given in the Hebrew text, in view of the fact that the Israelites employed at least two calendars during prolonged periods of their history: a Nisan calendar commencing in the spring, and a Tishri calendar beginning some six months later in the autumn.[4]

The Gezer calendar, as translated by Albright, which is closely associated with the various seasons of the agricultural year, dates from the period of the early divided monarchy, and would imply that the Tishri year was probably introduced not later than the time of Solomon.[5] There seems little doubt, however, that the spring or Nisan calendar is the more primitive, being attested in considerably earlier sources (Exod. 12:2; 13:4; 23:15; 34:18). This tradition of a dual calendar usage need occasion no particular surprise among occidentals: in the modern busi-

---

[1] Cf. M. Noth, *Überlieferungsgeschichtliche Studien I* (1943), pp. 61ff.

[2] *BHI*, p. 163.

[3] Cf. W. F. Albright, *BASOR*, No. 100 (1945), pp. 16ff.

[4] Cf. J. Morgenstern, *HUCA*, I (1924), pp. 13ff., X (1935), pp. 1ff., XX (1947), pp. 1ff., XXI (1948), pp. 365ff.

[5] W. F. Albright, *BASOR*, No. 92 (1943), pp. 16ff.; cf. R. A. S. Macalister, *The Excavation of Gezer* (1912), II, pp. 24ff.

ness world it is common for a fiscal and civil calendar to exist together without coinciding and in religious circles the ecclesiastical calendar and the civil one co-exist, but are related to different calendrical bases and patterns.

Further problems arise from the fact that the Hebrew chroniclers employed two different systems for computing regnal years. As described by Thiele, an ante-dating pattern, popular in Egypt and used by the scribes of Israel until about 789 B.C., reckoned the accession year twice, partly as the terminal year of the dead king and partly as the first year of his successor, while a post-dating or accession-year scheme of computation thought of the new reign as commencing with the beginning of the first month of the following New Year, a method current in Assyria, Babylon, and Persia. According to the latter system, any given year of a reign is always one year lower than its counterpart in the ante-dating or nonaccession-year scheme. Thus the first year of an accession-year pattern would correspond to the second year of the ante-dating form of chronological computation. It is obviously important for the scholar to know precisely which system has been employed at any given time, and whether that system has continued without change or modification throughout the period under study.[6]

The majority of the older chronologists computed the regnal years of the Hebrew kings in terms of a Nisan-to-Nisan year,[7] although Kleber used a Tishri-to-Tishri calendar for establishing his chronology of the Israelite kings.[8] Mowinckel and Morgenstern assumed that both Israel and Judah adopted a Tishri-to-Tishri calendar for the purpose of reckoning regnal years, while Begrich maintained that a Nisan-to-Nisan basis of computation was adopted at a later period, perhaps as a result of pressure exerted by the religious traditions.[9] From the evidence of I Kings 6:1, 37 it would appear that the Tishri-to-Tishri year was the basis of reckoning in the days of Solomon, although the months in Kings and elsewhere were reckoned from Nisan, irrespective of whether the year itself was begun in the spring or the autumn.[10] The totals arrived at invariably reflect the inclusive system of calculation, in which fractions

[6] *MNHK*, pp. 16ff. Cf. *Zondervan Pictorial Bible Dictionary* (1963), pp. 168ff.

[7] E. g. C. F. Keil, *Commentary on the Book of Kings* (1857), I, p. 206, W. J. Beecher, *The Dated Events of the OT* (1907), pp. 11ff., J. Lewy, *Mitteilungen der vorderasiatische-aegyptischen Gesellschaft*, XXIX, No. 2 (1924), pp. 2ff.

[8] *Biblica*, II (1921), pp. 15ff.

[9] S. Mowinckel, *Acta Orientalia*, IX (1941), pp. 175ff. J. Morgenstern, *Occident and Orient* (Gaster Anniversary Volume, 1936), pp. 439ff., and in *HUCA*, X (1935), pp. 1ff. J. Begrich, *Die Chronologie der Könige von Israel und Juda und die Quellen des Rahmens der Königsbücher* (1929), pp. 70ff.

[10] 1 Kgs. 8:2; 2 Kgs. 25:25; Exod. 12:2; Lev. 23:5; 24:27; Num. 9:1, 5; 28:16; 29:1, 7; Jer. 41:1, 8; 2 Chron. 5:3; 7:10; 29:3; Ez. 6:19; Neh. 1:1, *et al.*

of units were incorporated as though they were full units of the group under consideration.

Synchronisms with events recorded in extra-Biblical sources are naturally very important in establishing dates for the various rulers of Israel and Judah. Thus it is a matter of record that Shishak of Egypt invaded Jerusalem in the fifth year of Rehoboam (1 Kgs. 14:25; 2 Chron. 12:2); that Shalmaneser III fought a battle at Qarqar on the Orontes in his sixth year (853 B.C.) against Ahab and Benhadad; that Tiglathpileser III besieged Damascus and received tribute from Menahem of Israel (2 Kgs. 15:19) and subsequently from Jehoahaz (2 Kgs. 16:7ff.); and that Sennacherib attacked Jerusalem in the fourteenth year of King Hezekiah (2 Kgs. 18:13; Isa. 36:1). Since most of these events are mentioned in cuneiform annals, there is a firm measure of control extant for the corresponding periods of Hebrew history.

Synchronisms within the lists of the kings of Israel and Judah present problems when compared with the recorded lengths of the reigns themselves. As Thiele has pointed out, if a chronology is established in terms of the length of reign, the synchronisms do not coincide, and *vice versa*.[11] Scholars have frequently been forced to choose between the two, with results which have failed to do proper justice to the situation. Thus Wellhausen, Ewald, Bleek, Stade, and others ultimately concluded that the chronological records of the Hebrew kings were of no value whatever for the construction of an accurate chronology.[12] By contrast, other scholars have declared that, despite certain transcriptional and other errors, both the synchronisms and the lengths of the individual reigns are basically accurate, and that the data on which the Biblical records were constructed are sufficiently reliable to make an adequate chronology.[13]

Attempts to establish a chronology for the Hebrew kings have usually fallen into two distinct patterns. On the one hand the figures of the Massoretic text have been followed closely, usually by conservative scholars, in independence of contemporary Near Eastern chronology. This has resulted in a system that, for the early Hebrew kings, is at least fifty years longer than the chronology of neighboring nations would allow. As opposed to this "high" dating, other scholars have introduced a "low" chronology which surmounts the difficulty of the additional half-

[11] *MNHK*, p. 9.

[12] J. Wellhausen, *Jahrbücher für deutsche Theologie*, XX (1875), pp. 607ff. H. Ewald, *The History of Israel* (1876), I, pp. 206ff., II, pp. 20ff., 297ff. F. Bleek, *Einleitung in das AT* (1878), pp. 263ff. B. Stade, *Geschichte des Volkes Israel* (1889), I, pp. 88ff., 558ff.

[13] F. Rühl, *Deutsche Zeitschrift für Geschichtswissenschaft*, XII (1894), pp. 44ff.; *PIOT*, pp. 393ff.; *MNHK*, pp. 14f.

century by disregarding the computations of the Massoretic text to some extent in favor of synchronisms with the known chronology of other ancient Near Eastern peoples. While the latter is perhaps a more desirable course of action for the occidental methodologist, it must be remembered that the Biblical material was probably quite accurate originally, and that the lack of mechanical agreement between the figures of the Massoretic text and the synchronized events of contemporary Near Eastern history is most probably due either to alterations of the text in process of transmission, to the operation of now-unknown scribal principles of computation and reckoning, or to both factors.[14]

Whatever the chronological reconstruction of the monarchy, it has generally been found necessary to leave a margin of one or two years for the various reigns, and greater precision cannot be expected until further and more detailed chronological material is available. The reign of David has been assigned to ca. 1001/00-961/60 B.C., and the fact that its length is a compound figure implies that David actually ruled for forty years. Solomon was co-regent with David for a short period prior to his own accession, which can be dated about 961 B.C., from a synchronistic reference to Hiram, king of Tyre, in Josephus,[15] or 962 B.C., as proposed by Rowton.[16] If Solomon is credited with the full forty years allowed to him by the Massoretic text, his rule would terminate about 922 B.C.

A dating-sequence that places David and Solomon a decade earlier has been urged by some scholars[17] as a corrective to the theory of Albright, which was based on an incorrect interpretation of a reference to a lunar eclipse of a premonitory nature allegedly occurring in the reign of Takeloth II of Egypt, which apparently did not take place at all.[18] Thus the dates that Albright suggested for Shishak (ca. 935-915 B.C.) and the beginning of the Twenty-Second Dynasty should be raised by some ten years, making the commencement of the dynasty of Shishak about 945 B.C. and his invasion of Palestine, preserved in relief on a wall at Karnak, about 925 B.C.[19] This in turn would place the death of Solomon at approximately 931/30 B.C., and his accession at ca. 971/70 B.C. The date for the latter is thus somewhat later than the sequences suggested by T. H. Robinson, H. R. Hall, H. P. Smith and R. Kittel, who assigned it to 976 B.C., about 975 B.C., 973 B.C., and 972

---

[14] Cf. R. Kittel, *History of the Hebrews* (1896), II, pp. 235f.

[15] *AJ*, VIII, 3, 1. Cf. *Contra Apionem*, I, 126.

[16] M. B. Rowton, *BASOR*, No. 119 (1950), pp. 20ff. Cf. *ARI*, p. 130.

[17] E.g. K. A. Kitchen and T. C. Mitchell, *NBD*, pp. 217ff.

[18] W. F. Albright, *BASOR*, No. 130 (1953), pp. 4ff., No. 141 (1956), pp. 26f.; cf. R. A. Caminos, *The Chronicle of Prince Osorkon* (1958), pp. 88f.

[19] Cf. *ARE*, IV, sect 712ff., M. Noth, *Zeitschrift des Deutschen Palästina-Vereins*, LXI (1938), pp. 227ff., *VT*, suppl. vol. IV (1957), pp. 57ff.

B.C. respectively.[20] Coucke, Jirku, and Lusseau and Collomb assigned the accession of Solomon to the year 971 B.C.[21]

As Thiele has shown, there are good reasons for believing that the scribes employed a nonaccession-year system of computation in Israel, whereas for the kings of Judah an accession-year system, following the Babylonian pattern, was used in chronological reckoning with the exception of the rulers from Jehoram to Joash, where a nonaccession-year scheme was adopted.[22] It also seems highly probable that about the time of Amaziah of Judah, the scribes of Israel began to reckon in terms of an accession-year pattern, along with the scribes of Judah, who appear to have been using it somewhat prior to the days of Jehoram. There is some evidence also for the existence of co-regencies, and this is frequently to be found in the double datings furnished by the Hebrew scribes. Thus the accession of Joram (Jehoram) of Israel was dated in the second year of Jehoram the son of Jehoshaphat king of Judah (2 Kgs. 1:17) on the one hand, and in the eighteenth year of Jehoshaphat king of Judah (2 Kgs. 3:1) on the other. This points to a co-regency existing between Jehoshaphat and his successor Jehoram, which was mentioned subsequently in Kings (2 Kgs. 8:16).

As far as the possibility of interregna in Israel and Judah is concerned, there does not appear to be any evidence at all to indicate that such periods ever existed during the divided monarchy in either the northern or the southern kingdom. One other point in the matter of methodology is worthy of mention at this juncture. When the scribes of one kingdom synchronized the reign of their king with that of a neighboring ruler, they naturally employed their own system of computation for both monarchs, and did not use the foreign scheme for the foreign king.

The foregoing principles, as developed and illustrated by Thiele, are soundly established upon a correct ancient Eastern methodology, and when applied to the lists of kings found in the Massoretic text reflect a pattern of internal consistency as well as a substantial degree of harmony with the chronologies of neighboring kingdoms. By relating the Hebrew king-lists to cross-references in such invaluable sources as the Assyrian *limmu* or eponym lists[23] and the canon of Ptolemy,[24] it is possible to

[20] T. H. Robinson, *A History of Israel* (1934), I, p. 463; H. R. Hall, *The Ancient History of the Near East* (1936), p. 516; H. P. Smith, *OT History* (1911), p. 499; R. Kittel, *Geschichte des Volkes Israel*, II, p. 271.

[21] V. Coucke in *Supplement au Dictionnaire de la Bible* (ed. L. Pirot and A. Robert), I, col. 1247; A. Jirku, *Geschichte des Volkes Israel*, p. 146; H. Lusseau and M. Collomb, *Manual d'Études bibliques: II, Histoire du peuple d'Israël* (1945), p. 867.

[22] *MNHK*, pp. 17ff.

[23] A. Ungnad in *Reallexikon der Assyriologie* (ed. E. Ebeling and B. Meissner, 1938), II, pp. 412ff.; G. Smith, *The Assyrian Eponym Canon*, pp. 28, 42ff.

[24] F. K. Ginzel, *Handbuch der mathematischen und technischen Chronologie* (1906), pp. 138ff.; J. Hontheim, *Zeitschrift für katholische Theologie*, XLII (1918), pp. 463ff., 687ff.

secure certain synchronisms. The earliest of these is during the reigns of Ahab and Jehu of Israel and the period of Shalmaneser III of Assyria, which assists in insuring two fixed dates in Hebrew chronology. Thus it is now possible to state that the year 853 B.C. saw the death of Ahab and the accession of Ahaziah, and to observe that the death of Joram and the accession of Jehu occurred in 841 B.C.[25]

First Kings 14:25 records another important synchronism, dating the invasion of Judah by Shishak in the fifth year of the rule of Rehoboam. Unfortunately it is not easy to ascertain the corresponding year in the reign of Shishak, since the evidence furnished by Egyptian records in relation to this matter is somewhat ambiguous. According to Albright the reign of Shishak was to be dated *ca.* 935-915 B.C., as was observed above, making for a probable date of *ca.* 918 B.C. for the invasion of Judah.[26] The tentative chronological scheme at which Albright arrived, however, was based on the assumption that many of the numbers relating both to synchronisms and lengths of reigns became corrupt in process of transmission. However, once they had received the imprimatur of the "great work of the Deuteronomist" the numbers in the text were transmitted with "astonishing accuracy."[27] Instead of following the comparatively simple system of computation that he conceded to have existed in the recording of Hebrew regnal years, Albright found it necessary to resort to a series of complicated adjustments which in the end did not harmonize with the Biblical evidence. This is a rather arbitrary procedure, to say the least, especially in view of the fact that Thiele has solved the problem in an eminently satisfactory manner by employing ancient Near Eastern methodology and relating it to the evidence furnished by the Massoretic text. Not even an appeal to the chronology of the kings of Tyre can sustain the arguments of Albright, as Thiele has demonstrated.[28]

One or two modifications may be suggested for the pattern established by Thiele in connection with his objection to the synchronisms of the twelfth year of Ahaz and the accession of Hoshea of Israel (2 Kgs. 17:1), the equating of the third year of Hoshea with the accession of Hezekiah of Judah (2 Kgs. 18:1), and the correlating of the fourth and sixth years of the reign of Hezekiah with the seventh and ninth years of Hoshea (2

25 *MNHK*, pp. 50, 66. D. N. Freedman, *BANE*, p. 210; W. F. Albright, *BASOR*, No. 100 (1945), pp. 19, 21. Cf. A. T. Olmstead, *JAOS*, XXXIX (1915), pp. 344ff., XLI (1921), p. 374, *History of Assyria* (1923), pp. 134ff.; H. R. Hall, *The Ancient History of the Near East*, p. 449; T. H. Robinson, *A History of Israel*, I, p. 296.

26 W. F. Albright, *BASOR*, No. 130 (1953), pp. 4ff., No. 141 (1956), pp. 26f.; and followed by Bright, *BHI*, pp. 174 n. 26, 183 n. 43, 190 n. 61, 208 n. 15, 209 n. 1, 213 n. 14, 263 n. 31, 263 n. 32.

27 W. F. Albright, *BASOR*, No. 100 (1945), p. 19 n. 12.

28 E. R. Thiele, *VT*, IV (1954), pp. 188ff., *MNHK*, pp. 120ff., 181ff.

Kgs. 18:9f.).[29] Thiele assumed that these were years of sole reign, leaving a period of twelve or thirteen years[30] for which no proper place could be found in his chronological scheme. The mystery attaching to this situation is dispelled, however, when it is realized that these references simply continue the pattern of co-regencies established in the cases of Asa and Jehoshaphat, Jehoshaphat and Jehoram, Amaziah and Azariah, Azariah and Jotham, and Jotham and Ahaz. Thus Ahaz was co-regent with Jotham for a period of about twelve years (ca. 744/3-732 B.C.), while Hezekiah was co-regent with Ahaz from 729-716/15 B.C., and Manasseh was co-regent with Hezekiah from 696/95-687/86 B.C. There is nothing especially unusual about such a situation: there is a precedent in the example of David and Solomon.

The identity of the various Benhadads of Damascus mentioned in the Old Testament presents certain problems for chronology. The first of these, Benhadad I, who is styled "son of Tabrimmon, son of Hezion, king of Aram" (1 Kgs. 15:18), was described in identical terms in the inscription on the Melqart *stele,* which can be dated by epigraphy between 875 and 825 B.C.[31] It was in the thirty-sixth year of the divided monarchy that Baasha of Israel attacked Judah (2 Chron. 16:1ff.), making it necessary for Asa to seek the assistance of Benhadad I of Aram. This would imply that Benhadad I was already ruler of Damascus by about 895 B.C., or even slightly earlier.[32]

The Benhadad who opposed Ahab (1 Kgs. 20:1ff.) from about 874/3-853 B.C. died by the hand of Hazael in the days of Joram (ca. 852-841 B.C.). Hazael then succeeded Benhadad about 843 B.C., and was firmly in control of the Damascene regime when he was mentioned in the annals of Shalmaneser III of Assyria in 841 B.C.[33] The question which arises is whether this Benhadad is in fact to be identified with the Benhadad who was an ally of Asa. Albright accepted this identification, followed by Unger, Bright and others, and assigned a possible date of about 850 B.C. for the Melqart *stele* on the basis of the style of lettering employed.[34] However, the reference of 1 Kings 20:34 would seem to imply that Omri had been defeated in battle at an earlier period by a Benhadad who was the father of Benhadad, the contemporary of Ahab.

[29] Cf. *MNHK*, pp. 122ff.; 182ff.

[30] *MNHK*, pp. 120ff.; cf. Thiele in *A Stubborn Faith* (ed. E. C. Hobbs, 1956), pp. 39ff.

[31] Cf. W. F. Albright and L. della Vida, *BASOR*, No. 87 (1942), pp. 23ff., No. 90 (1943), pp. 30ff.; M. Black in *DOTT*, pp. 239ff.

[32] Cf. *MNHK*, pp. 57ff.

[33] M. F. Unger, *Israel and the Aramaeans of Damascus* (1957), p. 75.

[34] *Ibid.*, pp. 59ff., 141f.; Albright, *BASOR*, No. 87 (1942), p. 27; *BHI*, p. 221.

This latter Benhadad was referred to in the annals of Shalmaneser III for 853 B.C.[35] and 845 B.C.[36] under the name Adad-idri (Hadadezer).

On the basis of this evidence, any attempt to posit a single Benhadad who ruled for the lengthy period from about 900-843 B.C. would seem to be somewhat arbitrary. Two distinct individuals appear to be involved, and as such may be assigned reigns of *ca.* 900-860 B.C. and *ca.* 860-843 B.C. respectively. A third Benhadad was the son of Hazael who murdered Benhadad II (2 Kgs. 8:15), and fought against Shalmaneser III in 841 B.C. He was the contemporary of Jehoash of Israel, and was mentioned on the contemporary *stele* of Zakir, king of Hamath and Lu'ash.[37]

Of a rather different nature is the apparent discrepancy between the twenty years of reign credited to Pekah in 2 Kings 15:27 and the seven or eight years, terminating in 732/31 B.C., accorded to him by the Assyrian Eponym Chronicle. In this instance careful attention should be given to the tradition underlying the Biblical record, which indicates that the reign of Pekah was reckoned from 752 B.C., the year following the death of Jeroboam II. This may well imply that during the troubled period in which Zachariah, Shallum, and Menahem ruled over Israel, Pekah had seized control of Gilead, and had built up a kingdom in Transjordan which threatened the security of Israel. If such was actually the case, the chronology in Kings recorded the entire period of his rule, including that over Israel succeeding Pekahiah.

The annals of Sargon of Assyria show that the fall of Samaria occurred in 722 B.C.[38] Assyrian retribution upon Israel occurred as a result of an attempted conspiracy on the part of Hoshea with "So, king of Egypt." This enigmatic Egyptian ruler has been variously identified with Osorkon IV (*ca.* 727-716 B.C.) and with one of the rulers of the Delta region, Tefnakht (*ca.* 727-720 B.C.). The Egyptian commander of 720 B.C., mentioned in cuneiform records, was originally thought to have been named Sib'e, but as Borger has shown, the name should actually have been read as Re'e, a form which cannot be related to "So."[39] It may be that "So" was an abbreviated form of Osorkon in the same manner that "Sese" was a shortened version of Rameses. On the other hand, it may be, as Yeivin has suggested, a Hebrew transcript of the Egyptian word for "vizier," making "So" a high official under Osorkon IV.[40]

[35] D. J. Wiseman, DOTT, pp. 46ff.

[36] ANET, p. 280, ARAB, I, sect. 658ff.

[37] M. Black, DOTT, 242ff.

[38] Cf. ANET, pp. 284f.; MNHK, pp. 141ff.; Tadmor, JCS, XII (1958), pp. 22ff., 77ff.

[39] J. Borger, JNES, XIX (1960), p. 53.

[40] S. Yeivin, VT, II (1952), pp. 164ff.

A chronological table from the division of the monarchy to the fall of the northern kingdom will summarize much of the foregoing discussion:

TABLE 8: THE MONARCHY TO 722 B.C.

ISRAEL	JUDAH	Albright[41]	Thiele	Proposed Chronology
Jeroboam I		922-901	931-910	931/30-910/09
	Rehoboam	922-915	931-915	931/30-913
	Abijah	915-913	913-911	913-911/10
	Asa	913-873	911-870	911/10-870/69
Nadab		901-900	910-909	910/09-909/08
Baasha		900-877	909-886	909/08-886/85
Elah		877-876	886-885	886/85-885/84
Zimri		876	885	885/84
Tibni			885-880	885/84-880
Omri		876-869	885-874	885/84-874/73
	Jehoshaphat	873-849	873-848	873/72-848
Ahab		869-850	874-853	874/73-853
Ahaziah		850-849	853-852	853-852
Jehoram		849-842	852-841	852-841
	Jehoram	849-842	853-841	853-841
Jehu		842-815	841-814	841-814/13
	Ahaziah	842	841	841
	Athaliah	842-837	841-835	841-835
	Joash	837-800	835-796	835-796
Jehoahaz		815-801	814-798	814/13-798
Joash		801-786	798-782	798-782/81
	Amaziah	800-783	796-767	796-767
Jeroboam II		786-746	793-753	793-753
	Azariah	783-742	791-740	792/91-740/39
	Jotham	750-735	750-732	750-732/31
Zechariah		746-745	753-752	753-752
Shallum		745	752	752
Menahem		745-738	752-742	752-742/41
Pekahiah		738-737	742-740	742/41-740/39
Pekah		737-732	740-732	752-740/39
	Jehoahaz	735-715	735-715	735-716/15
Hoshea		732-724	732-723	732/31-723/22

It is possible to work out dates to within a year for the southern kingdom from the time of Hezekiah until the capture of Jerusalem by the Babylonians. A synchronism with Assyrian history has enabled scholars

[41] *BASOR*, No. 100 (1945), pp. 16ff.

to establish a date of 701 B.C. for the attack of Sennacherib on Jerusalem, which the Biblical records placed in the fourteenth year of Hezekiah (2 Kgs. 18:13; Isa. 36:1).[42] Thus his accession would occur in 716/15 B.C., having regard to the fact that he had been co-regent with Ahaz from 729 B.C. Such a precise synchronism indicates that the underlying Assyrian and Hebrew sources were based upon an absolute chronology. It is a remarkable testimony to the accuracy of both the Assyrian and the Hebrew records, in view of the fact that the preceding point of synchronism between Hebrew and Assyrian records had occurred a century and a half earlier in their respective chronologies.

Although the accession date of Hezekiah can now be considered established, other aspects of his reign present certain difficulties for chronology. The fall of Samaria (722 B.C.) occurred during the sixth year of his reign (2 Kgs. 18:10), whereas the invasion of Judah in 701 B.C. occurred in the fourteenth year of the same monarch. However, these events become compatible on the assumption that Hezekiah was co-regent with Ahaz from about 729 B.C., and that he succeeded to sole rule about 716 B.C. Thus the two apparently different dates would be recorded in terms of the beginning of the co-regency and from the commencement of his reign as sole monarch respectively. Although Hezekiah was credited with a twenty-nine-year rule, certain questions have been raised as to its actual duration. From 2 Kings 19:35-36 it would appear that the last recorded event of his reign was the deliverance of Jerusalem from the Assyrians under Sennacherib in 701 B.C. However, another reference in Kings (2 Kgs. 19:9; cf. Isa. 37:9) to Tirhakah, the ruler of Ethiopia, has given rise to the view that Judah was invaded by Sennacherib a second time about 688 B.C.

Many scholars have maintained that the mention of Tirhakah is an anachronism, and that the statement in 2 Kings 19:37 implies that Sennacherib died shortly after his return to Nineveh. On this basis they have postulated a subsequent unsuccessful Assyrian campaign against Jerusalem between about 689 and 686 B.C.[43] Tirhakah, equated with the pharaoh Taharqa of the Twenty-Fifth Dynasty of Egypt, reigned for a period of twenty-six years, ca. 690-664 B.C. If he commanded the Egyptian forces that Sennacherib defeated at Eltekeh in 701 B.C. while besieging Jerusalem, he was obviously not the pharaoh at that period, but only the commander of the army.[44] The Kawa temple inscriptions seem to imply that Tirhakah was only twenty years old when he came from Nubia to Lower Egypt as co-regent for six years with his brother Shebitku about 690/89 B.C., which would indicate that he was only nine

[42] E. Schrader, *The Cuneiform Inscriptions and the OT* (1885), I, pp. 307ff.
[43] Following the suggestion of Albright, *JQR*, XXIV (1933-1934), pp. 370f., *BASOR*, No. 130 (1953), pp. 8ff., No. 141 (1956), pp. 23ff.
[44] *BHI*, p. 283.

years of age in 701 B.C.[45] On the basis of this interpretation, Albright, Bright, and others have assumed that the contact between Tirhakah and the Assyrians must be dated to about 689 B.C., and consequently have felt that the hypothesis of a second Assyrian attack against Hezekiah suited the chronology rather better than otherwise.

In the first instance it should be noted that the theory of Macadam, which placed the birth of Tirhakah about 709 B.C., making it impossible for him to have led troops against Sennacherib and the Assyrians in 701 B.C., has been refuted by Leclant and Yoyotte, who have shown that Tirhakah could have been as old as twenty-two years by 701 B.C., and thus able to lead military forces in the field.[46] Furthermore, the usually accepted six-year co-regency period has been proved to be incorrect as the result of the studies of Schmidt.[47] The title of Tirhakah as "king of Ethiopia" would relate to a period from about 690 B.C. or later, constituting a prolepsis so as to make the situation perfectly clear to readers of the Biblical account.

If a second Assyrian campaign is postulated for about 687 B.C., there are two major difficulties to be faced. The first is that the Old Testament narrators have conflated descriptions of two separate campaigns into one account, a theory for which there is absolutely no evidence in the Hebrew text. The second requires a military campaign by Sennacherib and the Assyrian forces which is nowhere mentioned in the extant Assyrian annals or the Babylonian Chronicles. Although it is impossible to be absolutely precise on this matter at the present time, it is not unduly out of harmony with the facts of the situation to suppose that the Biblical records were actually describing a single campaign of Sennacherib against Hezekiah in 701 B.C.[48]

As far as the closing years of the southern kingdom are concerned, extra-Biblical sources have furnished a precise date of 605 B.C. for the accession of Nebuchadnezzar II and the battle of Carchemish.[49] Nebuchadnezzar actually ascended the throne of Babylon on September 6, 605 B.C. (cf. 2 Kgs. 24:12; 25:8), although the first official year of his reign commenced with the following New Year, in accordance with

[45] Cf. M. F. L. Macadam, *The Temples of Kawa* (1949); J. M. A. Janssen, *Biblica*, XXXIV (1953), pp. 23ff.

[46] Macadam, *op. cit.*, I, pp. 18ff. J. Leclant and J. Yoyotte, *Bulletin de l'Institut Français d'Archéologie Orientale*, LI (1952), pp. 17ff.

[47] G. Schmidt, *Kush*, VI (1958), pp. 121ff.

[48] Cf. W. Rudolph and A. Alt, *PJB*, XXV (1929), pp. 59ff.

[49] D. J. Wiseman, *Chronicles of Chaldean Kings (626-556 B.C.) in the British Museum* (1956). Cf. J. P. Hyatt, *JBL*, LXXV (1956), pp. 277ff.; H. Tadmor, *JNES*, XV (1956), pp. 226ff.; E. R. Thiele, *BASOR*, No. 143 (1956), pp. 22ff.; Albright, *BASOR*, No. 143 (1956), pp. 27ff.; D. N. Freedman, *BA*, XIX, No. 3 (1956), pp. 50ff.

Babylonian custom.[50] As Wiseman has shown, the Babylonian capture of Jerusalem can be dated with complete accuracy from cuneiform sources to March 15/16, the second day of the month Adar, in 597 B.C.[51] On this basis the reign of Jehoiakim can be assigned to 609-597 B.C., and the rule of Jehoiachin to a three-month period at the beginning of 597 B.C. After this date there are certain difficulties connected with the computation of the Hebrew civil year and the years of Zedekiah and Nebuchadnezzar II.

The first year of Zedekiah must evidently be regarded as 597 B.C., with his regency terminating in 587 B.C., according to the pattern of calculation for the years of the captivity as found in Ezekiel.[52] In such an event the second attack on Jerusalem occurred in 587 B.C., and not a year later as Thiele has suggested.[53] Gedaliah was appointed chief administrator of Judah by Nebuchadnezzar in 587 B.C., and continued in this office until he was murdered about 582 B.C. by a refugee officer.

The chronology of the kingdom of Judah from the time of Hezekiah to the death of Zedekiah is related to the foregoing discussion in Table 9.

TABLE 9: CHRONOLOGY OF JUDAH

Ruler	Albright	Thiele	Proposed Chronology
Hezekiah	715-687	715-686	716/15-687/86
Manasseh	687-642	696-642	697/96-643/42
Amon	642-640	642-640	643/42-641/40
Josiah	640-609	640-608	641/40-609
Jehoahaz II	609	608	609
Jehoiakim	609-598	608-597	609-598
Jehoiachin	598	597	598-597
Zedekiah	598-587	597-586	597-586

B. THE CAPTIVITY AND RETURN FROM EXILE

1. Darius the Mede. Although the general chronology of the exilic period is well established, the attempt to identify Darius the Mede necessitates certain adjustments in matters of detail. For those who, with Rowley, assume that Darius the Mede is a "fictitious creature," there is no real problem of chronology involved.[54] However, those who dismiss

---

[50] So Jer. 52:28f., which follows the Babylonian accession-year system of computation.

[51] D. J. Wiseman, *Chronicles of Chaldean Kings*, pp. 32ff.

[52] Cf. Albright, *BA*, V, No. 4 (1942), pp. 49ff.

[53] *MNHK*, pp. 169ff.; cf. Thiele, *BASOR*, No. 143 (1956), pp. 26f.

[54] H. H. Rowley, *Darius the Mede and the Four World Empires of the Book of Daniel* (1935), p. 59.

the historicity of Daniel 6 have to cope with what they regard as confusions on the part of the second-century B.C. author of the work in the matter of Neo-Babylonian and Persian chronology.[55] These scholars hold to the view that the person who wrote Daniel confused the fall of Babylon in 539 B.C. with that of 520 B.C. under Darius I Hystaspes (522-486 B.C.), made that monarch the predecessor instead of the successor of Cyrus the Great (539-530 B.C.), assumed that Xerxes (486-465/64 B.C.) was the father rather than the son of Darius I, and assigned Darius to Median rather than to Persian ancestry.

If, however, the suggestion of Whitcomb is accepted that Darius the Mede can be identified with Gubaru, the governor of Babylon under Cyrus, the chronology of the period can be settled without undue difficulty.[56] The edict of Cyrus, which was promulgated in 538 B.C., has been shown to be substantially historical as a result of modern archaeological discoveries, and constitutes one of the earliest acts of Cyrus after establishing the Persian empire.[57] The chronology of this period is generally accepted as recorded in Table 10.

TABLE 10: THE PERSIAN EMPIRE

Ruler	Date B.C.
Cyrus	539-530
Cambyses	530-522
Darius I	522-486
Xerxes I	486-465/64
Artaxerxes I	464-423
Darius II	423-404
Artaxerxes II	404-359
Artaxerxes III	359/58-338/37
Arses	338/37-336/35
Darius III	336/35-331

2. *Ezra and Nehemiah.* The most pressing problem for Biblical chronology during this period involves the work of Ezra and Nehemiah, and turns in particular upon the date when Ezra commenced his work in Jerusalem. Of the three current positions adopted on this question the traditional view holds that Ezra was sent to Jerusalem in 458 B.C. on the instructions of Artaxerxes I (464-423 B.C.).[58] The precise position

[55] So J. A. Montgomery, *Daniel* (*ICC* series, 1927), p. 65; R. H. Charles, *A Critical and Exegetical Commentary on the Book of Daniel* (1929), pp. 145f.; *DILOT*, pp. 498ff.; *PIOT*, p. 757.

[56] J. C. Whitcomb, *Darius the Mede* (1959), pp. 5ff. Cf. Albright, *JBL*, XL (1921), p. 112n.; D. J. Wiseman, *NBD*, pp. 293f.

[57] Cf. R. de Vaux, *RB*, XLVI (1937), pp. 29ff.; W. F. Albright, *Alexander Marx Jubilee Volume* (1950), pp. 61ff.

[58] Cf. J. Stafford Wright, *The Date of Ezra's Coming to Jerusalem* (1947), pp. 5ff.

which Ezra held in the Persian administration (cf. Ez. 7:6) has been a matter of some debate, but it most probably corresponded to the office of Secretary of State for Jewish Affairs.[59] At all events, his mission to Jerusalem had as its ultimate objective the proper observance of the Jewish law on the part of the returned community. After an initial period of activity Ezra dropped out of sight, presumably because he returned to Persia with a report which dealt with the situation in Judaea, and only reappeared in 444 B.C. in association with the work of Nehemiah in Jerusalem.

The second view, which is held by many scholars at the present, takes issue with the traditional standpoint and reverses the positions of Ezra and Nehemiah in the chronological scheme. According to this theory it was Nehemiah who came to Jerusalem about 445 B.C., and Ezra who arrived in 398 B.C., following the death of Nehemiah. This opinion lays claim to support from three passages of Scripture. Ezra 9:9 speaks of a city wall in the time of Ezra, whereas the wall was apparently constructed only by Nehemiah. Ezra 10:1 mentions a large assembly of people in Jerusalem, as opposed to Nehemiah 7:4, which indicates that the city was even then sparsely populated. A final citation (Ez. 10:6) mentions Johanan, son of Eliashib, as the contemporary of Ezra. According to Nehemiah 12:22-23, Johanan was the grandson of Eliashib. From the papyri discovered at Elephantine it also appears that Johanan was High Priest in 408 B.C., thus making Ezra later than Nehemiah on this basis. The view that Ezra was to be dated about 398 B.C. in the seventh year of Artaxerxes II was first propounded tentatively by Vernes and developed by Van Hoonacker over a period of thirty-five years.[60] This theory was contested vigorously by all German scholars except Hölscher, who also rejected it subsequently.[61] However, it found support among a number of French and English scholars, who felt that such a view satisfied the need for the reconstruction of events in the late fifth and early fourth centuries B.C.[62]

A third theory regarding the relative position of Ezra and Nehemiah was proposed by Albright, who had wavered for some time between the opinions of Van Hoonacker and the view that, while Ezra should be

[59] H. H. Schaeder, *Iranische Beiträge*, I (1930), pp. 14ff., *Esra der Schreiber* (1930), pp. 39ff.

[60] M. Vernes, *Précis d'Histoire juive* (1889), p. 582n. Cf. Van Hoonacker, *Le Muséon*, IX (1890), pp. 151ff., 317ff., 389ff.; *RB*, IV (1895), pp. 180ff., X (1901), pp. 5ff., 175ff.; *Une communauté Judéo-Araméenne à Éléphantine en Égypte, aux VIe et Ve siècles avant J. C.* (1915), pp. 19ff.; *RB*, XXXII (1923), pp. 481ff., XXXIII (1924), pp. 33ff.

[61] G. Hölscher in *Die Heilige Schrift des AT* (ed. Kautzsch and Bertholet, 1910), II, pp. 451f.; cf. *ibid.* (1923 ed.), II, pp. 491ff., 500f.

[62] For a partial bibliography see *RSL*, pp. 133ff., as corrected and supplemented in *BJRL*, XXXVII, No. 2 (1955), pp. 549f.

dated after Nehemiah, both belonged to the period of Artaxerxes I rather than Artaxerxes II.[63] This theory attempted to compromise between the Biblical tradition that the work of Ezra and Nehemiah overlapped and the opinions of Van Hoonacker and his supporters that Ezra followed Nehemiah. Albright finally arrived at a date of 428 B.C. for the beginning of the work of Ezra, taking the reference to the "seventh" year (Ez. 7:7) as haplography for "thirty-seventh," a literary device which he supposed had been undertaken in order to avoid a threefold repetition of the Hebrew letter שׁ and which had the effect of placing Ezra in the thirty-seventh year of Artaxerxes I.[64] While this date is alleged to be more in harmony with the situation in Jerusalem towards the end of the fifth century B.C. as reflected in the Elephantine papyri, it is still simply a fact that the number proposed by Albright can command absolutely no textual support, as Freedman has rightly observed, and thus it can hardly be employed as a valid basis for argument.[65]

Not all the objections that have been marshalled against the traditional position are quite as persuasive as their advocates have been led to believe. The nature of the wall which was in existence when Ezra arrived in Jerusalem has been one of the prime points at issue in the general debate, and the situation allows for a significant difference of opinion. The word in question, *gādhēr*, occurs nowhere else in Ezra and Nehemiah, and in other instances of its occurrence in the Old Testament it is used of a fence surrounding a vineyard (Ps. 80:13; Isa. 5:5) or a wall of stones without mortar (Num. 22:24; Prov. 24:31; Ezek. 42:7, 10) of varying height.[66] Consequently it has been suggested that the wall of Ezra 9:9 was not a completed city wall[67] but perhaps the kind of preliminary structure which was mentioned in the letter to Artaxerxes (Ez. 4:12), and which was subsequently abandoned (Ez. 4:21ff.; Neh. 1:3).[68] It is at least possible that this "wall" may have even preceded the visit of Ezra to the city by a few years, and have constituted an unsuccessful attempt by the returned community to furnish some sort of physical protection for the dwellers in Jerusalem.

[63] Cf. *FSAC*, p. 324.

[64] W. F. Albright in *The Jews, Their History, Culture, and Religion* (ed. Finkelstein, 1949), I, p. 64 n. 133. Cf. *The Archaeology of Palestine and the Bible* (1932), pp. 169ff., 218f.; *BPAE*, p. 112 n. 193.

[65] D. N. Freedman, *BANE*, p. 213.

[66] Cf. H. Kaupel, *Biblische Zeitschrift*, XXII (1934), pp. 89ff.; A. Fernández, *Biblica*, XVI (1935), pp. 82ff., XVIII (1937), pp. 207f.; H. Kaupel, *Biblica*, XVI (1935), pp. 213f.

[67] W. M. F. Scott, *ET*, LVIII (1946-47), pp. 263ff.; cf. C. T. Wood, *ET*, LIX (1947-48), pp. 53f.

[68] J. Stafford Wright, *The Date of Ezra's Coming to Jerusalem*, p. 18. On the walls of Nehemiah see M. Avi-Yonah, *Israel Exploration Journal*, IV (1954), pp. 239ff. On their position see L.-H. Vincent, *Jérusalem de l'Ancien Testament* (1954), I, pp. 237ff., pl. LXI; B. Mazar, *BA*, XXXIII, No. 2 (1970), pp. 49ff.

The argument that Jerusalem was apparently heavily populated in the time of Ezra (Ez. 10:1) but much less so during the period of Nehemiah (Neh. 7:4) turns largely on the nature of local circumstances. Whereas Nehemiah appears to have been concerned with the actual dwelling-places of the inhabitants of Jerusalem, it is clear from Ezra 10:7ff. that the congregation that assembled to hear the words of Ezra was drawn from a larger area than that of the city and its immediate environs, and which may in point of fact have been coextensive with the terrain occupied by the returned exiles.[69]

In any event this is not a particularly cogent argument for the priority of Nehemiah, which has been urged on an additional ground, namely the fact that the name of Nehemiah precedes that of Ezra in Nehemiah 12:26. For Albright, who followed Van Hoonacker on this point, this constituted the most decisive passage in favor of a Nehemiah-Ezra chronological sequence.[70] However, as Rowley has shown, the verse in question need indicate no more than that the chronicler assumed that Ezra and Nehemiah were contemporaries, and in consequence it need carry little weight as an argument for a later date for the period of Ezra.[71]

The references to Nehemiah as the contemporary of Eliashib the High Priest (Neh. 3:1, 20, 21; 13:4, 7)—whereas the son (or descendant) of Eliashib, a man named Johanan (Jehohanan) was contemporary with Ezra—constitute a more serious objection to the traditional standpoint. According to Nehemiah 12:22, 23, Johanan was in fact the grandson of Eliashib, and as shown by the Elephantine papyri occupied the office of High Priest in Jerusalem in 408 B.C.[72] Thus the high priesthood of his grandfather must have occurred some thirty years earlier, placing Nehemiah towards the middle of the fifth century B.C.[73] A subsequent reference (Neh. 13:28) indicates that Joiada, the son of Eliashib and the father of Johanan, had become High Priest, which in turn might suggest a date of about 432 B.C. for Nehemiah.

In this connection it is important to avoid the assumption that Johanan was High Priest in the time of Ezra, since this is not warranted by the Hebrew text of Ezra 10:6. If, as Josephus claimed, Joiakim was the High Priest when Ezra visited Jerusalem, there would be good reason for the lack of mention of Johanan in this capacity.[74] It may be, as Schofield has suggested, that the situation which involved the family of Joiada, the son of Eliashib, led to the High Priest's being deposed in favor of Johanan.[75]

---

[69] However, 1 Esdras 8:88 (92), parallel to Ez. 10:1, reads ἀπό 'Ιερουσαλὴμ instead of the Massoretic text מישראל.

[70] Albright, JBL, XL (1921), p. 121; Van Hoonacker, RB, X (1901), p. 197.

[71] RSL, p. 144; BJRL, XXXVII, No. 2 (1955), p. 550 n. 4.

[72] Cf. A. Cowley, Aramaic Papyri of the Fifth Century B.C. (1923), pp. 111ff.; ANET, p. 492.

[73] H. H. Rowley, BJRL, XXXVII, No. 1 (1955), pp. 176f.

[74] AJ, XI, 5, 5; cf. Neh. 12:10.

[75] J. N. Schofield, The Religious Background of the Bible (1944), p. 167.

However, considerable caution is called for in any discussion of the activities of Johanan, since the latter was a widely used name at that period, and this fact must constitute yet another element which contributes to the uncertainty and confusion surrounding this particular phase of Hebrew history. That Nehemiah may have been mentioned before Ezra in one particular passage (Neh. 12:26) has actually little bearing upon the larger chronological problem, since it appears fairly obvious that Nehemiah would in any event have taken precedence in his own memoirs in his capacity as civil governor of Judaea.

While the chronological situation for the period of Ezra and Nehemiah is far from complete, due as much to the lack of corroborative extra-Biblical sources as to any considerations of dislocation or disarrangement within the text itself, there seems to be little justification for abandoning the traditional order of Ezra and Nehemiah for a sequence which is beset with at least as many problems of chronology. As Bright has cautiously concluded, it appears best to avoid a dogmatic approach in the light of the available evidence.[76] Hence it is possible to envisage the traditional sequences of chronology as being at least as probable as any other.

3. *Intertestamental chronology.* After the death of Alexander the Great (331-323 B.C.), the chronology of the Greek period (331-65 B.C.) and subsequent times presents few difficulties for events in the Old Testament. Table 11 summarizes the situation for Syria and Egypt up to the death of Antiochus VII.

TABLE 11: THE GREEK PERIOD

Syria	Egypt	Date B.C.
	Ptolemy I	323-285
Seleucus I		312-281
	Ptolemy II	285-247
Antiochus I		281-261
Antiochus II		261-246
	Ptolemy III	247-222
Seleucus II		246-226/25
Seleucus III		226/25-223
Antiochus III		223-187
	Ptolemy IV	222-205
	Ptolemy V	205-182
Seleucus IV		187-175
	Ptolemy VI	182-146
Antiochus IV		175-163
Antiochus V		163-162
Demetrius I		162-150
Antiochus VII		139-129

[76] *BHI*, p. 376.

In 198 B.C. Palestine passed out of Egyptian control and came under the jurisdiction of the Syrian rulers. Syrian domination continued until 63 B.C., when Pompey established Roman rule in Palestine and made Judaea a protectorate. The chronology for this particular period, taken to 4 B.C., is given by Table 12.

TABLE 12: FROM THE MACCABEES TO HEROD

Event	Date B.C.
Maccabees in Judaea	167-140
Judas Maccabaeus	166-161
Jonathan Maccabaeus	160-143
Dead Sea Community	*ca.* 150
Simon Maccabaeus	143-135
John Hyrcanus I	135-104
Aristobulus I	104/03
Alexander Jannaeus	103-76
Hyrcanus II and Salome	76-67
Hyrcanus II and Aristobulus II	67-40
Pompey	63
Herod the Great	40-4

Part Four

THE OLD TESTAMENT TEXT AND CANON

I. THE HISTORY OF HEBREW WRITING

The study of the Hebrew text in its own right is a matter of great importance, since the judgments that are made by scholars in this field are basic to all other areas of Old Testament investigation. As a discipline textual criticism is independent of the history and early growth of the Scriptural writings, as well as of the formation of the canon.[1] The primary concerns of this study are the transmission of the text, the rise and development of revisions, the nature and scope of scribal activities during the process of transmission, the incidence of vocalization, and the emergence of the Massoretic text.

The ultimate aim of the textual critic is to recover the text of Scripture as nearly as possible in its original form. However, this laudable objective cannot always be realized, for none of the original drafts of the Old Testament compositions has survived, and the copies that exist have of course been subjected both to the frailty of human nature and the ravages of the centuries. There are undoubtedly numerous instances in which the original text will never be known, and many others in which cogent arguments can be adduced for the adoption of one of several plausible variants.

Contrary to the contentions of Wellhausen, who maintained, against archaeological evidence already available in his day, that writing did not appear among the Hebrews until the early monarchy, they had the means of producing written records at their disposal from very early times. From at least 3100 B.C. in the ancient Near East, writing was regarded as one of the high-water marks of culture and human progress. Writing may have been developed originally by the Sumerians in order to meet their administrative and economic needs,[2] although there appear to have been even earlier forms of written communication. At any rate, the cuneiform Sumerian corpus of logograms, syllabic signs, and determinatives was adopted and expanded by the Akkadians during the first half of the third millennium B.C. as a vehicle for expressing their own Semitic language. In the second millennium it was taken over with

[1] B. J. Roberts, *The OT Text and Versions* (1951), p. 1.
[2] R. J. Williams, *IDB*, IV, p. 909.

some modifications by the Horites and Hittites, and in the first half of the first millennium B.C. it also became the literary medium of communication of the Urartians of Armenia, following well-established Near Eastern patterns of linguistic expression. In addition, the Mesopotamian system of cuneiform writing also influenced the development of two other scripts, namely, the Old Persian syllabic and the alphabetic script of Ras Shamra.[3]

During the neo-Assyrian period (900-612 B.C.) the Aramaic language, written in a cursive alphabetic script, was also employed in parts of Mesopotamia, as is indicated by the presence of certain Aramaic notations on some cuneiform tablets.[4] However, the origin of Aramaic, in which some sections of the Old Testament (Dan. 2:4-7:28; Jer. 10:11; Ezra 4:8–6:18, 7:12-26) were written, antedates this period by many centuries. It may be that the influence of proto-Aramaic was enhanced in the third millennium B.C. by the nomadic invaders from the north-Arabian deserts who are mentioned in Assyrian inscriptions from the time of Tiglathpileser I onwards,[5] with whom the Pentateuch (Gen. 24:3ff.; 25:20; 28:2ff.; Deut. 26:5) associated the ancestors of Israel. By the twelfth century B.C. such groups were established in communities all along the Tigris and Euphrates from the Persian Gulf to northern Syria, and southward through Palestine into northern Arabia.[6]

What is perhaps the oldest extra-Biblical specimen of Aramaic may well be the Melqart *stele*,[7] dated in the ninth century B.C. Somewhat later are the inscriptions from Zenjirli, one of which mentions Tiglath-pileser III, dating from the eighth century B.C. In addition to the Aramaic notations on Assyrian and Babylonian tablets mentioned above, an important contribution to the history of the Aramaic language comes from the fifth-century B.C. colony of Jewish mercenaries stationed on the island of Elephantine in the Nile near Aswan.

[3] On the development of writing see J. H. Breasted, *AJSL*, XXXII (1916), pp. 230ff.; R. P. Dougherty, *JAOS*, XLVIII (1928), pp. 109ff.; H. Jensen, *Die Schrift in Vergangenheit und Gegenwart* (1935); J. G. Février, *Histoire de l'Écriture* (1948); H. Tur-Sinai, *JQR*, XLI (1950-51), pp. 83ff., 159ff., 277ff., G. R. Driver, *Semitic Writing: From Pictograph to Alphabet* (1944, rev. ed. 1954); D. Diringer, *The Alphabet* (1948), *The Story of the Aleph Beth* (1960); I. J. Gelb, *A Study of Writing* (1952).

[4] Cf. J. H. Stevenson, *Assyrian and Babylonian Contracts with Aramaic Notes* (1902).

[5] A. Jeffery, *IDB*, I, p. 186. Cf. J.-R. Kupper, *Les Nomades en Mésopotamie au Temps des Rois de Mari* (1957), pp. 147ff., 196; M. McNamara, *Verbum Domini*, XXXV (1957), pp. 129ff.; A. Dupont-Sommer, *VT* suppl. I (1953), pp. 40ff.; S. Moscati, *The Semites in Ancient History* (1959), pp. 66f.

[6] R. A. Bowman, *IDB*, I, pp. 191f.

[7] *ANET*, p. 501; *DOTT*, pp. 239ff.; M. Dunand, *Bulletin du Musée de Beyrouth*, III (1941), pp. 65ff.; W. F. Albright, *BASOR*, No. 87 (1942), pp. 23ff.

Earlier scholars were accustomed to divide Aramaic, which is actually a general term employed to describe a number of Semitic dialects closely related to Hebrew, into an eastern and a western group. It was also formerly assumed, in the absence of indications to the contrary, that western Aramaic was of late origin. By employing this as a criterion, Driver and others assigned a late date to Daniel.[8] Utilizing subsequent evidence, however, R. D. Wilson showed the fallacies of this argument, pointing out that the alleged distinction between eastern and western forms of Aramaic did not exist in the pre-Christian period.[9] The presence of Aramaic elements in the cuneiform compositions from Ras Shamra, as illustrated particularly by the consonantal shift from z to d in the relative pronoun and elsewhere, attests further to the antiquity of the tongue. Consequently, it is no longer possible to argue for a later date for a given composition on the basis of Aramaic words and expressions in it.

In the light of subsequent studies[10] it now appears more desirable to divide the development of Aramaic into four periods: (1) *Old Aramaic,* the language of the north-Syrian inscriptions, dating from the tenth to the eighth centuries B.C.; (2) *Official Aramaic,* which was widely used in the Assyrian (*ca.* 1100-605 B.C.), Neo-Babylonian (605-539 B.C.), and Persian (539-331 B.C.) periods; (3) *Levantine Aramaic,* which probably came into prominence in Syria and Palestine after 721 B.C.; and (4) *Palestinian Jewish Aramaic proper,* which in New Testament times consisted of several dialects (cf. Matt. 26:73). Of particular importance for the text of the Aramaic sections of the Old Testament, as well as for the dating of the books in which they occur, is the Official Aramaic, which apparently was the *lingua franca* in the government offices of the Assyrians. Official Aramaic became popular because it was better known outside Mesopotamia than the native cuneiform and because it was of a simple and quite static nature.

In consequence a good deal of care has to be exercised when attempts are made to date Old Testament documents in which Aramaic is found in view of the prolonged usage which the language enjoyed. The incidence of Aramaisms frequently indicates an early rather than a late date, as exemplified in Genesis 31:47 by the Aramaic name (יְגַר שָׂהֲדוּתָא) given by Laban to the stone heap that Jacob designated by the corre-

---

[8] *DILOT,* pp. 502f., following Th. Nöldeke, *ZDMG,* XXI (1867), pp. 183ff., XXII (1868), pp. 443ff., XXIV (1870), pp. 85ff., XXV (1871), pp. 129f., *Die Semitische Sprachen* (1899), pp. 35ff., in *EB,* I, col. 282; C. H. H. Wright, *A Comparative Grammar of the Semitic Languages* (1890), pp. 15f. Against this see G. L. Archer, *A Survey of OT Introduction* (1964), pp. 125ff.

[9] R. D. Wilson, *A Scientific Investigation of the OT* (1926), pp. 105ff., *Biblical and Theological Studies by the Members of the Faculty of Princeton Theological Seminary* (1912), pp. 261ff. Cf. H. H. Rowley, *JRAS* (1933), pp. 777ff.

[10] Cf. H. L. Ginsberg, *AJSL,* L (1933), pp. 1ff., LII (1935), pp. 95ff.; R. A. Bowman, *JNES,* VII (1948), pp. 65ff.; J. Kutscher, *EB* (1955), I, col. 584ff.

sponding Hebrew form (גלעד). Among other traces of early Aramaic structures in the area of Paddan-aram[11] during the second millennium B.C. are those materials contained in Egyptian texts from the New Kingdom period (1570-1150 B.C.), which followed the Aramaic rather than the Canaanite form when speaking of Aram-naharaim.[12]

Although Official Aramaic was comparatively static in nature, it nevertheless underwent considerable orthographic modification in the fifth century B.C. Such procedures were not uncommon in antiquity, as can be illustrated by the *Instruction of the Vizier Ptahhotep*,[13] written about 2400 B.C. in Old Egyptian[14] and revised by 1900 B.C. to include predominantly Middle Egyptian grammatical forms. Resultant "late" words or spellings of proper names merely date the particular scribal revision in which they occur, and not the manuscript itself, a point apparently not appreciated by H. H. Rowley in his criticism of Wilson.[15] Thus as Rosenthal has pointed out, the criteria that liberal scholars adduced as evidence for the late date of Daniel and Ezra are nothing more than the result of a process of modernizing in spelling which was carried out in the fifth century B.C.[16]

There can no longer be any doubt from archaeological sources that writing was a feature of life in Syria and Palestine from the earliest occupational periods. Certainly by the time of Moses there were several well-established means of linguistic expression for purposes of transmitting written communications. From the evidence presented by the Tell el-Amarna letters it is clear that Imperial Akkadian was the *lingua franca* of the age. In pharaonic Egypt the native tongue had been written in hieroglyphic pictographs from a period just prior to 3000 B.C., and shortly thereafter it was represented also by means of hieratic script, a non-pictorial, cursive form of hieroglyphic employed by scribes for purposes of rapid writing. The Canaanites of the Late Bronze Age (*ca.* 1500-1200 B.C.) employed a native cuneiform language, Ugaritic, which has very close affinities with Biblical Hebrew, as well as a linear alphabetic variety of writing. The latter is best exemplified in a *stele* from Balu'ah in ancient Moab, and although the script is badly weathered it is perhaps the same as that occurring on stone and bronze tablets unearthed at Gebal (the Byblos of the Greeks and the Gubla of the Akkadians). These "pseudo-hieroglyphic" inscriptions, as they have been designated, have not yet been read satisfactorily. They are thought to

---

[11] Cf. W. F. Albright, *Archiv für Orientforschung*, VI (1931), p. 218 n. 4.

[12] I. J. Gelb, *Hurrians and Subarians* (1944), p. 74.

[13] *ANET*, pp. 512ff.; cf. *FSAC*, p. 79.

[14] Cf. G. Fecht, *Die Habgierige und die Maat in der Lehre des Ptahhotep* (1958), pp. 49f.

[15] Rowley, *The Aramaic of the OT* (1929), pp. 23ff.

[16] F. Rosenthal, *Die Aramäische Forschung* (1939), p. 676; cf. K. A. Kitchen, *NBD*, p. 58.

date from a period between the eighteenth and fifteenth centuries B.C.

About twenty-five inscriptions recovered in 1904 from the turquoise mines of Serabit el-Khadem in the Sinai peninsula, which in antiquity were controlled by the Egyptians, have demonstrated that for some time prior to the period of Moses an early form of alphabetic script existed, variously named proto-Sinaitic, early Canaanite, and proto-Phoenician. These inscriptions were discovered by Sir Flinders Petrie, who dated them about 1500 B.C.[17] Albright deciphered the inscriptions in 1947 and traced their origin to the use of an alphabetic script by Semitic slaves brought in from Canaan to work the turquoise mines in the days of Thotmes III.[18] Other scholars, however, have expressed a preference for a date in the Middle Kingdom rather than in the Empire (New Kingdom) period. Nevertheless, for the present a date of about 1500 B.C. seems quite acceptable. The inscriptions are generally regarded as containing letters derived from Egyptian hieroglyphs, although the number of different signs, possibly a little more than thirty, indicates that the script is of a non-Egyptian alphabetic character. Potsherds found at Gezer, Lachish, Beth-shemesh, and Hazor, which bear analogous signs, may well constitute a witness to the widespread use of the script in Palestine during this period.

In summary it can be said that by 1500 B.C. the alphabet, as distinct from cuneiform writing and Egyptian hieroglyphs, came into use in Syria and Palestine, perhaps out of a need to find a less complicated form of writing than those in vogue at the time. Far from being illiterate, therefore, the inhabitants of the Syria-Palestine area were making use of at least five systems of writing during the Late Bronze Age.

While there are some gaps in present knowledge concerning the development of the Palestine linear script, it would seem that the Sinaitic variety was followed closely by that of Ugarit. A later stage of the proto-Canaanite can be discerned in a number of inscriptions from Byblos, Beth-shemesh, and Lachish, dated between the thirteenth and twelfth centuries B.C.[19] These latter serve to link the proto-Sinaitic inscriptions[20] with the tenth-century B.C. Phoenician material from Byblos on the sarcophagus of Ahiram (ca. 1000 B.C.). The proto-Phoenician script was apparently adopted between the eleventh and tenth centuries B.C. by the Aramaeans, who introduced *matres lectionis* (literally "mothers of reading"), the use of certain letters to indicate the

---

[17] W. F. M. Petrie and C. T. Currelly, *Researches in Sinai* (1906), pp. 129ff.

[18] Cf. *AP*, pp. 188f., also *BASOR*, No. 110 (1948), pp. 6ff.; F. M. Cross, *BASOR*, No. 134 (1954), pp. 15ff.

[19] Cf. R. H. Pfeiffer, *AJA*, XLI (1937), pp. 643f.; J. W. Flight in E. Grant (ed.), *Haverford Symposium on Archaeology and the Bible* (1938), pp. 114ff.

[20] Cf. J. T. Milik and F. M. Cross, *BASOR*, No. 134 (1954), p. 9.

presence of final long vowels, a feature that appeared from the ninth century B.C. on in Moabite and Hebrew texts. In Hebrew, for example, ו, י and ה, were used to indicate ū, ī, and ā, respectively. Eighth-century B.C. Aramaic inscriptions developed this device further to indicate medial long vowels, and ultimately 'aleph was employed on rare occasions as a vowel-letter. Hebrew script, both lapidary (inscribed on stones) and cursive, was a descendant of the Phoenician, and remained constant in the number and phonic value of its letters.

Although the evidence is too scattered both chronologically and geographically for a detailed palaeographic and epigraphic study, it is sufficient to indicate that the early Hebrew alphabet was constant throughout the millennium of its usage, dating from the Gezer calendar in the tenth century B.C.[21] Thus Diringer concluded that hardly any of its letters changed its form so radically during that time that a layman could mistake its identity, a phenomenon which is probably unique in the history of ancient writing.[22] The cursive script that many Old Testament writers would have employed at an early period was no doubt that found on the inscribed arrowheads and other smaller sources from about 1000 B.C.[23] The earliest group of texts is that from Samaria, assigned to the reign of Jeroboam II, and exhibits a clear flowing script which is quite obviously the work of professional scribes.[24] Word-dividers were commonly utilized in Aramaic, Moabite, and Hebrew inscriptions, and in the case of the Samaritan corpus the unvocalized words were separated by means of small strokes or dots. The script was very similar to that of the Siloam inscription, and by the time that the Lachish ostraca were written it had developed only slightly in form.

Unlike the Hebrew, the Aramaic script exhibited a degree of individual development from about 1000 B.C. The texts recovered from Arslan Tash and Tell Halaf indicate that there was still a close resemblance between the Phoenician linear script and the Aramaic character as late as 850 B.C. In the seventh century B.C. the increasingly cursive style was evident in the inscription on the Bar-Rekub *stele*,[25] on clay tablets, and on a papyrus letter sent from Philistia to Egypt about 604 B.C.,[26] which was written in a more archaic hand than many of the Elephantine papyri. In these texts it is common to discover archaic and late Aramaic forms existing side by side, as in Jeremiah 10:11.

[21] W. F. Albright, *BASOR*, No. 92 (1943), pp. 16ff.

[22] D. Diringer, *BA*, XIII, No. 4 (1950), p. 84.

[23] Cf. J. T. Milk, *BASOR*, No. 143 (1956), pp. 3ff.

[24] *ANET*, p. 321; *DOTT*, pp. 204ff.; *WBA*, p. 158; Y. Yadin, *Studies in the Bible* (1960), pp. 9ff.

[25] J. B. Pritchard, *The Ancient Near East in Pictures* (1954), p. 460.

[26] D. J. Wiseman, *Chronicles of Chaldean Kings (626-556 B.C.) in the British Museum* (1956), p. 28; *DOTT*, pp. 251ff.

By the late third century B.C. a semi-formal script had emerged in Persian Aramaic, similar in character to the Aramaic scripts of Palmyra and Nabataea, which seem to have come into vogue about this period.[27] Early in the second century B.C. modified forms of the Aramaic characters, which by that time had diverged considerably from the Phoenician, were adopted by the Jews, the first stages of which can be seen in the Nash Papyrus, *ca.* 150 B.C., and this was subsequently known as "square" character. Phoenician forms continued in use for some time, however, being found frequently on coins from the second century B.C. to the second century A.D., and surviving in some of the Dead Sea Scrolls. In a more elaborate fashion the Phoenician characters were perpetuated in the script utilized by the Samaritans. The use of special final forms for certain letters in the Aramaic "square" script can be traced back to some Egyptian papyri of about 300 B.C., but at first such letters were not commonly employed.

The formal Hebrew character developed quickly during the Herodian period (30 B.C.-A.D. 70), and after that time its progress could be traced by means of dated commercial and legal documents.[28] The manuscripts and fragments from Qumran and the Wadi Murabba'at exhibited a variety of scripts ranging from Palaeo-Hebrew to the formal and cursive hands of Early Jewish, with some Greek and Latin scripts in addition. Until vowel signs were developed after the fifth century A.D. there was no attempt made to indicate the vocalization of the Hebrew consonants, aside from the use of the *matres lectionis.* Neither a Palestinian nor a Babylonian system of supralinear vowels met with quite the success accorded to the Tiberian method, which was introduced at the end of the eighth century of our era. This was subsequently adopted as the best system for pointing the Hebrew text, and is still employed in modern Hebrew Bibles.

Writing materials varied considerably, to some extent depending upon climate and local conditions. Since stone was relatively scarce in Mesopotamia, cuneiform inscriptions on this substance were restricted to royal texts or *stelae* such as that bearing the Code of Hammurabi. Clay tablets were the commonest vehicles of written communications in Mesopotamia for many centuries, whereas in Egypt it was papyrus which claimed this distinction from about 3000 B.C. Because of the abundance of stone in Egypt it was customary to carve hieroglyphic texts on *stelae* and on the walls of innumerable temples and tombs. Metal was much less commonly used as writing material than either stone or clay, although cuneiform inscriptions in Sumerian, Akkadian, and Old Persian have been discovered on objects made of gold, silver, copper, and bronze. Gold is men-

[27] D. J. Wiseman, *NBD*, p. 1349.
[28] F. M. Cross, *BANE*, pp. 136ff.

tioned in Exodus 28:36 as a writing-surface; stone is also referred to several times in the Old Testament in this connection (Exod. 24:12; 34:1; Deut. 4:13; 27:2f.; Josh. 8:32; Job 19:24). The use of broken pottery as writing material was widespread throughout the ancient Near East, although potsherds were of limited value to the Mesopotamians, since they could only be utilized for a script like Aramaic, which was written with pen and ink rather than with a stylus. Wood in one form or another was also employed as a means of receiving writing (Num. 17:2f.; Ezek. 37:16f.; cf. Isa. 8:1; 30:8; Hab. 2:2), as were leather and parchment.

The use of tanned animal skins for purposes of writing dates back to the early third millennium in Egypt, and lasted until the Arab conquest in the seventh century A.D. It is very possible that the prophecies of Jeremiah were written upon a leather scroll (Jer. 36:4, 23) (as were some of the Qumran Scriptures), although papyrus may have been employed on that occasion. This latter may be indicated by the fact that the deed of purchase signed by the prophet (Jer. 32:10ff.) was undoubtedly a papyrus document of the kind found at Elephantine, and also by the use of *chartion* (36:2, 4, 6, 14—LXX chapter 43) and *chartēs* (Jer. 36:23—LXX chap. 43) in the LXX version of Jeremiah 36, both of which denote a sheet of papyrus. Although hides were tanned by the Hebrews (cf. Num. 31:20; 2 Kgs. 1:8), the Old Testament itself does not mention writing on leather. However, the Talmud preserved an ancient tradition that the Mosaic Torah was written upon the hides of cattle.[29] According to Josephus, the Pentateuchal manuscript from which the LXX was translated was written upon leather, although there is little evidence for such a statement.[30]

The widespread use of Egyptian papyrus in Syria long before the time of the early Hebrew monarchy can be appreciated from the report of Wen-Amon, an Egyptian official who had been sent on a journey to Byblos about 1100 B.C. Among other matters contained in his report to the authorities of the temple of Amon at Karnak[31] is a reference to five hundred rolls of papyrus that had been delivered to the Syrian ruler in partial payment for a load of timber required for the ceremonial barge of Amon.

In the light of all available evidence there is absolutely no ground for regarding the Old Testament references to writing in the time of Moses (Exod. 17:14; 24:4; 39:14, 30; Deut. 27:3; 31:24; cf. Josh. 18:4ff.) as anachronisms, in the manner favored by many adherents of the Wellhausenian theories. It is clear that at any period from the time of Moses

---

[29] *Maccoth*, 5.
[30] *AJ*, XII, 2, 11; cf. the *Letter of Aristeas*, III, 176.
[31] *ANET*, pp. 25ff.

onwards, the ancient Hebrews were capable of producing their own written records. Indeed, it will be shown in a subsequent chapter that there are excellent reasons for thinking that the bulk of Genesis was brought from Mesopotamia in the form of written tablets, and supplemented by the addition of the narratives concerning Joseph. Although there is no explicit statement in the Old Testament to the effect that Moses was literate, the references to his writing activities would seem to leave little doubt as to the facts of the case. As one who was presumably educated in court circles, Moses would be familiar with Egyptian writing and literary methods, and in all probability with Akkadian cuneiform, which from the beginning of the Amarna Age had constituted the official language of diplomacy in Egypt.

The foregoing discussion shows that peoples of the same cultural background as the Hebrews were literate from the fourth millennium B.C. onwards, though naturally not uniformly so. From the second millennium B.C. throughout the ancient Near East men were being trained in schools not only as scribes for business and professional purposes, but also as expert copyists. It seems improbable that from the time of Moses onwards the Hebrews should have been significantly less advanced than their contemporaries in this respect (cf. 2 Sam. 8:17), or that they were less scrupulous in the transmission of their sacred texts than were the Egyptians or the Mesopotamians.[32] Indeed, the prolonged Hebrew tradition of reverence for the text of Scripture indicates that the opposite was in fact the case (cf. Deut. 4:2; Jer. 26:2).

On this basis it is no longer necessary to assume that an extended period of oral transmission is a necessary prerequisite to the written form of many if not all of the Old Testament documents, as is common in liberal circles.[33] Modern scholars have largely misunderstood the purpose and function of oral transmission in the ancient Near East. The firm tradition of the Mosaic period, as well as of ancient peoples other than the Hebrews, was that any events of importance were generally recorded in written form quite soon after they had taken place. Some notable incidents were perpetuated in song and story also, doubtless for many centuries, but the principal purpose of oral transmission was the dissemination of the pertinent information to the people of the day and age in which the events occurred. Only as one generation was succeeded by another did the various elements represented by oral transmission approach anything like a sequence in time. Consequently it is entirely fallacious to assume, as many modern scholars have done, that an oral form of a narrative was the necessary and normal precursor of the written stage. There can be little doubt that in many cases both oral and

---

[32] Cf. W. J. Martin, *The Dead Sea Scroll of Isaiah* (1954), pp. 18f.

[33] Cf. E. Neilson, *Oral Tradition* (1954); B. S. Childs, *Memory and Tradition in Israel* (1963).

written traditions existed side by side for lengthy periods.[34] While one tradition may have been reinforced or corrected by reference to the other on specific occasions, the two were certainly free to pursue an independent if not an entirely unrelated course.

[34] H. S. Nyberg, *ZAW*, LII (1934), pp. 241ff. and *Studien zum Hoseabuch* (1935), pp. 7f., however, held that little of the Old Testament was in fixed written form until the post-exilic period.

II. THE OLD TESTAMENT TEXT

A. THE TRANSMISSION OF THE HEBREW TEXT

1. Pre-Massoretic developments. Although great care was taken by the Jews in the preservation and transmission of their Scriptures, it is important to notice that the details of the text were not standardized at the time when the canon of the Old Testament took its final form. The manuscripts from Qumran have shown that in the immediate pre-Christian period there were several types of text in circulation, some with readings different from those in the traditional Massoretic text. During the first two centuries or so before the time of Christ, the responsibility for preserving and transmitting the Hebrew text that later came to be known as Massoretic devolved upon the ancient scribes, or *Sopherim*, designated in this manner according to the Talmud,[1] because they counted scrupulously the letters in the Torah. In the immediate pre-Christian period the Jewish authorities gave a great deal of thought to the preservation of the Old Testament text in as pure a form as possible, a concern prompted as much by the existence of manuscript variants as by differences between the Hebrew and LXX texts. Their concern was brought into clear focus as a result of controversy with the Christians, which made it important for them to have a standard Biblical text not merely as an assured basis for theological polemic but also for the discovery of the divine will as revealed in the very words of the Scriptures themselves.

During the second century the movement for establishing an authoritative text of the Hebrew Bible gained momentum, largely through the enthusiasm of the notorious anti-Christian Rabbi Aqiba (d. *ca.* A.D. 132). More than his contemporaries he realized how important the existence of a fixed text of Scripture was for Jewish apologetics, as well as for Halakic and Haggadic exegesis. To him was credited the saying that "the accurate transmission (*massoreth*) of the text is a fence for the Torah."[2] He developed the verbal exegetical method of his teacher

---

[1] *Qiddush.* 30a; B. J. Roberts, *The OT Text and Versions*, p. 31; G. L. Archer, *A Survey of OT Introduction*, pp. 54f.

[2] *Pirqe Abot* III, 17.

Nahum of Gimzo, with whom he studied for twenty-two years, and utilized it to discover hidden truths and spiritual meanings in apparently unimportant Hebrew particles. The elaborate methods of Rabbi Aqiba were reflected in the work of Aquila, a pagan from Sinope, who first embraced Christianity and then at a later time became a Jew. About A.D. 130 Aquila prepared a new literal Greek version of the standard Hebrew text, undertaken with only little regard for either Greek syntax or idiom. Quite apart from its literary deficiencies it incurred the anger of Christians because it departed from the tradition of the LXX in preferring "young woman" for "virgin" in Isaiah 7:14.

Even though there was most probably a standardization of the Hebrew text in the time of Rabbi Aqiba, the resultant Scriptures still contained many divergent readings, variations in orthography, and the like. The scribes who functioned at this time indicated by means of certain marks those passages in the text about whose soundness they were in doubt. At a fairly early period the text was divided into sections, either according to logical breaks in the narrative or on the basis of passages used for liturgical readings. The subdivision of Biblical books into verses took place under the scribes also, although the current chapter divisions are comparatively recent in origin.[3]

2. The work of the Massoretes. The work of the scribes came to an end about the beginning of the sixth century after Christ, and in their place arose the Massoretes. Although scholars have argued about the correct spelling,[4] the name itself went back to Mishnaic times[5] (as has been seen in Aqiba's epigram above) and carried with it the general sense of a transmitted tradition. The Massoretes were the custodians of the sacred traditional text, and were active from about A.D. 500 to 1000. They continued and completed the objectives of the *Sopherim* and the rabbis by definitely fixing a form of the Hebrew text, which subsequently became known as Massoretic. Accordingly they concerned themselves with the transmission of the consonantal text as they had received it, as well as with its pronunciation, on the basis that the text itself was inviolable and every consonant sacred.

---

[3] C. D. Ginsburg, *Introduction to the Massoretico-Critical Edition of the Hebrew Bible* (1897), p. 25; cf. G. F. Moore, *JBL*, XII (1893), pp. 73ff.

[4] For the oscillation between *massorāh* and *māsorāh* see Bergsträsser, *Hebräische Grammatik* (1918), p. 15, H. H. Rowley, *JTS*, XLII (1941), p. 26, B. J. Roberts, *The OT Text and Versions*, pp. 40ff., P. Kahle, *Historische Grammatik der Hebräischen Sprache* (ed. Bauer and Leander, 1922), pp. 71ff., H. L. Strack, *Realencyklopädie für protestantische Theologie und Kirche* (1896-1909), XII, pp. 393ff., H. Wheeler Robinson, *The Bible in its Ancient and English Versions* (1940), pp. 26ff.

[5] *Sheqal.* VI, 1; *Pirqe Ab.* I, 1; III, 14.

The detailed statistical work that the Massoretes undertook on each book included the counting of verses, words, and letters, establishing the middle of a book (a procedure which was useful in the case of bifid, or two-part, compositions), noting peculiarities of style, and other similar matters. This information was included in the *Massorah finalis* or concluding notes, with which each book of the Massoretic Bible concluded, and it is printed in this way in modern versions of the text. Some of the observations of the Massoretes which were connected with unusual transcriptional forms of certain letters of the alphabet may, as Pfeiffer has observed,[6] have been based upon critical tendencies. The Massoretes replaced the earlier oral transmission of such textual peculiarities by means of Massorah marginals, or marginal notes, written either on the side (*Massorah parva*) or in larger form in the top and bottom margins (*Massorah magna*) of the manuscript. The material of the concluding notes is similar in character to that of the marginal notes, and contains such information as the number of sections, verses, and words in the particular book, along with aids for memorizing these facts.

Since it was the avowed aim of the Massoretes to transmit the Hebrew text in a form unchanged from that which they had received, they left the sacred consonants entirely untouched. But where their training and experience persuaded them that corrections or improvements could be made to passages that contained corruptions, they recorded the amended form by means of a marginal note, a procedure that avoided any alteration of the inviolable written text. The preferred reading was known as *Q^ere*, meaning "that which is to be read," as contrasted with the sacred consonantal text, the *K^ethibh* or "written" Scripture. The *Q^ere* on occasions may have constituted a genuine variant reading, since it is by no means unusual for copyists to supply such material in the process of their work. On the other hand there are many instances of Massoretic marginal readings that can only be described as conjectural. Although scholars differ in their computations, it has been estimated that there are about five thousand variations in the Massoretic text, of which some three thousand five hundred are orthographic.[7]

At first the Massorah was transmitted orally, but by the sixth century the activities of different Massoretic schools in endeavoring to fix the text and its pronunciation led to the custom of accentuation and vocalizing by means of vowel "points." Shortly after the beginning of the tenth century the Babylonian and Palestinian systems of placing the vowels above and between the consonants gave way to the Tiberian method of placing the vowel points under the Hebrew consonants (with the excep-

---

[6] *PIOT*, p. 83; cf. K. Albrecht, *ZAW*, XXXIX (1921), pp. 160ff.
[7] *PIOT*, p. 93.

tion of one vowel sign).[8] The latter system, which was adopted by the western Massoretes, was an elaborately designed and carefully regulated method, which in certain instances required that the conditional pronunciation of specific words be corrected according to its rules.[9]

While the Tiberian vocalization is not infrequently considered to be characterized by a mechanical inertness, it should be remembered that some of its artificiality may have been occasioned by the work of subsequent grammarians, who subordinated the flexibility of the system familiar to the Massoretes of Tiberias to the interests of grammatical schematizing. The fact that there are evidences of numerous inconsistencies and irregularities in the pointing appears to indicate the existence of a degree of liberty that was lost when the Massoretic tradition came to an end in the twelfth century.

The western Massoretes did not exhibit complete harmony among themselves, however, and in the first half of the tenth century two principal Massoretic families flourished in Palestine, that of ben Asher and that of ben Naphtali. Each family prepared a standard copy of the Massoretic Bible, whose minor textual differences[10] have no bearing upon the meaning of the passages concerned. Five generations of the family of ben Asher worked on the Hebrew text,[11] of whom the most famous were ben Asher himself and his son Aaron. The former copied a codex of the prophets in A.D. 895, and furnished it with vowel points and a *Massorah*. This celebrated manuscript is now in the Qaraite synagogue in Cairo. Aaron ben Moshe ben Asher was responsible for providing the pointing and a *Massorah* for a complete Biblical codex written by an unknown Massorete at the beginning of the tenth century, a copy of which was kept in the Sephardic synagogue at Aleppo. A subsequent copy of the ben Asher text was made about A.D. 1010 in Cairo by Samuel ben Jacob, and this important manuscript of the whole Hebrew Bible is in Leningrad.

---

[8] On the contribution of the Babylonian and Palestinian schools, see Ginsburg, *op. cit.*, pp. 197ff.; P. E. Kahle, *Masoreten des Ostens* (1913), *Theologische Studien und Kritiken*, LXXXVIII (1915), pp. 399ff., *Masoreten des Westens* (1927), I, pp. 23ff., II (1930), pp. 66ff., *ZAW*, XLVI (1928), pp. 113ff., *Theologische Rundschau*, V (1933), pp. 227ff., *The Cairo Geniza* (1947), pp. 44ff.; R. Gordis, *The Biblical Text in the Making: A Study of the Kethib-Qere* (1937), pp. 70ff.; B. J. Roberts, *The OT Text and Versions*, pp. 53ff.

[9] On the problem of pronunciation, see Kahle, *Masoreten des Westens*, I, pp. 43ff.; W. E. Staples, *AJSL*, XLIV (1928), pp. 6ff.; A. Sperber, *HUCA*, XII-XIII (1937-1938), pp. 103ff.; Kahle, *The Cairo Geniza*, pp. 88ff.; E. F. Sutcliffe, *Biblica*, XXIX (1948), pp. 112ff.

[10] Ginsburg, *op. cit.*, pp. 241ff.; S. H. Blank, *HUCA*, VIII-IX (1931-1932), pp. 229ff.; Kahle, *Masoreten des Westens*, II, pp. 45ff.; L. Lipschütz, *Ben-Ascher—Ben-Naftali. Der Bibeltext der tiberienischen Masoreten* (1937).

[11] Kahle, *The Cairo Geniza*, p. 55; M. H. Goshen-Gottestein, *Biblical and Other Studies* (1963), pp. 80ff.

The family of ben Naphtali is not quite as well known, since the text that they sponsored did not gain particular favor, and is only preserved in part.[12] The Reuchlin codex of A.D. 1105 at Karlsruhe is one of the best representatives of the ben Naphtali approach to the problems of the Hebrew text. A major contribution to the virtual oblivion of their efforts was the decree of Maimonides (d. A.D. 1204) in the twelfth century that the text and vocalization of the ben Asher manuscripts were to be regarded as standard from that time on.

The ben Asher text, influenced by that of ben Naphtali, fixed the pronunciation more exactly by means of the accentual system, although it was unable to exclude completely certain foreign influences which affected the vocalization. This resulted in differences between the ben Asher manuscripts and what later came to be the official text of the Old Testament. It was only during the fourteenth century of our era that the process of mutual assimilation was completed.[13] Its result was the Hebrew *textus receptus* of the late Middle Ages, a text of mixed character that formed the basis of most manuscripts of the Hebrew Bible. It was found in the medieval rabbinic Bibles, which contained the Aramaic Targums and the commentaries of such authoritative rabbis as Kimchi, Rashi, Ibn Ezra, and others, in addition to the text.

The first printed editions[14] of parts of the Hebrew Bible were issued in 1477, perhaps at Bologna; the first complete Bible appeared in Soncino in 1488, followed three years later by a second in Naples, and in 1494 by a third in Brescia. The first Rabbinic Bible was produced by Felix Pratensis and published in Venice by Daniel Bomberg in 1516-1517. It served as the basis for the second Rabbinic Bible, the four-volume work of Jacob ben Chayyim in 1524-1525, also published by Bomberg. The importance of this work was recognized almost immediately, for it furnished a revised text based upon the study of earlier manuscripts and editions. Although the resultant text was decidedly eclectic in character, it was accepted as virtually standard and remained authoritative through the nineteenth century. Subsequent Rabbinic Bibles (published in Venice in 1546-48, 1568, and 1617-19) followed the ben Chayyim text, but the Buxtorf edition, published in Basel in 1611, as well as the one issued in 1618, contained a hybrid type of text based on ben Asher and the Complutensian Polyglot, which was issued under papal sanction at Complutum in 1514-1517.

The urge to draw upon texts that antedated that of ben Chayyim was evident in the first critical edition of the Bible issued in 1720 by J. H. Michaelis, who consulted manuscripts containing variants from the popularly accepted text. Collections of variants were made in 1776 by

---

[12] D. R. Ap-Thomas, *A Primer of OT Text Criticism* (1947), p. 13.
[13] O. Eissfeldt, *Einleitung in das AT* (1934), p. 706.
[14] Cf. C. D. Ginsburg, *op. cit.*, pp. 779ff.

Kennicott, and in the eighteenth and nineteenth centuries by J. B. de Rossi, Baer and Delitzsch. In the twentieth century a critical text was issued by C. D. Ginsburg.[15] The textual revision by J. Athias and J. Leusden in 1661-67 of the manual edition of J. Buxtorf, published in 1611 and based upon the ben Chayyim and Complutensian Polyglot texts, was perpetuated in the widely circulated editions of A. Hahn (1832, 1833, 1868) and M. Letteris of Vienna (1852). The latter was adopted as its text by the British and Foreign Bible Society, who reprinted it from 1866 onwards. A nineteenth-century critical edition of the Old Testament text (which was never completed) was edited by Haupt and published in the United States.[16] It exhibited a variety of colors in its pages as a means of distinguishing the various literary sources that the proponents of the Graf-Wellhausen analytical method claimed to have isolated from the various books. The Hebrew text was printed in an unvocalized form, and was accompanied by critical notes.

The first two editions of the Kittel Hebrew Bible were based generally upon the ben Chayyim text, but furnished variant readings from the ancient versions along with some conjectural emendations.[17] In the third edition Paul Kahle printed the ben Asher text in its purest form, along with a critical apparatus giving variant readings.[18] This return to the ben Asher text was of great importance in the history of the study of the Massoretic tradition, and its validity was confirmed in the Snaith edition of the Hebrew Bible, about which more will be said subsequently.

3. *The Qumran texts.* Until the discovery of the Dead Sea Scrolls in 1947, the critical study of the Old Testament text was hampered by the fact that the earliest Hebrew manuscripts only went back to about A.D. 900.[19] The discovery in 1890 of a number of ancient manuscripts in the scroll-depository or *genizah* of the Old Synagogue in Cairo did not prove to be as significant as was first thought.[20] Some of the manuscripts recovered from this cache contained supralinear punctuation, but the high estimates of their value for the vocalized Massoretic text were diminished somewhat when it was discovered that there was a marked

---

[15] B. Kennicott, *Vetus Testamentum Hebraicum cum variis lectionibus*, 2 vols. (1776-78); J. B. de Rossi, *Variae lectiones Veteris Testamenti ex immensa manu scriptorum editorumque codicum congerie haustae*, 4 vols. (1784-88), *Scholia critica in Veteri Testamenti libros seu supplementa ad varias sacri textus lectiones* (1798); S. Baer and F. Delitzsch, *Textum Masoreticum accuratissime expressit e fontibus Masorae variae illustravit* (1869); C. D. Ginsburg, *The OT, Diligently Revised according to the Massorah and the Early Editions, With the Various Readings from Manuscripts and the Ancient Versions*, 4 vols. (1926).

[16] P. Haupt, *The Sacred Books of the OT* (1894-1904).

[17] R. Kittel, *Biblia Hebraica* (1906-12).

[18] R. Kittel-P. Kahle, *Biblia Hebraica* (1937).

[19] The most important are described by Ginsburg, *Introduction to the Massoretico-Critical Edition of the Hebrew Bible*, pp. 469ff.

[20] Cf. P. E. Kahle, *The Cairo Geniza*, pp. 1ff.

lack of consistency in vocalization. This factor, as well as the almost complete absence of variation from the traditional consonantal text, showed that at the time the manuscripts were written the vocalization was of secondary importance to the accurate transmission of the text. Some of the Biblical manuscripts may date from a little earlier than the ninth century although it is far from easy to establish a date for many of the scrolls.[21]

So bleak were the prospects of getting any nearer to the original Hebrew autographs that F. G. Kenyon wrote in 1939:

> There is, indeed, no probability that we shall ever find manuscripts of the Hebrew text going back to a period before the formation of the text which we know as Massoretic.[22]

This discouraging prospect was changed dramatically by the unexpected discovery of the scrolls in the Qumran caves. When arguments concerning the authenticity and date of the materials had subsided, it became obvious that the Biblical scrolls and fragments had at one blow advanced the extant textual sources by a millennium, and as such made the manuscripts of priceless value both for the textual critic and the palaeographer.[23] The identity of the sect that had preserved this material became somewhat less of a problem when it was found that a mutilated manuscript from 4Q had affinities with an ancient Jewish work known as the Zadokite Document, dated between the tenth and twelfth centuries after Christ, and first discovered in the *genizah* of the Old Synagogue at Cairo in 1876.

The Biblical manuscripts from Qumran have unquestionably confirmed the general tradition regarding the tremendous care exercised in the transmission of the Hebrew Scriptures, and have made it evident that much more respect must be accorded to the Massoretic text than had previously been the case in some quarters. Early studies of the Qumran scrolls showed that they followed the tradition of the Massoretes more consistently than that of the LXX Greek,[24] and contained reflections of ancient sources in the matter of spelling and name-forms.[25]

---

[21] For arguments against dating any manuscripts earlier than about the first half of the ninth century see J. L. Teicher, *JJS*, I (1949), pp. 156ff., II (1950), pp. 17ff.

[22] F. G. Kenyon, *Our Bible and the Ancient Manuscripts* (1939), p. 48.

[23] Cf. S. A. Birnbaum, *The Qumrân (Dead Sea) Scrolls and Palaeography* (1952).

[24] Cf. C. Kuhl, *VT*, II (1952), pp. 307ff.; R. Barthélemy, *RB*, LX (1953), pp. 18ff.; K. Elliger, *Studien zum Habakuk-Kommentar vom Toten Meer* (1953), pp. 78ff.; F. M. Cross, *BASOR*, No. 132 (1953), pp. 15ff.; R. de Vaux, *RB*, LX (1953), pp. 268ff.; P. Kahle, *Theologische Literaturzeitung*, LXXIX (1954), pp. 82ff.; J. Muilenburg, *BASOR*, No. 135 (1954), p. 32; S. Loewinger, *VT*, IV (1954), pp. 155ff.; M. Burrows, *The Dead Sea Scrolls* (1955), pp. 304ff.

[25] Cf. M. Burrows, *JBL*, LXVIII (1949), pp. 204f.; D. Beegle, *BASOR*, No. 123 (1951), pp. 26ff. For a study of superior readings in 1QIsaᵃ, see W. H. Brownlee, *The Meaning of the Qumrân Scrolls for the Bible* (1964), pp. 216ff.

The orthography of the large Isaiah scroll (1QIsa^a) has certain phonetic characteristics that are less prominent in the Massoretic text, and point to some degree of deviation from the tradition of the immediate pre-Christian period. Compared with the received text it is particularly marked by *scriptio plena* forms, by the full suffix endings of the second- and third-person masculine plural and the second-person masculine singular, and also in certain verbal forms. While some scribal corrections are noticeable in the scroll, they had the effect of bringing the text, rather than the spelling of particular words, into line with the Massoretic tradition, although not uniformly so.

It appears that 1QIsa^a furnished a contemporary phonetic spelling designed to make the reading of the Hebrew text considerably easier without at the same time actually altering the time-honored pronunciation. This contrasted with the procedures adopted in the fragmentary Sukenik scroll (1QIsa^b), which followed the older form of spelling employed prior to the destruction of the Second Temple. There are numerous textual divergences in 1QIsa^a from the Massoretic tradition, and while some may perhaps constitute improvements upon the *textus receptus*, others are quite clearly the result of textual error and corruption.[26] Of the thirteen readings adopted in the RSV on the basis of the text of 1QIsa^a, five of them are entirely without support from other ancient versions. The 1QIsa^b scroll contained a few readings that disagreed with the Massoretic text, and it is interesting to note that two of them (1QIsa^b 53:11, 12) reinforce the LXX tradition as against that of the Massoretes. Even more notable is the fact that 1QIsa^a also followed the reading preserved by the LXX in both these passages, since such a circumstance might well point to the possibility of error in the transmission of the Massoretic text itself. Apart from the two instances mentioned above there are nine other textual divergences in 1QIsa^b, all of which appear capable of explanation on grounds other than that they constitute genuine variants. The list collated by Loewinger[27] contained about three hundred alleged divergences, but most of these were concerned with the insertion of the consonants (ו) and (י), a phenomenon that has already been noticed in connection with some of the manuscripts from the Cairo *genizah*.

Quite aside from their importance in reflecting the transitional phases of Hebrew orthography,[28] the Qumran Biblical scrolls are of great value for indicating how Hebrew was pronounced just prior to the Christian era. This has been a matter of considerable discussion in scholarly

---

[26] Cf. M. Burrows, *BASOR*, No. 111 (1948), pp. 16ff., No. 113 (1949), pp. 24ff.
[27] S. Loewinger, *VT*, IV (1954), pp. 155ff.
[28] Cf. M. Burrows, *The Dead Sea Scrolls*, pp. 109ff.

circles,[29] since nobody can be absolutely certain as to precisely how the various tongues of antiquity were enunciated, and any information that contributes to the elucidation of this matter is certainly welcome. In another direction the scrolls have demonstrated the incorrectness of those views, long current in scholarly circles, which maintained that Hebrew had become a dead language prior to the second century B.C., since the manuscripts show conclusively that Hebrew persisted in some areas as a living language, despite the fact that most Palestinian Jews spoke Aramaic in one dialect form or another.[30]

Earlier studies in the relationship between the Hebrew text and the LXX[31] received considerable stimulation from the discoveries at Qumran,[32] particularly when fragments of 1 Samuel recovered from 4Q showed that the manuscript represented the same general tradition as that of the Hebrew text underlying the LXX version.[33] The divergences from both the Massoretic and Greek texts indicated that the fragments preserved a number of original readings that were not represented in either the Massoretic or Greek traditions.[34] Thus the 1 Samuel text from 4Q contained the phrase, "he shall become a *nazir* for ever" in 1 Samuel 1:22, a clause that had been lost to both the Hebrew and the Greek by haplography, a form of scribal omission common in antiquity in which a letter, syllable, or word is written only once when it should be written more than once. Such material is of immense importance for the history of the Old Testament text, since it points to a stage of development prior to the standardization of the literary tradition.

From the evidence presented by the Qumran discoveries it appears that there were at least three distinct types of Biblical text in circulation among the Jews of the Second Commonwealth.[35] This development,

[29] Cf. B. J. Roberts, *The OT Text and Versions*, pp. 47ff.; M. L. Margolis, *AJSL*, XXVI (1910), pp. 62ff.; E. A. Speiser, *JQR*, XVI (1925-26), pp. 343ff., XXIII (1932-3), pp. 233ff., XXIV (1933-4), pp. 9ff.; E. Brønno, *Studien über hebraische Morphologie und Vokalismus auf Grundlage der Mercatischen Fragmente der zweiten Kolumne der Hexapla des Origenes* (1943); P. E. Kahle, *The Cairo Geniza*, pp. 86f.

[30] Cf. M. Black, *NT Studies*, III (1957), pp. 305ff.

[31] Cf. J. Fischer, *Zur LXX Vorlage im Pentateuch* (1926); G. Bertram, *Theologische Rundschau*, III (1931), pp. 283ff., X (1938), pp. 69ff., 133ff.; F. X. Wutz, *Systematische Wege von der LXX zum hebräischen Urtext* (1937); J. Ziegler, *ZAW*, LIX (1944), pp. 107ff.; H. M. Orlinsky in H. R. Willoughby (ed.), *The Study of the Bible Today and Tomorrow* (1947), pp. 144ff.; I. L. Seeligmann, *The LXX Version of Isaiah* (1948); P. Katz, *Theologische Zeitschrift*, V (1949), pp. 1ff.

[32] Cf. D. Barthélemy, *RB*, LX (1953), pp. 18ff.; P. Kahle, *Theologische Literaturzeitung*, LXXIX (1954), pp. 82ff.; H. S. Gehman, *VT*, III (1953), pp. 141ff., IV (1954), pp. 337ff.; J. W. Wevers, *Theologische Rundschau*, XXII (1954), pp. 85ff., 171ff.

[33] F. M. Cross, *BASOR*, No. 132 (1953), pp. 15ff.

[34] Cf. J. M. Allegro, *The Dead Sea Scrolls* (1956), pp. 57ff.

[35] Cf. W. F. Albright, *Samuel and the Beginnings of the Prophetic Movement* (1961), p. 11.

which already has done much to shake the foundations of traditional literary criticism, depending as it did upon a standard "fixed" text, has made it clear that the Massoretic form was representative of only one body of Hebrew literary tradition. Even the Torah existed in a number of textual forms, contrary to the views held by some scholars of an earlier generation, as has been demonstrated conclusively by the fragments of the Pentateuch recovered from 4Q.[36]

B. THE RESTORATION OF THE HEBREW TEXT

1. The Samaritan Pentateuch. In addition to the Qumran scrolls and fragments, valuable as they are, other sources are also available for the task of restoring the text of the Old Testament. Of great importance in this respect is the Samaritan Pentateuch, which is unquestionably derived from a very ancient textual source. The Samaritans were regarded by the Jews as the descendants of Mesopotamian expatriates whom Sargon had settled in and around Samaria after the collapse of the northern kingdom in 722 B.C. (2 Kgs. 17:24ff.). Other colonists were subsequently introduced to the community by Esarhaddon and Ashurbanipal (cf. Ez. 4:2, 10). Whatever knowledge of Judaism they possessed was dismissed by the Jews as being rather coincidental and certainly superficial, and in consequence they were regarded as being at best only one degree removed from the Gentiles. The Samaritans themselves held quite a different theory of their origins, tracing their descent from those Israelites who had remained loyal to God when the Ark of the Covenant was deposited at the rival shrine of Shiloh (Judg. 18:1) instead of being placed on Mount Gerizim, which they claimed was its true location.[37] The infamy of constructing a second temple on an incorrect site was perpetrated by Ezra, who in the Samaritan view falsified the sacred text and thereby persuaded the returning exiles to erect the second temple in Judaea.

Quite obviously both views have elements in their favor. The Biblical account of the exchange of population after the fall of Samaria is supported in its general content by the Assyrian annals,[38] although it is quite probable that the time sequences indicated in 2 Kings have been compressed somewhat as the narrative now stands. In point of fact the colonization seems to have taken place over a number of years and under successive Assyrian rulers. Thus the Hamathites were probably only transported to Samaria after Sargon had suppressed an uprising in Hamath in 721 B.C., while the Cutheans may well have arrived in Samaria under Ashurbanipal rather than under Shalmaneser V.

---

[36] F. M. Cross, *BASOR*, No. 141 (1956), pp. 9ff.

[37] Cf. T. H. Gaster, *IDB*, IV, p. 191; J. Macdonald, *The Theology of the Samaritans* (1964), p. 17.

[38] *ARAB*, II, sect. 55.

Against this it should be pointed out that there is much to support the Samaritan claim to be an ancient Jewish sect, despite the fact that their testimony to this effect frequently appeared in an exaggerated form. Whereas Sargon only displaced 27,290 people, a contemporary record from Hebrew sources (2 Kgs. 15:19)[39] placed the number of wealthy landowners at 60,000, while the Chronicler (2 Chron. 34:9) spoke of a "remnant of Israel" still resident in Ephraim and Manasseh about a century later, in the period of Josiah (640-609 B.C.). This would seem to imply that on the fall of Samaria the artisans and peasants were left behind, and it was with these that the Mesopotamian immigrants evidently intermarried to produce the mixed population that subsequently took the name of Samaritans. On such a view, therefore, the enmity between the Jews and the Samaritans which became so marked at a later period was actually nothing more than a perpetuation of the ancient animosity which had existed between Judah and Israel.

As Gordon has shown,[40] there is considerable evidence for the theory that the principal shrine for Hebrew worship should have been located in Samaritan territory rather than in Judaea. Joshua 8:30ff.[41] records that after the fall of Ai, Joshua erected a shrine on Mount Ebal, and at its consecration one half of the people assembled nearby while the other half gathered on the twin peak of Mount Gerizim, which stood at the other side of a narrow pass. It is significant to realize that the shrine that Joshua built on Mount Ebal was the only one to be erected in accordance with the specific instructions of Moses (Deut. 27:4). The importance of the site may be adjudged from the order which Moses gave that the Law should be inscribed upon the stones of the altar there (Deut. 27:8), and that the penalties which would follow breaches of the Law should be proclaimed solemnly from the slopes of Mount Ebal (Deut. 11:29; 27:13; Josh. 8:33f.). It appears probable that Moses intended the center of Hebrew devotion to be located on Mount Gerizim, as the Samaritans insisted, and not at Jerusalem, which was a Jebusite stronghold until the time of David. As a matter of record, the capital of the united nation was chosen with political rather than religious considerations in view, while the Temple itself was an adjunct to the royal palace, and not in itself a primary structure.

Despite their own traditions involving Mount Gerizim and the first return from exile, the Samaritans offered to assist in rebuilding the post-exilic Temple in Jerusalem (Ez. 4:2). However, these "adversaries of Judah and Benjamin" were rebuffed by Zerubbabel; and with the coming of Ezra and Nehemiah the tensions increased considerably. The Samaritans, being of mixed ancestry, felt the weight of the religious

---

[39] Cf. R. Brinker, *The Influence of Sanctuaries in Early Israel* (1946), p. 214.
[40] *IOTT*, pp. 132f.
[41] Cf. G. F. Moore, *Judaism* (1927), I, pp. 25f.

reforms under Ezra; and the situation reached a climax when Nehemiah expelled the grandson of the High Priest, who had married the daughter of Sanballat (Neh. 13:8, 28, 30).[42] Josephus recounts a similar incident, making Sanballat responsible for the construction of the Samaritan temple on Mount Gerizim.[43] Sanballat was one of the chief opponents of Nehemiah, and according to the Elephantine papyri was the governor of Samaria in 407 B.C. If Josephus' story is true (a circumstance which is discounted by most modern scholars),[44] it may either be a distinct though similar narrative,[45] or the result of misunderstanding on the part of Josephus of several of the details, which appears more likely. However, he was doubtless correct in dating the construction of the Samaritan temple about 330 B.C.[46]

The Samaritans had their own version of the Hebrew Pentateuch, the only canonical material that they acknowledged, which they regarded as contemporary with the origins of the sect itself. Their text was independent of Jewish tradition. From the Judaistic point of view it could be thought most probably to have arisen with the return of a deported Hebrew priest whose task was to instruct the newly established inhabitants of Samaria in the Law of God, after a plague of lions had terrorized them (2 Kgs. 17:26ff.). The Samaritans' claim that their oldest Pentateuchal manuscript goes back to Abishua, the great-grandson of Aaron (1 Chron. 6:3f.), is obviously exaggerated; but the canon of the Samaritan Pentateuch long antedated the schism at the time of Nehemiah, since it constituted the Bible of the Samaritan community both before and after that period.[47]

The conservative nature of the group, combined with the tenacity with which they adhered to their particular theological standpoint,[48] resulted in the preservation of the contents of their Bible very much as it was from the beginning. Since the Samaritan community, of which a few

---

[42] For the continuing relations between Jews and Samaritans see J. A. Montgomery, *The Samaritans* (1907), pp. 71ff.; cf. M. H. Segal, *Asaf Anniversary Volume* (1953), p. 412.

[43] *AJ*, XI, 7, 2; XI, 8, 2ff. Cf. H. H. Rowley, *BJRL*, XXXVIII (1956), pp. 166ff.

[44] H. Willrich, *Juden und Greichen vor der makkabäischen Erhebung* (1895), p. 6; A. H. Sayce, *HDB*, IV, p. 391; F. Vigouroux, *Dictionnaire de la Bible* (1912), V, col. 1443; G. F. Moore, *Judaism*, I, p. 24; E. Sellin, *Geschichte des israelitisch-jüdischen Volkes* (1932), II, p. 169; M. Noth, *The History of Israel* (1960), p. 354.

[45] The view that there were two Sanballats was supported, among others, by H. Petermann in J. J. Herzog (ed.), *Real-encyclopädie für protestantische Theologie und Kirche* (1860), XIII, p. 366; W. F. Albright, *JBL*, XLI (1920), p. 122; M. Gaster, *The Samaritans: Their History, Doctrines and Literature* (1925), p. 30; C. C. Torrey, *The Second Isaiah* (1928), pp. 457f., *JBL*, XLVII (1928), pp. 380ff.; W. F. Lofthouse, *Israel after the Exile* (1928), pp. 33, 235f.

[46] Cf. L. E. Browne, *Ezekiel and Alexander* (1952), pp. 3, 22ff.

[47] Roberts, *The OT Text and Versions*, p. 188.

[48] Cf. J. Macdonald, *The Theology of the Samaritans* (1963), pp. 40ff.

families still survive in the neighborhood of Nablus, was neither large nor widely dispersed, the possibility of the incidence of textual corruptions and recensional divergences was always at a minimum. Thus, aside from deliberate alterations to the archetypal text, the Samaritan Pentateuch bears witness to one of the ancient text-forms of the Hebrew Pentateuch, which was current at least as early as the fifth century B.C., and which may possibly go back as far as the period of the undivided monarchy.

There is naturally considerable doubt about who was responsible for modifying the text of the Hebrew Pentateuch upon which the Samaritans drew for their belief that divine worship should be held on Mount Gerizim alone, since there are evidences that a similar tradition among the Hebrews themselves was subsequently expunged.[49] However, in other respects it is abundantly clear that the Samaritan scribes altered the text of the Pentateuch to suit their own historical and theological interests. In order to enhance the prestige of Mount Gerizim, they added a lengthy interpolation after the Decalogue in Exodus 20:17 and Deuteronomy 5:21, consisting in the main of material from Deuteronomy 11:29f. and 27:2-7, in which "Mount Gerizim" was substituted for "Mount Ebal." Disregarding geographical considerations the Samaritans changed the reference in Deuteronomy 11:30 from "over against Gilgal" to "over against Shechem." Dogmatic interests were responsible for the alteration of the familiar Deuteronomic phrase "the place which the Lord your God will choose" so that the verb read "has chosen," a device achieved by the omission of the initial consonant.[50] Other changes were orthographic and grammatical and did not affect the meaning of the words, such as the use of the *matres lectionis* and the elimination of some unusual constructions and anthropomorphisms.

The antiquity of the archetype appears evident from the confusion found in the oldest extant manuscript between the consonants ר and ד, and also between the letters מ and נ, a situation that would normally not have arisen in a post-exilic archaizing type of script. Confusion of this sort is much more likely to have occurred in the very early angular Sidonian characters, in the letter-forms of the Moabite Stone, or in the Siloam inscription from the time of Hezekiah. Word-dividers in the Samaritan Pentateuch were of a kind commonly employed in early Aramaic, Moabite, and Hebrew inscriptions, which points to an early date for the prototypal manuscript. The Samaritans evidently did not enunciate their gutturals. This may constitute a dialectical peculiarity indicating that their pronunciation dated from the time of Ahab and his successors in Israel, when the non-guttural Phoenician was popular in

[49] Cf. E. Meyer, *D'e Israeliten und ihre Nachbarstämme* (1906), pp. 543ff.; C. C. Torrey, *Ezra Studies* (1910), pp. 321ff.; G. M. Mackie, *HDB*, II, pp. 160f.
[50] *PIOT*, p. 102; E. König, *HDB*, V, p. 70.

the northern kingdom[51] as opposed to the Judaean dialect preserved in the Massoretic text. According to some estimates the fixation of the Samaritan Pentateuch in its ornate archaizing script took place in the first century B.C., [52] but Greenberg, among others, preferred a date in the fourth century B.C.[53] The style of the letters is akin to Palaeo-Hebrew script, and the extant manuscripts of the Samaritan Pentateuch show that this ancient version possessed a developed vocalization and an unusual form of paragraph division.[54]

Although there are some indications of a process of textual refinement, it seems reasonably clear that the Samaritans did not possess a body of professional scribes as such at any given period in antiquity. This fact is apparent from the nature of the variations, which are hardly compatible with serious textual study. According to the estimate of Kahle, the Samaritan Pentateuch differed from the Massoretic text in some 6,000 instances, and of these it agreed with the LXX as against the Massoretic text in 1,900 occurrences.[55] Whether the Samaritan Pentateuch has preserved a better reading than the Massoretic text in all cases is very doubtful, even though Kahle was of the opinion that the Samaritan version constituted the best-preserved text of the Hebrew Pentateuch.[56] Probably the most assured readings are those in which the Samaritan Pentateuch is supported by the LXX and by the Greek text underlying certain New Testament passages (Acts 7:4, 32; Heb. 9:3, 4).[57]

As has been noted above, many of the changes in the text of the Samaritan Pentateuch are either willful, accidental, or the product of a misunderstanding or ignorance of grammar and syntax. Of a rather different nature is the tradition concerning the chronology of the genealogies in Genesis, particularly chapters 5 and 11, where the Samaritan Pentateuch presents a record that is independent of both the Massoretic text and the LXX. It would seem that each one of these three texts represents a different recension of the original Hebrew, and at present there is no means of determining which one of the three is either original or correct. Josephus appeared to prefer the LXX chronology

[51] Cf. A. Sperber, *HUCA*, XII-XIII (1937-38), pp. 151f.

[52] *FSAC*, pp. 345f.; F. M. Cross, *The Ancient Library of Qumran and Modern Biblical Studies* (1961), p. 172.

[53] M. Greenberg, *JAOS*, LXXVI (1956), pp. 161ff. Cf. B. D. Eerdmans, *The Religion of Israel*, p. 236.

[54] Cf. E. Robertson, *Catalogue of the Samaritan Manuscripts in the John Rylands Library at Manchester* (1938), cols. xxi and following; cf. his *Notes and Extracts from the Semitic Manuscripts in the John Rylands Library, III. Samaritan Pentateuch Manuscripts* (1937).

[55] P. E. Kahle, *Theologische Studien und Kritiken*, LXXXVIII (1915), pp. 399ff.; cf. A. Sperber, *HUCA*, XIV (1939), pp. 161ff.

[56] P. E. Kahle in H. Bauer and P. Leander, *Historische Grammatik der Hebräischen Sprache*, p. 73.

[57] Cf. P. E. Kahle, *The Cairo Geniza*, pp. 144ff.

over that of the Massoretic text, while the Samaritan form was adopted by the *Book of Jubilees* and in Acts 7. The opinion that all three texts were in circulation among the Jews during the pre-Christian period has received support from the Qumran discoveries. Each one may have represented the tradition of some specific locality or scribal school. The vitality and persistence of the Samaritan version was emphasized by the recovery from the caves of the Wadi Qumran of a fragment of Exodus, in which the Samaritan text was written in Hebrew script.[58]

While the peculiar readings of the Samaritan Pentateuch can usually be accounted for by scholars, its agreements with the LXX against the Massoretic text are more difficult to explain. It seems quite probable that both the Samaritan Pentateuch and the LXX reached back to a Hebrew textual tradition that differed from that of the Massoretes in significant areas, since in those instances where the Samaritan Pentateuch and the LXX coincide, the text is usually preferable to that preserved by the Massoretes. A Greek translation of the Samaritan Pentateuch, known as the *Samaritikon*, was cited by Origen in his *Hexapla*, and it is now known that this translation was made from the Samaritan text by translators who were familiar with the text of the LXX and even employed it on occasions.[59] This material may perhaps constitute the source of some of the readings common to the Samaritan Pentateuch and the LXX, though in general it must be remarked, as Kenyon has observed,[60] that there is no satisfactory proof that either the LXX or the Samaritan Pentateuch was corrected from the other; thus, their independent evidence is extremely difficult to explain except, perhaps, on the basis of a Hebrew textual tradition or traditions other than that of the Massoretes. It may be that when corrections to the Hebrew and Samaritan Pentateuchs had to be made, an Aramaic targum was employed for the purpose,[61] due to the close similarity between the Samaritan dialect and the Aramaic language. But this suggestion too is beset with problems, for there are considerable internal differences between all known manuscripts of the Samaritan-Aramaic targum as well as divergent views regarding its origin.[62]

Quite aside from other considerations, there are numerous traces in the LXX of the influence of the Aramaic targums, making the problem of the agreements between the Samaritan Pentateuch and the LXX one of considerable complexity. It seems clear that, despite the antiquity of the archetype and the attempts of certain modern scholars to reinstate the

---

[58] Cf. P. W. Skehan, *JBL*, LXXIV (1955), pp. 182ff.; J. M. Allegro, *The Dead Sea Scrolls*, pp. 68f. and pl. 23.

[59] Roberts, *The OT Text and Versions*, pp. 194f.

[60] *Our Bible and the Ancient Manuscripts*, p. 51.

[61] Cf. L. Goldberg, *Das Samaritanische Pentateuchtargum, eine Untersuchung, seine handschriftlichen Quellen* (1935).

[62] Cf. P. E. Kahle, *The Cairo Geniza*, pp. 36ff.

Samaritan Pentateuch,[63] the text of this version must be employed with great care in any attempt to improve upon the readings of the Massoretic text.[64]

2. *Aramaic targums.* Another valuable source for the study of the Hebrew Old Testament is furnished by the Aramaic targums. "Targum" is a Hebrew word, not occurring in the Old Testament, used to describe an Aramaic paraphrase or interpretative rendering of some portion of the Old Testament. The targums became necessary in the post-exilic period, when Aramaic gradually replaced Hebrew in importance as the spoken language. With the increasing value placed upon Scripture, particularly the Torah, as the basis of faith and a guide to proper living, it became urgent that the ancient writings be rendered in a way that the common people could understand. Thus there grew up in the synagogues the custom of furnishing an oral Aramaic translation as a companion to the portion which had been read from the Torah. Written translations were frowned upon, however, as the Jerusalem Talmud indicates,[65] in an evident desire to avoid any ostensible parity between the original text and a rendering into the vernacular.

This practice of paraphrastic explanation may possibly date back to the time of Nehemiah, since the Hebrew word פֹרשׁ in Nehemiah 8:8, which is generally translated "clearly," more probably means "with interpretation," as the RSV footnote indicates. At all events, the custom was well established long before the birth of Jesus Christ. The official synagogue interpreter was known in the Jerusalem Talmud as *methurgeman*, and his paraphrase was designated *targum*, from the verb *targēm*,

---

[63] E.g. J. Bowman, *BJRL*, XXXIII (1951), pp. 211ff., XL (1958), pp. 298ff.; *Annual of Leeds University Oriental Society*, I (1959), pp. 43ff.; *PEQ*, XCI (1959), pp. 23ff.

[64] Enthusiasm greeted the first copy of the Samaritan Pentateuch that reached Europe in 1616 through Pietro della Valle, after its discovery in Damascus. Morinus' account of it (1623) claimed that it was in every way superior to the Massoretic text, and his opinion was quickly adopted by many scholars (cf. Kenyon, *Our Bible and the Ancient Manuscripts*, p. 50). The text was first printed in the *Paris Polyglot* (1632), after which it enjoyed considerable popularity, although dissident scholarly opinions were expressed with increasing frequency as to its value for textual criticism. In 1815 Gesenius (*De Pentateucho Samaritani origine, indole et auctoritate commentatio philologico critica*) demonstrated conclusively the superiority of the Massoretic text; subsequently the Samaritan Pentateuch began to decline in importance. Von Gall's five-volume critical edition of 1914-1918 (*Der Hebräische Pentateuch der Samaritaner*) was of limited value for scholarly purposes, as it drew upon only a comparatively small number of late medieval manuscripts. Earlier editions had been published by Walton in the *London Polyglot* (1675), Kennicott (*Vetus Testamentum Hebraicum cum variis lectionibus*, 2 vols., 1776-1780), and Blayney (*Pentateuchos Hebraeo-Samaritanus charactere Hebraeo-Chaldaico editus cura et studio Beniamini Blayney*, 1790). Some authorities have preferred Blayney's edition to that of Von Gall; cf. C. W. Dugmore, *JTS*, XXXVI (1935), pp. 131ff.

[65] *Megill.* IV, 1.

226

"to translate." While these renderings were oral, there are good grounds for holding that they soon acquired a degree of fixity, so that when they were ultimately committed to writing there was an adequate amount of traditional material available for the use of the Jewish scribes. Because the targums were originally oral, there is no single standard version, and this results in considerable divergences when targumic material is quoted by ancient authorities. It is thought probable that traces of early written targums can be seen to underlie the quotation from Psalm 22:2 in Matthew 27:46 and Mark 15:34,[66] as well as in one instance that occurs in Ephesians 4:8, corresponding to the targum of Psalm 68:19. The Babylonian Talmud mentions a targum to Job that was current in the days of Gamaliel I;[67] this is perhaps the same as that recovered from 11Q. Aside from this material from the first century after Christ, the earliest targums were probably committed to writing in the fifth century. At the present, targums exist for the Pentateuch, the Prophets, and part of the Writings, with the notable exceptions of Daniel, Ezra, and Nehemiah.

The most familiar of the three targums to the Pentateuch is the revised recension known as targum Onkelos, which is an Official Aramaic version of the Hebrew text. The identity of the author has been a matter of considerable discussion from early times,[68] with the Babylonian Talmud claiming him as a proselyte of the first century of our era,[69] whereas the Jerusalem Talmud confused him with Aquila,[70] the author of a Greek version of the Old Testament. Whatever his true identity, it seems probable that he produced his work about A.D. 145. This targum was conservative, adhering closely to the original Hebrew. Perhaps it was because of this very tendency that it acquired an authoritative position among contemporary Jews. The oldest targum to the Pentateuch is the so-called Palestinian Pentateuch targum, written in the kind of idiomatic Aramaic that was used in Palestine as early as the first century of the Christian era. It was formerly known only through fragments, but within recent years it has been identified in its entirety in a Vatican manuscript, Codex Neofiti I, an edition of which is in preparation at the time of writing.[71]

The official targum to the Prophets bore the name of Jonathan ben Uzziel, who, according to Jewish tradition, was a disciple of Hillel in the first century of the Christian era. Just as Onkelos furnished an official recension for the Pentateuch, Jonathan endeavored to produce a stand-

---

[66] Cf. A. Wikgren, *Journal of Religion*, XXIV (1944), pp. 89ff.

[67] *Shabb.* 115a.

[68] Cf. E. Silverstone, *Aquila and Onkelos* (1931), pp. 122ff.; Kahle, *The Cairo Geniza*, p. 117.

[69] *Megill.* III, 1.

[70] *Megill.* I, 11.

[71] Cf. A. D. Macho, *Estudios bíblicos*, XV (1956), pp. 446f.

ard form for the Prophets. He was more interpretative than Onkelos, however, although he was stricter in his rendering of the historical books of Joshua, Judges, Samuel, and Kings than of the Latter Prophets. Of some interest is the theological tendency to interpret certain passages messianically, particularly Isaiah 53.[72] One of the early Palestinian or "Jerusalem" targums to the Pentateuch was erroneously attributed during the fourteenth century to the activities of Jonathan, and is still frequently referred to as "pseudo-Jonathan." It was a rather fanciful composition which utilized the incidents contained in the original text as a vehicle for the folk legends which had grown up around the personages and circumstances of the narratives.

It is quite likely that, of the extant targums on the Hagiographa, none is older than the fifth century of the Christian era, and many of them are considerably later. Most probably they were originally composed for purposes other than public use in the synagogues or schools, since there was by that time no particular need for Aramaic translations.

Although the targums are useful both for the light which they shed upon traditional Jewish interpretations and the manner in which such activities were undertaken, they are of limited value for the textual critic because of their uncertain witness to the general Massoretic tradition. Unless the divergences of the targums are confirmed by readings from other versions it is frequently the case that they merely reflect targumic characteristics, and do not in fact testify to the presence of corruptions in the Hebrew text. Furthermore, there is no critical edition of the targums available,[73] a deficiency that constitutes a serious obstacle to textual study.

3. *The versions.* Since the Massoretic text cannot be regarded as the original form of the Hebrew, it is necessary to appeal to other sources in addition to the Hebrew variants in order to ascertain if possible what the original Hebrew text really read at disputed points. Valuable assistance in this direction is provided by versions, or translations from the Hebrew into another language. These are of great importance in any attempt to assess the nature of the Hebrew text, since they were often based upon traditions that were somewhat different from, and frequently more primitive than, the one preserved by the Massoretes.

a. *The Septuagint.* By far the most important version of the Old Testament is the LXX or Alexandrian Version, since it was associated by tradition with the activities of the Jewish community at Alexandria in Egypt. The origin of the name "Septuagint" (in full, "Interpretation of the Seventy Men [or Elders]") is unknown. Originally it applied only to the Pentateuch as rendered into Greek. A legendary explanation is found

---

[72] Cf. C. R. North, *The Suffering Servant in Deutero-Isaiah*, p. 11.
[73] For available editions see B. J. Roberts, *The OT Text and Versions*, pp. 212f.

in a letter written about 100 B.C., purporting to be from a certain Aristeas to his brother Philocrates during the reign of Ptolemy II Philadelphus (285-247 B.C.).[74] This document related how the monarch, having been persuaded by his librarian to secure a translation of the Hebrew prophecies for the royal library, appealed to the High Priest at Jerusalem, who responded by sending seventy-two elders to Alexandria with an official copy of the Law. Over a period of seventy-two days these men made a complete translation of the Torah, working independently during the day and comparing their results in the evening so as to arrive at a rendering that would be satisfactory to all concerned. This translation was then read to the Jewish community amid scenes of great enthusiasm, and was subsequently presented to the king. This story was embellished both by Jewish and Christian writers to the point where, in the fourth century, it was firmly believed that the translation comprised the entire Hebrew Bible, and that each scribe, working independently, had produced a rendering which was identical with those of his collaborators.[75] A fragment from the writings of an Alexandrian Jewish philosopher named Aristobulus, whose work is generally attributed to the period 170-150 B.C., was preserved by Eusebius and Clement of Alexandria, and dealt with the supposed origins of the LXX.[76] According to Aristobulus, portions of the Hebrew Scriptures relating to Israelite history had been translated into Greek at an earlier period, but by contrast the entire Torah was rendered into Greek in the reign of Ptolemy II Philadelphus through the efforts of Demetrius of Phalerum. Less plausibly, he claimed that Homer, Hesiod, Pythagoras, Socrates, and Plato were familiar with portions of the Pentateuch.

The most that can be said assuredly about these traditions is that about 250 B.C. the Torah was translated into Greek at Alexandria, either as a means of impressing and converting the heathen,[77] or of supplying the expatriate Jews in Alexandria with a Scriptural version in the vernacular[78] for purposes of worship or private study. This constituted the original LXX; the remainder was translated in piecemeal fashion. The canonical books had been rendered into Greek a little before 117 B.C., for they are referred to by the grandson of Ben Sira in the Prologue to Ecclesiasticus. The Apocrypha was completed at the beginning of the Christian era and interspersed among the canonical books. Finally the name "Septuagint" was extended to cover the entire corpus of translated material. This name, derived from the Latin *septuaginta*, meaning "sev-

---

[74] *APOT*, II, pp. 83ff.

[75] H. B. Swete, *An Introduction to the OT in Greek* (1900), pp. 13f.

[76] Eusebius, *Praep. Evang.* XIII, 12; Clement, *Strom.* I, 22, 148.

[77] Philo, *Vita Mosis*, II, 5f.; cf. J. Juster, *Les Juifs dans l'empire romain* (1914), I, p. 253.

[78] So F. Buhl, *Kanon und Text des AT* (1891), pp. 114f.; H. B. Swete, *An Introduction to the OT in Greek*, p. 19.

enty," hardly coincides with the tradition of seventy-two translators preserved in the *Letter of Aristeas,* and it may be that the term either arose or gained currency because of some popular association with the "seventy elders" of Exodus 24:1 and 9, with the seventy members of the Sanhedrin, or with the seventy apostles mentioned in the ministry of Christ (Lk. 10:1).[79]

While the evidence from Qumran[80] makes it obvious that the LXX had a long and involved prehistory, it seems unlikely that underlying the LXX there was a rendering of the Hebrew into Greek letters, as Wutz proposed.[81] Undoubtedly there were in existence transliterations of the Hebrew text into the Greek alphabet, analogous to the Samaritan Pentateuch, as an initial step towards helping Hellenistic Jews who could not follow the Hebrew script to understand the portions that were read aloud in the synagogues.[82] While the LXX does in fact employ Greek transliterations on occasions, particularly in the case of names, it is improbable that the LXX utilized such transcriptions to any significant extent. Thackeray suggested that the earliest portion of the Old Testament to be translated into Greek was the Torah, and that this was followed by Isaiah, parts of Samuel and Kings, the remainder of the Prophets, and finally by the Writings.[83] The balance of Samuel and Kings was thought to have been added by a later translator from Ephesus, whose Greek style resembled that of Theodotion.

Questions concerning the existence and nature of a "proto-LXX" have been raised by the fact that quotations from Greek sources in the New Testament writings and in the work of Josephus and Philo do not correspond verbally with the present LXX text.[84] This circumstance has been taken as implying that there were a number of early Greek texts in existence prior to the work of the LXX translators. Accordingly Kahle suggested that the *Letter of Aristeas* referred, not to a new translation, but to a revision of certain renderings already in existence in order to produce a standard Greek Bible for the benefit of Jews in the Hellenistic Diaspora.[85] Kahle styled this collection of renderings a "Greek targum," and pointed out the diversity of readings which it embraced. For him

[79] Cf. H. M. Orlinsky, *The Septuagint: The Oldest Translation of the Bible* (1949), p. 4.

[80] Cf. F. M. Cross, *BASOR,* No. 132 (1953), pp. 15ff., No. 141 (1956), pp. 9ff.; *IB,* XII (1957), pp. 655ff.

[81] Cf. F. X. Wutz, *ZAW,* XLIII (1925), pp. 115ff., *Die Psalmen textkritisch untersucht* (1925), *Die Transkriptionen von der Septuaginta bis zu Hieronymus* (1933), and *Systematische Wege von der LXX zum Hebräischen Urtext* (1937).

[82] H. M. Orlinsky, *JQR,* XXVII (1936-37), p. 140 n. 10.

[83] H. St. John Thackeray, *ISBE,* IV, pp. 2722ff. and *The Septuagint and Jewish Worship* (1921).

[84] For a survey of the problem see H. H. Rowley, *JQR,* XXXIII (1943-44), p. 497.

[85] Cf. Kahle, *The Cairo Geniza,* pp. 132ff.

230

the LXX as used by the Christian Church was not necessarily the one mentioned in the *Letter of Aristeas*, but was more probably one of the current translations into Greek, which the Christian Church ultimately adopted as its canonical Greek version of the Hebrew Old Testament. By this time the term "Septuagint" had been expanded to include the entire Old Testament and Apocrypha, whereas for Aristeas it had merely signified the Pentateuch. This view was developed by Sperber, who postulated the existence of a transitional period when Greek was used both for transcription and translation purposes to help the Hellenistic Jews of Egypt to read the Hebrew Scriptures.[86] This situation gave rise to sporadic attempts at translation, leading to the existence of at least two Greek renderings of the Old Testament which can be identified from quotations in the New Testament, whose writers regularly employed Greek versions instead of the Hebrew for their citations.

Although these theories may well throw important light upon the transmission of the text they are extremely difficult to demonstrate with facts, as Orlinsky has pointed out,[87] particularly where the postulate of at least two original and independent Greek renderings of the Hebrew Bible is concerned. Such arguments are rendered even less valid if, as some New Testament scholars suggest, it can be shown that many of the quotations in New Testament writings were derived originally from an Aramaic source or sources, or perhaps even from oral traditions, from memory, or from private translations. Again it should be observed that, while there are a few significant disagreements between manuscripts of the LXX, there are very many more agreements of such a character to indicate beyond reasonable doubt that the various manuscripts belong to the same family. Furthermore, the kind of variant to which Kahle appeals can more probably be accounted for as revisions of a basic LXX text than as remnants of rival translations or back-readings from New Testament authors.

It should be remembered, of course, that there is no definite proof that the early Christian Church ever regarded any particular Greek Old Testament text as standard,[88] and that, as the evidence from Qumran indicates, there was a good deal of freedom in the use of textual types during the immediate pre-Christian period. Yet in the days prior to Origen there was in existence a form of text which constitutes the LXX version, as made evident by the Chester Beatty papyri and the Scheide papyri.[89] While there are certain differences in New Testament usage, there is no doubt that of all the Greek versions the LXX was employed

---

[86] A. Sperber, *Orientalische Literaturzeitung*, XXXII (1929), cols. 533ff. and in *JBL*, LIX (1940), pp. 193ff.

[87] H. M. Orlinsky, *JBL*, LIX (1940), pp. 530f.

[88] B. J. Roberts, *IDB*, IV, p. 590; D. W. Gooding, *NBD*, pp. 1259f.

[89] Cf. Roberts, *The OT Text and Versions*, pp. 148f.

predominantly and that it enjoyed independent existence in the period just prior to the time of Christ.

The language of the LXX is by no means the normal Hellenistic Greek as represented by the papyri of Egypt and other sources, any more than is its counterpart in the New Testament. Even the most idiomatic renderings reflect certain obvious Hebraisms, and there are a great many passages which are little better than transliterations of the Hebrew. In numerous respects the Greek rendering of the Pentateuch is superior to the remainder of the work, and this may well indicate the degree of esteem in which the Pentateuch was held by the translators. Although the finished form of the Pentateuch exhibits a great many variations from the original, with some omissions and displacements in Exodus and Numbers, the parent LXX text corresponds largely to the Massoretic Hebrew. However, the divergence of the LXX text in some of the historical books, notably Samuel, as indicated by the fragments from Qumran,[90] points to the existence of a Hebrew text-type or types different from that of the Massoretes. This departure may have been encouraged by the fact that, outside the Pentateuch, some books appear to have been divided between two or more translators who were working simultaneously. Other books were translated at different times by persons who employed divergent methods and vocabulary; as a result, there is reasonably good *Koine* Greek in sections of Isaiah, Joshua, and 1 Maccabees, moderate Greek in Chronicles, the Psalter, Jeremiah, Ezekiel, the Minor Prophets, and parts of Kings, and very literalistic Greek in Judges, Ruth, the Song of Solomon, and some other sections of Kings. On occasions the translators showed no scruples about interpreting the text to make it conform to their own theological predilections, as with Judges 9:9, where the translation was altered in LXX Codex Vaticanus to enable men to "glorify God."

Wholesale adjustments are found in Jeremiah, where the LXX text was only about seven-eighths as long as that of the Hebrew, and in Job, where the LXX text was augmented from the version of Theodotion to correspond roughly to the length of the Hebrew. The text of Esther appears in two forms in the Greek Bible, one of which is the ordinary LXX and the other the recension of Lucian. Both of these contain interpolations which have no parallels in the Hebrew. The LXX translation of Daniel was so free that it was replaced about the first century of our era with a translation that is generally attributed to Theodotion, although it may well antedate him. The problem of the relationship between the LXX and the Hebrew text of Ezra, Nehemiah, and Chronicles is complicated by the presence of the apocryphal books of 1 and 2 Esdras. From these brief remarks it will be evident that the LXX as

---

[90] F. M. Cross, *BASOR*, No. 132 (1953), pp. 15ff.

a whole is of decidedly uneven quality, and although there are many instances in which it may well point to a more primitive reading than that contained in the Massoretic text, its use requires considerably more caution than might be apparent from the views of certain enthusiastic advocates of the LXX.

b. Other Greek versions. During the second century after Christ a few non-LXX Greek revisions of the Old Testament were undertaken in an attempt to reflect the contemporary Hebrew text. The first of these was Aquila's, produced about A.D. 130. It adhered firmly to the Massoretic tradition, and rejected in particular the witness of the LXX. Its author was a Hellenist who had become a convert to Judaism. His work was widely quoted by the patristic writers and also by some rabbinic authorities. Extant citations of his version were published from 1859,[91] augmented from palimpsests recovered from the *genizah* of the Old Synagogue in Cairo.[92] Owing to its extreme literalness and fidelity to the Massoretic text, this version met the need of the Greek-speaking Jews for a new Greek rendering of their Scriptures. Aquila translated the Hebrew with almost mechanical accuracy, and this procedure led to a version which was far removed from the Greek idiom. He was violently anti-Christian, and did not hesitate to render certain messianic passages in a manner widely different from that in the LXX, the treasured version of the Christian Church. In spite of this tendency, however, his fidelity to the Hebrew text won for his work the respect of such patristic authorities as Origen and Jerome. As may well be imagined, the translation was marked by many peculiarities, not least of which was the consistent imposition of Hebrew grammatical and syntactical structures upon the Greek. According to Reider, while Aquila followed the Massoretic text closely, he diverged from it on an average of once in three verses.[93] The identification of Aquila (who is not to be confused with the Aquila of Acts 18:2 *et al.*) with Onkelos (see above p. 227) is supported in part by marked resemblances between their translations.

Half a century later another rendering of the Old Testament in Greek was produced by a contemporary of Aquila named Theodotion, a proselyte who hailed from Asia Minor.[94] He used for his version a Hebrew text that was considerably closer to the Massoretic text than was the parent of the LXX, and as a result the book of Job exceeded the LXX rendering

---

[91] F. Field, *Origenis Hexaplorum quae supersunt; sive Veterum Interpretetum Graecorum in totum Veterum Testamentum Fragmenta* (2 vols., 1867-74).

[92] F. C. Burkitt, *Fragments of the Books of Kings According to the Translation of Aquila* (1897); C. F. Taylor, *Hebrew-Greek Cairo Genizah Palimpsests from the Taylor—Schechter Collections* (1901); cf. Kahle, *The Cairo Geniza*, p. 13.

[93] Cf. J. Reider, *JQR*, IV (1912-13), pp. 321ff., 577ff., VII (1915-16), pp. 287ff.

[94] For the priority of Theodotion over Aquila see H. M. Orlinsky, *JQR*, XXVI (1935-36), p. 143 n. 14.

by about one-sixth. His translation was more idiomatic than Aquila's, and was esteemed more highly by the Christians than by the Jews of that period. Theodotion's version of Daniel actually came to replace the old LXX rendering of that prophecy, a circumstance that is usually attributed to the influence of Origen.

A third Greek version dating from the end of the second century or the beginning of the third century A.D. was that made by Symmachus, who according to Christian tradition was a Jewish convert to Ebionite teaching. Fragments of this translation have survived in portions of the *Hexapla* and in the writings of patristic and rabbinic authors. Apparently the author made use of earlier Greek versions, but on the whole he exhibited a decided preference for the work of Aquila. He followed rabbinic exegetical customs in attempting to remove many of the Old Testament anthropomorphic expressions, and the result of his labors was an independent translation of the Old Testament into decidedly better Greek than that of either Aquila or Theodotion.

Manuscript discoveries in the Wadi Murabba'at caves have brought these versions into prominence again within recent years. Of particular interest was the recovery of a leather scroll in Greek containing fragments of the minor prophets Jonah, Micah, Nahum, Habakkuk, Zephaniah, and Zechariah.[95] Barthélemy dated the manuscript from the end of the first century after Christ, and found that it constituted a revision of the LXX from the pre-Christian era and was similar to that which formed the basis of the renderings by Aquila, Theodotion, and Symmachus. This scroll would thus indicate that in the second century of the Christian era there was current among both Christians and Jews a common textual form acceptable to both parties, which was itself a revision of the earlier LXX translation.[96]

Prior to the work of Origen, several Greek versions existed side by side, some of which are known only from fragments of the *Hexapla*.[97] This great work was compiled by Origen in an attempt to bring some sort of order to the rather chaotic textual situation of his day. His revision of the Greek Old Testament, which was completed by about A.D. 245, contained six parallel columns representing respectively the Massoretic text, the Hebrew text transliterated into Greek letters, the version of Aquila, the translation of Symmachus, his own revision of the LXX, and the translation of Theodotion. For the Psalter he also furnished the versions which he named *Quinta, Sexta,* and *Septima,* the first two of

[95] Cf. D. Barthélemy, *RB*, LX (1953), pp. 18ff., 85f.; P. E. Kahle, *Theologische Literaturzeitung*, LXXIX (1954), cols. 82ff.; J. M. Allegro, *The Dead Sea Scrolls*, pp. 178f. For a detailed refutation of the views of Kahle see Barthélemy, *Les Devanciers d'Aquila, VT* suppl. X (1963).

[96] B. J. Roberts, *IDB*, IV, p. 583.

[97] Cf. B. J. Roberts, *The OT Text and Versions*, p. 127.

which, according to Kahle,[98] he had discovered in Jewish *genizahs*. Taking the current Hebrew text as his basis, he proceeded with his revision by choosing from all the available Greek manuscripts those readings which accorded most closely with the Hebrew. Where his text was deficient in relationship to the Hebrew he inserted appropriate sections derived mainly from the version of Theodotion, and marked by critical signs. Those portions of his text containing readings that were absent from the Hebrew were retained, but were marked by means of other critical signs employed according to the usage of Aristarchus (third century B.C.). Finally, those passages in the Greek Bible that did not follow the order of the Hebrew[99] were rearranged so as to accord with the Massoretic pattern, and, incidentally, the corresponding columns of Aquila and Symmachus.

It is probable that the last four columns of the *Hexapla* were subsequently issued independently in a form known as the *Tetrapla*.[100] Since it lacked the Hebrew sections, it was a more manageable work. Against the view of Orlinsky that the *Tetrapla* was not a separate four-column work but only a variant designation of the *Hexapla*,[101] it should be noted that the text of the *Tetrapla* contained emended errors of translation and corrections of textual corruptions in the LXX,[102] which would indicate that it was a later work with, ostensibly, a separate existence.

By any standards the *Hexapla* was a monumental accomplishment. The original manuscripts, which were seldom copied owing to their size, were kept for safety in Caesarea, and were probably destroyed when that city was overrun by the Arabs in A.D. 638. The fifth column of the *Hexapla*—the LXX—was copied the most frequently of any, for it was highly esteemed from the beginning of the fourth century and given wide circulation in Palestine through Eusebius and Pamphilius.[103] Al-

---

[98] *The Cairo Geniza*, p. 164; cf. H. M. Orlinsky, *JQR*, XXVII (1936-37), pp. 137ff.

[99] E.g. Exod. 35-40; 1 Kgs. 4-11, 20-21; Jer. 25-50.

[100] Cf. Eusebius, *Hist. Eccl.*, VI, 16; *PIOT*, p. 109.

[101] *BA*, IX, No. 1 (1946), p. 27 n. 10.

[102] Cf. O. Procksch, *ZAW*, LIII (1935), pp. 240ff., LIV (1936), pp. 61ff.; O. Pretzl, *Byzantinische Zeitschrift*, XXX (1930), pp. 262ff.

[103] The Hexaplaric text of Genesis 31 to Judges 21, marked with the Aristarchean critical signs, was contained in the fourth/fifth-century Codex Colberto-Sarrauianus, parts of which are in Leningrad, Paris, and Leyden. Hexaplaric readings were also recorded as notes in the margins of Codex Marchalianus (sixth century) and Codex Coislinianus (seventh century) and in several cursives of the medieval period. Hexaplaric fragments were incorporated into the Sixtine edition of the Greek Bible by Petrus Morinus; see J. Reider, *JQR*, V (1913-14), p. 330. The same material was published by Drusius in 1622 and Lambertus Bos in 1709. A more comprehensive collection was made by de Montfaucon in *Origenis Hexaplorum quae supersunt, multis partibus auctiora quam a Flaminio Nobilio et Joanne Drusio edita fuerint* (vol. II, 1713); this was superseded by Field's *Origenis Hexaplorum quae supersunt; sive Veterum Interpretetum Graecorum in totum Veterum Tesamentum*

though Origen's recension of the LXX constituted a landmark in textual study, it did not dispossess other forms of the LXX text. In Syria and Asia Minor a recension prepared by the Antiochene presbyter Lucian of Samosata (d. A.D. 312) enjoyed great esteem for a considerable time. Lucian appears to have revised the Hexaplaric text at least in part by combining variants into conflated readings, substituting synonyms for certain LXX words, and imposing a more polished literary style on the LXX. While the resultant text of the Prophets was of generally poor quality, that of the historical books is of particular value, being frequently based upon a Hebrew text superior to the one preserved by the Massoretes. Paul de Lagarde edited what he believed to be something approximating to the Lucianic text of the LXX, and regarded his work as constituting a step further back into the involved history of the LXX.[104] However, he appears to have overlooked the possibility that Lucian may actually have possessed a type of text containing better Hebrew readings, or that he may have arrived at his renderings with the aid of an earlier non-LXX form of translation. Thus the Lucianic version may possibly be another Greek rendering of a variant Hebrew original, at least in part, and not a strict revision of the Alexandrian text as such.[105]

In Egypt a third recension was in common use, prepared by Hesychius of Alexandria (d. A.D. 311).[106] Although this revision is mentioned by Jerome in the *Prologus Galeatus,* little is known either about the reviser or the procedure upon which his work was based. Contrary to most scholars, Kahle and Sperber held that the texts of Lucian and Hesychius were not revisions of the LXX, but instead constituted independent translations.[107] Sperber also maintained that as late as the time of Origen there were two different translations of the Old Testament into Greek that were circulating separately and were known as "Septuaginta."[108] However, since the principal materials available for the reconstruction of the Lucian and Hesychian recensions are to be found mainly in

---

Fragmenta (2 vols., 1867-74), which, although restricted to poor copies and collations of manuscripts, was a work of great importance. The only remnants of a transmission of the *Hexapla* in manuscript form are the "Mercati fragments," which were discovered by Cardinal Mercati in Milan at the end of the nineteenth century in a palimpsest manuscript. It contained portions of the Psalter from the last five columns of the *Hexapla*. A representative portion of Psalm 45 (LXX) was published by Klostermann in 1896 (*ZAW*, XVI, pp. 334ff.; cf. Kahle, *The Cairo Geniza,* p. 88).

[104] P. de Lagarde, *Librorum Veteris Testamenti canonicorum pars prior graece edita* (1883).

[105] Cf. G. F. Moore, *AJSL*, XXIX (1913), pp. 37ff.

[106] Cf. Eusebius, *Hist. Eccl.,* VIII, 13; A. Sperber, *JBL,* LIV (1935), pp. 73ff.

[107] Kahle, *Theologische Studien und Kritiken,* LXXXVIII (1915), pp. 410ff. Sperber, *JBL,* LIV (1935), pp. 75ff.

[108] *JBL,* LIX (1940), p. 279.

patristic citations, there would seem to be inadequate manuscript evidence for making too forthright a claim for these versions as independent renderings of the LXX.

Attempts at a critical reconstruction of the LXX, insofar as this is possible, are based upon manuscripts of the Greek Bible. A major classification of such material was begun by Rahlfs,[109] which was superior to its precursors, although it was not absolutely exhaustive. The earliest manuscript material is fragmentary, and consists of scraps of papyrus dated between the second and fourth centuries after Christ. One of the oldest extant LXX manuscript fragments is the Rylands papyrus, discovered in 1917 and published in 1936 as *John Rylands Library Papyrus Greek 458*.[110] It contained Deuteronomy 23:24–24:3; 25:1-3; 26:12, 17-19; 28:31-33, and was written in a fine book-hand of the second century B.C.[111] This text preceded the revisions of Aquila, Symmachus, and Theodotion by some three centuries, and the later recensions by five centuries. It is thus an extremely important witness to the nature of the early LXX text. Other valuable papyrological material includes the Chester Beatty papyri,[112] the Freer Greek manuscript at Washington, and the Berlin Genesis.[113] Of the great uncial manuscripts containing both the Old and New Testaments the most important is the fourth-century Codex Vaticanus, to which portions of the Scheide Biblical papyri are related textually.[114] Although it is by far the best extant copy of the LXX and constitutes the basic text of the editions of the Greek Bible currently in use, a study of the manuscript makes it clear that there is a striking lack of uniformity in the quality of the text itself. For Judges it furnished an Egyptian version made early in the fourth century,[115] while for Daniel, Ezra, Nehemiah, and Chronicles it followed the translation of Theodotion.[116] Though the text of Codex Vaticanus does not belong properly to the Hexaplaric recension, there are numerous instances in which it has obviously been corrected from it.[117] Another

[109] *Verzeichnis der griechischen Handschriften des Alten Testaments für das Septuaginta-Unternehmen aufgestellt* (1914).

[110] C. H. Roberts, *Two Biblical Papyri in the John Rylands Library, Manchester* (1936).

[111] F. G. Kenyon, *The Text of the Greek Bible* (1949 ed.), pp. 41f.

[112] F. G. Kenyon, *The Chester Beatty Biblical Papyri* (1933-7), fasc. i-vii, *Our Bible and the Ancient Manuscripts*, pp. 64ff.; A. C. Johnson, H. S. Gehmann, and E. H. Kase, *The John H. Scheide Biblical Papyri* (1938).

[113] H. A. Sanders and C. Schmidt, *The Minor Prophets in the Freer Collection and the Berlin Fragment of Genesis* (1927); H. A. Sanders, *Facsimile of the Washington Manuscript of the Minor Prophets in the Freer Collection* (1927).

[114] Cf. H. S. Gehmann, *JAOS*, LVIII (1938), pp. 92ff.; J. Ziegler, *ZAW*, LX (1945-8), pp. 76ff.

[115] G. F. Moore, *A Critical and Exegetical Commentary on the Book of Judges* (1903), p. xlv.

[116] C. C. Torrey, *Ezra Studies*, pp. 66ff.

[117] F. C. Burkitt, *JTS*, X (1909), p. 445.

important uncial from the fourth century is Codex Sinaiticus, discovered in 1844 by Tischendorf and ultimately purchased in 1933 from Russia by the British government.[118] Much of the Old Testament is missing from this manuscript, and according to Noth it may never have existed in a complete form.[119] Fragments of the Pentateuch are followed by portions of Chronicles, Ezra, Nehemiah, and several of the prophetical works. In general the text of Codex Sinaiticus is similar to that of Vaticanus, to which it is not greatly inferior.

A more complete uncial is that known as Codex Alexandrinus, an early fifth-century manuscript preserved in the British Museum. This uncial has far fewer gaps than Codex Sinaiticus, omitting in the main portions of Genesis, 1 Samuel, and the Psalter.[120] It exhibits an independent type of text that was revised according to the *Hexapla*, although there are some scholars who maintain that it represents a distinct translation of the LXX and not just a corrected form.[121] Another great uncial, the palimpsest known as Codex Ephraemi Rescriptus, now in Paris, was probably originally written in the fifth century, but only parts of the Old Testament have survived, amounting in all to some sixty-four leaves. Other uncial and minuscule codices contain only limited sections of Old Testament material.[122]

c. Latin versions. In any attempt to establish the text of the LXX it is important to utilize a number of other ancient versions from the early

[118] *The Mount Sinai Manuscript of the Bible* (1934). British Museum.

[119] *Die Welt des AT* (1940), p. 216.

[120] F. G. Kenyon, *The Text of the Greek Bible*, pp. 49, 82.

[121] Cf. A. Allgeier, *Die Chester Beatty Papyri zum Pentateuch* (1938), p. 35.

[122] For a history of the printed texts of the Greek Bible see H. B. Swete, *An Introduction to the OT in Greek*, pp. 171ff. Among these texts are the Complutensian Polyglot (1514-1517); the Aldine edition (1518-1519), based on manuscripts in Venice; the Sixtine edition (1587), based on Codex Vaticanus. This was reproduced substantially in the Walton *London Polyglot* (1654-1657), the *Vetus Testamentum Graecum Cum Variis Lectionibus* (ed. R. Holmes and J. Parsons, 5 vols., 1798-1827), the editions by Tischendorf from 1850 on, and in several others. J. E. Grabe published an edition of Codex Alexandrinus in Oxford between 1707 and 1720. Paul de Lagarde undertook a new edition of the LXX (1882), but this so-called "Göttingen Septuagint" was actually an attempt to restore the recension of Lucian in its original form. After Lagarde's death (1891), his work was carried on, with important modifications, by Rahlfs and his school at Göttingen. Seven volumes of this planned sixteen-volume work have appeared since 1926. Rahlfs' edition is based on that of Holmes and Parsons and the *Larger Cambridge Septuagint* (ed. A. E. Brooke, N. McLean, H. St. J. Thackeray, 1906ff.), both of which follow Codex Vaticanus, as did H. B. Swete's three-volume edition published between 1887 and 1907. Distinct from this project is Rahlfs' *Septuaginta* (2 vols., 1935), a convenient edition of the LXX whose value is somewhat limited by the eclectic nature of the text, which was based primarily upon Codices Vaticanus, Sinaiticus, and Alexandrinus, with selections from other sources provided in a small critical apparatus.

Christian period, which were translated from the Greek into a variety of European and Oriental languages in order to meet the needs of the inhabitants of countries where Greek was not spoken. One of the most prominent of these versions is the Old Latin, which originated with the work of Pope Victor (*ca.* A.D. 190), and was soon firmly established in North Africa with the writings of Tertullian (A.D. 160-230) at Carthage. In this region Latin supplanted Greek as the language of the Christian Church, as it did also in the northern provinces of Italy.[123] Presumably the first Latin translations of the LXX came into existence in the second half of the second century, although nothing is known about their origins. There are citations from these early Latin renderings in Tertullian and Cyprian (d. A.D. 258), although these differ in important areas. However, the first Latin translations of the LXX are of great significance because they go back to the text as it existed prior to the revisions of the third and fourth centuries, and therefore furnish valuable evidence for the reconstruction of the LXX text. Latin interpreters of the Greek were not wanting either in second-century southern Gaul or third-century Rome, and their activities led Augustine to complain about the "*infinita varietas*" of Latin translations and variant readings.[124]

The Old Latin or "Itala"[125] version of the Old Testament was probably made in Africa, and fragments of this material, recovered principally from patristic citations, were collected and published by Sabatier.[126] The Lyons manuscript of the Pentateuch was published in three volumes in 1881.[127] The presence of an Old Latin recension in Lyons indicates that there was a European Old Latin family as well as an African one, though whether the former was an independent version or merely a revision of the latter is unknown. The European Old Latin furnished a more polished rendering than its African counterpart and had apparently been revised with reference to the LXX text. The most significant section of the Old Latin is the Psalter, which was commonly employed in ecclesiastical liturgies.

The vocabulary of the Old Heptateuch was studied by Billen;[128] fragments of the Pentateuch at Munich were edited by Ziegler.[129] A sixth-century palimpsest at Würzburg containing fragments of the Pen-

---

[123] H. F. D. Sparks in H. Wheeler Robinson (ed.), *The Bible in its Ancient and English Versions*, p. 101.

[124] *De Doct. Christ.* II, 11.

[125] Cf. F. C. Burkitt, *The Old Latin and the Itala* (1896), p. 5 and *JTS*, XI (1910), pp. 260ff.

[126] P. Sabatier, *Bibliorum Sacrorum Latinae versiones antiquae, seu Vetus Italica et caeterae* (3 vols., 1739-49).

[127] U. Robert, *Pentateuchi versio latina antiquissima e codice Lugdunensi* (1881); cf. H. A. A. Kennedy, *HDB*, III, pp. 47ff.

[128] A. V. Billen, *The Old Latin Texts of the Heptateuch* (1927).

[129] L. Ziegler, *Bruchstücke einer vorhieronymianischen Übersetzung des Pentateuch* (1883).

tateuch and some passages from the Prophets was published by Ranke in 1871.[130] The task of making a comprehensive collection of Old Latin texts was begun by Fischer in 1949,[131] who based his collection principally upon the work of Denk. While there are many instances in which the Old Latin furnishes a source for the pre-Origen LXX, it is generally conceded to be of only limited value in the criticism of the Massoretic text.

The Vulgate, a revision of the Old Latin undertaken by Jerome at the behest of Pope Damasus in A.D. 383, was an attempt to remedy the chaotic textual situation that had arisen from the manifold contemporary interpretations of the LXX.[132] Jerome commenced his work with a revision of the Old Latin Psalter, which on completion in A.D. 383 was incorporated forthwith into the Roman liturgy by Pope Damasus.[133] A second edition based upon the *Hexapla* became known as the *Psalterium Gallicanum*, because it was first adopted in Gaul. Jerome then revised the remainder of the Old Testament books, but apart from the Psalter and a recension of Job only fragments of Proverbs, Ecclesiastes, and Canticles have survived. The remaining books apparently disappeared before they were published.

The translation was far from uniform, and although Jerome adhered to the Hebrew he frequently followed the LXX, Aquila, Symmachus, and Theodotion, particularly where the original presented doctrinal difficulties for Christians.[134] Despite these efforts his translations from the Hebrew were declared heretical by Rufinus (d. A.D. 410), and their necessity questioned by Augustine (d. A.D. 430). Even when his work received the sanction of Gregory the Great (d. A.D. 604), the text was treated with a noticeable lack of care, so that it required successive revisions during the medieval period.[135] It is apparent that even greater caution is required when the Vulgate is employed for purposes of textual criticism than is the case for many other ancient versions.

d. Syriac versions. After the LXX, the oldest and most important rendering of the Hebrew Scriptures into other languages is the Syriac version. This translation, used by the Syriac Church, has been described since the ninth century by the term *Peshitta* or "simple." It must not be confused with the Syro-Hexaplaric version. Like the LXX it was the

---

[130] E. Ranke, *Par palimpsestorum Wirceburgensium Antiquissimae Veteris Testamenti Versionis Latinae Fragmenta* (1871).

[131] B. Fischer, *Vetus Latina, die Reste der altlateinischen Bibel nach Petrus Sabatier neu gesammelt und herausgegeben von der Erzabtei Beuron* (1949).

[132] Cf. H. J. White, *HDB*, IV, pp. 872ff.

[133] The authorship by Jerome of the *Psalterium Romanum* was contested by D. de Bruyne, *Revue Bénédictine*, XLII (1930), pp. 101ff., but accepted by A. Allgeier, *Biblica*, XII (1931), pp. 447ff.

[134] Cf. F. Stummer, *Einführung in die Lateinische Bibel* (1928), pp. 99ff.

[135] *Ibid.*, pp. 125ff.

product of many hands, and it is possible that some portions of the Old Testament translations reached back to pre-Christian times, although many scholars have maintained that the version itself was Christian in origin.[136] There is at present no direct information about the date of the translation or the authors of the work. This circumstance is hardly surprising, since details concerning the origin of the Syriac version were unknown as early as the time of Theodore of Mopsuestia (d. A.D. 428). It seems probable, however, that some earlier Jewish translations were utilized in the compilation of the work, since the Syrian Christian Church contained many Jewish members. Further evidence for this is found in the way that the translation of Chronicles paraphrases freely and avoids anthropomorphisms in a manner characteristic of the targums. Nöldeke went so far as to affirm that the Peshitta of Chronicles was in fact a Jewish targum,[137] but this cannot be proved.

Kahle has conjectured that the Old Testament, or at least some portions of it, were translated into Syriac for the benefit of the Jewish royal family of Adiabene in the middle of the first century of the Christian era.[138] Whatever the date of origin, it seems probable that the Pentateuch was the first portion to be translated; and it was subsequently revised to constitute the present Syriac Pentateuch. Linguistic affinities between the Palestinian Aramaic targum and the Syriac version of the Pentateuch possibly indicate that the Peshitta Pentateuch originated in a district where eastern Aramaic, of which Syriac is a dialect, was spoken, and which had some contact or relationship with Jerusalem.[139] The most probable region would be that of Adiabene, a province of Syria situated east of the Tigris, which was converted to Judaism about A.D. 40. Since the Palestinian Aramaic targum, written in the dialect of Judaea, was in use in Palestine at that period, it appears quite probable that it was transposed into the Syriac dialect spoken in Adiabene. Further examination indicates that manuscripts of the Peshitta Pentateuch existed at an early period in two recensions, one literal and the other more like a targum. According to Barnes the literal translation was the older, since the Syriac Church authorities were more familiar with that type of text.[140] However, this view appears inadequate when it is remembered that the Syrian Fathers such as Aphraates and Ephraem did not always quote the literal rendering. It is therefore

---

[136] E.g. F. Buhl, *Kanon und Text des AT*, p. 187; E. König, *Einleitung in das AT*, p. 122; *PIOT*, p. 120. This view was opposed by F. C. Burkitt, *EB*, IV, col. 5025; J. Bloch, *AJSL*, XXXV (1919), pp. 215ff.; A. Baumstark, *Geschichte der syrischen Literatur* (1922), p. 18; Kahle, *The Cairo Geniza*, p. 180; A. Bentzen, *Introduction to the OT*, I, pp. 72f.; C. Peters, *Le Muséon*, XLVIII (1935), pp. 1ff.

[137] T. Nöldeke, *Die Alttestamentliche Litteratur* (1868), p. 263.

[138] *The Cairo Geniza*, pp. 179ff.

[139] Cf. A. Baumstark, *ZDMG*, XIV (1935), pp. 89ff.

[140] *JTS*, XV (1914), p. 38.

considered more likely that a targum was revised during the second century in order to bring it into conformity with the ancient Hebrew text.

The Peshitta can scarcely be described as a homogeneous piece of translation, varying as it does from literal to paraphrastic renderings. Proverbs and Ezekiel are distinctly reminiscent of the targums, while the Psalter is translated in a free fashion, and along with Isaiah and the Minor Prophets shows clearly the influence of the LXX.[141] Job was translated from the original Hebrew, and is unintelligible in parts due to corruptions in textual transmission and the influence of other versions. Chronicles, as has been noted, is paraphrastic in character, and according to Fraenkel was translated by Jews in Edessa in the third century and added as a supplement along with the contents of the Apocrypha.[142]

The oldest surviving manuscript of the Peshitta dates from about A.D. 464, and there are several extant sixth-century manuscripts of the Psalms and Isaiah. The most important manuscript, Codex Ambrosianus, which comprises the entire Old Testament, is in Milan. This manuscript, which uses the western Syriac form of the text, was published in a photo-lithographic edition by Ceriani in 1874.[143] Other Syriac translations include a Jerusalem rendering of the Old and New Testament made in the sixth century, of which only a few fragments of the Old Testament have survived. It was evidently made from the LXX, and was intended for the religious worship of the Palestinian-Syriac Melchite Church. The language was Palestinian Aramaic, written in Syriac characters. A translation of the entire Bible from Greek into Syriac was commissioned about A.D. 508 by Philoxenus of Mabbug, but no Old Testament portions other than fragments of the Psalter have survived. According to Baumstark, the latter were based on a Lucianic recension of the text of Isaiah.[144]

Another Syriac version of the Old Testament was made in A.D. 617 at the request of the Patriarch Athanasius by Paul, bishop of Tella. It followed the text of the LXX column of the *Hexapla* with slavish exactness, and is known as the Syro-Hexaplaric version. It retained the Hexaplaric signs in marginal notes, and supplied readings from Aquila, Symmachus, and Theodotion. Some fragments of the Syro-Hexapla were collected by Lagarde[145] to supplement earlier manuscripts, particularly the edition published by Ceriani in 1874. Within recent years a number

---

[141] Cf. W. E. Barnes, *JTS*, II (1901), p. 197.

[142] S. Fraenkel, *Jahrbücher für Protestantische Theologie* (1879), pp. 508ff., 720ff.

[143] A. M. Ceriani, *Translatio Syra Pescitto Veteris Testamenti* (1874).

[144] A. Baumstark, *Geschichte der syrischen Litteratur*, pp. 144f.

[145] *Bibliothecae Syriacae I. Veteris Testamenti Graeci in sermonem Syriacum versi fragmenta octo* (1892).

of new fragments of this recension were discovered among some manuscripts in London.[146] The Syro-Hexapla is not merely of value for restoring the Hexaplar text of the LXX, but also for recovering the original LXX text of Daniel. No complete scientific edition of the Syriac Old Testament exists as yet, although critical texts of certain canonical books such as the Psalter, Isaiah, Canticles, and Ezra have been published. The main edition of the Peshitta was prepared by a Marcionite, Gabriel Sionita, for inclusion in the 1645 *Paris Polyglot,* but unfortunately it was based upon inadequate manuscript sources. This text was followed in the Walton *London Polyglot* of 1657, and also by Lee in the 1821 and later editions published by the British and Foreign Bible Society under the title *Vetus Testamentum Syriace.* The Urmia edition, representing the eastern Syriac text, was published in 1852, and in many instances followed the readings of Nestorian manuscripts.

From about A.D. 300 on numerous translations of the LXX into different vernacular dialects appeared among the Coptic Christians of Egypt, the Ethiopic Church, the Armenians, and the Arabs. These versions were subsequently revised and expanded and became in turn the basis of later translations as the need was dictated by missionary expansion and other considerations.

[146] M. H. Goshen-Gottestein, *Biblica,* XXXVI (1955), pp. 162ff.

III. TEXTUAL CRITICISM

A. SEMITIC PHILOLOGY

Within recent years important aids to textual criticism have been furnished by inscriptional and manuscript discoveries. These include valuable proto-Hebrew Ugaritic texts, northwest Semitic documents of the Late Bronze and Early Iron Ages, ostraca such as those from Lachish, Aramaic papyri from the fifth century B.C., and, of course, the Dead Sea Scrolls. Archaeological material of this sort is of immense value in studying the history of the Hebrew language against its northwest Semitic background.[1] The dramatic advances that have been made possible by recent dicoveries can be appreciated in the light of the complaint by Gesenius, who in the fifth edition (1822) of his *Hebräische Grammatik* noted a total lack of historical data for the earlier stages of the development of the language. Even a century later, the Bauer-Leander *Historische Grammatik der Hebräischen Sprache* showed that little progress in the historical understanding of the language had taken place, despite the decipherment of the Phoenician inscriptions by Gesenius and the important contribution made by the 1907 edition of the Tell el-Amarna tablets.[2]

Some light was thrown upon the nature of early Hebrew in 1926, when Bauer collected and published all the personal and geographical names from Old Babylonian documentary sources that had been held to reflect a west-Semitic speech.[3] In the same year Sethe published his decipherment of the celebrated "Execration Texts," inscribed in Egyptian upon vases suitable for smashing.[4] Aside from the implications of this material for processes of sympathetic magic, it has been observed that among the names of potential rebel vassals listed on the vases are about thirty Palestinian and Syrian chieftains, mentioned in conjunction with the

---

[1] Cf. W. L. Moran, *BANE*, pp. 54ff.

[2] J. A. Knudtzon, *Die El-Amarna Tafeln* (vol. I, 1907, vol. II, 1915).

[3] T. Bauer, *Die Ostkanaanäer, Eine philologisch-historische Untersuchung über die Wanderschicht der Sogenannten "Amoriter" in Babylonien* (1926).

[4] K. Sethe, *Die Ächtung feindlicher Fürsten, Völker und Dinge auf altägyptischen Tongefässscherben des mittleren Reiches* (1926).

territory over which they ruled. All appeared to be of the same type, and reflected substantially the same language as that studied by Bauer in connection with the cuneiform sources.[5] They are generally regarded as having come from the period between 1925 and 1875 B.C.[6]

Similarly inscribed figurines were found at Sakkarah from a slightly later period,[7] and on examination proved to be identical linguistically with the earlier texts published by Sethe. More than thirty northwest Semitic names, mostly of females, were contained in the Hayes list published by Albright,[8] and assigned to the eighteenth century B.C. While these 150 or so personal names from Syria and Palestine in the period 1900-1700 B.C.[9] may not appear particularly significant in themselves, they are of great value, since they are substantially the same as those found in the more abundant cuneiform sources. The orthographic principles governing Egyptian transcriptions were laid down in the fundamentally important treatise *The Vocalization of the Early Egyptian Syllabic Orthography* by W. F. Albright (1934). This threw additional light upon early Canaanite designations of individuals and places.

Study of the history of northwest Semitic was unexpectedly enriched by the tablets excavated at Mari from 1933,[10] as well as by similar material from Alalakh[11] and Tell Chagar Bazar,[12] which contained invaluable information for the study of philology and grammar. The Mari texts in particular furnished hundreds of personal and geographical names, and through deviations in vocabulary and idiom from the current Babylonian these have supplied material of great importance for estimating the nature of northwest Semitic speech in the patriarchal period. Considerable diversity of opinion exists in connection with this particular subject,[13] and there is a pressing need for an authoritative synthesis of the material now available.

As with the Amarna tablets, it was a chance discovery that led to the excavations at the site of ancient Ugarit. While the native Amorite speech of Mari was similar to, though not identical with, the Hebrew of

[5] W. L. Moran, *BANE*, p. 56.

[6] Cf. G. Posener, *Princes et pays d'Asie et de Nubie* (1940), pp. 31ff.; W. F. Edgerton, *JAOS*, LX (1940), p. 492 n. 44; Albright, *BASOR*, No. 88 (1942), p. 32.

[7] Posener, *op. cit.*, pp. 40ff.

[8] *JAOS*, LXXIV (1954), pp. 222ff.

[9] For studies see Albright, *JPOS*, VIII (1928), pp. 223ff., *BASOR*, No. 81 (1941), pp. 16ff., 30ff.; J. Simons, *Handbook for the Study of Egyptian Topographical Lists Relating to Western Asia* (1937); M. Noth, *Zeitschrift des Deutschen Palästina-Vereins*, LXV (1942), pp. 9ff.

[10] For early reports see *SRA*, XVI (1935), pp. 1ff., 117ff., *et al.*; for transliterations and translations of texts, *Archives royales de Mari* (1950-54), I-VI; for a bibliography to 1950, *Studia Mariana* (1950), pp. 127ff.

[11] Cf. C. L. Woolley, *Alalakh* (1955); D. J. Wiseman, *The Alalakh Tablets* (1953).

[12] Cf. C. J. Gadd, *Iraq*, VII (1940), pp. 35ff.

[13] W. L. Moran, *BANE*, p. 57.

the patriarchal period, the language of the Ugaritic texts consisted of a Hurrian dialect and a previously unknown northwest Semitic tongue closely akin to pre-Mosaic Hebrew. The importance of the archaic Canaanite dialect for the writings of the Old Testament, and particularly the Psalms, was immediately apparent, as has been observed in an earlier chapter. The contribution of this material to the study of Hebrew grammar was of great value also, for it was soon realized that the Massoretic text had preserved peculiarities in Canaanite grammar and speech-forms, whose nature and significance had passed into oblivion after the close of the Amarna Age, and which had been regarded as textual corruptions by the critical scholars of the nineteenth century. Not the least benefit for the grammarian is the information which this ancient literary corpus has furnished with regard to the problems connected with the Hebrew verbal system.[14]

Although the professional student of Hebrew palaeography and epigraphy cannot boast of a wealth of material such as is available in cuneiform, he does possess many hundreds of inscriptions that have made available a fund of new knowledge of enormous value for a study of the Old Testament text. Many of the inscriptions on stone were written in various dialects of Canaanite[15] as well as in north-[16] and south-Arabic, and their importance for the history of the north-Semitic alphabet has been shown previously. Equally valuable were the discoveries of inscribed ostraca at Samaria and Lachish.[17] The former comprised administrative documents recording shipments of wine and oil to Samaria in the time of Jeroboam II, and contained numerous personal names and place-designations, some of which also appeared in the Old Testament. The latter are of value for the textual critic because of the incidence of scribal errors, the use of the *scriptio defectiva* rather than the fuller forms of the Massoretic tradition, the presence of a dot as a word-divider, and the fact that the language of the ostraca is to all intents and purposes the kind of classical Hebrew familiar from the Old Testament writings.

---

[14] *Ibid.*, pp. 61ff.

[15] Cf. J. W. Flight in *Haverford Symposium on Archaeology and the Bible* (ed. E. Grant), pp. 114ff.; A. M. Honeyman, *OTMS*, pp. 264ff.

[16] Cf. F. V. Winnett, *BASOR*, No. 73 (1939), pp. 3ff.; W. F. Albright, *BASOR*, No. 66 (1937), p. 30.

[17] For Samaria see W. F. Albright, *PEF Quarterly Statement* (1936), pp. 211ff., *BASOR*, No. 73 (1939), p. 21; D. Diringer, *Le inscrizioni antico-ebraiche palestinese* (1934), pp. 21ff.; *ANET*, p. 321; *DOTT*, pp. 204ff. For Lachish see H. Torczyner, *The Lachish Letters* (1938); J. W. Jack, *PEF Quarterly Statement* (1938), pp. 165ff.; K. Elliger, *PJB*, XXXIV (1938), pp. 30ff., *Zeitschrift des Deutschen Palästina-Vereins*, LXII (1939), pp. 63ff.; J. Hempel, *ZAW*, LVI (1938), pp. 126ff.; R. de Vaux, *RB*, XLVIII (1939), pp. 181ff.; D. W. Thomas, *JTS*, XL (1939), pp. 1ff.; Albright, *BASOR*, No. 82 (1941), p. 21.

When the antiquity of the Qumran scrolls was demonstrated to the satisfaction of the majority of scholars, the palaeographers and textual critics realized that they had in their possession materials which at once advanced textual sources to a completely unexpected extent. The large manuscript of Isaiah (1QIsa^a) proved of particular value in this connection, since it differed in certain respects from the Massoretic text, including the wider use of the *matres lectionis* and the preservation of some readings not found in the Massoretic tradition but supported by the LXX and other ancient versions. Subsequent studies of the Qumran Biblical material[18] have shown something of the extent to which these documents testify independently to the traditions lying behind the Massoretic form, and have furnished powerful support for the general trustworthiness of the Massoretic text. In addition to earlier materials, the palaeographer now has at his disposal a variety of scripts including palaeo-Hebrew, early Jewish, and Greek hands, written both in formal and cursive styles. There is thus a significant corpus available for purposes of typological analysis and for fixing absolute dates within the relative systems furnished by such analyses.

As with many other aspects of Biblical study, much of the groundwork of palaeographical method was laid by Albright, whose analysis of the Nash Papyrus constituted a model of its kind.[19] Palaeographic study of the Qumran material led to conclusions as to the date of the materials from 1Q, which were subsequently confirmed by carbon-14 dating of linen scraps from the same source.[20] In a reply to certain critics of advanced palaeographic methods, Birnbaum furnished an excellent conspectus of the science.[21] Presently he is in process of issuing his major work on Hebrew palaeography, an attempt to deal with the various

---

[18] E.g. F. M. Cross, *JBL*, LXXIV (1955), pp. 147ff.; P. W. Skehan, *CBQ*, VIII (1955), pp. 38ff., XXII (1960), pp. 47ff., *VT*, suppl. IV (1957), pp. 182ff.; H. M. Orlinsky in *A Stubborn Faith* (ed. E. C. Hobbs, 1956), pp. 117ff., *JBL*, LXXVIII (1959), pp. 26ff.; Cross, *The Ancient Library of Qumran and Biblical Studies* (1958), pp. 179ff.; M. Martin, *The Scribal Character of the Dead Sea Scrolls* (2 vols., 1958); B. J. Roberts, *BJRL*, XLII (1959), pp. 132ff.; W. J. Brownlee, *The Meaning of the Qumran Scrolls for the Bible*, pp. 5ff.

[19] *JBL*, LVI (1937), pp. 145ff.; cf. G. Margoliouth, *JE*, VIII, pp. 304, 312; N. Peters, *Die älteste Abschrift der zehn Gebote, der Papyrus Nash* (1905).

[20] Albright, *BASOR*, No. 118 (1950), p. 6; J. C. Trever, *BASOR*, No. 113 (1949), p. 23, *Smithsonian Report* (1953), pp. 425ff.; S. A. Birnbaum, *BASOR*, No. 115 (1949), p. 22; E. L. Sukenik, *Megilloth Genuzoth*, I, pp. 14f. These methods were contested by Kahle, *Die hebräischen Handschriften aus der Höle* (1951), p. 22 *passim;* J. L. Teicher, *JJS*, II (1951), pp. 67ff.; O. H. Lehmann, *PEQ*, LXXXIII (1951), pp. 32ff.; E. R. Lacheman, *JQR*, XL (1949-1950), pp. 15ff.

[21] S. A. Birnbaum, *The Qumran Scrolls and Palaeography. BASOR*, Suppl. Stud. 13-14 (1952).

phases through which Hebrew scripts have passed, which is expected to become definitive in its field.[22]

Within recent years comparative Semitic philology has gone hand in hand with the Qumran discoveries in increasing scholarly confidence in the substantial trustworthiness of the Massoretic tradition. In the light of the fuller information that scholars now possess concerning northwest Semitic languages generally, it has become apparent that much of the zealous emendation of the Hebrew text undertaken by adherents of the Graf-Wellhausen theories on what was the flimsiest of ground or no ground at all can no longer be justified on a philological basis, or any other, for that matter. As Thomas has pointed out, what were formerly imagined to be impossible Hebrew forms can now be explained quite satisfactorily by comparison with some other Semitic tongue.[23]

The foundations of modern Semitic philology were laid in the nineteenth century by the monumental labors of several scholars, among them Gesenius, who deciphered the Phoenician alphabet, and Rödiger, who studied the Minaeo-Sabaean alphabet. Among the numerous subsequent studies are included works on grammar, lexicons, and studies of the Amarna tablets.[24]

---

[22] *The Hebrew Scripts* (vols. I, II, 1954). Other valuable contributions to the field have been made by Cross, *JBL*, LXXIV (1955), pp. 147ff., *BANE*, pp. 133ff.; N. Avigad, *Scripta Hierosolymitana*, IV (1957), pp. 56ff.; and Milik, *DJD*, II, pp. 67ff.

[23] In *Record and Revelation* (ed. H. W. Robinson, 1938), p. 400; *OTMS*, p. 242.

[24] Gesenius' *Hebräisches und Chaldäisches Handwörterbuch* first appeared in 1812; Rödiger published the fourteenth to twenty-first editions of Gesenius' Grammar between 1845 and 1872. An edition of Gesenius' lexicon was published by F. Buhl in 1915, entitled *Hebräisches und Aramäisches Handwörterbuch über das AT*. Other nineteenth-century contributions included F. Delitzsch, *Prolegomena eines neuen Hebräisch-Aramäischen Wörterbuch zum AT* (1886), *Assyrisches Wörterbuch zur gesampten bisher veröffentlichen Keilschriftliteratur* (1887-90), and *Assyrische Grammatik* (1889); A. H. Sayce, *Assyrian Grammar for Comparative Purposes* (1872), *Principles of Comparative Philology* (1874), and *Introduction to the Science of Language* (1879); W. Wright, *Lectures on the Comparative Grammar of the Semitic Languages* (1890); H. Zimmern, *Vergleichende Grammatik der semitischen Sprachen* (1898); Th. Nöldeke, *Die Semitischen Sprache* (1899); E. Kautzsch, *Grammatik des Biblisch-Aramäischen* (1884); K. Marti, *Kurzgefasste Grammatik der Biblisch-Aramäischen Sprache* (1896); E. König, *Historisch-kritisches Lehrgebäude der Hebräischen Sprache* (vol. I, 1881, vol. II, 1897) and *Hebräisch und Semitisch* (1901); and P. de Lagarde, *Uebersicht über die im Aramäischen, Arabischen und Hebräischen übliche Bildung der Nomina* (1889). Early twentieth-century studies included Delitzsch, *Philologische Forderungen an die hebräische Lexicographie* (1917); H. Torczyner, *Die Entstehung des semitischen Sprachtypus* (1906); Brockelmann, *Grundriss der vergleichenden Grammatik der semitischen Sprachen* (1908); and D. O'Leary, *Comparative Grammar of the Semitic Languages* (1923). The linguistic form of the Tell el-Amarna tablets was studied by F. Böhl, *Die Sprache der Amarnabriefe* (1909), and F. Ebeling, *Das Verbum der El-Amarna-Briefe* (1910). Numerous Hebrew and Aramaic grammars and lexicons have appeared, among them G. Dalman, *Grammatik des Jüdisch-Palä-*

Taken together all these works—earlier and later—have shown that the Massoretic text, although admittedly faulty at certain points, is a remarkable testimony to scribal fidelity in the transmission of the Hebrew Scriptures, and in general constitutes a witness whose reliability is of a deservedly high degree.[25] While it is now apparent that there were several types of Hebrew text circulating in the pre-Christian period, it is evident that some of the supposed departures from the Massoretic text exhibited by ancient versions such as the LXX are not as real as they purport to be. Sometimes a translation may exhibit certain variations from the traditional meaning of the Hebrew words in a manner that seems to suggest that the translators were working from a divergent Hebrew text. However, comparative philological studies can frequently trace such idiosyncrasies to their source and demonstrate that the divergence in question is more apparent than actual.[26] No scholar would deny, of course, that there are important divergences between the Massoretic text, other pre-Christian texts, and the ancient versions, in which

---

stinischen Aramäisch (1905); Brown, Driver, and Briggs, *A Hebrew and English Lexicon of the OT* (1906); H. L. Strack, *Grammatik des Biblisch-Aramäischen* (1921); A. B. Davidson, *Hebrew Grammar* (rev. ed., 1921); H. Bauer and P. Leander, *Historische Grammatik der hebräischen Sprache* (vol. I, 1922); P. P. Joüon, *Grammaire de l'Hébreu Biblique* (1923); W. B. Stevenson, *Grammar of Palestinian Jewish Aramaic* (1924); Bauer and Leander, *Grammatik des Biblisch-Aramäischen* (1927); Leander, *Laut- und Formenlehre des Ägyptisch-Aramäischen* (1928); and L. H. Gray, *Introduction to Semitic Comparative Linguistics* (1934). A number of treatises have been published dealing with particularized aspects of Semitic speech, e.g. E. König, *Stilistik, Rhetorik, Poetik in Bezug auf die biblische Litteratur komparativisch dargestellt* (1900); S. Landesdorfer, *Sumerisches Sprachgut im AT* (1916); A. Jirku, *Die Wanderungen der Hebräer* (1924). In 1940 Zorell and Semkowski began the publication of their *Lexicon Hebraicum et Aramaicum Veteris Testamenti;* this was followed in 1948 by the outstanding *Lexicon in Veteris Testamenti Libros* of Köhler and Baumgartner. G. R. Driver began his important contributions to philological study in 1920; for a select bibliography of these see *Hebrew and Semitic Studies Presented to G. R. Driver* (ed. D. W. Thomas and W. D. McHardy, 1963), pp. 191ff. In Germany M. Noth's *Die Israelitischen Personennamen im Rahmen der gemeinsemitischen Namengebung* (1928) superseded all previous works on the subject of Israelite personal names from philological, semantic, and other standpoints. Interest in Semitic philology has been sustained through such studies as Z. S. Harris, *Grammar of the Phoenician Language* (1936) and *Development of the Canaanite Dialects* (1939); C. F. A. Schaeffer, *Ugaritica* (from 1939); R. de Langhe, *Les Textes de Ras Shamra-Ugarit et leurs rapports avec le milieu biblique de l'Ancien Testament, I-II* (1945); and C. H. Gordon, *Ugaritic Grammar* (1940) and *Ugaritic Handbook* (1947); as well as the manifold contributions of Noth, Albright, Winton Thomas, Margolis, Orlinsky, and many other scholars.

[25] Cf. D. W. Thomas, *The Recovery of the Ancient Hebrew Language* (1939), p. 37.

[26] D. W. Thomas in *OTMS*, pp. 242f.

readings superior to those of the Massoretes have been preserved. Even conjectural emendation of the Hebrew is a legitimate discipline when carried out under properly controlled conditions, and not as an arbitrary exercise designed to furnish textual support for some conjectural scheme.

B. MODERN EDITIONS OF THE HEBREW BIBLE

At the beginning of the twentieth century the study of Old Testament textual criticism was in decline, and it remained in this condition for the next few decades.[27] Orlinsky[28] correctly laid much of the blame for this unfortunate situation on Rudolf Kittel's celebrated *Biblia Hebraica*. This work, issued in 1906 and 1912, was based on the ben Chayyim text, and superseded both Oort's *Textus Hebraici emendationes quibus in Vetere Testamento Neerlandice vertendo* (1900), which was popular at that time in parts of Europe, and the earlier Hebrew editions of A. Hahn (1832) and M. Letteris (1852), the latter being the text used by the British and Foreign Bible Society (1866). The Kittel Bible tacitly emended the ben Chayyim text, and furnished footnotes that contained conjectural emendations and variant readings from ancient sources such as versions. The critical apparatus received high praise from scholars such as S. R. Driver, though this, characteristically, was tempered with some caution.[29] Very soon, however, as Orlinsky has remarked,[30] scholars began to regard the apparatus as more sacred and authoritative than the Massoretic text itself, and where choice was involved they tended to accept the emendations in preference to the Hebrew text. A third edition of *Biblia Hebraica* was published by Paul Kahle in 1937, based upon what Kahle regarded as the purest form of the ben Asher text, the Leningrad manuscript B 19a, dated A.D. 1008. Different scholars contributed a critical apparatus containing selected variant readings from manuscripts and the ancient versions, but unfortunately this collection of notes was only a slight improvement upon its predecessors.[31]

[27] This state of affairs prompted complaints by scholars of the caliber of Rowley, *Society for Old Testament Study Book List*, X (1955), p. 640, and Orlinsky, *BANE*, p. 114, that little interest was shown in textual criticism proper, apart from such occasional articles as M. L. Margolis, *Proceedings of the American Philosophical Society*, LXVII (1928), pp. 187ff.; J. Reider, *HUCA*, VII (1930), pp. 285ff.; Orlinsky, *BA*, IX, No. 2 (1946), pp. 22ff., and in *The Study of the Bible Today and Tomorrow* (ed. H. R. Willoughby), pp. 141ff.

[28] *BANE*, p. 114.

[29] *Notes on the Hebrew Text of the Book of Samuel* (1913), p. xxxv n. 6.

[30] *BANE*, p. 114.

[31] Orlinsky in *The Study of the Bible Today and Tomorrow*, p. 151; *BA*, IX, No. 2 (1946), pp. 24ff.

The first important scholar to criticize this curious situation was C. C. Torrey, who made a scathing attack on the methods used to amass this apparatus.[32] Torrey's views were shared by Montgomery, who in his *Critical and Exegetical Commentary on the Book of Daniel* (1927) ignored the apparatus completely. These opinions were also elaborated by Margolis, who made it clear that the Kittel critical apparatus was completely unreliable for scholarly purposes.[33] Orlinsky also took the same stand in 1934, and has continued his criticisms of this collection of material since that time.[34] Ziegler and Katz have been equally forthright in their warnings as to the complete inadequacy of the Kittel apparatus.[35]

Ignoring these weighty criticisms, the Privilegierte Württembergische Bibelanstalt published in 1951 an introduction by Würthweim to the critical apparatus of the Kittel Hebrew Bible, and this work was translated into English six years later.[36] Criticisms of the German version were rejected quite calmly in the foreword to the English edition, indicating that at least some English and continental European scholars were satisfied with an inadequate and incorrect critical apparatus. Quite obviously, any attempt at textual criticism that employs such a faulty device can only produce indifferent, if not absolutely incorrect, results.

In contrast, textual studies in the LXX version have not been hampered to the same extent by a poor critical apparatus, although Margolis[37] claimed to have discovered errors in the apparatus of the *Larger Cambridge Septuagint*, and also in the edition by H. B. Swete. The recovery of Hebrew and Greek Biblical materials from Qumran has stimulated interest in the restoration of the original Greek text of the LXX, the one from which, according to Lagarde, all existing manuscripts and recensions of the Greek Old Testament arose. This theory received support from scholars such as Albright, Margolis, B. J. Roberts, Marcus, Allgeier, Orlinsky, and others.[38] Although the principles laid down by

[32] *The Second Isaiah* (1928), pp. 214f.

[33] *AJSL*, XXVIII (1912), p. 3; cf. H. M. Orlinsky, *Max Leopold Margolis: Scholar and Teacher* (1952), pp. 34ff.

[34] *JQR*, XXV (1934-35), pp. 271ff.; cf. his statements in *JBL*, LXIII (1944), p. 33, LXIX (1950), p. 153 n. 5, *JQR*, XLIII (1952-53), pp. 330, 340, *BANE*, pp. 114ff., and *A Stubborn Faith* (ed. E. C. Hobbs), pp. 117ff.

[35] J. Ziegler, *ZAW*, LX (1944), pp. 108ff. P. Katz in *The Background of the NT and its Eschatology* (ed. W. D. Davies and D. Daube, 1956), pp. 176ff., *VT*, IV (1954), pp. 222f.; for a bibliography see J. W. Wevers, *Theologische Rundschau*, XXII (1954), pp. 86, 90.

[36] *Der Text des AT, eine Einführung in die Biblia Hebraica von Rudolf Kittel* (1951): E. tr. P. R. Ackroyd, *The Text of the OT; an Introduction to Kittel-Kahle's Biblia Hebraica* (1957).

[37] *JBL*, XLIX (1930), pp. 234ff.

[38] Cf. Orlinsky in *Max Leopold Margolis: Scholar and Teacher*, p. 43n.

Lagarde were challenged by Kahle and Sperber,[39] these scholars have themselves been criticized by Orlinsky, Katz, Cross, and others.[40]

According to the hypothesis that Lagarde postulated concerning the archetype of the Scriptures, the Jews possessed a standard authoritative text of the Hebrew Bible from the early part of the second century of the Christian era that was based upon a single master scroll and constituted the text upon which all subsequent medieval manuscripts of the Hebrew Bible depended.[41] Lagarde was followed by Gordis and Orlinsky among others,[42] but his opinions failed to secure firm scholarly support, probably because his theory was overstated. At the same time it has been recognized from the evidence presented by the Qumran texts that at the end of the first century after Christ a uniform Hebrew tradition had begun to appear and that despite textual differences it was handed down in a remarkably consistent form from that time onwards.

Whereas early reports on the textual relationship between the Qumran Hebrew scrolls and the LXX tended to emphasize the agreement of the Hebrew, particularly 1QIsaᵃ, with the LXX as against the Massoretic text, subsequent research disclosed that the Wadi Qumran material did not in fact diverge in favor of the LXX as frequently as had at first been supposed.[43] Recent studies in this and other aspects of textual research have gone far towards showing that the LXX has, with the Massoretic text, acquired very considerable respect as a source for the recovery of the pre-Massoretic Hebrew in disputed areas, although, as has been stated above, the LXX still needs to be used with considerable care.[44]

[39] Kahle in *Theologische Studien und Kritiken*, LXXXVIII (1915), pp. 432ff. and *The Cairo Geniza*, pp. 174ff.; Sperber in *JBL*, LIV (1935), pp. 73ff. and *Studien zur Geschichte und Kultur des Nahen und Fernen Ostens* (ed. W. Heffening and W. Kirfel, 1935), pp. 39ff.; cf. his statements in *HUCA*, XIV (1939), pp. 153f., XVII (1943), pp. 293ff., and *PIOT*, p. 79.

[40] Orlinsky, *JAOS*, LXI (1941), pp. 81ff., *BANE*, p. 121; Katz, *Theologische Zeitschrift*, V (1949), pp. 1ff., *Studia Patristica*, I (1957), p. 353; Cross, *The Ancient Library of Qumran and Modern Biblical Studies*, p. 170 n. 13.

[41] P. de Lagarde, *Anmerkungen zur griechischen Uebersetzung der Proverbien* (1863), pp. 1ff.; cf. Orlinsky, *On the Present State of Proto-Septuagint Studies* (1941), p. 84; W. Robertson Smith, *The OT in the Jewish Church* (1892), p. 57 n. 2.

[42] Gordis, *The Biblical Text in the Making: A Study of the Kethibh-Qere*, pp. 44ff.; Orlinsky, *JAOS*, LXI (1941), pp. 84ff.

[43] Cf. J. Muilenburg, *BASOR*, No. 135 (1954), pp. 32f.; M. Burrows, *More Light on the Dead Sea Scrolls*, pp. 144ff.; P. W. Skehan, *BASOR*, No. 136 (1954), pp. 12ff. and *VT* suppl. IV (1957), pp. 148ff.

[44] Among recent studies are Orlinsky, *The LXX, The Oldest Translation of the Bible* (1949); I. Soisalon-Soininen, *Die Textformen der Septuaginta-Übersetzung der Richterbuches* (1951); D. H. Guard, *The Exegetical Method of the Greek Translators of the Book of Job* (1952); H. S. Gehman, *VT*, III (1953), pp. 141ff., IV (1954), pp. 337ff.; J. W. Wevers, *Theologische Rundschau*, XXII (1954), pp. 85ff.,

Since the publication of the third edition of *Biblia Hebraica* one or two noteworthy attempts have been made to issue an authoritative text of the Hebrew Bible. In 1933 the British and Foreign Bible Society decided to publish a new text to replace the worn-out plates of the Letteris Bible. The editing of it was given to N. H. Snaith, who consulted certain Spanish Hebrew manuscripts in an attempt to come as close as possible to the true ben Asher tradition. The publication of the text was delayed by World War II and its aftermath until 1958. A brochure issued at that time by the British and Foreign Bible Society[45] stated that the text was based upon the first hands of certain Spanish Hebrew manuscripts in the British Museum, together with the Shem Tob manuscript from the library of the late David Sassoon. The work was not a revision of the Letteris text, nor was it connected in any way with the ben Chayyim text that had been edited for the Bible Society by C. D. Ginsburg in the first decade of the 1900s. Following the policy of the Society, the Bible contained no footnotes or apparatus apart from the official Massoretic notes. Although the text was not based upon that of Kahle to any significant extent, the conclusions at which Snaith arrived supported the contentions of Kahle concerning the true nature of the ben Asher tradition.

An edition of the Old Testament that was corrected on the basis of the Massorah of ben Asher was published under the title *Hebrew Bible: Jerusalem Edition* in 1953. Associated with the late M. D. Cassuto, who died two years before the publication of the work, it was not so much a new Bible as a photographic reproduction of the 1908 Ginsburg edition, to which some corrections had been added on the basis of textual notes left behind by Cassuto at his death. The choice of the Ginsburg text was unfortunate—particularly for a scholar such as Cassuto who had an unrivalled first-hand knowledge of the ben Asher codex—because Ginsburg had frequently been influenced by the number rather than by the quality of the manuscripts which supported important variant readings in the text. Compounding this unhappy situation was the hurried and careless technical work of the printer, which resulted among other things in an irregular number of lines per page and in numerous misprints. Since the notes made by Cassuto himself were based upon the Letteris edition of the Hebrew Bible, the finished work presented certain confusing aspects for students of the text.

171ff.; D. W. Gooding, *Recensions of the LXX Pentateuch* (1955); O. Eissfeldt, *Einleitung in das AT* (1956 ed.), pp. 822ff.; G. Zuntz, *ZAW*, LXVII (1956), pp. 124ff., *Classica et Mediaevalia*, XVII (1956), pp. 183ff.; G. Gerleman, *Studies in the LXX: Proverbs* (1956); H. M. Orlinsky, *BANE*, pp. 117ff.; F. M. Cross, *The Ancient Library of Qumran and Modern Biblical Studies*, pp. 168ff.

[45] For similar material see *VT*, VII (1957), pp. 107ff.

An edition of the complete Hebrew Bible known as the *Koren-Jerusalem Bible* was issued in 1962, preceded in 1959 by the publication of the Torah in Israel and the United States. In announcing this work, Dr. Haim Gevaryahu, chairman of the Israeli Society for Biblical Research and director of the World Jewish Bible Society, remarked that it was the first edition of the Hebrew Bible ever to be set, printed, and published in Jerusalem. Furthermore, this was the first time in over four centuries that Jews had undertaken to print and publish a Hebrew Bible. The text appears to differ only slightly from that of the Massoretes, although there are occasional variations in matters of spelling and punctuation.

In 1955, through the persistence of M. Goshen-Gottestein, the Hebrew University of Jerusalem undertook to place the textual study of the Old Testament on an entirely new basis by abandoning the eclectic character of the Kittel Bible and furnishing all the available evidence, whether valuable or not, for the purpose of recovering the genuine original Hebrew insofar as that objective was possible. This Bible was planned, like the *Biblia Hebraica,* to consist of two parts, the text and an apparatus, each of which was to be a scientific product in its own right. A large part of the Aleppo codex, believed destroyed in 1948 during Arab riots at Aleppo, is now in Israel, and has become available for scholarly study. The editors of the Hebrew University Bible believe that the codex is the original manuscript produced by Aaron ben Asher and recommended by Maimonides. Since only about two-thirds of this venerable source escaped destruction during the riots, it will be necessary for the editors to rely upon other ancient manuscripts that are as close as possible to the Aleppo codex. When completed this magnificent enterprise will present the purest variety of the traditional text in its most scientific form, and will furnish a full critical apparatus to replace the highly selective ones found in editions of the Kittel Bible.

C. Scribal Errors in Transmission

The account of the manner in which the Massoretic tradition was transmitted makes it apparent that there were times when scribal interference with the text was undertaken in accordance with theological presuppositions or liturgical requirements. These emendations must be differentiated from pure scribal error, however, since they constitute part of the legitimate historical development of the text. Nevertheless, the Massoretic scribes were aware of the fact of accidental textual corruption. One trace of their attempts to preserve the sacred text from error can be seen in the elongated form of the five *literae dilatabiles* (ת, ם, ל, ה, א) and some other consonants, which were lengthened in shape in order to fill vacant space at the ends of lines and thus avoid incorrect repetition of syllables or words.

254

In the light of present knowledge concerning the conditions under which the ancient scribes made copies of Biblical manuscripts, it is nothing short of miraculous that so few mistakes were made in the transmission of the text. For the most part the errors that do exist fall into definite categories of transcriptional error, which can also be recognized in other ancient works. Although a full discussion of types of scribal error is outside the scope of the present work,[46] the principal varieties can be described briefly as follows.

Purely scribal mistakes in copying the text arose at an early period when the Canaanite script was still in use, and resulted from confusion between consonants that exhibited a similar archaic form. Such mistakes usually involved the consonants *beth* and *daleth* (Gen. 9:7), *kaph* and *mem* (2 Kgs. 22:4), *'aleph* and *daleth* (2 Chron. 22:10), *nun* and *pe* (1 Chron. 11:37). When the square Aramaic script was introduced, confusion between ד and ר (Gen. 41:3, 19), ה and ח (Isa. 13:2), י and ו (Isa. 30:4), ה and ת (Ps. 49:15), and other consonants became increasingly common. Other instances of this kind may possibly be due to textual peculiarities in the parent manuscripts, and may not represent actual scribal error at all.

The absence of word-division in the Canaanite and early Aramaic scripts frequently led to corruptions of the text. Thus in Isaiah 2:20 the word for "to the moles" (לחפרפרות) was wrongly divided in the Massoretic tradition to comprise two words, "to a hole of rats" (לחפר פרות). A common scribal mistake arises when the consonant ו, occurring at the end of a verb, is attached erroneously to the beginning of the next word as though it were the conjunction "and" (1 Sam. 14:21). In Joel 2:1-2 an incorrect sentence-division assigned the words "for it is near" to the end of verse one rather than to the beginning of verse two, as the metrical structure requires. The introduction of the *matres lectionis* occasioned considerable textual variation, which was, however, minor. Occasionally such consonants appeared in a wrong context (e.g. Num. 21:1; 1 Sam. 10:5; Jer. 2:25), and when copied by the Massoretes produced a pointing that varied from the original as it might be reconstructed from ancient versions.

Distinct from the foregoing, which arose primarily from a misunderstanding of the text, are those corruptions which involved a definite alteration, whether accidental or deliberate, of the Hebrew consonants. The rearrangement of letters known as metathesis involves the reversing of their proper position, as in the Hebrew of Psalm 49:12, where the Massoretic text reads קרבם ("their inward parts") instead of the obvious

---

[46] Cf. A. Geiger, *Urschrift und Übersetzungen der Bibel* (1857); F. Perles, *Analekten zur Textkritik des AT* (1895); F. Delitzsch, *Die Lese- und Schreibfehler im AT* (1920). J. Kennedy in *An Aid to the Textual Amendment of the OT* (ed. N. Levison, 1928), should be used with caution.

form קברם ("their grave"). Transposition of consonants can be seen in Amos 6:2, where the Hebrew reads, "*Is their* border wider than *your* border?", thus supplying the wrong answer. Quite clearly the respective suffixes of the two nouns have been transposed accidentally, with the result that *your* must be read for *their* and *vice versa*. The acrostic form of Nahum 1:6 transposes the first two words, so that the second must be regarded as actually coming first in order to supply the ו needed for the acrostic.

Errors of confusion can be subdivided into *aural* and *visual* classes, depending on whether the scribe was writing from dictation or from sight. Aural errors are those in which the scribe substitutes one letter for another similar one on the basis of sound (e.g. 1 Sam. 2:16; 1 Kgs. 11:22); in visual errors consonants of like form are confused (e.g. Isa. 14:4). Conjectural emendation, or the restoration of the Hebrew or Greek text to a state that, in the opinion of the scribe, conveyed the best sense, was resorted to in cases of lacunae or gaps in the exemplar, or where the faded ink made the reading illegible. Quite frequently the general sense of the context left little doubt as to what was intended, although in at least one instance the inadequacy of this procedure can be demonstrated from internal evidence. Apparent illegibility of the text in 2 Samuel 22:33 led the scribe to emend the line to read, "God is my refuge," influenced possibly by verse two of the chapter. However, the duplicate form of the verse in Psalm 18:32 makes it clear that the original read, "God was girded with power," a reading that is supported by the versions.

An interesting variant arising from wrong word-division and pointing can be seen in Amos 6:12, where the Massoretic text reads, "Does one plow with oxen (*babbᵉqarim*)?" This obviously gives an answer that was not intended, and some versions, such as the AV and RV, have accordingly inserted the word "there" in order to make some sort of sense. Clearly the copyist read two words as one, so that the Hebrew should have been divided up into *bᵉbhaqar yam* ("with an ox [the] sea") to read, "Does one plow the sea with an ox?" Less sophisticated alterations are found in Jeremiah 27:1, where "Jehoiakim" should read "Zedekiah," as indicated by the context and as corrected by several ancient versions. Abbreviated forms frequently led to error also, as in Isaiah 5:19, where the consonant ה, representing the Divine Name, was absorbed into the preceding word.

Another common scribal addition to the text is that of *dittography*, in which the copyist wrote a letter or an entire word twice instead of once. Thus initial consonant ל in the word for "thy garment" found in the Massoretic text of Isaiah 63:2 should be omitted on such grounds, and the text of Ezekiel 48:16 should be similarly amended to omit the second "five." Scribal glosses were commonly employed in antiquity to explain rare words in the text, as in Isaiah 51:17, 22, where the word כוס

("cup") was inserted in order to convey the proper meaning of the unfamiliar קבעת, a Ugaritic term meaning "libatory vessel." Scribal corrections made in the margins of manuscripts were sometimes incorporated into the text, and this may explain the phrase "an evil divine spirit" in 1 Samuel 18:10, where "evil" may have been intended as a marginal improvement upon or correction of "divine."

Where there are apparently unnecessary words in the text, their presence may point to the readings of two different manuscripts or groups. This may possibly underlie the awkward rendering in 1 Samuel 28:3, where the phrase "in his city" appears to be a variant of "in Ramah" which was incorporated into the narrative, presumably on the authorship of an independent manuscript source. A more developed form of this situation consists of the conflation or blending of different accounts of the same incident, as in Zechariah 12:2, where the mention of "Judah" and "Jerusalem" seems to have combined two sets of textual possibilities.

Scribal omissions can be posited in all instances in which the Massoretic text is shorter than the original appears to have been, and each of these mistakes seems to have been unintentional. The resultant losses vary from the omission of a single letter, as in 2 Samuel 22:41, where the meaningless תתה should read נתתה ("thou hast given")—as in the duplicate section in Psalm 18:41—to the omission of the phrase "let us go into the field" after the Massoretic reading, "And Cain said unto his brother Abel . . ." in Genesis 4:8, which was retained by several ancient versions.

Haplography, or the failure to repeat a letter, syllable, or word, can be contrasted with instances of *homoiosis*, where the same or similar letters or words are accidentally repeated. In Genesis 32:23, *hû'* should read *hahû'*, "on that night"; in Judges 20:13 the word *b^enê* should precede "Benjamin" to read, "And the Benjamites were not willing." Haplography is also commonly found in cases of similarity between the last consonants of two words or the last words of two phrases, and is known as *homoioteleuton*. This phenomenon occurs when the eye of the scribe jumps across the contents of a section enclosed between identical or closely related words, and can be seen in 1 Samuel 14:41, where it is evident from the ancient versions that an entire section has been omitted.[47] Similar examples of the loss of a passage between identical words can be seen in 1QIsa^a 4:5f.; 16:8f.; and 23:15.

D. THE ROLE OF THE TEXTUAL CRITIC

While the avowed aim of the textual critic is to recover the original Hebrew form, it must always be remembered, as Winton Thomas has

---

[47] D. R. Ap-Thomas, *A Primer of OT Text Criticism*, pp. 40f.

pointed out,[48] that this objective is essentially ideal, and in actual fact cannot be attained to a large extent. Indeed, the very concept of an "original Hebrew" raises certain pressing theoretical and practical questions, even if it is granted that at least some of the Old Testament documents existed at one time in a single textual form. Aside from the strictly ben Asher manuscript, it is at least possible that even the Massoretic text itself was never completely free from mixed readings. However, the pressing need for the textual critic is to come to grips with the pre-Massoretic text, hypothetical though this may be from some points of view. For this purpose he will find the Massoretic tradition an indispensable starting-point for assessing the text-types from Qumran on the one hand and those underlying the ancient versions on the other.

Textual critics have generally proceeded on the principle that the more ancient the document is, the greater is its authority. This dictum must be modified by the realization that, given two manuscripts of different antiquity, the older one may have been copied from a comparatively recent and inferior exemplar, while the other may reach back to a considerably earlier and better text. Furthermore, the character of the text as it occurs in different manuscripts must also be borne in mind, since particular copyists have been known to be amenable to certain typical errors.[49] Again, it should be recognized that the incidence of divergences might not necessarily indicate textual corruption so much as the existence of variant textual forms, especially insofar as peculiarities of dialect are involved.[50] Textual corruptions can also be eliminated by comparative means, although it must be remembered here that sheer numerical preponderance can never be decisive in itself. No matter how many representatives there may be of the same archetype, they can obviously count as only one witness to the nature of the text.

As has been noted earlier, the Qumran discoveries have enhanced the prestige of the LXX considerably in matters of textual criticism. Some of the Qumran scrolls occasionally agree with the LXX against the Massoretic text in places where the LXX was thought to paraphrase and be unsupported by any Hebrew tradition. Even here, however, it must be urged that the readings of the Biblical scrolls from Qumran need not necessarily be good ones simply because they may antedate or differ from those of the Massoretic text. Merely to compare individual LXX readings with their counterparts in the traditional Hebrew text can lead to an unbalanced view of the essential worth of the LXX version. It is true, of course, that the Qumran discoveries have lent considerably more stature to the historical books of the LXX, but, as with all translations of the Hebrew, it has become apparent that the attitudes and techniques of

---

[48] *OTMS*, p. 259.
[49] Cf. J. Hempel, *ZAW*, XLVIII (1930), pp. 191ff.
[50] Cf. B. J. Roberts, *JJS*, I (1949), pp. 147ff.

the translators need to be studied carefully before the superiority of a part or the whole of their work is conceded. Such controls have placed the LXX in a rather different light from that of an earlier period, and in the future will insure that the proper precautions are taken in its use.

It seems most probable that all future critical reconstructions of the text will be rather eclectic, with each variant reading being judged upon its merits in the light of all the available textual evidence. While this procedure obviously involves a certain degree of subjectivity, it will be controlled to a large extent by the vast body of knowledge that is now available from such disciplines as epigraphy, lexicography, and comparative linguistics. If on examination it is found that either the Samaritan Pentateuch or the LXX, for example, offers a better rendering than that of the Massoretic Hebrew, the textual critic will be governed accordingly. He will also be sufficiently instructed in his discipline to avoid the mistaken view espoused by some contributors to the critical apparatus of the *Biblia Hebraica* that a divergent LXX reading, when retranslated into Hebrew, necessarily represents the "original" pre-Massoretic Hebrew. Textual emendation will still be necessary, but this procedure can no longer be undertaken in the spirit of gay abandon that characterized some areas of Old Testament scholarship in earlier generations. The textual critic is in some respects a responsible interpreter of the text, particularly in those places where the Hebrew is badly corrupted. He will, however, subject himself to those controls that safeguard the integrity of the Hebrew text and the versions, and such tentative emendations as are suggested will be given their proper place in the critical apparatus, and will not be presented to the unsuspecting reader as an authoritative rendering of the text.

However inviting and relatively harmless his work may be thought to be as a discipline, the textual critic will not be content with merely producing as perfect a restoration as possible of the one complete, though textually faulty, Hebrew recension that has been handed down by tradition. If the doctrine of inspiration means anything at all for the written Word of God, it surely refers to the original autographs, since subsequent copyists, however gifted or diligent, were not themselves inspired. The true objective of the textual critic, therefore, should be the restoration of the Hebrew to the point where it is as near as possible to what the original author is deemed to have written. Such an endeavor will confront all the present difficulties of the Massoretic text with every device of modern scholarship, and will make full and proper use of those ancient translations that are known to have been based upon Hebrew exemplars of one family or another. The exercise of the purely subjective factor will itself be governed by adequate controls, and the end-result will constitute an impressive attempt to reconstruct a genuine pre-Christian Old Testament text, thus making the ancient Word of God more intelligible to its modern readers.

IV. THE OLD TESTAMENT CANON

A. The Growth of the Canon

The study of the Old Testament canon can properly commence with the observation that all the major world religions have as their legacy a collection of writings that the devout regard as the word of God to a greater or lesser extent, and therefore as containing authoritative norms for faith and practice. Not all adherents of the various religious faiths existing in the modern world maintain that their Scriptures are necessarily inspired, but in any event they normally regard them as enshrining the highest degree of religious authority. The Hebrew Scriptures, emerging as they did over a lengthy period of time and from widely diverse circumstances, constituted the official collection of Jewish religious literature. Portions of this material were originally oral, and represented the communication of revealed truth from God to man. Some historical sections were in written form from the beginning, and there is no doubt that certain portions of the Hebrew Scriptures co-existed in written and oral forms for prolonged intervals.

To speak of a "canon" of Scripture is to employ the Greek term κανών in one of its special senses. The word itself was derived from such Semitic cognates as the Assyrian *qanû*, the Ugaritic *qn*, and the Hebrew *qaneh*. These were borrowed in turn from the Sumerian GI-NA, which originally meant a "reed" (Job 40:21). In this sense the term passed into Greek, Latin, and other languages to indicate something of a reed character or structure. In a figurative sense it implied anything straight and upright, and in Greek it was used, among other things, to describe a rule, standard, paradigm, model, boundary, chronological table, and a tax assessment. The Greek and Latin Church Fathers applied the word κανών in a general sense to Biblical law, an ideal or exemplary man, articles of faith, Church doctrines, a catalog or list, a table of contents, and an index of saints.[1] It is possible that Origen may have used the designation "canon" in the sense of the divinely inspired books of Scripture, although there is no direct evidence that it was applied to the Bible

---

[1] Cf. A. Souter, *Text and Canon of the NT* (1912), pp. 154ff.

as such any earlier than *ca.* 352, when Athanasius (d. A.D. 373) used it in this precise sense in the *Decrees of the Synod of Nicea*, No. xviii.

The earliest designation of the books of the Old Testament as the "holy books" or "holy writings" occurred in the work of Josephus, *ca.* A.D. 100. For him the essential characteristic of canonical Scripture was that it constituted divine pronouncements of unquestioned authority that originated within the prophetic period and were therefore under divine inspiration. It was also to be distinguished from every other form of literature because of its intrinsic holiness; the number of canonical writings was strictly limited, and its verbal form was inviolable.[2] These views were completely in accord with the pronouncements of official Judaism as they were ultimately crystallized in the Talmud. While in Greek usage the term κανών appears at first to have denoted the catalog of sacred literature as such, the Latin Fathers employed the designation for Scripture itself, thus indicating that this literary corpus vested with divine authority constituted the rule for faith and life.

Although the Jews of the immediate pre-Christian period venerated their national literature, and in particular regarded the Torah as the authoritative guide to godly living, they were somewhat indiscriminate in their acceptance of material that could be considered as "holy writ." The nearest approach to the idea of canonicity was expressed in the Mishnah,[3] where it was stated that those writings which accorded with such a concept "render the hands unclean." The meaning of this phrase is at best rather uncertain, and numerous explanations have been adduced for it. It may have been intended to insure greater caution against the profanation of the sacred scrolls by careless handling, but it seems more likely that, regarding the sacrosanct nature of the canonical writings, it described a situation whereby contact with such scrolls demanded ritual ablutions after handling in order that conditions of ceremonial purity might be maintained.[4] The term was ultimately extended to include all the writings in the canonical list determined by the rabbinic authorities, thereby distinguishing such compositions from non-canonical works.[5]

While there is a distinct sense in which it can be asserted that it was Christian theism that specifically related the ideas of inspiration and authority to the concept of Biblical canonicity, using the latter term to embrace the writings of the New Testament as well as those composi-

---

[2] *Contra Apionem*, I, 38ff.; cf. Hölscher, *Kanonisch und Apokryph* (1905), p. 4; S. Zeitlin, *Proceedings of the American Academy for Jewish Research*, III (1932), pp. 121ff.

[3] *Yad*. III, 5.

[4] Cf. G. F. Moore, *Judaism*, III, pp. 65ff.; S. Zeitlin, *An Historical Study of the Canonization of the Hebrew Scriptures* (1933), p. 19; M. Haran, *Tarbiz* (1956), XXV, pp. 245ff.; cf. *Yad*. IV, 6; *Zab*. V, 12; *Shabb*. 13a, 14a.

[5] Cf. L. Blau, *Zur Einleitung in die Heilige Schrift* (1894), pp. 21, 69ff.

tions which were venerated by the Jews, it must never be forgotten that later Jewish tradition also adopted the view that every word of Holy Writ was inspired by the divine Spirit. In each instance this Spirit was believed to have rested upon a prophet, and in consequence every Old Testament book was attributed to the activity of a prophetic author. For the Christian the use of the term "Old Testament canon" signifies that the Old Testament is to be regarded as a closed collection of books, inspired by the Spirit of God (2 Tim. 3:15), having a normative authority, and valid as the rule for faith and life. The final provision is important for the Christian, since it serves to emphasize the unity of the revelation in both Testaments, and also witnesses that there are important aspects of the Old Testament self-disclosure of God in history that are binding upon both Christians and Jews for all time. This is in direct contravention of the view, popular in some quarters, which asserts that the Christian ethic can commence with the Sermon on the Mount rather than with the events on Mount Sinai and earlier phases of Hebrew covenantal history.

In any discussion of the Old Testament canon it is of importance to distinguish between that of the Hebrew Bible and its counterpart in other versions of Scripture. The degree of difference in the idea of a canon of sacred writings can be seen by reference on the one hand to the Samaritan version, in which only the Pentateuch was accorded canonicity, and on the other to the LXX, which included the writings known as the Apocrypha. Furthermore, while in many versions the books listed were generally the same as those of the Old Testament canon, the order and number were apt to differ considerably, as was the length of certain of the compositions. The Hebrew canon comprises twenty-four books arranged in three major divisions which are designated the Law, the Prophets, and the Writings respectively. By contrast, the various Christian Bibles, following the general pattern of the Greek and Latin versions, recognized thirty-nine books as canonical, dividing Samuel, Kings, Chronicles, and Ezra-Nehemiah into two books each, and regarding the Minor Prophets as twelve separate works.

The very fact that the canon exists at all in its present form is a striking testimony to human activity and cogitation under divine guidance. Unfortunately it is virtually impossible to be more specific than this about the processes by which the Old Testament canon, or parts of it, became acknowledged as authoritative. While the Bible legitimately ought to be allowed to define and describe canonicity, it has in point of fact almost nothing to say about the manner in which holy writings were assembled, or the personages who exercised an influence over the corpus during the diverse stages of its growth. Historical investigation is no more fruitful in uncovering significant information about the activities of synods or other authoritative bodies with regard to the formation of the Old Testament canon than any other form of study. For the Hebrew Scriptures, however, this circumstance need not occasion particular surprise, since they are of a self-authenticating character, and do not derive their authority either from individual human beings or from corporate ecclesiastical pronouncements. As Ridderbos has pointed out,[6] the various books possessed and exercised divine authority long before men ever made pronouncements to that effect. Ecclesiastical councils did not give the books their divine authority, but merely recognized that they both had it and exercised it.

The concept of a divine norm or rule reaches far back into Hebrew history. Adam, Noah, and Abraham received specific commandments from God that served as their rule of faith and life, and which were enshrined in written form at an early period. During the Mosaic age specific collections of laws were put into writing, as indicated by the formulation of the Book of the Covenant (Exod. 24:4ff.) and the composition of the essentials of Deuteronomy (Deut. 31:9ff.). The latter was of particular importance, because it was placed in close proximity to the highly sacred Ark of the Covenant to constitute the divine witness to the people. Its position was an indication of the sacredness and divine authority attaching to this legal code, which was required to be read in the presence of the nation (Deut. 31:11). To insure equity in Israel, the king was to be given a copy of it, and he was to regulate his decisions according to its contents (Deut. 17:18ff.). Even a revered figure such as Joshua was commanded to adhere to its precepts (Josh. 1:8).

In subsequent periods of Hebrew history the Mosaic Torah was considered to be the divine rule for faith and life (1 Kgs. 2:3; 2 Kgs. 14:6), and the people were urged continually to obey its injunctions. In this connection the prophets played an important role, for they reminded their hearers that the misfortunes and calamities that overtook them were divine judgments for disobedience of the Law, and made it clear that further infractions could only result in drastic punishment. While the prophets urged deference to the Law, and frequently based their own utterances upon its doctrinal themes, they also regarded the words that they themselves spoke under the influence of the divine afflatus as of equal authority with the Torah, arising as they did from the same inspirational source. Popular disregard of their pronouncements was held to bring an equal measure of divine wrath upon the heads of the offenders as did disregard of the Law.

The exalted position that the Torah occupied in Hebrew national life as the standard for faith and practice is reflected in the attitude adopted by the Old Testament writers towards their sources. Unlike many authors in other nations and at different periods, the Hebrews treated their source material with profound respect, preferring to copy the sections

[6] *NBD*, p. 187; cf. E. J. Young in *Revelation and the Bible* (ed. Carl F. H. Henry), p. 157.

that they needed as literally as possible rather than quoting them freely from memory. Because their sacred literature was an essentially vital and relevant corpus, and because it still had to attain to the degree of fixity that became a concomitant of canonicity, it was possible for the ancient Hebrews to interpolate additional material into their writings, to replace one law by another when altered circumstances made such a procedure necessary,[7] or to engage in whatever revisions were considered desirable and proper at the particular time.

The belief that God could reveal His will by means of a holy book was thus an early and indelible feature of Israelite religious life. This concept did not originate, as Eissfeldt imagined,[8] from a belief in the word of an inspired person—the *torah* of the priest or the utterance of the prophet—so much as from the fact that what the inspired individual said constituted the *verba ipsissima* of God, and was accepted as such even though its implications were not always taken to heart. By uniform tradition the early normative communications of God to Israel took the form of laws, which were committed to writing by and large within the contemporary situation. On two occasions Israel solemnly pledged herself to obey the Book of the Law that God had given through Moses, first during the reign of Josiah (2 Kgs. 23:2ff.; 2 Chron. 34:30ff.), subsequent to the discovery of an ancient legal code of unknown content, second during the period of Ezra and Nehemiah (Ez. 7:6, 14; Neh. 8:1ff.), when the "Book of the Law" comprised at the very least a part of the Pentateuch.

It is impossible in the light of present knowledge to state with any degree of certainty exactly when the Pentateuch was finished in its extant form, although there seem to be substantial grounds for thinking that it was virtually complete by the death of Samuel.[9] What can be said, however, is that from the very beginning of its existence high authority was attached to its contents, and as a result it is little wonder that it became the first major section of the Hebrew Scriptures to be accorded unquestioned acceptance prior to subsequent formal canonicity. It is evident that the Torah in general, and Deuteronomy in particular, goes back in principle to an early period of Israelite life from the presence of a formula of imprecation warning against adding anything to its contents or detracting from it in any way (Deut. 4:2; 12:32). So specific a command, which is reflected only once in other parts of the Old Testament (Prov. 30:6), was employed in a considerably more elaborate form at the end of the laws of Hammurabi,[10] where impreca-

[7] For such modifications compare Num. 26:52-56 with 27:1-11, 36:1-9; Num. 15:22-31 with Lev. 4:1ff.

[8] *Einleitung in das AT*, p. 615.

[9] Cf. R. Brinker, *The Influence of Sanctuaries in Early Israel*, pp. 216ff., 224.

[10] *ANET*, pp. 178f.

tions were directed at any who would endeavor to alter the law. Hammurabi's law was codified under the stated patronage of the deity Shamash and mediated by a great leader of the state to the people, who were given due warning to pay careful heed to its contents. As far as Hebrew religious tradition was concerned, the fundamental precepts of the Mosaic Torah were manifested to Israel through the agency of a divinely appointed leader of the populace. Thus the idea of a revealed, authoritative, and mediated written code was by no means novel both before and during the Mosaic era. The fact and existence of the Mosaic Torah at an early period furnished the foundations for all subsequent religious writing in Israel, and as such supplied one element of the concept of canonicity.

It may be, as Bentzen has suggested,[11] that another germinal aspect relating to the formation of a canon of Scripture is what von Rad has called the "historical *credo* of Israel"[12] as it occurs in certain types of Old Testament literature.[13] Some caution should be urged in entertaining this idea, however, since it would be comparatively easy to assume that such a *credo* constituted the skeletal form that was subsequently clothed by the religious traditions of an Israelite "amphictyony" and enriched by the "laws of the state." It must be remembered, accordingly, that the *credo*, if it can be legitimately conceived of as such, was only one element in a tradition that was already rich in literary material (as will be argued subsequently in the present work) and had as its authoritative written foundation the legislation given to Moses on Mount Sinai.

It is clear, therefore, that the Torah did not only mark the beginning of a body of national literature (a fact that, in the event, is rather incidental to more pressing spiritual considerations) but also constituted the normative expression of the divine will for the Hebrew people. By its very nature it established a basis for doctrine and life upon which subsequent expositors of revealed religion leaned heavily. So deeply rooted were the traditions as to the antiquity and sanctity of the Mosaic enactments that the term "Torah" was applied not only to the first five books of the developing canon, but also to the entire corpus of the Hebrew Scriptures at a later period. This designation, which occurs in 2 Esdras 19:21, and in John 10:34 under the form *nomos*, arose from the belief, popular in rabbinic circles, that the Prophets and the Writings were to be included in the Torah, since Holy Writ in its entirety constituted the Word of God. Since, however, "Torah" was the title of the first and principal section of the Biblical writings, it is also conceivable that it

[11] *Introduction to the OT*, I, p. 24.

[12] G. von Rad, *Das Formgeschichtliche Problem des Hexateuchs* (1938), pp. 3ff.

[13] Exod. 15:1ff.; Deut. 26:5-9 (cf. 6:20-24); Josh. 24:2-13; Ps. 136:1ff.

was transferred to the entire collection as a means of indicating its inspiration and canonicity.

The second major section of the canon, the Prophets, was commonly subdivided into two parts. These were the "Former Prophets," consisting of the books of Joshua, Judges, Samuel, and Kings, and the "Latter Prophets," which comprised Isaiah, Jeremiah, Ezekiel, and the Twelve. The authority that the Former Prophets acquired is readily understandable when it is realized that these writings describe the manner in which the provisions of the Covenant agreement were applied to the conditions in the land of Canaan. As chronicles of the relationships between God and His people, these documents were without doubt drawn up by individuals of official standing in Israel, and so in many respects would have a secular as well as a religious authority.

By their very nature the compositions of the Latter Prophets were held to be authoritative from their earliest appearances, although initially, at least, the number of those who venerated them as writings whose tenor and spirit were akin to that of the Torah was probably quite small. Almost certainly their authority was enhanced greatly when the predictions of disaster that many of them contained found fulfillment in the exile, and the victims of that catastrophe were forced to think of other aspects of the prophetic message. That the individual prophets themselves felt that they stood in a firm and unified spiritual tradition can be seen from the manner in which they ascribed authority to their predecessors either by quoting from their utterances, alluding to incidents in the Torah (e.g. Jer. 4:4; 5:15, 17; 11:4), or rebuking the nation for not listening to previous prophecies (Zech. 1:4ff.; Hos. 6:5). Undoubtedly some of this material was set down in written form during the lifetime of most if not all of the individuals concerned, as were the prophecies of Jeremiah. If the reference in Daniel 9:2 to "the books" is to a collection of prophetic writings, as seems most probable, it would imply that these works were regarded as having divine authority, and were thus akin to the Pentateuchal compositions.

The third major division of the canon, known as the Writings or Hagiographa, comprised eleven compositions of diverse character emanating from various facets of Hebrew life. The collections of psalms that formed the basis of the Psalter were important both for private and public devotions and for their associations with the sanctuary and the cultus and the revered name of David, the traditional father of Hebrew psalmody. In the same manner, the connecting of the proverbs with Solomon and the growth of the Wisdom Literature from the utterances and traditions of the Hebrew sages led to the acceptance of important elements of this division of the canon as constituting authoritative moral and spiritual pronouncements that participated fully in the divine spirit expressed in the Torah. Historical and prophetic writings such as those attributed to Daniel, Ezra, and Nehemiah were also accepted as being in

266

keeping with the religious tenor of other aspects of the national literature, as were the Chronicles, which were compiled with a specific theological standpoint in view. These and other books were regarded properly as holy writings because of their association with the cultus, the national history and tradition, and revered personages of the past. If the Prophets can be said to have derived some of their authority from their consonance with the teachings of the Torah, the Writings did also, springing as they did from the very warp and woof of the Hebrew spiritual fabric.

There are some grounds for assuming the antiquity of a twofold rather than a threefold division of the canon, in which the Old Testament Writings were subsumed under the second major section because of the similarity of some of the compositions to the works of the prophets, with the result that the canon was simply thought of in terms of the Law and the Prophets. References in certain of the Qumran scrolls, to be mentioned subsequently, indicate that the sectaries themselves thought in terms of a twofold division, as did some of the copyists of later LXX manuscripts.

The foregoing outline of the conjectured growth of a canonical corpus of Old Testament writings is, of course, general and is based in part upon the rather scanty internal information that the Old Testament furnishes with regard to the assembling and the relationships of the various canonical books. From the purely Jewish standpoint there is a distinct sense in which the concept of canonicity can only have been crystallized and implemented when there were sufficient works in the corpus of Hebrew literature from which a selection could be made, since not all Hebrew writings were accorded canonicity. As far as the historical books were concerned, the finished product alone rather than the underlying sources constituted the preferred choice. In the sense that they were incorporated in some manner into the final production the sources themselves could be considered canonical, but the most obvious reason for the overall attitude consisted in the comparative availability of the extant work as contrasted with that of the source material. Public acceptance was thus one important criterion of canonicity. The feelings of the readers regarding canonicity were governed, of course, by the considerations of essential consonance with the spirit of the Torah and the other factors referred to above.

B. Speculation About the Canon

The completed Jewish canon consisted of twenty-four books as follows: five of the Pentateuch, eight books of the Prophets—Joshua, Judges, Samuel, Kings, Isaiah, Jeremiah, Ezekiel, the Minor Prophets, and eleven Writings—Psalms, Proverbs, Job, Song of Solomon, Ruth, Lamentations, Ecclesiastes, Esther, Daniel, Ezra, and Chronicles. From the Greek translation by Aquila it is seen that Samuel and Kings formed one book each; the Twelve were also known as a single work in the time of Ben Sira (Ecclus. 49:10). The division of the Prophets into "Former" and "Latter" was evidently introduced by the Massoretes. Later Jewish tradition gave great prominence to the activity of prophets in the formulation of the canon of Scripture, and held that every word of Holy Writ was inspired by the Spirit of God. Because this Spirit was believed to have rested in every case upon a prophet, it followed that the authorship of such Biblical books ought to be attributed to prophetic functioning.

1. Baba Bathra. The classical passage for the sequence of the books in the Babylonian *Baba Bathra* 14b proceeded on this assumption, discovering the prophetic author either in the titles or the sequence of the works themselves. Thus Moses, Joshua, Samuel, Ezra, and the Prophets were credited with having written the compositions attributed to them; in addition Moses was regarded as the author of Job, whose hero was held to have been his contemporary. The last eight verses of the Pentateuch were thought to have been composed by Joshua. Samuel was given credit for the authorship of Judges and Ruth. Jeremiah was believed to have written Kings and Lamentations, and Ezra the scribe was regarded as the author of Chronicles. There was thus an unbroken chain of prophets from Moses to Malachi, into which company David and Solomon were also placed. The Psalms were credited as a whole to David, while Proverbs, Canticles, and Ecclesiastes were assigned to the literary activity of Solomon. Esther alone was not attributed a prophetic author, but this omission was more apparent than real since Jewish tradition venerated Mordecai as a prophet contemporary with Haggai, Zechariah, and Malachi and he was held to have prophesied at the time of Darius I. In any event, the position of Esther was safeguarded by the tradition that the Great Synagogue had numerous prophets among its members, who took upon themselves the right to have the Esther scroll written down.[14] Quite clearly, then, one dominant criterion of canonicity for the ancient Jews was the attribution of a work to prophetic authorship, so that a composition such as Ecclesiasticus, in which the identity of the author was known to be non-prophetic, presented absolutely no problems as far as canonicity was concerned.

In summary, from the Jewish standpoint only those works which could properly claim prophetic authorship had a legitimate right to canonicity, and out of this corpus there was a decided preference for finished works rather than for source material of prophetic origin. The relationship of the particular author to the theocracy was also an important determining consideration.[15] Moses was naturally a towering figure in the Old Testament economy generally, since he occupied a pre-eminent position as the faithful servant of God (cf. Num. 12:1ff.). In virtue of being as-

---

[14] Cf. *Yom. 80a; Shabb. 104a; Megill. 2a.*
[15] Young in *Revelation and the Bible,* pp. 165f.

sumed as the author of the Pentateuch as a whole, and the real contributor of a significant amount of its contents, his literary products formed the foundation on which the entire Old Testament corpus was based.

Although the second section of the Hebrew canon, the Prophets, comprised material written by men standing within the spiritual tradition of Moses, these individuals were nevertheless inferior in stature to the great lawgiver himself. In the theocracy, therefore, their position in the affections of the Jews is shown by the division that incorporated their writings into a second major group of sacred literature, different in content from the Torah but akin in moral and spiritual quality. Although there are some respects in which the attribution of prophetic stature to certain of the authors of compositions in the Hagiographa imposes a strain upon the concept of prophetism, it may well be that the writers concerned were thought of in the ancient Hebrew sense as mediators between God and the nation, or as representatives of God in their capacity as spokesmen to the people (cf. Exod. 4:16; 7:1; Deut. 18:15ff.). At all events they appear to have been accorded a position of considerable importance in the traditions of the Israelites, quite aside from being regarded as inspired by the Holy Spirit of God. Perhaps it was this that led to a twofold division of the canon into the Law of Moses and the Prophets, in which some, if not all, of the compositions subsequently designated by the technical term *K^ethubhim* or "Writings" were included.

Whatever the motivation governing the curious and sometimes rather uncritical kind of rabbinic speculation in matters of Scripture, the threefold division of the canon was well established in the early Christian era. The New Testament makes it clear that the canon familiar to Jesus Christ was identical with the one which exists today. None of the Apocrypha or Pseudepigrapha is ever cited by name, much less accorded the status of Scripture, whereas Daniel is specifically quoted as a prophetic composition in Matthew 24:15. The three chief divisions were enumerated in Luke 24:44 as the Law, the Prophets, and the Psalms. Usually the New Testament writers only mentioned the first two sections (cf. Matt. 5:17; Lk. 16:16), but quite obviously they included the Hagiographa with the Prophets just as the Talmudic teachers did (due perhaps to the lack of a current technical term for the Hagiographa).

From the words of Jesus in Matthew 23:35 and Luke 11:51, it can be inferred that Chronicles was regarded as the last book in the Hebrew canon at that time. The murder of Abel is recorded in the first canonical writing (Genesis); that of Zechariah is contained in the final book of the Hebrew Scriptures (2 Chronicles 24:20). Of course no chronological order is intended to be conveyed by the words of Jesus, since innocent blood was shed after the killing of Zechariah (Jer. 26:23). The reference in Matthew could possibly be to the prophet Zechariah, who was the son of Berechiah (Zech. 1:1), although there is no independent evidence to the effect that he was martyred. Alternatively, some have supposed that

269

the reference is to the martyrdom of Zechariah the son of Jehoiada (2 Chron. 24:20-22), and that the error of the father's name was due either to the Evangelist himself, or, since it does not occur in the best manuscript of Luke, to the addition of a copyist.

Further evidence of a threefold division of the canon is provided by Josephus,[16] who enumerated five books of Moses, thirteen prophetical writings, and four books of hymns to God and precepts for human behavior. Probably Josephus arrived at the number thirteen for the second division of the canon by including Ruth with Judges and Lamentations with Jeremiah, and regarding the Minor Prophets as a unified book in the manner current in the time of Ben Sira. A threefold canon of Scripture was also given attestation in the writings of Philo, particularly in his *Contemplative Life*, written about A.D. 40.[17] Although some doubt was thrown on the genuineness of this work by nineteenth-century scholars, there is, as Cohn has demonstrated,[18] no substantial ground for such an attitude. Philo mentions by title the Law, the Prophets, the Psalms and other books, but does not refer to Ezekiel, Daniel, or the five Megilloth (Canticles, Ruth, Lamentations, Ecclesiastes, and Esther) in his extant works. But Philo's failure to name these books cannot be taken as proof that they were not in his canon of Scripture, for as Blau has pointed out,[19] the silence of Philo concerning Ezekiel is most probably accidental, since even Ben Sira mentioned the book attributed to that prophet. Consequently, there seems no good ground for questioning the assertion of Siegfried[20] and others that the canon known to Philo was essentially the same as that current at the present time.

An even earlier attestation of the threefold division is to be seen in the Prologue to Ecclesiasticus, dated about 132 B.C., in which specific mention was made of the Law and the Prophets (or prophecies) as well as "the others which follow after them." Since the author of the Prologue stated that his grandfather Jesus ben Sira, the compiler of Ecclesiasticus *ca.* 190 B.C., had long given himself to a careful study of the "law and the prophets and the other books of the fathers," it is legitimate to assume that this threefold division went back at least to the beginning of the second century B.C. A reference in 2 Maccabees, which was extant by about the middle of the first century of the Christian era and may have been compiled as early as 100 B.C., spoke of the founding of a library by Nehemiah, who "gathered together the books concerning the

---

16 *Contra Apionem*, I, 8.
17 *De Vita Contemplativa*, II, 475.
18 *Einleitung und Chronologie der Schriften Philo's* (1899), p. 37.
19 *JE*, III, p. 146.
20 *Philo* (1875), p. 61. Cf. H. E. Ryle, *The Canon of the OT* (1904), pp. 158ff.

kings and the prophets, and those of David, and the epistles of the kings concerning holy gifts" (2 Macc. 2:13f.).

The Torah was not mentioned in this collection, since its wide circulation made references to it unnecessary. However, there can be no doubt about the second part of the canon, which was unmistakably specified by "books concerning the kings," that is, Joshua, Judges, Samuel, and Kings, and by "the prophets," namely, Isaiah, Jeremiah, Ezekiel, and the Minor Prophets. Since the Hagiographa had not at that time received its technical designation, the contents were referred to as "those of David," that is, the Psalms, using as a title the first and most important book of the collection. But if the expression "the books of the kings concerning holy gifts" indicates the royal letters mentioned in Ezra and Nehemiah,[21] then the Hagiographa as a whole would seem to be implied by reference to the Psalms and Ezra-Nehemiah-Chronicles as the first and last books respectively.

As mentioned above, the classical definition of the sequence of canonical Hebrew Scriptures was the *baraitha* or unauthorized gloss in the Talmudic tractate *Baba Bathra*. There are reasons for believing that the gloss is of second-century B.C. origin, for at that time there was considerable discussion as to which books of Scripture belonged to the same section, and therefore were to be written in one roll. With the exclusion of interpolated comments[22] the *baraitha* is as follows:

> The order of the prophets is Joshua, Judges, Samuel, Kings, Jeremiah, Ezekiel, Isaiah, the Twelve (Minor Prophets). That of the Kethubhim is Ruth, Psalms, Job, Proverbs, Ecclesiastes, Song of Solomon, Lamentations, Daniel, the roll of Esther, Ezra, Chronicles.
>
> Who wrote the books? Moses wrote his book, the section about Balaam, and Job; Joshua wrote his book and the last eight verses of the Torah; Samuel wrote his book, Judges, and Ruth. David wrote the Psalms at the direction of the Ten Ancients, namely through Adam [Ps. 139:16; Ps. 92?], Melchizedek [Ps. 110], Abraham [Ps. 89], Moses [Pss. 90-100], Heman [Ps. 88], Jeduthun [Ps. 62, Ps. 77?], Asaph [Pss. 50, 73-83], and the three sons of Korah [Pss. 42, 49, 78, 84, 85, 88]. Jeremiah wrote his book, the Book of Kings, and Lamentations; king Hezekiah and his council wrote Isaiah, Proverbs, Song of Solomon, and Ecclesiastes; the men of the Great Synagogue wrote Ezekiel, the Twelve Prophets, Daniel, and Esther. Ezra wrote his book and the genealogy of Chronicles down to his own period. Nehemiah completed it.

From the fact that Moses is mentioned as the author of the Torah it may be gathered that the five books of the Law were originally designated in the collection to which the gloss referred. However, because of the familiarity of the Jews with the Torah through contemporary synagogue usage, it could well have been regarded as comprising a single

---

[21] For the view that they were letters from the Persian kings relating to gifts for the Temple see G. Ch. Aalders, *Oud-testamentische Kanoniek* (1952), p. 31.

[22] For the full form, translated from G. A. Marx—G. Dalman, *Traditio Rabbinorum Veterrima* (1884), see H. E. Ryle, *The Canon of the OT*, pp. 284ff.

work whose component parts needed no specific enumeration. Since the gloss does not specify the books according to their origin, succession, and age, it can only have considered the order of the Biblical writings insofar as they belonged to the same section of the canon. Yet it seems clear from the gloss that the "Former Prophets" had been credited with a fixed sequence of considerable antiquity concerning which there was no doubt in the minds of the rabbinical authorities. This was evidently occasioned by the way in which the writings from Joshua to Kings carried on the narrative of Hebrew history from post-Mosaic times (cf. 2 Macc. 2:13). The order of the "Latter Prophets" was irregular, and in the majority of manuscripts the only uniformity occurred in the placing of the Twelve Minor Prophets at the end of the list of books. According to Ginsburg there were no fewer than eight varying sequences of the Hagiographa.[23]

The *baraitha* in its fuller form is certainly a curious piece of writing, containing as it does some strange and occasionally impossible traditions regarding the composition of certain books of the Hebrew canon. While it has often been held to have had an important bearing upon the history of the canon, its contents demonstrate that it can throw no light at all upon the processes by which the canon achieved its final form. The unusual order of Jeremiah, Ezekiel, and Isaiah was explained by Talmudic authorities on the basis of a principle of internal consistency. Kings ended with destruction, and as such was appropriately succeeded by the prophecy of Jeremiah, which began and concluded with desolation also. Despite the fact that Ezekiel commenced with destruction, it ended with consolation, while all of Isaiah consisted of a consoling theme. In this way destruction appropriately followed upon destruction, and consolation upon consolation. This explanation is patently artificial, and it seems most probable that the prophetical books were actually arranged according to their size, a principle that appears to have been followed also in the accumulation of Mishnaic treatises.

2. *Apocrypha, Septuagint, and patristic sources.* It seems highly improbable that there was ever any specific enumeration of the books of the canon in Jewish literature generally. Early estimates were apt to vary somewhat; Second Esdras gives the number as twenty-four,[24] whereas Josephus computed the number as twenty-two.[25] In his preface to Samuel and Kings, Jerome mentions twenty-two books, but he finally arrived at a total of twenty-four, whereas Origen adhered to the number suggested by Josephus.[26] Since both Origen and Jerome studied under

[23] *Introduction to the Massoretico-Critical Edition of the Hebrew Bible* (1897), p. 7.

[24] 2 Esdr. 14:44ff. Variant readings (94, 204, 84, 974) agree in containing the number "4."

[25] *Contra Apionem*, I, 8.

[26] In Eusebius, *Hist. Eccl.*, VI, 25.

Jewish teachers, it appears probable that the synagogue authorities themselves were somewhat undecided on the matter. The *baraitha* seems to favor twenty-four books, if Ruth formed one roll along with Judges or Psalms, and if Lamentations was included with Jeremiah on another roll, thus making twenty-two rolls but twenty-four books. The latter number was mentioned specifically in some Midrashic passages, and according to Strack[27] it was also known in antiquity in certain non-Jewish circles.

Scholars generally assume the arrangement of the books as given in *Baba Bathra* to be essentially the original one, and that of the LXX to be secondary. This view is by no means undisputed, however. Although the antiquity of the threefold division of the canon is never seriously questioned, it is obviously difficult to ascertain the order and contents of a section referred to as "the prophets" (Lk. 24:44), for example. In this general connection some reference may be made again to Origen and Josephus. The latter stated that the number of sacred books received by the Jews was twenty-two, which he distinguished from other works and enumerated as the five books of Moses, thirteen compositions in which the prophets described Hebrew history from the immediate post-Mosaic period to the reign of the Persian monarch Artaxerxes I, and four books containing hymns of praise and regulations for social behavior.[28] It seems reasonably certain that Josephus combined Ruth and Lamentations with Judges and Jeremiah respectively in his computation, as suggested above, and that in so doing he was following a well-established Palestinian tradition.

Origen, who also held that the Jews accepted twenty-two books as their Scriptural canon, showed considerably greater conformity to the order of the LXX in his enumeration of the canonical writings than did Josephus and some rabbinical authorities.[29] However, he did not follow the LXX listing slavishly, and there are significant differences between the two. It is at least reasonable to conclude from Origen's testimony that the order of the canon in *Baba Bathra* did not command unquestioned assent in Palestine during that period.[30] From the evidence presented by the Qumran texts it would seem probable that there were several different forms of the canon in existence by the first century of the Christian era, which is in harmony with the rather fluid picture of the pre-Massoretic text as indicated by the Qumran scrolls.

Any assessment of the LXX canon of the Old Testament must note that the Greek manuscripts exhibit significant differences, both in the

---

[27] In J. J. Herzog (ed.), *Real-Encyklopädie für Protestantische Theologie und Kirche* (1896), IX, p. 757.

[28] *Contra Apionem*, I, 8.

[29] In Eusebius, *Hist. Eccl.*, VI, 25.

[30] Cf. A. Jepsen, ZAW, LXXI (1959), pp. 114ff. and *Theologische Literaturzeitung*, LXXIV (1949), pp. 65ff.

number of the books that they contain and the order in which they are arranged. Such a situation would appear to reflect an earlier Palestinian Jewish tradition, and indicate the secondary nature of the LXX canon. It is of significance that Philo followed the Jewish rather than the Alexandrian tradition in his estimate of the content of Scripture. It would seem that the differences between the Hebrew and the LXX canons lie not so much in a wider interpretation of the canon by the Alexandrian Jews because they thought in terms of a much broader view of inspiration, as in the fact that the Jews in Alexandria (and the Diaspora generally) did not distinguish as sharply between the canonical and non-canonical works as their Palestinian counterparts did. Had they done so it is highly probable that the early Christian Church would have looked a little more critically at the excess of the Hebrew canon that they used in the LXX version.

A criticism of the originality of the Hebrew order was made by Katz,[31] who maintained that the earliest attestation of the Hebrew selection of books was related to the period of the reconstitution of Judaism after the destruction of the Temple. He further claimed that the evidence for twenty-four as the number of Old Testament canonical books was scanty, and that twenty-two was the proper and correct total as known in Palestine. In order to disprove the originality of the Hebrew order of books, he maintained that the arrangement Ezra-Nehemiah-Chronicles was artificial, a position that, in the view of the present author, is extremely difficult to justify, even if the Chronicler is considered to be someone other than Ezra. As has been remarked above, it is quite likely that in early times several forms of the canon existed side by side, preserving the same threefold division but varying to some degree in content. The fact that the Old Testament books were written down on separate rolls would contribute to this diversity and indeed would serve as a hindrance to the appearance of a fixed order of books. The canon of the LXX evidently reflected this general state of affairs, and perpetuated it in some ways, thus showing its dependence upon the traditions of the Palestinian Jews.

Although neither the *baraitha* nor the Hellenistic Jews of Alexandria can furnish proper information relating to the compilation of the Hebrew canon, it is interesting to note that for many centuries the view was current that the canon of the Old Testament was formulated and completed within the lifetime of Ezra. This tradition drew for its Biblical foundation upon Ezra and Nehemiah (cf. Ez. 7:10, 25; Neh. 8:1ff.; 9:3), and was given currency not merely by *Baba Bathra*, which credited Ezra with the compilation of his own book and the genealogy of Chronicles to his own time, but also to some extent by the opinions of Josephus. About

---

[31] *Zeitschrift für die Neutestamentliche Wissenschaft*, XLVII (1956), pp. 191ff.

A.D. 95 Josephus recorded that the history of the origin of the world up to the reign of Artaxerxes I had been described in the Jewish holy writings, and added that although the story had subsequently been carried towards his own time, this latter material did not deserve the same confidence on the part of the reader, since the succession of the prophets was not fixed accurately.[32] From this statement it can be inferred with great probability that during the lifetime of Ezra the historical books of the Old Testament, and perhaps some portions of the Hagiographa as well, were circulating in their extant form.

Second Esdras, a Jewish apocalyptic composition whose central section seems to have been written by an unknown Jew at the end of the first century of the Christian era, preserved the tradition that in the thirtieth year after the destruction of Jerusalem (557 B.C.) Ezra was inspired to dictate ninety-four books to five scribes within a period of some forty days. Of this corpus twenty-four books were to be made available for general perusal, while the remaining seventy, evidently consisting of apocalyptic material, were to be restricted to the wise men (2 Esdr. 14:18ff.). Presumably the twenty-four books were the same as those mentioned by other writers—with Ruth and Lamentations as separate works which had been incorporated, for various reasons, with Judges, Psalms, or Jeremiah. Another apocryphal work, 2 Maccabees (ch. 2:13ff.), contains a letter purporting to have been written by Palestinian Jews to the Hellenistic Jews of Alexandria. This epistle mentions the nature of the library said to have been assembled by Nehemiah. If it is genuine, it would be dated 165 B.C., but many scholars have denied its authenticity and assigned it to the first century B.C. While these passages may be nothing more than attempts to project into the age of Ezra and Nehemiah certain tendencies that were only evident at a later period, it must not be forgotten that the middle of the fifth century B.C. was a time when considerable interest was shown in the codification of Hebrew sacred literature. On the other hand, neither the Talmud nor Josephus specifically credits Ezra with a special function in the formulation of the Old Testament canon, even though Baba Bathra mentions his literary activity.[33] The tradition that ascribes to Ezra an important role in the creation of the Old Testament canon only appears to go back with certainty as far as the account in 2 Esdras, and the nature of this material is such that it is difficult to ascertain its historical value. Despite this fact it may well be that the narrative was based upon a genuine tradition of collection and assemblage of Scriptural materials in the fifth century B.C., whether by Ezra, Nehemiah, or some of their followers. In the same way it is at least possible that an historically reliable tradition is at the root of the information furnished by 2 Macca-

---

[32] *Contra Apionem*, I, 8.
[33] Cf. E. Bickermann, *RB*, LV (1948), p. 398.

bees. Whatever may be the facts of this situation, it is simply a matter of record that little is known about the development of the canon in the period immediately following the time of Ezra and Nehemiah. As has been observed previously, Ben Sira knew of the threefold division of the Old Testament canon, and attached high authority to the various sections. He was familiar with at least some of the Writings, though to what extent he was conversant with all of them is uncertain. In the narratives about the Maccabees there are numerous references to the sacred books of the Jews,[34] although it is impossible in the nature of the case to be certain as to the extent to which such a corpus corresponded to the Old Testament canon.

By the time of Christ, it would seem, the Old Testament existed as a complete collection. The evidence presented by the New Testament writers indicates that the Old Testament as a whole was referred to as "the Scriptures"[35] or "the Scripture"[36] at that period to designate a familiar and unified group of inspired and authoritative writings. In particular, the specific designation of "Old Testament" was applied by the primitive Church to this corpus of Holy Writ to convey the sense of a completed assemblage of Scriptural compositions (2 Cor. 3:14). New Testament authors commonly alluded to the Scriptures in terms of two categories—the Law and the Prophets. Support for this position has been provided by the discoveries from Qumran, where in four instances the Community Rule or Manual of Discipline (1QS, I:3; VIII:13ff.) and the Zadokite Fragment (CDC, V:21; VII:15ff.) referred to the Old Testament writings in precisely the same two categories. That this twofold canon included all the present works appears obvious from the fact that the Qumran community cited most of the Old Testament books, including those later classified in the third section of the canon. On this evidence alone there would seem to be considerable ground for a theory of the antiquity of a twofold division of the Old Testament canon.

Naturally it is impossible to determine in detail the contents of the canon in the time of Christ, although, as has been mentioned above, one reference (Matt. 23:35, Lk. 11:51) would imply that the canon terminated with Chronicles at that time. The fact that Esther, Ecclesiastes, Canticles, Ezra, Nehemiah, Obadiah, Nahum, and Zephaniah are not cited by New Testament authors does not in itself indicate that these compositions were not considered to constitute part of the Old Testament at that particular period, since being quoted in the New Testament is not a necessary condition of canonicity for an Old Testament book.

If this assemblage of sacred writings was substantially the same in the days of Jesus Christ as it is at the present, such a canon was "closed"

---

[34] E.g. 1 Macc. 1:56f., 4:30, 7:41, 12:9.
[35] Matt. 26:54; John 5:39; Acts 17:2, *et al.*
[36] John 2:22; Acts 8:32, *et al.*

more by common consent and popular acceptance than by formal decree on the part of the rabbinic or early Christian authorities. In connection with this latter concept an appeal has sometimes been made to the work of the "men of the Great Synagogue," who were referred to in the Talmud.[37] Unfortunately it is far from clear as to precisely who these men were. According to some theories they belonged to a generation that included Haggai, Zechariah, Daniel, and Esther, a view that Ryle repudiated as "ignorant tradition."[38] In the view of Elias Levita (d. A.D. 1549), these men, along with Ezra, united in one volume the twenty-four books of the canon, which until that time had circulated separately, and classified them in three divisions, determining the order of the Prophets and the Sacred Writings.[39]

Although Levita's arrangement differs from the order listed in *Baba Bathra,* his view gained currency in the sixteenth century, and for the next two hundred years was accepted as orthodox. From the middle of the seventeenth century, however, the nature of the "Great Synagogue" was disputed, and in the nineteenth century Kuenen argued strongly that the "Synagogue" was none other than the great assembly at Jerusalem described in Nehemiah 8:1ff., which pledged itself to the acceptance of those conditions enunciated by Ezra the scribe from the ancient Jewish law.[40] On the basis of the available evidence[41] it would seem that if such a body of men as was envisaged in *Baba Bathra* actually existed, its activity was confined to the period of Ezra and that it extended to only four books, not the entire Old Testament canon. When it is said that they "wrote" Ezekiel, the Twelve Prophets, Daniel, and Esther, what is meant is clearly that they were engaged in editing such works, probably with a view to incorporating them into a sacred canon.

3. *The "Council of Jamnia."* It has also been suggested that pronouncements that defined the limits of the Old Testament canon were made by a formal council of Jewish authorities held towards the end of the first century after Christ at Jamnia or Jabneh. Desirable though such an event might have been, it is far from certain that there ever was a Council or Synod of Jamnia in the strictest sense. To speak of such a body as though it was responsible for closing the Old Testament canon

[37] *Bab. Bath.* 14b, 15a.
[38] *The Canon of the OT,* p. 290.
[39] E. Levita, *Massoreth Hammassoreth* (1867 ed.), p. 120; cf. A. Bentzen, *Introduction to the OT,* I, p. 27.
[40] Kuenen in K. Budde (ed.), *Gesammelte Abhandlungen* (1894), pp. 161ff. He was followed, among others, by W. Robertson Smith, *The OT in the Jewish Church* (1881), pp. 156ff., 168f.; *DILOT,* p. vii; K. Budde, *EB,* I, cols. 654f. The tradition was defended by C. H. H. Wright, *The Book of Koheleth, Commonly Called Ecclesiastes* (1883), pp. 475ff.; S. Krauss, *JQR,* XI (1898-99), pp. 347ff.
[41] Cf. E. Bickermann, *RB,* LV (1948), pp. 397ff.

by fixing its limits as they had been arrived at by A.D. 90 is to beg the entire question, as Moore has pointed out.[42] As far as the facts of the situation are concerned, very little is known about the supposed Synod of Jamnia. After Jerusalem was destroyed by the forces of Titus in A.D. 70, Rabbi Johanan ben Zakkai obtained permission from the Romans to settle in Jamnia, where he proposed to carry on his literary activities. The location soon became an established center of Scriptural study, and from time to time certain discussions took place relating to the canonicity of specific Old Testament books including Ezekiel, Esther, Canticles, Ecclesiastes, and Proverbs.[43] There can be little doubt that such conversations took place both before and after this period, and it seems probable that nothing of a formal or binding nature was decided in these discussions, even though, as Rowley had indicated,[44] the various debates helped to crystallize and establish the Jewish tradition in this regard more firmly than had been the case previously.

If it is questionable as to how far one can speak correctly of the Council of Jamnia, it is even more doubtful if the participants in the discussions were actually concerned with the problem as to whether certain books should be *included* in the canon of Scripture or not. Rather, as Young has pointed out,[45] the conversations seem to have centered upon the question as to whether specific books should be *excluded* from what was to be regarded as the Scriptural corpus. Certain compositions were generally accepted as inspired and authoritative, even though they reflected the Jewish tradition in a somewhat peculiar fashion: Esther did not mention the Divine Name; Ecclesiastes seemed partly Epicurean to some authorities and out of harmony with contemporary Jewish philosophy; and the Song of Songs, though credited to Solomon, appeared to be nothing more than a composition dealing with the vagaries of human passion and physical love.

The fact is that the works under discussion were already accorded canonical status in popular esteem, so that, as Stafford Wright has stated,[46] the "Council" was actually confirming public opinion, not forming it. The conversations that took place were strictly academic, and in consequence it is very questionable if the doubts that they raised in connection with certain compositions actually represented the general attitude of the populace as a whole to any significant extent. Certainly Ezekiel, to mention but one topic of dispute, must have been accepted as Scripture long before the rabbis of Jamnia undertook to examine its status. It ought to be concluded, therefore, that no formal pronounce-

---

[42] *Judaism,* I, pp. 83ff.; cf. W. W. Christie, *JTS,* XXVI (1925), pp. 347ff.
[43] Cf. *Yad.* III, 5; G. Lisowsky, *Jadajim* (1956), pp. 9, 57.
[44] *The Growth of the OT* (1950), p. 170.
[45] *Revelation and the Bible,* p. 160.
[46] *EQ,* XIX, No. 2 (1947), pp. 93ff.

ment as to the limits of the Old Testament canon was ever made in rabbinic circles at Jamnia.

4. Modern theories. The manuscript discoveries at Qumran provide little information about the origin and limits of the Old Testament canon. The library of the sectaries included numerous religious compositions other than those normally accepted by the Jews, but as far as the content of the Hebrew canon is concerned, the only work missing in the early discoveries was Esther.[47] One reason for this omission from the Qumran collection of scrolls may be that it was deliberately rejected by the sectaries.[48] On the other hand, the absence of the manuscript could be entirely a matter of chance, and the book may yet be discovered in the fragments which at the time of writing have still to be examined and evaluated.

As far as the available evidence goes, it is clear that while the Old Testament does not furnish any significant information about the manner in which the canon arose, or the extent of the Prophets and the Writings at any given period of their history, it does bear testimony to the existence from early times of an authoritative literature to which appeal was made in varying ways and which, with subsequent additions, was venerated as Holy Writ. This vague internal testimony has been more than offset by the precision of modern critical scholarship, which has furnished a number of theories as to the growth and content of the Old Testament canon. These views have generally emphasized the concept of the Biblical canon in terms of purely human acceptance of a national literature, taking no particular cognizance of the divine inspiration or authority of the canonical writings.

Such approaches are a product of their age in the sense that, for the most part, they are firmly wedded to the outlook and tenets of the Graf-Wellhausen school. Thus Ryle[49] maintained that a Hebrew national literature was in existence long before there was any canon as such. While the latter was assembled in three successive stages, due notice had to be taken of the literary antecedents of the various books, the redaction to their extant form, and finally the elevation of these works to a position in the national canon of Scripture. For Ryle, as for all liberal scholars, the Pentateuch in its finished form was the end-product of a prolonged period of growth during which various supposed documents were brought together and edited. When Ezra read what Ryle and others thought to be the Pentateuch in the presence of the assembled multitude, this Law was acknowledged as binding upon the people and was deemed canonical as a result. However, such a canon was inade-

---

[47] F. M. Cross, *BASOR*, No. 141 (1956), pp. 9ff., 56ff.

[48] So H. L. Ginsberg in *Israel: Its Role in Civilisation* (ed. M. Davis, 1956), p. 52.

[49] *The Canon of the OT*, pp. 29ff.

quate, for considerable interest had been aroused during the time of Nehemiah in preserving the utterances of the prophets. These books were subsequently canonized perhaps between 300 and 200 B.C., possibly as a result of the threat which Hellenistic culture was posing to traditional Judaism. When the prophetic portion of the canon was closed, other writings such as Ecclesiastes were assembled, and their popularity during the Maccabean period led to their being recognized as authoritative. Ryle maintained, with some others,[50] that the entire collection was deemed canonical by about A.D. 100, and related this activity to the Council of Jamnia.

A modification of this view appeared in the work of Hölscher, who thought that one mark of canonicity consisted in the fact that the very holiness of the books distinguished them from every other form of literature, a suggestion made considerably earlier by Josephus. Hölscher[51] did not subscribe to the idea of a threefold canonization of Scripture, but suggested instead that the concept of the canon arose because Greek culture and the growth of Greek literature presented a serious challenge to the religious traditions of Judaism. Equally pressing was the widespread dissemination of Jewish apocryphal material, so that in being compelled to separate the genuine from the spurious the Jewish religious authorities were forced to accept the idea of a canon of Scripture. The Torah was highly venerated from the seventh century B.C., but even when it had reached its final form about the end of the fourth century B.C. it was still not accorded canonicity. The same situation existed for the Prophets, which in the opinion of Hölscher were added periodically to the larger corpus up to the middle of the second century B.C. The testimony of Ben Sira could not be regarded as evidence that the prophetical canon was closed by that time,[52] but instead served to indicate the particular works which had come to be regarded with special veneration by about 190 B.C. For Hölscher, proof that the idea of a canon had not arisen at that time was furnished by the fact that Ben Sira could speak of himself as the latest of all the Biblical writers (Ecclus. 33:16), and deck out his utterances in the style of the ancient prophets.[53] Plausible as the latter objection sounds, it does not explain precisely why Ecclesiasticus failed to gain acceptance into the Old Testament canon, nor does it recognize the fact that Ben Sira was not standing in the tradition of the prophets, but of the ancient Hebrew sages.

[50] E.g. Wellhausen, *Einleitung in das AT,* pp. 550f.; F. H. Woods, *HDB,* III, p. 614; K. Budde, *EB,* I, cols. 671f.

[51] *Kanonisch und Apokryph,* pp. 4ff.

[52] This view was adopted by F. Buhl, *Kanon und Text des AT* (1891), p. 12, Ryle, *The Canon of the OT,* p. 113, and others.

[53] Hölscher, *Kanonisch und Apokryph,* p. 20.

A similar view of the formation of the canon was adopted by Oesterley and Robinson,[54] who acknowledged their indebtedness to Hölscher, and maintained that the concept of relative holiness provoked the idea of a canon of Scripture. The feeling that some books were more holy than others could not, in their view, have arisen all at once. Indeed, it was only gradually and by general consent that certain works came to have a special sanctity attached to them.[55] Oesterley and Robinson followed Hölscher again in maintaining that there had never been three successive stages in which the principal collections of books were in turn recognized as canonical in the strictest sense. For them the fixing of the Biblical canon was a piecemeal affair, and was governed in part by the spread of Hellenism and the impact of Jewish apocryphal literature upon the nation. The canon was supposed to have been formulated finally about A.D. 100, and when completed was recognized by the Jews as binding and authoritative. But, as Anderson has pointed out,[56] a theory of this sort seems to attribute too much to an assembly whose very existence has been questioned, and for which the evidence is neither precise nor complete. Any denial of a threefold stage in the organization of the canonical Hebrew Scriptures must take cognizance of the veneration associated with the Law on the part of both Jews and Samaritans, and the fact that, for the latter, the Torah alone was canonical. This is not to say, however, that a more detailed tripartite division of Holy Writ did not ultimately emerge from a clarification in definition and usage of a corpus of Scripture which was in general thought of in terms of two preponderant sections, the Law and a collection of prophetical writings.

According to Bentzen,[57] the reading of the Law in the time of Ezra and Nehemiah probably signified the introduction of the form of the Torah which was current in Babylonian Jewish circles at that particular period. Basing his views upon the critical analysis of the Pentateuch he maintained that even if the latter was not complete, comparatively little could have been lacking. In any event, the idea of a normative law-book occurred as early as the reform of King Josiah in 621 B.C., a time which was of particular importance for the formation of the idea of a holy written law. Even earlier, however, was the ancient concept of law as given by a god, and also, following von Rad,[58] the ancient *credo* of Israel.[59] Nevertheless, these ideas did not lead to the fixed concept of a canon, the oldest portion of which was established when the various

---

[54] *IBOT*, pp. 5ff.

[55] *Ibid.*, p. 2.

[56] *A Critical Introduction to the OT* (1959), p. 13.

[57] *Introduction to the OT*, I, pp. 22f.

[58] *Das Formgeschichtliche Problem des Hexateuchs*, pp. 3ff.

[59] A similar position was adopted by G. W. Anderson, *A Critical Introduction to the OT*, p. 13.

alleged strata of the Pentateuch were unified in the post-exilic period. For Bentzen the prophetic section of the Old Testament canon commenced when Isaiah (8:16) imposed upon his disciples the obligation to be the bearers and preservers of his words, and when Jeremiah instructed his secretary Baruch to commit his prophecies to writing. The exile was of great importance in that it sealed the prophetic utterances with the stark confirmation of history. The post-exilic prophets, who stood in the tradition of their predecessors (cf. Zech. 1:4; 7:7), had their writings regarded as canonical somewhat before 200 B.C., while the Hagiographa, the most vaguely defined portion of the canon, was probably complete by the time the prologue to Ecclesiasticus was written. Plausible as this theory may appear, it unfortunately fails to take account of the fact that the Samaritans venerated the Torah as canonical from at least the time of Ezra and Nehemiah, if not indeed considerably earlier, and that it was the Jewish and not the Babylonian form of the Law that they accepted as authoritative. Again like many another liberal scholar, Bentzen assigns too late a date to many of the writings in the Prophets and the Hagiographa, and thus finds it necessary to consider the Synod of Jamnia important in the fixing of the Old Testament canon.

A modification of the views expressed by Ryle occurred in the writings of R. H. Pfeiffer.[60] He maintained that the first instance of canonization in human history occurred when Deuteronomy, discovered during the reign of King Josiah, was venerated as the Word of God and respected as a norm for human behavior. But apart from this, other literary works in Israel were being combined and edited about 650 B.C. to comprise a national epic. A century later the canonized Deuteronomy was interpolated into the corpus of this material, with the result that the latter also came to be regarded as canonical. About 200 B.C. the so-called "Priestly document" was inserted into this combined work, and it also attained to canonicity as a result. Unhappily this theory not merely reflects all the weaknesses associated with the developmental theory of Pentateuchal origins, but assumes quite gratuitously and without any evidence that the lawbook recovered from the Temple in the time of Josiah actually constituted the book of Deuteronomy, a position for which there is not the slightest factual justification. Even a casual reading of the text will be sufficient to indicate that the finding of the Temple scroll was in fact the rediscovery of an already authoritative book, of which both Josiah and Hilkiah had heard previously, but which had been lost. Pfeiffer maintained an inadequate view of the concept of canonicity, as would seem evident from his assertion that a book could apparently exist from 650 to 550 B.C. as a mere national epic, and then suddenly span the gap separating the secular from the sacred to become the Word of God. Furthermore, Pfeiffer's assumption that the Jewish scribes would incor-

60 *PIOT*, pp. 50ff.; *IDB*, I, p. 503.

porate non-canonical material with that which was deemed canonical reflects a fundamental misunderstanding of the entire Jewish attitude towards Scripture.

Critical authors have been apt to maintain that the Law, in part or whole, attained to canonical status through the activities of Ezra and Nehemiah.[61] Since, however, Ezra was described as an "adept scribe in the Law of Moses" (Ez. 7:6), it is apparent that the Mosaic enactments had already become an object of professional study in their own right prior to his time. Furthermore, the whole purpose of Ezra in going up to Jerusalem with the permission of Artaxerxes was to insure that the precepts of the Law were carried out. Ezra 7:14, 23, 25, 26 shows clearly that the Law was already in existence, and that its commands required the wholehearted obedience of the people. There is consequently no evidence whatever that Ezra, in virtue of his position in the community, was about to impart to certain already existing religious writings of the Hebrews a degree of moral and spiritual authority that they had not possessed at an earlier time.

In the same way it is incorrect to see Nehemiah 8–10 as an account of the canonization of Scriptural writings.[62] The "book of the Law of Moses" that Ezra read at the request of the people, which resulted in a solemn act of religious renewal, owed its authority to the fact that it was an ancient document believed to have constituted material revealed by God to Moses. Rather than being an occasion on which the opinions of men were given in such a way as to assign canonical stature to a written composition by common resolve, it demonstrated that it was the inherent authority of the book itself that, when properly received, subjected the assembled throng to the judgment of God and recalled the populace to the observance of the ancient religious precepts.

If these considerations apply to Ezra and Nehemiah, they are of equal force for the "men of the Great Synagogue" and the Council of Jamnia— assuming that the latter was a properly constituted body. What these groups did, if anything, was to approve as canonical works that which had for long been venerated as authoritative. Even though doubts had arisen concerning Ecclesiastes and the Song of Solomon, the weight of tradition was such that they were included in the corpus of Scripture without undue difficulty.

The fundamental issue that divides liberal scholars from their more conservative counterparts appears to be their rejection of inspiration as the ultimate determining principle of the extent of the Old Testament canon. For liberal scholars the formation of the Scriptural corpus was nothing more than a type of human activity in which certain books were

---

[61] E.g. S. Zeitlin and S. Tedesche, *The Second Book of Maccabees* (1954), p. 113.

[62] So Ryle, *The Canon of the OT*, pp. 80ff.

regarded as canonical because they had demonstrated their pragmatic value in religious usage. However, such a theory has to face the fact that, although works such as Ecclesiasticus and 1 Maccabees had undoubted value for Judaism, they failed to secure a place in the canon of Scripture. Even if the concept of conformity to the spirit and ideals of the Torah is held to be the determining factor in the formation of the canon, as is commonly maintained by some writers, the problem still needs to be taken one stage further back by accounting for those principles which resulted in the canonization of the Law.

In contradistinction to the liberal outlook, the available evidence supports the position that the Old Testament writings, being divinely inspired, were consequently authoritative and were accepted as such from the period of their initial appearance. The Spirit of God that inspired these compositions also worked in the hearts and minds of the chosen people to testify to them that the writings were in fact the divine Word. It was this witness, in conjunction with the conscious human response, that was evidently the ultimate determining agent in the formulation of the canon. Had the question of canonicity merely rested upon purely academic decisions without an acknowledged concept of inspiration, it is impossible to see how the Jews could ever have come to accept the Old Testament books as being of divine authority. If considerations of positive affectivity had been dominant in the process of endeavoring to arrive at some form of canonical delineation it is very doubtful that more than a fraction of the extant canon would ultimately have proved to be acceptable, since the majority of the Old Testament compositions were severely critical of the ancient Hebrews in one way or another.

There is little doubt that matters relating to inspiration were responsible for furnishing at least some of the criteria by which certain compositions were assigned by the rabbinic authorities to the third division of the Hebrew canon. As has been noticed earlier, Jewish tradition maintained that all the Old Testament authors were prophets. Not all the contributors to the *K^ethubhim* or Sacred Writings could claim this distinction, however; for example, Daniel was a statesman rather than a classic mediator between God and a theocratic nation. His position in the third division of the canon was apparently justified by the fact that works in the *K^ethubhim* were deemed to have been written by individuals who were not prophets in the strictest sense of the word, but who nevertheless wrote under divine inspiration.[63]

It has been already observed that numerous questions were raised at different times among rabbinic authorities concerning the canonicity of certain highly esteemed compositions. In particular, discussion centered

---

[63] Cf. N. Schmidt, *JE*, III, p. 152; R. L. Harris, *Zondervan Pictorial Bible Dictionary* (1963), p. 145.

upon Ezekiel, Esther, and the three works attributed popularly to Solomon—Proverbs, Ecclesiastes, and Canticles. The opposition to Ezekiel was only temporary, and apparently arose because the priestly nature of the program outlined in the concluding nine chapters of the prophecy was thought to be in conflict with the tenor of the Pentateuch. Those who questioned its suitability for inclusion in the canon wished to prevent its use as authoritative Scripture, but the work was ultimately rehabilitated by the labors of a certain Hananiah ben Hezekiah ben Garon, who "spent three hundred jars of oil to release it."[64]

Tannaite scribes of the second century B.C. were eager to include the Esther scroll in the canon of Scripture, and in the end the issue turned upon the question as to whether or not the work actually constituted a revealed composition. If the latter proved to be the case and the book was found to have proceeded from other than divine inspiration, it could not properly be given a place in the list of Scriptural writings.[65] Despite considerable uncertainty on the matter,[66] it was ultimately agreed, with Rabbi Simeon (150 B.C.), that Esther "defiled the hands," and as such it was deemed canonical. The opposition to Proverbs was comparatively slight, and was based for the most part upon apparent internal inconsistencies. Similar objections were levelled against Ecclesiastes,[67] although in this case it was felt that the quasi-Epicurean tone of the book was out of harmony with the religious traditions of Judaism.[68] The canonicity of Ecclesiastes was supported, among others, by the followers of Hillel, while the most vigorous opposition apparently came from the strict school of the Shammaites.[69]

According to Rabbi Simon ben Menasya, the Song of Solomon "defiled the hands," since it was inspired by the Holy Spirit of God.[70] Regarding this work it can be said in general that it does not appear to have evoked any specific statement to the contrary. That there was prolonged, and perhaps acrimonious, discussion concerning Canticles, however, is apparent from the drastic step taken by Rabbi Aqiba about A.D. 100 to rehabilitate the Song in his celebrated pronouncement that "he who, for the sake of entertainment, sings the Song as though it were a profane song, will have no share in the future world."[71] There can be little doubt that the popularity of works such as Esther, Ecclesiastes, and

---

[64] Cf. *Shabb.* 13*b*; *Men.* 45*a*.
[65] Cf. *Yom.* 29*a*; *Megill.* 7*a*.
[66] Cf. *Sanhed.* 100*a*; *Megill.* 19*b*.
[67] *Shabb.* 30*b*.
[68] *Levit. Rabb.* XXVIIIff.
[69] Cf. H. Graetz, *Koheleth* (1871), p. 149.
[70] *Tosef. Yad.* II, 14.
[71] *Sanhed.* 101*a*; *Megill.* 7*a*.

Canticles in connection with Jewish feast days furnished powerful support for their claim to canonicity.

While certain books were the subject of periodic discussion in this regard, there was no controversy at all in connection with the books of the Apocrypha, for everyone was agreed that they were non-canonical.[72] The reason appears to have been that the works themselves simply gave no evidence whatever of having been divinely inspired. As Green and others have pointed out, some of these writings contain egregious historical, chronological, and geographical errors, quite apart from justifying falsehood and deception and making salvation dependent upon deeds of merit.[73] Although the books of the Apocrypha can quite obviously claim to possess much that is in harmony with the spirit of the canonical compositions, there are numerous instances in which they diverge sharply from the latter.

The lengthy processes by which the canon of the Old Testament arrived at its present form cannot be traced with anything approaching exactitude, and only the most general of principles can be enunciated reasonably satisfactorily. Without doubt the element of divine inspiration was a profoundly important consideration for the Jews, particularly in the immediate pre-Christian period. Equally true is the fact that, from its beginnings, the Pentateuch was considered authoritative because it contained the divine revelation to Moses, and as a direct result it was regarded as the standard to which other writings were to be related.[74] The Torah must obviously have possessed what amounts to canonical authority long before it was accorded such by the Hebrews, otherwise the nation of Israel would have been under no obligation to accept its precepts as the norm for moral and spiritual behavior. The fact of this recognition was thus the effect rather than the cause of the "canonical" status associated with the Torah from early times. It is apparent from the evidence presented by the Samaritan Pentateuch that the Torah commanded a high degree of veneration even prior to the early post-exilic period, and that during the time of Ezra and Nehemiah its authority was accepted anew by the nation.

As far as the prophetic literature is concerned, the evidence is even more scanty, for there is no record in the Old Testament either of formal recognition or acceptance by the people of any of the works contained in the second and third divisions of the Hebrew canon. The fact that some portions of the Hagiographa are older than certain of the prophecies might imply that the second division of the canon remained "open" until

[72] Cf. L. Ginzberg, *JBL*, XLI (1922), pp. 115ff.
[73] W. H. Green, *General Introduction to the OT, The Canon* (1899), pp. 195f.
[74] Cf. G. Wildeboer, *The Origin of the Canon of the OT* (1895), p. 97.

much of the Hagiographa was in existence. Whether this was actually the case or not, the determining principle of canonicity for the Jewish religious authorities appeared to be that of divine inspiration. Even here there are certain difficulties in interpretation, however, for the medieval scholars were accustomed to assert that the three divisions of the canon corresponded to three degrees of inspiration. The highest of these was that of Moses, who communicated directly with God: the second was that attributed to the prophets, who wrote by the spirit of prophecy; while the lowest was that of the other writers, who were inspired by the Holy Spirit of God.[75] Such a differentiation is, of course, completely unsupported by the Scriptures themselves. The prophets believed that they stood firmly in the Mosaic tradition and that their own words possessed equal moral and spiritual authority with the pronouncements of the great lawgiver. Furthermore, the alleged distinction between the spirit of prophecy and the Holy Spirit is purely imaginary.

While the "men of the Great Synagogue" and the Council of Jamnia may possibly have played some small part in the growth of the canon in its final stages, there is insufficient evidence to show that their disputations resulted in any significant fixing of its limits. If the views of those liberal writers who regard the canon as having been "closed" about A.D. 100 are unacceptable because their dating is far too late, the theories of those conservative scholars who would place the closing of the Old Testament canon about 400 B.C.[76] are equally improbable, simply because such a date appears to be too early. In all its essentials the canon was most probably complete by about 300 B.C., and while discussion concerning certain component parts was continued well into the Christian era, the substance of the canon as it existed a century-and-a-half after the time of Ezra and Nehemiah remained unaffected by these controversies.

Supplementary Literature

Blau, L. *Masoretische Untersuchungen.* 1891.

———. *Zur Einleitung in die Heilige Schrift.* 1894.

Fritsch, C. T. *The Anti-Anthropomorphisms of the Greek Pentateuch.* 1943.

Fürst, J. *Der Kanon des Alten Testaments nach den Überlieferungen in Talmud und Midrasch.* 1868.

[75] F. Buhl, *Canon and Text of the OT* (1892), pp. 37f.

[76] So E. B. Pusey, *Daniel the Prophet* (1891), p. 294; W. H. Green, *General Introduction to the OT, The Canon,* pp. 38, 78, 117; J. H. Raven, *OT Introduction,* p. 33.

Kahle, P. *Der Hebräische Bibeltext seit Franz Delitzsch.* 1961.

Lofthouse, W. F. *The Making of the Old Testament.* 1915.

Loisy, A. *Histoire critique du texte et des versions de la Bible.* 2 vols., 1893-1895.

Margolis, M. L. *The Hebrew Scriptures in the Making.* 1922.

Price, I. M. *The Ancestry of our English Bible.* Rev. ed. 1956.

Ryle, H. E. *Philo and Holy Scripture.* 1895.

Tyle, R. H. *The Canon of the Old Testament.* 1904.

Part Five

OLD TESTAMENT HISTORY

I. THE STUDY OF OLD TESTAMENT HISTORY

A. HISTORY AND HISTORIOGRAPHY

In its most comprehensive sense history may be said to furnish a description of phenomena in process of continuous change: of all that has happened in human life and in natural life. Such a definition provides a proper basis for both the activities of the historian of science and of the chronicler of various phases of human endeavor. Thus anything that changes in any way, that happens or appears to happen, falls within this broad purview.

In a more restricted sense the concept of history involves a controlled, scientific, descriptive consideration of certain facets of this universal process of change. As a result, history has frequently been thought of in a twofold sense: first, a study of chronological and literary forms as a record of events, and secondly, in possibly a more dynamic manner, as the events themselves, implied, for example, by the expression "makers of history." In the former sense its predominant concern is the basic aims of inquiry and statement; in the latter its appeal to the sense of drama in the human personality has occasionally resulted in the interpretation of processes and movements—sometimes in the absence of specifically written narratives—in terms that have come close to epic proportions.[1]

It may well be this tendency that has led to the familiar charge that historians are chiefly concerned to record only events that result from the activities of the "history-makers," and consequently ignore or treat inadequately large areas of cultural and social development that would be very important to one writing from a different standpoint. In the best sense of the term, the objective of history, as a branch of research or inquiry in the field of the humanities, is the investigation of human activities in a given period or periods of the past[2] with a view to discerning the nature and significance of man's achievements.[3]

[1] The writings of chroniclers from Herodotus to the nineteenth-century English historians furnish ample illustration of this attitude.

[2] Cf. R. G. Collingwood, *The Idea of History* (1946), p. 9.

[3] The term ἱστορία was first employed by the sixth-century B.C. Ionians to describe their search for knowledge in the widest sense. It was used at that time to convey the basic impression of inquiry or investigation into a subject in order to obtain

The modern scientific approach to historiography distinguishes two phases in the work of the historian. First, there is a period of investigation in which the facts are ascertained as carefully and accurately as scientific method will permit. Second, there is a descriptive task, involving the presentation of an interpretation of the material accumulated in a systematized, acceptable literary form. This stage inevitably brings aesthetic considerations to bear upon the finished product. Unlike many earlier authors modern historiographers have managed to avoid a heavy reliance upon subjective descriptions of sources far removed from the original events, and they now possess an important array of valuable ancillary tools in such sciences as linguistics, philology, sociology, anthropology, and archaeology.

As Albright has pointed out, the task of the historian is by no means complete when he has accumulated a vast store of properly authenticated historical data.[4] There must be at least some mental reflection upon the problems posed by historical events if the material collected by painstaking research is to become history in the most genuine sense of the word. This, in the last analysis, is a philosophical exercise,[5] which may often be characterized by legitimate moral overtones, for life tends to move in recognizable configurations, thus demanding from the histori-

---

specific information or knowledge (Herodotus, *Hist.*, II, 118). This understanding of the term led Aristotle to designate his *Natural History* by the expression Ἀι περὶ τῶν ζῴων ἱστορία which the natural historian Theophrastus (*ca.* 320 B.C.) imitated in entitling his work 'Η φυτῶν ἱστορία. The knowledge that was obtained as a result of pursuing an investigation was also described as ἱστορία by Herodotus (*Hist.*, I, 1; II, 99) and Hippocrates (*Vet. Med.*, XVI). The earliest use of the word in the sense of a narrative, history, or written account of an individual inquiry can also be traced to Herodotus (*Hist.*, VII, 96; cf. Aristotle, *Rhet.*, I, 4, 13; *Poet.*, IX, 1). By the fourth century B.C. the word ἱστορικός (narrator) had replaced to a large extent the earlier ἱστορέων (inquirer after knowledge), and in the writings of Aristotle (e.g. Poet., IX, 2) it was employed as a substantive to mean "a historian." In Plutarch (*Themist.*, XIII) the phrase τὰ ἱστορικά was interpreted as "histories." Polybius (*ca.* 170 B.C., II, 62, 2) utilized ἱστοριόγραφος, an expanded form of the earlier Greek term, to designate a "writer of history" in the sense of one who pursued inquiry into historical facts; Plutarch (II, 898A) distinguished between this function and that of the narrator (συγγραφεύς) himself. From this it is clear that history as a branch of scientific research activity commenced properly with the work of Herodotus in the secular field. This distinguished writer of antiquity was both narrator and historian. With Aristotle came the application of ἱστορία to the finished literary product enshrining the data accumulated during a prolonged search for knowledge instead of to the inquiry antecedent to the written result. Since that time *historia* has universally been accepted as a form of literature.

[4] *FSAC*, p. 82.

[5] Thus provoking Voltaire's comment, "Il faut écrire l'histoire en philosophe." Cf. H. Butterfield, *Christianity and History* (1949), pp. 28ff.; C. A. Beard in H. Meyerhoff (ed.), *The Philosophy of History in Our Time* (1959), pp. 142ff.; G. J. Renier, *History, Its Purpose and Method* (1950), p. 253.

an certain conclusions that will necessarily transcend to some extent the data themselves.

Modern historiography has rejected the assumption that the actuality of history can be identical with, or even closely akin to, that of the physical world. History therefore cannot properly be regarded as an exact science, even though it may employ scientific techniques in the execution of its objectives. Yet it can quite legitimately be deemed to constitute a valid interpretation of human affairs, and as such the historian's opinion is an inevitable factor in the larger picture. Since he is dealing with the activities of a species whose character is based in morality, he has every right to include moral considerations in his estimate of the human situation.

The problem of historical interpretation was met in the late nineteenth and early twentieth centuries by such widely divergent approaches as those of Marx and Lenin, Oswald Spengler, and Arnold Toynbee. Marxism rejected the Hegelian notion that the causal force in history subsisted in the process itself, supplying history with its own meaning. For Marxist materialism the only reality was matter in motion, and the Hegelian dialectic was no longer regarded as furnishing the metaphysical clue to the significance of history. Marx conceived of historical processes as having definite meaning and an attainable goal, which would be realized dialectically and would be characterized by material and economic progress in an emerging classless proletariat.

Spengler was an able advocate of the nineteenth-century view that natural law was the valid framework of reference for historians, but he departed from the optimistic evolutionary concepts of progress popular with historians of that century generally and emphasized that decay and doom were the inescapable fate of all civilizations. Spengler maintained that every culture passed through a quasi-biological cycle of birth, progress, and ultimate degeneration,[6] an approach that led him to adopt a concept of naturalistic determinism that was the antithesis of the Kantian and Hegelian notion of progress and freedom as the goals of history. Although Spengler emphasized the importance of the cultural contribution that each epoch of history made to its successors, his failure to comprehend the meaning of history correctly arose from his substitution of a biological metaphor of society for the dynamics of historical processes.

Arnold Toynbee grappled with the problems posed by the forces of cultural change in a significantly different manner by appealing to the *élan vital* of Henri Bergson for a clue to the puzzle as to why civilizations should rise and fall. Starting from the general premise that a definite

---

[6] O. Spengler, *Der Untergang des Abendlandes* (1920), I, p. 153.

forward or upward movement is discernible in history,[7] he adduced a theory that implied that civilizations flourish as long as they meet the challenges confronting them with adequate responses. Despite the attractive development and presentation of this theory, it has failed to answer why there should be a particular time in the history of every culture when a challenge is no longer able to be met successfully, so that degeneration results.

The foregoing represent different reactions to the positivistic German school whose interpretative principles were established through the writings of L. von Ranke, Th. Mommsen, and E. Meyer in the nineteenth century. For those men the task of the historian lay in reconstructing as accurately as possible a picture of what actually took place in the past. Ranke was concerned to let the facts speak for themselves—"*wie es eigentlich gewesen*"—in apparent unawareness that facts so frequently need to be interpreted if they are to be at all meaningful historically. Yet although positivistic method has led in some quarters to a cult of scientific historicism, its emphasis upon accurate verification of facts and classification of data is of supreme importance for any branch of historical study. While it is true to say that it is virtually impossible to envisage a philosophy of history without postulating some sort of generally purposive evolutionary process, it must also be realized that such an outlook is at best only theoretical, and need not correspond to the facts of a situation in a given age or time. Frequently the kind of evolutionary development assumed to be normative by biologists like Darwin is neither completely valid for their own discipline nor for other fields of study to which the principle may be applied.

Any holism that purports to see a continuous and progressive development in the unfolding stream of world history from the comparatively simple existence of primitive peoples to the complexities of modern civilization requires a certain manipulation of the facts. Geological studies have shown conclusively that the flora and fauna in existence at the beginning of each new era occurred in their most developed and highly differentiated forms, and subsequently degenerated through the successive periods of the era until they approached extinction, a situation that was quite the opposite of the process contemplated by philosophically minded nineteenth-century biologists. In the ancient Near East the culture of the Sumerians apparently came on the historical scene in a fully developed form and exerted a vast influence in Mesopotamia before succumbing to the incursions of the Akkadians and Elamites. An even more spectacular example of this tendency is furnished by the culture of ancient Egypt, which burst upon the scene in full flower at the

[7] A. Toynbee, *A Study of History* (1934), I, p. 196; III, p. 216. For a survey of this approach see W. F. Albright, *History, Archaeology and Christian Humanism* (1964), pp. 241ff.

beginning of the Old Kingdom period (2700-2200 B.C.) and gradually degenerated (apart from such notable revivals as that experienced at the beginning of the New Kingdom period, 1570-1150 B.C.) until its grandeur was lost irretrievably in the Ptolemaic period.

The most instructive scheme of interpretation is always a servant rather than a master. Particular caution must be exercised whenever any attempt is made to adduce a philosophical interpretation of sequences that can be touted as valid for all civilizations in all ages. Too frequently such approaches are strictly the product of the western mind, and the application of their categories to ancient oriental civilizations is not necessarily valid and in specific instances decidedly untrue. As Albright has wisely remarked, historical and sociological configurations are less rigid than those of the physical sciences, so that the mechanical principles applicable to the latter must be related to the former more as analogies rather than as rigorous demonstrations.[8] Only in this sense is it possible for terms such as "continuum," "operational method," "integration," and the like to be employed, and always on condition that the limitations of this type of procedure are fully recognized. Thus it is of vital importance for the historian to be acutely aware of the need for a proper methodology. If the information upon which he relies cannot survive critical examination of its accuracy, it is clearly not an adequate basis for his general principles. The historian must be determined to face the implications of *all* the available evidence, whether or not it conflicts ultimately with any of his predetermined theories. Too much of what has been allowed to pass as history in recent years has actually consisted of ingenious attempts to arrange factual data so as to make them conform to some preconceived *schema*. This tendency has been as noticeable in the field of Old Testament study as in the writings of Spengler and Toynbee.

B. SEMITIC HISTORIOGRAPHY

Since modern occidental methods of historical interpretation may present decided problems when imposed upon oriental cultures, particularly those of antiquity, it is probably wise to consider the historical outlook and methods of compilation of the Near Eastern cultures on their own terms also, lest the historiographical attempts of antiquity unwittingly be assessed in terms of the scientific methods of more recent times, with equally unfortunate results. The Sumerians were the first peoples who not merely made history, but actually recorded it. Basic to their cultural concepts were the associated ideas of *nam* and *me* (approximating roughly to "essence" and "dynamism"),[9] the activities of

---

[8] *FSAC*, p. 117.
[9] Cf. E. A. Speiser, *IHANE*, p. 37; T. Jacobsen, *JNES*, V (1946), p. 139 n. 20, approximates *me* to *modus operandi*.

which underlay all cultural functioning. Unfortunately it is at present impossible to determine the role these factors played in the Sumerian idea of history. However, this should not necessarily be taken as an indication that these ancient Mesopotamians were oblivious to the happenings of the past, for the eager manner in which they recorded all kinds of details concerning occurrences in former times furnishes clear indications to the contrary. For the Sumerians history was the very warp and woof of life as manifested in a temporal continuum of past, present, and future events, so that the process of historical appreciation was a matter of personal experience of life rather than the analysis of sources or the formulation of principles. Fortunately for purposes of control, the available source material recurs at different stages of Mesopotamian civilization. It consists of such direct historical references as king-lists,[10] chronicles,[11] and annals, along with literary compositions based upon historical happenings that had been overlaid with myth and legend. Dated bricks, official inscriptions commemorating the erection of palaces and temples,[12] and foundation deposits were also available for those who were interested in the study of the past. The latter sources proved to be of especial value to Babylonian monarchs of a subsequent era who were possessed of antiquarian tastes, as Ashurbanipal (669-627 B.C.) and Nabonidus (556-539 B.C.).

One reason that has been adduced for the preoccupation of later rulers with Mesopotamian antiquities is that they desired to learn how to interpret the present and the future in the light of past experience.[13] This objective was no doubt aided greatly by the extremely conservative attitude adopted towards the traditional values of ancient Mesopotamia. The profoundly superstitious outlook of these peoples virtually demanded that the course of terrestrial events should be governed by antecedent celestial decisions, a prominent feature in their myths and legends. In this sense, therefore, history was of a theocratic order, although, as the mythological cycles indicate, the latter was not absolute, since divine authority was not infrequently modified by other considerations.[14]

Like the Mesopotamians, the ancient Egyptians had no single term for "history" or the "idea of history." Nevertheless, they were at least as

[10] See the Weld-Blundell prism, probably written during the Third Dynasty of Ur; S. Langdon, *Oxford Editions of Cuneiform Texts* (1923), II; G. A. Barton, *The Royal Inscriptions of Sumer and Akkad* (1929); T. Jacobsen, *The Sumerian King List.* Assyriological Studies XI (1939).

[11] The Weidner Chronicle recounts the first two post-diluvian dynasties at Kish and Uruk and the Akkadian dynasty of Sargon I; H. G. Guterbock, ZA, XLII (1934), pp. 47ff.

[12] It is not easy to see how Collingwood, *The Idea of History*, p. 11, can dismiss these as lacking "the character of science," since they expressed the facts of the situation as the ancient Sumerians knew them.

[13] *IHANE*, pp. 48f.

[14] *IHANE*, pp. 55f.

296

interested in the record of their national past as were the Mesopotamians.[15] Events deemed worthy of being handed down to posterity were carefully preserved by royal command, and some of these records reach back into the predynastic period (4500-2900 B.C.). The earliest of these sources is a fragment dating from *ca.* 2550 B.C., made long after the particular events themselves.[16] One portion of this is the celebrated Palermo Stone, a diorite monument that no doubt originally contained lists of the rulers over the two predynastic kingdoms of Upper and Lower Egypt, which were subsequently united under Menes of Thinis at the beginning of the Protodynastic period (*ca.* 2900-2760 B.C.).[17]

The famous Turin papyrus of Kings,[18] written about the thirteenth century B.C. and comprising a list of more than three hundred kings of Egypt, was of unusual interest because its compilers had attempted to trace the rulers back to the celestial deities from whom they were popularly supposed to have descended. Four other shorter king-lists, dating from the New Kingdom period, seem to have preserved a genuine collection of names from the particular epochs with which they dealt.[19] Several genealogical lists, covering many generations and varying considerably in size, have also been dated from the latter part of the dynastic period. To the extent that the references to individuals can be verified from other contemporary sources, the contents of the genealogies appear to be reasonably accurate as they now stand.

Along with the Narmer Palette, which was recovered in 1898 from the temple at Hierakonpolis,[20] the macehead excavated from the same site,[21] and the royal annals of the Old Kingdom period, there are numerous smaller tablets of ivory and wood that contain a wide variety of observations of a historical character. From the Old Kingdom period also came the pyramids, which in every sense of the term can be held to constitute monuments to the historicity of the rulers whose corpses they were designed to protect. Numerous inscriptions recovered from the walls of private tombs have also preserved a wealth of autobiographical material, some of which goes back to a very early period of Egyptian life.

Despite the abundance of historical source-data, the Egyptians do not appear to have manifested too much concern for historiography itself, for

---

[15] Cf. Herod. *Hist.*, II, 77.

[16] Cf. J. T. Shotwell, *The History of History* (1939), I, p. 79.

[17] *LAP*, pp. 70, 74, and pl. 27; Finegan, *Handbook of Biblical Chronology* (1964), pp. 77ff.

[18] Published in 1938 by G. Farina, *Il papiro dei re;* cf. A. Gardiner and J. Černý, *The Turin Canon of Kings* (1952).

[19] *IHANE*, pp. 7ff.

[20] J. E. Quibell, *Hierakonpolis* (1900), I, p. 10 and pl. 29.

[21] *Ibid.*, pp. 8f. and pl. 26B; II (1902), pp. 40f.

no histories have survived from the dynastic period.[22] It was only in the time of Manetho (third century B.C.) that any systematic attempt at historical formulation was undertaken, and even so the result was less in the tradition of Egyptian historical interest than in the Greek view of the significance of events. Although the myths and religious texts make clear their subservience to the deities, there seems in general to have been a less developed sense of dependence upon theocratic rule among the ancient Egyptians than was the case in Mesopotamia. This tendency may have been due in part to the greater stability of the Egyptian temperament[23] and the decidedly static quality of their general world-view, which was one result of their comparative geographic isolation. The ancient Egyptians had never laid claim to a tradition of migration to the land of the Nile; and because they considered themselves to have been the original inhabitants of the terrain, they proudly assumed the title of "men," a situation that reflected with some distaste upon their heterogeneous neighbors to the west, the east, and the south.

One serious drawback to a study of Egyptian history generally is that the treasury of source material, abundant though it frequently is, fails to furnish a consistently illuminated picture of ancient Egyptian times and events. While those intervals of national history that have been well represented by extant records tend quite naturally to occupy the attention of historians, the areas that are deficient in such testimony have been unduly neglected in historical study. An additional obstacle which stands in the way of a proper interpretation of events in ancient Egypt is the fact that the great majority of the historical monuments erected in that country and duly inscribed with a record of happenings were actually intended as official propaganda for transmitting to posterity that projection of the glory and power that the pharaohs thought proper for the occasion. As such they are not really the kind of material upon which an objective historical study ought to be based, a situation which has caused not a little embarrassment among unwary exponents of the Egyptian past. As with other ancient Near Eastern countries, it must also be remembered that in Egypt a great many crises of revolution, inner strife, political intrigue, and military defeats in foreign wars were either passed over in silence or else were interpreted in such a manner that the monuments conveyed impressions that were thoroughly distorted and invariably manipulated so as to reflect creditably upon the Egyptians themselves.

Like other peoples in the ancient world, the Egyptians had no fixed method for reckoning the passing of the years and ages. Events that they wanted to record in chronological order were usually associated with particular regnal years of the pharaohs, although in the earliest period

---

[22] *IHANE*, p. 20.
[23] *IAAM*, pp. 39ff.

these were not counted. As in ancient Babylonia, specific years were styled in terms of outstanding events that had occurred in them, so that one year came to be designated as "the year of fighting and smiting the northerners." This clumsy method was gradually superseded by a simpler one in which the reckoning was related to the regnal year, so that an event became dated in a particular year of a specific pharaoh. Finally, the priests compiled detailed lists of kings in which their names and either the designations or, later, the numbers of their regnal years were entered, and it is highly probable that these archives constituted the basis of the king-lists and the historical tables preserved by Manetho.

Important as the attempts of the Babylonians and Egyptians were in the recording of ancient Near Eastern life and times, they were far surpassed by the creative genius of the Hittite history-writers. Cuneiform sources from Boghazköy indicate clearly that the Hittites were supreme in the area of historiography in their day, and were only surpassed by the Hebrews and the Greeks. C. H. Gordon believes that these two nations emerged as the historians of the western world because they began their historiographic activities on a substratum of Hittite culture. He has remarked:

> It is no accident that Herodotus, the Father of History, came from Anatolia. The seeds of historical writings were planted by the Hittites back in the second millennium throughout their sphere of influence, spanning Halicarnassus and Zion.[24]

While the sources available for determining the idea of history among the ancient Hebrews are of an accredited literary nature, they are quite unlike the cuneiform and hieroglyphic inscriptions of Babylonia and Egypt. At least one Moabite ruler has a royal inscription; the Hebrews possessed none. In fact, there is almost nothing that approximates to a Hebrew inscription with the possible exception of the Siloam inscription and the Lachish and Samarian ostraca. Despite this lack of official records, however, there were a great many other sources in existence upon which the writers of the Old Testament books were able to draw. Some of this material was of considerable antiquity, and includes sagas, poems, historical narratives, genealogical tables, and certain legal formulations, many of which preserved in one way or another the characteristic Hebrew concepts of divine purpose and destiny in history.

The annals that underlie Kings and Chronicles are late in comparison with their Mesopotamian and Egyptian counterparts, and they point to the didactic nature of most Old Testament historical narratives. This resulted largely from the general Hebrew attitude that events were essentially *sub specie aeternitatis*. This religious approach is particularly

[24] *GBB*, p. 97.

prominent in Chronicles, where the ontological significance of the divine commonwealth is presented against an historical framework. For the ancient Hebrews the history that they, as the covenant people, experienced consisted inevitably of more than a mere series of rather coincidental occurrences or "happenings" (*Geschehen*). While history for them included the elements of "events" and "facts"[25] that underlie the categories described by German scholars as *Historie* and *Geschichte*, there was also a transcendent spiritual factor that the ancient Hebrew prophets and historians recognized consistently and associated with the outworking of the Covenant provisions towards a planned goal.

The Hebrew idea of history, therefore, was ultimately a theological one, and as such has frequently been spoken of by scholars as "sacred" or "salvation" history (*Heilsgeschichte*). However, since the Old Testament conveys the general impression of incompleteness in relation to the historical process, and points for its culmination to something beyond itself, the use of the term *Heilsgeschichte* as strictly applicable to Old Testament history is not altogether satisfactory. The predominant concern of the Old Testament was for the nature and manifestation of the divine revelation in and through Israel, but even so it is evident from the Hebrew understanding of history that the process of salvation was far from being accomplished when the extant works were formulated. Consequently the term *Heilsgeschichte* can only find its fullest meaning in the New Testament world-view where the atoning work of Christ gave the greatest degree of ontological significance to the dictum, "salvation is of the Jews" (John 4:22).

Since ancient Semitic historiography was influenced considerably by cultural attitudes and activities among others, the histories of these ancient peoples can be approached most satisfactorily when they are examined from the standpoint of the writers and their environment.[26] Elementary though this observation may appear, the facts of the case are that it is frequently far from easy for the occidental scholar to make such an approach, particularly if his training has been weighted heavily with literary-critical procedures and principles. However, there are still significantly large areas of the world where the attitudes and customs of nations and groups have undergone little fundamental change since the Late Bronze Age, despite the attempts of western nations to impose modern technology upon them. It is therefore instructive to realize, for example, that a good deal of light can be thrown upon the outlook and behavior of the ancient Semites by observing the way of life of the modern Bedouin Arab or the Turkish tribesman.[27]

---

[25] C. R. North, *IDB*, II, p. 608, has distinguished between these terms by defining a fact of history as an event together with the interpretation accompanying its recollection or recording. Cf. B. Albrektson, *History and the Gods* (1967).

[26] Cf. R. G. Collingwood, *The Idea of History*, pp. 163, 282ff.

[27] Cf. *IOTT*, p. 106 n. 10.

In much the same manner, an appreciation of the sociological impor-tance of such ancient institutions as the matriarchate will go far towards unravelling some of the mysteries implicit in narratives that depicted life in the early Hebrew monarchy. Attention has already been called to the importance of epigraphic material which, when integrated into the larger historical picture by means of stratigraphic, typological, and other forms of evaluation, can furnish very significant corroborative evidence. While it is important to avoid confusing the two concepts of history—as that which has happened and that which has been written down about what has happened—it should be remarked that it is not necessary for the facts furnished by internal evidence to be corroborated at all stages by the external evidence of archaeology and the like before they can be accepted as valid.

What must be examined with consistent care, however, is the manner in which the facts available to the historian have actually been reported. It is now realized that the ancient Near Eastern peoples approached the handling of their material far differently than do modern occidental chroniclers. The scribes of antiquity frequently—though not invariably—compiled their material towards the end of a particular sequence rather than at intervals during it,[28] and in ancient Sumeria the scribes always made more than one copy of any given composition.[29] Poetic material of varying kinds was often transmitted orally over long periods of time, frequently related to written forms of epics and similar works. The an-cients valued prose sources such as genealogies, since they preserved a record of past events like those of their modern counterparts in such widely diverse cultures as the modern Bedouin Arab, the inhabitants of Hawaii, the Malagasy people, and others.[30]

The use of numbers among the ancient Near Eastern nations varied sharply from current occidental practice. In contrast to the detail and precision of the West, the numbers employed in literary sources and inscriptions were generally exaggerated greatly. One example of this tendency can be furnished by the Sumerian king-list known as the Weld-Blundell prism,[31] which attributed reigns of completely dispropor-tionate length to eight kings who reigned in Eridu, Badtibira, Larak, Sippar, and Shuruppak.[32] It may well be that on occasion the scribes of Near Eastern antiquity utilized numbers in a symbolic, schematic, or epic fashion, which is decidedly at variance with common occidental

[28] This is particularly noticeable in the case of the Egyptian medical texts, such as the Ebers, Hearst, Kahun, Greater Berlin, and Edwin Smith papyri. However, it did not occur to the same extent in Babylonia.

[29] S. N. Kramer, *Sumerian Mythology* (1961), p. 23.

[30] Cf. *FSAC*, p. 72; *IOTT*, pp. 103f.

[31] Cf. *ANET*, pp. 265f.

[32] Cf. C. L. Woolley, *The Sumerians* (1928), p. 21.

practice.[33] Particularly noticeable in oriental compositions is the custom of exaggerating victories in the annals, probably an attempt to magnify the achievements of the rulers and peoples thus commemorated.[34] Conversely, an entirely different attitude was adopted towards defeat: all mention of the calamity was usually omitted. Apparently, therefore, the numerical references in ancient Near Eastern annals generally ought not to be assumed to be factually accurate or "reliable" in the usual occidental sense. Where parallel accounts occur in the Old Testament narratives, these can often furnish a useful measure of control on the records of pagan annalists, although such control is naturally by no means absolute.

Written and oral traditions existed side by side in antiquity, the former often serving as an aid to memory rather than as a substitute for it.[35] Since verse form is generally considered more satisfactory than prose structures for oral transmission, a good deal of the material handed down from generation to generation must have had some basis in poetic formulation. Scholars now recognize that both the prose and poetry of the Old Testament may be related to a limited extent to epic antecedents, and sometimes even modeled upon such structural patterns.[36] Furthermore, it is of some significance to note that the historiography of the Hebrews drew in part on the epic and dramatic forms of ancient Babylonia and Homeric Greece. For example, Old Testament historical writers frequently reconstructed the events of past days in the form of verbatim utterances, a characteristic epic device. One of the best examples of this tendency is seen in the speech of the Assyrian officer in 2 Kings 18:17-35, which occurs in a particularly dramatic historiographical expression, and lends added suspense to the narrative.

C. Modern Scholars and Old Testament History

It may be instructive to survey the attitudes of modern western scholars to the historical narratives of the Old Testament with a view to determining the extent to which they thought that the latter could be regarded as constituting an authentic record of the time. Prior to the period of Wellhausen, orthodoxy held that the Biblical accounts were divinely inspired and inerrant in consequence. Interest in Old Testament history as such did not begin until the seventeenth century when Archbishop J. Usher published his *Annales Veteris et Novi Testamenti*

---

[33] For symbolic interpretation see the attribution of 110 years, the Egyptian ideal of a full and fruitful life (cf. *ANET*, p. 414 n. 33), to Joseph (Gen. 50:26) and Joshua (Josh. 24:29; Judg. 2:8). A schematic interpretation is probable with the numerical reference in 1 Kgs. 6:1. For the epic approach cf. *IOTT*, pp. 293f.

[34] Compare the account of Sennacherib's siege of Jerusalem *ca.* 701 B.C. (*ARAB*, II, sect. 240) with the Biblical narrative in 2 Kgs. 18:14.

[35] *FSAC*, p. 64.

[36] Cf. *IOTT*, pp. 290f.

(1605). The chronological sequences which Usher propounded were subsequently associated with the text of the Authorized Version—though quite without authority. About seventy-five years later J. B. Bousset published his work entitled *Discours sur l'histoire universelle* (1681), and in 1716 the celebrated treatise of H. Prideaux was issued in two volumes under the title *The Old and the New Testaments Connected in the History of the Jews and Neighbouring Nations.*

English Deism produced at least one apologetic work dealing with the subject of Old Testament history: in 1727 S. Shukford wrote *The Sacred and Profane History of the World Connected.* On the continent M. F. Roos published his *Einleitung in die biblische Geschichte* in 1700, which furnished a good historical survey of the Israelites. The following century saw the rise of rationalism, and with it the publication of a work by L. Bauer in 1800 entitled *Geschichte der hebräer Nation.* H. Ewald set the tone of Old Testament historical writing for the nineteenth century with the publication in 1843 of his monumental five-volume *Geschichte des Volkes Israel.* What undoubtedly constituted the standard work of the advanced critical school in Europe was Wellhausen's *Geschichte Israels,* published in 1878, and known as *Prolegomena zur Geschichte Israels* after 1883. The position that he adopted was widely imitated, and its adherents included B. Stade (*Geschichte des Volkes Israel,* 1881), K. H. Graf (*Die geschichtlichen Bücher des Alten Testaments,* 1886), C. Piepenbring (*Histoire du Peuple d'Israël,* 1898), and C. H. Cornill (*Geschichte des Volkes Israel,* 1898). A more moderate account of Hebrew history was furnished by R. Kittel in his three-volume work *Geschichte des Volkes Israel,* published from 1888.

The rise of the nineteenth-century critical school, with its emphasis upon literary analysis and its evolutionary view of Hebrew origins, brought with it an extremely skeptical evaluation of the Old Testament historical narratives. Part of this was due to the Wellhausenian pattern of documentary analysis, which imposed a considerable gap between the form of the narratives and the events that they purported to describe, and part to the principles followed by the members of the Wellhausenian school, which did not permit them to regard the documents as reliable sources for the history of the times they chronicled. Since extra-Biblical archaeological data were deemed too scanty to be worthy of notice, and since comparatively little was known at that time about Near Eastern life in the second millennium B.C., the historians who had fallen under the influence of Wellhausen were thrown back upon the evolutionary philosophy of Hegel. Even when Hegelianism lost its appeal, the basic principle that the faith of Israel had its origins in rudimentary forms, which slowly and demonstrably progressed to the higher forms of belief culminating in monotheism, continued to be repeated tirelessly by the faithful adherents of liberalism. This position necessarily demanded a complete reconstruction of the history of Israel, in which the early traditions were relegated to the realm of myth and legend, the historicity of the patriarchs was denied, the campaigns of Joshua dismissed as fundamentally unhistorical, and the beginnings of Hebrew historiography assigned to a comparatively late period in the growth of the monarchy.

With the availability of much new archaeological information providing a good control for assessing the value and trustworthiness of the Biblical narratives, one might expect that a fundamental change in attitude towards the long-held evolutionary concepts of Hebrew history would have taken place by now among scholars. In point of fact, however, as Bright has stated, the major treatises dealing with Old Testament history still adhere to much the same developmental pattern as that cherished by an earlier generation.[37] This has been reinforced by a general uncritical acceptance of what many nineteenth- and early twentieth-century scholars liked to call "the most assured results of Biblical criticism." Even those who have acknowledged the antiquity and substantial historicity of the tradition underlying the documentary sources that they profess to recognize have been slow to afford such a development its proper place in their scheme of historiography.

Perhaps the most serious objection that can be levelled against contemporary writers in the field of Old Testament history is that so many have failed or have been reluctant to take into proper account those assured archaeological discoveries that are now available to scholars. Such was the case with the two-volume history written by Oesterley and Robinson, which, as Orlinsky has pointed out, did not make adequate use of factual archaeological material in existence at the time of writing, a deficiency that remained uncorrected in subsequent re-issues.[38] Equally guilty was A. Lods, whose two volumes on the historical background of Israelite life betokened a grave ignorance of important areas of archaeological discovery.[39] Not a few European scholars have run afoul of this unfortunate tendency, and reviewers of their work have been quick to comment on this fault. However, there is no excuse for this failure; while it may be perfectly legitimate for a scholar to propound views that issue from the standpoint of critical methodology, it is unscientific for him to ignore vitally important sources of information relating to his subject, whether they result in a modification of his basic position or not. A scholar who persists in this kind of procedure cannot command very much confidence among his colleagues.

Whereas at the end of the nineteenth century one of the most pressing questions of debate among Old Testament historians was the nature of

[37] *Early Israel in Recent History Writing* (1956), pp. 23f.

[38] W. O. E. Oesterley and T. H. Robinson, *A History of Israel* (2 vols., 1932); H. M. Orlinsky, *Ancient Israel* (1954), p. 178.

[39] A. Lods, *Israel from its Beginnings to the Middle of the Eighth Century* (1932) and *The Prophets and the Rise of Judaism* (1937).

304

the progression from polydaemonism to monotheistic faith in the experience of ancient Israel, the situation had changed by the middle of the twentieth century to the point where scholars were concerned to grapple with the entire question of the origins of Israel. Consequently the whole area of early traditions and methods by which they can be evaluated most effectively has been under constant examination in recent years, particularly by Albright and Noth. Part of the difficulty that liberal scholars invariably have to meet lies in their self-imposed assumption that the traditions in their extant written form are comparatively late. Although there are good reasons for believing that this view is in many respects erroneous, it is a necessary concomitant of the scheme of literary analysis as understood and practiced by Wellhausen and his successors.

What is needed, therefore, is a reliable methodological approach that will bridge the gap between the Biblical events and the extant written form of the narratives describing them, if the writing is not contemporary with the event or nearly so. Basic to any historiographical method for Alt and Noth is the Wellhausenian scheme of literary analysis, assisted by a rigorous application of the results of form-historical study. By this means they feel best equipped to trace the blocks of tradition that they have isolated to their most primitive form, after which they can begin to describe the manner in which the narrative may be thought to have assumed its normative state.[40]

[40] Thus Noth devoted the opening sections of *UP* to a careful exposition of the classical documentary theory of Pentateuchal origins, whose tenets he accepted. He then utilized an investigation of the tradition-history or *Überlieferungsgeschichte* of the Pentateuch on the assumption that the underlying sources had experienced a long history of transmission in one form or another before assuming their extant character. On the basis of the five distinct areas of tradition that he isolated according to the principles of form-criticism, Noth concluded that the traditions of the patriarchs had developed and been transmitted independently of the other Pentateuchal narratives, and that originally they had dealt with Jacob as the principal figure. Integral to the procedure of recognition and isolation of traditional elements were the *Haftpunkt*—the place from which the tradition was transmitted or with which it was originally associated—and the *Ortsgebundenheit*—the adherence of traditions to specific localities. One feature of the Alt-Noth school is the way in which the concept of aetiology, the analysis of stories purporting to account for ancient names or customs, has been employed as a means of identifying what are alleged to be accretions of the legendary in orally transmitted material; for the function of aetiology in historical tradition, see W. F. Albright, *BASOR*, No. 74 (1939), pp. 12ff. On this basis the narratives dealing with the meeting of Jacob and Esau at Mahanaim (Gen. 32:6ff.), or the wrestling at Penuel (Gen. 32:24ff.), are aetiological and therefore secondary material (*UP*, p. 104). While Noth, unlike Wellhausen, concedes that the patriarchs were historical personages and not mere eponyms, he has placed them on the desert fringe of Canaan rather than in a cultured Mesopotamian setting. Again, although he admits that Moses is historical, Noth seems to think that he had nothing to do with the Exodus or Wilderness wanderings, but rather was associated with a grave tradition (*Grabstradition*) in

While the methodology of the Alt-Noth school includes an insistence upon a rigorous examination of literary sources, it has largely resulted in what Bright has described as a "totally negative evaluation of the historical worth of the early traditions of Israel and . . . a surprising reluctance to call upon the results of archaeology in a measure to fill the void thus created."[41] There can be no doubt that the position maintained by this school is backed up by scholarly diligence and great erudition. An unfortunate weakness in their methodological procedures, however, is the fact that they are immediately ineffective for anyone who does not accept the documentary or phase-analyses of Alt and Noth. Because archaeological evidence is decidedly subordinated to *a priori* considerations, literary or otherwise, a grossly inadequate view of the Hebrew *Sitz im Leben des Volkes,* or life-situation, results. Their assessment fails from a purely theological standpoint, as Bright has indicated, to account for the phenomenon of Israel's being the "people of the faith." Furthermore, their historical estimate is primarily subjective.

When tested by normal procedures of interpretation, the archaeological material from the Middle Bronze Age points to certain social and historical configurations that Alt and Noth are unprepared to accept. Since for them all other material seems to be subordinated to theoretical considerations, it is not easy to see how their rather nihilistic position represents any significant advance upon the evolutionary hypotheses of Wellhausen. Despite the attention that the efforts of Alt and Noth to interpret the early historical traditions of Israel command, their position must be rejected as an invalid methodology, if for no other reason than that one of its basic presuppositions is in error. As C. H. Gordon has

---

Transjordan (*UP*, pp. 186f.). Interest in this suggestion was quickened in 1962 with the discovery of a pyramid-like structure by a South American archaeological team excavating to the south of 'Amman in Jordan. According to Julio Ripamonti, the leader of the expedition, the walls of the building were about 140 feet high and nearly 95 feet wide, thus representing the largest single building unearthed to date in either Canaan or Transjordan. It was dated to the Late Bronze Age, about 1250 B.C. On examination it was found to consist of an inner building, adjacent to which were twelve small chambers. Ripamonti associated the structure with the burial of Moses, and thought that it may have marked the place where he died. He further suggested the possibility that the twelve chambers represented the traditional number of the tribes of Israel. While this discovery remains to be evaluated at the time of writing, it is not impossible that a cenotaph was erected in Transjordan by the Israelites to commemorate the histor:cal Moses prior to the occupation of the Promised Land. Although Alt and Noth have demonstrated a considerably greater awareness of the nature and significance of archaeological discoveries than did Wellhausen and his more immediate successors, the use to which they have put this information is generally of a decidedly negative character. This is perhaps understandable, since for them much of the tradition has little if any historical value, and therefore there does not seem to be any point in invoking evidence to support it (e.g. *GI*, pp. 70f.).

[41] J. Bright, *Early Israel in Recent History Writing,* p. 55.

remarked, the material available must dictate the method to be employed;[42] and, as a result, it is difficult to repose any confidence in an approach to historiography which, on the basis of rigid *a priori* considerations, is unwilling to consider the total evidence at hand.

A much more satisfactory approach to the problems of Hebrew historiography has been provided by W. F. Albright, the foremost Biblical archaeologist of the twentieth century, who has brought an enormous amount of erudition and experience to bear upon a critical examination of the problems in hand. Under his influence the course of Old Testament studies has taken an entirely new turn, and his prodigious scholarly output from the decade following World War I is eloquent testimony to the virility of his attack upon outstanding difficulties. He has utilized as fully as possible the more adequate controls furnished by archaeological discoveries, and has included philology, sociology, anthropology, and other disciplines in his methodology. His work and that of his students is characterized by a high degree of academic competence combined with a charitable understanding of positions with which they find themselves unable to agree. Though Albright himself and some of his followers appear to concur in a kind of documentary analysis of the Pentateuch that has affinities with that propounded by Wellhausen, they are quick to recognize the breakdown of the classical pattern of source-analysis as the primary means of reconstructing Hebrew history and religion, and are willing to avail themselves of other cognate areas of information.

The significance of this approach is that its methodology is still largely valid even for those, such as the present writer, who reject the Wellhausenian literary analysis of Pentateuchal material, since this analysis, or something very much akin to it, is no longer vital to the success of the method of history-writing. In this sense Albright's approach is unlike the position adopted by Alt and Noth, whose disregard of important areas of evidence vitiates the validity of a great many of their conclusions. An excellent example of the method favored by the Albright school has been furnished by Bright, whose *History of Israel*, published in 1959, grapples with the problems of Hebrew origins and development in a remarkably satisfying manner, furnishing what is by far the best history of Israel since the work of Kittel. Bright marshals as much of the evidence as possible in executing his task, evaluates it critically and presents a coherent pattern that differs radically in significant areas from the history of Noth, written a decade earlier. Bright's book gained early acceptance as the standard English-language history of Israel, and although it must be used with caution at some points, it constitutes in general an important step forward in this area of Biblical study.

---

[42] *IOTT*, pp. 17f.

II. PROBLEMS OF OLD TESTAMENT HISTORY

On the basis of the foregoing remarks it is possible at this point to consider the historical background of significant periods of Hebrew history and the problems associated with them, utilizing for the purpose as much of the available material as is possible. It will be evident from the following survey that the contention of Wellhausen and his followers that the record of events in the Old Testament is basically tendentious, and consequently requires objective analysis, can no longer be sustained in the light of the facts. As professional students of the ancient Near East acquire even more information about the life and times of ancient cultures in the Biblical world, it becomes increasingly apparent that the Old Testament is a substantially accurate record of events based upon accredited historiographical procedures. That certain tendencies appear in the historical writings from time to time is well recognized, as is the fact that any history worthy of the name must exhibit specific emphases and points of view, whether it is an ancient composition or a modern work. This, incidentally, is one of the reasons for the superiority of ancient Hittite historiography over the dull cataloging and gross exaggeration of comparable Egyptian and Mesopotamian sources.

Perhaps a more serious objection to the approach of the Wellhausenian school is that their methodology, subjective as it was, constituted an entirely inappropriate medium for those precise purposes of objective analysis that they were at such pains to stress. Even more unfortunate is the failure of those who still subscribe to a greater or lesser extent to the methodology of Wellhausen to realize that the literary-critical naturalistic approach can never begin to do adequate justice to the grandeur of Hebrew history and religion as presented in the pages of the Old Testament.[1] In those areas where the writer indulges in a spiritual or metaphysical interpretation of events, it is made abundantly clear that the course of human affairs generally is under divine control, a proposition that cannot be accepted by those whose outlook is rigidly governed by *a priori* positivistic categories.

[1] Cf. *ARI*, p. 3.

That there are apparent inconsistencies and contradictions in ancient Hebrew life as recorded in the Old Testament narratives would scarcely be denied by anyone. Yet it is also true that equal inconsistencies and alleged discrepancies can be documented from virtually every period of human history, and not the least by any means from the modern age. As far as the ancient Near East is concerned, scholarly studies and archaeological discoveries have now advanced the corpus of knowledge concerning life in Bible lands to the point where it is far more correct to speak of "problems" in Biblical history or chronology than to think in terms of "contradictions." The one really acceptable methodology for the study of ancient Hebrew history and culture will embrace as full an understanding as possible of the Near Eastern *Sitz im Leben des Volkes* of antiquity and will then set the narratives of Hebrew life and times against this larger factual background with great caution. Only when this is done with all the care and restraint of modern Biblical scholarship will the true nature of Hebrew historiography become apparent to the contemporary mind, and the authors of the Old Testament be revealed as purposeful and responsible men.

A. The Patriarchal Narratives

Although some scholars have found no historical value in the patriarchal narratives, assuming with Wellhausen that Abraham, Isaac, and Jacob were either eponymous ancestors of clans or at most purely mythical figures,[2] others have begun to realize that the Genesis narratives can no longer be dismissed as mere Canaanite myths or legends.[3] While certain tribal names were treated in Genesis as designations of individuals, following general Semitic custom, and fitted into a genealogical sequence, it has been discovered impossible to carry through to a logical conclusion the theory that in the patriarchal traditions the experiences represented as being individual were actually personifications of group life, since Abraham, for example, conveys every impression of strict and distinct individuality.

It is true, of course, that there is to date no independent confirmation from extra-Biblical sources of the patriarchal narratives as they now stand, and equally true that there is much that will never be known about this particular phase of human history. Yet enough has been discovered by examining the archaeological sequences occurring in the Bronze Age to require a far more sympathetic evaluation of the Genesis tradition than was the case among earlier generations of scholars. This evaluation is based on objective study of the situation rather than on

[2] Wellhausen, *Prolegomena zur Geschichte Israels* (1895), pp. 322ff.; B. Stade, *Geschichte des Volkes Israel* (1887), I, pp. 145ff.; cf. E. Meyer, *Die Israeliten und ihre Nachbarstämme* (1906), pp. 249ff.

[3] E.g. E. Dhorme, *La Religion des Hébreux nomades* (1937), p. 69.

purely subjective considerations. All lines of evidence indicate that the cultural milieu of the patriarchal sagas[4] can be placed with complete confidence in the Bronze Age, and in particular within a period extending from 2000 to 1500 B.C.[5] Against a background of an advanced Mesopotamian civilization, the beginnings of Hebrew tradition were associated with the name of Abraham.[6] With the discoveries of texts at Mari and Nuzu has come the realization that the names current in the narratives of the patriarchs were of common occurrence, particularly in Amorite circles, both in Mesopotamia and Palestine in the second millennium B.C.[7] Thus "Abraham," under the syllabic forms *A-ba-am-ra-ma* and *A-ba-am-ra-am*, was in current usage considerably before the sixteenth century B.C., and may have occurred also in the Egyptian Execration Texts.[8] The Mari letters mentioned the city of Nahor, home of Rebekah, under the name Nakhur, which in the eighteenth century B.C. was ruled by an Amorite prince.[9] In an eighteenth-century B.C. Egyptian list the names Asher and Issachar have been found in cognate form.[10] The Nuzu texts, which mirrored the traditions and social customs of a predominantly Horite (Hurrian) group flourishing in northeastern Mesopotamia during the fifteenth century B.C., have thrown particular light upon patriarchal traditions that previously had been deemed inexplicable.[11] For example, the narrative dealing with the sale of the Cave of Machpelah to Abraham, which was assigned by the nineteenth-century critics to the latest of the Pentateuchal documents, is now known to have followed very closely the procedures laid down by Hittite law in cases of land transactions,[12] and is early rather than late in origin. The culture

[4] Terms such as "saga" and "tradition" occurring in the present work are used without prejudice as to the historical nature of the material under discussion.

[5] Among the many sources of information are included *FSAC*, pp. 236ff.; R. de Vaux, *RB*, LIII (1946), pp. 321ff., LV (1948), pp. 321ff., LVI (1949), pp. 5ff.; *LAP*, pp. 54ff.; H. H. Rowley, *BJRL*, XXXII (1949), pp. 3ff., reprinted in *The Servant of the Lord and Other Essays* (1952), pp. 271ff.; *WBA*, pp. 40ff.

[6] W. F. Albright, *JBL*, LVIII (1939), pp. 91ff.; *FSAC*, pp. 154f. For the view that Abraham was a merchant prince living in a north-Mesopotamian city see C. H. Gordon in D. W. Thomas and W. D. McHardy (eds.), *Hebrew and Semitic Studies presented to Godfrey Rolles Driver* (1963), p. 77; *GBB*, pp. 287f., in *JNES*, XVII (1958), pp. 28ff., and in A. Altmann (ed.), *Biblical and Other Studies* (1963), p. 8.

[7] *BHI*, p. 70.

[8] W. F. Albright, *BASOR*, No. 83 (1941), p. 34, No. 88 (1942), p. 36; cf. Albright in *JBL*, LIV (1935), pp. 193ff.; J. A. Wilson, *The Culture of Ancient Egypt* (1956), pp. 156f.

[9] Cf. G. E. Mendenhall, *BA*, XI, No. 1 (1948), p. 16.

[10] W. F. Albright, *JAOS*, LXXIV (1954), pp. 227ff.

[11] Cf. C. H. Gordon, *BA*, III, No. 1 (1940), pp. 1ff.; R. T. O'Callaghan, *CBQ*, VI (1944), pp. 391ff.; E. A. Speiser, *JBL*, LXXIV (1955), pp. 252ff.; A. E. Draffkorn, *JBL*, LXXVI (1957), pp. 216ff.

[12] M. R. Lehmann, *BASOR*, No. 129 (1953), pp. 15ff.; cf. *ANET*, p. 191.

and political milieu of the second millennium B.C. in Mesopotamia is also reflected by the migrations of the patriarchs, which were characteristic of many such contemporary movements along the length of the Fertile Crescent.

Despite the admission of Albright[13] that sporadic domestication of the camel might have gone back several centuries before the end of the Bronze Age, there are still writers who assume that the few references to camels in the patriarchal sagas (Gen. 12:16; 24:64) are anachronistic.[14] Prior to their full-scale domestication in the twelfth century B.C., camels were used to a limited extent as beasts of burden, a fact that is evident from their mention (GAM.MAL) in an eighteenth-century B.C. cuneiform list of fodder for domestic animals, discovered at Alalakh in northern Syria.[15] In addition, the excavations of Parrot at Mari uncovered the remains of camel bones in the ruins of a house belonging to the pre-Sargonic era (ca. 2400 B.C.).[16] A relief at Byblos in Phoenicia, dated in the eighteenth century B.C., depicts a camel in a kneeling position, thus indicating the domestication of the animal in Phoenician circles some centuries prior to the Amarna Age.[17] Albright's objection that the animal depicted on the relief had no hump and could not therefore be considered a camel was refuted by de Vaux, who pointed out that there was a socket on the back to which the hump and its load had been attached separately.[18] Other evidence for the early domestication of the camel consists of a jawbone recovered from a Middle Bronze Age tomb (ca. 1900-1600 B.C.) at Tell el-Farah,[19] and cylinder seals found in northern Mesopotamia, dating from the patriarchal era and depicting riders seated upon camels.[20] The foregoing ought to be sufficient to refute the commonly held view that references to camels in Genesis are "anachronistic touches" introduced to make the stories more vivid to later hearers.[21]

The same may be said, to a less demonstrable extent, about the allegation that the occurrence of Philistines in the patriarchal narratives

[13] *FSAC*, p. 165; cf. J. P. Free, *JNES*, III (1944), pp. 187ff.

[14] *BHI*, p. 72; *BANE*, p. 204; cf. R. Walz, *ZDMG*, CI (1951), pp. 29ff., CIV (1954), pp. 45ff.

[15] D. J. Wiseman and A. Goetze, *JCS*, XIII (1959), pp. 29, 37; D. J. Wiseman, *The Alalakh Tablets* (1953), No. 269:59; S. Moscati, *Rivista degle Studi Orientali*, XXXV (1960), p. 116; cf. W. G. Lambert, *BASOR*, No. 160 (1960), p. 42.

[16] A. Parrot, *SRA*, XXXII (1955), p. 323.

[17] P. Montet, *Byblos et l'Égypte* (1928), p. 91 and pl. 52.

[18] W. F. Albright, *JBL*, LXIV (1945), p. 288; R. de Vaux, *RB*, LVI (1949), p. 9 n. 4f.

[19] *Ibid.*, p. 9 n. 8. Cf. C. H. Gordon in *Biblical and Other Studies*, p. 10.

[20] The Tell Halaf sculptured relief (*LAP*, p. 55 and pl. 25) is far from being "one of the earliest known representations of the camel." For the early domestication of the camel in India see M. Wheeler, *The Indus Civilisation* (1953), p. 60.

[21] *BHI*, p. 72; K. A. Kitchen, *NBD*, pp. 181ff.

is also anachronistic.[22] While it is true that a significantly large body of Philistines settled in Palestine (a name that itself is derived from "Philistine") about 1187 B.C., after being repulsed by Rameses III in a naval battle, there are good reasons for believing that the Philistines were active in Canaan at a considerably earlier period. If the term is extended, as it can be quite legitimately, to include the Minoans and other Aegean peoples with whom the Philistines were connected, it must then be remembered that there is conclusive evidence of an expansion of Aegean trade in the Middle Minoan II period (*ca.* 1900-1700 B.C.), which left behind objects of Aegean manufacture at such places as Ugarit, Hazor, Lachish, and Abydos in Egypt. This commercial thrust alone would be sufficient to bring a number of pioneering Philistine trading-groups into Canaan and Syria, and the fact that they were most probably small in number during the patriarchal period would account for a general lack of mention in the annals of larger states. In this latter connection it is improbable that the members of such a mixed group as the Aegean peoples would be distinguished at all carefully by name in the Middle Minoan period, particularly since they were not in the cultural and military ascendency that was the case in the twelfth century. Nevertheless there are records of Philistine activity in the Near East at this period, including an eighteenth-century B.C. Mari text recording that a certain king of Hazor in Palestine sent gifts to Crete (*Kaptara*).[23] Pottery from the Middle Minoan period has been recovered from Ras Shamra (Ugarit), from Hazor, and in Egypt from Abydos and Memphis, all of which date between 1900 and 1600 B.C.[24] This is clear evidence for close contact between Aegean groups and the peoples of Palestine during the patriarchal period, a phenomenon that does much to explain why the Philistine settlements in Canaan experienced no linguistic difficulties when dealing with the native inhabitants.[25] It should also be remembered that ancient scribes frequently substituted current designations for earlier names when revising literary works, and it may be that at least some instances of the usage of "Philistine" in Pentateuchal material may be the result of this influence. Whether this was actually the case or not, there can be no doubt that the Philistines were active in Palestine and Egypt during the Middle Bronze Age.

From the standpoint of topography, the patriarchal sagas agree in essence with what is known about Middle Bronze Age life in Canaan also. Genesis represents the patriarchs as semi-nomadic herdsmen or

[22] E.g. B. W. Anderson, *Understanding the OT* (1957), p. 46 n. 3; *BHI*, p. 73, *et al.*

[23] A. Pohl, *Orientalia*, XIX (1950), p. 509.

[24] For Ras Shamra, see C. F. A. Schaeffer, *Ugaritica*, I (1939), pp. 54ff.; for Hazor, Y. Yadin *et al., Hazor II* (1960), p. 86 and pl. 115; for Egypt, H. J. Kantor in *Relative Chronologies in Old World Archaeology* (ed. R. W. Erich), pp. 10ff.

[25] *IOTT*, p. 108.

shepherds. In this connection it is important to note that the places mentioned as visited by Abraham are situated in an area whose annual rainfall is between ten and twenty inches. This is admirably suited to the requirements of sheep,[26] and substantiates the ancient tradition of the sagas in this regard. Furthermore, the patriarchs were associated by the narratives with sites in the densely wooded hill-country of Palestine (cf. Gen. 13:18; 26:23; 28:10; 33:18; 35:1; 37:17). As the investigations of Glueck in the Hashemite Kingdom of Jordan have demonstrated, Dothan, Shechem, Gerar, and Bethel were all inhabited between 2000 and 1700 B.C.[27] Hebron was founded "seven years before Zoan in Egypt,"[28] that is to say, about 1725 B.C., and while the exact age of Beersheba is uncertain, the wells at the site are unquestionably of great antiquity.

Evidence for an earlier rather than a later period of activity for Abraham has been furnished somewhat indirectly by considerations relating to the destruction of Sodom, Gomorrah, and the other "cities of the valley." Their sites may with great probability be located south of el-Lisan ("Tongue") peninsula in the southern part of the Dead Sea. Sodom itself may have been situated near the southern end of the valley, and had its name preserved in Jebel Usdum ("Mount of Sodom"), a mountain along the southern end of the west side of the Dead Sea about five miles long and more than 700 feet high, composed predominantly of crystalline salt. Further evidence supporting the suggested location has been provided by the site of Bab edh-Dhra', situated about five miles from and about five hundred feet above the shore of the Dead Sea southeast of el-Lisan. It had apparently been a pilgrimage place, and since no other traces of human habitation have been uncovered in this general region, it can be concluded that the homes of those who formerly frequented Bab edh-Dhra' must have come from what was once known as the Vale of Siddim. The presence of fertile fields around the mouths of the streams that flow into this southeast part of the Dead Sea lends credence to the belief that the entire area was one of great fertility in antiquity. The date of the catastrophe that overtook Sodom and the neighboring cities in the valley can be estimated roughly with reference to the pottery found at Bab edh-Dhra'—which indicated that the site had been frequented by pilgrims and others between 2300 and about 1900 B.C. The cessation of visits to Bab edh-Dhra' would most probably coincide with the destruction of Sodom and Gomorrah, since it was from the "cities of the valley" that the pilgrims

[26] N. Glueck, *BA*, XVIII, No. 1 (1955), p. 4.

[27] Glueck, *The Other Side of the Jordan* (1940), pp. 114ff. and *BA*, XVIII, No. 1 (1955), pp. 2ff.; *WMTS*, p. 71.

[28] Num. 13:22. Its original name may have been Kiriath-arba (Gen. 23:2; 35:27), hence the explanatory gloss of Gen. 13:18.

and other visitors came. The corollary to this is that evidence is here provided that Abraham was living about the end of the twentieth century B.C.

While the patriarchal narratives obviously need to be examined with care against the known background of contemporary life and times before they are used as sources for the history of the period, there can be little serious doubt on the basis of such an examination that the traditions they preserve are substantially historical. If, as many liberal scholars have assumed, the materials were transmitted orally, they may, as Albright has pointed out, have been subjected to processes of refraction and selection of elements suited for epic narrative, and this could well have ignored considerations of strict chronology.[29] But if, on the other hand, these materials have been transmitted as written texts on tablets, some of which were linked in series, they stand in the same general tradition as the Mari, Nuzu, and Alalakh sources, and in consequence they must be accorded a similar degree of historicity.

As has been noted in part three, some of the chronological problems associated with this general period are extremely complex, and there is at the time of writing no noticeable measure of scholarly agreement concerning them. Genesis 14 used to be utilized as a means of setting Abraham within the context of world history, but, although this material is now regarded by many scholars as constituting an ancient historical source, its significance for the chronology of the patriarchal period is still enigmatic in many respects.[30] However, the total picture presented by all the available evidence places the events of the sagas between the twentieth and sixteenth centuries B.C., and not in the Late Bronze Age of the sixteenth to thirteenth centuries B.C.

In discussing above the topography of the patriarchal narratives, it was noted that the pattern was consistent with the situation in the Middle Bronze Age rather than in other periods such as that of the Egyptian Empire (ca. 1570-1200 B.C.), when Palestine was an Egyptian dependency. Despite this assertion, however, it is impossible to say with certainty precisely when the ancestors of the later Israelites actually went down to Egypt and subsequently endured humiliating bondage. Nevertheless, some of the customs mentioned in Genesis 34-50 are particularly characteristic of the Second Intermediate period of Egyptian history (ca. 1776-1570 B.C.), during which the land was under the control of the invading Hyksos. Certain of the names prevalent in early Israelite circles, particularly in the tribe of Levi, reveal a connection with Egypt.[31] The antiquity of the tradition associated with the

---

[29] FSAC, pp. 68f., 72.

[30] BHI, pp. 75f.

[31] T. J. Meek, AJSL, LVI (1939), pp. 113ff.; J. G. Griffiths, JNES, XII (1953), pp. 225ff. The attempts of Noth, UP, pp. 178f., to dismiss this evidence are unconvincing.

names of the midwives attending Hebrew women in Egypt (Exod. 1:15) is confirmed by the fact that Shiphrah appears as a name in an eighteenth-century B.C. slave-list, and Puah occurs as a proper name in the Ugaritic texts.[32] A papyrus document dated about 1785 B.C. describes the prison system of the period, and on the *verso*, probably written some fifty years later, are listed 79 servants in an Egyptian household, of whom forty-five were Asiatics bearing characteristic west-Semitic names such as Menahem and Shiprah.[33] Finally, it is significant that Egyptian texts refer to the presence of captive 'Apiru in the land during the Empire period, who apparently had been brought as slave laborers to Egypt as early as the time of Amenophis II (*ca.* 1435-1414 B.C.), if not earlier, and among whom would almost certainly have been elements of the later Israelites.[34]

The local color of the narratives recounting the career of Joseph seems to accord with a period when Asiatic invaders dominated Egypt rather than with a time when native Egyptians were exercising rule over their own land. Under normal conditions the ancient Egyptians were never particularly tolerant towards politically ambitious foreigners in their midst, since they regarded their high offices of state as the perquisite of the Egyptian noble families. If, however, an enterprising and talented Semite such as Joseph had the political backing of the Hyksos conquerors, there would be little to prevent his rise to prominence in the land.[35] The Joseph narratives indicate that the territory of Goshen was near the Egyptian capital of Avaris, and that the Hebrews had ready access to the royal court, which would suit the conditions of Hyksos rule quite well. Further evidence of a connection between the patriarchal migration to Egypt and the Avaris era may be seen in the reference to Joseph's buying up land for the pharaoh during the famine years (Gen. 47:13ff.), a procedure that displaced the old landed nobility and created a new class of serfs. This reflects closely the social upheaval in Palestine during the Hyksos regime.[36]

B. The Date of the Exodus

There is no extra-Biblical evidence relating directly to the fact of the Exodus, but it is clear that a belief so firmly rooted in the religious tradition of Israel can hardly be explained in terms other than that this

[32] W. F. Albright, *JAOS*, LXXIV (1954), p. 229.

[33] W. C. Hayes, *A Late Middle Kingdom Papyrus in the Brooklyn Museum* (1955); K. A. Kitchen, *NBD*, p. 658.

[34] M. Greenberg, *The Hab/piru*, pp. 56f. For the mention of the Habiru in certain Egyptian texts see *ANET*, pp. 22, 247, 255, 261.

[35] H. M. Orlinsky, *Ancient Israel*, p. 33.

[36] Cf. G. Steindorff and K. C. Seele, *When Egypt Ruled the East* (1942), p. 88. The name "Hyksos" occurred in the Egyptian Execration Texts as early as 1960 B.C. in the form *hekau khasut*. For their Palestinian origin see A. Alt, *Die Herkunft der Hyksos in neuer Sicht* (1954), pp. 26ff.

stupendous liberating act of God occurred in reality. The precise spot where the *Yam Suph* was crossed cannot be identified with certainty,[37] but as Bright has commented, the specific location was as little central to the faith of Israel as is that of the tomb of Christ to the Christian faith.[38]

Attempts to establish a chronology for the Exodus have resulted in some of the most perplexing problems in the entire panorama of Hebrew history, as has been noted in an earlier chapter. Two principal views of the situation have arisen, one of which envisages a date in the fifteenth century B.C., while the other assigns the Exodus to the thirteenth century B.C. What is interesting about this diversity of opinion is that both positions can be supported to some extent from the Biblical narratives themselves. The earlier date furnishes problems for the chronology of the patriarchal period, for by applying the literal statements of Genesis it would appear that a period of 250 years elapsed between the arrival of Abraham in Canaan and the migration of Jacob to Egypt. If the statement that Israel was in Egypt for 430 years (Exod. 12:40) is to be considered independently of the Hyksos movement, it would place the entry of the patriarchs into Canaan some 645 years before the Exodus, giving a date for the birth of Abraham (cf. Gen. 12:4) about 2161 B.C. This event would have thus occurred somewhat before the founding of the Third Dynasty of Ur (*ca.* 2060-1950 B.C.), and judged by the trend of migratory movements in Mesopotamia subsequent to the twentieth century B.C. such a date seems to be a little early.

Genesis 15:13 predicted that the descendants of Abraham would be afflicted in a strange land for 400 years, a figure that was extended in Exodus 12:40 to 430 years.[39] The Massoretic reading in the latter reference is to be preferred to the LXX variant, which regards the 430 years as covering the patriarchal sojournings in Palestine as well as in Egypt, since the "selfsame day" (Exod. 12:41) at the end of this long interval of time was the anniversary of the entrance of Jacob and his family into Egypt. It would thus seem that a period of four hundred and thirty years ensued between the entry of Jacob into Egypt and the departure of the Israelites under Moses. The genealogy that appears to reduce the stay in Egypt to only two or three generations (Exod. 6:16ff.) was probably compiled under the influence of those principles of abbreviation and selectivity that seem to have governed other genealogies (e.g. Gen. 5 and 11).[40]

---

[37] Cf. M. Noth in *Festschrift Otto Eissfeldt* (ed. J. Fueck, 1947), pp. 181ff.; H. Cazelles, *RB*, LXII (1955), pp. 321ff.; *WBA*, pp. 60ff.

[38] *BHI*, p. 112.

[39] On the interpretation of the period as a conventional expression for an *era*, cf. C. H. Gordon, *New Horizons in OT Literature* (1960), p. 13.

[40] Cf. K. A. Kitchen and T. C. Mitchell, *NBD*, p. 214.

The fifteenth-century B.C. date for the Exodus can also be supported on arguments based on the chronological note in 1 Kings 6:1, stating that Solomon commenced building the Temple in the 480th year after the departure from Egypt. If this construction is to be dated about 961 B.C., the Exodus would thus have taken place *ca.* 1441 B.C. If this sequence is meant to be taken literally, it is a powerful argument for a fifteenth-century date.[41] However, while such a figure represents the unanimous testimony of the manuscripts, it can be questioned on other grounds, particularly when it is examined against the background of oriental symbolism.[42] The number 480 can be resolved into units of twelve generations of forty years each. A double cycle or *motif* may be involved in consequence, having the effect of relating the concept of a generation to each of the twelve tribes. If, however, the symbol of forty years as constituting a generation is reckoned more realistically in terms of the period extending from the birth of the father to the birth of his son, a figure of twenty-five years would be a more appropriate estimate for a generation, yielding about 300 years and bringing the Exodus into the mid-thirteenth century B.C.

Symbolic numerical configurations are a recognized element in oriental historiography. The New Testament genealogy of Jesus Christ found in Matthew 1:17 is divided into three sections of fourteen generations each. These extend from the time of Abraham to David, from David to the period of the Babylonian captivity, and from the deportation to the birth of Jesus.

In the same way, by placing the Exodus some four hundred and eighty years prior to the building of the Temple in Jerusalem, there emerges a pattern of twelve generations of High Priests between the erecting of the wilderness Tabernacle, which prefigured the Temple, and the actual construction of the Temple by Solomon. Again, another period of 480 years, or twelve generations of forty years each, extends between the building of the First Temple and its restoration under Zerubbabel. With reference to the 430 years of Exodus 12:40, another period of 480 years emerges by adding the fifty years between the building of the Bethel altar by Jacob (Gen. 28:18; 35:1ff.) and his descent into Egypt, thus furnishing a twelve-generation interval between the erection of the first altar and the commencement of formal worship in the Tabernacle. Quite clearly a systematized approach of this kind indicates that considerations other than those of purely literal chronology are in view.

Further support for a fifteenth-century date for the Exodus was adduced from the excavations of Garstang at Jericho, for, as has been

[41] J. W. Jack, *The Date of the Exodus* (1925), pp. 200ff.
[42] B. Couroyer, *L'Exode* (1952), p. 11.

observed earlier, he believed that he had uncovered conclusive evidence of destruction under Joshua, which he dated a little prior to 1400 B.C.[43] The city in question was the fourth in a series that Garstang identified alphabetically at different archaeological levels, beginning about 3000 B.C. City "D" was believed to have been constructed *ca.* 1500 B.C., and to have flourished for approximately a century before being destroyed. From the fact that diplomatic contact between Jericho and Egypt appeared to have ceased under Amenhotep III (*ca.* 1405-1368 B.C.), Garstang formed the opinion that the Exodus had occurred in the reign of the pharaoh Amenhotep II (*ca.* 1436-1414 B.C.).

These conclusions now have to be modified as a result of the work undertaken at Jericho since 1952 by Kathleen M. Kenyon.[44] Her discoveries have confirmed the belief that the city was one of the oldest occupational sites in the entire Near East, going back to the seventh millennium B.C., but they have also made it clear that the walls of City "D" belong properly to the third millennium B.C., about 2300 B.C. They apparently constituted part of a contemporary defensive complex, and as such have no relevance for the conquests of Joshua. Ceramic remains recovered from graves in the area indicated that Jericho was occupied considerably later than 1400 B.C., though it is not wholly clear by whom. It is unfortunate that most of the thirteenth- and twelfth-century levels of the mound have been removed by the local inhabitants or eroded by natural forces. As a result it is virtually impossible for archaeologists to determine with any accuracy the nature and extent of Jericho during this general period.

Although at the beginning of the twentieth century most scholars, liberal and conservative alike, dated the Exodus in the thirteenth century B.C., the discoveries of Garstang at Jericho, and the construction that he imposed upon them, stimulated interest in a fifteenth-century date to the point where other archaeological material was adduced as evidence for an early Israelite departure from Egypt. One such source consisted of a group of clay tablets from Tell el-Amarna. In 1887 a peasant woman, rummaging around in the ruins of el-Amarna, the site of the once-proud city of Akhenaton, had discovered about 370 tablets written in Babylonian cuneiform.[45] When translated they were found to deal with a wide range of social, personal, and political matters, including a series of diplomatic communications from Babylonian, Mitanni, and other rulers to Amenhotep III (*ca.* 1405-1368 B.C.) and Akhenaton (*ca.* 1370-1353 B.C.). About one hundred and fifty of the texts originated in Palestine, and the nature of their contents has enabled scholars to achieve a great

[43] J. Garstang, *Joshua-Judges* (1931), p. 146.

[44] For a survey of work at the site up to 1956 see R. K. Harrison, *The Churchman*, LXX, No. 3 (1956), pp. 157ff.; cf. K. M. Kenyon, *Digging Up Jericho* (1957).

[45] Cf. W. M. F. Petrie, *Tell el Amarna* (1894); J. A. Knudtzon and O. Weber, *Die El-Amarna Tafeln* (1915); S. A. B. Mercer, *The Tell el-Amarna Tablets* (1939).

deal of insight into the state of Palestine prior to the arrival of the Israelites.

Most of the Palestinian texts complained to the Egyptian authorities that the Habiru were overrunning the territory and occupying several of the walled cities in southern Canaan. One of these letters, requesting immediate aid from the Egyptian army, read as follows:

> To the king, my lord, say...The whole land of the king has revolted. There is not one governor that is loyal. . . . The Habiru are capturing the fortresses of the king . . . the Habiru are taking the cities of the king. . . .[46]

Particularly poignant was the plea of Abdi-Hiba, governor of Jerusalem, in a letter to the pharaoh Akhenaton, in which he begged for assistance against the marauding Habiru, stressing that continued Egyptian control of southern Canaan was in the balance:

> Let the king...send troops against the men who transgress against the king, my lord. If troops are provided (here) this year, then the lands...will (still) belong to the king, my lord; if there are no archers, the lands of the king, my lord, will be lost. . . .[47]

This material was interpreted in some academic circles as an account of the conquest of Joshua, written by those administrative officials in southern Palestine who were loyal to the Egyptian regime,[48] an assumption that rested in part on the equating of the Habiru with the invading Hebrews under Joshua.

A more critical reading of the tablets, however, shows that during the Amarna period the Canaanite princes, who had increased greatly in numbers, were endeavoring to obtain their liberty and expand the territory of their city-states by employing mercenary troops to overthrow their neighbors. It was for help against these semi-nomadic marauders, named SA.GAZ or Habiru in the texts, that the loyal princes were appealing to Egypt; and they were not requesting military reinforcements in order to fend off attacks by the Israelites under the leadership of Joshua. Since as few as fifty, or in one instance, ten, soldiers were thought necessary for the purposes of strengthening the defense of loyal strongpoints, the situation appears to have been one of internecine strife rather than invasion by a powerful united enemy.

Furthermore, in the light of other archaeological discoveries it does not seem possible to equate the Habiru with the Hebrews. The term "Habiru" is most probably west-Semitic, and may originally have denoted a social class rather than an ethnic group, although there is a variety of opinion on this matter. The Habiru were mentioned as early as the Third

---

[46] G. L. Robinson, *The Bearing of Archaeology on the OT* (1941), p. 58; cf. *ANET*, pp. 262ff.; *LAP*, pp. 98ff.

[47] Cf. J. A. Knudtzon, *Die El-Amarna Tafeln*, No. 286, lines 55ff.; *ANET*, p. 488.

[48] H. R. Hall, *The Ancient History of the Near East* (1926), p. 409.

Dynasty of Ur, and in the second millennium B.C. they were widely distributed through the ancient Near East. In Ugaritic texts they were designated by the term *'prm*,[49] and seemed to be of a heterogeneous ethnic background, as, indeed, was the case elsewhere. Hittite texts mentioned the Habiru as a social group somewhat above the slave class but not free citizens in the fullest sense of the term. Nevertheless, some texts from Mari and Alalakh convey the impression that the Habiru manifested certain attributes characteristic of an ethnic group, and in the Amarna tablets they are depicted as a separate ethnic entity bearing west-Semitic names.[50]

Albright has maintained that their designation was more properly 'Apiru, a form closely related philologically to 'Ibhrîm, the Biblical Hebrews, which also appears in the Egyptian texts.[51] There are other scholars, however, who have identified the Hebrews and the Habiru, but have disclaimed any connection between the Habiru and the 'Apiru—making, in the end, for a very complex situation.[52] From the available evidence it would seem that, while the 'Apiru were basically semi-nomads of the Near Eastern desert areas who lived and worked under sedentary conditions at various times, it is incorrect to think of all 'Apiru as Hebrews although they may, and perhaps did, include elements of the Hebrews.[53]

If the Habiru mentioned in the letter of Abdi-Hiba to Akhenaton were in fact the Hebrews of the conquest period under Joshua, it would be reasonable to expect some correspondence between the names of the Canaanite princes that occurred in the Amarna texts and the Palestinian chiefs mentioned in the Old Testament narratives, which—unfortunately for the theory of an early dating—is not the case. In point of fact, it would seem that the Amarna tablets and the Joshua narratives portray two quite different social and political settings. In the cuneiform texts the local Canaanite rulers were exploiting the disturbed political conditions of the time as a means of gaining their freedom, using bands of 'Apiru or Habiru mercenaries to that end. In the Joshua narratives, however, the Canaanite city-states were already independent and were

[49] Ch. Virolleaud, *BASOR*, No. 77 (1940), p. 32.

[50] Cf. J. Bottéro, *Cahiers de la Société asiatique*, XII (1954), pp. 10ff.; Greenberg, *The Hab/piru*, pp. 3ff.

[51] W. F. Albright, *The Archaeology of Palestine and the Bible* (1935), pp. 206f.; cf. *FSAC*, p. 240; *BASOR*, No. 77 (1940), p. 33; *Vocalisation of the Egyptian Sullabic Orthography* (1934), p. 42, VII. B. 4; *ARI*, p. 200 n. 8. Cf. T. J. Meek, *Hebrew Origins* (1960 ed.), pp. 11ff.

[52] Cf. H. H. Rowley, *From Joseph to Joshua* (1950), pp. 45ff.

[53] C. de Wit, *The Date and Route of the Exodus* (1960), p. 11. Cf. *BHI*, pp. 124f.; M. Noth, *Festschrift Otto Procksch* (1934), pp. 99ff.; J. Lewy, *HUCA*, XIV (1939), pp. 587ff., XV (1940), pp. 47ff.; E. Dhorme, *Revue de l'Histoire des Religions*, CXVIII (1938), pp. 170ff.; J. W. Jack, *PEQ* (1940), pp. 95ff.; H. H. Rowley, *PEQ* (1942), pp. 41ff.

in a position to make a coalition in order to oppose the advance of the invading Hebrews.

Because of this it appears difficult to reconcile the situation relating to the Habiru of the Tell el-Amarna tablets with the conquering activities of the Biblical Hebrews under the leadership of Joshua, and at the present it would seem unwise to make a positive identification of the Hebrews with either the Habiru, the 'Apiru, or both. It should also be noted that, although the origins of Israel were extremely complex, including the "mixed multitude" of Egypt, the Kenites of the Sinai peninsula, and the Gibeonites of the time of Joshua, the nucleus of Israel at the period of the Exodus consisted of the tribes or descendants of Jacob, who could trace their lineage back to him without any difficulty, and that any 'Apiru or Habiru who happened to be included in the larger number were present originally on a rather incidental basis.

Those scholars who supported a thirteenth-century B.C. date for the Exodus rested their theories in part upon the reference in Exodus 1:11 that implied that elements of the Hebrews were in bondage when the cities of Raamses and Pithom were being rebuilt or enlarged, thus making Seti I (*ca.* 1308-1290 B.C.) or Rameses II (*ca.* 1290-1224 B.C.) the pharaoh of the oppression. Excavations at the site of Tanis-Avaris by Montet revealed the reconstruction of the city under Seti I, while the presence of statues, *stelae*, and other artifacts bearing the names of Rameses II and his successors testified to the vigor of the New Kingdom period.[54] Contemporary Egyptian texts mention that some 'Apiru were employed to drag the huge blocks of masonry used at Avaris and at other sites for the construction of temples and public buildings.[55]

It is highly probable that many Hebrews who remained behind in Egypt during the Nineteenth Dynasty, long after the Hyksos had been expelled, were similarly organized into gangs of forced-laborers, and these would certainly include the ancestors of the later Israelites. That there were 'Apiru in Egypt as late as the time of Rameses IV is apparent from a contemporary inscription dated about 1160 B.C.[56] If there is any connection at all between the 'Apiru and the Hebrews, this need only mean that not all of the Hebrews in Egypt went out with Moses, or that other Hebrews settled in Egypt subsequent to the time of the Exodus.[57] A link with the Amarna era was furnished by the discovery of a *stele* recording that the city had been founded some four hundred years prior to the erection of the monument itself. Since the

[54] P. Montet, *Les nouvelles fouilles de Tanis* (1929-33).
[55] Cf. *WMTS*, pp. 74f.
[56] Cf. J. A. Wilson, *AJSL*, XLIX (1933), pp. 275ff.; B. Gunn, *AASOR*, XIII (1933), p. 38 n. 93.
[57] T. J. Meek, *Hebrew Origins*, p. 35; *WMTS*, p. 274.

monument has been dated about 1320 B.C., it points to a date for the establishment of the capital city of the Hyksos about 1720 B.C.[58]

The tradition preserved in Exodus that government store-cities were erected by the use of forced Israelite labor has been largely confirmed independently by excavations in Egypt. An ancient site in the Wadi Tumilat, Tell el-Retabeh, supposed to have been Raamses by Petrie who excavated it originally, is now known to have been Pithom.[59] Work at the site has uncovered some of the massive brickwork erected in the time of Rameses II, and since no traces of Eighteenth Dynasty construction or expansion were evident, it would appear that the Exodus tradition of forced labor referred to the days of Rameses II.

Tanis-Avaris, the Hyksos capital in the Nile delta,[60] was renamed the "house of Rameses" (*Per Re'emasese*) and bore this designation for two centuries (*ca.* 1300-1100 B.C.).[61] Its positive identification by Montet made it clear that the store-cities were not constructed under Thotmes III or Queen Hatshepsut—as was once thought—and designated by their later rather than by their earlier names.[62] If the Exodus tradition is to be taken at its face value, therefore, it would imply that Rameses II was the pharaoh of the oppression, and that the Exodus took place in the thirteenth century B.C.

On the basis of the Avaris era, scholars saw a connection between the Hyksos invasion of Egypt and the Hebrew occupation of the land of Goshen in the Nile delta area, as recorded in Exodus 12:40, which gave a 430-year sojourn for Israel in a foreign land. This usage was further alleged from the reference in Numbers 13:22 stating that Hebron was built seven years before Zoan (Avaris), and once again the Avaris period was employed as a medium for dating-sequences.[63] On this basis the Exodus would have occurred some 430 years· after the founding of Avaris-Tanis, or about 1300 B.C.

One important Egyptian source precludes a date very much beyond 1220 B.C. for the entry of the victorious Israelites into Canaan. This is the celebrated *stele* from the time of Meneptah (*ca.* 1224-1216 B.C.), which dated from the fifth year of his reign. It was discovered by Flinders Petrie in 1895 in the ruined temple of Meneptah in western Thebes, and consisted of a lengthy court poem describing the victories of

[58] *WMTS*, pp. 72, 75.

[59] Pithom was identified in 1883 with Tell el-Mashkuta by E. Naville, *The Store-City of Pithom* (1885), but the "store-chambers" which he claimed to have discovered proved on subsequent examination to be fortress emplacements.

[60] Cf. A. H. Gardiner, *Ancient Egyptian Onomastica* (1947), I, pp. 169ff.

[61] *FSAC*, p. 255.

[62] P. Montet, *Le Drame d'Avaris* (1940), pp. 18ff.; cf. S. Caiger, *Bible and Spade* (1936), pp. 66ff.

[63] R. M. Engberg, *The Hyksos Reconsidered* (1939), p. 49, has observed that this assertion has never been tested archaeologically.

Meneptah over Libya and the eastern Asiatic lands including Palestine. The *stele* described graphically the terror and submission of the neighboring peoples:

> The princes are prostrate, saying: Salaam!
> There is not one who holds up his head among the Nine Bows;
> Since the Libyans are defeated, the land of the Hittites is pacified.
> Canaan is plundered with every evil;
> Askalon is conquered; Gezer is held;
> Yenoan is made a thing of naught;
> Israel is destroyed: it has no seed-corn;
> Palestine has become a widow for Egypt.
> All lands are united in peace. . . .[64]

The name "Israel" was written on the *stele* with the determinative symbol that denotes "people" rather than "land" or "territory," which would imply sedentary occupation of western Palestine.[65] However, it is conceivable that this is a transcriptional error, since the *stele* contains other similar mistakes.

As Burrows has pointed out, some scholars experienced difficulty in interpreting the evidence of the Meneptah *stele,* which shows that Israel experienced a defeat under Meneptah about 1230 B.C., partly because they assigned too late a date for the Exodus itself.[66] For them the *stele* showed that the Israelites were already in Canaan when they should still have been wandering about in the Sinai peninsula. This led to efforts to show that only a portion of the Israelite people had gone into Egypt, and that the *stele* referred to the remainder who had never left Palestine in the first place.[67] While it may well be that the sojourn in Egypt and the events of the Exodus are most properly associated only with a limited group, as described principally in the Biblical narratives, there are good reasons for believing that all the tribes may have been in Canaan prior to 1230 B.C.

The work of Nelson Glueck in the Hashemite Kingdom of Jordan has shown that southern Canaan was in the middle of a nomadic upheaval during the Third Dynasty of Ur. The Middle Bronze Age sites that he excavated afforded convincing evidence of large-scale abandonment and destruction of towns and cities.[68] Before the end of the twentieth century the material culture of the area declined, and sporadic raids by marauding nomads from the east and south precipitated a decline in the density of human settlement. After 1850 B.C. an interruption of sedentary occupation of southern Transjordan resulted in the replacement of inhabitants of walled cities by semi-nomadic tribes, a state of affairs that

---

[64] W. Spiegelberg, *Zeitschrift für Aegyptische Sprache,* XXXIX (1896), pp. 1ff.
[65] *FSAC,* pp. 255f.
[66] *WMTS,* p. 274.
[67] Cf. T. J. Meek, *Hebrew Origins,* p. 31.
[68] N. Glueck, *The Other Side of the Jordan,* pp. 114ff.

lasted about five centuries.[69] No subsequent attempt to settle in walled towns was evident until about 1300 B.C.,[70] which would suggest that the Israelite victories over the Ammonites in Transjordan did not occur until after that time.

If a date *ca.* 1300 B.C. is assigned to the Exodus, the traditional period of the Wilderness wanderings would be sufficient to bring the Israelites into northern Moab a little before the middle of the thirteenth century B.C. Excavations at Lachish, Bethel, Debir, and Hazor have shown clear traces of destruction at thirteenth-century levels, indicating the rapidity of the Israelite advance as described in Joshua. It would seem therefore that the invasion of Canaan by the Hebrews was neither a typical irruption of tent-dwelling nomads who continued to pursue a semi-sedentary way of life long after the first invasion, nor was it a matter of gradual infiltration and assimilation, as many modern scholars have thought.

The highly complex nature of the problems associated with the dating of the Exodus may be conveniently summarized in terms of three distinct theories. The first, based upon the work of Garstang at Jericho, would date the fall of that city between 1400 and 1385 B.C.,[71] associate the Habiru of the Amarna letters with the invading Israelites under the leadership of Joshua, and interpose a century or more between the fall of Jericho and the overthrow of Bethel, Lachish, Debir, and Hazor. The second, following a thirteenth-century B.C. dating-sequence, would maintain that the Exodus took place shortly after 1290 B.C.,[72] and that this was followed by the invasion of Moab and Canaan a little prior to 1250 B.C. Computations of this sort are based in general upon the Avaris era. The third hypothesis, advanced by Rowley and supported to a large extent by Gordon,[73] would place the Exodus after the middle of the thirteenth century B.C. and the conquest at the end of that century. Such a view has the decided disadvantage of disrupting earlier chronological sequences to the point that the patriarchs appear on the historical scene somewhat later than the patriarchal period.

Each of the foregoing positions suffers from obvious disadvantages,[74] and serves to show the enormous amount of care that must be exercised

[69] Cf. W. F. Albright in *The Jews: Their History, Culture and Religion* (ed. L. Finkelstein, 1949), p. 5.

[70] Cf. N. Glueck, *BASOR*, No. 55 (1934), pp. 3ff., *AASOR*, XIV (1934), pp. 1ff., XVIII-XIX (1939), p. 268. These conclusions were confirmed by Albright at Tell Beit Mirsim, *AASOR*, XII (1932), pp. 52ff., XVII (1938), pp. 76ff., and by Sellers at Beth-zur. Cf. O. R. Sellers, *The City of Beth-zur* (1931), pp. 9ff.

[71] J. and J. B. E. Garstang, *The Story of Jericho* (1940), pp. 120ff.

[72] Cf. *FSAC*, pp. 255ff.

[73] H. H. Rowley, *BJRL*, XXII (1938), pp. 243ff., and in *IDB*, II, p. 752; cf. C. H. Gordon, *IOTT*, p. 131.

[74] *WMTS*, p. 79. For the view that the destruction of the "cities of the valley" substantiates an early rather than a late date for Abraham see J. P. Harland, *IDB*, IV, p. 397.

324

in any attempt to interpret and correlate archaeological data with a view to elucidating and establishing the larger historical pattern. The solution that appears to present the fewest difficulties would seem to envisage a period of time covered by the Late Bronze Age and the Nineteenth Egyptian Dynasty, with the actual Exodus occurring about 1280 B.C.

C. JOSHUA AND JUDGES

The dating-sequences that a scholar accords to the Exodus from Egypt transpose their own peculiar difficulties into the period of Joshua and Judges, as might well be expected. Those who assign a fifteenth-century B.C. date to the event note that the fall of Jericho was preceded by the Israelite occupation of Moab, which according to Jephthah (Judg. 11:26) extended over a period of three hundred years. By assigning a date of about 1100 B.C. to Jephthah, it was thus possible to place the initial occupation of Moabite territory at 1400 B.C. The attack of Joshua on Debir (Josh. 10:38f.) was interpreted in terms of the destruction of its inhabitants only, the fall of the city proper being considered to have been the work of Israelite forces under Othniel, the nephew of Caleb (Judg. 1:11ff.). Similarly, the final overthrow of Canaanite culture in Hebron was assigned to the period of the Judges (Judg. 1:10).

One of the chief difficulties with the thirteenth-century date of the Exodus espoused by Albright lies in the fact that Joshua apparently had no connection with the fall of Jericho, which by implication had been in ruins for at least fifty years before he crossed the Jordan.[75] However, one can only assume that the destruction of Jericho preceded the circuit of Edom and the invasion of Moab if he rejects some of the archaeological evidence and reverses the order of the Biblical record, which Albright regards in general as substantially historical. Since the archaeological findings at Jericho are at best somewhat inconclusive, the date of its fall ought not to be made the dominant consideration in determining either the date of the Exodus or the settlement in Canaan, although it is of some importance for the traditional Biblical record, which clearly regards Jericho as having immense strategic significance.

That the chronologies in the book of Joshua and Judges are sources of considerable difficulty has already been noted in part three. Attacks made by Noth and Möhlenbrink on the historicity of the conquest narratives have been subjected to devastating criticisms by Albright, who has maintained that the actual course of events followed more closely the sources underlying the Biblical tradition than modern attempts at reconstruction.[76] The first eleven chapters of Joshua present

---

[75] W. F. Albright, *BASOR*, No. 58 (1935), p. 18.
[76] M. Noth, *PJB*, XXXIV (1938), pp. 7ff. and *Kleine Schriften zur Geschichte des Volkes Israel* (1953), I, pp. 176ff.; K. Möhlenbrink, *ZAW*, LVI (1938), pp. 238ff.; W. F. Albright, *BASOR*, No. 74 (1939), pp. 11ff.

the traditional view of a rapid succession of forays in southern Canaan, followed by the liquidation of native opposition in the north. The remainder of the book and the first chapter of Judges, however, might convey an impression of a more piecemeal type of conquest, which on some occasions was actually reconquest, accomplished in part by individual tribes independently of the leadership of Joshua.

Some scholars who associated the Habiru incursions into Palestine with the Israelite overthrow of Jericho and the invasion of the hill-country of Ephraim under Joshua concluded that there must have been two distinct settlements in Palestine, perhaps separated by as much as a century and a half.[77] On the one hand was the settlement of the northern or Israelite group occurring from about 1400 B.C.; on the other was the southern or Judaean occupation, thought to have commenced by about 1200 B.C. The Biblical writers, it was maintained, foreshortened and dovetailed the two conquest narratives into one another as the achievement of a single people, a process that would account for the resultant confusion and inconsistency in the Biblical narratives.[78]

Examples of this tendency were adduced from the description of the reduction of Debir (Kiriath-sepher, identified with Tell Beit Mirsim), which in Joshua 10:38f. is attributed to the celebrated Israelite leader, whereas elsewhere (Josh. 15:15; Judg. 1:11ff.) its conquest is regarded as being the work of Othniel. The first 21 verses of Judges attribute the conquest of the south to Judah, whereas verses 22-36 record that northern Canaan was conquered by the Israelite tribes under Joshua. In point of fact, however, the confusion is less real than apparent, for Judges, while summarizing the conquest and occupation of Canaan, shows the extent to which the native inhabitants had been left in possession of their cities and had become resurgent after the death of Joshua. Thus it was necessary for the tribes of Judah and Simeon to advance south against the Canaanites (Judg. 1:4ff.) and overthrow Bezek, following this by attacks upon Hebron and Debir, which had been reoccupied since their destruction in the time of Joshua (Josh. 10:36, 39). Attempts to take Jerusalem from Jebusite control (Judg. 1:21) were not successful, although the attack against Hormah resulted in victory (Judg. 1:17), as did the campaign against the three Philistine cities (Judg. 1:18f.), despite the fact that in the latter case the cities were not held because of Philistine military superiority. The Joseph tribes were forced to reoccupy Bethel (Judg. 1:22ff.), which had revolted; and at this point further Israelite efforts to eradicate the native inhabitants failed. No more cities were taken (Judg. 1:27ff.), and the tribe of Dan was actually evicted from its allotted territory (Judg. 1:34) by the Amorites.

[77] T. J. Meek, *Hebrew Origins*, pp. 21f.
[78] Cf. C. F. Burney, *Israel's Settlement in Canaan* (1921), pp. 3ff.

Thus if a clear view of the conquest period is to be obtained, it is important to distinguish between the events that characterized it and those that occurred after the death of Joshua, when a resurgence of the native Canaanite population took place. The conquest can be illustrated by the facts of archaeological exploration at sites such as Bethel, Lachish, Debir, Hebron, Gibeah, and Hazor, which show clearly that these places were occupied or destroyed in the latter part of the Late Bronze Age. If this destructive activity is to be correlated with the campaigns of Joshua as outlined in the Biblical sources (Josh. 11:16ff.), it would appear that the land as a whole was occupied with comparative rapidity by the Israelite invaders, although not all of the fortified strongholds, including a belt of Canaanite resistance separating the northern and southern tribes, were reduced at that time (cf. Josh. 13:1).

There can also be little doubt from the findings of the excavators that many of the sites were later reoccupied by the dispossessed Canaanites, and subsequently changed hands a number of times in the period from the thirteenth to the eleventh centuries. As Wright has stated, the Biblical version of the campaigns of Joshua reflected success in attacking certain key royal Canaanite cities, but also portrayed the prolonged period of struggle for possession of the land, a situation in evidence for a considerable time after the death of Joshua.[79] As has been mentioned previously, a good deal of discussion has centered upon the problems raised by the narratives dealing with the Israelite conquest of Bethel and Ai in particular, and to a lesser extent with the role of Shechem in the conquest period.

The Biblical account seems to have envisaged Ai as an inhabited site with its own ruler, or at the very least as a defensive point—whether temporary or permanent—manned by troops under the control of a commander-in-chief, where the Israelites encountered initial opposition. The severity of this opposition is indicated by the reference in Joshua 8:33ff., in which a party of thirty thousand men, a number that may have been inflated according to ancient scribal traditions, was sent out to ambush "the city" from the west, while, according to verse 12, a second group of five thousand men was also dispatched to capture the site. Quite apart from the immediate problem raised by the size of the numbers mentioned, it seems clear that the narrative is not just a redactional version of one attack upon Ai, but that it does in fact describe the activities of two distinct ambush parties. The question then arises as to why the military tactics on that occasion should have required such an enormous force of soldiers for such an apparently limited objective. Surely from some points of view it would be more plausible for the thirty thousand men to be sent to Bethel while the five thousand were engaged in reducing the opposition at Ai.

---

[79] G. E. Wright, *JNES*, V (1946), pp. 105ff.

A rather clearer view of the situation can be obtained by an appreciation of the military exigencies that confronted both Joshua and the enemy commander of both Bethel and "the ruin" (Ai). Since the latter was so prominent in the narratives, it seems most probable that it was a strongpoint that controlled the eastern approaches to Bethel, overlooking as it does the valleys to the north and south. Since Bethel is in a reverse-slope position and Ai in a forward-slope position, any defending commander could be expected to move his principal defensive point forward to the ruin of Ai so as to take advantage of the terrain, and leave his reserve units in Bethel, along with the civilian population. This tactical move would doubtless be influenced by the presence of an established ridgeway track running from Ai to Bethel and making communication over the distance of less than two miles a matter of comparative ease.

The Israelite base camp was located north of Bethel and Ai in "dead ground" beyond the valley, which contained seasonal *wadis* (Josh. 8:11, 13). However, this location presented certain problems, so that even with as many as forty thousand troops at his disposal it must have occurred to Joshua that it would be inadvisable to attack Bethel only to leave his flank and rear guard open to a strong enemy force at Ai. On the other hand he must have realized that he could hardly attack the ruin itself without being observed from some considerable distance, thereby losing the element of surprise. The latter consideration was the more pressing, since a strong Israelite task-force had already been decisively thrown back at Ai (Josh. 7:2ff.). Accordingly Joshua seems to have decided to gain as much tactical advantage as possible under such conditions by surreptitiously placing large bodies of troops near Ai and Bethel, with the apparent intention of drawing the enemy defense by engaging in a decoy frontal attack and subsequently withdrawing, as though he was repeating his previous tactical mistake (Josh. 8:14f.). Thus it was necessary for the larger ambush of thirty thousand men (accepting these figures at their face value for the sake of the immediate discussion) to leave the base camp some thirty-six hours before the battle and move into position, unobserved and concealed, to the west of the ruin. In order to allow an adequate amount of time for this maneuver, the troops were allotted two nights to reach their appointed station (Josh. 8:9, 13). The smaller ambush of about five thousand men would experience considerably less difficulty in moving to the west of Bethel, and as a result they only needed to be dispatched on the eve of the battle (Josh. 8:12). Having briefed the ambushes, Joshua bivouacked in the valley north of Ai in full view of the enemy (Josh. 8:11ff.), leading the officer in command of the force stationed at the ruin to think that the Israelites were on the point of repeating their earlier mistaken tactics. Unaware of the ambush, the reserve troops in Bethel who witnessed the mock flight of the Israelites took off after them in hot pursuit (Josh. 8:15ff.). When the signal was given by Joshua, the thirty thousand soldiers arose to take the pursuing enemy forces in the rear, while the five thousand were left to sack and burn Bethel (Josh. 8:19f.).

This reconstruction of events is based upon the evidence afforded by the text, and takes note of the fact that "the city" and "the ruin" are apparently used interchangeably. Since the two words differ by only one consonant in the Hebrew (הָעִיר and הָעַי), there is an understandable degree of confusion in their specific application to Bethel as the city and to Ai as the ruin. In Joshua 8:12 it becomes necessary to read "Beth-aven" for "Bethel," with the eastern text K*thibh and the Lagarde edition of the LXX (cf. Josh. 7:2), and at the end of the same verse the Massoretic K*thibh must be preferred to the Q're. The presence of textual confusion in this verse is clearly indicated by the LXX, which has a shorter rendering, but in any case the suggested reading accords with the general sense of the military maneuver, and resolves any clash which might seem to be suggested in Joshua 8:9.

As far as Shechem is concerned, the difficulties are of a different order, and are related in part to the fact that Joshua has nothing to say about the conquest of central Palestine, which is a rather unexpected situation in view of the importance that the region assumed in subsequent Israelite history. The presence of Joshua at the covenant ceremonies celebrated at Shechem, which in early times was the capital of the region and the locale at which the tribes gathered (Josh. 8:24, 30ff.), has led many scholars to conclude that Shechem was at that time under the control of Hebrews who had either never been in Egypt in the first place and therefore did not take part in the Exodus, or that they had been part of an earlier exodus somehow connected with the movements of Hyksos after they had been expelled from Egypt about 1570 B.C. Some writers have even seen the Shechem area as the place where the later differences that arose between Israel and Judah originated. Be that as it may, it is clear from the Tell el-Amarna tablets that the district around Shechem was for at least a century before the time of Joshua in firm control of a military group that paid little heed to the Egyptian pharaoh and many of the petty Canaanite kings who had pledged him their loyalty. It has also been long a matter of recognition that in Genesis 34 there is a tradition of an early Hebrew relationship with Shechem that need not have been modified to any significant extent by the events of the sojourn in Egypt and the Exodus. Certainly the tradition of Joshua 24, in which the Israelite leader sealed the covenant with a united nation at a city which he had not had to reduce previously, would be explicable if there were already in existence at Shechem a mixed Canaanite and Hebrew group of clans, united in a covenant relationship and preserving the memory of an association with the Israelite movement.

329

Excavations conducted at el-Jib, identified with ancient Gibeon, between 1956 and 1959 uncovered the remains of a culture that goes back at least to Late Bronze Age IIb strata (1300-1200 B.C.), and was also well represented in Iron Age levels.[80] Subsequent excavations revealed the presence of five distinct occupational levels dating from about 2800 B.C. to approximately 100 B.C. While certain other sites may present problems in any attempt to correlate the conquest period archaeologically, the findings at el-Jib have at least shown that the occupational situation at Gibeon in the early days of the conquest was that represented in the book of Joshua (ch. 9:21ff.).

There can be little question that the accounts of the military campaigns furnished by the narratives of Joshua are selective. It may well be within the bounds of possibility that some of the battles that occurred during this important period were not included in the final form of the conquest tradition, perhaps because they were considered rather incidental to the general purpose of the author or compiler, namely, to demonstrate that the Israelites had finally occupied the land promised to their ancestors. There seems to be no valid reason for assigning the career of Joshua preserved by tradition to the realm of myth and legend, since all that the original authors were doing was giving the bulk of the credit for the victories in Canaan to their accredited military hero. Exactly the same device is employed by traditionist and historiographer alike in the present age, where, in some senses, the detailed and observed facts of the case might well point to other conclusions. All available evidence indicates that it was Joshua who was the strategic figure in the entire military scheme of things, and that under his inspired leadership the conquest of Canaan was accomplished, a feat that was to be remembered in subsequent times in something approaching epic terms.

Although the general trend of archaeological discovery has made a thirteenth-century B.C. date for the Exodus and conquest a matter of the highest probability, it has raised issues of chronology that affect the Judges period in particular. On the basis of the reference in 1 Kings 6:1 to the fourth year of Solomon, a figure of just under 400 years is obtained for the period covered by Joshua and the Elders, Judges, and Saul. If, however, the beginning of the conquest is assigned to about 1240 B.C. on archaeological grounds, a period of only 230 years or so intervenes between the military activities of Joshua and the accession of David, ca. 1010 B.C. Some scholars have attempted to shorten the Judges period by assuming that the narratives dealt with the exploits of more or less contemporary local heroes rather than with a chronological succession of national leaders, and as a result they have been able to compress the events between the time of Joshua and the rise of Saul into a period of

---

[80] Cf. J. B. Pritchard, VT, suppl. vol. VII (1960), pp. 1ff.

about one hundred and fifty years. Some caution should be urged with respect to the view that the Judges may have been nothing more than local heroes, since while their activities may have been confined to some specific area of the Promised Land, the deliverance that they achieved was certainly regarded by the book of Judges as being national in scope. No doubt at least some of the Judges and the crises with which they dealt were contemporary in incidence, and not strictly successive in point of time as might appear from a superficial reading of Judges.[81] The real problem lies not so much in this area, however, as in the methods of computation and compilation which were employed by the ancient Near Eastern scribes.

The difference between 400 or more years and 230 years, both of which are at least arguable possibilities in terms of occidental reckoning, is not nearly as important as the principles of compression or omission that ultimately dictated the form of the Old Testament narratives dealing with this and other similar periods of time. In antiquity the scribes normally tabulated each series of rulers and reigns separately, and did not compile synchronistic lists in the manner of current occidental chroniclers. The lack of cross-references between contemporaries in the period of the Judges can be paralleled by similar omissions for the history of Dynasties XIII to XVII in the Egyptian Turin Papyrus of Kings. In this Egyptian source, a total of some 450 regnal years has to be aligned to a period of about 216 years between ca. 1786 and 1570 B.C., a situation that illustrates the problems raised and the methods employed to resolve them.

Mesopotamian annals and Egyptian king-lists illustrate the tendency of ancient scribes and chroniclers to foreshorten historical sequences[82] and make selective use of data by exercising principles of omission and other methods of control over the sources. There seems therefore to be no valid reason for supposing that a different methodology was applied in general to a composition such as Judges. On the other hand, it is important for those grounded in occidental traditions of precise numerical expression to realize that the actual numbers as such—whether they occur in Biblical or extra-Biblical sources—need not be called into question, since they may well be accurate in themselves as they now stand. What is significant, however, is the manner in which these numbers were interpreted by the ancient scribes, a consideration that must always be borne in mind by modern readers. From the standpoint of the latter, however, it is obvious that the historical period in question presents difficulties both of chronology and of historical detail, and these cannot be resolved completely without fuller information.

[81] K. A. Kitchen and T. C. Mitchell, *NBD*, p. 216.
[82] Cf. J. E. McFadyen, *ET*, XXXVI (1924-25), pp. 103ff.

It would not be amiss to mention at this juncture the so-called amphictyonic relationship of the Israelite tribes after the period of the immediate territorial occupation of Canaan. The term "amphictyony" was derived from the twelve-tribe sacral leagues of the early centuries of the first millennium B.C. in Greece and Italy. This classical concept was applied by Noth and Alt to the organization of the Israelite tribes by Joshua at Shechem near Mount Gerizim (cf. Deut. 11:29; 27:12), where an association of the tribes was established around a central sanctuary, as a means of unifying their religious and political activity.[83] This arrangement was held by these scholars to be similar to the somewhat later amphictyonies such as the twelve-member Etruscan League of Voltumna, or the Greek League of Delphi, which functioned on much the same basis.

Despite the persuasive arguments of Noth and Alt, there is some doubt as to whether such an amphictyony ever existed in Canaan in quite this manner. In the first place, one ought to be able to see such an institution reflected in the social structure of the Philistine occupation of southern Palestine, since these peoples were already grouped into a confederacy for purposes of self-protection. There seem only to have been five major cities, however, with which were associated numerous smaller settlements (1 Sam. 6:18), which certainly does not conform to the overall classical Aegean picture of an amphictyony. The Philistines would certainly be expected to be organized in such a configuration, since their Aegean background could well have given them at least some degree of familiarity with it. This contention would still have validity, even though in its developed form the amphictyony was slightly later than the general period under discussion, since the very existence of the Philistines as a group depended to no small extent upon some such compact social structure. Even though the geography of southern Canaan was favorable to this kind of organization, there is no evidence that the Philistines were grouped in the amphictyonic pattern of Aegean nations. According to the Biblical sources they lived in five independent cities ruled over by lords or governors who acted in concert for the good of the nation as a whole, and were able to overrule dissident or imprudent decisions made by an individual governor (1 Sam. 29:1ff.).

In actual fact it is more probable that the associations of twelve-member tribes originated in Semitic rather than in Greek circles. Traces of early groups of this kind can be seen in Genesis, where there are enumerated twelve Aramaean tribes (Gen. 22:20ff.), the twelve Ishmaelite tribes (Gen. 25:13ff.), and the twelve tribes of Edom (Gen. 36:10ff.). It is well known that the *motif* of configuration in terms of six or twelve is of Sumerian, and not Greek, origin. Further traces of

---

[83] M. Noth, *Das System der zwölf Stämme Israels* (1930), pp. 39ff. A. Alt, *Kleine Schriften zur Geschichte des Volkes Israel,* I, pp. 278ff.

federations among neighbors of the Israelites, based upon the number six rather than twelve, can also be seen in the six sons of Keturah and in a list of Horite clans (Gen. 36:20ff.). The idea of a central shrine around which houses and other buildings were grouped represented the earliest attempts at social organization in Mesopotamia, as is indicated by the archaeology of the Mesopotamian Neolithic period. It is only a comparatively small step from this basic Semitic concept to the organization of the twelve tribes around a central sanctuary, and subsequently to the Greek amphictyony, which was established on the basis of an accredited religious authority. As represented in Judges, the association of Israelite tribes was at best of a loosely knit variety, and dependent in a significant measure upon the Philistine economy, due to the technological inferiority of the Hebrew peoples.

Although the Hebrews were without a formally organized government like those of neighboring lands, it must not be presumed on that account that the only authority that the Judges claimed was of a moral or spiritual order. This opinion is an incorrect conclusion from the suggestion of Alt that leadership in the period of the Judges was based solely upon acknowledged possession of charismatic gifts. As C. H. Gordon has shown, the Judges were not elevated to positions of leadership simply because they were thought to display inspirational qualities or certain mystic attributes of personality.[84] It is now evident from the nature of Mycenaean kingship and its counterpart among the Hebrews that the Judges followed the pattern familiar in Aegean circles of appointment or selection from the ruling class. While it was possible for inspiration alone to elevate the more inferior members of the aristocracy, it is never recorded as having descended upon those individuals whose fathers were of a lowly and non-aristocratic status in the Heroic Age. Thus, while Jephthah was the son of a woman who occupied a decidedly inferior position in the social scale, he was actually an aristocrat from the side of his father Gilead, whose status conferred upon him the privilege of membership in the warrior class or גבורי חיל.[85] In spite of the kind of leadership that the Judges provided, however, the forces that operated on the side of internal disruption during this period were as serious a menace as the Philistines, Amalekites, or Midianites, for the geographical structure of the country favored territorial groupings and the resultant perpetuation of distinctive dialects, local customs, and special political attitudes.

Even when the central Tabernacle was definitely established at Shiloh, there were a number of other shrines in existence with which groups or alliances of tribes were associated from time to time. Thus the central shrine could not have exercised the cohesive force predicated of those

---

[84] *GBB*, pp. 295ff.

[85] C. H. Gordon, *Christianity Today*, VII, No. 12 (1963), p. 579.

associated with Mediterranean amphictyonies. The very fact that there were so many places where religious veneration was in evidence seems yet another reason for doubting whether there was in fact any twelve-tribe amphictyony of the kind envisaged by Alt and Noth in existence at this period. It should also be observed that the renewal of the Covenant (Josh. 24:1ff.) was a feature of the Wilderness wanderings (Deut. 27:1ff.), and did not take its rise from Greek configurations. It would therefore seem prudent, with Bright, to relate the origin of the social structure of the Israelite tribes to Sinai rather than to Greek political or religious patterns of organization.[86] Alt and his followers are undoubtedly correct in their attempts to bring the social structure of the Joshua-Judges period within the traditions of the Heroic Age, but against this it has to be noted that the concept of "twelveness" was depicted by the narratives of Joshua and Judges as a normal outgrowth of the kind of tribal system that functioned during the period of the Wilderness wanderings, making it much more probable that the organization of Israel in Canaan subsequent to the conquest was of independent origin.

D. The Monarchy

With the commencement of the Iron Age about 1200 B.C., problems of historiography and general chronology become much less confused. The humble beginnings of the kingdom under Saul have been amply illustrated by the excavations of Albright at Gibeah. The rustic simplicity of the buildings unearthed and the presence of cultivated land in the area point to the limited nature of the regal power, and furnish a striking contrast to the wealth and military vigor of subsequent times. The Biblical traditions that associate David with music and psalmody have also been verified from archaeological sources. These indicate that Palestine had been noted for its musical attainments for a number of centuries before the time of David. The Beni-Hasan tableau, which can be dated about 1900 B.C., depicts visiting Palestinian nomads walking behind their animals in Egypt to the accompaniment of a lyre,[87] while inscriptions on Egyptian monuments dated some 350 years later refer to examples of Canaanite music.[88]

The religious poetry of the Ugaritic texts has been shown to have close affinities with the phraseology of the Hebrew Psalms.[89] From the same sources come references to a class of Temple personnel designated by the term *sarim*,[90] who exercised functions similar to those of the Hebrew singers during the monarchy and later times. Some of the servants of

---

[86] *BHI*, pp. 145f.
[87] *LAP*, p. 83.
[88] *ARI*, pp. 125ff.
[89] J. H. Patton, *Canaanite Parallels in the Book of Psalms* (1944).
[90] C. H. Gordon, *Ugaritic Handbook* (1955), p. 272, No. 1934; cf. No. 1991.

David, who were designated in 1 Kings 4:31 (cf. 1 Chron. 2:6) by the term אזרח meaning "aboriginal" or "native sons," and who possessed Canaanite names such as Heman, Chalcol, and Darda, were engaged in various forms of musical activity. As such they were described by the phrase "sons of Mahol," a Hebrew term closely related to the Greek ὀρχήστρα, used of a semi-circular area in which the Greek chorus danced,[91] and meaning "members of the orchestral guild." A further reflection of this musical interest became apparent when Megiddo was excavated and the treasure room of the royal palace was uncovered. From this area was recovered a plaque inlaid with ivory, depicting a royal personage seated on a throne. He was drinking from a small bowl, and was being entertained by a court musician who stood before him plucking the strings of a lyre.[92]

The report of the Egyptian envoy Wen-Amon about 1080 B.C. furnishes graphic illustration of the manner in which trade and commerce were expanding in Palestine at that period.[93] With the large-scale domestication of the camel about the twelfth century B.C. there came a significant growth in the volume of the import and export trade in the country. Tribes such as Dan and Asher participated in maritime activity (cf. Judg. 5:17), and the general widening of Mediterranean trade was such that merchant shipping was organized into convoys in order to afford better protection against pirates, freebooters, and other raiders.[94] Archaeological excavations in different Mediterranean lands have confirmed the Biblical traditions that speak of the maritime activity characteristic of the days of Solomon, and the part which Phoenician shipbuilders played in it, a matter that has been noted in an earlier chapter.

It may well have been the threat posed by the technological advances of the Solomonic period to the domestic economy of Arabia which prompted the visit of the Queen of Sheba (Saba) to Jerusalem. Older historians were consistently accustomed to assign this regal personage to the area of myth and legend, but this was because comparatively little was known at that time about the history of the Sabaeans. Originally nomads, these people had become sedentary by the time of Solomon,[95] and had established a kingdom in the region of modern eastern Yemen. As such they exercised a good deal of control over the caravan-routes

[91] Cf. Plato Apol. 26E.
[92] WBA, p. 94.
[93] ANET, pp. 25ff.
[94] B. Maisler, BASOR, No. 102 (1946), p. 10.
[95] ARI, pp. 132ff.; W. F. Albright, BASOR, No. 128 (1952), p. 45, JBL, LXXI (1952), pp. 248f.; G. W. van Beek, BA, XIV, No. 1 (1952), pp. 5f.; R. L. Bowen and F. P. Albright, Archaeological Discoveries in South Arabia (1958). pp. 215f. For the history and archaeology of southern Arabia see G. W. van Beek, BANE, pp. 229ff., and BASOR, No. 151 (1958), p. 16.

between northern India, Mesopotamia, and Palestine. When Solomon acquired control of the northern end of the trading-routes and sought to extend this to the frontier areas of Transjordan also, he posed an immediate threat to the economic interests of southwestern Arabia in particular. The situation was aggravated even further by the expansion of his maritime trade, which brought serious competition to the overland caravan-routes for the first time. It was the urgency of this matter that prompted a Sabaean queen to undertake an arduous journey of about twelve hundred miles by camel. Although the oldest Sabaean inscriptions only go back as far as the eighth century B.C., it is known from cuneiform sources that queens governed large tribal confederacies in northern Arabia from the ninth to the seventh centuries B.C., and that they largely dropped out of the historical picture in southern Arabia after the sixth century B.C.[96] There would therefore seem to be no valid reason for dismissing the account of the visit made by the Sabaean queen to Solomon as legendary (1 Kgs. 10:1ff.).[97]

The unsettled nature of conditions in Palestine following the death of Solomon depicted by the Biblical narratives has also been reinforced by archaeological discovery. The invasion of the country by Shishak I of Egypt in 925 B.C. was part of a larger military campaign designed to restore the fortunes of Egypt in the Near East, a fact made clear by the Shishak inscription on the temple walls at Karnak. With typical oriental exaggeration this inscription depicted the victorious Egyptian pharaoh leading the Asiatic peoples to a state of slavery.[98] A fragment of a *stele* from the period of Shishak was unearthed at Megiddo, and showed the extent of his conquest in the Negeb and Transjordan regions.[99]

While Shishak was busily occupied in subjugating Palestine, the Aramaean dynasty of Damascus was increasing in vigor after rather humble and uncertain beginnings. According to 1 Kings 15:18ff. the succession of rulers was traced back to "Hezion, king of Syria," and this lineage was largely confirmed in 1940 by the discovery of the inscribed *stele* of Benhadad I at a site in Syria some five miles north of Aleppo.[100] Unfortunately this artifact failed to identify the individual described as "Rezon, son of Eliadah," who according to 1 Kings 11:23f. attacked and occupied Damascus in the Solomonic period and subsequently established a Syrian dynasty. The name Rezon has been thought to be a

[96] J. A. Montgomery, *Arabia and the Bible* (1934), p. 180. For an untechnical account of explorations in southern Arabia see W. Phillips, *Qataban and Sheba* (1955).

[97] Cf. E. Ullendorff, *BJRL*, XLV (1963), pp. 486ff.

[98] M. Noth, *Zeitschrift des Deutschen Palästina-Vereins*, XLI (1936), pp. 227ff.; cf. B. Mazar, *VT*, suppl. vol. IV (1957), pp. 57ff.

[99] W. F. Albright, *AASOR*, XXI-XXII (1943), p. 29 n. 10.

[100] Cf. M. Dunand, *Bulletin du Musée de Beyrouth*, III (1941), pp. 65ff.; W. F. Albright, *BASOR*, No. 87 (1942), pp. 23ff., No. 90 (1943), pp. 30ff.

corruption of Hezion, the *Hadyan* of the Benhadad *stele*, or, alternatively, a title meaning "prince."

Before the *stele*[101] was discovered, it was customary to distinguish at least three Damascus rulers named Benhadad. The first was an ally of Asa when Baasha of Israel attacked Judah (2 Chron. 16:1ff.); the second was his son, identified with Hadadezer (Adadidri) (1 Kgs. 20:34), who fought against Shalmaneser III between 853 and 845 B.C.; the third, the son of the Hazael who murdered Benhadad II (2 Kgs. 8:15), fought against Shalmaneser III in 841 B.C. It was one of these persons who left the Melqart *stele*, and the usual attribution is to Benhadad I.[102] Since the *stele* is mutilated and the patronymic is lost, it is difficult to be certain either about the mention or the identity of Rezon, or even about the attribution of the *stele* to Benhadad I. The general position adopted by the Albright school[103] was to subsume the three individual Benhadads under one name, Benhadad I, and to assign a forty-year period (*ca.* 880-842 B.C.) to his reign.[104] If the Benhadad of Ahab and Joram is the same individual as the Benhadad of King Asa, he would have reigned for approximately fifty-seven years, *ca.* 900 to 843 B.C., which, though not without parallel, would certainly be rather unusual. If, however, Benhadad I died about 860 B.C., his successor, Benhadad II (Adadidri), would then be contemporary with Ahab. From the style of the script Albright assigned a median date of about 850 B.C. for the *stele*, but this estimate is at best rather tentative, and is certainly not an assured basis for identifying three Benhadads as a single person. For the present, therefore, the evidence furnished by the Melqart *stele* must be regarded as inconclusive in this matter.

Independent testimony to the events that occurred in the reign of Menahem of Israel (752-742/41 B.C.) has been furnished by Assyrian sources. The cuneiform annals of Tiglathpileser III, an enterprising leader who usurped the Assyrian throne about 745 B.C. and instituted a series of campaigns against Syria and Palestine, recorded the manner in which King Menahem (2 Kgs. 15:17ff.) was compelled to become tributary to the Assyrian regime.[105] The head of this resurgent kingdom, who was known to the Israelites as Pul, though probably originally named Pulu,[106] appeared subsequently on the Israelite scene as an ally of Ahaz of Judah (732/31-716/15 B.C.) in the face of an attack upon the latter by a Syrian-Israelite coalition (2 Kgs. 16:7). Tiglathpileser III marched

[101] *DOTT*, pp. 239ff. and pl. 15; *ANET*, p. 501.

[102] W. F. Albright, *BASOR*, No. 87 (1942), pp. 23ff.

[103] Cf. M. Unger, *Israel and the Aramaeans of Damascus* (1957), pp. 59ff., 141f.

[104] So *BHI*, p. 221. For views supporting the existence of three Benhadads see M. Vogelstein, *Fertile Soil* (1957), pp. 7ff.; J. Gray, *I and II Kings* (1963), pp. 374f.

[105] *ARAB*, I, sect. 816.

[106] Cf. E. R. Thiele, *JNES*, III (1944), p. 156.

against the alliance, captured Galilee, placed Damascus under siege, occupied the Philistine plain and took a large number of prisoners.[107] Further Assyrian inroads occurred about 727 B.C. under Shalmaneser V (727-722 B.C.), the successor of Tiglathpileser III, and under Sargon II (722-705 B.C.), when Samaria refused to pay tribute to Assyria. Samaria fell in 722 B.C.,[108] not in 721 B.C. as Bright states,[109] and its collapse was described in the usual graphic terms in the Khorsabad annals.[110]

To the present, no archaeological discoveries have provided conclusive evidence for the captivity of Manasseh in Babylon (2 Chron. 33:10ff.). However, cuneiform sources have preserved a reference to a visit which he made to Nineveh about 678 B.C. at the command of Esarhaddon:

> I summoned the kings of Syria and those across the sea—Baalu, king of Tyre, Manasseh, king of Judah...Musurri, king of Moab...twenty kings in all. I gave them their orders. . . .[111]

Contrary to the argument that Manasseh could not have visited Babylon at that time in any case because it was in ruins is the fact that, according to cuneiform records, Esarhaddon rebuilt Babylon following its destruction at the hands of Sennacherib.[112] The name "Manasseh, king of Judah" appears on the prism of Esarhaddon,[113] and also on the prism of Ashurbanipal,[114] as part of a list of twenty-two tributaries of Assyria. A parallel to the Chronicles account of the captivity of Manasseh is furnished by the capture and subsequent release of Necho, pharaoh of Egypt, by Ashurbanipal, as preserved on the Rassam cylinder.[115] Since a revolt in support of Shamash-Shum-Ukin, the governor of Babylon who posed a serious military threat to Assyrian power, occurred during the reign of Manasseh, it may well be that the latter was involved to some extent in a move to overthrow Assyrian rule in the Near East.[116]

E. CAPTIVITY AND RETURN

The historicity of the Babylonian captivity of Judah has been amply verified from archaeological sources, a fact that demonstrates the incorrectness of those views that maintained that there was neither a significant exile nor a great return.[117] Excavations at Lachish, Debir, Beth-

---

[107] *ARAB*, I, sect. 801f.; 2 Kgs. 15:29ff.
[108] *MNHK*, pp. 121ff.; H. Tadmor, *JCS*, XII (1958), pp. 22ff., 77ff.
[109] *BHI*, p. 258.
[110] *ARAB*, II, sect. 55; *ANET*, pp. 284f.
[111] *ARAB*, II, sect. 690.
[112] *ARAB*, II, sect. 646f.
[113] *ANET*, p. 291.
[114] *ANET*, p. 294.
[115] *ANET*, p. 295.
[116] Cf. *ANET*, pp. 297ff.
[117] So C. C. Torrey, *Ezra Studies* (1910), *The Chronicler's History of Israel* (1954); S. A. Cook in *The Cambridge Ancient History* (1925), III, pp. 394ff.

shemesh, Beth-zur, and other sites have shown conclusively that there was an almost complete break in the urban life of the southern kingdom of Judah consequent upon the Babylonian incursions, which terminated in 581 B.C. Pottery remains recovered from contemporary levels have indicated the existence of a phase that preceded the more developed Persian ceramic types of the fifth century B.C. From the Palestine Shephelah have come stamped jar-handles dating between 598 and 587 B.C., while excavations at Lachish, Tell en-Nasbeh, and artifacts recovered from the site of the Ishtar Gate in Babylon have furnished conclusive proof of the devastation and depopulation of Judah and the presence of Jewish exiles in Babylon from 597 B.C. on.[118]

The New Empire period (612-539 B.C.) of Babylonia presents certain problems of identification and historicity that have long been a source of discussion. One of these involves the relationship between Nabonidus and Belshazzar in the light of certain statements in Daniel. Nabonidus, the last king of Babylon (556-539 B.C.), was of priestly lineage; his mother was probably the high priestess of Sin, the moon-deity.[119] Nabonidus was a man of considerable culture, who restored the temple of the moon goddess at Ur and maintained a small museum of antiquities in the temple precincts, part of which came to light when Woolley's excavations unearthed its foundations.[120] Nabonidus also instructed his emissaries to collect ancient inscriptions and other similar artifacts from various locations in Mesopotamia, and was responsible for the compilation of a chronology of Babylonian rulers.

The priests of Marduk, patron deity of Babylon, resented many of the religious innovations that Nabonidus introduced, and regarded his revival of long-forgotten rites and ceremonies as bordering upon impiety. Before commencing a series of campaigns in Cilicia and Syria about 554 B.C.,[121] he made Bel-shar-uṣur (Belshazzar) his *maru restu,* or firstborn son, regent of the empire; and about 552 B.C. he transferred his royal residence to the oasis of Teima in the Arabian desert, southeast of Edom. Whether his reasons for this change were religious or commercial is difficult to say with certainty.[122] At all events he remained there for

[118] For the Shephelah see *DOTT*, p. 224; H. G. May, *AJSL*, LVI (1939), pp. 146ff.; W. F. Albright, *JBL*, LI (1932), pp. 77ff.; for Lachish *WBA*, pl. 128; *DOTT*, pp. 223f.; for Tell en-Nasbeh *DOTT*, p. 222; for the Ishtar Gate R. Koldewey, *Das Wieder Erstehende Babylon* (1925), pp. 90ff.; W. F. Albright, *BA*, V, No. 4 (1942), pp. 49ff.

[119] Cf. *Recueil Édouard Dhorme. Études bibliques et orientales* (1951), pp. 325ff. This view was opposed, among others, by J. Lewy, *HUCA*, XIX (1945-46), pp. 405ff.

[120] *UC*, pp. 153, 156f.

[121] W. F. Albright, *BASOR*, No. 120 (1950), pp. 22ff.; *ANET*, p. 305.

[122] Cf. R. P. Dougherty, *JAOS*, XLII (1922), pp. 305ff., *AJA*, XXXIV (1930), pp. 296ff.; W. F. Albright, *BASOR*, No. 82 (1941), p. 14; J. Lewy, *HUCA*, XIX (1945-46), pp. 434ff.; C. C. Torrey, *JAOS*, LXXIII (1953), pp. 223f.

about ten years, and erected lavish buildings after the Babylonian manner.[123] Nabonidus was apparently so preoccupied with affairs at Teima that he neglected to visit Babylon in order to observe the New Year festival, an important event that formed the climax of the annual Babylonian cultic rites. Such dereliction of duty was sacrilegious, to say the least, and appears to have contributed to the increasing state of tension and unrest which was current in the empire.[124]

The reference in Daniel 5:30 to Belshazzar as the last king of Babylon can now be understood against this background. Belshazzar was unique in Babylonian antiquity as an example of a crown prince who was officially recognized as co-regent. Two extant legal documents recording oaths taken by the life of Nabonidus the king, and Bel-shar-uṣur the crown prince, dating to the twelfth and thirteenth years of Nabonidus, are without parallel in cuneiform sources.[125] The fact that Belshazzar was mentioned in Daniel 5:18 as a "son" of Nebuchadnezzar is in full accord with Semitic usage, which frequently employed the designation "son" as synonymous with "descendant." Nitocris, mother of Belshazzar, was apparently the daughter of Nebuchadnezzar,[126] thus making Belshazzar his grandson by strict lineal reckoning.

Although the official dating of documents from this period employs the regnal years of Nabonidus, Daniel most probably dates events by reference to the years of co-regency (Dan. 7:1; 8:1). An inscription from Harran assigned a ten-year period for the Arabian exile of Nabonidus,[127] and this, along with other sources, would imply that the royal personage (Dan. 5:30) who was killed in 539 B.C. was in fact Belshazzar. The position of Daniel as "third" in the political echelon is now shown to be correct, and indicates that he was a prominent officer of state (Dan. 5:16, 29). The result of all this is that earlier assertions by critical scholars to the effect that Belshazzar was unhistorical[128] have been shown to be entirely erroneous, and to have been advanced on the basis of an imperfect knowledge of the historical situation. Equally invalid are the objections of Rowley to the designation of Belshazzar as a ruler of the Neo-Babylonian empire, a situation which he described as "a grave

---

123 *LAP*, p. 190.

124 For cuneiform sources from this period see S. Smith, *Babylonian Historical Texts Relating to the Capture and Downfall of Babylon* (1924), pp. 27ff., 98ff.

125 A. L. Oppenheim, *IDB*, I, pp. 379f.

126 R. P. Dougherty, *Nabonidus and Belshazzar* (1929), pp. 59ff., 194.

127 C. J. Gadd, *Anatolian Studies*, VIII (1958), pp. 35ff.

128 E.g. F. W. Farrar, *The Book of Daniel* (1895), pp. 54ff. Cf. H. Ewald, *A History of Israel* (1880), V, p. 52, who identified Belshazzar with Nabonidus, and A. H. Sayce, *The Higher Criticism and the Monuments* (1895), pp. 526f., who denied a familial relationship between Belshazzar and Nebuchadnezzar. A summary of the evidence for the historicity of Belshazzar is contained in J. A. Montgomery, *A Critical and Exegetical Commentary on the Book of Daniel* (1927), pp. 66ff.

historical error."[129] Cuneiform sources have shown that Belshazzar was associated with Nabonidus in governing the kingdom, but in a subordinate capacity, for they speak of him specifically as *mar sharri* or "son of the king," and never as *sharru* or "king."

The other important problem of identification concerns what Rowley has styled "the fiction of Darius the Mede," a man who, according to Daniel 5:30, 31, came to power after the death of Belshazzar.[130] Since Darius the Mede is not mentioned outside the Old Testament narratives, and since the cuneiform inscriptions do not record the existence of any king between Nabonidus-Belshazzar and the accession of Cyrus, the historicity of Darius the Mede has been denied by many liberal scholars, and the accounts concerning his reign have been held to be a conflation of confused tradition.[131] But because these narratives bear all the marks of accredited historical writing, other scholars have taken them as genuine products of the period, particularly since there is a noticeable lack of historical material from the Neo-Babylonian age that might otherwise invalidate such an approach, or at the least introduce considerable modifications.

The discovery of one of the Nabonidus texts at Harran, inscribed in Babylonian cuneiform, referred to the "king of the Medes" in the tenth year of the reign of Nabonidus (546 B.C.). D. J. Wiseman identified this ruler with Cyrus the Persian, assuming that he used the title "king of the Medes" in addition to the more customary designation of "king of Persia, king of Babylonia, king of the lands."[132] Thus Wiseman would translate Daniel 6:29 as "in the reign of Darius, even in the reign of Cyrus the Persian."[133] While Cyrus was related to the Medes through his mother Mandane, it was the custom of the Achaemenid kings to trace their lineage to Persian origins in the victories of Achaemenes over Sennacherib in 681 B.C. Thus the reference to the "seed of the Medes" (Dan. 9:1) must imply that the paternal ancestry of Darius was Median. This, as Rowley has pointed out, would not describe Cyrus the Persian accurately.[134] Again, Cyrus is nowhere spoken of as the "son of Ahasuerus," being in actual fact the son of Cambyses, king of Anshan (Elam).

Arguing from cuneiform sources, Winckler, Riessler, and Boutflower equated Darius the Mede with Cambyses, the son of Cyrus, a procedure that elicited from Rowley the observation that it was "the only effort to harmonise the Book of Daniel with known history that can claim the

---

[129] *JTS*, XXXII (1931), pp. 12ff.
[130] *RDM*, p. 59.
[131] *Ibid.*, p. 175; cf. *IOTT*, p. 286.
[132] *Christianity Today*, II, No. 4 (1957), pp. 7ff.
[133] *DOTT*, p. 83; cf. D. J. Wiseman, *Notes on Some Problems in the Book of Daniel* (1965), pp. 12ff.
[134] *RDM*, p. 17.

slightest plausibility."[135] Boutflower argued that in the first year of Cyrus after the fall of Babylon, Cambyses stood in the same relationship to his father as Belshazzar had done to Nabonidus, and that Cambyses was subsequently appointed by Cyrus as the successor of Belshazzar. However, Dubberstein showed that several of the tablets dated to the first year of Cambyses had suffered from confused scribal dating-systems, and deduced that Cyrus had made Cambyses co-regent just prior to leaving for what proved to be his final campaign in 530 B.C. Thus Cambyses was not known as "king of Babylon" at a time shortly after the city fell to Cyrus, and therefore could hardly be identified with Darius the Mede. Indeed, as Dubberstein pointed out, to postulate a dual reign at the commencement of the rule of Cyrus rather than at the end is completely unsupported either by the cuneiform texts or by tradition.[136]

Whitcomb has proposed a more acceptable alternative solution to the problem, also based upon cuneiform sources.[137] He noted that the majority of translations of the Nabonidus Chronicle made since the time when it was first published by T. G. Pinches[138] have failed to distinguish between two separate individuals, Gubaru and Ugbaru, mentioned in lines 15 to 22 of Column III of the Chronicle, and instead have identified them with the Gobryas mentioned by Xenophon.[139] The translation by Sidney Smith, published in 1924,[140] however, made such a distinction and suggested that the chronicler intended to differentiate between Ugbaru of Gutium and Gubaru, the former being the Gobryas of Xenophon, who died after the fall of Babylon; whereas the latter was subsequently appointed by Cyrus as governor of southern Babylonia.

Whitcomb has suggested very plausibly that Ugbaru, the governor of Gutium, was the one who led the Persian troops to victory in Babylon in 539 B.C. and died some three weeks after this event, possibly from wounds. Gubaru was then appointed governor of Babylon and the region beyond the river by Cyrus, a position which he appears to have held for at least fourteen years,[141] and was mentioned in the book of Daniel under the designation of Darius the Mede. This theory has the undoubted merit of being based upon an accurate reading of the Nabonidus Chronicle rather than on secondary sources, and makes it clear that at

[135] H. Winckler, *Altorientalische Forschungen* (1899), 2. Reihe, II, p. 214; P. Riessler, *Das Buch Daniel erklärt* (1902), pp. xiv, 53; C. Boutflower, *JTS*, XVII (1916), pp. 48ff., and *In and Around the Book of Daniel* (1923), pp. 142ff.; *RDM*, p. 12.

[136] W. H. Dubberstein, *AJSL*, LV (1938), p. 419.

[137] J. C. Whitcomb, *Darius the Mede* (1959), pp. 5ff.

[138] In *Transactions of the Society of Biblical Archaeology*, VII (1882), pp. 139ff.

[139] *Cyropaed.* IV, 6; VII, 5, 26ff.

[140] *Babylonian Historical Texts Relating to the Capture and Downfall of Babylon*, p. 121.

[141] A. T. Olmstead, *History of the Persian Empire* (1948), pp. 56, 71.

the very least the whole problem connected with Darius as an accredited historical personage has to be re-opened, whatever the nature of his true identity may ultimately prove to be.

Although Rowley brought a good deal of learning to bear upon his efforts to show the fundamentally unhistorical nature of Darius the Mede, his labors were largely vitiated by the fact that he based his arguments upon inaccurate and unreliable secondary sources. As a result, when writing of Gobryas, he had in mind, as Whitcomb has shown,[142] not only a combination of the Gubaru and Ugbaru mentioned in cuneiform sources, but also the Gobryas of Herodotus[143] and Xenophon, and the "Gaubaruva, son of Mardonius a Persian" in the Behistun Inscription. Clearly such a composite character never existed in history, but this is very different from saying that therefore Darius the Mede is unhistorical also.

Failure to note that the translation by Pinches contained certain inaccuracies leading to the identification of a single, so-called Gobryas in the Nabonidus Chronicle[144] resulted in the fact that many scholars tried to relate Darius the Mede with such a Gobryas and also with the individual mentioned by Herodotus and Xenophon. This view can be traced to its earliest phases in a period long before the Nabonidus Chronicle was known to exist, being first represented in the writings of Des-Vignoles and subsequently expounded, among others, by Babelon, Pinches, Wright, R. D. Wilson, and Albright.[145] When the translation by Sidney Smith distinguished accurately between Ugbaru and Gubaru, it became apparent for the first time that two different persons were being described, thereby making it possible for Gubaru to be identified without undue difficulty with Darius the Mede.

The historicity of events mentioned in such compositions as Ezra and Nehemiah has been substantially vindicated by archaeological discoveries also, as is the case with many other periods of Hebrew history. Whereas older authors frequently argued that there was no evidence to indicate that Cyrus ever made a decree about 538 B.C. of the kind mentioned in Ezra 1:2ff.; 6:3ff.,[146] subsequent researches have enabled

---

[142] J. C. Whitcomb, *Darius the Mede*, p. 26.

[143] *The Persian Wars* III, 70ff.

[144] As perpetuated, for example, by A. L. Oppenheim, *ANET*, p. 306.

[145] A. Des-Vignoles, *Chronologie de l'histoire sainte et des histoires étrangères qui la concernent depuis la Sortie d'Égypte jusqu'a captivité de Babylone* (1738), II, pp. 517ff. E. Babelon, *Annales de philosophie chrétienne*, N.S. (1881), IV, pp. 680f. T. G. Pinches, *HDB*, I, p. 559. C. H. H. Wright, *Daniel and His Prophecies* (1906), pp. 135ff. R. D. Wilson, *PTR*, XX (1922), pp. 177ff. W. F. Albright, *JBL*, XL (1921), p. 112n.

[146] E.g. W. O. E. Oesterley and T. H. Robinson, *A History of Israel*, II, pp. 75, 81; cf. M. Noth, *GI*, pp. 306f.

scholars to show beyond doubt that the edict of Cyrus was genuine,[147] and to estimate the effect which its promulgation had upon the captive elements in the Babylonian population. According to Ezra 6:1ff., the second decree, a *dikrona* or memorandum of a royal decision, was discovered in the archives at Achmetha (Ecbatana), where Cyrus is known to have stayed for a time during 538 B.C., his first regnal year.

The most serious problem connected with this period, however, is perhaps not one of historicity as much as of chronology, and deals with the general order of events as reflected in Ezra and Nehemiah. Part of the difficulty lies in the fact that these works have passed through certain phases of transmission, which has resulted in the availability for study of slightly different recensions. In the main, however, the problem turns upon the actual time when Ezra came to Jerusalem, since the dating of Nehemiah's activity does not present quite the same degree of difficulty. The traditional view that Ezra preceded Nehemiah, arriving in Jerusalem in 458 B.C., with Nehemiah coming upon the scene as civil governor in 445 B.C. in order to rebuild the walls and resolve certain economic difficulties, was first challenged by A. van Hoonacker,[148] who rearranged the Biblical text in an attempt to straighten out what seemed to him to be a thoroughly confused picture of events. Van Hoonacker advocated the view that Nehemiah preceded Ezra.[149] There is little

---

[147] Cf. H. H. Schaeder, *Ezra der Schreiber* (1930); R. de Vaux, *RB*, XLVI (1937), pp. 29ff.; E. Bickermann, *JBL*, LXV (1946), pp. 244ff.

[148] A. Van Hoonacker, *Le Muséon*, IX (1890), pp. 151ff., 317ff., 389ff., *RB*, IV (1895), pp. 186ff., X (1901), pp. 5ff., 175ff., XXXII (1923), pp. 481ff., XXXIII (1924), pp. 33ff.

[149] In this he was followed, among others, by M. J. Lagrange, *RB*, V (1908), pp. 343ff., IV O.S. (1895), pp. 193ff.; L. W. Batten, *A Critical and Exegetical Commentary on the Books of Ezra and Nehemiah* (1913), pp. 28ff.; W. E. Barnes, in *The People and the Book* (ed. A. S. Peake, 1925), pp. 293f.; V. Coucke, in *Supplément au Dictionnaire de la Bible* (ed. L. Pirot and A. Robert, 1928), I, cols. 1269f.; W. L. Wardle, in *Record and Revelation* (ed. H. W. Robinson, 1938), p. 127; and H. Daniel-Rops, *Histoire sainte: le peuple de la Bible* (1943), pp. 348ff., 455. The complexity of the situation can be illustrated by the manner in which the views of W. F. Albright have been modified from time to time. In 1921 he inclined to the views of Van Hoonacker, *JBL*, XL (1921), pp. 104ff.; in 1932 he adopted the opinion expressed earlier by Kosters, *Het Herstel van Israël* (1893), pp. 124ff., that Ezra belonged properly to the 32nd year of the reign of Artaxerxes I Longimanus (464-423 B.C.), *The Archaeology of Palestine and the Bible*, p. 219. In the first edition of *FSAC*, p. 248 (1940), he reverted to the standpoint of Van Hoonacker; in the second edition six years later, p. 336, he once more adopted the view of Kosters, although he assigned Ezra to the 37th year of Artaxerxes; cf. Albright, *BA*, IX, No. 1 (1946), pp. 10ff.; cf. J. A. Bewer, *The Literature of the OT* (1922), p. 281. In 1950 he still adhered to this position, in *The Jews: Their Culture, History and Religion* (ed. L. Finkelstein), I, pp. 53, 64; cf. *FSAC* (1957 ed.), p. 324, *BPAE*, pp. 90, 112 n. 193. At no time, however, did these opinions go unchallenged, and despite the assertions of Albright, *FSAC*, p. 324, and others that this position represented the consensus of scholarly thought, it was vigorously opposed by such authorities as Sellin, *Geschichte des israelitisch-jüdischen Volkes*

doubt that the rather confused historical tradition in Ezra and Nehemiah has conceded a degree of legitimacy to both standpoints, and in some quarters has led to more confident claims than the state of the evidence would seem to warrant, thus meriting the caution urged by Noth in this regard.[150]

Certain objections to the traditional view that have been described as "well-nigh insuperable"[151] are not quite as serious as some scholars have imagined. Olmstead has shown that the conditions of travel in the Persian empire about 458 B.C. were by no means as unsafe as has been alleged by those who oppose the priority of Ezra over Nehemiah.[152] Furthermore, the immediate task of Ezra as depicted in the book bearing his name was not to proclaim the binding nature of a new law-book[153] as much as to regulate the religious life of the returned community on the basis of a long-established tradition enshrined in the Torah. If by the "failure" of his mission there is meant the absence of initial success, then the inability of Ezra to organize the life of the theocracy in terms of the precepts of the Law on his first visit to Jerusalem is not quite as unbelievable as Bright would suppose.[154] To attribute such a result to personal deficiencies on the part of Ezra ignores an important reciprocal factor, namely the moral turpitude of the Jews in Judaea, whose norms of behavior he was endeavoring to regulate. In point of fact the activities of Ezra anticipated a situation that occurred under Nehemiah in 433 B.C., under strikingly parallel circumstances. Accordingly it would be no more correct to imply that the initial reforms of Nehemiah failed because abuses arose during his temporary absence from 433 B.C. than it would be to regard the first mission of Ezra as a failure simply because the old conditions that he had attempted to suppress showed signs of resurgence during his absence from Jerusalem. It may well be, of course, that Ezra had aroused local antagonism because of a promise of success rather than failure in his mission, and one explanation of his departure from Judaea could be that his political enemies had managed to secure his recall. A more probable alternative, however, is simply that at the end of a two-year period of duty Ezra returned to the central

---

(1932), II, pp. 134ff.; Kittel, *Geschichte des Volkes Israel* (1923), III, ii, pp. 567ff.; Eissfeldt, *Einleitung in das AT* (1934), p. 597; Weiser, *Einleitung in das AT* (1939), pp. 246ff.; R. de Vaux, in *Supplément au Dictionnaire de la Bible*, IV, cols. 765f.; J. Stafford Wright, *The Date of Ezra's Coming to Jerusalem* (1947); and E. J. Young, *An Introduction to the OT* (1949 ed.), pp. 369ff. To cite additional authorities on this whole question would merely serve to emphasize the wide divergence of opinion that has arisen in this particular area of Old Testament study.

[150] *GI*, p. 277.
[151] *BHI*, p. 377.
[152] A. T. Olmstead, *History of the Persian Empire*, p. 306.
[153] J. Stafford Wright, *The Date of Ezra's Coming to Jerusalem*, p. 26.
[154] *BHI*, p. 378.

administrative bureau in his capacity as Secretary of State for Jewish Affairs in order to present to his Mesopotamian superiors a report on the situation in Judaea.

Arguments for a reversal of the traditional chronology based upon certain passages in Nehemiah (e.g. 12:26, 47) cannot properly be used for purposes of demonstrating chronological sequences, since in his capacity as *tirshatha* or civil governor it would be natural for Nehemiah to give precedence to his own activities when compiling his memoirs. Equally important for the traditional view is the observation of Gordon that an impractical religious enthusiast, such as Ezra was depicted to have been, would need the forceful administrative backing of a disciplined person of the caliber of Nehemiah in order to offset the mistakes and inadvertencies of too enthusiastic an approach to the contemporary social and religious scene.[155] In the last resort it must be realized that no chronological reconstruction is completely free from difficulties, as will be observed subsequently, and this is due in part to the rather confused nature of the Biblical narratives and the lack of specific extra-Biblical confirmation for the date of Ezra. However, it appears to the present writer to be unwise for scholars to jettison the traditional position in matters of chronology in order to adopt one beset with even more uncertainty.

There are very few Jewish documents indeed that can be dated in the fourth century B.C., and the situation is made worse for the historian by the fact that neither Egyptian nor Babylonian sources furnish any information about their Jewish colonies, as contrasted with the state of affairs existing in the late fifth century. It is known, however, that in the late Persian period the Jewish state was recognized by the Persians as a religious commonwealth[156] that, like its north-Syrian counterpart of Hierapolis, was permitted to levy its own temple taxes and issue its own silver coinage based upon the *darkemon* standard mentioned in 1 Chronicles 29:7.[157] Seal impressions have been recovered from jars of this period, and although some of the wording is obscure, it would seem to indicate that the jars were employed for the purpose of collecting some sort of levy.[158]

According to Hecataeus of Abdera, there was a movement of thousands of Jews to Egypt as voluntary immigrants and mercenaries during the reign of Ptolemy Lagi, about 300 B.C. This proved to be a most impor-

---

[155] *IOTT*, p. 270n.

[156] *BHI*, p. 394.

[157] The "daric," known to the Jews from the post-exilic period at least (Ez. 2:69; 8:27; Neh. 7:70f.), as employed here indicates that the current monetary term equivalent to the Davidic amount was being used by the Chronicler.

[158] N. Avigad, *JPOS*, XIV (1934), pp. 178ff., *BASOR*, No. 53 (1934), pp. 20ff., No. 109 (1948), pp. 21f., No. 148 (1957), pp. 28ff., *Israel Exploration Journal*, VII (1957), pp. 146ff.

tant step in the process of Hellenizing the Jews subsequent to the conquests of Alexander the Great. This tradition was shown to be substantially correct by the excavations of Sellers at Beth-zur in 1931, where a coin was discovered bearing the name of Hezekiah, in all probability the high priest mentioned in this connection by Hecataeus.[159] As the *Letter of Aristeas* indicates,[160] it is most probable that Ptolemy I had brought many Jews back as prisoners from one or more of his military exploits in Palestine,[161] and this would help to account for the presence of so many Jews in Egypt during this general period. Be that as it may, the existence of a large Jewish community led ultimately to the translation of the Scriptures into Greek, a task that commenced with the rendering of the Torah into the vernacular in the third century B.C. The result of this activity was a version that opened the way for more adequate communication between Jews and Gentiles, and which for many in the primitive Christian Church constituted Scripture *par excellence.*

This historical panorama of the Seleucid period is well attested by a variety of sources, as is the era of the Roman domination of Palestine from 63 B.C. Important historical sidelights have been thrown upon this age by the discoveries in the neighborhood of the Wadi Qumran, and these testify in part to the turbulence and unrest that characterized this phase of Jewish history. Its close was marked in A.D. 70, when the Jewish Commonwealth was overthrown by the armies of Imperial Rome.

---

[159] Cf. O. R. Sellers and W. F. Albright, *BASOR,* No. 43 (1931), pp. 2ff.; A. T. Olmstead, *JAOS,* LVI (1936), pp. 243f.; F. M. Abel, *RB,* XLIV (1935), pp. 577f.

[160] Cf. vss. 4, 12.

[161] Pseudo-Aristeas, writing in the second third of the second century B.C., used considerably older material. Cf. E. Bickermann, *Zeitschrift für die Neutestamentliche Wissenschaft,* XXIX (1930), pp. 280ff.; M. Hadas, *Aristeas to Philocrates* (1951), pp. 98f.

Part Six

OLD TESTAMENT RELIGION

I. THE EVOLUTIONARY HYPOTHESIS

Prior to the nineteenth century, such study as was expended upon the subject of Old Testament religion tended to deal with the various elements of the Hebrew faith as units of one institutional corpus. This great body of belief took its rise under Moses at Sinai and was influenced over the centuries by a number of factors, many of them being of an adverse, pagan nature. A prolonged declension from the monotheistic ideals of the Torah led ultimately to divine retribution upon Israel in the Babylonian exile. On returning to Judaea, the Jewish people were found to be purged of all idolatrous tendencies, and for the remainder of the Old Testament period they followed a theocratic pattern of life, to a greater or lesser degree, according to the rituals and ceremonies of the ancient law.

With the rise of the Positivist approach under Auguste Comte (1798-1857), there came an emphasis upon the application of historical method to the study of religion. In part this constituted a reaction against some of the early nineteenth-century speculations about the nature of religion in general. Comte and his followers were concerned with real facts, as opposed to the abstractions of metaphysics or what they regarded as the figments of theological speculation. Their methodology was founded upon the premise that positive science explains natural phenomena in terms of verifiable laws of succession and resemblance, and they repudiated any suggestion that natural events could be understood by such theological devices as the intervention of supernatural beings in the stream of history, or the mutual relationships of hypostasized concepts. Although this type of view is open to serious criticisms, the Positivists attracted the attention of many learned individuals who had previously entertained grave doubts about the intellectual integrity of theological attitudes such as those that characterized Roman Catholicism.

Consequently the scholars who were affected by this naturalistic approach began to study the data of the various religions against the more factual background of their culture and history. This method bore increasing fruit as literary and archaeological sources shed new light on ancient faiths. In studying a given religion, Positivist historians made it

351

their dominant concern to familiarize themselves with all its facets; and, consistent with their view that historical processes were entirely naturalistic, they rejected any alleged supernatural causation. Because religion for them was thus but one manifestation of human culture, all faiths and creeds could be studied on the same general level; and the religion of the Old Testament could be compared with other similar expressions of the human spirit in the ancient Near Eastern world and examined in terms of the same methodological attempt to trace origins, stages of growth, environmental influences, and the like.

A. WELLHAUSEN'S STUDY OF OLD TESTAMENT RELIGION

The study of Old Testament religion took a somewhat different turn as a result of Julius Wellhausen's speculative ideas about the development of Hebrew history. Starting from the Positivist premise that religion was merely an offshoot or product of human cultural activity, he applied the evolutionary philosophical concepts of Hegelianism to a study of the faith of Israel. On the view that little could be known for certain with regard to Hebrew history and religion prior to the beginning of the monarchy, Wellhausen rejected the idea that the Torah as a whole was the starting-point for the history of Israel as a community of the faith. Instead, he adopted a naturalistic view of its origins and development and assumed that the Law constituted primarily a priestly program of religious observances for post-exilic Judaism. True to Hegelian principles, normative Judaism was regarded as a synthesis that resulted from the dialectic of the pre-prophetic Israelite faith (thesis) and the prophetic reaction to that faith (antithesis). Thus on this view the religion of the Old Testament evolved gradually through the phases of popular, prophetic, and priestly belief and practice. At the other end of the historical process, Wellhausen posited the kind of naturalistic origin for Hebrew religion that was also accorded to other faiths of antiquity, particularly to those existing in primitive societies. This procedure involved the use of metaphors of growth and development culled from biological sources, which assumed that the most primitive of the Hebrew religious notions were to be found in the earliest datable sections of the Old Testament while the more advanced concepts could be discovered in passages that emerged from a considerably later period in the chronological sequence.

Looking at primitive society in much the same way as the Positivists did, and being aware of some of the findings in the area of comparative religion, Wellhausen discerned among the Hebrews traces of such typical primitive phenomena as animism, totemism, tabu, polydaemonism and ancestor worship. These facets of religious activity he assigned to the area of patriarchal religion, and held that they were normative during the pre-monarchical period. The eighth- and seventh-century prophets applied themselves to this situation in an attempt to raise the level of religious appreciation to the point where monolatry (the worship of one of a number of available gods) was replaced by henotheism (belief in one god without denying the existence of others). The exile purified Hebrew faith and removed lingering idolatrous elements, so that ethical monotheism, the crown of the religious edifice, was the attested result. This reconstruction of various alleged stages in the development of Hebrew religion gave great prominence to the prophets, but at the same time it detracted from the significance of the events at Sinai and the religious activities of an even earlier period.

Since almost nothing was known of the life and times of the patriarchs at that point, there was little to prevent Wellhausen from assuming that patriarchal religion was scarcely more than crude superstition. Wellhausen, Robertson Smith, and Stade had investigated other aspects of Semitic religion, particularly the customs and beliefs of the pre-Mohammedan Arabs, as a means of illustrating the religious usages of the primitive period of Hebrew history.[1] On the basis of their findings they attributed certain of the phenomena of primitive religion to the pre-Mosaic period.

For Wellhausen the earliest stages of Hebrew religion represented in the Pentateuch furnished clear indications of animism, a term coined by E. B. Tylor to express the belief cherished in primitive society that every object having sufficient innate activity to affect the behavior of an individual was animated by a life and will of its own.[2] Such objects included running water, rolling stones, and waving tree branches[3]— though in some instances movement was not necessary in order for the object to receive attention.[4] Old Testament examples of this alleged tendency included the terebinths of Moreh (Gen. 12:6), Mamre (Gen. 13:18; 18:1), and Shechem (Gen. 35:4), the maççebhah or large stone mentioned in Joshua 24:26 and Judges 9:6, the tamarisk trees of 1 Samuel 22:6 and 1 Kings 13:14, and a great many references to wells and springs of water (e.g. Gen. 14:7; Num. 21:17f.; Josh. 18:17; Judg. 15:18f.).

A slightly later stage of development for Wellhausen consisted in polytheism, the belief in a multiplicity of male and female goddesses. He devoted the first 68 pages of his *Reste Arabischen Heidentums* to cataloging the names of ancient Arab deities along with their functions, and on

---

[1] J. Wellhausen, *Reste Arabischen Heidentums* (1887); W. Robertson Smith, *Lectures on the Religion of the Semites* (1889); B. Stade, *Geschichte des Volkes Israel* (1886), I, pp. 358ff.; cf. C. G. Montefiori, *Lectures on the Origin and Growth of Religion as Illustrated by the Religion of the Ancient Hebrews* (1892).

[2] *Primitive Culture: Researches into the Development of Mythology, Philosophy, Religion, Language, Art and Custom* (1903 ed.), I, pp. 23, 425; cf. J. B. Noss, *Man's Religions* (1949), pp. 17f.

[3] Cf. J. G. Frazer, *The Golden Bough* (1927), I, p. 208, II, p. 172; E. O. James, *ERE*, XII, p. 708a; E. S. Hartland, *ERE*, XI, p. 864a.

[4] R. H. Codrington, *The Melanesians* (1891), p. 183.

this basis he was able to associate polytheistic tendencies with such Old Testament concepts as place names connected with God (*El*, Josh. 15:11; 19:14; 2 Kgs. 14:7, *et al.*), the Baals (Num. 25:3; 32:8; Judg. 3:3, *et al.*), sanctuaries (Num. 21:28; Deut. 32:13; 2 Kgs. 17:9; Jer. 7:31, *et al.*), or elements of pagan Canaanite religion (Judg. 3:7; 1 Kgs. 15:13; 2 Kgs. 21:7, *et al.*).

Wellhausen envisaged an even more advanced stage of primitive religion in totemism. The term *totem* is strictly North American Indian in origin, but it is used by anthropologists and students of primitive religion to signify the belief that the members of a clan or tribe are related to some group of plants or animals in a rather impersonal manner.[5] In their examination of the Old Testament Wellhausen and his followers detected totemistic remnants in such personal and place names as Simeon (hyena?), Rachel (רחל, ewe), Caleb (כלב, dog), Shaalbim (שעלבים, foxes), and Eglah (עגלה, calf)[6] in addition to certain references that implied the existence of animal-cult worship as a survival of an earlier totemistic phase (e.g. Isa. 66:3, 17; Jer. 2:27; Ezek. 8:10). A totemistic interpretation was also accorded to personal names that incorporated elements of divine designations such as *El* or *Yah*, on the ground that the individuals who possessed such names believed themselves to be descended from a god, just as the members of a clan that bore the name of an animal thought that they were the offspring of that particular totem animal.

From the study of primitive religions Wellhausen found that tabu was closely associated with totemism. The imposition of tabus[7] is almost universal among primitive peoples; inherent bans exist involving sacred personages, rituals, and ceremonies, a wide variety of non-religious activities including parturition and death, and sometimes even specific objects or places.[8] Wellhausen found many parallels for these attitudes in ancient Near Eastern life, including sacred persons and consecrated things. Ideas of "holiness" and "uncleanness" constituted important tabus among ancient Semitic peoples.[9] Robertson Smith saw particularly close parallels between the varieties of prohibited food in Leviticus and the tabus relating to diet which occurred among heathen Semites general-

---

[5] W. Robertson Smith, *Kinship and Marriage in Early Arabia* (1903 ed.), p. 219; E. S. Hartland, *ERE*, XII, pp. 406b-407; E. Durkheim, *The Elementary Forms of the Religious Life* (1926), pp. 88ff.; J. B. Noss, *Man's Religions*, pp. 24f., 26.

[6] B. Stade, *Geschichte des Volkes Israel*, I, pp. 398, 409; G. B. Gray, *Hebrew Proper Names* (1896), pp. 86ff.

[7] *Tabu* is a Polynesian word meaning "marked off." Cf. R. R. Marett, *The Threshold of Religion* (1909), p. 127.

[8] J. B. Noss, *Man's Religions*, pp. 15f.

[9] Cf. S. A. Cook in W. Robertson Smith, *Lectures on the Religion of the Semites* (1927 ed.), pp. 548ff.; M. Jastrow, *Die Religion Babyloniens und Assyriens* (1912), II, pp. 896f., 933ff.

ly.[10] However, it should be noted that Old Testament tabus dealt with more than the rules concerning food laid down in Leviticus 11:1ff. and Deuteronomy 14:7ff. They embraced a number of other considerations in religious and secular affairs, and if violated they required some kind of purificatory ceremony in order to restore the individual to favor with God (cf. Lev. 6:27ff.; 11:32ff.; 1 Sam. 21:4ff., 2 Sam. 11:4).

A further development of totemism and tabu was seen by Wellhausen and his school in ancestor worship. For them the totem-ancestor gradually developed into a human ancestor, and subsequently into a divine being.[11] In the Old Testament, ancestor worship was naturally contemplated in terms of mourning customs for the departed and the sanctity of burial sites (cf. Gen. 23:1ff.; 35:8; Josh. 24:32, et al.), as well as tribal or personal names such as Baal-gad (Josh. 11:17; 12:7; 13:5), which contained the name of the deity. Scholars of that period also detected traces of ancestor worship in the existence of the "teraphim" or "household-gods" (Gen. 31:19, 30; 1 Sam. 19:13, 16). By connecting this ancient Semitic term with the Hebrew רפאים or "shades of the departed," they propounded the theory that the teraphim represented defunct ancestors,[12] who were venerated superstitiously by the living.

These early stages of spiritual growth, thought to be discernible in both primitive religions and the worship of the pre-Mosaic period, gave way to the more localized tribal god of the pre-prophetic period in Israel, and ultimately—through the work of the prophets—to the ideals of ethical monotheism, which were held to be the final stage of Hebrew religious development. Like many other scholars since his time, once Wellhausen had formulated his evolutionary theory to his own satisfaction—based though it was on only a small part of the evidence—he displayed a complete indifference towards subsequent anthropological or archaeological discoveries, even though they demanded a substantial modification of his original position.[13] Instead, he continued to propound his views as though his conclusions were final and irrevocable. In this mental frame of egotistical inflexibility he was followed slavishly by his adherents, with the possible exception of Kittel, who employed Posi-

[10] W. Robertson Smith, *Lectures on the Religion of the Semites* (1889), pp. 218ff., *Kinship and Marriage in Early Arabia*, p. 311.

[11] Cf. Wellhausen, *Reste Arabischen Heidentums*, pp. 183ff.; Stade, *Geschichte des Volkes Israel*, I, pp. 387ff.; G. Hölscher, *Geschichte der Israelitischen und Jüdischen Religion* (1922), pp. 24ff.; S. A. Cook in W. Robertson Smith, *Lectures on the Religion of the Semites* (1927 ed.), pp. 508ff., 544ff.

[12] F. Schwally, *Das Leben nach dem Tode* (1892), pp. 358ff.; C. Piepenbring, *Histoire du Peuple d'Israël* (1898), p. 28. For the connection with necromancy see W. O. E. Oesterley, *Immortality and the Unseen World. A Study in OT Religion* (1921), pp. 125ff.

[13] H. F. Hahn, *OT in Modern Research*, p. 86. For the archaeological material available for Wellhausen and his school see H. V. Hilprecht, *Explorations in Bible Lands during the Nineteenth Century* (1903).

tivist categories of approach along with the results of the most recent archaeological discoveries to probe into the origin and growth of the Hebrew people. One immediate effect of Kittel's work was to clarify the religious as well as the historical background of the Old Testament peoples, giving prominence to the patriarchal age as the period when Hebrew religious activities took their rise.

B. REACTIONS AND MODIFICATIONS

The high development of Semitic Babylonian civilization even long before the patriarchal period implied that the religious ideas that could have been brought to bear upon Abraham, Isaac, and Jacob were far more complex than Wellhausen had ever imagined. Accordingly it was necessary to take this new material into account when estimating the nature and origin of the Hebrew faith. This was undertaken by the brilliant Orientalist Hugo Winckler, who was the first to publish a critical edition of the Tell el-Amarna tablets.[14] Subsequently he endeavored to interpret the life of the ancient Near East during the fifteenth and fourteenth centuries B.C.[15] Unfortunately Winckler was unable to exercise proper control over his sources, with the result that his findings furnished an inaccurate picture of Near Eastern culture during the Amarna Age.

Winckler formulated what soon became known as the "pan-Babylonian" theory, which assumed that all the oriental peoples of antiquity had subscribed to concepts about the nature of the universe and man that were dominated by the religious ideas of the Babylonians. From this position it was only a short step to the claim that a great many of the cultural and religious forms that occurred in the Old Testament were in fact dependent on this ancient intellectual and spiritual corpus, a position that Winckler adopted in the second volume of his *Geschichte Israels*, published in 1900. The furor over this theory[16] was overshadowed by the controversy that flared up two years later when Friedrich Delitzsch took the "pan-Babylonian" theory of Winckler a dramatic step further. In his celebrated *Babel und Bibel*, published in 1902, Delitzsch propounded the view that anything of significance in the cultural and religious life of the Hebrews had been derived from Babylonian sources, and that there was little or nothing original about the spirituality of the Old Testament generally. The theories espoused by Delitzsch met with sharp opposition from Egyptologists, who at that time were fully per-

[14] H. Winckler, *Der Tontafelfund von El-Amarna* (2 vols., 1889-90), *Die Tontafeln von Tell el-Amarna* (1896).

[15] H. Winckler, *Das alte Westasien* (1899).

[16] Cf. S. A. Fries, *Moderne Darstellungen der Geschichte Israels* (1898), pp. 11ff.; O. Weber, *Mitteilungen der vorderasiatischen Gesellschaft*, XX (1915), pp. 13ff.; L. W. King, *History of Babylon* (1915), pp. 291ff.; S. A. Cook in *The People and the Book* (1925), pp. 58ff.

suaded that human culture had taken its rise in the Land of the Two Kingdoms.[17] Under the onslaught of criticism the theory subsided, being maintained only by Jeremias.[18] Nevertheless Delitzsch's work had one profoundly important benefit to Old Testament study, namely, it compelled all future investigators of Hebrew history to consider their subjects against the larger background of ancient Near Eastern life and thought.

As far as the followers of Wellhausen were concerned, the theories of Winckler and Delitzsch ran counter to all received concepts of the progressive unfolding of spirituality from rudimentary beginnings. What could not be denied, however, was the fact that even the archaeological evidence of the day pointed unmistakably to an advanced cultural and religious milieu in Babylonia that antedated the patriarchal period considerably. As Hahn has pointed out, the only escape from such a dilemma was to attempt to discover the particular elements of thought and behavior that could have been taken over by the ancient Hebrews from neighboring cultures, and to ascertain the extent to which these specific derivations had affected the nature and growth of Hebrew religion.[19]

It was clear that the methodology adopted by Winckler, Delitzsch, and Jeremias was inadequate for this task, and several years elapsed before Hermann Gunkel, an outstanding exponent of the religio-historical approach, attacked the problem once more. By bringing the comparative method to bear upon the issues of historical criticism, and by attempting to interpret the Old Testament religious concepts on their own terms, the excesses of the "pan-Babylonian" school were avoided and better control was obtained over Near Eastern archaeological material. Old Testament ideas were treated seriously in their own right, and Gunkel maintained that once they had been traced in outline through the Hebrew sources they could then be compared and contrasted with their counterparts in other oriental literary sources.[20] This method proved to be a further criticism of the Wellhausen school, for it emphasized the origin and growth of the fundamental religious concepts rather than the provenance and formulation of alleged documentary sources, and the subordination of the development of Hebrew faith to theories of philosophical and biological evolutionism.

Important also in this connection was the work of Gressmann, who took pains to point out the relationship of Hebrew religious thought to the mythological and eschatological patterns found in ancient Near

---

[17] Cf. W. L. Wardle, *Israel and Babylon* (1925), pp. 302ff.

[18] A. Jeremias, *Das AT im Lichte des alten Orients* (1904) and *Handbuch der altorientalischen Geisteskultur* (1913).

[19] H. F. Hahn, *OT in Modern Research*, p. 91.

[20] H. Gunkel, *Die Religionsgeschichte und die alttestamentliche Wissenschaft* (1910).

Eastern literature. Although Gressmann did not abandon entirely the methods and results of the Wellhausen school of literary criticism, he followed Gunkel[21] in maintaining that the mythological concepts apparent in prophetic eschatological passages were most probably the result of early contact between Babylonia and the Hebrews, and did not emerge from the exile period as Wellhausen and his followers had suggested.[22] Gressmann drew more consistently upon Egyptian sources for the origin of Hebrew religious concepts than had others before him, and although he did not actually prove that the cultural influences upon which Hebrew religious ideas were allegedly based were early, he made it clear that they could certainly be considered earlier rather than later in incidence, in contrast to what the Wellhausen school held.

More conservative scholars disapproved of the extent to which the religio-historical school envisaged the influence of ancient pagan cultures upon the development of Hebrew religion. Thus Reischle and Clemen cautioned against the tendency to overlook the distinctive features of Hebrew religion in favor of detecting pagan elements within the larger structure.[23] In particular they urged the intrinsic value of those aspects which were peculiar to the religious activities of the Hebrews, especially in view of the fact that the faith of Israel had survived those of her pagan neighbors. Some of these criticisms were unfortunately rather beside the point, for as Gunkel showed, the purpose of the religio-historical method of study, when properly applied, was to bring into sharp relief the greatness of Old Testament religion.[24] There can be no doubt, however, that Gunkel thought that certain portions of the Hebrew literature borrowed Babylonian myths directly, for example, in the accounts of creation and the Flood, although he contended, like many other scholars since his time, that in the process the elements characteristic of Babylonian polytheism had been removed and the finished product given a distinctive monotheistic cast.

A more emphatic rejection of the evolutionary development of Hebrew religion as expounded by Wellhausen and his adherents came from Paul Volz. A conservative member of the religio-historical school, Volz argued from the Mosaic authorship of the Decalogue to the fact that the precepts of ethical monotheism, attributed by Wellhausen to the general exilic period, were in fact promulgated by Moses to the Hebrews at

[21] H. Gunkel, *Schöpfung und Chaos in Urzeit und Endzeit* (1895), pp. 135ff., *Deutsche Rundschau*, CXV (1903), pp. 267ff.

[22] H. Gressmann, *Der Ursprung der israelitisch-jüdischen Eschatologie* (1905), pp. 238ff.

[23] M. Reischle. *Theologie und Religionsgeschichte* (1904), pp. 50ff.; C. Clemen, *Die religionsgeschichtliche Methode in der Theologie* (1904), pp. 20ff.

[24] H. Gunkel, *Deutsche Literaturzeitung*, XXV (1904), pp. 1100ff.

Mount Sinai.[25] He based his views in part on the comparative study of ethical sections in the Egyptian *Book of the Dead*,[26] which can be dated at least to the beginning of the Amarna Age, and also on a series of Babylonian incantation tablets which were compiled between 1500 B.C. and 1150 B.C.[27] Since such ethical material was already extant somewhat prior to the Mosaic period, Volz saw no intrinsic difficulty in attributing the ethical monotheism of the Decalogue to the work of Moses.

A similar position was maintained by Baentsch, who argued from what he thought was an innate monotheism in the ancient texts of Babylonia— speculative though he admitted this form to be—to a general tendency towards monotheism among the peoples of the ancient Near East.[28] This phenomenon was also present among the Hebrew tribes, who were subsequently welded into a spiritual unit by the events consequent upon the Sinai revelation, and who at that time espoused a genuine monotheistic faith. Despite such well-attested Egyptian 'monophysitic' tendencies as the "solar monotheism" of the Old Kingdom period and its revival under Amenhotep IV during the Amarna Age,[29] it is doubtful that monotheism was ever implicit in the religious movements of the orient to the degree that Baentsch assumed. Nevertheless, his arguments concerning the nature of Mosaic monotheism are not, as Hahn has implied, inadequate because he did not accommodate his theories to the accepted canons of contemporary historical criticism.[30] The fact that the mixed multitude of the Hebrews may have manifested somewhat more than a semi-sedentary phase of culture when they entered Palestine need not imply that they consistently incorporated the better developed cultural facets of Canaanite civilization, including the "advanced legislation" of the local communities, into their own way of life as a means of spiritual progression, as the Wellhausen school had supposed. Although the Hebrews were evidently inferior technologically at the commencement of the settlement period, as archaeological discoveries in Palestine have demonstrated, the superiority of their ethic, derived from the

---

[25] P. Volz, *Mose: ein Beitrag zur Untersuchung über die Ursprünge der israelitischen Religion* (1907), pp. 60ff.

[26] As J. H. Breasted, *Development of Religion and Thought in Ancient Egypt* (1959 ed.), pp. 293f., has pointed out, no *Book* as such existed between 1500 and 1100 B.C., but rather a collection of papyrus mortuary texts which were collated subsequently. The section entertained by Volz was the *Negative Confession* in chapter 125.

[27] The celebrated deprecatory spells of "burning," known as the Series *Shurpū*. For the date see A. Schott, *Die Vergleiche in den akkadischen Königinschriften* (1926), *ZDMG*, LXXXII (1928), p. lvii; W. von Soden, *ZDMG*, LXXXIX (1935), pp. 156ff.; *FSAC*, pp. 288ff.

[28] *Altorientalischer und israelitischer Monotheismus* (1906), pp. 30ff.

[29] Cf. *IAAM*, pp. 8f., 65f.

[30] *OT in Modern Research*, p. 101.

events at Sinai, was made the source of appeal time after time by prophetic figures from the period of Samuel onwards, particularly on those occasions when the orgiastic polytheism of the pagan Canaanites was a point at issue. If further proof were needed, the antiquity of Tabernacle worship as the religious focus of the Sinai revelation, to be discussed subsequently, and its perpetuation in the Solomonic Temple, points to the distinctiveness and virility of Hebrew monotheism in the midst of unprepossessing environmental circumstances. Though it is well known that there was a great degree of religious and social fusion between the Canaanites and the Israelites, it is faulty historical criticism to suggest that the Hebrew faith advanced to monotheism by way of the pagan rituals of Canaan.

The work of Rudolf Kittel, which represented a significant modification of the position adopted by Wellhausen, was nonetheless not as conservative in outlook as that of Baentsch. Kittel did not subscribe to the view that Moses taught a "genuine monotheism," although he recognized certain historical elements in the Mosaic traditions. On the basis of careful study of what was known at that period about Canaanite culture, he deduced that there may have been some tendency towards monotheism implicit in the religious thought of Canaan.[31] Starting with the worship of El as a supreme being at the pagan shrines, Kittel argued towards an analogous form of devotion during the patriarchal period as the basis for the later Mosaic concepts of the nature and function of deity. This, however, was not the ethical monotheism of the later prophets, but was at best a form of monolatry which failed to emphasize the uniqueness of the divine character. Although he differed from the Wellhausen school in recognizing that a declension from the high levels of Mosaic religion occurred at the beginning of the settlement period, he nevertheless subscribed to the belief that the ethical monotheism of the prophets evolved from the monolatry of Moses.[32]

A similar cautious position was adopted by Ernst Sellin, a brilliant contemporary of Kittel.[33] He, too, parted company with the Wellhausen approach to the extent of placing in an earlier age certain religious ideas that literary-critical orthodoxy had assigned to a much later period. At the same time he left room for the possibility of growth and development within the corpus of Israelite spirituality, which he dated from the Mosaic era. Following Hegelian methodology to a certain degree, Sellin, like Kittel, saw the enrichment of rudimentary Mosaic teaching through the interaction of the advanced spirituality of the Hebrew religious leaders on the one hand, and the continued declension of popular

[31] R. Kittel, *Geschichte des Volkes Israel* (1912 ed.), I, pp. 187ff.
[32] *Ibid.*, pp. 549ff.
[33] E. Sellin, *Alttestamentliche Religion im Rahmen der andern altorientalischen* (1908).

religion on the other. From this emerged a developing synthesis of religious belief that culminated in the advanced ethical teachings of the prophets.

The attempts that Kittel and Sellin made to emphasize the persistence of Mosaic ideals among minority religious groups during the settlement period and the monarchy served as an effective counterbalance to the stress laid by the critical school upon the presence of demonstrable Canaanite evidence in Hebrew religious life. Equally important was their insistence that significant aspects of the faith of Israel were to be considered as early rather than late. But unlike Volz or Baentsch, they did not quite appear to possess a view of the advancement of contemporary civilization that would have enabled them to assign distinctive monotheistic elements to the faith of Moses. In this respect, however, they were reasonably consistent, since by accepting the dating-sequences assigned by the Wellhausen school to the Mosaic Torah they could hardly do more than attribute a very small amount of the Pentateuch to the great Hebrew leader himself, or regard the monotheistic elements as other than prophetic in origin.[34]

[34] Subsequent studies of OT religion were based largely on the developmental theories of the Wellhausen school, although such a forthright exponent of the literary-critical methods as Gustav Hölscher, *Geschichte der israelitisch-jüdischen Religion* (1922), tended to follow Kittel and Sellin in emphasizing the *Sitz im Leben des Volkes* of the ancient Near East, and in attributing certain facets of Hebrew history to a comparatively early period. In the English-speaking world the views of Wellhausen were popularized by such writers as Addis, *Hebrew Religion* (1905); H. Wheeler Robinson, *The Religious Ideas of the OT* (1913); J. P. Peters, *The Religion of the Hebrews* (1914); G. A. Barton, *The Religion of Israel* (1918); H. P. Smith, *The Religion of Israel* (1914); R. L. Ottley, *The Religion of Israel* (1926); and others.

II. RECENT STUDIES IN HEBREW RELIGION

A. THE RAS SHAMRA TEXTS

Following the lead of Kittel and Sellin, scholars began to look for further traces of Canaanite religious influence during the settlement period and the monarchy upon the faith of Israel. Unfortunately, extra-Biblical sources available to these scholars were extremely sparse, and inscriptions that were available from Syria prior to World War I added very little to what was already known. Anthropological speculations based in part upon the nature of ruined Canaanite shrines proved to be of limited value in determining the character of Canaanite religion.[1]

However, an entirely new and unexpected source of information concerning the culture of ancient Canaan came to light with the discovery in 1929 of a great many cuneiform tablets at Ras Shamra, the Ugarit of the Amarna Age, on the coast of northern Syria. The first tablets were published in 1930 by C. F. A. Schaeffer, and were found to have been written in two languages, one a Hurrian dialect and the other an ancient Canaanite tongue closely resembling pre-Mosaic Hebrew. In the eleven campaigns at the site prior to World War II,[2] many hundreds of tablets were unearthed whose contents placed the culture of ancient Canaan in an entirely new perspective.[3] Since it is no longer possible to discuss the religion of early Israel without reference to Phoenician-

---

[1] Cf. S. A. Cook, *The Religion of Ancient Palestine in the Second Millennium B.C.* (1908); W. C. Wood, *JBL*, XXXV (1916), pp. 1ff., 163ff.

[2] For early reports see part two, section I, footnote 34 (p. 90); R. de Vaux, *RB*, XLVI (1937), pp. 526ff.; A. Bea, *Biblica*, XIX (1938), pp. 435ff., XX (1939), pp. 436ff.; a bibliography is found in C. F. A. Schaeffer, *Ugaritica: Études relatives aux découvertes de Ras Shamra* (1939), I, pp. 153ff.

[3] Cf. C. F. A. Schaeffer, *The Cuneiform Texts of Ras Shamra-Ugarit* (1939); R. de Langhe, *Les textes de Ras Shamra-Ugarit et leurs rapports avec le milieu biblique de l'Ancien Testament* (2 vols., 1945); C. H. Gordon, *Ugaritic Handbook* (1947), sect. II, pp. 129ff.; G. R. Driver, *Canaanite Myths and Legends* (1956); C. F. A. Schaeffer, *Ugaritica*, III (1956); J. Gray, *The Legacy of Canaan* (1957); H. L. Ginsberg, *ANET*, pp. 129ff.

Canaanite[4] cult-worship, a short résumé of the discoveries at Ugarit is desirable.

The sacrificial and ritual texts have furnished the most satisfactory guide to the names of the Ugaritic deities, although an assessment of their interrelationship has been hampered by the extraordinary fluidity of function and individuality of the gods mentioned in the tablets. Thus it is not always easy to ascertain the extent to which specific deities were related to one another mythologically, or even to determine whether they were consistently male or female at specific times—a confusion which contrasts curiously with the gods of the Hittite, Babylonian, and Egyptian pantheons.

The Canaanite generic term for deity was 'el, probably from an original 'ilum; and, according to the customs obtaining in the Amarna Age, the gods were designated as members of a class or guild by the terms 'elim or Bene 'el. The supreme deity of the Phoenician-Canaanite pantheon was known as El, that is the god, corresponding to El 'Elyon or El Shaddai in the patriarchal age of Hebrew history. El was at best a rather obscure figure—probably more so than the Egyptian Re or the Sumero-Akkadian Anu—and he was generally depicted as inhabiting a remote area of the cosmos known as the "Source of the Two Deeps," from which he supplied life-giving water to the earth.[5] He was known by the titles "father of man" (abū adami) and "father of years" (abū shanima), and on a stele found at Ras Shamra, he was depicted with hands outstretched in blessing over the ruler of Ugarit.[6]

The consort of El was the goddess Asherat (Ashirat), known to Israelite tradition as Asherah, a deity who was also worshipped by the Amorites and southern Arabians. Although the role of El was generally inactive, one of the myths depicts his seduction of two women, who were banished to the desert once they had given birth to their children, named "dawn" (Shahru) and "sunset" (Shalmu).[7] The active figure of the Canaanite pantheon was Baal (Haddu), offspring of El and Asherat; he was venerated as the overlord of rain and storm.[8] As the acknowledged king of the gods his titles included the names Aliyn (the Pre-

---

[4] For the cultural unity of these peoples see W. F. Albright, *Studies in the History of Culture* (Waldo Gifford Leland Volume, 1942), pp. 11ff., and the revised form in *BANE*, pp. 328ff.; C. Virolleaud, *Annales de l'Université de Paris*, VIII (1933), pp. 397ff.

[5] The word for deep is תהום, as in Gen. 1:2 *et al.* Note the importance of the water-deity Ea in Babylonian cosmogony and the place of the Nile in Egyptian life; cf. R. Dussaud, *Revue de l' Histoire des Religions*, CIV (1931), pp. 358f.

[6] *LAP*, pl. 60.

[7] Compare the Akkadian *sheru*, Hebrew שׁחר, "dawn"; Akkadian *shalam shamshi*, "sunset."

[8] Compare the eminence of the weather-god Hatti in the Hittite pantheon.

vailer)[9] and Zabul (Earthly Lord),[10] the former occurring with great frequency in Ugaritic poetry. He was also known as the "Son of Dagon," who was the chief deity of Ashdod (1 Sam. 5:1ff.),[11] and who was honored at shrines in Ugarit and the Gaza region (cf. Judg. 16:23).

Fertility goddesses played a far more important part in the cultus at ancient Ugarit than anywhere else in the Near East. As represented in the mythological texts, the relationships existing between Anath, Asherah, and Astarte (Ashtaroth) were particularly complex. The primary function of all three was sexual or procreative, although their warlike attributes were considered almost equally important. A thirteenth-century B.C. Egyptian text spoke of Anath and Astarte as "the great goddesses who conceive but do not bear," but at Ugarit they were regarded sometimes as virgins (*batulu*, Heb. בתולה) and on other occasions as mothers of all life.[12]

Ritual prostitution was a notable feature of Phoenician-Canaanite cultic worship, which frequently functioned at the lowest levels of moral depravity. As a sacred prostitute the goddess bore the title "the holiness of . . . ," in which the word *qudshu* was employed to denote dedication to the service of a deity.[13] The militant, even bloodthirsty, character of the Canaanite goddess Anath is made clear from the cuneiform sources, which represent her on occasions as wallowing fiendishly in human blood.[14] Asherah, who bore the title "She Who Walks in the Sea,"[15] was also referred to by the appellation *qudshu* in the Amarna Age, and was spoken of as the consort of Baal. Canaanite deities were generally depicted in human form, although some artistic representations conceived of them as birds or animals.

The Canaanite goddesses had as their major responsibility the fecundity of animals and man and this function was enshrined in the form of a myth that purported to account for the cyclic pattern of natural forces. Thus Baal, representing rain and vegetation, was killed every spring by Mot (Death) or by the "Devourers," who then dominated the climatic situation during the parched months from April to the end of October. In the autumn, the warrior-consort of Baal overcame death in a vicious struggle, and restored Baal to life. Virility overtook the land in early spring when Baal mated with either Anath or Ashtoreth.

---

[9] Cf. W. F. Albright, *BASOR*, No. 70 (1938), p. 19.

[10] Cf. Albright, *JPOS*, XII (1932), pp. 191f., XVI (1936), pp. 17f.

[11] *Dagon* is probably a corruption of *Dagan*, an ancient Akkadian vegetation deity; cf. *ARI*, p. 74.

[12] Cf. M. Burrows, *BASOR*, No. 77 (1940), pp. 6f.

[13] Cf. *Mélanges syriens offerts à M. R. Dussaud* (1939), I, p. 118 n. 2; *BASOR*, No. 78 (1940), pp. 26f.

[14] Cf. *Baal Epic* II, 7ff.; *UL*, pp. 17f.; C. Virolleaud, *La déesse 'Anat* (1938), pp. 13ff.; J. Aistleitner, *ZAW*, LVII (1939), pp. 205ff.; *FSAC*, pp. 233f.

[15] *ARI*, pp. 77f.

As Gordon has pointed out,[16] however, it must not be assumed that Baal can be identified with the Dying God, whether Tammuz or some other deity, as earlier anthropologists thought.[17] The Canaanite myths do not contain an annual cycle of death and revival on the part of Baal, but instead represent him as a fertility deity rather than as a seasonal deity. Furthermore, Baal was not necessarily integral to the fertility rituals, for he is not mentioned in one text dealing with the inauguration of a seven-year fertility cycle.[18]

It will be apparent from the foregoing considerations that the primary concern of Canaanite worship was that of insuring the fertility of the land, of flocks and herds, and of the human populace. Male and female prostitution were commonly practiced under the guise of religion at the various centers of worship.[19] The bulk of Canaanite religious activity was carried out at the "high places," where there were sacrificial altars (cf. 1 Sam. 9:12; 1 Kgs. 3:4). The best example of such an altar is found at Megiddo and dates from about 1900 B.C.[20] In the immediate vicinity of this altar were considerable quantities of animal bones comprising the remains of sacrifices which had been offered at this popular "high place."

Objects of religious veneration which were used in Canaanite cult-worship included the sacred post or *'asherāh*, which may have been a wooden emblem or image connected with the goddess Asherah.[21] This cult-object was associated with stone pillars or *maççebhôth*, which were quite possibly intended as representations of Baal or El. Excavations at various Palestinian sites have uncovered small altars of incense of the kind common in Canaan after 1100 B.C. They were made of limestone and carried projections or "horns" on each corner. The earliest of these was found at Megiddo in a shrine of the Israelite period dated in the early tenth century B.C.[22]

From Palmyra in northern Syria came an altar of incense with the term *hamman* inscribed on it, revealing the original use of the artifact.[23] A well-preserved Canaanite temple unearthed at Lachish in thirteenth-century B.C. levels appeared to have been destroyed by the Israelites while still in use as a sanctuary.[24] Despite the fact that the walls furnished evidence of having sustained heavy damage by fire, they were in sufficiently good condition to make it clear that they had originally

[16] *UL*, pp. 3f.
[17] J. G. Frazer, *The Golden Bough*, II, pp. 118f.; IV, pp. 5ff.
[18] Text 52, *UL*, pp. 58ff.
[19] Cf. *FSAC*, pp. 234f.
[20] G. E. Wright, *BA*, XII, No. 2 (1950), p. 31, pl. 6.
[21] *ARI*, p. 78.
[22] *WBA*, p. 114.
[23] Thus the reading "altar of incense" should be subsituted for "sun image" in Lev. 26:30; 2 Chron. 14:5 and 34:4, 7; Isa. 17:8 and 27:9; and Ezek. 6:4, 6.
[24] Cf. Sir Charles Marston, *The Times*, July 8, 1939.

been plastered and equipped with benches or shelves for storing sacrificial offerings. At the front of the building the archaeologists excavated a raised platform which may originally have accommodated an idol, and perhaps a small sacrificial altar in addition. To the rear of the temple were clearly defined areas for storage, as well as small apartments for the priests, a feature commonly found in the larger shrines. Debris from the sacrifices revealed the presence of many bones from birds and animals, all of them taken from the right front leg of the species.

While this custom reflects the provisions of Levitical law (Lev. 7:32) concerning the peace offerings, which provided that the right shoulder should become the perquisite of the priest, with the remainder presumably being consumed by the assembled worshippers at a festal meal, it should not be thought that the Levitical provisions were comparatively late enactments incorporated into Hebrew religion from pagan sources, or that the temple uncovered at Lachish was in fact an accredited Israelite shrine. As Albright has pointed out, the upper portion of the right foreleg was prescribed specifically by Assyro-Babylonian sacrificial rituals, indicating that the preference for this particular part of the animal was general throughout ancient western Asia,[25] and therefore can hardly be denied to the culture of the Hebrews at a comparatively early period. The almost complete absence of burned bones at the site of the Canaanite temple at Lachish pointed to the fact that the sacrificial meal had been boiled (cf. 1 Sam. 2:12ff.). From a study of the Ugaritic texts it is apparent that Canaanite sacrificial rituals were much more diversified than those among the Israelites, and a far wider range of animals was employed as offerings. These included bullocks, small cattle and birds, wild bulls, stags, fallow deer, and wild goats.[26]

So far comparatively few idols of any size have been unearthed in Syria or Palestine, which contrasts sharply with the situation in other areas of the ancient Near East. However, engravings of deities on stone have come to light, as well as small metal images of male gods, which are referred to in the Old Testament (e.g. Lev. 19:4; Ps. 106:19; Isa. 30:22; Hab. 2:18). Containers of incense and pottery models of pigs, bulls, and birds were commonly associated with Canaanite worship, as were cult-objects such as lilies (representing sex-appeal) and serpents, which were symbolic of fertility. A center dedicated to the worship of Anath was excavated at Gebal (Byblos), an extremely important site in ancient Phoenicia, which was noted for its fertility rites and ceremonial prostitution. Plaques recovered from Ras Shamra depicted the nakedness and fecundity of this same goddess. Terra-cotta figurines of Astarte have been unearthed at a great many sites throughout Palestine, and they invariably portray a naked woman with exaggerated sexual features.

[25] *FSAC*, p. 236.
[26] *ARI*, p. 92.

As was the case in ancient Near Eastern society generally, the Canaanite priesthood played an important part in the organization and control of social life at Ugarit. The king was the head of the community-state, which was organized along theocratic lines. Following Mesopotamian custom, certain of the priests were assigned to full-time duty with the military forces as staff astrologers. Such priests were required to furnish a prognosis for battles upon examination of various parts of sacrificial animals in accordance with the normal priestly procedures. On occasions the course of events in a battle was such that it required a fresh opinion on the basis of a further consideration of the omens, making the position of staff astrologer one of great importance for the fortunes of Ugarit.[27] The priestly hierarchy as a whole was controlled by a "chief of the priests" or *rabbu kahinima* in the fourteenth and thirteenth centuries B.C.[28]

Despite various references in the Old Testament to human sacrifice in the Heroic Age and later times (cf. Judg. 11:31ff.; 2 Kgs. 3:26f.; Mic. 6:7), including the Moloch rituals (cf. Lev. 18:21; 20:1ff.; Jer. 7:29ff.; Ezek. 16:20ff.; 23:37ff.; Am. 5:26) and the remains of child-sacrifices discovered by Garstang under the foundation stones of the gates of ancient Jericho, there is no indication from the Ugaritic texts that human sacrifice was either peculiarly acceptable to the deity, or that it was even practiced to any significant extent in the cultus. This is important in view of the testimony by Roman writers that the Carthaginians, who had migrated from northwest Canaan in the ninth century B.C. and later periods, practiced human sacrifice consistently until the fall of Carthage.[29]

It seems quite evident that the Canaanites shared with the Hebrews and other Semites the belief that, when a person died, he went to a place beneath the earth known as Sheol or "the pit." Here he continued in some sort of vague, shadowy existence in company with the "shades" of those who had preceded him. Thus it is not surprising to find that Canaanite burial customs were similar to those of the Hebrews, the Hittites, and other neighboring nations, with the notable exception of Egypt. Members of a family normally shared a common burial place, as was also the case in Hebrew patriarchal times.[30] With them were interred weapons, jewelry, pottery containers, and other objects thought to be needed in the underworld. When recovered from burial sites, such

---

[27] *IOTT*, p. 82.

[28] *ARI*, p. 108.

[29] Cf. L. Poinssot and R. Lantier, *Revue de l'Histoire des Religions*, LXXXVIII (1923), pp. 32ff.; S. A. Cook, *The Religion of Ancient Palestine in the Light of Archaeology* (1930). For the origins of human sacrifice see E. Meyer, *Geschichte des Altertums* (1909 ed.), I, ii, p. 345; E. A. Westermarck, *The Origin and Development of the Moral Ideas* (1906), I, pp. 434ff.

[30] Cf. the Cave of Machpelah, Gen. 25:9; 49:31; 50:13.

artifacts have proved to be of immense value in contributing to an understanding of contemporary social and religious customs in ancient Canaan.

B. STUDIES OF THE UGARITIC TEXTS

Although it was clear almost from the very beginning that the discoveries at Ras Shamra would require radical revision of the Wellhausenian evolutionary scheme of Hebrew religious development in important areas, the writers of that time tended to treat the subject much as Wellhausen himself had done. Thus Oesterley and Robinson, in their *Hebrew Religion: Its Origin and Development*, originally written in 1930 and subsequently revised in an enlarged edition in 1937, followed the classical liberal theories in assuming that the growth of Hebrew religion passed from a primitive state, associated with the patriarchs, through a phase in which the tribal deity was localized in the pre-prophetic era, and culminated in the highest stage of development, that of the cosmic monotheism of the latter part of Isaiah.[31]

These authors reflected the pattern of critical orthodoxy so faithfully that G. E. Wright was prompted to complain that one-fourth of their book was given over to the description of the supposed animistic and magical background of Israelite religion. "Yet we now know that. . .the authors are dealing neither with patriarchal nor with pagan religion of the day, but chiefly with Stone Age survivals and relics."[32] In addition, the section dealing with the religion of Canaan[33] treated the Ras Shamra discoveries in a most inadequate fashion, and seemed blissfully unaware of the tremendous importance of the Ugaritic cuneiform sources for the Amarna period as a whole. Other writers such as Jack and Hooke drew attention to similarities and differences in Canaanite and Hebrew religious rituals, but they also failed to appreciate the extent to which the discoveries constituted a criticism of the orthodox Wellhausenian position.[34] As the study of the Ugaritic material progressed, the character of certain aspects of Canaanite religion came into clearer focus. Of considerable importance in this connection was the nature of the deity El. Although some scholars had noted a monotheistic tendency in the Ugaritic worship of El,[35] following to a certain extent the position adopted by Baentsch and in a more modified form by Kittel, it soon

---

[31] A similar position was adopted by I. G. Matthews, *The Religious Pilgrimage of Israel* (1947), pp. 7ff.

[32] Wright, *The OT Against Its Environment* (1950), p. 12 n. 6.

[33] Oesterley and Robinson, *Hebrew Religion: Its Origin and Development*, pp. 170ff.

[34] J. W. Jack, *The Ras Shamra Tablets* (1935); S. H. Hooke, *The Origins of Early Semitic Ritual* (1938).

[35] E.g. Jack, *The Ras Shamra Tablets*, p. 13.

became evident that Canaanite cult-worship was crude, orgiastic, and polytheistic in character.[36] No longer could it be regarded as having exerted a direct influence upon the wilderness religion of the Hebrews, but it was instead seen as the indigenous faith of Canaan for some time before the Hebrew occupation of the Promised Land.[37]

Attention was also drawn to the fact that certain of the mythological patterns contained in the Ras Shamra literature were reflected to a limited degree in various parts of the Old Testament.[38] Thus the references to the monster Leviathan (Job. 3:8; 41:1ff.; Pss. 74:14; 104:26; Isa. 27:1; Ezek. 29:3ff.)[39] and the dragon Rahab (Job 9:13; 26:12; 38:8ff.; Pss. 87:4; 89:10; Isa. 30:7; 51:9), the female monster of chaos closely allied mythologically with Leviathan, were seen to have been derived from Canaanite literary sources rather than from Babylonian myths, as Gunkel and others had supposed. In the rush of claims for a direct influence of Ugaritic religious forms upon their Hebrew counterparts it was not noticed that early Hebrew tradition was entirely free from such Canaanite influence, which is indicated by the fact that in the Hebrew account of world-beginnings there is no narrative describing a conflict between the Creator and a dragon. Although the curbing of the unruly forces of chaos at the creation is depicted in Genesis poetically in terms that, under certain conditions, could perhaps be applied to Rahab (cf. Job 9:13; 26:12; 38:8ff.), the general imagery in the Old Testament narratives was invariably transferred from the creation setting current in Babylonia to the narrative of the redemption of Israel from Egypt (cf. Ps. 89:10; Isa. 51:9), with the result that the term "Rahab" became synonymous with that country (Ps. 87:4; Isa. 30:7; cf. Ezek. 29:3). Again, it should be observed that although there is an undeniable literary and linguistic relationship between the cuneiform sources from Ugarit and many sections of the Hebrew Bible, it remains true that the characteristic mythological forms of the ancient Near East found no place in Old Testament literature. As Gordon has remarked, the mythology of Canaan constituted little more to the Hebrew writers than a literary background upon which to draw for poetic images.[40]

The Ras Shamra texts were also considered to give support for Sigmund Mowinckel's theories about the presence of a cultic myth underlying an annual New Year enthronement of God as King in Jerusalem, on the

---

[36] R. Dussaud, *Revue de l'Histoire des Religions*, CIV (1931), pp. 353ff.; J. A. Montgomery, *JAOS*, LIII (1933), pp. 101ff.; *ARI*, pp. 71ff.

[37] W. Baumgartner, *Theologische Zeitschrift*, III (1947), pp. 81ff.; *FSAC*, p. 271.

[38] Cf. T. H. Robinson in S. H. Hooke (ed.), *Myth and Ritual* (1933), pp. 172ff.

[39] For comparison with the Ugaritic *lotan* see C. F. Pfeiffer, *EQ*, XXXII (1960), pp. 208ff.

[40] *IOTT*, p. 82.

analogy of the Babylonian *akitu* festival.[41] This suggestion had been followed principally by Schmidt, and received development and modification by S. H. Hooke and his followers, who attempted to prove that certain clearly defined myths and rituals had been the common property of the ancient Near East.[42] These scholars endeavored to show that what had been the spring festival in Mesopotamia was adapted to the cultural milieu of the Hebrews so as to constitute the three main festival occasions of unleavened bread, the feast of weeks, and the festival of tabernacles. In support of this theory they adduced the fact that at different places in Mesopotamia the *akitu* festival was celebrated at various times during the year, particularly in the spring and autumn.[43] The Myth and Ritual school associated with Hooke assigned particular importance to an enthronement rite as it was thought to have obtained during the Hebrew monarchy, since the figure of the king was central in the ritual act that renewed the unity of the people with its kingly deity. But, as Pedersen had pointed out, certain of these ideas were at variance with the concepts that Israel entertained concerning its kingship.[44] Considerations of this nature, combined with the realization that there were decided limits to the knowledge of what constituted pre-exilic ritual practices among the Hebrews, led many to conclude that Hooke and his followers had greatly exaggerated the importance and influence of Mesopotamian religious *motifs* upon the cultic practices of the Hebrews, and had adhered too closely to the subjective thinking of Mowinckel in attempting to make the facts conform to their theories.

A similarly cautious approach was adopted by Hvidberg in a study of certain of the cuneiform sources from Ras Shamra.[45] He concluded that, while in some areas of Palestine, and possibly in northern Israel, the degree of religious syncretism had become such that God was mourned ritually as dead and then greeted as risen in the manner associated with the Baal fertility ceremonies, the Old Testament furnished absolutely no evidence for this idea. What was in fact celebrated were the saving acts

[41] Cf. S. Mowinckel, *Psalmenstudien II. Das Thronbesteigungsfest Jahwäs und der Ursprung der Eschatologie* (1922), pp. 200ff.; *RHPR*, LX (1926), p. 409; K. H. Ratschow, *ZAW*, LIII (1935), pp. 176ff.; A. S. Kapelrud, *Norsk Teologisk Tidsskrift*, XLI (1940), p. 57. For a study of divine kingship as the unifying factor of mankind and the world of nature see H. Frankfort, *Kingship and the Gods: A Study of Ancient Near Eastern Religion as the Integration of Society and Nature* (1948).

[42] H. Schmidt, *Die Thronfahrt Jahves* (1927); S. H. Hooke (ed.), *Myth and Ritual* (1933), *The Labyrinth* (1935), and *The Origins of Early Semitic Ritual* (1938). For a formulation of this theory see *Myth and Ritual*, pp. 1ff.

[43] *Myth and Ritual*, pp. 46f.; cf. S. A. Pallis, *The Babylonian Akitu Festival* (1926), pp. 27ff.

[44] J. Pedersen, *Israel: Its Life and Culture*, p. 442; cf. O. Eissfeldt, *ZAW*, XLVI (1928), pp. 81ff.; C. R. North, *ZAW*, L (1932), pp. 8ff.

[45] F. F. Hvidberg, *Graad og Latter i det Gamle Testamente* (1938), pp. 115ff.

of God on behalf of His people, and the thing that was renewed was the Sinaitic Covenant. It remained for C. H. Gordon to point out that the texts from Ras Shamra said nothing about any annual death and resurrection of Baal,[46] and that the notion that the agricultural year in Canaan was divided into a fertile and sterile season was false. Since Baal was thus not indispensable as far as fertility rituals were concerned, he is to be considered a seasonal rather than a fertility deity.[47]

The Scandinavian scholar Ivan Engnell argued from traces of divine kingship that he observed in the ancient Near Eastern nations other than Israel to the view that the king as a cultic figure was identical with the dying and resurrected vegetation deity and also with the creator-god. For Engnell the process of religious syncretism was accomplished with penetrating thoroughness in the early monarchy, and was still evident at a much later period.[48]

An attack upon certain of the presuppositions of both the Scandinavian scholars and the Myth and Ritual school was made by N. H. Snaith, who in a study of the so-called "enthronement psalms" renounced the idea that they were in any way connected with the New Year festival, and related them instead to sabbath worship, assigning them to a distinctly post-exilic date.[49] In a subsequent treatise on the New Year festival itself he repudiated the suggestion that the festival was held twice each year, and stated flatly that there was no Old Testament evidence for associating the New Year feast with divine kingship.[50] He was critical of the way in which Mowinckel had reconstructed Hebrew ritual to accord with the Babylonian *akîtu* ceremonies, and denied that the kings of Israel ever acted as substitutes for the deity in cultic rites.

Although there might well be some difference of opinion as to the date of the "enthronement psalms," there can be little doubt that Snaith was correct in pointing out the distinctive nature of the Hebrew festivals. It is noteworthy in this connection that the Old Testament feasts did not adopt the ancient Near Eastern pattern of confessional and purificatory rites followed by joyous ceremonies,[51] since the seasonal festivals of the Hebrews differed radically in origin, purpose, and nature. In Mesopotamia and Ugarit the cultic rites were intended in part to honor the gods of the pantheon, so as to insure the fertility of the land for another year. For the Hebrews the festive seasons constituted a manifestation of divine beneficence and demonstrated that God was the supreme provider for the needs of His people, who acknowledged His gifts with gratitude.

[46] On one occasion only was he killed (Text 67:II) and was subsequently revived (Text 49:III).

[47] *UL*, pp. 4f.

[48] *Studies in Divine Kingship in the Ancient Near East* (1943).

[49] *Studies in the Psalter* (1934).

[50] *The Jewish New Year Festival* (1947).

[51] T. H. Gaster, *Thespis* (1961 ed.), pp. 26ff.

Whereas in the pagan cultic rites people approached the deity superstitiously and called attention to their needs, the seasonal feasts of the Hebrews proclaimed the reverse of this process, and showed that the divine Creator was working consistently for the requirements of His creatures, for whom He was morally responsible.

There can be little denial of the fact that attempts to see traces of enthronement and vegetation rites in various portions of the Old Testament have led to extreme and even fanciful interpretations of the Hebrew text. Morgenstern envisaged 2 Samuel 15:30ff. in terms of David in his role as the deity of the annual crop leading a solemn procession up the Mount of Olives, where he would stay according to the cultic rites for the seven-day feast of unleavened bread, which was followed immediately by the New Year.[52] Then with the resurrection of the deity accomplished, the king would return in solemn procession to his capital and reascend the throne.

That this is a completely forced and unrealistic interpretation of what actually transpired on that occasion is immediately apparent on a plain reading of the text. Far from participating in a solemn religious festival, David was fleeing from his capital for his life because he was on the point of being usurped as king by his rebellious son Absalom. The sound of the trumpet (2 Sam. 15:10) had no connection whatever with the *shôphār* heralding the beginning of a festival, but was the signal that would climax many months of treachery and intrigue. The entire event bore all the characteristics of a political coup, and the turbulent emotions that marked the flight of David across the Wadi Kidron to Jericho and the Jordan fords were completely removed from the atmosphere of a Hebrew festal occasion.

C.   W. F. ALBRIGHT

The work of W. F. Albright has done much to clarify certain of the issues in the study of Hebrew religion. After surveying the various religious systems of the ancient Near East, he concluded that the deities that made up the pantheons of Babylonia, Egypt, Anatolia, and Canaan were personified universal natural forces which functioned in a designated sphere or manner.[53] The reflection of these peoples upon the cosmic activities of a high god led almost immediately to their belief in his universal dominion, a tendency particularly noticeable in Egyptian thought, although it was not completely absent from Mesopotamian literature.[54] Once men had recognized that the many and various deities were simply manifestations of a single god, Albright argued that it was only a comparatively short step to some kind of henotheism, where the

---

[52] J. Morgenstern, *IDB*, III, p. 545.
[53] *FSAC*, pp. 192, 213; cf. *JBL*, LIX (1940), pp. 102ff.
[54] *FSAC*, pp. 214f.

worshipper focused his adoration on a single deity.[55] He traced two specific stages by which the Mesopotamians moved towards an empirical monotheism,[56] though he observed that such monotheistic tendencies were partial or ineffective. In Egypt, however, he maintained that monotheism had been achieved by about 1400 B.C., when the universal sun-god Amun-Re was divested of mythological accretions and revered as the only deity.[57] However, in this connection it must be remembered that the so-called monotheism of Akhenaton comprises nothing more than the selection of the solar disc as the prime power within nature.

Albright denied that there was any substantial basis for an "El" monotheism among the pre-Mosaic western Semites, and envisaged Moses as monotheistic in the sense that he taught "the existence of only one God, the creator of everything, the source of justice...who has no sexuality and no mythology, who is human in form but cannot be seen by human eye and cannot be represented in any form. . . ."[58] Even though Albright admitted to being hampered in dealing with the subject by the fact that the literary sources were comparatively late in origin[59]— an obstacle furnished by an uncritical acceptance of the Graf-Wellhausen postulates—he felt that the tradition was sufficiently well attested both by the Hebrew Bible and by the nature of second-millennium B.C. religion in the Near East to be considered essentially historical.[60]

Albright's view was a decided advance upon the position of Sellin, who had attributed to Moses only a germ of the ethical monotheism that was represented by the teaching of the Hebrew prophets. It also marked a distinct break with liberal orthodoxy in that it took the historical traditions of the Old Testament much more seriously than had been the case previously. Naturally his views aroused opposition among those who preferred to think that the Old Testament record of the Hebrew past could not be regarded as history in the generally accepted sense, and who were thus unable to think of the Biblical narratives as other than warped or tendentious accounts of remote traditions and events.[61]

There can be little question, however, that Albright presented strong arguments for what he considered to be Mosaic monotheism, and although it would be gratifying to have still more evidence than is available, it remains true that the situation that Albright has depicted represents substantially the religion of the Mosaic age.

[55] P. 192.
[56] P. 217.
[57] P. 219.
[58] P. 272; cf. *JBL*, LIX (1940), pp. 91ff.
[59] *FSAC*, p. 257; cf. T. J. Meek, *JBL*, LXI (1942), p. 34.
[60] *ARI*, p. 96.
[61] Cf. the criticisms of M. Burrows, *JQR*, XXXIII (1942-43), pp. 475f.; W. Eichrodt, *Theology of the OT* (1961), I, p. 221 n. 1.

D. Yehezkel Kaufmann

By far the most important treatise since the time of Wellhausen to deal with the origin and nature of Hebrew religion was the eight-volume work published by Yehezkel Kaufmann between 1937 and 1956.[62] In it he adopted a position diametrically opposed to that of Wellhausen and the German school of Biblical criticism, asserting that Israelite monotheism did not at all evolve slowly out of crude polytheism through the concerted efforts of a priestly caste, but was from the very beginning a characteristic of the people of Israel under the religious guidance of Moses. This position was all the more surprising because Kaufmann accepted the principles of higher criticism as such, although he protested against the arbitrary delineation of sources and supported the strictures of the Uppsala school against the "debaucheries of literary criticism."[63] Thus he was in general accord with the consensus of earlier critical opinion that Deuteronomy belonged to the time of Josiah,[64] although he criticized the liberal view that Joshua and Judges contained little or no authentic historical information, stressing that the city-lists in Joshua reached back to the very days of the conquest and settlement.[65] By applying somewhat of the same literary and historical criticism as that favored by the Graf-Wellhausen school, Kaufmann argued from a comparison of the various legal codes to the fact that the Priestly legislation antedated its Deuteronomic counterpart instead of elaborating upon its contents, and thus stood nearer in time to the Jehovistic-Elohistic sources.[66] In addition he also maintained that the Priestly sources reflected an age when the "congregation of Israel" was a military rather than an ecclesiastical body, and concluded that its ideology was independent of prophetic teaching,[67] pointing instead to a period of origin that antedated many of the other Pentateuchal sources.

Kaufmann expressly rejected the conventional Wellhausenian views of the origins of Hebrew monotheism. He maintained that Israelite religion was an original and indigenous product whose monotheistic *Weltanschauung* had no antecedents in ancient near Eastern paganism (*KRI*, p. 2). For Kaufmann Hebrew monotheism was not so much a theological dogma nurtured carefully in prophetical circles over several generations, but an idea that was absolutely basic to the national culture of the Hebrews, which it permeated from the very beginning. While historical relations could be traced between paganism and Israelite religion, the latter

---

[62] Y. Kaufmann, ‏תולדות האמונה הישראלית: מימי קדם עד סוף בית שני‎. Translated and abridged by M. Greenberg, *The Religion of Israel: From Its Beginnings to the Babylonian Exile* (1960).

[63] *BACP*, pp. 2f.

[64] Cf. *KRI*, pp. 172ff.

[65] *BACP*, pp. 24f.

[66] Cf. *KRI*, pp. 167ff., 175ff.

[67] Y. Kaufmann, ZAW, XLVIII (1930), pp. 23ff., LI (1933), pp. 35ff.

was never genuinely polytheistic in nature. Kaufmann maintained that the Old Testament narratives conceived of pagan gods in a different manner from that current among the votaries of Near Eastern deities, so that where alien gods were mentioned in the text in company with the God of Israel, it was the latter alone who was consistently depicted as an active divine Being (pp. 10f.). Thus when the Hebrew God did battle with the "gods of the nations," the objects of His wrath were idols, and not militant foreign deities (pp. 12f.).

Pentateuchal prohibitions against pagan religions generally depicted them in terms of mere fetishism, whether the underlying sources were early or late, and hence prohibited the manufacture of alien deities and the worship of such material objects. Where prohibitions against the veneration of beings other than the God of Israel were recorded (Exod. 22:19; Lev. 17:7; cf. KRI, pp. 63ff.), the point at issue was not that foreign active deities were mentioned, but rather that specifically Israelite divine beings and demons were being envisaged. Any mention of alien gods in the Pentateuch was invariably a reference to idols and nothing more (p. 18). Since this was so, the non-involvement of the Old Testament writers with the mythological materials (pp. 20, 60ff.) and polytheism of pagans required a fresh examination of the conventional notions of Israelite idolatry and, by implication, the general character of Hebrew monotheism itself.

As encountered in the Old Testament literature, the concept of idolatry included magic, divination, idol cults, necromancy, and other manifestations of pagan religion. For Kaufmann the question of Israelite idolatry turned upon whether God was worshipped in Israel as just one of many deities, whether He was associated with a mythological pantheon, or whether Hebrew idolatry was of a genuinely syncretistic variety (pp. 137f.). On the basis of an examination of the sources, Kaufmann concluded that the popular form of idolatry did not constitute a genuine polytheism, but was instead a "vestigial idolatry," comparable to the rather superstitious belief in amulets, spells, and other semi-magical influences that persist in certain levels of monotheistic faith to the present day (p. 142). The popular type of idolatry depicted in the prophetical literature consisted of a magical, fetishistic, non-mythological veneration of imported images along with a certain amount of private cult-worship. On the basis of the readiness of the Hebrews to eradicate Baal worship from their midst on request, Kaufmann claimed that in the popular religious consciousness there was always the underlying conviction that the Lord was God (p. 145). At the same time there lurked in Israel the lingering suspicion that images and cultic rites could lay legitimate claim to a degree of magical efficacy. In sum, Israelite idolatry was to be construed as a vulgar phenomenon characterized by fetishistic, magical, and ritualistic elements, which, because of the lack of a basic pagan mythology, never attained to the level of a cultural force among the Hebrews (pp. 147f.).

Historical monotheism, as interpreted in terms of the Divine Name, a prophetic mission, and the struggle of the nation with idolatry, was not characteristic of the patriarchal period, when none of these elements occurred in the Hebrew records (p. 222). Even the people of Israel who constituted the real bearers of historical monotheism did not inherit their faith from the patriarchal age in the strictest sense, for it was under Moses that the monotheistic concept came into being, at which time there occurred the beginnings of religious tension between Israel and the pagan world. Since the basic concept of Hebrew religion had no roots in paganism, Moses must have been the first to originate it (p. 225). But although Israelite religion was fundamentally different from every other variety of pagan cultic worship, the fact that it was born in the midst of thriving alien cultures virtually assured some degree of influence by Near Eastern paganism. For Kaufmann, however, Hebrew religion was not governed so much by the environmental background of antiquity as by the fact that, in process of incorporating certain pagan materials into its religious corpus, the faith of Israel generated a fresh spirit and a new ethos never contemplated by paganism. It surpassed the monotheistic tendencies of Egypt and Babylonia in that it postulated the existence of a God who transcended nature, whose will was supreme in the universe, who was free from bondage to myth and magic, and was not subject to matters of compulsion or fate (pp. 226f.), rather than merely reducing the arithmetic number of available deities.

This high view of deity, accompanied by the sense of mission fostered by the Sinai Covenant, provided a powerful stimulus towards unity among the Israelite tribes during the time of Joshua. For Kaufmann this underlay the entire conquest period, which he thought of as a unified movement, carried out by a confederation of tribes who were consciously following a national plan of conquest (p. 245). This same preconceived scheme also formed the background to the tribal battles described in the early chapters of Judges. As evidence, Kaufmann adduced the fact that the eras of the conquest and settlement were singularly free from inter-tribal territorial disputes, despite the chaos and internecine strife of the Judges period.

At this time secular authority was vested in the "primitive democracy" of the Elders, a survival of the inter-tribal group of Elders that had arisen during the days of Moses and Joshua (p. 256). The specifically spiritual direction which that age took was the responsibility of those religious figures who emerged periodically to emphasize the fact that the God of Sinai continued to rule His people through His appointed messengers. Kaufmann denied that the Judges were local heroes who were subsequently given national status by the editor of the book of Judges (p. 257), arguing from the general absence of a distinction between

376

national and local events to the possibility that a local deliverance could well have assumed the proportions of national relief. Equally emphatic was his rejection of the view that temples and priesthoods alike were taken over by the Israelites from Canaanite precursors in the land despite the religious syncretism of the period. Israelite temples did not antedate the Hebrew patriarchs, and the sanctity of particular locations from that time arose from the revelations given by God to the ancestors of the Israelites when they were aliens in Canaan.

Kaufmann traced four distinctive phases in the historical development of Hebrew religion. The first, constituting the age of Moses, Joshua, and their generation, was non-idolatrous. This was succeeded by an idolatrous interlude which lasted throughout the Judges period, and was followed by a third phase of loyalty to God in the early monarchy. From the time of Solomon there was a second prolonged interval of an idolatrous nature, culminating in the exile (p. 260). The monarchy was thought of as the direct successor to the "apostolic kingdom of God," operative from the time of Moses, and the somewhat different traditions concerning the way in which Saul was elected to kingship (cf. 1 Sam. 7; 8; 10:17ff.; 12) were held to reflect faithfully an aspect of the contemporary historical situation (p. 264). The involvement of Solomon in the cultic rites of his pagan shrines marked the turning-point of the religious and political fortunes of the monarchy, and subsequent historians raised the vestigial idolatry, which had always persisted among the vulgar, to the level of national sin so as to account for the political decline which followed the days of Solomon (p. 270).

The extent to which the Baal cult constituted a vital danger to the ethos of Hebrew religion was depreciated by Kaufmann (pp. 274f.), who also dissociated the prophetic orders (בני נביאים) that arose after the time of David from the ecstatic figures who appeared in the narratives connected with the work of Samuel. He followed the general pattern of critical opinion in maintaining that the lasting historical significance of Josiah's reform constituted an important step towards the priestly concept of a book of Torah as the regulating medium of national life (p. 290), an ideal that was to become normative with the formulation of the Pentateuch in the post-exilic period (p. 448).

There can be little question that, particularly for the formative period of Hebrew religion, the researches of Kaufmann constitute an extremely important contribution that will richly repay careful study. But while it presents a challenging criticism to certain facets of the traditional liberal interpretation of the origin and development of Hebrew religion, it is still based to a large extent upon the evolutionary premises of the Graf-Wellhausen school, particularly as regards literary sources. Perhaps it is this curious degree of contrast which has led at least one critic to describe the methodology of Kaufmann as eccentric.[68] On the other hand he appears to be following what can be considered a basically legitimate procedure in attempting to interpret the religious symbols of the Hebrew world from within, rather than in examining them in the light of pagan models and counterparts insofar as these existed.[69] As C. H. Gordon has remarked in another connection, by reading *out of* texts it is possible for scholars who understand the general content to derive much more from the sources than comparativist scholars who read so much *into* them.[70]

Nevertheless there is a certain unconscious inconsistency in the general approach adopted by Kaufmann towards his source materials. Concerning the period of the conquest, for example, he stresses that his views "do not flow from the assumption that the stories of the Bible are historical reports"[71] and that "the events of the Conquest are shrouded in a mist of legend."[72] Yet his conclusions as to the course of events are almost identical with what is narrated in Joshua. Precisely what happened to the unhistorical and legendary elements in the process has not been stated. The main difficulty undoubtedly resides in the fact that, while Kaufmann was able to detach himself intellectually from certain propositions of the Graf-Wellhausen school regarding the development of Hebrew religion and suggest some radically different views, he was not in effect weaned from the basic evolutionism of that body of theorists.

The literary strata that Kaufmann has distinguished in the Old Testament look remarkably like the sources that the Graf-Wellhausen school purported to uncover, with the possible exception of the early Near Eastern materials in Genesis.[73] Even if Kaufmann had preferred to avoid the Graf-Wellhausen categories of literary analysis, which he apparently did not, he could have followed the lead of those scholars who utilized the methods of form-criticism in their studies. But aside from noting that Genesis constituted a stratum in itself, whose material was, on the whole, most ancient, Kaufmann does not appear to have applied form-critical techniques to the sources under study.

Kaufmann, like Alt and Noth, is remarkably selective—to say the least—in his consideration of the archaeological evidence for the pre-exilic period. Because he pays little or no attention to this extremely important source of information, he tends to present the conquest in terms of a concerted onslaught by a unified and highly coordinated Israelite task-force under the leadership of one gifted commander. A careful reading of Joshua will make it plain that even the Biblical material falls somewhat short of this exalted conception, while a consid-

---

[68] J. Bright, *Early Israel in Recent History Writing*, p. 73.
[69] *KRI*, p. 3.
[70] *UL*, p. 4 n. 1.
[71] *KRI*, p. 247 n. 3.
[72] *BACP*, p. 91.
[73] *KRI*, p. 208.

378

eration of the archaeological evidence relating, for example, to the fall of Jericho and Ai, gives some indication of the complexity of the problem in a way that Kaufmann was unable to entertain. It is this precise lack of attention to archaeological matters that, in the view of the present writer, led to an inadequate assessment of the character and extent of Canaanite Baal worship, and a resultant deficiency in the estimate of its pervasive influence in Hebrew life.

The dissatisfaction of Kaufmann with the general dating-scheme assigned by traditional liberalism to the Pentateuch and the earlier historical books was reflected by his attempts to redate them in accordance with the principles of criticism upon which he proceeded.[74] Thus he maintained the Priestly material was more ancient than the Deuteronomic composition,[75] although the latter contained some very early passages and was divisible on grounds of style into "early" and "late" forms. He criticized the Graf-Wellhausen school for their complete indifference to the cuneiform literature of Mesopotamia extant in their day, which if considered would have placed Israelite religious origins in proper perspective by relating them to Assyrian rather than to the much later Bedouin culture.[76]

Kaufmann assigned the composition of Joshua to the beginning of the Judges era and held that it was compiled from such sources as the *Book of Yashar*, the city- and border-lists of that period, and priestly material including, among other items, a list of Levitical cities. Though Joshua and Judges bear the marks of Deuteronomic editing, he rejected any suggestion that they belonged properly to the time of Josiah, and maintained that only the legislation in Deuteronomy that referred to the unification of the cult could be dated in the seventh century B.C. Kaufmann denied any trace of Deuteronomic redaction in Samuel, and argued from the presence of a reference to cultic unification in 1 Kings 3:2 to the fact that the book was compiled after the reign of Josiah. By implication the absence of allusions to unification of the cult in Joshua, Judges, and Samuel (except for an explanatory gloss in Josh. 9:27) showed that they dated from an earlier period.

The redating of the historical books in this manner is certainly at variance with the general position adopted by liberal orthodoxy, and accordingly has come under considerable criticism. While many scholars now concede that there are very ancient sources in Deuteronomy, few would follow Kaufmann in his suggestion that there existed an "early" and a "late" form of Deuteronomy, differentiated on purely stylistic grounds. Furthermore, on any basis, it is incorrect to state that the book

---

[74] *KRI*, pp. 153ff.
[75] Cf. *ZAW*, XLVIII (1930), pp. 32ff.; *BACP*, pp. 3f.; *VT*, IV (1954), pp. 307ff.; *KRI*, pp. 175ff.
[76] *KRI*, p. 205 n. 16.

that was found in the Temple at the time of Josiah was Deuteronomy "as has long been recognized."[77] In point of fact there is not a shred of evidence for this view. The precise nature of the code is uncertain, and in all probability it constituted only a small section of the Mosaic law, which may have incorporated some of the ancient Passover material.

By abandoning considerations of style in favor of internal evidence,[78] Kaufmann has certainly cast doubt upon the efficacy of the former as one of the traditional elements of literary criticism, and for this alone his work has been received with misgivings by liberal scholars. However, his use of internal evidence is hampered partly by an indifference to archaeological data and also by the necessity for a continual reference to the general trends of liberal criticism, from which he is not by any means weaned. This results in some rather bizarre attempts to demonstrate the authenticity and reliability of the Biblical narratives by relating them to his own canons of interpretation and criticism, a procedure that does not endear him to either liberal or conservative scholars.

[77] *KRI*, p. 208.
[78] *BACP*, p. 7.

III. INFLUENCES ON THE RELIGION
OF THE HEBREWS

A. THE METHODOLOGICAL APPROACH

Some attempt must now be made to reconstruct in outline the nature of Hebrew religious activity from the earliest periods on in the light of what is known about such phenomena in primitive cultures, bearing in mind the results of archaeological activity in the Near East. It is now generally recognized by scholars that the methodological approach adopted by Wellhausen in his evaluation of the growth of Hebrew religion left much to be desired. As indicated elsewhere, Wellhausen was strongly influenced by the pronounced Hegelianism of Vatke; and taking his cue from biological concepts current in the evolutionism of his day, he concluded that if monotheism was the highest form of Hebrew faith, it must have emerged at the latest phase of development. Similarly, those sections of the Old Testament that could be regarded as early must contain the most primitive traces of religious activity, sometimes barely distinguishable from pure superstition. In complete contrast to the Biblical view, which attributed monotheism to the earliest of the Hebrew ancestors, Wellhausen saw the mature faith of Israel as an outgrowth of the animistic and totemistic trends of patriarchal worship, which slowly evolved into monotheism under the influence of the literary prophets. In conformity with this theory, any comparatively advanced theological concepts found in "early" narratives were relegated to the activities of editors during the prophetic and subsequent periods.

As was the case with the Wellhausenian theories of literary criticism, the criteria by which the development of Israelite religion was judged would certainly have been greatly modified—perhaps even abandoned completely in some areas—if Wellhausen had paid greater attention to the evidences of ancient Near Eastern culture as revealed by the archaeological activity of his day. Wellhausen made some concessions to comparative study by surveying the nature of primitive Bedouin religion. But he made his fundamental error in thinking that Hebrew culture generally arose from comparatively late Bedouin origins and in rejecting the archaeological evidence of social and religious activity in the civilizations of Mesopotamia and Egypt, which he deemed irrelevant for the history of Israelite religion. It seems unfortunate, to say the least, that such a pioneer in the field of Old Testament scholarship should have been content to erect his theoretical formulations on only a portion of the available evidence, particularly when the cuneiform sources from Mesopotamia and the hieroglyphic inscriptions from Egypt were already being studied by scholars with reference to the religion of the Hebrews. As the result of a much wider acquaintance with Near Eastern archaeology, it is now possible to say, with Kaufmann, that the prehistory of Israelite religion is not to be sought in primitive or Bedouin sources, but in the mellowed civilizations of the ancient Near East.[1]

Again, it is extremely doubtful that it is justifiable to apply the metaphors of growth and progress that Wellhausen borrowed from biological sources to religious phenomena. Comparative studies in the area of religious development have shown clearly that "primitive" and "advanced" conceptions of deity can co-exist in the mind of any one individual without apparently being mutually exclusive.[2] Furthermore, the way in which Wellhausen thought of the growth of Israelite religion from rudimentary beginnings to an advanced monotheism is completely contrary in significant areas to the Old Testament interpretation of its own history. This attitude of course requires that the Biblical narratives be taken at something like face value, a procedure that is still anathema to many liberal scholars, or at best is regarded as fraught with danger for all save the most wary. At the risk of repudiating the evolutionism of an earlier phase of Old Testament scholarship, however, it should be observed that the Old Testament narratives saw the historical process as anything but an ordered and progressive development like that contemplated by Wellhausen. Instead, the Old Testament writers consistently thought of their history as a dynamistic confrontation of humanity by the divine Word against a background of revealed monotheism.

Fundamental to this activity was the reminder that, as a supremely moral Being, God would judge the nation for its lack of fidelity to the terms of the Sinaitic Covenant, and that, if the nation persisted in its reprobate ways, it would be rejected as the social instrument of divine revelation to the world. Complementary to this, however, was the self-consistency of God, which required that He should not utterly cast off the people with whom He was bound by the Covenant relationship, but rather that He should purify and re-create them as a unified instrument for conveying His blessing to mankind. To the objection that these conclusions represent the shape into which Hebrew historical material was cast by later scribes and interpreters, it must merely be said that such a view results from an uncritical acceptance of *a priori* evolutionary

---

[1] *KRI*, p. 221.
[2] Cf. I. Engnell, *Gamla Testamentet*, I, p. 111; E. O. James, *The OT in the Light of Anthropology* (1934), pp. 83ff., *Comparative Religion* (1938), p. 11.

and literary-critical theories of sources, which require the appearance of ethical monotheism at the end, rather than at the beginning or during the middle of the process. Modern scholarship is no longer able to sustain the sharp contrast between the Prophets and the Law that was commonly asserted by the older school of liberal criticism.

Whatever may be thought of the difference in degree between the monotheistic outlook of the Mosaic period and the corresponding teaching contained in the prophetical writings, there can be little doubt, as Anderson has stated, that the latter was already in large measure implicit in the older faith.[3] One unfortunate result of the application of growth-metaphors to Old Testament study is the common misunderstanding that requires the subject always to be appraised in terms of an ascending series of values. The dynamistic interpretation of history that the Old Testament narratives contained meant that, as a result of the mighty acts of God, the elect people were challenged to reconsider the significance of their Covenant relationship to Him. This standpoint, as Wright has indicated, cannot easily be accommodated to a single metaphor such as that of growth.[4] The plain fact is that history cannot be viewed either as a collection of chance occurrences or as a chain of mechanically related happenings. Historical sequences are composed, rightly or wrongly, of a vast complex of interacting social, political, and religious patterns that are in continuous flux. As such they cannot be compressed into the framework of a strictly deterministic theory, nor can they be interpreted satisfactorily in terms of so rigid a method as that of Hegelian dialectic,[5] useful though these approaches may be for certain phases of historical investigation.

B. Animism

Recent investigation shows that the interpretation of the earliest phases of Hebrew religion in terms of animism, polydaemonism and the like, which was basic to the Hegelian-Wellhausenian concept,[6] requires considerable modification. It is now evident from the comparative study of ancient Near Eastern literature and from archaeological sources that animism disappeared from the oriental world centuries before the Hebrew patriarchs appeared upon the historical scene. As Wright indicated in his criticism of the developmental theme expounded by Oesterley and Robinson, the animism and polydaemonism which were thought to have characterized the religious activities of the patriarchs and their pagan contemporaries were in fact survivals from the Neolithic period.[7] Just as

[3] *OTMS*, p. 290.
[4] *The OT Against Its Environment*, p. 11.
[5] *ARI*, p. 3.
[6] *FSAC*, p. 88.
[7] *The OT Against Its Environment*, p. 12 n. 6.

is the case with the perpetuation of ancient elements in more modern religions, it is now regarded as extremely doubtful that the true meaning of these remnants was appreciated at all during the later stages of their existence, so that their continued survival was predominantly the result of religious conservatism.

These considerations have been brought into clearer perspective as a result of archaeological activity in Mesopotamia, where accredited temples dating from the end of the fifth or the beginning of the fourth millennium B.C. have been unearthed from the 'Ubaid period at sites such as Tepe Gawra, Eridu, and Uruk. The earliest Chalcolithic shrines at Tell Halaf consisted of a single circular chamber, whereas somewhat later structures were comparable to those of the pre-pottery Neolithic phase at Jericho, with a rectangular anteroom built into the main structure. From these ruins were recovered rough models of domestic animals, as well as a number of human figurines which generally depicted the nude female body with exaggerated sexual organs in a manner similar to that encountered among the Aurignacians and other cave-dwellers.[8]

Pre-pottery Neolithic levels at Jericho yielded a building that appears to have been a shrine. Among other relics it contained some plastic studies of groups of human beings, each containing what seems to have been a father, mother, and child.[9] These artifacts alone should suggest that an animistic phase had long since passed, a conclusion that is reinforced by the highly developed polytheism that characterized the religions of Egypt and Mesopotamia in the third millennium B.C. The Mesopotamians of this period had already applied categories of personality to the great cosmic powers that dominated their pantheon, and were worshipping them in temples that were regarded as the earthly residence of the deities.[10] In Egypt, the authoritarian head of the pantheon was the creator and sun-deity Re, whose cult had flourished in Lower Egypt prior to the First Dynasty and had influenced the conception of kingship in that area.[11] In Canaan, the supreme being was the deity El, whose offspring Baal wielded executive power among gods and men alike. Thus the stage of Hebrew religious formulation represented by the patriarchal period must be related to a comparatively sophisticated cultural situation, far different from the primitive superstitions that Wellhausen associated with the early Bedouin tribes.

Modern anthropological research has also demonstrated the antiquity of human belief in "High Gods," whose powers were considered to be

---

[8] *FSAC*, p. 132.
[9] *FSAC*, p. 135; *LAP*, p. 122.
[10] T. Jacobsen in *Encyclopedia of Religion* (ed. V. Ferm, 1945), pp. 770f.
[11] Cf. G. Roeder, *Urkunden zur Religion des alten Ägypten* (1915), p. 108.

universal.[12] In ancient Mesopotamia the adherents of polytheism described their reactions to the universe and their deities in what has been called "mythopoeic" language.[13] By viewing happenings as individual events, they personalized the qualities and will of the phenomena with which they were confronted, and cloaked their essential truth by means of a literary structure approaching the form of a myth, or better still, of an allegory. Since natural occurrences were understood in terms of human experience, the confrontation of man by environmental forces involved a mode of cognition far transcending that normally accorded animism in primitive cultures.

For the Babylonians this premise found its logical conclusion in the *akîtu* festival, a yearly re-enactment of a ritual designed to secure for the participants an identification with the ruling powers of the cosmos, and an assurance that the life of society was once again in harmony with the activities of nature.[14] Even in its earliest form, such a religious expression represented a much more advanced stage than was implied by the animistic concepts of Wellhausen. There may be some ground for the belief that, as Hooke suggested, an animistic phase of Mesopotamian religion can be seen in the Babylonian preoccupation with the spirits of the deceased, and perhaps also in connection with the amulets and clay figurines recovered by archaeologists from Babylonian sites.[15] However, it should be noted that, in connection with the latter, the "teraphim" were apparently related in some manner to rights of primogeniture in cultures such as those of Mari and Nuzu, and this may well indicate other than purely animistic origins.[16]

There seems to be little doubt that alleged remnants of animism discovered in Hebrew religion by some modern writers have been greatly exaggerated, if not actually misinterpreted. Although it is true that in the religion of Israel, as with the faith of other peoples, there may be a number of primitive survivals whose precise origin defies explanation, an attempt to construct from their incidence what might be regarded as a system of early Hebrew religion is no more valid than it would be to apply the same process to the known religions of Near Eastern antiquity. The accredited animistic traces that may be discerned in these systems belong to the remote past, and as far as the sophisticated culture of the patriarchal period in Mesopotamia is concerned, it is probable that the original meaning of most animistic survivals had even then been long obscured with the passing of time.

[12] E.g. W. Schmidt, *High Gods in North America* (1933), pp. 129ff., *Der Ursprung der Gottesidee* (1926-34), I, pp. 632ff., V, pp. 473ff.
[13] T. Jacobsen, *IAAM*, pp. 8ff.
[14] *Ibid.*, pp. 199f.
[15] S. H. Hooke, *Babylonian and Assyrian Religion* (1953), p. 23.
[16] *IOTT*, p. 117.

Even though it may be agreed that such Old Testament place names as En Mishpat and En-gedi indicated important sources of water, it is surely going beyond the available evidence to suggest that they constituted oracle-wells or that they were subsequently venerated as sites where a divine revelation had been given. In Palestine, where copious supplies of fresh water are seldom assured, any well is an important location, and the idea of "decision" inherent in the ancient name "En Mishpat" need commemorate nothing more than the kind of pastoralist agreement that took place between Abraham and Lot (Gen. 13:7ff.).

Certainly there are no real grounds for thinking that the patriarchs named such sites against a background of animistic superstition, since it is quite probable that they took over the traditional designations from the Canaanites in the first instance, and subsequently renamed them. The attempt to explain the name Beer-Sheba as "well of seven spirits" is fanciful, and Driver was correct in associating the name with the plurality of wells in that district.[17] The true significance of the designation, which means "well of the oath" (Gen. 21:31), was amply illustrated by Robertson Smith, who showed that the Hebrew term "to swear" (שׁבע) means literally "to come under the influence of seven things."[18]

Similar misinterpretations may well apply to sites associated with the names of trees, such as Elon Moreh or Elon Meonenim. The first of these was apparently a familiar landmark in Shechem, and from the reference in Genesis 12:6 it would seem to have derived its name from Canaanite sources. If the tree in question was in fact an evergreen, its value as a shady resting-place in the heat of the day will be immediately evident to any who have travelled in Palestine. The fact that Abraham here received a divine manifestation and later erected an altar to mark the site is coincidental, since he also received other revelations at locations unconnected with trees, and which were also marked by means of wayside altars. In connection with the second, or "diviner's terebinth," mentioned in Judges 9:37, the reference is again to Canaanite origins, and although it may be that apostate Israelites of the Judges period participated in soothsaying at that site, there is no factual evidence for such a supposition, or for the view that the location, which is unknown, had any connection, animistic or other, with the worship of the patriarchal period.

A similar criticism may be levelled against the kind of theory maintained by Robertson Smith in connection with the well addressed in the poetic fragment in Numbers 21:17f.[19] Arguing from late Bedouin counterparts, he held that the well was being venerated as the embodi-

---

[17] G. A. Smith, *EB*, I, col. 518, following A. von Gall, *Altisraelische Kultstätten* (1898), pp. 44ff.; S. R. Driver, *The Book of Genesis* (1904), p. 215.

[18] *Lectures on the Religion of the Semites*, p. 182.

[19] *Ibid.*, p. 169 n. 3; cf. H. Gressmann, *Mose und seine Zeit* (1913), pp. 349f.

ment of a supernatural force.[20] In point of fact, the stanza that commemorated the occasion when an underground source of water was successfully tapped need have no more significance than that attached to the rejoicing which takes place in modern times when an arduous effort of excavation for a water supply is similarly rewarded. This little section of poetry appears to be of the same general kind as the vintage lyrics sung by those who were treading out the grapes at the harvest season (cf. Isa. 16:10; Jer. 25:30). The fact that this fragment occurred in a poetic section should be sufficient warning against mistaking for animism what may probably be nothing more than poetic license. Since the ancient Egyptians regularly personified a wide range of objects without at the same time assigning to them the structure of divinity,[21] it may well be that the original author of the passage in Numbers was following precisely the same literary practice, thereby testifying indirectly to the antiquity of the composition.

Equally suspect is the assertion, commonly found among an earlier generation of interpreters of early Hebrew religious tendencies, that a reference to activity related in some manner to trees indicates a clear survival of animism. Thus a person such as Deborah the prophetess, who dispensed judgment for Israel from the shade of a palm tree in the hill-country of Ephraim (Judg. 4:4f.), or King Saul, who held court under a pomegranate tree (1 Sam. 14:2), received inspiration not from the balanced exercise of ratiocinative activity but from the rustling of the leaves above, and this was thought to indicate the nature of the decision to be given. The inadequacy of such a view is immediately apparent from the fact that there is no suggestion anywhere in the Old Testament that prophets or prophetesses were unable to function in the absence of certain material concomitants. The staff of Moses constituted the symbol of his authority and was not the source of his inspiration or power. In the same way, the mantle of Elijah was a characteristic of the man himself, and when it was assumed by Elisha it merely constituted a token of the fact that the inheritance of the first-born (cf. 2 Kgs. 2:9) was henceforward to typify his prophetic activities. The literary sources make it clear that Deborah was a stern adherent of the Sinai Covenant, who never countenanced the paganism of the indigenous population for one moment. Similarly, the early days of the reign of Saul were completely devoid of idolatry, as the narratives that describe the period indicate, and it was only at the very end of his life, when under acute stress and beset by a serious psychotic condition, that he indulged in an activity which he had previously banned from his kingdom (1 Sam. 28:3ff.).

[20] Cf. Oesterley and Robinson, *Hebrew Religion: Its Origin and Development*, p. 38.

[21] *IAAM*, p. 41.

For these and other similar occurrences in the Old Testament there would seem to be a much simpler and more logical explanation. In the countries of the Near East, an outdoor situation is much more tolerable in the shade of a leafy tree than in the heat of a burning sun, a scorching desert wind, or even the doubtful shelter of a tent-doorway. Indeed, it is almost impossible to overestimate the value of trees in that part of the world, a fact that appears to have been impressed upon the minds of its ancient inhabitants, judging from the appreciative references to trees in the Bible and other Near Eastern literature. Unfortunately, simple explanations of this kind seldom commend themselves to those who are determined to find evidence in the written sources for preconceived notions or *a priori* theories in connection with the alleged animistic and polydaemonistic background of patriarchal and early Hebrew religion generally.

C. Totemism

The success of Robertson Smith's attempts to accommodate totemistic concepts to the growth of early Hebrew religion was questioned from the time that his *Kinship and Marriage in Early Arabia* appeared in print. Two of his most noteworthy critics were Lagrange and König, who pointedly repudiated any suggestion that any remnants of totemism could be found in the Old Testament narratives.[22] It must be admitted that the gravest deficiency of a theory of a totemistic stage in Hebrew religious development was its imperfect understanding of the nature and distribution of totemism in primitive religions. Although totemism occurs in such widely diverse parts of the world as North America, Australia, and Africa, it cannot on that account be regarded as a universal stage of religious development.[23] From variations of procedure with respect to the venerated animal or plant species in various parts of the world, it would appear that in some instances totemism is a social custom rather than a religious one. Generally speaking, anthropologists incline to the belief that, where totemism flourishes, it fosters the growth of more advanced spiritual concepts by lending a degree of religious sanction to interpersonal obligations and tribal loyalties.

The Wellhausenian school did not realize fully that the fact that animals were sometimes associated mythologically or otherwise with the gods of a national religion did not necessarily prove that such a religion had passed through a totemistic phase. For them it was comparatively simple to point to the place of animals in the cults of Egypt and Greece, without at the same time appreciating that such a phenomenon need only indicate a primitive animal worship. The religion of ancient

---

[22] M. J. Lagrange, *Études sur les Religions sémitiques* (1903), pp. 112ff.; E. König, *Geschichte der alttestamentlichen Religion* (1924), pp. 72ff.
[23] G. Galloway, *The Philosophy of Religion* (1914), p. 97.

Egypt in particular was taken as a prime example of developed totemism, especially since all the early deities were associated with some specific plant or animal that constituted the visible aspect of social unity.[24] Yet when the literary sources of ancient Egypt were studied carefully, it became apparent that nothing comparable to the totemism of Australia, North America, or Africa had ever existed in Egypt.

As Frankfort has pointed out, the characteristic features of totemism, such as the claim of descent from the totem, its sacrifice among certain tribes so as to provide a ceremonial feast for the clan, and the insistence upon exogamy, the prohibition of marriage within the clan, cannot be discovered in Egyptian sources.[25] Although early Egyptian religion might have possessed the basic attitudes from which some form of totemism or fetishism could have emerged, it seems more probable that it was in fact simple animal worship, since in Egypt the animal as such appears to have possessed enormous religious significance, regardless of its specific nature. This contention is reinforced by the consideration that during those periods when religion passed through phases of decadence, animal worship came very much to the fore in Egypt, as evidenced by the numerous cemeteries filled with mummified cats, crocodiles, dogs, bulls, and other animals.

If there are grounds for questioning the existence of a genuine totemistic phase in the religious development of ancient Egypt, there are even more reasons for disputing its existence in Mesopotamia. Whereas most early Egyptian name-deities were associated in some manner with an animal or plant, there is virtually no trace of this phenomenon in early Mesopotamian religion. The names of a few Sumerian deities such as Shagan, the serpent-god, and Gud, the bull-deity, reflected some vague linking of animals and gods,[26] but in the main the Sumerian deities were anthropomorphic in character.[27] Whether one studies the Sumerian spiritual tradition or its modification by the later Babylonians, the religion of Mesopotamia conveys the impression of having appeared in a comparatively advanced stage of development from the time of its inception. Certainly it contains nothing that would correspond strictly to a totemistic phase as part of that process of growth.

In the light of these observations it would appear very unlikely that specifically totemistic survivals can be demonstrated in the Old Testament. Having regard to the elements necessary for proof of the existence of totemism in any race or culture,[28] it must be observed at once that nowhere in the Old Testament does the concept that the members of a

---

[24] J. Černý, *Ancient Egyptian Religion* (1952), pp. 19ff.

[25] H. Frankfort, *Ancient Egyptian Religion* (1961 ed.), p. 9; cf. *FSAC*, pp. 178f.

[26] *ARI*, p. 27.

[27] *FSAC*, pp. 192f.

[28] W. Robertson Smith, *Kinship and Marriage in Early Arabia*, p. 219.

particular stock have been derived from the blood of an eponym animal appear. Nor is there any evidence of the belief that the members of a clan with an animal name such as Simeon (*hyena?*) were actually the offspring of the totem animal. Despite the elaborate explanations that G. Buchanan Gray offered for the origin of proper names among the ancient Hebrews,[29] the fact is that very little is known for certain about the process. In view of the absence from the Old Testament writings of the two most important elements in any totemistic system, namely, the claim of descent from the totem and its ceremonial sacrifice among certain tribes, it seems improbable that clan names became in certain cases personal designations "with the break-up of the totem clan system" as Gray suggested.

Biblical records from the patriarchal period indicate that certain individuals were likened to animals with regard to temperament or characteristic attitudes; these included Judah (Gen. 49:9), Issachar (Gen. 49:14), Dan (Gen. 49:17), Naphtali (Gen. 49:21), and Benjamin (Gen. 49:27). In the same way others were compared with the behavior of water, such as Reuben (Gen. 49:4), or with a spreading tree beside a well, as in the case of Joseph (Gen. 49:22). When Hagar received an announcement from the divine messenger, she was promised that her son Ishmael would be "a wild ass of a man" (Gen. 16:12), a complimentary designation indeed, since the wild ass had its habitat in the desert areas and as such was the choicest beast of the entire hunt.[30] In each instance the emphasis appears to have been on the character or physical attributes of the animal or plant concerned and has no reference, overt or explicit, to either animism or totemism. Again, however, a plain reading of the text in the light of the social customs of that remote age will hardly satisfy those who are determined to find evidence for their theories in the Old Testament narratives.

D. Tabu

It is possible to adduce from Semitic sources a number of usages that might fall under the heading of tabu, such as lists of animals associated with certain deities.[31] However, it is a mistake to suppose that similar lists in Leviticus (11:2ff.) and Deuteronomy (14:4ff.) reflected a primitive tabu against human consumption of sacred animal species. In these Biblical sources the concern was essentially a dietetic and hygienic one, of a kind completely unique and entirely lacking in other ancient Near Eastern literature. Before the forbidden species were enumerated there was set forth the general principle by which those deemed suitable for human consumption could be recognized empirically. There was no need

---

[29] *Hebrew Proper Names*, pp. 85ff.
[30] *IOTT*, p. 105.
[31] Cf. M. Jastrow, *Die Religion Babyloniens und Assyriens*, II, pp. 896f., 933ff.

for either magic or priestly counsel in this matter, and when the list is examined in the light of modern medical science it is seen to be of a remarkably advanced nature, embodying fundamental principles of health and human well-being.

Those species that were prohibited are liable to parasitic infection of various kinds, and as such are unsuitable for food, particularly where the danger of epidemic disease is an ever-present reality.[32] The attempt made by Robertson Smith to relate the Levitical prohibitions to pagan tabu concepts by stating that "the unclean creatures therefore are the divine animals of the heathen; such animals as the latter did not ordinarily eat or sacrifice"[33] is vitiated by the observation that the clean species in the Levitical lists were also prominent in the religious veneration of pagan cult-worship, showing that considerations other than those of tabu were being envisaged by the ancient author.

E. ANCESTOR WORSHIP

Since the time of Wellhausen the extent to which traces of ancestor worship can be detected in the Old Testament has been a matter of much controversy. In the main, those who supported this position related it to a totemistic phase, in which the totem-ancestor gradually developed into a human progenitor who subsequently became divine.[34] On the other hand there were scholars who disputed the interpretation of the data adduced in support of ancestor worship, and maintained that the evidence admitted of a different explanation. Thus Vincent argued from the available archaeological material that the care for the dead, rather than a cult-worship of the deceased, was the prepossessing concern of the relevant Old Testament narratives.[35]

Margoliouth conceded that the importance of practices relating to the dead had been greatly exaggerated, and stated flatly that there was no ground for assuming that ancestor worship was the only or even the chief religion of pre-Mosaic Israel.[36] Kautzsch, following Carl Gruneisen, denied that traces of a primitive ancestor worship could be found in the Old Testament, and pointed out that the mourning customs

---

[32] Cf. A. R. Short, *The Bible and Modern Medicine* (1953), pp. 40ff.; R. K. Harrison, *IDB*, II, pp. 543f.

[33] W. Robertson Smith, *Kinship and Marriage in Early Arabia*, p. 311.

[34] Cf. R. Goldhizer, *Culte des Ancêtres chez les Arabes* (1885), p. 15 *passim;* B. Stade, *Geschichte des Volkes Israel*, I, pp. 387ff.; *Biblische Theologie des AT* (1905), I, pp. 104ff.; J. Wellhausen, *Reste Arabischen Heidentums*, pp. 183ff.; G. Hölscher, *Geschichte der Israelitischen und Jüdischen Religion* (1922), pp. 24ff.; S. A. Cook in *Lectures on the Religion of the Semites*, pp. 508ff., 544ff.; S. A. Cook, *The Religion of Ancient Palestine in the Second Millennium B.C. in the Light of Archaeology and Inscriptions* (1908), pp. 57ff.

[35] A. Vincent, *Canaan d'après l'Exploration Récente* (1907), pp. 288ff.

[36] G. Margoliouth, *ERE*, I, p. 449.

belonged to different grades of thought, with some of them defying all attempts at explanation.[37]

Oesterley enumerated the mourning practices which he regarded as indicative of the remnants of ancestor worship among the Hebrews, including the cutting of the hair, the wearing of sackcloth, baring of the feet, fasting, and the like.[38] What he did not make clear was that, when the Hebrew prophets were inveighing against mourning customs, they were in fact condemning specific Canaanite elements such as laceration.[39] Pentateuchal sources regarded both contact with the dead and formal mourning itself as occasioning ritual or ceremonial defilement. Levitical law permitted the Aaronic priesthood to mourn by rending the clothing, weeping, and allowing the hair to flow freely (Lev. 21:1ff.), but these privileges were forbidden to the High Priest (Lev. 21:10f.). Both priests and people were prohibited from lacerating bodily tissues, trimming off the corners of the beard and the sides of the head, eating tithes as an act of mourning, or offering them on behalf of the dead (cf. Lev. 21:5; 29:27f.; Deut. 14:1; 26:14), all of which were associated with heathen Canaanite worship. Weeping and lamentation, the use of ashes, and the wearing of sackcloth were not prohibited by Hebrew ceremonial law.

The use of tribal or personal names in which an element of the designation of deity occurred is not necessarily an indication of a prior stage of ancestor worship, as some scholars have imagined. While the origin of certain of these names in the Hebrew Bible is unknown, others clearly reflect an association with a theophany or some other significant event. Thus Ishmael, meaning "God hears," was significant to Hagar because of the assurance it carried that God had heard her cry of affliction (Gen. 16:10), and despite the fact that the generic designation "El" formed part of the name, it carried no connotation whatever of the divinity of any ancestor. Even compound forms such as Baal-gad (Josh. 11:17; 12:7; 13:5) designated territory which had been named jointly in honor of the Canaanite storm-deity and the god of Fortune (cf. Isa. 65:11), and had no reference whatever to intermediate human ancestors.

An equally indiscriminate use of evidence is that by Oesterley and Robinson, who argued from the association of altars with the general location of the burial places of Sarah (cf. Gen. 13:18; 18:1; 23:1), Deborah (Gen. 35:8), and others to the postulate that, among ancient peoples, if the grave of an ancestor was a sanctuary, it meant that the

---

[37] E. Kautzsch, *HDB*, extra vol., p. 614; C. Gruneisen, *Der Ahnenkultus und die Urreligion Israels* (1900).

[38] W. O. E. Oesterley, *Immortality and the Unseen World*, pp. 141ff.

[39] For Ugaritic epic parallels cf. *DOTT*, p. 130.

ancestor was being worshipped.[40] This is by no means the case, for it surely indicates that the god of the sanctuary was the foremost object of worship, and that the dead were interred in the locality precisely because it had sacred associations. Thus the deceased members of the family were by implication committed into the care of the deity, and if anything of a more developed nature is to be understood by such activity, the tendency of thought is not so much a reflection of ancestor worship as a groping of the human mind towards some concept of life after death.

In general it may be observed that there is an all-too-common confusion between respect for the departed and a cult of ancestor worship in the minds of certain scholars. Many peoples, both ancient and modern, indulge in burial customs whose significance can be easily and inadvertently misinterpreted, and it is particularly unfortunate when contemporary tendencies and attitudes are projected into the past in an attempt to explain ancient customs. In this connection the contribution of archaeology serves as an important corrective. Although there are many instances where it can throw no light whatever upon archaic attitudes, there are others where it serves to clarify the issue for the occidental mind. One of these is connected with the teraphim as alleged survivals of ancestor worship. From archaeological data it is evident that in the patriarchal period the teraphim were small portable idols the possession of which indicated, among other things, inheritance rights.[41]

F. The Limitations of These Influences

Any attempt to assess the nature of pre-Mosaic religion will need to take cognizance of the much wider range of evidence in the comparative study of religion than was available for Wellhausen and his immediate followers. There will probably be few who would dispute the view expressed by Waterhouse that Tylor made a "brilliant guess" in formulating the concept of animism as one of the most primitive stages of religion.[42] On the other hand there will be those who will urge that Tylor was much too comprehensive and speculative in his conjectures, and that the application of his theories to Semitic religion by Robertson Smith was too rigid, and went beyond the available evidence. More recent study has shown that any dynamistic or animistic phase which may have existed in

[40] W. O. E. Oesterley and T. H. Robinson, *Hebrew Religion: Its Origin and Development*, p. 100.

[41] C. H. Gordon, *IDB*, IV, p. 574, *BA*, III, No. 1 (1940), pp. 1ff.; *IOTT*, pp. 116f.; A. E. Draffkorn, *JBL*, LXXVI (1957), pp. 216ff.

[42] E. S. Waterhouse, *The Dawn of Religion* (1936), p. 31.

ancient Near Eastern life had ended centuries before the patriarchal period commenced, as has been observed earlier.

Furthermore, the concept of animism as understood classically has been modified significantly with regard to the nature of Mesopotamian and Egyptian religion. Elements of life that were personified have been shown to represent the counterpart of an emotional or dynamic reciprocal relationship in which the "I" of selfhood was confronted not by an "it," but by a "Thou" of the phenomenal world. The scope of this relationship can be gathered from the remark of Wilson to the effect that it is difficult to think of any phenomenon with which ancient man might not have had a "Thou" relationship, as exemplified by Egyptian scenes and texts.[43] Or, as Frankfort himself commented, "Primitive man simply does not know an inanimate world. For this very reason he does not 'personify' inanimate phenomena nor does he fill an empty world with the ghosts of the dead, as 'animism' would have us believe."[44] No longer is it merely a question of human behavior's being affected by anything that possessed such innate activity as to suggest that it was animated by its own life and motivating force. Now it is clear that the initiative lay with man, who tended to personalize phenomena, and in the process of confrontation assigned categories of individuality and will to the manifold aspects of life surrounding him.[45]

If it is increasingly difficult to interpret pre-Mosaic religion in terms of animism, it is even more so in terms of totemism, for which there appears to be very little warrant in the early Biblical narratives. As far as the theory of an underlying phase of ancestor worship is concerned, the available evidence lends itself to more than one interpretation, and as a result the extent of its influence in early Israelite religion is very questionable. Although the elements of tabu and polytheism that marked ancient Near Eastern religious life are reflected in varying degrees in the Old Testament records, this is not to say that the restrictions upon Hebrew life established by religious sanction were derived in principle or content from Near Eastern sources, nor that Israelite religion had at one time passed through a polytheistic stage.

Though there may be aspects of early Hebrew religious life that present certain similarities to animism, it seems fairly assured in the light of more recent study that they were not understood by the ancients in the sense attributed to them by the Wellhausenian school. Indeed it is probable that many of the ancient ritual practices of Mesopotamia and Egypt had long outlived their original

[43] J. A. Wilson, *IAAM*, p. 41

[44] *IAAM*, pp. 5f.

[45] *ARI*, p. 27.

significance before the patriarchs appeared on the historical scene, a point that has been mentioned above. In the view of what is known about the highly developed cultural forms of Near Eastern antiquity, it seems best to conclude with Kaufmann that the "initial level [of Israelite religion] was not magical, totemistic, animistic, or demonistic; it originated among developed theistic religions."[46]

[46] *KRI*, p. 221.

IV. THE HISTORY OF OLD TESTAMENT RELIGION

Although the narratives of the Pentateuch convey the impression that the Hebrew patriarchs followed a monotheistic religious tradition, it is made evident in Joshua 24:2 that they were involved in Mesopotamian polytheism to some extent at least.[1] Certainly the Biblical narratives lend no support to the idea that Abraham originated the idea of monotheism, or that he established a monotheistic cult within the framework of his own society. Instead, Abraham was portrayed as the ancestor of that nation which was destined to become monotheistic. Although much is known about the religious practices and beliefs of the contemporary Mesopotamians, little detailed material concerning patriarchal religion is forthcoming from the Genesis narratives. This is rather unfortunate, since they constitute the only records of patriarchal faith and practice, although certain other elements of the corpus can be illustrated from contemporary Mesopotamian sources.

The patriarchs were clearly depicted as objects of divine revelation (Gen. 12:1, 7; 15:1), who were convinced of the necessity for a personal faith-relationship with the Deity. Once this had been established, the patriarchs could look confidently to their God for protection and sustenance throughout life (Gen. 15:4ff.; 17:1ff.; 28:11ff.). On receipt of divine guidance they had no option but to obey the revealed will of God (Gen. 22:3ff.). Circumcision was adopted as a religious rite to mark out specifically those who were included in the Covenant relationship. This act appears to have had a particular significance in designating the ancestors of Israel as a distinctive unit, since it is known that, unlike the Egyptians, the ancient inhabitants of Babylonia and Assyria did not practice the rite.[2] The closeness of their relationship with the Deity caused the patriarchs to commemorate divine beneficence in the names of certain of their offspring, or in the designations of specific localities where a revelation had been given (Gen. 16:11, 14; 32:30; 35:15). The

---

[1] Contrary to J. Muilenburg, *IB*, I, p. 296, who assigned patriarchal religion to a Canaanite milieu.

[2] J. P. Hyatt, *IDB*, I, p. 629.

pattern of worship during the patriarchal age included sacrifice and the offering of prayer to God (Gen. 12:8; 26:25).

The emphasis upon the special quality of the relationship between the individual patriarchs and the Deity seems to have been preserved in the particular names for God that were a feature of this period. As Bright has indicated, the religion of the patriarchs was quite different in character from the paganism of the surrounding nations.[3] The personal deity of the clan-chief was the god of the entire clan, as illustrated by such archaic titles for God as the "Shield" of Abraham (cf. Gen. 15:1; 31:53), the "Kinsman" of Isaac (Gen. 31:42),[4] and the "Champion" of Jacob (Gen. 49:24). As Alt has shown, the deliberate choice of God by each successive generation of patriarchs represents an extremely ancient religious concept that is thoroughly consistent with the Biblical tradition.[5] The place of the deity as the "father" or "brother" of the worshipper was also enshrined in such personal names as Abiram ("the Exalted One is my father"), Abimelech ("the King is my father"), and Ahiram ("the Exalted One is my brother"). It was to such a deity that the clan members, following the lead of the patriarchal head, gave supreme if perhaps not always complete devotion.

Hebrew personal names containing some appellation of deity and clan have been paralleled by a similar usage in Mesopotamia during the Old Akkadian period (ca. 2360-2180 B.C.) and in the Amorite names occurring between 2100 and 1600 B.C.[6] Albright has concluded that the pre-Mosaic religion of the Hebrews envisaged the deity in terms of mountain-imagery. For example, the name El Shaddai may have meant originally "the god of the mountains."[7] Albright interprets this against the general Mesopotamian background of the patriarchs, where among the Amorites the mountain-deity Hadad, associated with winds and storms, was a venerated member of the pantheon. However, he also recognized that the God of the patriarchs was not restricted to one particular locality, but to a family that stood in a special relationship of obedience and faith to Him and whose interests He was pledged to protect.[8] Thus, whatever the pagan antecedents of El Shaddai and other analogous terms may have been, if any, there was for the patriarchs no concept of nature-religion as such and no hint that the deity had ever been displaced from an association with a specific locality in favor of a

[3] J. Bright, *IDB*, II, p. 561.
[4] Cf. *FSAC*, p. 248.
[5] Cf. A. Alt, *Der Gott der Väter* (1929), pp. 40ff.; W. F. Albright, *JBL*, LIV (1935), pp. 188ff.
[6] *FSAC*, pp. 243ff.
[7] *FSAC*, pp. 245f.
[8] Cf. B. W. Anderson, *IDB*, II, p. 412; H. G. May, *JBL*, LX (1941), p. 113, *The Journal of Bible and Religion*, IX (1941), pp. 155ff.

connection with a particular social group, in the manner in which Alt had thought of the growth of primitive tribal religion.[9]

Although Albright is probably correct in asserting that there was no "El-monotheism" current among the early western Semites, there is no evidence for his contention that early Hebrew popular religion was organized in terms of a triad of father, mother, and son, after the Neolithic pattern of plastic statues in triads.[10] At no time in patriarchal religion was there the slightest hint of a female component of deity, and the same is true of the period of the Sinai Covenant. Though the God of the Hebrews might be associated with several titles, there was never any suggestion as to plurality or multiplicity in the personage of the Deity. Insofar as plural forms occurred in Hebrew names for God or in titles relating to the Godhead, they were not so much vestigial remains of an earlier stage of polytheism as grammatical structures designed to emphasize the majesty of the God who was being described. Although Alt tended consistently to associate the primitive deity with a particular locality, he was nevertheless correct in assuming that the divine appellations compounded with "El" in the patriarchal narratives were genuinely pre-Israelite in nature.[11] The antiquity of this practice in west-Semitic religion has been further illustrated by the presence in Ugaritic literature of the titles *Elyon, Olam,* and *Ro'i* as designations of deity.

The traditions that underlie the religious attitudes of the patriarchs can thus be seen to be of great antiquity. In essence their faith involved a sense of personal relationship with the Deity, an awareness that implicit obedience to the divine will was an essential element in the continuity of that relationship, and a degree of spiritual insight that enabled them to assess the nature and significance of the divine promises. Vivid though the patriarchal experience of God appears to have been, it is very doubtful if it can be described consistently as a "real blood relationship between a family or clan and its god" as Albright has done.[12] Albright's language is reminiscent of the attempts of other scholars to establish a totemistic phase in Hebrew religion, an approach which he has repudiated elsewhere.[13] The only blood relationship that existed between a worshipper and the Deity during the patriarchal period was strictly poetic, as represented in certain of the proper names discussed above; and this situation did not hold good for all families or clans by any means. Although the patriarchs worshipped the same deity under a variety of names, he was no mere local numen but the patron of the clan. Despite alleged monotheistic tendencies in the second-millennium

[9] Alt, *Der Gott der Väter,* p. 33.
[10] FSAC, pp. 173, 247.
[11] Alt, *Der Gott der Väter,* pp. 49ff.
[12] FSAC, p. 249.
[13] FSAC, p. 93.

B.C. religious life of Mesopotamia, it does not seem possible to describe the patriarchs as anything more than monolatrists.

B. THE RELIGION OF MOSES

The origin of historical monotheism must thus be considered in the light of those events which occurred in the Mosaic era. The Biblical sources for this period have been assigned a much greater degree of historicity within recent years than was formerly the case in some scholarly circles. Unfortunately it is still true that others are hampered by an uncritical acceptance of the Wellhausenian dictum that Pentateuchal sources are relatively late and represent a long tradition of oral transmission. Be that as it may, there can be little doubt that Moses established the religious system of Israel, and that the uniform witness of Old Testament tradition to this fact is reliable.

Equally certain is the form of the Divine Name יהוה, which was revealed to Moses. Although this tetragrammaton is often thought to have been pronounced *Yahweh,* following Greek transcriptions such as those of Clement of Alexandria and Theodoret, the fact is that the original pronunciation is unknown, and all attempts to reconstruct it have so far proved conjectural.[14] A shorter form of the Divine Name may have circulated either as "Yah," "Yahu," or "Yo," and although some have thought that one or another of these may have been earlier than the tetragrammaton, the presence of the latter in ancient poetic fragments of the Old Testament as well as in extra-Biblical material such as the Moabite Stone seems to imply that the four-letter form was the original. Attempts to show that the sacred name was known before the time of Moses by adducing as evidence Akkadian personal names such as *Yaum-Ilu* (Mine is the god), or the alleged presence of "Yo" in one of the texts from Ugarit[15] have been unsuccessful to date.

The Kenite hypothesis, which suggested that Moses learned of the Divine Name through marriage into the family of Jethro (Exod. 2:15ff.) and subsequent initiation into the Midian cult of *YHWH,* has certain elements in its favor, but it lacks decisive evidence in terms of the text. In the first instance it is clear that the God of Israel was explicitly the God of the patriarchs, and not exclusively of their Kenite cousins. Secondly, the traditional translation of the revelation of the name *YHWH* in Exodus 6:2f. is open to certain objections. As W. J. Martin has shown, it is possible that the patriarchs did in fact know the name *YHWH,* assum-

---

[14] On this general problem see W. F. Albright, *JBL,* XLIII (1924), pp. 370ff., XLIV (1925), pp. 158ff., XLVI (1927), pp. 175ff., LXVII (1948), pp. 379f.; G. R. Driver, *ZAW,* XLVI (1928), pp. 7ff.; O. Eissfeldt, *ZAW,* LIII (1935), pp. 59ff.; J. Obermann, *JBL,* XLVIII (1949), pp. 301ff.; J. Gray, *JNES,* XII (1953), pp. 278ff.; G. R. Driver, *JBL,* LXXIII (1954), pp. 125ff.; D. Goitein, *VT,* VI (1956), pp. 1ff.; *FSAC,* pp. 258ff.

[15] C. Virolleaud, *La déesse 'Anat* (1938), pp. 97f. and pl. XIII.

ing that there was an elliptical interrogative present in the verse.[16] The passage in question would thus read, "I suffered myself to appear to Abraham, to Isaac, and to Jacob, as El Shaddai, for did I not let myself be known to them by my name *YHWH*?"

An alternative suggestion has been made by J. A. Motyer, who retranslated the verse as follows: "And I showed myself to Abraham, to Isaac, and to Jacob in the character of El Shaddai, but in the character expressed by my name Yahweh I did not make myself known to them."[17] This interpretation is important in recognizing the dynamic character of nomenclature as understood by the peoples of the ancient Near East, where names were so frequently connected with specific functions or with facets of personality. Furthermore, it does not deny to the patriarchs the knowledge of the name *YHWH*, but merely prohibits them from appreciating the significance of what the name implied. As Davidson long ago pointed out, the author of Exodus 6 did not mean to deny that the tetragrammaton was older than Moses or unknown before his day.[18] What he was attempting to show was that it had no divine authorization prior to the Mosaic period, but that in speaking to Moses God appropriated it and authorized it as part of His fuller self-manifestation. Even in its present state the Hebrew text makes it clear that the name *YHWH* was old, since it does not say, "My name *YHWH* was not known to them," but "as to my name *YHWH*, I was not known by them," or "as to my name *YHWH* I did not become known to them." On these grounds alone there would seem to be room for the view that the patriarchs knew of the name *YHWH*, without at the same time being aware of its significance.

The provenance and meaning of the tetragrammaton have been the subject of repeated philological discussion for many decades. Numerous scholars adhered to the view that a causative interpretation of the verb-stem הוה was the only one to supply the real sense of the term. Against those who objected that a causative connotation was too abstract a concept for that period of historical development, Albright pointed out quite properly that such an idea can be illustrated amply from the pre-Mosaic texts of Mesopotamia and Egypt.[19] However, more recent philological research has made it clear that the name is in fact a regular substantive word in which the root הוה is preceded by the preformative י. As a proper noun the tetragrammaton is thus the designation of a Person and stands in contrast to such titles as *El Shaddai* and *El Elyon*.

---

[16] W. J. Martin, *Stylistic Criteria and the Analysis of the Pentateuch* (1955), pp. 18ff. For examples of this form see P. Joüon, *Grammaire de l'Hébreu Biblique* (1923), p. 495.

[17] *The Revelation of the Divine Name* (1959), pp. 11ff.

[18] *The Theology of the OT* (1904), p. 68.

[19] *FSAC*, p. 260.

Among the ancient Semites the concept of a "name" had a real bearing upon the functions and personality of the individual involved. While *YHWH* was in fact the God of the patriarchs (Exod. 3:15), His newly revealed name involved a considerably wider ideological setting. God was soon to be understood by the fledgling nation of Israel as a living Person who by virtue of the Covenant of Sinai was in intimate moral and spiritual relationship with those who accepted and obeyed His revealed precepts. Unlike other oriental deities He stood alone, without consort or offspring, and was not restricted to any one geographical location, but was the controller of all cosmic forces. While the Covenant was consistently related by tradition to the Sinai region, there was no special cult associated with this particular location, as was the case in Canaan and elsewhere. Attempts to regard *YHWH* as a derivation from an original volcanic deity are unconvincing, since there are no volcanoes, extinct or active, anywhere in either Sinai or Midian. As Morgenstern showed, the language of the Old Testament theophanies is so frequently drawn from weather phenomena, fire, earthquakes, and the like, that the imagery must properly be connected with the divine glory rather than with a localized volcano.[20]

Basic to the Mosaic religious tradition was the anthropomorphic conception of God that represented the divine personality in a manner suggesting human form to the individual worshipper. Equally emphatic, however, were the aniconic strictures emerging from the Mosaic period, which flatly prohibited the representation of deity in tangible form. So basic was this enactment to the whole of Hebrew religious tradition that almost no images or idols that can possibly be identified as representations of *YHWH* have been excavated from archaeological sites in Palestine, a situation which is truly remarkable in view of what the Old Testament writers had to say about the prevalence of idolatry in certain periods of Hebrew history.

The Covenant at Sinai was the logical extension of the revealed personality of God, since it incorporated Israel into the larger scope of divine activity and furnished her with a sense of election and mission. The personal relationship between a god and his people, inherent in the name *YHWH*, was thus made characteristic of Hebrew religion by the contractual nature of the Covenant. It drew the Israelites within the scope of the mighty divine acts, and gave them a sense of historical perspective and destiny that was unique among the nations of the ancient Near East. It also revealed the Deity as a supremely moral and ethical Being, beneficent towards His obedient people yet manifesting Himself as a jealous and wrathful God when the principles of the Covenant relationship were threatened by apostasy. As a righteous Deity, *YHWH* regulated the social and spiritual life of His people, and de-

[20] ZA, XXV (1910), pp. 139ff., XXVIII (1913), pp. 15ff.

manded that the relationships of Hebrew community life should be governed by dynamic concepts of equity and morality. The idea of a Torah or body of doctrine of an authoritative order can be attributed with complete confidence to the period of Moses, since as Erman has shown, the followers of the Aten cult in Egypt used the term *sbayet* or "teaching" to designate the traditional corpus of knowledge or instruction in a manner closely allied to the later Latin *doctrina*.[21]

The extent to which Moses can be regarded as a true monotheist has been a subject of much discussion among scholars. As was observed earlier, any animistic phase that may have been present in ancient Near Eastern religion had long since been transcended in the patriarchal period,[22] while empirical unitary tendencies in the thought of the Mesopotamians concerning their deities had been in existence from at least the fourth millennium B.C.[23] Ringgren detected two processes in the thought of the ancient Mesopotamians concerning the nature and functioning of the deities in their pantheon. Arguing from a primitive belief in "High Gods," he postulated a process of separation in which certain qualities of an original High God, such as his truth and righteousness, were split off, personified, and venerated as divine. Complementary to this process in some respects was a tendency towards unification, whereby different deities could be regarded as manifestations of a supreme Being who had absorbed their characters and functions.[24]

Despite this, however, as has been observed above, the Hebrew patriarchs can hardly be described as monotheists in the generally accepted sense of the term. Furthermore, it has to be recognized that much of the discussion regarding monotheism has been colored by Hellenic rather than Semitic categories of thought. It is also important to notice, as Anderson has indicated, that Hebrew monotheism is not to be traced to any particular characteristic, but rather to an entire complex of factors inherent in the religion of the Mosaic age.[25] While Moses was not regarded as specifically rejecting all other gods, this attitude was certainly implicit in his belief that there was only one existent deity, the creator of the world, who exercised control over both the processes of nature and the fortunes of man. In that sense Albright could speak of the religion of Moses as monotheistic, taking care, however, to distinguish such a faith from the monotheistic connotations of the Maccabean and

---

[21] A. Erman, *Die Religion der Ägypter* (1934), pp. 121f. On the etymology of *Torah* see G. Oestborn, *Törä in the OT*, pp. 4ff.

[22] G. E. Wright in H. R. Willoughby (ed.), *The Study of the Bible Today and Tomorrow* (1947), p. 90.

[23] *FSAC*, p. 177.

[24] H. Ringgren, *Word and Wisdom* (1947), pp. 20ff.

[25] B. W. Anderson, *OTMS*, p. 291.

Christian eras.[26] In the view of the present writer there seems little justification for not attributing monotheism to Moses, although care should be taken not to understand that concept in a speculative Hellenic sense. A more accurate designation of the situation might well be framed in terms of an empirical ethical monotheism.[27]

C. THE TABERNACLE AND CANAANITE INFLUENCES

Considerable modification of the critical position adopted by Well-hausen with regard to the Tabernacle is now required as the result of recent archaeological study. In his *Prolegomena* Wellhausen took the view that the wilderness Tabernacle was nothing more than the idealization of the Temple. As such, the narratives describing it were historical fiction, and even the intrinsic possibility of the existence of such a structure was a matter of the gravest doubt. In this position he was followed by other scholars,[28] who regarded it generally as the work of some post-exilic priestly compiler, or else as a late idealization of a considerably less complex tent in terms of the Solomonic structure.[29] This opinion, however, was by no means uniform, for as long ago as 1919 Lammens explored late Arabic sources much as Wellhausen had done, and argued from the presence of the old-Arabic *qubbah* to the possibility of some kind of palladium or tent-shrine in the Mosaic period.[30] This view was subsequently adopted by Morgenstern, who showed that, among the Arabs of the pre-Mohammedan period, images or cult-objects of the tribal deity were kept in a small tent normally made of red leather, which was sometimes carried into battle in order to arouse the patriotic instincts of the warriors.[31] An Aramaic inscription from Palmyra contained the word *qubbah*, which was intended as a designation of some kind of sacred tent;[32] bas-reliefs and terra cottas from that area depicted what seem to be portable tent-shrines of the kind carried by camels. On this basis the *qubbah* would appear to have been in use among the Palmyrenes in the early centuries of the Christian era. Although these parallels were comparatively late, Cross and Bright felt sufficient confidence in the ancient tradition preserved by this evidence

[26] *FSAC*, pp. 271f. For criticisms of his position see T. J. Meek, *JBL*, LXI (1942), p. 34; M. Burrows, *JQR*, XXXIII (1942-43), pp. 475f.
[27] Cf. H. H. Rowley, *The Rediscovery of the OT*, p. 88; *ET*, LXI (1949-50), pp. 333ff.
[28] E.g. A. Bentzen, *Introduction to the OT* (1948-49), II, p. 34; R. H. Pfeiffer, *Religion in the OT* (1961), p. 77f.
[29] K. Galling, *Exodus* (1939), pp. 128ff.
[30] H. Lammens, *Bulletin de l'Institut Français d'Archéologie Orientale*, XVII (1919), pp. 39ff.
[31] J. Morgenstern, *HUCA*, V (1928), pp. 81ff., XVII (1942-43), pp. 153ff., XVIII (1943-44), pp. 1ff., *The Ark, the Ephod and the "Tent of Meeting"* (1945); cf. E. Nielsen, *VT*, suppl. vol. VII (1959), pp. 61ff.
[32] H. Ingholt, *Berytus* (1936), I, pp. 85ff.

to assign a tent-shrine to the Davidic period, and Albright held that it was captious to refuse a Mosaic date to the Ark of the Covenant and the Tabernacle, since they were of desert origin and in any event foreign to sedentary Canaanite custom.[33]

It should be noted, however, that the nomadic Arabic parallels adduced above are comparatively late and that much earlier evidence for prefabricated religious structures is now available. As Cross has shown,[34] the fragmentary Phoenician histories of Sanchuniathon, dating from the seventh century B.C., referred to a portable shrine drawn by oxen, and a bas-relief dating from the period of Rameses II about 1285 B.C. showed the tent of the divine king deposited in the middle of the Egyptian military encampment.[35] The cultic use of a tabernacle was familiar to the people of Ugarit, as attested by one of the texts that spoke of King Krt practicing certain rituals in a tent,[36] despite the fact that, as Gordon has pointed out, his was an age of roofed houses.[37] Gordon himself adduced this evidence against the idea that the Biblical Tabernacle was a retrospective adaptation of the Temple to pre-Solomonic times as maintained by the Wellhausenian school. The Ugarit sources may well indicate that the Canaanite deity El could have had some such portable shrine as a regular feature of his cult in the Amarna Age,[38] and if this was actually the case it would reflect the practices of a prior nomadic phase in Canaan.

Examples of even earlier prefabricated structures from Egypt have been collected by Kitchen,[39] the most outstanding of which was the splendid portable bed-canopy of Queen Hetepheres I dated about 2600 B.C.[40] It consisted of beams at the top and bottom which were separated by means of vertical rods and corner posts on three sides of a rectangle. The beams and rods were fitted together by means of tenon joints in such a manner that it could be erected and dismantled very quickly, as with the Hebrew Tabernacle. In addition, the structure was overlaid with gold leaf, and had hooks for the hanging of draperies. The prevalence of such canopies in ancient Egypt between 2850 and 2200 B.C. has been indicated by a number of sculptures from the Fourth, Fifth, and Sixth Dynasties in tomb-chapels[41] as well as by the recovery

---

[33] F. M. Cross, *BA*, X, No. 3 (1947), pp. 45ff. *BHI*, pp. 146f. *FSAC*, p. 266.

[34] *BA*, X, No. 3 (1947), pp. 55, 60f.

[35] Ch. Kuentz, *La Bataille de Qadech* (1928-34), pls. 34, 39, 42.

[36] *The Legend of Krt*, 159; *UL*, pp. 66ff.

[37] *UL*, pp. 5f.

[38] Cf. W. F. Albright, *BASOR*, No. 91 (1943), pp. 39ff., No. 93 (1944), pp. 23ff.

[39] K. A. Kitchen, *The Tyndale House Bulletin*, Nos. 5-6 (1960), pp. 8ff.

[40] Cf. W. S. Smith, *The Art and Architecture of Ancient Egypt* (1958), pls. 30a, 34; L. Cottrell, *The Lost Pharaohs* (1950), p. 128, fig. 23.

[41] G. A. Reisner and W. S. Smith, *A History of the Giza Necropolis* (1955), II, p. 14.

of canopy poles in fragmentary condition from a royal tomb of the First Dynasty at Saqqara.[42]

An analogous specifically religious structure, dating from the third millennium B.C. in Egypt, was the "Tent of Purification," to which the bodies of deceased royalty and high court officials were taken for ritual purification before and after the processes of embalming. As depicted in the scene from the walls of Old Kingdom tombs, these portable buildings were made from a framework of vertical pillars linked by means of horizontal bars, and surrounded by hangings of cloth.[43]

From the Eighteenth and Nineteenth Dynasties, the period of the sojourn of the Israelites in Egypt, come other illustrations of the ancient tabernacle principle. At Karnak, Tuthmosis III erected a stone structure about 1470 B.C. in the huge temple of Amun, which was in effect a replica of a large tent-shrine supported on the traditional wooden pillars.[44] From the tomb of Tutankhamun, about 1340 B.C, was found a complete set of four prefabricated coverings overlaid with gold leaf, which were placed concentrically over the coffins of the dead king.[45] These rectangular shrines were carefully fitted together by means of mortice and tenon joints and assembled in the royal burial chamber.

In view of this evidence there seems to be no adequate reason for denying the existence of a structure such as the Tabernacle to the Hebrews of the Mosaic period. Against the older objection that the Hebrews of that era did not possess the skills necessary for fabricating a structure comparable to that described in Exodus,[46] it need only be remarked that the Egyptians placed a high value upon Semitic craftsmanship in precious metals when it came to exacting tribute from subjugated areas of Syria and Palestine, as illustrated by a number of tomb-scenes.[47]

In their turn the discoveries at Ras Shamra have necessitated a drastic revision of the views of traditional Wellhausenism with regard to the evolutionary nature of Canaanite religion.[48] No longer is it permissible

[42] W. B. Emery, *Great Tombs of the First Dynasty* (1949), I, p. 58, fig. 30.

[43] As pictured in A. M. Blackman, *Rock Tombs of Meir* (1952), V, pls. 42, 43.

[44] J. Lange and M. Hirmer, *Egypt: Architecture, Sculpture, Painting in 3000 Years* (1956), pls. 137, 138, 139.

[45] As pictured in P. Fox, *Tutankhamūn's Treasure* (1951), pls. 18, 21.

[46] So S. R. Driver, *The Book of Exodus* (1911), pp. 426f.; A. H. McNeile, *The Book of Exodus* (1917), p. lxxxi.

[47] D. J. Wiseman, *Illustrations from Biblical Archaeology* (1958), p. 34, fig. 29.

[48] Much of the reason why Wellhausen repudiated the Biblical tradition concerning such cultic objects as the Ark of the Covenant and the Tabernacle lay in the fact that they did not conform to his idea of how the cult developed. It would be permissible to argue, as Wellhausen and his followers did, towards a rigid unilinear development of Hebrew religious institutions if it were also possible to grant the validity of the *a priori* evolutionary concepts of Hegelianism. Unfortunately Wellhausen based his theories on the developmental *Zeitgeist* of the nineteenth

to conceive of Baal in a developmental fashion as a spirit that became associated with a particular locality and ultimately came to discharge the functions of a vegetation deity. In the same way, a careful study of the Baal epic and other literary sources from Ugarit has made it evident that it is impossible to regard the title "Baal" as a generic name for a host of local deities each of which exercised jurisdiction over an allotted extent of territory.

It has now become plain that Baal was accorded the status of a "High God" in the cult-worship because of his prominence in the Canaanite pantheon. He was in fact venerated as a cosmic deity who wielded executive power, and who was worshipped in various communities under his own name or under the designation Hadad, the god of wind and storm.[49] Descriptions of Canaanite religion prior to the discovery of the Ugaritic material which pictured it as a primitive form of nature-worship having little or nothing in the way of a priesthood or organized ritual, are now known to be completely inadequate. The Ras Shamra literary material has shown that, while Canaanite religious beliefs and practices exhibited an appalling depravity, the cult possessed an elaborate pantheon that compared favorably with those of the Babylonians, Egyptians, or Hittites, and was characterized by a highly organized priesthood which functioned at a great many temples and shrines throughout Canaan. Some indication of the virility of this degenerate religion can be

---

century, and reinforced his arguments from biological concepts like those fostered by Darwin and Wallace. A closer comparison of historical processes indicates that, instead of pursuing an unfaltering unilinear course, they are apt to swing with an oscillatory movement that is sometimes as vigorous as it is unpredictable; cf. *ARI*, pp. 107f., 204 n. 37. Again, arguments from the field of biological study would be valuable as analogies, provided that the biological concepts themselves were completely assured. Unfortunately the Darwinian theory of organic evolution is as replete with incorrect premises and faulty conclusions as is the Graf-Wellhausen theory of Pentateuchal origins. Thus Darwin assumed that his self-motivating, self-developing scheme of organic evolution known as "Natural Selection" would demonstrate conclusively that organisms became progressively more complex and highly differentiated as a result of slow, almost imperceptible variations over a prolonged period of time. However, as Haldane has pointed out, the usual course followed by an evolving line has been one of degeneration; *The Causes of Evolution* (1932), p. 167. The fallacy of the Darwinian unilinear developmental hypothesis was demonstrated conclusively by Leo Berg, who assembled a vast amount of evidence from zoology, botany, and palaeontology to show that the development of organisms was based on law, not on chance variation as Darwin had assumed, and that it progressed by violent leaps, major mutations and paroxysmal movements rather than by slow and almost unnoticeable variations; *Nomogenesis* (1926), pp. 19 *et al.* In the light of this evidence alone it merely remains to be said that, although it may have been considered valid in the nineteenth century for one unproved empirical hypothesis to invoke a related but equally undemonstrated conjectural theory for support, such a procedure can no longer be entertained methodologically in the light of a far vaster range of knowledge.

[49] *ARI*, pp. 73f.; *BPAE*, pp. 26f.; *FSAC*, pp. 230f.

gathered from the fact that certain aspects of its rituals even succeeded in infiltrating the highly conservative religions of Egypt and Babylonia, where they were identified with their local cultic counterparts. Despite the fundamental importance of the Ugaritic discoveries both for establishing the true nature of Canaanite cult-worship and for providing an instructive background to the religion of the pre-exilic Hebrews, there are still some writers, such as Kaufmann, who tend to minimize or underestimate the basic depravity of Canaanite religion.

As Albright has shown, the traditions concerning the nature of Hebrew cultic personnel have been complicated by certain entirely gratuitous assumptions.[50] The orthodox Wellhausenian view was that, since the place that the High Priest occupied in the cultic activity of the monarchy was comparatively insignificant, there was in fact no High Priest in the period of the Judges, and Biblical statement to the contrary reflected the editorial extrapolation and theological interests of a much later period.[51] It is now known that the ancient Egyptians assigned great importance to the position of High Priest both during and after the fifteenth century B.C. In the Twenty-First Dynasty, the highest officials of the country under the pharaoh included the High Priest of Amun of Karnak, and the Viziers for Upper and Lower Egypt;[52] in the time of Hatshepsut, the Vizier for Upper Egypt was also the High Priest of Amun. At Ugarit, the cultus was headed by a High Priest during the Amarna Age, and he carried the designation of *rabbu kahinima* or "chief of the priests."[53] In view of the latter circumstance it hardly appears necessary to derive the Hebrew word כהן or "priest" from Arabic sources as Wellhausen did, since the term was most probably of Canaanite origin.[54] The fact that the Biblical writings purporting to come from the Judges period spoke only of the High Priest as "the priest" is merely a reflection of Akkadian usage, as Albright has pointed out.[55] In reality the figure of the High Priest is far removed from the Wellhausenian concept of a royal personage who mirrored the functions of the post-exilic religious leaders, for it reflects instead the conditions of the military encampment of the wilderness period, which was subservient to the authority of Moses, not of Aaron.[56] There is thus no reason for denying the priest at Shiloh the eminence attributed to him by the Biblical narratives, nor is there

[50] *ARI*, pp. 107f.

[51] W. Robertson Smith and A. Bertholet, *EB*, III, cols. 3837ff.

[52] Cf. G. Lefebvre, *Histoire des Grands Prêtres d'Amon de Karnak jusqu'à la XXIe Dynastie* (1929); G. A. Reisner, *JEA*, VI (1920), pp. 28ff., 73ff.

[53] *FSAC*, p. 282.

[54] Cf. G. B. Gray, *Sacrifice in the OT* (1925), p. 183; A. Haldar, *Associations of Cult Prophets Among the Ancient Semites* (1945), pp. 162ff.

[55] *ARI*, p. 108.

[56] *KRI*, pp. 184ff.

adequate ground for refusing to consider the Tabernacle as essential to Hebrew religious activity during the Judges period.[57]

Indeed, as Albright has remarked, the only reason for the Wellhausenian school's consistent disregard or rejection of the straightforward Biblical account of the central Tabernacle at Shiloh was that it did not fit into their theory of the progressive centralization of the cult.[58] It is true, of course, that there was a comparative lack of emphasis upon the office of the High Priest during the monarchy, but when the kingdom collapsed with the exile, the High Priesthood rose once again to a position of prestige. While recognizing the problems associated with the origin of the Levites, Albright concluded that they had first a functional, and subsequently a tribal significance.[59] He also accepted the historicity of Aaron, and held that there was no adequate reason for not considering Zadok in the Aaronic line, in contrast to the opinion of Rowley,[60] who regarded Zadok as a Jebusite priest of the pre-Davidic Jerusalem sanctury of Nehushtan.

D. THE SACRIFICIAL SYSTEM

No discussion of the religion of Israel would be complete without some mention of the sacrificial system. Scholars have adduced many parallels from neighboring peoples in an attempt to explain Israelite sacrifice. Robertson Smith employed pre-Islamic nomadic Arab sources to reconstruct a theoretical "Semite" for whom the sacrificial meal, involving some kind of communion with the deity, constituted the original sacrificial form.[61] The "pan-Babylonian" school, which flourished at the turn of the twentieth century, looked to the higher civilization of Mesopotamia for the origin of sacrifice, and stressed the developed ritual of propitiatory sacrifice which was practiced there,[62] apparently unaware that the Babylonian rituals lacked the moral and religious characteristics of expiation found in Hebrew sacrifice. Theories of Canaanite origin for the Hebrew rituals were favored by Dussaud, who discovered parallels in the Carthaginian sacrificial tariffs and, more particularly, in the Ugaritic

---

[57] Cf. Josh. 18:1; 1 Sam. 2:22, et al.

[58] FSAC, p. 282.

[59] ARI, pp. 109f.; cf. T. J. Meek, Hebrew Origins (1960 ed.), pp. 121ff.; R. de Vaux, Les Institutions de l'Ancien Testament (1960), II, pp. 195ff.

[60] JBL, LVIII (1939), pp. 113ff.

[61] W. Robertson Smith, Encyclopaedia Britannica (1886), XXI, pp. 32ff., Lectures on the Religion of the Semites (1894 ed.), pp. 54, 256, 360, following J. Wellhausen, Prolegomena to the History of Israel (1885), pp. 62ff.

[62] Cf. P. Haupt, JBL, XIX (1900), p. 61; H. Winckler, Religionsgeschichtlicher und Geschichtlicher Orient (1906), pp. 20ff.; J. Jeremias, EB, IV, col. 4120; A. Jeremias, The OT in the Light of the Ancient East (1911), II, p. 49.

texts.[63] With the publication of this material the so-called Myth and Ritual school stressed the sedentary background even more firmly, and the result was a developed pattern of myth and ritual centered in the person of the king.[64]

The first serious suggestion in critical circles that the beginnings might go back as far as the nomadic patriarchs was made by Alt, who argued from Nabataean and Palmyrene Arab veneration of the "gods of the fathers" to the principle that the patriarchs had engaged in a form of monolatrous worship of clan-deities expressed syncretistically by the phrase "the god of Abraham, the god of Isaac, and the god of Jacob."[65] Whereas Maag thought that the zebhaḥ or sacrificial communion meal predominated at that time, Vriezen maintained that the 'ōlāh or burnt offering was more common, a position supported to some extent by Genesis 22:7.[66] When Jacob journeyed to Egypt (Gen. 46:1) he offered slain sacrifices (זבחים), probably of an expiatory variety; and subsequent generations were called to similar sacrifice in the wilderness (Exod. 5:3), which necessitated the use of animal victims and which was differentiated from the kind offered by the Egyptians (Exod. 8:26).

In contrast to the current trends in Old Testament scholarship, which have placed little emphasis upon the personality or work of Moses in relationship to the origin of the developed sacrificial system in the Pentateuch, the uniform witness of Biblical tradition saw the entire pattern of cultic sacrifice as divinely imposed through the agency of Moses. In addition to the three festive occasions prescribed in the Book of the Covenant (Exod. 23:15f.), a number of others were entertained as part of Israelite life, and some of these celebrations (e.g. Judg. 6:25ff.; 11:30ff.; 1 Sam. 1:3) were evidently of non-Mosaic origin. A wealth of detail surrounds the legislation for sacrificial offerings in the Mosaic code, but for practical purposes they could be divided into two groups, animal and vegetable.

Flour, cakes, parched corn, and libations of wine for the drink offerings constituted the normal vegetable sacrifices and were frequently offered in conjunction with the thanksgiving made by fire (Lev. 4:10-21; Num. 5:11; 28:7-15). Acceptable animals were unblemished oxen, sheep, and goats, not under eight days old and not normally older than three

---

[63] R. Dussaud, Le sacrifice en Israël et chez les Pheniciens (1914), p. 7; cf. S. Langdon, JBL, XXIII (1904), pp. 80ff.; Dussaud, Revue de l'Histoire des Religions, CVI (1932), pp. 285ff., Les découvertes de Ras Shamra et l'Ancien Testament (1937), pp. 109ff.

[64] S. H. Hooke, Myth and Ritual (1933), pp. 1ff., The Origins of Early Semitic Ritual (1938).

[65] A. Alt, Der Gott der Väter, pp. 67ff.; cf. V. Maag, VT, suppl. vol. VII (1960), pp. 131ff.; cf. H. H. Rowley, Worship in Ancient Israel (1967), pp. 14f.

[66] V. Maag, VT, VI (1956), pp. 14ff.; T. C. Vriezen, An Outline of OT Theology (1958), p. 26; cf. R. J. Thompson, Penitence and Sacrifice in Early Israel outside the Levitical Law (1963), p. 66, NBD, pp. 1114f.

years. In cases of poverty, doves could be offered as a sacrifice (Exod. 12:5; Lev. 5:7; 9:3f.), but wild animals and fishes were not acceptable, and human sacrifice was expressly prohibited (Lev. 18:21; 20:25). The offerings were presented to the officiating priests in the outer court of the sanctuary, but occasionally were sacrificed elsewhere (Judg. 2:5; 1 Sam. 7:17). In all such ritual procedures, whether animal or vegetable, the worshipper had to present himself in a state of ritual purity (Exod. 19:14). During animal sacrifice the worshipper identified himself with his offering by laying his hand upon it and dedicating it to the purposes of atonement through vicarious sacrifice, subsequent to which the blood was sprinkled near the altar. On the Day of Atonement the collective sins of inadvertence on the part of the nation were confessed and forgiven, and on that occasion only the priest entered the Most Holy Place. The Hebrew sacrificial system was intended only for sins of inadvertence, accident, ceremonial defilement, and the like, and there could be no atonement for transgressions committed in a spirit of sheer obduracy (Num. 15:30). A more detailed survey of the various kinds of sacrificial offerings and the prescriptions concerning them will be undertaken subsequently in the present work.

E. The Religion of the Monarchy

The period of the Judges, which saw continuous national idolatry characterized by an alarming degree of Canaanite religious infiltration, was followed by an abrupt change in the pattern of Hebrew religious life. Throughout the reigns of Saul and David, and for the early part of the Solomonic regime, there emerged a period of loyalty to the Deity of the Sinaitic Covenant in which serious attempts were made to suppress the idolatrous practices of Canaanite cult-worship. The Davidic dynasty was confidently expected to usher in a new era of Israelite life of an enduring quality (2 Sam. 7:5ff.), because it was firmly rooted in loyalty to the God of the Covenant.

Probably the most characteristic religious feature of the period was the erection of the Temple at Jerusalem in the early days of Solomon. From the available evidence there can be no doubt that Phoenician skill was drawn upon heavily in the design and building of the Temple, although the general pattern of the wilderness Tabernacle was basic to the structure. Similar sanctuaries, reflecting strong Phoenician influence and built between 1200 and 900 B.C., have been unearthed in different parts of northern Syria, particularly at Tell Tainat (Hattina). Columns such as the two free-standing pillars known as Jachin and Boaz were a common architectural feature in Syrian shrines of the first millennium B.C., and at a later time they occurred in Assyrian and western Mediterranean temples also. The copper laver of the wilderness period (Exod. 3:17ff.) was replaced by an elaborate metal basin fashioned from bronze, and resting upon four groups of four bronze oxen oriented in terms of the

compass points. There are reasons for thinking that the basin had mythological associations, and it may be that the removal of the oxen from
the pedestal by Ahaz (2 Kgs. 16:17) was an attempt to repudiate these
connections with paganism.[67] The cherubim or winged sphinxes, made
from olive wood and overlaid with gold leaf, were a characteristic
Syro-Phoenician decoration, while the latticed windows placed near the
ceiling of the Holy Place were also a feature of Phoenician architecture.

The tradition that associated music and psalmody with the Davidic
age generally has been verified by archaeological discoveries, which
show decisively that for centuries previously the people of Palestine had
been renowned for their musical interests. Palestinian nomads on a visit
to Egypt were depicted in the Beni Hasan tableau as walking behind
their animals to the accompaniment of music.[68] Other Egyptian sources
from 1550 B.C. refer to examples of Canaanite music,[69] while Ugaritic
texts are replete with religious poetry, some of it being distinctly parallel
in phraseology to the Hebrew Psalter. From the same sources come
references to a class of temple personnel known as "sarim,"[70] who
closely resembled the Hebrew singers of the monarchy and later periods.
The Biblical writings indicate that some of the servants of David who
functioned in this manner possessed Canaanite names, for example, Chalcol and Darda (1 Kgs. 4:31; 1 Chron. 2:6). They bore the designation "Sons of Mahol," that is to say, members of the orchestral guild, and
were regarded as native Canaanites.[71] Excavations at Megiddo uncovered one plaque inlaid with ivory, showing a royal personage seated on a
throne and drinking from a small bowl. His attendants included a musician, who stood before him plucking the strings of a lyre.[72]

With the later days of Solomon came a resurgence of Canaanite
idolatry, and when the kingdom began to function as two separate units,
the breach between the religious life of the north and south was accentu-
ated. According to references in Kings, the initiator of idolatry in the
north was Jeroboam ben Nebat, who set up golden calves in Bethel and
Dan, instituted a non-Levitical priesthood, and appointed a new festival
to be celebrated in the eighth month (1 Kgs. 12:26ff.; 14:9). The denunciation of the calves by Ahijah, the prophet from Shiloh, is not a late and
biased viewpoint as some would imagine,[73] but a contemporary judgment that saw in the infamous calves the establishing in the north of a

---

[67] Cf. *ARI*, pp. 148f.; *KRI*, p. 268.
[68] *LAP*, p. 83.
[69] *ARI*, pp. 125ff.
[70] C. H. Gordon, *Ugaritic Handbook* (1955), p. 272, No. 1934; cf. No. 1991.
[71] *ARI*, p. 210 n. 96. The term אזרח in Exod. 12:19, 48; Num. 9:14; 1 Kgs.
5:11, *et al.* means "aboriginal," "a native of the place."
[72] *WBA*, p. 94.
[73] So *KRI*, p. 270.

counterpart to Egyptian bull-worship as a means of rivalling the spiritual influence of the Temple in Jerusalem.

It has been suggested by certain scholars that Jeroboam was governed to some extent by the cultic traditions of the Canaanites, Arameans, and Hittites in formulating his own religious patterns. Albright has shown that these peoples invariably depicted their deities as seated on a throne borne on the backs of animals or standing upright on such beasts.[74] On this basis the calves made by Jeroboam may perhaps have been winged, and as such may merely have constituted variant forms of the cherub. Consequently, this suggestion continues, they were only the vehicle of deity and not an actual representation of the god.[75] Insofar as he adopted this motif, Jeroboam intended the bulls to represent the pedestal upon which the invisible deity stood, rather than constituting objects of veneration in themselves, although they may have ultimately been regarded as such.

This theory appears plausible enough at first sight in view of the introduction of Canaanite cult-objects, fertility grove rituals, high places for pagan deities, and other forms of gross idolatry into the religion of the northern kingdom. However, it is important to note that Jeroboam I was under no illusions regarding the nature of the images that he had fashioned, for he spoke of them as "thy gods, Israel, which brought thee up out of the land of Egypt" (1 Kgs. 12:28) and deliberately offered sacrifices to the calves as deities in Bethel (1 Kgs. 12:32). That other Israelites adopted precisely the same attitude towards the calves is made plain by Hosea, who said of the Samarian idol, "A workman made it; it is not God" (Hos. 8:6). These considerations, which reflect different phases of contemporary opinion in Israel on the subject, seem much nearer to the facts than the speculations of Albright and his followers.

The basic reason for contemporary denunciations of the religious practices current in the northern kingdom (1 Kgs. 13:1ff.; 14:14ff.) is that bull-worship encouraged the syncretism of *YHWH*-veneration with the depraved fertility cult of Baal, and as such posed a serious threat to the entire ethic of the Sinai Covenant. As far as the religion of the northern kingdom was concerned, the royal cult instituted by Jeroboam set the pattern for all successive reigns. As the memory of the Sinai Covenant and its implications became progressively diminished, the dissolute cultic exercises of Canaan gained a stranglehold upon the worship of the northern kingdom. Society disintegrated increasingly, and with the perversion of justice came a whole host of social iniquities.[76]

[74] *FSAC*, pp. 299f.; cf. *WBA*, pl. 97.
[75] Cf. H. Th. Obbink, ZAW, XLVII (1929), pp. 268f.
[76] J. Bright, *IDB*, II, p. 565; *BHI*, pp. 241ff.

F. THE PROPHETS AND LATER JUDAISM

To a lesser extent the southern kingdom of Judah suffered from the oscillation between periods of religious laxity that encouraged Canaanite idolatry, and the attempts to institute a thoroughgoing reformation of national worship. The rise of the literary prophets marked a resurgence of the Covenant faith, and brought a new vitality to the old religious tenets. As Bright has correctly observed, these prophets are not to be described, as has often been done, in terms of great spiritual pioneers who discovered ethical monotheism.[77] On the contrary, it is now clear that they were heirs to a spiritual tradition that was already centuries old. Their attacks upon the social and religious abuses of the day were made in the light of the Covenant provisions that themselves were firmly rooted in the historical past of the nation. The eighth- and seventh-century B.C. prophets added nothing that was specifically new and distinctive to the traditional *Torah* or "teaching," but instead concentrated upon a re-examination or a fresh interpretation of Mosaic tenets. In this way it was possible for the empirical ethical monotheism of the Mosaic age to be proclaimed in an elaborated form with vigor and conviction by the prophet Isaiah, who made explicit for his day that which was already implicit in the older religious tradition.[78]

As the last days of Judah approached, it fell to the prophets to meditate upon the process of divine justice. Jeremiah held no hope for the nation since the provisions of the Covenant had been broken. He rejected outright the superstitions of popular religion, which clung blindly to the permanence of the Jerusalem Temple and the dynasty of David (Jer. 7:1ff.; 21:12ff.), claiming instead that God had renounced His Temple and abandoned the sinful nation to its doom. While Jeremiah rejected the official cult, he prepared the people for the ordeal of spiritual survival in Babylonia without tangible cult-objects by insistence upon character and motive in relation to both worship and life (Jer. 4:4). He maintained that, by an act of divine clemency and grace, a new and purified people would emerge from the ordeal of exile, upheld spiritually by the promise of a New Covenant (Jer. 31:31ff.), and freed from the destructive claims of a pagan faith.

The non-sacrificial type of worship that Jeremiah had contemplated became a reality among the exiled Jews in Babylonia. Under the uncompromising leadership of Ezekiel they were directed to a rigid monotheism and a high standard of personal and social morality. It was due in no small measure to the efforts and example of Ezekiel that pagan practices ceased to all intents and purposes among the Jews in Babylonia, whereas their Egyptian counterparts, who had disregarded the warnings of Jeremiah, continued to indulge in syncretistic observances of a distinctly

[77] J. Bright, *IDB*, II, p. 566.
[78] Cf. G. W. Anderson, *OTMS*, p. 290.

413

pagan character. Since the Babylonian Jews were unable to participate in the worship of the cultus as in former days, the exile marked an important turning-point in their religious development. Open-air meetings by the Kabar irrigation-canal replaced gatherings in the Temple and its precincts; a non-sacrificial worship emphasized confession, fasting, prayer, and the reading of the Law, and initial improvisations were developed to the point where the faithful community aimed at as great a spiritual differentiation from the pagan Babylonians as was possible. With the development of house-gatherings and the increased importance attached to the knowledge and observance of the Torah, there was laid the basis for subsequent synagogue-worship, an institution that owes its origin to the diligence of Ezekiel.[79]

With the return from exile and the building of the Second Temple came the growth of Judaism proper. It assumed the characteristic form of a theocracy, in which the divine will was proclaimed to the commonwealth through the mediation of the priesthood. The emphasis upon the Covenant, the Torah, and other distinctively Jewish institutions was of material assistance in repudiating the incursions of Hellenism, although at the same time it stimulated tension between the particularistic and universalistic insights of the ancient faith. Careful attention to ritual requirements in worship was held to constitute an invaluable safeguard against any further infiltrations of paganism, although none of the post-exilic prophets ever suggested that correct ritual performances could be regarded as an acceptable substitute for proper moral and spiritual attitudes.

Characteristic of developed Judaism was the emphasis laid upon the keeping of the Torah. To clarify obscurities in the written Law to make it more applicable to certain tangible situations, there grew up a corpus of oral law which gradually acquired a degree of veneration comparable to that assigned to the Mosaic enactments. This traditional law was also employed to safeguard the provisions of the Torah proper, lest they be broken through ignorance or inadvertence. For Judaism, the Law exemplified the ideal concept of a people dedicated to the service of God. While cultic rites never lost their prominence in the post-exilic period, the emphasis in religious activity shifted to the point where Judaism became a religion of the book,[80] in which the highest degree of virtue subsisted in the study and observance of the written Law (cf. Pss. 1:2; 19:7ff.; 119:1ff.). It is this aniconic character, so typical of the age of Moses and so lacking in subsequent eras, recaptured by the stern disciplines of the exile and fostered during the turbulent post-exilic period, which has been perpetuated over the centuries since the dispersion of ancient Judaism to form such a prominent feature of contemporary Jewish faith.

[79] R. K. Harrison, *A History of OT Times* (1957), pp. 197ff.
[80] J. Bright, *IDB*, II, p. 570.

Part Seven

OLD TESTAMENT THEOLOGY

I. THE HISTORY OF OLD TESTAMENT THEOLOGY

A. PRIOR TO THE EIGHTEENTH CENTURY

Until the beginning of the eighteenth century, Old Testament theology was subsumed under the wider study of Christian dogmatic theology. The progressive unfolding of divine truth in the Old Testament was viewed in the light of the Christian dispensation; the Law was considered a shadow of good things to come (Heb. 10:11). Consequently, theological interpretations of the Old Testament tended to presuppose the conclusions of Christian dogmatists and were confined mainly to looking to the Hebrew Scriptures for support or confirmation of the particular concepts under consideration.

While the earliest Christians cherished the text of the Old Testament, particularly in its Greek form, as their Bible, they tended to interpret it along apocalyptic lines.[1] Because of the far-reaching differences between the oriental Semitic mind and the culture of the Hellenistic world, the early Christians recognized that not all the concepts expressed in the Old Testament were in absolute harmony with the outlook of the nascent Christian era.[2] This divergence of standpoint received fresh emphasis when the works of the Law were set in contradistinction to the character of divine grace, as in the theology of Paul. Further accentuation of this distinction came from the increasing spread of the Christian Church into the Gentile world. Nonetheless, the primitive Christians were committed to a loyal acceptance of the Old Testament teachings because of their adherence to the concept of the verbal inspiration and inerrancy of both its Hebrew and Greek texts.

A further problem arose when heretical doctrine began to make an impact on Christian thought. Marcion's repudiation of the Old Testament led a great many Christians to minimize the alleged differences between the two Testaments, and to explain the Old Testament in a symbolic or allegorical manner. When this procedure was ridiculed by the Gnostics it became necessary to emphasize the Incarnation as the

---

[1] E. Stauffer, *Die Theologie des NT* (1947), pp. 2ff.
[2] Cf. R. M. Grant, *Interpretation*, V (1951), pp. 186ff.

focal point in the revealed scheme of divine salvation. This approach saw the Mosaic covenant and the redemptive act of Christ on Calvary as marking appropriate stages in the historical process. Thus Irenaeus was able to balance the different emphases of the Old and New Testaments and at the same time insist upon the fundamental unity of the divine plan for the salvation of humanity.[3]

The rise of this kind of apologetic made it increasingly difficult for the Christian Church to treat the Old Testament as an object of legitimate historical study. The dogmaticians needed the allegorical method of Old Testament interpretation for attacks upon Gnosticism and pagan doctrines in general. This method was carried to its greatest point of development by the Alexandrian school of exegetes, who under Philonic influence strove to discover in the Old Testament all the Christian dogmas in allegorical or figurative form. Clement of Alexandria stressed the existence of hidden truths behind the literal verbal forms;[4] Origen argued from the presence of discrepancies and textual difficulties to the presence of an underlying spiritual truth.[5]

At Antioch a divergent form of interpretation arose in opposition to that of Alexandria. Following the tradition of Bishop Theophilus, who flourished about A.D. 180, the Antiochene school studied the grammar and syntax of the Hebrew and Greek texts, and eschewed the allegorical method in favor of a literal interpretation of the Scriptural writings. In consequence the Antiochene expositors gained a much more balanced insight into the historical nature of the Old Testament revelation. Under Diodorus of Tarsus (A.D. 330-392), close attention was given to the study of Israelite history with a view to discerning the genuine meaning of the extant text, and this tradition was continued to a greater or lesser degree in the writings of Theodore of Mopsuestia and John Chrysostom.

In the west, Jerome was influenced to a considerable extent by the Antiochene school, as exemplified by his interest in the original text of the Old Testament that his task of translating the Scriptures required. Although this period of ecclesiastical history was not characterized by historical criticism,[6] Jerome followed the Antiochenes in attempting to study the text of Scripture from an accredited historical standpoint. With that school he also acknowledged the existence of typological meanings that transcended the bare form of the words themselves.

When Augustine broke with Manichaean canons of Scriptural interpretation, he adopted the allegorical methods popular in Alexandria. Like Jerome he displayed little interest in critical or historical problems.

---

[3] *Adv. Haer.* IV, 9, 2.
[4] *Strom.* VI, 15, 125ff.
[5] *De Princip.* IV, 2, 9; IV, 3, 1ff.; cf. K. Grobel, *IDB*, II, pp. 719f.
[6] Cf. R. M. Grant, *Journal of Religion*, XXV (1945), pp. 183ff.

Although he was primarily concerned with theological issues, he did not attempt to systematize the doctrinal themes of Scripture. However, he made a concerted effort to envisage the theology of history in Books XV-XVII of his celebrated treatise *The City of God*, but this was undertaken more from the standpoint of the apocalyptic interpretation of an earlier generation than from considerations of historical reality.[7]

Although the way in which the early patristic writers used the text of the Bible was in many senses quite different from that of modern expositors, there can be no doubt that they were Biblical theologians in the best sense of the term. For the most part the Fathers adhered to the Scriptures as a textbook of revealed truth, whose propositions could be used to support their own doctrinal inferences. They accepted the inspiration of Scripture without, however, propounding any particular theory of inspiration.[8] Quite frequently they stated that the Logos or the Spirit spoke through the various authors, but in the main the patristic writers were content to acknowledge the existence of both divine and human agencies without formulating any concept of their interrelationship. Perhaps it was because of the fact of inspiration that the Fathers were prepared to find such depths of mystery in the Bible. Certainly for them there was nothing accidental or irrelevant in the Scriptural record, nothing inherently absurd or trivial, and nothing that could be regarded as unworthy of God himself. The common belief of the Fathers that the Old Testament was in principle a Christian book led to their widespread use of the theory of prefiguration, which for them reinforced the unity of the Biblical revelation. The Old Testament was not so much a "schoolmaster unto Christ" as it was a foreshadowing of spiritual realities that were subsequently to be displayed openly, and therefore Christ was the key that would unlock all the Scriptures. Upon this theoretical basis the exegesis of the Old Testament was undertaken by writers such as Origen, Jerome, Chrysostom, and Augustine. Despite the excesses that resulted from this kind of approach, the Fathers held firmly to the conviction of the primacy and sufficiency of Scripture for both the divine revelation and the salvation of humanity.

During the medieval period the Old Testament was frequently the ground of appeal when Scriptural support was required for the theocratic concept of the Church. A great many Old Testament passages were employed to sustain the dogmas of medieval ecclesiasticism, a purpose to which the exegesis of the text was completely subordinated.[9] Such an approach opened the entire field of Old Testament doctrine to gross subjectivism; and this situation was abruptly challenged by Martin Luther, who emphatically repudiated any suggestion that the interpretation of

[7] Cf. E. Jacob, *Theology of the OT* (1958), pp. 15f.
[8] H. E. W. Turner, *The Pattern of Christian Truth* (1954), pp. 260ff.
[9] H. Pope in *St. Thomas Aquinas* (ed. A. Whitacre, 1924), pp. 125ff.

419

Scripture was the prerogative of the pope.[10] However, Luther's theological position allowed him to hold certain books of the Biblical canon in greater esteem than others, and he tended to regard the Old Testament as having been superseded to a large extent, although he was quick to adduce its message in support of the New Testament gospel. Certain of his commentaries on the Old Testament showed that he was well aware of the importance of historical method in the study of Scripture, but despite this recognition he was apparently unable to see in the Old Testament writings anything approaching progression in the content of divine revelation.

Calvin, on the other hand, was convinced that a developing revelation was enshrined in Scripture, although his views had nothing in common with the tenets of a much more modern process-theology. He held that the promise to Adam was the dawning of that bright light that illumined the world at the Incarnation.[11] While agreeing with Luther in preferring the "superior excellence of the New Testament" to that of the Old,[12] Calvin linked the two closely together to present a unified dispensation characterized by the proclamation of the law and the gospel. Although he recognized the presence of typological material in certain of the Old Testament rites, Calvin generally avoided the allegorical method of interpretation in consonance with his belief that the natural and obvious meaning of Scripture was in fact the true one. His pre-eminence as an expositor lay in his expressed purpose to subordinate philological, historical, and other considerations to the one aim of discovering and expounding the divine message as contained in the text.

The progressive character of revelation also received emphasis in the works of another Reformed theologian, Johannes Cocceius (1603-1669), a celebrated Hebrew philologist.[13] He was one of the leading exponents of Covenant theology, and in his *Summa Doctrinae de Foedere et Testamento Dei* (1648) he maintained that the relationship between God and man was as much covenantal in nature before the fall as after it. The *foedus naturale* existed prior to the human fall from grace; and it was succeeded by the *foedus gratiae*, the fulfilment of which necessitated the coming of Christ in the flesh. In consequence the Covenant of grace was unfolded both historically and spiritually, with the result that the destiny of old Israel found its logical conclusion in the growth of the Christian Church. While Cocceius invoked an extensive typology in order to arrive at these conclusions, his approach gave a new direction to Biblical study by showing that it was no longer legitimate to suppose

---

[10] *Werke*, VI, pp. 388ff.

[11] *Institutes*, II, 11, 20.

[12] *Ibid.*, II, 11, 12.

[13] His most valuable work in this field was his *Lexicon et Commentarius Sermonis Hebraici et Chaldaici* (1669).

that the Old Testament was merely a repository of proof-texts for the support of ecclesiastical dogmas. Instead, the Bible as a whole was to be considered as a legitimate object of study in its own right, and as a source that could inform—not merely support—the Christian faith.

The work of J. A. Bengel (1687-1752), the greatest Biblical exegete of the eighteenth century, marked a further stage in the development of an historical interpretation of Scripture. Although his major works were concerned with the New Testament, Bengel stressed the continuity of the Old and New Covenants, holding to the view that Scripture contained a unified dispensational scheme grounded in the history of ancient Israel, which looked for its fulfillment in the mission of the Christian Church. Bengel maintained an independent attitude towards the dogmatic orthodoxy of his time, and arrived at his theological conclusions by applying grammatico-historical rules to the text of Scripture.

A revival of interest in Biblical studies in Germany resulted from the Pietist movement within the Lutheran Church, which gained impetus towards the end of the seventeenth century. The forerunners of Pietism included the theosophic mystic Jakob Boehme (1575-1624) and Johann Arndt (1555-1621). More directly, it arose as a result of the work of Philip Jacob Spener (1635-1705), who combined the Lutheran emphasis on Biblical doctrine with the Reformation appeal for vigorous Christian living. His proposals were embodied in his *Pia Desideria,* or *Earnest Desires for a Reform of the True Evangelical Church* (1675), which maintained that the life of the Church would be enriched by an emphasis upon conversion and sanctification rather than by a mere correctness of doctrine. Although Pietism had waned by the middle of the eighteenth century, its individualistic emphasis helped to prepare the way for new and more radical modes of thought.[14]

B. THE RISE OF RATIONALISM

The influence of European rationalism upon the study of Scripture also assisted in liberating it from the impediments of medieval dogmatism, and in its own way made possible a further stage of development in the growth of Biblical theology as an independent entity. The break with medievalism came with the formulation of a distinction between dogmatic and Biblical theology in 1787 in an academic lecture by Johann Philipp Gabler entitled *Oratio de justo discrimine theologiae biblicae et dogmaticae regundisque recte utriusque finibus.* Whereas dogmatic theology consisted of definite propositions that were held to be delivered by authority and drew upon Scripture for support,[15] Biblical theology, as depicted by Gabler, was considered as an historical science whose pur-

[14] For the influence of Pietistic theologians see A. Ritschl, *Geschichte des Pietismus* (1886), III, pp. 62f.

[15] Cf. H. Martensen, *Christian Dogmatics* (1866), p. 1.

pose was to describe what the writers of the Old and New Testaments thought concerning divine things.

Biblical theology became from that time on an academic discipline in its own right, but the influence of German rationalism upon its growth was such that the native genius of the ancient Hebrews was seldom permitted to penetrate the rigid and artificial mold imposed upon it by rationalistic philosophy. Although there is a sense in which the rationalist movement can be said to have assisted in the objective and methodical study of the Old Testament writings, the ancient Hebrew Scriptures were generally the object of hostile criticism imposed less by an examination of the sources against an oriental background than by the accepted canons of European philosophical speculation. Typical of this approach was Bauer's *Theologie des Alten Testaments* (1796), which, although it purported to trace the development of religious concepts from the earliest days of the Hebrew people to the beginning of the Christian era, merely succeeded in furnishing a depreciatory evaluation of certain Biblical themes, shaped predominantly by the belief that the pure truth of Scripture had to be disentangled from the local and temporal disguises that it had assumed in the text.

A more historical approach, accompanied by a somewhat greater insight into the essential content of Biblical theology, became evident in the work of De Wette,[16] who based his methodology upon the rationalistic principles expounded by Eichhorn, Geddes, and Vater. De Wette's outlook demonstrated an independence of rationalism at least to the extent that he was able to adopt a more flexible view of historical evolution.[17] At the same time he adduced criticisms of Kantian skepticism concerning metaphysical issues. De Wette followed the contemporary historical pattern, which had come to regard the exile as the division between Hebraism and Judaism; and he was rationalistic in his approach to the extent that he desired to separate dogma from the outmoded forms in which the Bible, and particularly the Old Testament, presented it. De Wette recognized that the Old Testament recorded the history of the Hebrew theocracy and noticed a difference between the Mosaic revelation and its implementation at a later period. He accorded only a limited degree of canonicity to the Old Testament, however, and conceded that the nature of life and thought presented in it was largely strange to the western world.

The theological writings of Schleiermacher—especially his two-volume *Der Christliche Glaube nach den Grundsätzen der Evangelischen Kirche* (1821)—did not recognize De Wette's demand that the Old Testament

[16] W. M. L. De Wette, *Lehrbuch der Christlichen Dogmatik, I: Biblische Dogmatik des Alten und Neuen Testaments* (1813).

[17] O. Pfleiderer, *The Development of Theology in Germany Since Kant and Its Progress in Great Britain Since 1825* (1890), pp. 77ff.

be interpreted in a strictly historical manner. Instead Schleiermacher emphasized the points of divergence between the Old and New Testaments. For Schleiermacher the former was largely polemical, and he accorded inspiration as commonly understood only to the messianic prophecies. He took the view that the best elements of Old Testament thought, such as monotheism, could also be discovered in Greek philosophy, and he maintained that Christian doctrine would only benefit when the practice of adducing Old Testament proof-texts was abandoned.

A more serious treatment of Hebrew history and religious thought took place in the writings of Hegel,[18] who in his categorizing of the three religions of spiritual individuality regarded the Jewish faith as that of exaltedness (*Erhabenheit*). Judaism was not an accident of history, as Schleiermacher supposed, but a necessary component in the development of Christianity, which Hegel regarded as the "absolute religion." Hegelian evolutionism was synthesized with the critical findings of Eichhorn and De Wette by Wilhelm Vatke, who in 1835 published the most elaborate treatise to that time on the development of Old Testament religion.[19] Half a century later Wellhausen acknowledged his debt to Vatke's work, declaring that it was the most significant attempt ever made to understand ancient Israel in strictly historical categories. Vatke maintained the basically unhistorical character of the Mosaic society, and saw in the Torah the product of a state that was already in existence. Deuteronomy was held to be one result of the religious reformation initiated by Josiah, and the latest portions of the Pentateuch were thought to have emerged from the exilic period. Vatke held that the religion of the Hebrews evolved from comparatively primitive and unhistorical beginnings into the monotheistic faith that characterized the religion of Judaism.

Equally typical of Hegelian idealistic thought was B. Bauer's treatise on the problem of Old Testament revelation.[20] He interpreted religion in terms of divine self-consciousness, which was in the process of evolution to more highly differentiated levels. Its fullest development could only be attained when all obstacles to growth were overcome, at which time the content of the history of revelation would become apparent. Since religion was essentially historical, it too passed through various stages in an ascending pattern, and this was motivated by the degree of antithesis that any particular stage of religious development exhibited in relationship to the ultimate goal.

[18] Especially in his posthumous *Philosophy of Religion*. Cf. K. Fischer, *Geschichte der neueren Philosophie* (1909), VIII, 2, pp. 985f.

[19] W. Vatke, *Die Biblische Theologie wissenschaftlich dargestellt, I, Die Religion des AT nach den kanonischen Büchern entwickelt* (1835).

[20] B. Bauer, *Kritik der Geschichte der Offenbarung, I, Die Religion des AT* (1838).

From Hengstenberg, a contemporary of Schleiermacher at Berlin, came a reaction against the higher critical views of Eichhorn and De Wette, with their concomitant unorthodox theological interpretations. In his study of Christology he adhered firmly to traditional views of the authority of Scripture.[21] While recognizing current theories of the origin and growth of the Hebrew Scriptures, he repudiated vigorously the various divisive theories of the critical school. Although he anticipated later Biblical theologians in his stress upon the fundamental unity of the two Testaments, his meticulous rebuttal of the arguments commonly raised against the Mosaicity of the Pentateuch were out of harmony with the critical tastes of the day; and consequently his theological views were largely ignored outside his own immediate circle.

Within the same general tradition, however, was the work of Hofmann,[22] a New Testament scholar who developed his position against the background of the Old Testament. His purpose was to justify the inspiration and authority of the Bible by the use of historical method rather than by dogmatic pronouncement, and he envisaged the entire Old Testament in terms of "redemptive history" or *Heilsgeschichte*. Hofmann viewed each area in the historical process as carrying within itself the seed of the subsequent period, which it anticipated. For him history and prophecy were intimately related, and he reflected the Hegelian outlook in the course of his maintaining that Jesus Christ was the goal of history. Thus his "history of salvation" constituted an accredited historical process that developed through progressive stages until it attained its terminal phase in the Incarnation of Jesus Christ. Consequently, human salvation was firmly rooted in history, and this demonstration provided a stable foundation upon which a theology of the Old Testament could be erected.

The pattern of the historical presentation of revealed religion that Hofmann had established was continued with marked success by Oehler. In 1845 he published a historical *Prolegomena* as a foundation for his posthumous *Theologie des Alten Testaments* (1873) which quickly became a classic. Like Hofmann, Oehler reflected Hegelian influence in his view that life was a continuum in which the earlier stages could only be understood in terms of the final phase of the entire process. Although he rejected the traditional Christian interpretation of the Old Testament, Oehler held that the Hebrew Scriptures were preparatory to the New Testament and could only be explained ultimately in the light of the Incarnation and Atonement. Oehler maintained that the Old Testa-

---

[21] E. W. Hengstenberg, *Christologie des AT* (3 vols.; 1829-35); E. tr. R. Keith, *Christology of the OT* (1836-39). A similar position was maintained by H. A. C. Hävernick, *Vorlesungen über die Theologie des AT* (1848).

[22] J. C. K. von Hofmann, *Weissagungen und Erfüllungen im AT und NT* (2 vols., 1841-44) and *Der Schriftbeweis* (1852).

ment recorded the historical process by which God reconciled the world to Himself; and in consequence his Old Testament theology was basically a theology of history, demonstrating God's progressive manifestation to the world, which ultimately aimed at recapturing for man the pristine spiritual fellowship with God and the gift of eternal life. With this laudable aim in view Oehler proceeded according to a strictly historical interpretation. He refused to assign to the Old Testament authors concepts that had been imposed upon them by later Christian interpreters; yet he viewed the content of their thought as an essential contribution to the growth of Christianity, in which the historical process of revelation culminated. Despite the subjectivity that must inevitably accompany such an approach, Oehler was correct in emphasizing the importance of proper historical method and in rejecting some of the more eccentric interpretations of the Old Testament that had been popular since the time of the Alexandrian school.

Three years before Oehler died, an important contribution to the methodology of Old Testament theological study was made by Diestel, who suggested that the best approach to this problem would be to combine three lines of inquiry which had previously been pursued either singly or in inadequate combination.[23] The first of these was an approach from the purely historico-cultural perspective seeking to set Israel firmly against her Near Eastern background. For Diestel this by itself had resulted in an imbalanced evaluation of Hebrew religious worth. The second involved applying a philosophy of religion in order to estimate the nature and extent of Hebrew spiritual growth. This method had previously been clouded with a good deal of subjectivism. Third, Diestel urged that the eternal verities of Israelite religion should be studied in the light of the *Heilsgeschichte* presented in the Old Testament writings. Diestel's methodological synthesis envisaged the fullest revelation of God in Jesus Christ, and, by implication, the conscious activity of God in human history. He was firm in his insistence that obscurities and apparent discrepancies must not be allowed to interfere with the attainment of the soundest possible historical and spiritual evaluation of the divine self-revelation through ancient Israel, arrived at by using all the means at the disposal of scholarship.

Diestel was far ahead of his time in proposing such a method, for it was nearly three-quarters of a century before scholars began to heed his advice and apply his principles. The Biblical writers of his day were for the most part obsessed with the evolutionary and literary-critical concepts that were to blossom with the work of Graf and Wellhausen. Already the developmental approach was being applied to Old Testament theology in a manner that reduced it to a study of the history of

---

[23] L. Diestel, *Geschichte des AT in der Christlichen Kirche* (1869).

Hebrew religion,[24] although Schultz followed Oehler in emphasizing the unified nature of the Old Testament as a preparation for the coming of the divine kingdom on earth.[25] The barrenness of eighteenth-century Old Testament studies began to bear its scant fruit at this time in the increasingly secularized approach to Hebrew history as reflected, for example, in the writings of Ewald.[26] Curiously enough, the theological speculations of Ewald tended to revert to the ecclesiasticism of an earlier age.[27] He maintained that the Bible was but one means of coming to know the divine revelation, and that the fellowship of the Christian Church and the personal practice and experience of the fear of God were equally valid sources. The Bible was the supreme source of revelation for the Christian Church, but it was merely a means to an end and as such should not be overestimated. In the usual Hegelian manner Ewald discerned progress in the religious ideas of the Old Testament, and his highest praise for the ancient Hebrew Scriptures was the fact that they were indispensable to the New Testament revelation. However, his general views served to subordinate the Bible to the Christian Church and to individual spiritual experience, as Kraeling has indicated.[28] As far as Old Testament theology was concerned, his approach came perilously close to the scholastic attitude that regarded the Old Testament as a legitimate source of proof-texts to support dogmatic pronouncements.

Although Wellhausen's views concerning the nature and development of Hebrew religion had great influence on contemporary theological estimates of the Old Testament, not all scholars regarded the developmental process in quite the same manner. The moderate critic Ernst Sellin stressed that it was in the Mosaic period that the characteristic Hebrew religious institutions originated, and he urged that correspondingly less emphasis should be placed upon the supposed emergence of religious concepts in the exile and later periods.[29] In conjunction with Kittel[30] he modified the Wellhausenian conception that Hebrew religion had developed through the popular, prophetic, and priestly stages respec-

---

[24] E.g. A. Kayser, *Die Theologie des AT im ihrer Geschichtlichen Entwicklung dargestellt* (1886). The 1903 edition, revised by K. Marti, was retitled simply *Geschichte der israelitischen Religion*. Cf. C. Piepenbring, *Théologie de l'Ancien Testament* (1886).

[25] H. Schultz, *Alttestamentliche Theologie: Die Offenbarungsreligion auf ihrer vorchristlichen Entwicklungsstufe* (1896).

[26] H. Ewald, *Geschichte des Volkes Israel* (5 vols., 1843-55).

[27] H. Ewald, *Die Lehre der Bibel von Gott oder Theologie des Alten und Neuen Bundes, I, Die Lehre vom Wort Gottes* (1871).

[28] *The OT Since the Reformation* (1955), p. 86.

[29] E. Sellin, *Beiträge zur israelitischen und jüdischen Religionsgeschichte* (2 vols., 1896); *Die alttestamentliche Religion im Rahmen der andern altorientalischen* (1908).

[30] R. Kittel, *Geschichte des Volkes Israel, II: Das Volk im Kanaan* (1895).

tively, to stress that different levels of religious insight had existed at the same time among the Israelites, and went on to show the nature of the religious conflicts that resulted from this situation. August Dillmann supported the theological position of Oehler and Schultz,[31] but in general the trend among European scholars of that period was to depict the development of Old Testament religion in intimate relationship to the history of the Hebrew people.[32]

The historical standpoint was also prominent in the posthumous work of A. B. Davidson, who denied that there was a theology as such in the Old Testament, and preferred instead to treat his subject as the "history of the religion of Israel as represented in the Old Testament."[33] For Davidson the Old Covenant was not so much a foreshadowing of the New as the introduction of the divine kingdom in embryonic form. The purpose of Old Testament theology, as he saw it, was to exhibit the organic development of the religious life that God sought to stimulate in His ancient people. The truths contained in the Old Testament about the divine kingdom were manifested in terms of the history and religious institutions of Israel. These, however, did not necessarily prefigure the birth of the Christian Church, although the latter constituted the climax of the Old Testament revelation. Davidson's work suffered more than similar treatises on Old Testament theology because it was posthumous. In the earlier part of the book he rejected the traditional division of his subject into theology, anthropology, and soteriology, but at a later stage he accepted this pattern as the basis for formulating his study.[34] Whether this was due to poor editorial work by S. D. F. Salmond (as Porteous has suggested),[35] to the confused state of the manuscript sources left by Davidson, or to the fact that the later adoption of the traditional division represented a substantial change in the opinions of the author, is impossible to say.

C. RECENT STUDIES

It is noteworthy that for the next two decades a theological interpretation of the Old Testament was precluded by the constant emphasis upon the study of Hebrew religious history, and only a very limited number of works succeeded in presenting the religious concepts of the Old Testa-

[31] A. Dillmann, *Handbuch der alttestamentlichen Theologie* (1895).

[32] E.g. B. Stade, *Geschichte des Volkes Israel* (2 vols., 1887), *Biblische Theologie des AT, I* (1905); R. Smend, *Lehrbuch der Alttestamentlichen Religionsgeschichte* (1893); E. Riehm, *Alttestamentliche Theologie* (1889); R. V. Foster, *OT Studies: An Outline of OT Theology* (1890); W. H. Bennett, *The Theology of the OT* (1896).

[33] A. B. Davidson, *The Theology of the OT* (1904), p. 11.

[34] *Ibid.*, pp. 30ff.; cf. pp. 12ff.

[35] *OTMS*, p. 315; cf. H. Wheeler Robinson, *ET*, XLI (1929-30), p. 247.

ment as such.[36] A reaction to the critical position towards Old Testament theology came in 1922 with the work of König, a brilliant Hebraist and long-time opponent of the Wellhausen school.[37] He took a high view of the reliability of the Old Testament sources, and brought to bear upon his task the exact historical and grammatical procedures for which he was renowned. While he did not adhere to the current evolutionary interpretation of Hebrew history, he did follow the customary pattern of describing the history of Hebrew religion, after which he dealt systematically with the dominant concepts that helped to shape the Israelite nation. He firmly rejected anything that seemed to him to savor of allegorical exegesis, and sought instead for explanations in harmony with a rational and historical interpretation of the text.

Rudolf Kittel had already called for a systematized presentation of the religious values of the Old Testament in a theological rather than a purely historical context, and this challenge was taken up by Steuernagel, who in the Marti *Festschrift* attempted to resolve the confusion between Old Testament theology as such and the history of Old Testament religious concepts, arguing that the former was necessary in order to comprehend the significance of the data supplied by the latter.[38] A short article by Otto Eissfeldt in 1926 warned of the inherent dangers in compounding the historical investigation of Israelite religion with the view that the faith of the Old Testament was essentially a matter of divine revelation, as was being attempted by the proponents of dialectic theology.[39] For him the study of Old Testament theology was a perfectly legitimate exercise in itself, although it would be conditioned by the religious approach of the individual scholar. Eissfeldt explained the tension between the historical and theological attitudes towards the investigation by stating that the former constricted the breadth and depth of the revelation amenable to faith, whereas the latter imposed limitations upon the diverse nature of the historical data. There were thus two approaches to the subject: the historical attitude, which was basically one of inquiry and knowledge, and the outreach of faith, which saw in the Old Testament writings the true religion of divine revelation. Since he held that it was impossible to demonstrate revelation as such within the realm of historical events, it was obviously necessary to keep both approaches to the problem quite separate. Consequently, the study of Old Testament theology must be undertaken in a systematic manner

---

[36] E.g. M. Hetzenauer, *Theologia Biblica, I: Vetus Testamentum* (1908); R. B. Girdlestone, *OT Theology and Modern Ideas* (1909); H. Wheeler Robinson, *The Religious Ideas of the OT* (1913); A. C. Knudson, *The Religious Teaching of the OT* (1918); C. F. Burney, *Outlines of OT Theology* (1920).

[37] E. König, *Theologie des AT kritisch und vergleichend dargestellt* (1922).

[38] Kittel, ZAW, XXXIX (1921), pp. 84ff.; Steuernagel, BZAW, XLI (1925), pp. 266ff.

[39] ZAW, XLIV (1926), pp. 1ff.

rather than in the form of a purely historical presentation so as to present the living truth implicit in the Hebrew Scriptures. The Christian writer, however, need not feel under any obligation to find each central Old Testament theme fulfilled in the New Testament, and where Old Testament concepts did not find such fruition, their literary sources could then be regarded as co-equal in the matter of authority with the New Testament writings.

Unfortunately, Eissfeldt's important contribution ignored the fact that revelation is inextricably connected with the historical process as its given sphere of operation. Therefore any imposed dichotomy between historical investigation and theological interpretation is basically false, if for no other reason than that it would remove faith from the immanent historical situation in a manner completely foreign to the Old Testament *Heilsgeschichte*. If Eissfeldt were correct in insisting upon separating faith and knowledge, Old Testament theology would assume a purely confessional character, a situation that would immediately impose severe restrictions upon the acceptability of the findings. In order for Old Testament theology to have any validity at all as an accredited discipline, it could not be hampered by such limitations. An additional disadvantage to applying Eissfeldt's kind of approach is that the same sort of subjective evaluation that brought such confusion and chaos to the findings of the Graf-Wellhausen school would almost certainly be rampant in the field of Old Testament theology. In sum, if the recommendations of Eissfeldt were followed, two independent branches of study would emerge, one of which would examine the manifold data of Old Testament religion objectively, in a manner acceptable to scholars of any religious persuasion, and the other which would be a purely confessional presentation of Old Testament truths arranged systematically.[40]

In 1929 Walter Eichrodt published an article in which he also devoted some attention to the demands of dialectical theology for something in excess of a mere historical investigation of the phenomena of Hebrew religion.[41] However, he went further than Eissfeldt in asserting that it was the scholar's responsibility to expose the structure of Old Testament religion and demonstrate the interrelationship of its component parts so as to uncover those elements which were constant in Old Testament religion. Eichrodt was aware of the extent to which subjective factors operated in historical research, and he felt that the philosophy of history of the Christian Old Testament student ought to have the New Testament revelation as its goal, so that the principles of selectivity employed by the research worker would be governed accordingly.

Within the next few years a number of books dealing with Old Testament theology were published in Europe. In 1933 Sellin followed

[40] Cf. G. von Rad, *Theologische Blätter*, XV (1936), pp. 30ff.
[41] ZAW, XLVII (1929), pp. 83ff.

the classical pattern, first rejected and then adopted by Davidson, of dealing successively in his study with the doctrines of theology, anthropology, and soteriology.[42] For Sellin such an investigation of the Old Testament was part of the larger discipline of Christian theology, and accordingly he traced the progress of the religious current from the time of Moses until it reached its highest point of development in the revelation of Jesus Christ. Three years later Köhler followed the same basic pattern, but found that the concept of divine kingship served to unify the Old Testament writings.[43] His treatment was more comprehensive than Sellin's and was notable for the opinion that revelation in the Old Testament constituted a progressive unfolding of many and varied truths, and did not merely consist of one body of doctrine.

W. Eichrodt parted company with the traditional arrangement of doctrinal material.[44] His contribution was important because it seized upon a much-neglected theme, the Covenant, as the central concept from which the basic unity of outlook exhibited in the Old Testament writings derived its impetus. In distinction from the members of the Graf-Wellhausen school, Eichrodt ascribed the Covenant concept to Moses,[45] and asserted that it exercised a consistent influence over all other aspects of Old Testament religion. For Eichrodt, God was not merely the sovereign deity of the Israelite monarchy, but One who by a definite agreement had incorporated the Hebrew people into the Kingdom of God. In his attempt to describe the fundamental unity of Old Testament religion Eichrodt did not neglect the possibility of historical development in Old Testament belief, and stressed that the very incompleteness of the Old Testament at certain stages pointed to the emergence of the New Testament revelation in Christ. However, he regarded the connection between the two Testaments as neither accidental nor purely historical. Rather it was an organic connection resulting from the activity of the one God whose kingdom was founded on the law, prophecy, and the gospel. Eichrodt was doubtless correct in thinking that the Old Testament was not particularly amenable to systematic treatment, and although he only applied his unifying principle to the first volume of the triad, he made it clear that the spiritual values of the Old Testament could be interpreted in terms of religious institutions historically evaluated.

[42] E. Sellin, *Alttestamentliche Theologie auf religionsgeschichtlicher Grundlage, II: Theologie des AT* (1933).

[43] L. Köhler, *Theologie des AT* (1935), E. tr. A. S. Todd, *OT Theology* (1957). Cf. Köhler in *Theologische Rundschau*, VII (1935), pp. 255ff., VIII (1936), pp. 55ff., 247ff.

[44] W. Eichrodt, *Theologie des AT*, I (1933), II (1935), III (1939); cf. his *Man in the OT* (1951).

[45] Cf. *JBL*, LXV (1946), pp. 205ff.

430

Of a very different nature was the work of Wilhelm Vischer, which made no secret of its attempt to discern Christian doctrine in the Old Testament.[46] Vischer's approach had much in common with the historical method, but he tended to look for a typological interpretation as a means of revealing the eternal significance of the material for both Testaments. He attempted to systematize the "eternal truth" of the Old Testament as the foundation for the New Testament revelation of God in Christ, and his work is much the best representative of this school of thought.

The theme that Old Testament religion was in fact a developing living relationship between God and man that was completed with the coming of Christianity had been expounded by Baumgärtel, and was dealt with briefly by Lindblom in an Old Testament symposium.[47] The latter maintained that the concept of deity held by the Hebrews was so unique and central to their faith that it differentiated it from the religions of the surrounding nations. Having compared the Old Testament idea of God with contemporary pagan concepts of deity, Lindblom related it organically to the New Testament doctrine of God. Despite obvious differences in the two ideas, he maintained that much of the Old Testament material regarding God had specific value for the Christian Church, and his emphasis upon the purposiveness of the divine nature led him to the conclusion that God was guiding the world to a specific goal in history.

In the same symposium Artur Weiser stressed the importance of discerning the original meaning of the Old Testament through careful exegesis.[48] The dynamic view of reality evident in the Hebrew Scriptures was bound up with a degree of encounter or some movement that involved a decision of faith. The very nature of this experience precluded a formal systematization of concepts by the Hebrews in terms of a "doctrine" of God. The task of the Old Testament exegete was to relate the existence and the destiny of modern man to analogous situations occurring between men and God in Hebrew history. While the sense of progress towards a goal would be identical, the Christian had the decided advantage of a fuller revelation of the divine nature and will.

The general philosophy of revelation was discussed by Wheeler Robinson in 1938, and was followed by an examination of the characteristic doctrines of God, man, sin, grace, and the judgment of history, from Old Testament sources.[49] A posthumous work by the same author was pub-

[46] W. Vischer, *Das Christuszeugnis des AT*, I (1934), II (1942); E. tr. of vol. I, *The Witness of the OT to Christ* (1949).

[47] F. Baumgärtel, *Die Eigenart der alttestamentlichen Frömmigkeit* (1932). J. Lindblom in *Werden und Wesen des Alten Testaments* (ed. P. Volz, F. Stummer and J. Hempel, 1936), pp. 128ff.

[48] *Ibid.*, pp. 207ff.; cf. Weiser, ZAW, LXI (1945-48), pp. 17ff.

[49] *Record and Revelation* (1938), pp. 303ff.; cf. his *Redemption and Revelation in the Actuality of History* (1942), pp. 95ff.

lished in 1946, which had been intended as a prolegomenon to a projected volume on Old Testament theology, and which developed certain
lines of approach indicated by Davidson's *Theology of the Old Testament.*[50] The period between World Wars I and II had witnessed a
searching re-evaluation of liberal humanism in Europe and elsewhere. In
consequence a number of books emerged that sought to show in varying
ways that the essential message of the Old Testament was still
strictly relevant to the troubled twentieth century of the Christian era.
Those who endeavored to furnish an interpretation of Old Testament
theology did so predominantly in terms of the permanent ideas of the
Hebrew Scriptures, tacitly abandoning the realm of pure historical criticism as largely irrelevant for the purposes in view. The result of this was
an increased emphasis upon the nature and relevance of the "abiding
values" of the Old Testament for the modern reader.[51]

At the beginning of World War II the Roman Catholic theologian
Paul Heinisch pursued the classical dogmatic themes in a systematized
account of Old Testament theology.[52] Subsequent publications in English continued to stress the relevance of the Old Testament for the
modern age, and under the influence of neo-orthodoxy they endeavored
—with varying degress of success—to relate the theological interpretation
of specific areas of the Old Testament to the original day and age, then
to the period covered by the entire Bible, and finally to the culmination
of the divine revelation in Jesus Christ.[53] Characteristic of the neo-
orthodox movement was the conviction that the pattern of the divine
purpose for mankind was unfolded gradually by means of specific
creative experiences in the stream of historical events,[54] whose logical
culmination occurred in the New Testament.[55]

---

[50] Robinson, *Inspiration and Revelation in the OT.*

[51] E.g. S. A. Cook, *The OT: A Reinterpretation* (1936); *The "Truth" of the Bible*
(1938); H. H. Rowley, *The Relevance of the Bible* (1942); G. E. Wright, *The
Challenge of Israel's Faith* (1944); R. B. Y. Scott, *The Relevance of the Prophets*
(1944); R. Calkins, *The Modern Message of the Minor Prophets* (1947); C. A.
Simpson, *Revelation and Response in the OT* (1947); A. G. Hebert, *The Authority
of the OT* (1947); G. P. Baker, *The Witness of the Prophets* (1948); W. A. L.
Elmslie, *How Came Our Faith: A Study of the Religion of Israel and Its Significance
for the Modern World* (1949).

[52] P. Heinisch, *Theologie des AT* (1940); E. tr. W. G. Heidt, *Theology of the
OT* (1955).

[53] Cf. H. Cunliffe-Jones, *The Authority of the Biblical Revelation* (1945).

[54] Cf. H. Wheeler Robinson, *Record and Revelation in the Actuality of History,*
pp. 304ff.

[55] Cf. W. J. Phythian-Adams, *The Call of Israel* (1934), *The Fulness of Israel*
(1938), *The People and the Presence* (1942); C. H. Dodd, *History and the Gospel*
(1938); F. G. Lankard, *The Bible Speaks to Our Generation* (1941); H. Wheeler
Robinson, *Redemption and Revelation in the Actuality of History* (1942); H. H.
Rowley, *The Rediscovery of the OT* (1946); C. H. Dodd, *The Bible Today*
(1946); W. A. Smart, *Still the Bible Speaks* (1948); B. W. Anderson, *Rediscovering
the Bible* (1951).

Another posthumous work on Old Testament theology was that of Otto Procksch, which represented the final stage of much earlier study by the author.[56] Following Hofmann he adopted a Christocentric attitude towards history, and like Sellin distinguished the permanent elements of Hebrew thought from the more transient ones in the light of the yardstick supplied by the Christian gospel. Procksch began with a history of Israelite religion, and followed this by a more systematized grouping of concepts in which the divine Covenant was associated in a threefold manner with the people of Israel, with mankind, and ultimately with the world.[57] A similar emphasis upon the fundamental unity of the Old and New Testaments was made by Vriezen, who stressed the importance of the Christocentric interpretation of the Old Testament narratives.[58]

Two American publications issued just after World War II continued the theme of the unity of Scripture. Millar Burrows wrote a manual of practical theological studies on the whole Bible, which, although it did not furnish a particularly vigorous picture of Hebrew religion, at least succeeded in expounding the most important concepts against a background of their original context and significance.[59] The other work, by Otto Baab, recognized the existence of stages of development in Hebrew religion, but regarded these as constituting aspects of the fundamental unity of religious experience in the community of Israel.[60] The major doctrines were discussed in the order commonly employed in dogmatic theology, and in the process Baab was careful to point out the importance of personal spiritual insight for the understanding of Old Testament doctrines.[61]

A reflection of the attitudes of Eichrodt appeared in the writings of another American scholar, R. C. Dentan, who utilized the neo-orthodox concept of revelation to relate the history and ideology of Old Testament religion to that of the New Testament.[62] A British writer, N. W. Porteous, in a survey of Old Testament theological writings since the time of Davidson, observed that a theology of the Old Testament will not attempt to obscure the fact that Christ did not merely decode the Old Testament but fulfilled it.[63] Any endeavor to use the word "theology" for

[56] O. Procksch, *Theologie des AT* (1950); cf. his study in *Neue kirchliche Zeitschrift*, XXXVI (1925), pp. 485ff., 715ff.
[57] W. Eichrodt, *Theologie des AT*, I, p. 6n., borrowed this pattern from Procksch.
[58] Th. C. Vriezen, *Hoofdlijnen der Theologie van het Oude Testament* (1949).
[59] M. Burrows, *An Outline of Biblical Theology* (1946).
[60] O. J. Baab, *The Theology of the OT* (1949).
[61] Cf. Baab in *The Study of the Bible Today and Tomorrow* (ed. H. R. Willoughby, 1947), pp. 401ff.
[62] R. C. Dentan, *Preface to OT Theology* (1950, rev. ed., 1963).
[63] *OTMS*, p. 344; the survey is found on pages 311ff.

a history of human beliefs about God would fail to bring out the fullest sense implicit in the term.[64]

In a book published in 1952, G. E. Wright appeared to reflect von Rad's theory, which saw the Hebrew recognition of divine acts in their history in terms of a confession or *Heilsgeschichtliches Credo*.[65] For Wright, Old Testament faith comprised a recital of such "mighty acts" as the deliverance at the Red Sea and the Covenant event at Sinai. While he showed that the basic beliefs of the Old Testament were given meaning for the early Christian Church through typological means, he adopted a very conservative attitude towards the use of typology generally, preferring to restrict it to what was envisaged by the New Testament authors. This approach appears to have the double demerit of reviving an outmoded form of Biblical dogmatic theology, and making the ancient Hebrew faith confessional in nature. Old Testament religion is to all intents and purposes reduced to a series of thankful reminiscences concerning past historical events, and on this basis would seem to take little cognizance of such important themes as soteriology or divine judgment. Equally unfortunate is the apparent inability of Wright to think of the divine election of Israel as integral to the concept of the Covenant. But in any event, theology as recital is much too restricted to do proper justice to the manifold facets of Old Testament thought concerning the divine nature and purpose. Supremely for Hebrew tradition it was the metaphysic of Sinai that gave meaning and purpose to history, and not *vice versa*. As Fichte remarked in a somewhat different connection, "only the metaphysical can save; never under any circumstances the historical."[66] Certainly the Old Testament writings make it clear that recollection of the characteristic divinely motivated saving events served to

[64] Problems connected with Old Testament theology were also discussed in European works that were not specifically theological in character. In a study of the literary strata of the prophetic character of Deuteronomy, H. Breit outlined some of the principal ideas occurring in the book; *Die Predigt der Deuteronomisten* (1933). G. von Rad attempted a similar task in his discussion of the Hexateuchal priestly material, *Die Priesterschrift im Hexateuch* (1934). Noth examined the theological character of Pentateuchal law in *Die Gesetze im Pentateuch: ihre Voraussetzungen und ihr Sinn* (1940). Three years later Von Rad gave a broad consideration to some of the issues involved in formulating a theology of the Old Testament; *Theologische Literaturzeitung*, LXVIII (1943), col. 225, cf. in *Werden und Wesen des AT*, pp. 138ff. He maintained that the Old Testament writings constituted a testimony to continuous divine action in history, and emphasized the *kerygma* of the prophetic utterances. The importance that he assigned to prophecy and its fulfilment can be gauged from the fact that he was in agreement with the limited use of typology in this connection. The seeming nihilism of Noth was reflected in his *Geschichte und Gotteswort im AT* (1950), in which he adduced historical difficulties confronting those who attempted a thorough treatment of Old Testament theology.

[65] G. E. Wright, *God Who Acts: Biblical Theology as Recital* (1952); cf. *IB*, I, pp. 354ff.

[66] Quoted by E. Brunner, *Offenbarung und Vernunft* (1941), p. 394.

furnish a perspective for faith, and never at any time constituted the form or content of faith itself. However, Wright was correct in maintaining that the variety of thought occurring in the Old Testament was unified by the overall concern for the meaning of historical events and the place of Israel within the stream of history. What he does not seem to have made clear, however, is that there is a distinct sense in which the objective written record is at once a description and an interpretation of many of the historical events that it narrates. The Old Testament theologian, therefore, must be prepared to deal alike with the "event-concept" and the "written-concept," and if the latter is rejected or attenuated on the basis of nineteenth-century "objective historicism," the former is immediately open to a great deal of subjective speculation.

A similar emphasis upon the "acts of God" was made in 1955 by Edmond Jacob,[67] who maintained that the faith of the Old Testament was not centered upon concepts of Deity as such, but upon appreciation of and response to the actions of God in history. Jacob adopted a threefold division of his subject which dealt successively with the divine nature and attributes, the activity of God in history and human life, and the concepts of sin, redemption, eschatology, and the consummation of divine activity in history. His work was based upon a moderate critical position, but perhaps because of its inherent assumptions it failed to emphasize the place of the Covenant in the religious life of the nation, and also neglected the status of the cult in Israelite faith generally. It should be said that his presentation suffered from the deficiencies common to those scholars who have based their interpretation of Old Testament religion upon divine acts rather than on Biblical thought as such.

An approach to Old Testament theology from the standpoint of Pauline soteriology was undertaken by F. Baumgärtel in 1952, who held that the Christian gospel was the ultimate standard by which the Old Testament ought to be judged theologically.[68] Employing an objective historical method of interpretation, he claimed that the character of the Old Testament was that of promise rather than prophecy, the expectation being realized in Jesus Christ. The modern Christian, Baumgärtel affirmed, could not utilize typology as the Early Church did in order to make the Old Testament relevant, but instead he ought to relate himself to the Old Testament *Heilsgeschichte* from the standpoint of his experience of Christ. Forgiveness through the Cross presupposed the divine judgments on sin depicted in the Old Testament. Although Baumgärtel made a valiant attempt to bring the theology of the ancient Hebrew

---

[67] E. Jacob, *Théologie de l'Ancien Testament* (1955); E. tr. A. W. Heathcote and P. J. Allcock, *Theology of the OT* (1958).

[68] F. Baumgärtel, *Verheissung: Zur Frage des evangelischen Verständnisses des AT* (1952); cf. in *Theologische Literaturzeitung*, LXXVI (1951), cols. 257ff., and in *Geschichte und Altes Testament, Albrecht Alt zum 70. Geburtstag* (1953), pp. 13ff. Cf. J. Bright, *The Authority of the Old Testament* (1967), pp. 72f.

435

Scriptures beyond the bounds of mere historicism into the present experience of the individual Christian, he failed to give an adequate place to the strictly prophetic element in the Old Testament writings, particularly where such passages were of a messianic character.

A major work on Old Testament theology from the standpoint of Roman Catholicism was published in 1954 by Van Imschoot.[69] The plan of his book reflected the influence of Köhler and Eichrodt, particularly in the first volume, which dealt with the nature and attributes of Deity, the concept of election, and the character of the Covenant relationship. The second volume was concerned with the doctrine of man, and discussed his origin, nature, destiny, and duties. The author managed to avoid the deficient views of sin and its consequences that are apparent in the theological writings of Köhler and von Rad. Van Imschoot rejected Köhler's opinion that the cultus was a human attempt at self-redemption, characterizing it instead as an aspect of human duty towards God. Van Imschoot does not appear to have been as successful as Eichrodt in presenting the essential unity of Israelite faith, despite his emphasis upon the Covenant relationship. Although his work constituted a careful synthesis of Biblical material it suffered from certain of the deficiencies associated with dogmatic methodology.

A comprehensive study of Old Testament theology based on the general approach of Alt and Noth was published in 1957 by von Rad.[70] This masterly application of form-critical method to the problems of Old Testament theology was based on the presupposition that the principal task at hand was the reiterating of the historical character of the Hebrew faith as the witness of ancient Israel, itself a creation of the amphictyony, to the mighty acts of God. In so doing von Rad repudiated the Israelite "world of faith" envisaged by Eichrodt in favor of retelling in its historical form the Old Testament *Heilsgeschichte*. For von Rad the Hexateuch came into being from an arrangement in confessional form of various groups of traditions that were largely contradictory and conflicting. The figure of Moses emerged but dimly, since the traditions about the normative founder of Hebrew faith were held to be far from easy to reconcile with one another.

Von Rad accorded separate treatment to the prophetic writings, because the message contained in them not only presupposed the earlier historical traditions but involved other issues as well. For him the entire consideration turned upon the assertion that the soteriological concepts enshrined in the older traditions had proved inadequate, and in consequence would subsequently be replaced by a fresh series of divine "mighty acts." Von Rad discussed the nature of the prophetic utterances

[69] P. Van Imschoot, *Théologie de l'Ancien Testament*, I (1954); II (1956).

[70] *Theologie des AT, I, Die Theologie der geschichtlichen Überlieferungen Israels* (1957); E. tr. *OT Theology*, I (1962); II (1965).

generally in relationship to the idea of revelation, and followed this by a treatment of the individual prophets and their teachings. The second volume ended with a section dealing with problems of interpretation and the use of the Old Testament narratives in the books of the New Testament.

Von Rad's work was characterized by a pronounced authoritarian tone, an arbitrary subjectivity of judgment, and a distinct reluctance to consider other points of view on the subject of Old Testament theology. Von Rad conveyed the impression that other approaches than his own were unhistorical because they resulted in a static theological picture, and did not furnish the concept of an ongoing revelation in the stream of historical encounter. The kind of form-criticism that he employed might well raise serious questions as to its validity, especially where it led the author to treat primary elements of the narrative as though they were secondary. For example, it is difficult to see how, if in fact the creation narrative is to be regarded as a secondary element, it can be connected realistically with the *Heilsgeschichte* on his theory.

An even more formidable objection to his general methodology is the question whether the concept of *Heilsgeschichte* is, after all, the best category for exercising control of the source material in any interpretation of Old Testament thought. Again, serious objections must be raised with respect to the claim that the earliest Jehovistic faith was given its normative expression in terms of "short historical creeds." Although it is a commonplace of the Alt and Noth school to emphasize the importance of the amphictyony and to relate the beginnings of Israel to this type of ancient social organization, the shortcomings of a view that deliberately flouts the uniform tradition of Israel regarding its origins must be apparent even to the most casual reader. In any event it is far from certain, as Kaufmann has shown, that the political organization of the Hebrews during the settlement period corresponded to the type of Greek social structure envisaged by Alt and Noth.[71]

Von Rad displayed the kind of insight necessary for producing a true theology of the Old Testament in his determination to show that such a theology was related to the history of the divine acts of salvation. His crucial error, however, consisted in using the critically reconstructed testimonies of Israel to such deeds as the foundation for his theology. Surely a genuine Old Testament theology can only be possible when the ancient Hebrew Scriptures are recognized as constituting nothing less than the oracles of God. For von Rad, however, a sufficient basis for theology was furnished by the witness of Israel to what it believed to be the historic acts of divine mercy. While the presentation that von Rad furnished was generally consistent with the form-critical principles adopted, there must remain grave doubt as to the validity of the methodology upon which the work was based.

[71] *KRI*, p. 256.

The most notable British contribution to Old Testament theology since the time of Davidson was made in 1959 by G. A. F. Knight, who stands firmly in the orthodox liberal tradition of esteem for the Old Testament as the Word of God but insistence on a thoroughgoing reconstruction of the literature along critical lines as a necessary preliminary to theological assessment.[72] Knight exhibits traces of the influence of von Rad and Wright in seeing the "God Who Acts" supremely at work on behalf of His people during the Exodus and the exile. His approach is marked by distinct anthropological overtones that emphasize the pictorial images of the Hebrew mind and show their continuity of expression in the New Testament. Knight seems to assign a position of secondary importance to the Sinai Covenant, and almost completely neglects the covenant associated with Abraham. He prefers to stress the living nature of God rather than attempt a more formal examination of the divine attributes, in the conviction that God was ever active on behalf of His people Israel so as to secure their ultimate salvation and the concomitant blessings for the world.

Knight views with disfavor the Christological interpretation of certain passages of the Old Testament to the exclusion of others, since for him the Hebrew Scriptures as a whole are messianic. Thus a Christian theology of the Old Testament is meaningless without the person of Jesus Christ as its culmination. Though Knight presents his case with considerable erudition, his conclusions are rather vague, and he seems to stress the reality of the Israelite religious experience without giving proper attention to those divine attributes that afforded permanent meaning to that experience. Rather curious is his statement that God "became one flesh with Israel,"[73] which has distinctly Christian overtones, and cannot be demonstrated from the Hebrew Scriptures themselves.

To the present writer Knight seems to display an inadequate appreciation of the extent to which Israelite religious life constituted failure rather than success in its experience of God, a deficiency that is hardly balanced by the statement that Christ was the perfect embodiment of the true Israel, the union of divine and human, however correct the latter might be. In common with some other modern authors Knight pays comparatively little attention to the Temple cultus and its elaborate ritual, and as a result it is hardly surprising that his treatment of the entire question of sacrifice is completely inadequate. It is unfortunate that Knight passes over the nature of the divine attributes so casually, since not merely were these of fundamental importance for the great Hebrew prophetic figures, but, indeed, for the very ethos of the nation of Israel. Any serious attempt to come to grips with a theology of the Old Testament must include a discussion of the attributes of God, particular-

---

[72] G. A. F. Knight, *A Christian Theology of the OT* (1959).
[73] *Ibid.*, p. 205.

ly in the light of the fact that the "wholly other" concept of the neo-orthodox theologians has gone far towards making God quite obscure.

The earlier contributions of Muilenburg to the history and content of ancient Hebrew religion are reflected in a work published in 1961.[74] Like Knight and other liberal writers, Muilenburg's thought presupposes the acceptance of the results of European critical scholarship with a concomitant rearrangement of the Hebrew literature to conform to the precepts of the Wellhausen school. At the same time his inquiry is moderate and well disciplined within this context, emphasizing that the primary responsibility of the scholar is to ascertain the original meaning of the particular passage under study without being unduly influenced by subsequent historical or doctrinal developments. For the Christian, however, the history and religion of ancient Israel find their logical continuation and fruition in the New Covenant. Accordingly, while an evaluation of isolated passages may afford some insight into the divine activity through Israel, the fullest significance of Old Testament faith can only be appreciated as a result of contemplating a linear movement of Biblical thought culminating in the atoning work of Jesus Christ.

Muilenburg was able to avoid many of the difficulties arising from a standpoint that emphasized human religious experience rather than divine revelation. Thus he consistently depicts God as a real Person who transcended human conceptions of Himself, and emphasizes the Covenant as the motivating factor in all considerations of ethical behavior. His general conclusions are the result of careful scholarly inquiry, and his work constitutes one of the most adequate representations of the moderate critical approach to the problems of ancient Hebrew faith.

American conservative scholars who addressed themselves to the theology of the Old Testament include J. H. Raven, who in 1933 issued a work which, while it appeared to deal primarily with Hebrew religion, did in fact constitute an accredited Biblical theology.[75] The book was deficient, however, in that it only considered developments up to the period of Manasseh. The conservative traditions of Princeton Theological Seminary were continued by O. T. Allis of Westminster Theological Seminary, who in 1945 published an anti-dispensational study of the prophetic writings,[76] and also by the works of E. J. Young.[77] While the theological writings of John Murray dealt with Biblical doctrines in the wider sense, they included considerations of more specific Old Testa-

---

[74] His earlier contributions are found in *The Vitality of the Christian Tradition* (ed. G. F. Thomas, 1945), pp. 1ff., and in *IB*, I, pp. 291ff. These were reflected in his *The Way of Israel: Biblical Faith and Ethics* (1961).

[75] *The History of the Religion of Israel* (1933).

[76] *Prophecy and the Church* (1945).

[77] *My Servants the Prophets* (1952); *Studies in Isaiah* (1954); *The Study of OT Theology Today* (1958).

439

ment themes.[78] Similar to these were the theological studies of G. Vos, who dealt with the major areas of Old Testament theology without actually considering all the doctrines generally envisaged by orthodox dogmatic theology.[79]

Aside from works devoted primarily to the problems encountered in Old Testament theology, a number of semantic studies have enriched the general discipline in important areas of detail.[80] Valuable contributions have been made by German authors in the Kittel *Theologisches Wörterbuch zum Neuen Testament*, which, although it was not concerned specifically with Old Testament concepts, dealt in varying degrees with the Hebrew antecedents of certain Christian doctrines.[81]

Certain of the principles upon which the Kittel *Wörterbuch* was based met with heavy criticism from James Barr,[82] who argued from the standpoint of sound linguistic method that the nature and function of language should not be the victim of unscientific lexicographical speculation. Barr accused contemporary writers in the general field of Biblical theology of uncritical procedures, pointing specifically to the disputed area of the relationship between the Biblical languages and Biblical thought. In particular he focused attention on the problems raised by the kind of semantic approach that ascribed to the Biblical writers a thought-structure based on areas of meaning assigned to specific words. As a necessary preliminary to sound etymological study for Biblical theology, he asserted, it was of paramount importance for Scriptural *statements* to be relied upon, rather than isolated Biblical *words*. In questioning the linguistic presuppositions and methods of Biblical theologians, Barr showed the dangers inherent in an incautious use of the traditional distinctions between Greek and Hebrew modes of thought,[83] maintaining that such contrasts were not infrequently employed *a priori*.

---

[78] *The Covenant of Grace* (1953); *Redemption, Accomplished and Applied* (1955); *The Imputation of Adam's Sin* (1959).

[79] *Biblical Theology* (1948).

[80] One of the most important of these works was N. Glueck's *Das Wort ḥesed im alttestamentlichen Sprachgebrauch als menschliche und göttliche gemeinschaftsgemässe Verhaltungsweise*, BZAW, XLVII (1927). The trend that he established was followed in the writings of Dodd, *The Bible and the Greeks, I: The Religious Vocabulary of Hellenistic Judaism* (1935); J. Pedersen, *Israel: Its Life and Culture* (vols. I, II, 1926; III, IV, 1940); J. J. Stamm, *Erlösen und Vergeben im AT: eine begriffsgeschichtliche Untersuchung* (1940); A. R. Johnson, *The One and the Many in the Israelite Conception of God* (1942) and *The Vitality of the Individual in the Thought of Ancient Israel* (1949); N. H. Snaith, *The Distinctive Ideas of the OT* (1944); and G. Oestborn, *Tōrā in the OT: A Semantic Study* (1945).

[81] Some of the Biblical studies have been issued separately in English in the series entitled *Bible Key Words*.

[82] *The Semantics of Biblical Language* (1961).

[83] *Ibid.*, pp. 8ff.

In consequence the linguistic evidence was generally made to conform to a particular philosophical or theological assumption.[84] This all-too-familiar Wellhausenian pattern raised the question as to whether the interests of Old Testament theologians would not be served more adequately by an emphasis upon the differences between the Old Testament as such and its ancient Near Eastern environment.

In pointing to scholars whose observations on Biblical languages and thought had not been grounded in a proper method of linguistic analysis, Barr called attention to the misuses of etymologies in general[85] and to the underlying presuppositions of the Kittel *Wörterbuch* in particular.[86] His predominant complaint was that the authors of various articles tended to read into Scripture certain theological concepts that could not properly be deduced from the actual linguistic form of the text itself.[87] He also criticized the preoccupation of the *Wörterbuch* with the history of ideas rather than with the specific meanings of words,[88] resulting in the treatment of ordinary semantic criteria as something approaching developed theological concepts. As a corrective he urged the grouping of terms by related semantic fields rather than by roots, and their comparison with synonyms and antonyms[89] as well as the study of phrases or sentences, rather than the individual words, as the true vehicles of theological concepts.[90] Furthermore, he maintained that such presuppositions as eschatology or *Heilsgeschichte* should be subordinated to proper linguistic discipline so as to avoid the common tendency of loading the etymological history of a term with theological significance. In short, the meaning of Hebrew words in the Old Testament was to be determined by their use and context, not by their etymology.

Barr made no secret of the fact that he adopted a functional view of linguistic expression, and that his emphasis upon proper semantic method was designed to bring long-overdue canons of discipline to the study of Biblical terms.[91] While he conceded that many of the conclusions at which Biblical theologians had arrived were correct, he affirmed that the methods that they had utilized in this endeavor were not.

---

[84] *Ibid.*, pp. 23 *passim*.

[85] *Ibid.*, pp. 111ff.; as examples of improper methodology, T. Boman, *Das hebräische Denken im Vergleich mit dem Griechischen* (1954 ed.); E. tr. *Hebrew Thought Compared with Greek* (1960); J. Pedersen, *Israel, I-II* (1920), *III-IV* (1934), E. tr. *Israel: Its Life and Culture* (1926, 1940).

[86] Barr, *op. cit.*, pp. 206ff.

[87] E.g. Weiser, πίστις, VI, pp. 182ff.; W. Foerster, κτίζω, III, pp. 102ff.

[88] Barr, *op. cit.*, pp. 209, 229ff.

[89] *Ibid.*, p. 235.

[90] *Ibid.*, pp. 249, 265f.; cf. L. Bloomfield, *Language* (1933), pp. 27ff.

[91] *Op. cit.*, pp. 263ff.

Whether linguists generally will be in agreement with the position of Barr is naturally a matter of some doubt, linguistic debate being what it is. There can be little question, however, that this brilliant and determined attack upon poor methodology in Biblical linguistic studies will go far towards removing the obscurities and uncritical generalities so commonly associated with the exposition of leading Biblical ideas.

II. PRINCIPLES OF INTERPRETATION

A. THE BASIS OF OLD TESTAMENT THEOLOGY

From the foregoing discussion it is evident that a satisfactory theology of the Old Testament is far from an easy accomplishment.[1] Historical perspective and method in this field did not come into their own until the nineteenth century,[2] and were accompanied by what was regarded as an objective historicism, which, however, rejected the idea of an established written revelation of a final character. This turn of events was unfortunate since Biblical theology was immediately at the mercy of subjective and arbitrary forms of interpretation, which in a great many cases proved to be little more than philosophies of religion. On balance there would seem to be very little to choose between this situation and that which obtained at the height of the medieval period with regard to the theological interpretation of the Old Testament. It is true, of course, that the approaches and emphases were quite different in many respects, but the abuse of the Scriptural text was a feature common to both.

Although the neo-orthodox theologians redressed the imbalance to some extent by stressing the uniqueness of the history itself, they abandoned the traditional view of revelation as the communication to man of divine truth involving the moral and spiritual categories of life in favor of relating the unfolding of the divine purpose through specific experiences of encounter in the history of the chosen people. Although it is true that ordinary historical phenomena constitute part of the vehicle of revelation, there are dangers implicit in the assumption that a satisfactory theology can be built upon certain arbitrarily chosen manifestations of God in history. First of all, the theological presuppositions of the particular author will lead to a sharp difference of opinion as to precisely what constitutes a "saving act," and which of those thus available for discus-

---

[1] For some of the problems connected with Biblical and OT theology generally see E. Ebeling, *JTS,* VI (1955), pp. 210ff.; J. D. Smart, *The Interpretation of Scripture* (1961); J. van der Ploeg, *Une théologie de l'Ancien Testament est-elle possible?* (1962).

[2] Cf. A. Richardson, *The Bible in the Age of Science* (1961), pp. 49ff.

sion are to be taken as exemplifying the purpose of God in history. Clearly the approach adopted in this regard by a Jewish writer will differ radically from that of a Christian. Secondly, the view of a deity who acts in a voluntaristic manner is an essentially Greek one, and can be employed subjectively to associate events that have no organic connection with one another. As E. G. Kraeling has pointed out, there are many who will feel that any grouping of "saving acts" should be limited to the Incarnation, Crucifixion, and Resurrection of Jesus Christ, and that the Old Testament writings in general should be deemed prophetic of the work of the Saviour.[3]

Although it has brought a reaffirmation of many important principles, such as the priority of revelation over reason, the neo-orthodox movement generally has suffered from certain unresolved internal tensions. These are reflected in writings involving Old Testament theology. Following Schleiermacher, who maintained that God imparted life rather than dogma, and that He could not be known as He is in Himself but only in relationship to the existence of the individual human being, writers such as Kierkegaard called for a resolute individual commitment to the truth of a quality that would completely transform the whole of existence. From one point of view this position represented a salutary reaction against formal orthodoxy and shallow liberalism, but in other respects it resulted in a tendency to dispose its adherents towards a doctrine of revelation whose locus consisted in an immediate existential response to encounter, and not in an objective Scriptural content.[4]

Existential truth, as envisaged by Kierkegaard and his followers, may well be dominant in the transformation of concrete individual experience, but at the same time it is important to recognize that the source of truth is neither in mortal experience nor in human reason, but in a rational and objective divine revelation embodied in the Scriptures.[5] For this reason it is important to note, as Rowley has insisted, that an Old Testament theology should be based firmly upon Biblical thought rather than upon particular events in the history of Israel. Such a theology will avoid the dichotomy that Eissfeldt saw between faith and knowledge, for faith will have the same active character as knowledge; and it will lead to a proper appreciation of the spiritual issues involved without impairing the objective historical nature of knowledge. The vast majority of writers in this field have recognized that the Old Testament has a meaning that far surpasses its more immediate significance as the national literature of the ancient Hebrews; and if there are absolute and transcendent spiritual values in the Old Testament, it is surely legitimate for them to be grasped by the exercise of faith in a manner that does not

[3] *The OT Since the Reformation*, p. 280.
[4] C. F. H. Henry in *Baker's Dictionary of Theology* (1960), p. 459.
[5] Cf. G. H. Clark in *Revelation and the Bible* (ed. C. F. H. Henry, 1958), pp. 29ff.

compromise the historical situation. The trend of modern studies has been such that it is now no longer necessary to follow the older critical concept that the earlier stages of Old Testament thought were necessarily the most primitive. Instead, a new emphasis has been given to the substantial and unified nature of the corpus of Hebrew belief existing from comparatively early times. Anthropomorphic expressions, which were once regarded as typical of a rudimentary theological outlook, can now be esteemed symbolically as constituting rich and deep insights into the character of the Deity, expressed in a way to afford them the greatest permanence.

B. INTERPRETATIVE APPROACHES

The question as to what principles of interpretation are to be applied to the Old Testament writings will naturally be of some concern in the formulation of an Old Testament theology. Certain approaches are common to the Bible and other ancient literature, while others concern the Scriptural writings exclusively as the unique record of divine revelation in and through Israel. The interpretation of specific events or writings was, of course, a common feature of ancient life, and found a comparable place in the pages of the Old Testament. Thus the interpretation of dreams was recorded on occasions,[6] as well as the exposition of an older passage in one of later date (Jer. 31:29f. expounded in Ezek. 18:2ff.). On a general basis the various Biblical documents and any parts into which they can properly be subdivided must be studied not merely in their immediate verbal context but also against the background of the occasion, the place, and the human situation to which they belong.[7] This requires an understanding of the historical and geographical setting of ancient Near Eastern life—on its own terms and not those of artificial *a priori* postulates—and a firm grasp of the structure and literary idioms of the Biblical languages and their Near Eastern counterparts, as well as an appreciation of the kind of literature under study. The interpretation will naturally vary as the source material is found to be allegory, poetry, prophecy, or apocalyptic. The last named especially calls for the application of special rules of interpretation. An understanding of the historical background of the Old Testament will prevent the interpreter from applying the canons of Christian morality to the social and religious activities of the Middle and Late Bronze Ages. The significance of the prophetic movement will not be appreciated most fully until the religious, social, and political movements in contemporary Near Eastern nations are familiar to the interpreter. Mention should be made again of

---

[6] Gen. 40:8ff.; 41:1ff.; Dan. 2:36ff.; 4:19ff.; cf. E. L. Ehrlich, *Der Traum im AT* (1953).

[7] F. F. Bruce, *NBD*, p. 567.

the importance of the geographical setting[8] and the general *Sitz im Leben* of the ancient Hebrews as revealed by modern archaeological discoveries.[9]

1. Early exegetical approaches. In a more restricted sense the interpretation of the Old Testament involves not merely the separate documents or writings as such, but for the Jewish scholar their place in the entire corpus of Hebrew literature, and for the Christian their interpretation as part of the Bible. In emphasizing that sense of unity and internal harmony in Scripture that enables each part to be interpreted in the light of the whole, the Christian Church was merely applying a principle familiar to Jewish teachers. Traditionally the latter conceived of the Prophets and the Sacred Writings to a large extent as commentaries on the Torah.[10] Medieval Jewish exegetes developed a fourfold theory of interpretation, consisting of the *peshat* or obvious literal meaning of the text, the *remes* or allegorical significance, the *derash,* a meaning to be obtained by applying certain methodological rules, and the *sod* or mystical meaning of the text.

Christian patristic interpretation in Alexandria was influenced by the Biblical expositions of Philo in the direction of undertaking a massive allegorization of the text as a means of ascertaining the mind of the inspiring Spirit of God. In this way much in the Bible that was unacceptable to the intellect or unpalatable to the conscience could be regarded as proper and legitimate. This was as much a theological method as an attitude of faith, for as has been observed above, the Fathers generally were unable to regard anything in Scripture as useless. The Antiochene school, in contrast, paid much more attention to the historical sense of the text, and, while not rejecting the allegorical method completely, pursued a more realistic exegetical course. Medieval Christian interpreters could either work on a twofold basis involving the literal historical and the mystical spiritual sense, or in a still more highly differentiated fourfold form parallel to the Jewish canons of exegesis: the *literal* connotation of the Biblical record, the *allegorical* interpretation that deduced doctrine from narrative passages, the *moral* understanding that held lessons for behavior and life, and the *anagogical* sense that found heavenly meanings in earthly facts. On such a basis the word *water* could mean literally a colorless liquid, allegorically baptism by water, moral purity, or anagogically eternal life in the celestial Jerusalem.[11]

[8] Cf. J. M. Houston, *Journal of the Transactions of the Victoria Institute,* LXXXVI (1954), pp. 62ff.

[9] Cf. L. Köhler, *Der Hebräische Mensch* (1953); E. W. Heaton, *Everyday Life in OT Times* (1956); P. R. Ackroyd, *The People of the OT* (1959); R. de Vaux, *Ancient Israel, Its Life and Institutions* (1962), *et al.*

[10] Cf. J. Weingreen, *BJRL,* XXXIV (1951), pp. 166ff.

[11] F. F. Bruce in *Baker's Dictionary of Theology,* p. 293.

Emphasis upon grammatico-historical exegesis and the primacy of the literal sense of Scripture characterized the Reformation period. Luther began in the old hermeneutic tradition of allegory, but later counselled interpreters against all but the most cautious use of allegorical method. Protestant interpretation generally was governed by the Reformation attitude that Scripture was amenable to a simple literal meaning and that it could never be subservient to a purely human authority.[12]

2. *Modern approaches.* Some modern interpreters have argued from the New Testament use of the Old Testament to establish four basic principles of interpretation.[13] These consist of the *historical,* which regards the Old Testament as an authentic and reliable chronicle of events, the *propositional,* in which Old Testament statements are either fulfilled in the New Testament or employed as a basis for doctrine or conduct, the *homological,* a mathematical concept employed to express the identity or correspondence between Old Covenant and New Covenant situations,[14] and the *illustrational,* in which historic material is employed to reinforce truth and emphasize moral lessons. These principles may be contrasted with such spurious approaches as the superstitious,[15] the rationalistic, the mythological, and the allegorical.

The latter raises the problem as to whether secret senses of Scripture can be said to exist independently, or whether they are valid only by derivation or implication from a primary sense. One form of allegorization which has experienced some degree of revival in the twentieth century is that of *typological* interpretation.[16] This involves the tracing of parallels or correspondences between the two Testaments in order to discern the fundamental meaning of the Old Testament passage in terms of its New Testament equivalent. In the primitive Church typology was employed in general to demonstrate the Old Testament prefigurations of the Christian dispensation, and as such was prophetic and Christocentric in nature.[17] If typology is to be employed at all as a method of interpretation[18] it should follow the cautious approach exhibited by the New Testament writers, who invariably saw the earliest stages in the Biblical demonstration of divine redemption as foreshadowings of later phases. By this means some of the more eccentric allegorical interpreta-

---

[12] Cf. B. Ramm, *Protestant Bible Interpretation* (1953).

[13] Cf. E. F. Kevan in *Revelation and the Bible,* pp. 285ff.

[14] Cf. F. W. Farrar, *The History of Interpretation* (1886), p. 218; W. J. Phythian-Adams, *The Way of At-one-ment* (1944), pp. 10f.; A. G. Hebert, *The Authority of the OT,* p. 219.

[15] Cf. Farrar, *The History of Interpretation,* p. 107.

[16] G. W. H. Lampe and K. J. Woollcombe, *Essays on Typology* (1957); Cf. W. A. Irwin, *ZAW,* LXII (1950), p. 6; R. Bultmann, *Theologische Literaturzeitung,* LXXV (1950), pp. 205ff.; C. Westermann (ed.), *Essays on OT Hermeneutics* (1963).

[17] W. Broomall in *Baker's Dictionary of Theology,* pp. 533f.

[18] Cf. H. H. Rowley, *The Changing Pattern of OT Studies* (1959), pp. 27f.

tions that arose in the patristic period and were perpetuated by subsequent generations will be avoided.

Any historically oriented Old Testament theology must somehow grapple with the problem of the ultimate meaning of Old Testament history. The standpoint of the author will naturally have considerable bearing upon the conclusions arrived at, but the issue will be particularly problematical for Jewish scholars. The list of those who have showed revived interest in the dynamic Biblical concepts of divine transcendence, of man under sin and grace, and of God as the Lord of History include few Jewish scholars. The neo-orthodox movement did at least serve their interests to the point where it was able to make portions of the Old Testament relevant to the needs of modern man, and this in itself was no small undertaking. But it has been largely unsuccessful in stimulating among Jewish scholars the counterpart to a "theology of crisis," and this is all the more surprising in view of the appalling tribulations suffered by European Judaism. Even Martin Buber concentrated more upon the history of religious thought in Israel than in formulating a theology of the divine-human encounter in Hebrew religion.[19]

a. Heilsgeschichte. For Jewish as for Christian scholars, the *Sitz im Leben* approach, though extremely valuable for historical and cultural investigation, is disappointing in its inability to do much more than point to its own situational context, which has only an indirect bearing upon the great doctrinal themes of the Old Testament revelation. Even more frustrating for Jewish writers must be the greatly overworked concept of *Heilsgeschichte*, which purports to discover the ultimate meaning of history in terms of a specific series of events. The "salvation" expressed by this idea can hardly be said to have been achieved within the period of Old Testament history, either actually or ideally, and if *Heilsgeschichte* can have any meaning at all for Jewish scholars, it must be at best rather potential and tentative. Christian theologians have enjoyed a considerably greater advantage in this respect, for they have been able to perceive in the Person of the Incarnate Christ the climax of the divine purpose of human redemption. While this supreme point of revelation to man was historically oriented in a manner analogous to that of the Torah and prophecy, it partook in a special way of the character of eschatological fulfilment. From its inception the Christian Church accepted the new revelation as being in organic connection with the old, though transcending and consummating it. Christian tradition has consistently emphasized that the Old Testament finds its fullest meaning and expression in terms of the work of Christ as a specific and unique redemptive act. This latter transferred to a universalistic setting the divine revelation that had been given earlier to a particular community,

---

[19] M. Buber, *Das Kommende, I: Das Königtum Gottes* (1932), *The Prophetic Faith* (1949); cf. *Ich und Du* (1923), pp. 10ff., 25.

and thus the Christian Church was made the supreme organ of divine witness. In fulfilling the Law and prophecy it was the function of Jesus Christ to create a people for Himself, the spiritual heirs and successors of Old Israel, and through them to usher in the final stages of the *Heilsgeschichte.* Insofar as an existential aspect can be demonstrated, Old Testament theology as such will have value for Jewish scholars. But an understanding of the Old Testament as an end in itself can hardly do justice to the great covenantal theme of the prophet Jeremiah (31:31ff.) and its continuation by Ezekiel (34:25ff.; 37:26), or to the concept of the emergent Mighty Ruler (Ps. 103:19; Isa. 40:10) as Messiah and Divine Servant (Isa. 9:6f.; 42:1ff.; 52:13ff.), to the outpouring of the Divine Spirit (Joel 2:28ff.) or the creation of new heavens and a new earth (Isa. 65:17).[20] In all of these there is latent the promise of activity that never actually came to fruition in the Old Testament period, but which for the Christian are essential elements in the fuller concept of *Heilsgeschichte.*

The manner in which the term *Heilsgeschichte* has been employed by certain neo-orthodox writers calls for some caution in its use. As "holy history," the "history of salvation," or "saving history," the word would appear to describe an accredited Biblical situation with a certain accuracy. There are few who would question the assertion that Scripture constitutes a record of happenings set in an historical framework, which for the Christian interpreter moved towards a specific climax within the stream of history and time. Though there is a sense in which any event in history can be attributed generally to divine working, it is important to recognize that the great saving acts of Hebrew history were of a special character, wrought for the benefit of a particular people. A genuine *Heilsgeschichte* will have as its overall consideration the relationship between God and man, but always with a specific concept of redemption in view. The perceptive scholar will take pains to distinguish between redemption and salvation as theological concepts, and will be aware that neither were realized within the period of Old Testament history. An approach of this kind will also recognize the existence of human sin, from which man needs to be redeemed, as well as the accomplished fact of the redemption itself in terms of the atoning work of Jesus Christ.

Quite obviously a purely historical kind of investigation can scarcely do justice to a situation that is basically theological in nature, as neo-orthodox scholars have recognized. Thus any accredited "salvation history" must have the topics of sin and redemption firmly established as central themes in the history of the Hebrew people. Through them it

---

[20] This deficiency is illustrated in the work of Samuel Sandmel, *The Hebrew Scriptures: An Introduction to Their Literature and Religious Ideas* (1963), p. 193, who rather helplessly concluded that the "Suffering Servant" was a "stray poem that quite unaccountably came to be included in the Book of Isaiah."

must relate these concepts to human history as a whole. In this way the basic concern of the Old Testament will be paramount, and will not ultimately be subsumed under what may be considered to be a more urgent task, namely that of reconstructing and rewriting the historical material according to some specific analytical scheme, as von Rad and others have done. While method is of great importance in any constructive endeavor, especially in the field of Old Testament theology, it must always remain the servant of the scholar, and not his master.

Neo-orthodox writers have further complicated the situation regarding the understanding of *Heilsgeschichte* by making a distinction between *Geschichte* and *Historie*. For these authors the supra-temporal or supra-historical realm is more properly described as *Geschichte*, which makes it possible for certain situations normally regarded by orthodox theologians as falling within time and space to be interpreted as purely parabolic or spiritual in nature. Thus for Barth, the resurrection of Jesus Christ is not to be understood historically in the traditional sense, but as a supra-temporal *Geschichte*, belonging to the realm of faith and as such outside purely factual or scientific demonstration.[21] In the same manner the Old Testament narrative of the fall of man into sin is to be assigned to the supra-historical area, and not regarded in the orthodox sense of *Historie*. This standpoint is in diametric opposition to the consistent witness of both Judaism and Christianity, which insist that man fell *in* time rather than *into* it. *Heilsgeschichte* should narrate the various aspects of the divine revelation to men against a strictly historical background, assessing objectively the acts of God on behalf of mankind, and seeing the climax of human redemption in the work of Christ on the Cross. There is a distinct sense in which *Heilsgeschichte* must always remain a limited and incomplete concept, having regard to the eschatological aspects of salvation in Christ.

b. Myth, saga, and legend. The neo-orthodox assumption that certain portions of the Scriptural narratives are supra-historical or nonhistorical has been accompanied by the widespread use of terms such as saga, legend, and myth in an attempt to assign proper character to particular parts of the Old Testament. Barth appears to have distinguished between myth on the one hand, and saga or legend on the other, by regarding myth as hostile to the substance of the Biblical testimony, whereas legend, even when its historical character was a matter for debate, is not necessarily in opposition to the witness of Scripture.[22] Brunner, however, utilized the term "myth" for those categories that Barth described as legend.

The recovery of much of the literature that was widely circulated in the ancient Near East has disproved the assertion of W. Robertson Smith

[21] K. Barth, *Kirchliche Dogmatik*, IV, 1, pp. 331ff.; IV, 2, pp. 118ff.
[22] Cf. K. Barth, *Kirchliche Dogmatik*, I, 1, pp. 368ff.

that, strictly speaking, mythology was no essential part of ancient religion.[23] It is now known that scientific and philosophical categories of thought were long antedated by myth-forms, and that the inhabitants of the Near East in antiquity utilized what has been called "mythopoetry" as a substitute for abstract logical thinking.[24] Old Testament critical scholars had for generations pointed to what they considered to be the mythological nature of certain portions of the Hebrew Scriptures, and although the extent to which Israelite literature was influenced by these modes of thought has proved debatable, it seems difficult to imagine on purely rational grounds that the Old Testament writings could remain completely untouched by mythological tendencies in the ancient Near East. The extent to which this is apparent in the Old Testament has been estimated by T. H. Gaster in terms of direct parallels to pagan myths, allusions to gods and ancient heroes, and the use of poetic imagery.[25] Ugaritic texts have illustrated the manner in which natural forces such as the wind[26] and thunder[27] were employed in the literary expressions current in the Amarna Age. The concept of the sun as winged (Mal. 4:2) was familiar from Egyptian usage.[28] References to demonic figures such as Lilith (Isa. 34:14) and Resheph (Hab. 3:5; cf. Job 5:7) reflect Canaanite folklore in an analogous manner. Allusions to epics of ancient deities have been seen in hints found in various parts of the Old Testament relating to a primordial revolt in heaven (cf. Ps. 82:6; Isa. 14:12ff.), or in references to astral bodies (Job 38:31f.; Am. 5:26).

In all the foregoing instances, however, the mythological content as such is so attenuated as to justify the conclusion that it was merely employed as dead verbal imagery whose origins were even then almost completely forgotten. A more direct parallel to pagan mythological ideas has been envisaged in the scattered references to divine conflict with some kind of monster, variously named Leviathan (Job 3:8; Ps. 74:14; Isa. 27:1),[29] Rahab (Job 9:13; 26:12f.; Ps. 89:10; Isa. 30:7; 51:9f.), Tannin, i.e. "Dragon" (Job 7:12; Ps. 74:13; Isa. 27:1; 51:9), Yam, i.e. "Sea" (Job 7:12; Ps. 74:13; Isa. 51:10; Hab. 3:8), and Nahar, i.e. "River" (Ps. 93:3; Hab. 3:8). This has been held to constitute the Hebrew version of the Ugaritic myth dealing with the victory of Baal over the dragon Yam, the spirit of rivers and streams,[30] a theme paralleled in the Mesopotamian narrative of the conflict between Marduk and Tiamat, in

[23] *The Religion of the Semites*, p. 19.
[24] *IAAM*, pp. 7f.
[25] *IDB*, III, pp. 481ff.
[26] Cf. T. H. Gaster, *Thespis* (1961 ed.), p. 168.
[27] Cf. F. Rück in Hommel *Festschrift* (1917), pp. 279ff.
[28] Cf. B. Perring, *Archiv für Orientforschung*, VIII (1933), pp. 281ff.; V. Christian, *ibid.*, IX (1934), p. 30.
[29] Cf. G. R. Driver in *Studi orientalistici (Levi della Vida Festschrift)*, I (1956), pp. 234ff.
[30] T. H. Gaster, *Thespis*, pp. 153ff.; *UL*, text 137, p. 14.

the old Hittite story of the struggle between the storm-deity and the dragon Illuyankas,[31] in the Sumerian myth narrating the triumph of Ninurta over the monster Asag,[32] in the fight between Horus of Behdet and the "Caitiff,"[33] and other similar Near Eastern legends.[34]

When those Old Testament passages which are commonly cited as references for these myths are examined carefully, they fall into two distinct groups. The first category preserves pagan folklore concerning monsters, a feature that has remained a consistent part of the tradition of more modern peoples. Such references are to be found principally in the poetical writings and in Isaiah. The second category, also predominantly poetical, has as its primary purpose not so much the preservation of ancient mythology as the demonstration of divine superiority over every aspect of nature and life. The fact that an extant vocabulary was utilized in this connection merely shows that there was never any new or specific terminology of divine revelation. The difference between Israelite and pagan usage consisted supremely in the manner in which traditional terminology and thought-forms were interpreted. In this connection it will be readily observed that pagan myths and deities were frequently held up as the object of ridicule among the Hebrews, and served as symbols of all that was alien to the true Hebrew genius.[35]

It further appears evident that where pagan myths were reflected in the Psalms and in the prophetic writings, they had already been subjected to a considerable process of what might be described as demythologizing. In at least one dramatic instance (Ps. 74:12ff.) the language of myth was employed to refute conclusively the very beliefs that had been responsible for the rise of myth-forms, and to assert the absolute sovereignty of God. Again, in Isaiah 51:9ff., which is rich in poetic imagery of all kinds, the mythology of the ancient Near East was applied both to the Exodus from Egypt and to the projected return from exile to demonstrate the supreme power of God as exemplified in mighty acts of restoration. In Amos 9:3 Leviathan is depicted as the servant of God rather than His enemy (cf. Ps. 104:26), indicating a similar transformation of a pagan mythological concept. It would appear, then, that where

---

[31] Cf. *ANET*, pp. 125f.

[32] S. N. Kramer, *Sumerian Mythology* (1961), pp. 78ff.

[33] Cf. A. Blackman and H. W. Fairman, *JEA*, XXI (1937), pp. 26ff., XXVIII (1942), pp. 32ff., XXIX (1943), pp. 3ff.

[34] For the principal Egyptian texts see *ANET*, pp. 2ff.; for Akkadian myths, *ANET*, pp. 60ff.; *DOTT*, pp. 3ff.; for Ugaritic myths, *ANET*, pp. 129ff., *UL*, pp. 9ff., *DOTT*, pp. 128ff. Cf. *IAAM*, pp. 50ff., 157ff., S. H. Hooke (ed.), *Myth, Ritual and Kingship* (1958); E. O. James, *Myth and Ritual in the Ancient Near East* (1958); J. R. Clarke, *Myth and Symbol in Ancient Egypt* (1959); T. H. Gaster, *Thespis* (1961).

[35] Thus the text of Hosea 8:6 can now be understood to mean, "Who is the bull-deity El? He is the one made by an artisan, and is not a god at all," replacing the meaningless מישראל ("from Israel," AV, RV; "in Israel," RSV) by מי שר אל.

452

the language of myth was countenanced in the Old Testament writings, it carried with it a very different meaning for the Hebrews than for the pagan nations of the Near East. As a literary phenomenon, the usage of mythological allusions is widespread in many later cultures, and the fact that such references might appear in literary productions is no indication that the writer is necessarily committed to any underlying theology, or that he does more than merely approve of the suitability of the allusion as part of the process of human communication.[36]

In any event, the Old Testament passages which appear to reflect the myths of the ancient world are of a poetic and highly figurative nature, making a literal interpretation of them both unwise and unwarranted. The "leviathan" of Job 41:1ff. is ultimately nothing more than a crocodile, and as such can hardly be considered a primeval foe of Jehovah. The conflict of Isaiah 27:1 is a future one, and "leviathan" is either the Assyrian or the Babylonian empire, or possibly both. In Isaiah 30:7, "Rahab" is explicitly Egypt, an illusion which is repeated elsewhere. In point of fact there is never once any clear statement in the Old Testament that the foes of Jehovah were regarded as mythological deities of any kind whatsoever.

By far the most challenging area of myth has been that connected with the early chapters of Genesis, which has been a matter of concern for both Old Testament scholars and neo-orthodox theologians. The recovery of Mesopotamian creation and flood narratives persuaded many writers that the Genesis accounts were comparatively late compositions, stripped by post-exilic priestly interests of their Babylonian paganism, and presented in a demythologized form as the accredited Hebrew tradition of the creation and deluge. However, further study of the situation has shown that these conclusions represented an over-simplification of the entire matter, and that in actual fact the problems of interrelation are infinitely more complex than the earlier scholars imagined. To no small degree what is involved is the occidental understanding of the oriental concept of myth. Unfortunately western understanding in this case has been dominated by the classical Greek mythological forms, which were marred by highly personified and individualized ideas of a distinctly static nature. Scholars assumed, quite erroneously, that the Greek understanding of myth was characteristic of ancient Near Eastern attitudes as a whole in this matter; however, the situation was entirely different, for the peoples of Mesopotamia and Egypt regarded everything in the world of nature as pulsating with life; and they regularly distinguished these natural forces as personal simply because they had experienced a direct encounter with them. For the superstitious inhabitants of Mesopotamia in particular and to a certain extent for the Egyptians, it was evident from the beginning that man was

---

[36] Cf. *IOTT*, pp. 81f.; D. F. Payne, *Genesis One Reconsidered* (1964), p. 14.

swamped by the interaction of prodigious natural forces with which he had to coordinate his activity if he was to survive. Thus to apply the concept of personification as encountered in the Greek myths to Mesopotamian mythology is misleading, since the deities and other supernatural entities of the latter were nothing more than the forces of nature as experienced personally. Their very existence depended entirely upon the presence and activity of natural phenomena, and although later literary developments in the legendary cycles tended to assign a greater degree of individuality to the deities than the situation warranted, the fact remains that even at the highest level the gods of Mesopotamia seldom if ever gained a true personality independent of the functioning of natural forces.[37] While some Greek philosophers, notably Thales and the Milesians, held that everything was "full of gods," they were merely describing a vague pantheism which bore no real relationship either to the Homeric heroes, to the cosmological speculations of the sixth-century B.C. Ionian thinkers generally, or to the contemporary revival of religious thought, which revered the personifications of those subterranean powers allegedly responsible for the sustaining and renewing of vegetable life.

c. Creation and fall. It is significant that to the present no Canaanite cosmogonic myths have been discovered. There can be little doubt, however, that such material would have followed the dominant pattern established by the Sumerians and adopted by the Babylonians and other peoples of the ancient Near East. Even Egyptian cosmogonic mythology, peculiar as it was to the local scene, conformed to the same basic concepts expressed by the Sumerians and Babylonians. What is of importance for the student of Mesopotamian cosmogony, however, is that the myths show no concern with creation in the accredited sense at all. An underlying monistic concept pervades all these writings that deal with creative activity, which in general describes in mythological form the evolution of an ordered cosmos from a primeval chaos. In a manner that was never clearly explained, the creator-deities emerged from the chaos, managed to conquer it and formulate it into some sort of order, and manipulated the process to the point where man finally appeared at the end, being especially for the Sumerians almost an afterthought of divine creativity.

The similarities between *Enuma elish* and the creation narratives in Genesis can be summarized by saying that both commence with something analogous to a watery chaos and conclude with the Creator in repose, and the sequence of creative events follows the same general order. However, it is a scientific axiom that in all questions of comparison the differences are more important than the similarities, and in the light of this principle it is apparent that a comparison furnishes no real

---

[37] Cf. *ARI*, pp. 91f.

parallels between the Genesis creation narratives and *Enuma elish*. At one period it was customary among critical scholars to stress the similarities between the deluge narrative of the Gilgamesh Epic and its counterpart in the Biblical writings, with the inference that there were similar parallels in the Genesis creation narratives and *Enuma elish*.[38] Aside from the fact that this assumption is completely unwarranted by the nature of the evidence, such an attitude failed to realize that the Genesis Flood narrative was dealing essentially with the problem of certain events within historic time, and did not have as its immediate concern the composition of legendary poetic material. While there are few who would question the ultimate Mesopotamian background of the Biblical creation and deluge narratives, the relationship of either or both to extant Mesopotamian mythological cycles such as *Enuma elish* or the Epic of Gilgamesh is very much an open question.[39]

The Genesis narratives of human creation and fall used to be described as myths because of their alleged desire to explain aetiologically the reason for existing human customs and attitudes, the behavior of serpents, and similar phenomena.[40] But subsequent research has shown that the subjects of myth among ancient Near Eastern peoples were the essential powers of the universe as experienced personally, and not questions of human custom or the behavior of certain animal species. The prime concern of the Mesopotamians of antiquity was to insure that they remained firmly on the side of those powers that had brought order from chaos, with the expectation that such a favorable state of affairs would continue to exist. Where the form of myth served its supreme purpose was in narrating in a memorable way the universal facts of life to which man had to adjust himself. Thus, as Frankfort has pointed out, the myths of the ancient Near East recounted events in which the people who formulated them, and indeed their successors, were involved to the extent of their entire existence.[41] Although they were products of the imagination, they were not mere fantasy, and as such must be distinguished carefully from legend, saga, fable, and fairy tale.

The Mesopotamian myths presented their images and imaginary actors with a compelling authority that perpetuated the essential reality of the I-Thou relationship. For the Babylonians, myth constituted a form of poetry that transcended mere poetic function and proclaimed a complex truth. Acts of reasoning inherent in myth-form were designed to bring

---

[38] S. R. Driver, *Genesis* in Westminster Commentaries (1926 ed.), p. 30. H. Zimmern and T. K. Cheyne, *EB*, I, col. 938, *et al.*; cf. A. Richardson, *Genesis I-XI* (1953), pp. 17f.

[39] Cf. A. Heidel, *The Babylonian Genesis* (1951), p. 139; J. V. Kinnier Wilson, *DOTT*, p. 14; G. von Rad, *Genesis* (1961), p. 48.

[40] S. R. Driver, *Genesis*, p. 36; H. Gunkel, *Die Schriften des AT* (1911), p. 65; S. Mowinckel, *He That Cometh*, p. 11.

[41] *IAAM*, p. 7.

about a recognition of the truth that they sought to proclaim, and where ritual behavior was involved it merely served to illustrate and exemplify the basic concepts of reality underlying the visible drama.[42] The imagery of such myth must consequently never be confused with allegory, since it constituted the cloak of authoritative truth. Nor could it ever be separated from the thought-content, for the very important reason that the imagery was basic to the form in which the experience had become actualized, whether that form was dramatized or presented as simple poetry. Fundamental to the character of myth was the recognition of its underlying, essential truth by the initiated or the faithful, as opposed to its irrationality for the critical, unsympathetic, or skeptical observer.

The Biblical narratives of the creation and fall of man are particularly good examples of material that partakes of the basic character of ancient Mesopotamian myth. In an even wider sense they reflect the concern of the oriental mind regarding the communication of essential truth, namely to safeguard by every possible means that which is most precious, and protect it from the skeptical gaze of the profane by cloaking it in story form. If the structure of the story form was perpetuated in a way that led to a rejection of both the form and the content by the undiscerning, the basic truth embedded in it would at least have been protected from ridicule. The principle underlying this attitude was crystallized by Isaiah (6:9f.), and repeated by Jesus Christ in connection with the parabolic method (Matt. 13:14ff.; Mark 4:12; cf. John 12:40 and Acts 28:26f.).

Yet despite the fact that the narratives of creation exhibit the same attitude towards the presentation of truth as their Mesopotamian counterparts, they cannot properly be regarded as myths in themselves. Their precise origin is a matter of considerable speculation, and while some would suggest that they constituted "demythologized" Mesopotamian material, others would assert that they were unique products of the Hebrew religious spirit. Since a careful comparison with pagan mythology reveals only the most casual parallels between Mesopotamian and Hebrew accounts of creation, and in view of the fact that none of the characteristic elements of the Babylonian myths appears in the Genesis narratives, it would seem unwise to employ the term "myth" in order to describe the Biblical accounts of creation, the fall, and so on, especially in view of the fact that the concept of myth is misleading for the occidental mind because of Greek influences ascribing implicit untruth to myth. As has been remarked, this is the exact opposite of what the ancient inhabitants of Mesopotamia envisaged in their myth-forms.

The inadequacy of the term "myth" as descriptive of the Biblical presentation of faith was demonstrated by G. E. Wright, who em-

[42] *IAAM*, p. 8.

456

phasized the difference between the Biblical material and the polytheistic compositions of the ancient Near East.[43] He pointed out that the Old Testament narratives were historical accounts whose traditions were taken seriously in the presentation of the faith of Israel. There was no question of adjusting life to a divine cosmic pattern typical of polytheism, and furthermore, the Old Testament literature was not unreal in the sense that it was separated from the stream of normal human life. While the Biblical writers showed a distinct interest in nature, they did not regard it as necessarily constituting the life of God, who was invariably considered as an independent Being. As distinct from the gods of Mesopotamian and Egyptian polytheism, the God of the Hebrews demonstrated His personality and sense of purpose by means of significant continuous acts in history. Man himself was a creature of God, furnished with a sense of destiny and cautioned to formulate the pattern of his life within the context of divine promise and fulfilment in history. Thus the Old Testament can never be regarded as a typical mythology in part or in whole, because it proclaimed God as the Lord of History in contradistinction to the polytheistic patterns that made life and history in general dependent upon the rhythm of natural forces. The sense of historical movement that the Hebrews possessed was based upon the Covenant concept, and related metaphysical dynamism to specific events and periods within the temporal continuum of Israelite life. As such it is diametrically opposed to myth, which in its classical occidental form is timeless and static, and therefore unsuitable for use in connection with Old Testament material.

The general problem of terminology in this regard was discussed by B. S. Childs, who felt that the definition of myth in terms of aesthetic, historical, form-critical, or philosophical categories was inadequate, and proposed that it should be construed in phenomenological terms.[44] This suggestion would seem to be hampered by certain difficulties from a terminological standpoint, if not an existential one. Richardson was considerably nearer the truth of the matter when he spoke of such material as symbolic and partaking of the nature of parable.[45] Unfortunately such a definition fails to convey the dynamic content inherent both in ancient Near Eastern mythology and in the Genesis narratives of the creation and fall. The present writer prefers to regard them as "religious drama," using the noun in the sense entertained by the Homeric verb $\delta\rho\acute{a}\omega$, in which activity was the paramount concern. This definition helps to preserve the form which is essential to the content, without at the same time casting any doubt, historical or otherwise, upon the basic truths en-

[43] *WBA*, pp. 102f.
[44] B. S. Childs, *Myth and Reality in the OT* (1960); cf. R. A. F. MacKenzie, *Faith and History in the OT* (1963), pp. 61ff.
[45] *Genesis I-XI*, pp. 27ff.

shrined in the narratives themselves. Certainly to follow the lead of Reinhold Niebuhr and other theologians, who apply to the early material in Genesis the concept of myth as a symbolical representation of nonhistorical truth, is to beg the entire question, and to ignore the distinct possibility that the so-called "myth" was for the ancient Hebrews an account of what were actually thought to have been the historical facts of the case.

It was to the credit of the neo-orthodox theologians that they repudiated the puerile view of the fall that regarded the Genesis account as a conglomeration of narrative material merely designed to explain certain circumstances of human society and animal behavior. However, they were unable to accept the concept of the fall as an historical event, a matter upon which Barth in particular was quite evasive.[46] Instead, they insisted that existential method was incompatible with the view of the fall as an occurrence in the remote past, maintaining that it was something that everyone commits. For this reason it was of paramount theological importance for anyone who was prepared to take a realistic view of human nature. For neo-orthodox thinkers the tradition of the New Testament as enshrined in Augustine and Calvin invited a conflict with modern scientific opinion.

By taking note of the attitude of neo-orthodox scholars generally towards the theological and historical problems of the Old Testament, one can find certain anomalies in their position. By emphasizing the subjective nature of the religious experience, neo-orthodoxy is in constant danger of minimizing the objective reality or "givenness" of the revelation itself. No one would deny the importance of an existential relationship with God, which was just as fundamental for the ancient Hebrew as it is for the modern Christian. On the other hand, it must also be recognized that human experience in this regard can never be considered to be coterminous with the objective revelation itself. As far as the fall is concerned, neo-orthodoxy has sought to existentialize the matter by asserting that it is something committed by everybody. This presumably would refer to conscious life and activity, which in turn involves the exercise of free choice. If, therefore, it is possible to share in the fall of man, it should be equally possible to resist participation in the sin of Adam through the equal exercise of such choice, unless *homo sapiens* is the victim of a rigid determinism. From this it would follow that man is able to assist in his own salvation by becoming to a considerable extent his own savior, a position far removed theologically from both the Old and New Testament teachings.

[46] Cf. E. Brunner, *Der Mensch im Widerspruch* (1937), p. 78n. For an orthodox analysis of Brunner's thought see P. K. Jewett, *Brunner's Concept of Revelation* (1954); see also C. Van Til, *The New Modernism, An Appraisal of the Theology of Barth and Brunner* (1946), *The Defence of the Faith* (1947); E. J. Carnell, *The Case for Orthodox Theology* (1962).

There are obvious overtones of Pelagianism in such an inadequate doctrine of man, for if there is neither transmitted corruption nor an implicit sense of guilt in human nature, there would appear to be no absolute necessity for the existence and operation of divine grace. What neo-orthodox theologians have failed to grasp clearly is that by the very act of birth the individual is placed immediately on the side of fallen humanity, and that this is a circumstance upon which individual choice has absolutely no bearing. Modern scientific studies in the realm of human personality have reinforced the Biblical conclusion that man is characterized by a typical egocentric orientation and that this is a transmitted feature of the species. On this matter the Biblical testimony is illuminating in pointing to a time when this condition did not obtain.

The Biblical and Augustinian doctrine of human fall involving an empirical event can never be regarded as scientifically obsolete, since science cannot make a final pronouncement upon it for lack of the kind of evidence with which the descriptive sciences deal. While neo-orthodox writers have rightly stressed the revelational character of the early narratives of Genesis, they have also denied the basically historical nature of revelation by refusing to consider the events that the narratives described as having in fact occurred in a time-space dimension. One would suspect that many exponents of this view have stumbled in characteristic occidental fashion over the form of the early Genesis accounts, confusing the issues of an historic fall with the narrative structure in which that truth was conveyed. As P. K. Jewett has pointed out, this "event-ness" is not simply the form of revelation but actually constitutes the revelation itself, with man falling, not into history, but in it.[47]

In the view of the present writer, to relegate the fall to the shadowy realm of a supra-temporal *Geschichte* or *Urgeschichte* is to adopt an unrealistic standpoint towards one of the most compelling and characteristic features of *homo sapiens* and to remove any substantial foundation for a doctrine of man that does justice to the Old Testament narratives. One unfortunate product of the neo-orthodox attitude towards the fall has been the embarrassing anomaly whereby the disobedience of the first Adam has been existentialized out of history, and the obedience of the Second Adam emphasized as a fact in time and held necessary to all true Christian faith.[48] Since there is a good deal of diversity in the theological pronouncements of representative writers in the neo-orthodox movement, and a certain inevitable distortion or modification of their views by their followers, the reader will recognize that the forego-

[47] In *Revelation and the Bible*, p. 49.
[48] P. K. Jewett in *Baker's Dictionary of Theology*, p. 377.

ing comments are rather general, and in certain particular circumstances might not be applicable to the opinions of some writers.

Any view of the primal history of *homo sapiens* as recorded in Genesis is almost certain to encounter some difficulty with the religious drama that constitutes the indispensable form of the narrative. That it contains what might appear to the occidental mind as bizarre elements that in reality were designed as safeguards for the inner truths has been noted earlier. What is seldom observed, however, is the presence in this and other Biblical narratives of a characteristic Near Eastern literary idiom known to modern scholarship as *merismus,* the relating of antonymic pairs as polar extremes to describe the totality of a particular situation, for example, the ancient Egyptian expression "evil-good," which meant "everything."[49]

Thus in the narrative of the fall, the phrase literally translated "good and evil" as applied to the Tree of Knowledge (Gen. 2:10) should be rendered more properly in a manner recognizing the inherent concept of *merismus.* Unfortunately the conservative nature of Biblical translations is generally such as to perpetuate traditional renderings, however inappropriate they may be in the light of subsequent discovery and research. Even A. M. Honeyman, in a discerning study of *merismus* in Biblical Hebrew, was influenced by tradition in this particular instance.[50] To be true to the idiom, therefore, the "tree" should be envisaged as the "tree of the entire range of moral knowledge." In the light of this the subtlety of the temptation becomes more evident. What was in fact offered to woman was an opportunity to know the entire moral sphere as God does, that is to say, intuitively. Aside from the gross deception involved, the temptation was the kind of flattering appeal to the alleged intuitive qualities of the female that few women would be able to resist. Unfortunately for mankind, the privilege of knowing the range of moral experience invariably carries with it certain harsh realities.

What applies to the narrative idiom in the description of the fall is also true in a rather wider sense of the whole question of evil. Thus it is no longer seen as necessary to envisage elements of an Iranian or other form of dualism when considering the relationship of evil to the Creator, as in Isaiah 45:7. If, as Temple has stated,[51] the most promising philosophies of religion are apt to come to grief upon this question,[52] it is also true that many theologies experience difficulties in ascribing the creation of evil to the Deity, save, perhaps, when dualistic tendencies are contemplated. There can actually be no question that the ancient Hebrews

---

[49] C. H. Gordon, *Archiv Orientální,* XVIII (1950), p. 202 n. 7.
[50] A. M. Honeyman, *JBL,* LXXI (1952), pp. 11ff.
[51] W. Temple, *Nature, Man and God* (1935), p. 356.
[52] A. M. Fairbairn, *The Philosophy of the Christian Religion* (1903), pp. 94f.

were firmly monistic in outlook, and could embrace such diverse concepts as peace and evil in a manner that depicted them as polar opposites in a comprehensive scheme of existence for which the one true God was ultimately responsible. Thus the emphasis was not upon the creation of evil as a specific metaphysical category; it was instead upon the totality of existence, of which evil constituted only one aspect. This understanding of the situation is obviously of great importance for any exposition of Old Testament theological concepts.

III. THE AUTHORITY OF SCRIPTURE

A. REVELATION

One of the great merits of neo-orthodoxy was that it repudiated the nineteenth-century liberal Protestant view of man in many of its facets and dethroned reason as the supreme arbiter of human life, giving priority instead to the concept of divine revelation. However, the movement fell short of the implicit Biblical view that revelation can be subordinated into the categories of general and special. Barth in particular was quite emphatic as to the inadmissibility of the former on the ground that it set up a second source of divine revelation alongside that of Christ. Brunner, on the other hand, upheld the concept of general revelation, maintaining that this did not destroy the image of God in the manner envisaged by Barth. Richardson dissented from both Barth and Brunner in repudiating their view that a saving revelation was to be found only in the Judeo-Christian tradition.[1] He maintained that general as well as special revelation partook of the nature of salvation, but that the former had become distorted through human sin and egocentric preoccupation, making the latter a spiritual necessity. However he denied the possibility of a simple continuity between general and special revelation, since the latter was a qualitatively new kind of existence. Richardson did not support the orthodox view that special revelation consisted of the disclosure of supernatural knowledge, but regarded it instead as the power to apprehend those spiritual truths communicated by means of general revelation.

As far as the Biblical evidence is concerned, the idea of general revelation as that contained in nature (cf. Pss. 19:1ff.; 29:3ff.), history, and conscience was supported on empirical grounds by Paul (cf. Acts 17:27ff.; Rom. 1:26f.; 2:14f.) to show that fallen man could not claim complete exemption from the revelation of God. While no one would suggest that the existence of the God of Israel could be deduced by means of formal logical reasoning on the basis of an empirical examination of the cosmos, the possibility of a general revelation to mankind

---

[1] *Christian Apologetics* (1947), pp. 127ff.

needs more than a passing thought if only because modern archaeological discoveries have shown the sophisticated nature of fourth-millennium B.C. life in Mesopotamia, and the concomitant highly developed concepts of a personal deity.

Special or particular revelation complements the distortion of any general manifestation of the nature and character of Deity by focusing attention upon divine redemption through the medium of the historical process, culminating in the work of Jesus Christ. Generally speaking, however, the Bible correlated general and special revelation by showing that the divine λόγος was both Creator and Redeemer, and by introducing special revelation to stress the guilt of humanity. Divine revelation was intimately bound up with the written word of God, which the Christian Church traditionally regarded as in itself constituting a form of revelation. Neo-orthodox writers have protested vigorously against the latter identification, preferring instead to regard Scripture simply as a witness to revelation, and to think of Jesus Christ alone as the Word of God. This attitude is completely unsupported by both Old and New Testaments, which emphasize the concept of divine revelation in the form of rational ideas (cf. Isa. 8:1; Jer. 18:5ff.; Hos. 2:1ff.; 1 Thess. 2:13), and which in any event distinguish between the λόγος of God as the Incarnate Word, and the ῥῆμα, which is the epistemological word of Scripture.

As one result of the neo-orthodox emphasis upon supernatural revelation in terms of a special divine disclosure, the whole question of the nature of revelation has assumed a position of central importance in theological discussion.[2] While it is ultimately the nature of the Christian revelation which is at issue, it is obvious that what the Old Testament has to contribute to this matter is basic to all other considerations. At the risk of some repetition, it should be remarked that the earliest Christian views concerning revelation proclaimed the self-disclosure of God in the Hebrew Scriptures. In the Early Church this attitude was enlarged to include the canonical writings of the New as well as of the Old Testament as constituting the tangible record of divine utterances bearing witness to the nature and purpose of Deity. The medieval insistence upon supplementing and authenticating the Scriptures by means of the *ecclesia docens* was repudiated by the Reformers, who held that, under the Holy Spirit, Scripture was self-authenticating and self-interpreting. Luther stressed the importance of approaching Old Testament doctrines against a background of sympathetic experience before undertaking any

---

[2] Cf. D. M. Baillie, *The Idea of Revelation in Recent Thought* (1956), pp. 1f.; H. D. McDonald, *Theories of Revelation. An Historical Study, 1860-1960* (1963); H. Schuster, *Offenbarung Gottes im AT* (1962).

interpretation of the narratives, emphasizing the importance of personal trust or *fiducia* in the Biblical revelation.[3]

With the seventeenth century a liberal humanism arose that reflected the tradition of the ancient Greek Sophists in elevating man and his reason as the sole standard of judgment and the final authority for faith. With the period of the Enlightenment in the following century this rationalistic subjectivism came into full flower, and with Kant there was formulated the denial of any factual knowledge involving the supra-sensible. The liberal theological interests of Schleiermacher sought to ransom Christianity from complete rationalism by introducing the con-cept of a mystical subjectivism, which, as far as Old Testament theology was concerned, was limited to the examination of certain human feelings or emotional reactions involving religious phenomena. For Schleiermach-er, revelation was not a disclosure of fundamental truth from God to mankind, but at best represented the progress of humanity towards a consciousness of God. Under the impact of nineteenth-century evolution-ism the Wellhausen school jettisoned the supernaturalism implicit in the outlook of the Hebrews in favor of a religious record rewritten in terms of the naturalistic principle of monolinear evolution.[4]

When the confident anthropocentrism of the nineteenth century went into eclipse, largely as the result of World War I, the vacuum began to be filled by the rise of the neo-orthodox movement proper and the dialectical theology of crisis associated with Barth. Against a background of existential method, the adherents of this position sought to resolve the problem of authority in religion by reasserting the priority of revelation over reason in theology, but doing so without becoming involved in what was regarded as orthodox obscurantism. Their concept of inspiration and the nature of the *kerygma* prevented them from identifying the words of Scripture with the Word of God, since its human dimension made the Bible fallible and liable to error. This standpoint has led many theolo-gians to reject, in part or in whole, the orthodox concept of Scripture as the divine communication to the Biblical writers of unique and other-wise inaccessible truths about the divine nature and purpose, and to think of revelation as the process by which God directed the historical sequences recorded in the Biblical narratives, and made individuals aware by one means or another of His existence and activity. Concomi-tant with this has been the abandonment of the traditional view that the Biblical revelation was largely propositional in character. This has led many scholars to the conclusion that the Bible is most adequately thought

---

[3] Cf. M. Reu, *Luther and the Scriptures* (1924), pp. 24ff.; B. B. Warfield, *Calvin and Calvinism* (1931), p. 83; J. Kostlin, *The Theology of Luther* (1897), II, p. 252.

[4] J. I. Packer in *Revelation and the Bible*, p. 92.

of as a fallible human response to revelation, and not as revelation in the sense of the communication of abstract moral and spiritual truths.

The majority of theological writers who do not observe the canons of orthodox thought on the question of revelation have envisaged two major foci in which man is confronted authoritatively and directly by revelation. The first is found in the sequence of historical events by which God disclosed Himself to the original witness of the "mighty acts," an emphasis that is of interest to those scholars who are primarily concerned with Biblical history.[5] The second "moment of revelation" consists in the repeated encounter in which the content of the original revelation is mediated to, and appropriated by, successive generations of the faithful; and this aspect is of primary concern to the writers in the fields of apologetics and systematic theology.[6] A further group of scholars, predominantly British, insist upon divine initiative in the matter of revelation without adopting the conclusions of Barth and Brunner, and in general deny that Scripture as such constitutes revealed truth.[7]

An ardent adherent of the naturalistic approach to the question of revelation in the Old Testament was W. A. Irwin. In a composite work published in 1947, he viewed religion as in the last analysis a social process, and as such identifiable with the divine working in human hearts everywhere, an activity that constantly urged mankind to higher

[5] E.g. C. H. Dodd, *History and the Gospel* (1938); H. Wheeler Robinson, *Redemption and Revelation in the Actuality of History* (1940), *Inspiration and Revelation in the OT* (1946); A. Simpson, *Revelation and Response in the OT* (1947); G. E. Wright, *God Who Acts* (1952); S. Mowinckel, *The OT as Word of God* (1959).

[6] E.g. K. Barth, *Kirchliche Dogmatik*, I, 1, p. 2, E. tr. *The Doctrine of the Word of God* (1956); F. W. Camfield, *Revelation and the Holy Spirit* (1934); J. Baillie and H. Martin (eds.), *Revelation* (1937); J. Baillie, *Our Knowledge of God* (1939); E. Lewis, *A Philosophy of the Christian Revelation* (1940); H. R. Niebuhr, *The Meaning of Revelation* (1940); Reinhold Niebuhr, *Moral Man and Immoral Society* (1932), *The Nature and Destiny of Man* (1941); E. Brunner, *The Divine-Human Encounter* (1944), *Revelation and Reason* (1947); N. F. S. Ferré, *Faith and Reason* (1946); R. Niebuhr, *Faith and History* (1949); P. Tillich, *Systematic Theology, I* (1953).

[7] These included John Oman, *Grace and Personality* (1925), *Vision and Authority* (1929), and *The Natural and the Supernatural* (1931); W. Temple, *Nature, Man, and God* (1934); J. Y. MacKinnon, *The Protestant Doctrine of Revelation* (1946); Alan Richardson, *Christian Apologetics* (1947); and D. D. Williams, *What Present-Day Theologians Are Thinking* (1952) and *Interpreting Theology 1918-1952* (1953). Treatments of the question of revelation from an orthodox standpoint were published by J. Orr, *Revelation and Inspiration* (1910); B. B. Warfield, *Revelation and Inspiration* (1927); John Murray et al., *The Infallible Word* (1946); Louis Berkhof, *Reformed Dogmatics: Introduction* (1932); T. Engelder, *Scripture Cannot Be Broken* (1944); L. S. Chafer, *Systematic Theology* (1948); Geerhardus Vos, *Biblical Theology* (1948); and C. F. H. Henry, *Remaking the Modern Mind* (1948), *The Protestant Dilemma* (1948), and (ed.) *Revelation and the Bible* (1959).

goals.[8] Divine revelation was thus fully human and natural, and to be connoted only in terms of universal divine process. A special revelation in Israel could only be countenanced in the sense that the Bible stands supreme in the exaltation of its knowledge of God, in the nobility of its vision of human duty, and in its power to stimulate the imagination with a vision of possibilities that lie open to the human spirit. This attempt to minimize the supernatural experience of God, so prominent throughout Old Testament history, enshrined the worst features of philosophical naturalism by being aligned to a concept of evolutionary meliorism, and by refusing to treat the primary source material on its own terms. The logical outcome of such an unscientific procedure can only be the loss of a credible divine Word, and, indeed, of the concept of God Himself. If one commences a consideration of revelation from an anthropocentric standpoint, it is difficult to see how one can possibly avoid losing the essence of what historic Christianity has connoted by the general term, namely an activity of God.

Although neo-orthodoxy has performed a valuable service in emphasizing the reality of sin, its interpretation of revelation in terms of selective historical events, fallible records, and encounter with God can only end in subjectivism and in a mystical interpretation of Scripture that fails to do justice to the Biblical view of itself as the words and acts of God revealed through a controlled redemptive history and recorded in written form to constitute an authoritative basis for human thought concerning the divine. There is an avowed Schleiermacherian influence evident in the thought of most neo-orthodox writers, and this fact makes for obvious internal difficulties in their consideration of revelation. Not the least of these is the attempt to erect some superstructure of the supra-rational upon the foundations of philosophical rationalism. It is not easy to see how such theological writers can claim that they have substituted the Biblical conception of the Deity for the liberal Protestant one while still retaining the liberal understanding of Scripture as fallible, and remain consistent methodologically.[9]

While neo-orthodoxy in full flood denied the possibility of an authoritative verbal revelation as such, a matter of grave doubt for such writers as Brunner and Tillich, the tide has now turned to the point where it is no longer possible for scholars to dismiss out of hand the orthodox doctrine of Scripture as the Word of God on the ground that a revelation in words is not possible.[10] The fact of the matter is that the revelation of a personal Deity can only be properly effected through the medium of

[8] W. A. Irwin in H. R. Willoughby (ed.), *The Study of the Bible Today and Tomorrow* (1947), pp. 259ff.

[9] Cf. J. Lowe in *The Interpretation of the Bible* (ed. C. W. Dugmore, 1944), p. 113.

[10] Cf. V. Taylor, *The Person of Jesus Christ in NT Teaching* (1958), pp. 246ff.; A. M. Ramsey, *Durham Essays and Addresses* (1957), p. 32.

personal communication, the most characteristic form of which is verbal. While the order and functioning of nature and the events of history may be appealed to as valid means of revelation, they are at best inadequate in comparison to the proclamation of the divine word through law, prophecy, and the person of Jesus Christ. Furthermore, it should be noticed that according to uniform Biblical tradition, the revelation enshrined in the written records is substantially propositional in nature. Finally, on *a priori* grounds, there is no reason, as Reid has pointed out, why a divine disclosure such as that represented by the Biblical writings should not have the character of a body of divinely guaranteed truths.[11]

B. INSPIRATION

While a place has been found in modern theology for supernatural revelation, the same cannot be said for the concept of supernatural inspiration that would give validity and authority to the written record of the divine revelation. The orthodox doctrine of inspiration was formulated in the Early Church from Scriptural allusions to the work of the Holy Spirit in connection with the testimony of Scriptural writings (cf. Matt. 22:43; John 14:26; 2 Tim. 3:16; 2 Pet. 1:21 *et al.*). This attitude was in general harmony with that of contemporary Judaism, which adhered to a high view of inspiration, especially towards the Torah. For the Early Church, however, the objective inspiration of the written record was matched by a subjective enlightening of the human understanding, the latter being a peculiar function of the Holy Spirit. This conception helped to guard against any association with pagan ideas regarding inspiration, which tended to depreciate the human element and interpret inspiration as a purely psychological phenomenon.[12]

The Church Fathers accepted the inspiration and authority of the Scriptures as self-evident, and gave proper recognition to the place of the human element in the corpus of the Biblical writings generally. During the medieval period a high doctrine of inspiration was maintained, although the authority of Scripture was minimized considerably when the Bible was considered as only one source of Church doctrine. In repudiating this development, the Reformers reasserted the traditional view that God alone was the true author of Scripture, a matter that was particularly emphasized by Calvin.[13] Reformed theologians of the seventeenth century, while upholding the teaching of the Reformers regarding inspiration, tended to subsume the personality of the human author under that of the divine.[14] They also pushed the

---

11 *The Authority of Scripture* (1957), pp. 162f.
12 Cf. Plato, *Ion*, 533.
13 *Institutes*, I, 7, 2ff.
14 G. W. Bromiley in *Revelation and the Bible*, p. 213.

doctrine of verbal inspiration to extremes by insisting upon the inspired nature of the Massoretic pointing system, and made inerrancy the increasing basis of their doctrine of inspiration.

The rationalistic attacks upon the literary and historical material of Scripture, common in the following century, involved a rejection of the classic concept of inspiration to a greater or lesser degree, and a restatement of the situation in terms of conformity to the concepts of pure reason. The influence of Kant led to the subjective postulates of Schleiermacher, who subordinated the divine element to the human and understood inspiration as the activity of the common spirit of the faithful, which because of its intrinsic nature could bestow equal inspiration upon any great spiritual composition.[15] The mysticism of Schleiermacher, compounded by the influence of Hegel, who separated faith from reason, and Ritschl, who distinguished sharply between the scientific and the religious, provided a fertile soil from which the various forms of liberalism subsequently sprang.

Of the neo-orthodox writers Brunner in particular was hostile to the idea of verbal inspiration, which for him had deified the "letter" of the Bible to the point of imprisoning the Spirit between the covers of a book.[16] Brunner maintained that the prophetic utterances of the Old Testament came closest to the concept of verbal inspiration, though such a theory had clearly been demolished by higher criticism and evolutionary science.[17] Biblical infallibility was precluded on the ground of alleged errors and contradictions in the Scriptural narratives, which would point in general to a degree of restriction upon the activity of the Holy Spirit in the matter of inspiration. While Barth was less vehement than Brunner in his views on verbal or plenary inspiration, he too rejected the orthodox viewpoint in his attempt to formulate a concept of Biblical authority.[18]

In venturing to define the concept of inspiration, modern theologians do so with some hesitation, and on occasions with frank misunderstanding of what is involved. Thus some authors speak of "degrees of inspiration"—when probably they should be thinking of progressive revelation—oblivious to the fact that inspiration does not admit of degrees, any more than morality, honesty, and similar concepts do. In this connection it should be noted that the Bible as a whole, and not least the Old Testament, never enunciates any principle for distinguishing between those parts which are inspired, and therefore authoritative for faith and doctrine, and any ostensibly uninspired portions, which would conse-

[15] Schleiermacher, *Der christliche Glaube nach dem Grundsätzen der evangelischen Kirche* (1821-22), II, pp. 409ff.

[16] *Revelation and Reason* (1947), p. 145.

[17] *Ibid.*, pp. 133, 286f.

[18] Cf. Barth, *Zwischen den Zeiten* (1925), III, pp. 215ff.

quently not possess binding authority upon Jew or Christian. Other writers have tended to confuse the idea of Biblical inspiration with the divine illumination of the human mind that enables the revealed truths to be appropriated.[19] Even those who criticize the terms "verbal" and "plenary" as means of describing inspiration are not always clear as to what is to be understood by them.

Accordingly it should be recognized that the concept of the inspiration of Scripture must be evaluated in the light of what the Bible teaches about the term "inspiration." The text that constitutes the *locus classicus* of the doctrine occurs in 2 Timothy 3:16, which in the AV was translated, "All Scripture is given by inspiration of God...," a rendering that was modified in the RV to follow Tyndale in reading, "Every Scripture inspired of God. . . . "[20] The point at issue is the interpretation of the Greek word θεόπνευστος, a term that occurs nowhere else in Scripture. The sense of the word is passive rather than active, and the implicit movement is outwards rather than inwards. Thus the adjective speaks of being "out-breathed" rather than "in-breathed," so that to speak of Scripture as θεόπνευστος means that God has breathed out Scripture as part of His creative activity, not that it is "breathed-into" by God, or that it is inspiring, true though the latter may be in other connections. Because of the absence of the verb "to be" in the Greek, the way in which Tyndale construed the clause has found wide approval among liberal writers.[21] Even a casual glance at the Greek, however, will be sufficient to indicate that the first three words constitute a clause that embodies its own separate idea, and this is linked up with the development of that concept by means of the conjunction "and." This is a common Greek construction, and when translated should be rendered so as to indicate an elliptical verb "to be," as was done in the AV.

As against the complaint of Brunner that διδασκαλία should properly be rendered "teaching" rather than "doctrine,"[22] it must be remembered that the Latin word *doctrina* signified both teaching and doctrine, without prejudice as to the nature of either. Paul was making it clear that the sacred writings were God-breathed, and therefore valuable for both life and faith. On such a basis orthodoxy has understood inspiration to describe in a general manner the influence of the Holy Spirit upon the minds of certain individuals, making them media for the communication of revelation. With regard to Scripture itself, the term was employed

[19] E.g. J. Baillie, *The Idea of Revelation in Recent Thought*, p. 66.

[20] πᾶσα γραφὴ θεόπνευστος καὶ ὠφέλιμος πρὸς διδασκαλίαν . . . , where the adjective θεόπνευστος is in the predicative position. To translate καὶ here as "also" is inadmissible, since it constitutes the simple conjunctive particle "and." Cf. J. N. D. Kelley, *A Commentary on the Pastoral Epistles* (1964), pp. 202f.

[21] So S. Mowinckel, *The OT as Word of God*, p. 23.

[22] E. Brunner, *Revelation and Reason*, p. 9n.

actively to denote the means by which Scripture was produced, and passively to describe the inspired nature of the Biblical material.[23]

The method by which the written testimonies were produced under divine inspiration has frequently been misunderstood. As a result the views of some conservative scholars have been caricatured by more liberal writers.[24] Accordingly it should be made clear that nowhere does the Bible even countenance a concept of mechanical dictation or automatic writing, let alone propound it. Such an idea of divine inspiration belongs strictly to Philo, to the Talmud, and to some of the early Christian Fathers such as Augustine. But even Augustine was careful not to obliterate the human element so obviously necessary in any understanding of inspired writing.[25] It was only in the seventeenth century that continental Reformed dogmaticians began to incline to a theory of dictation,[26] but this tendency was certainly never a part of the theological scene in England, nor was it characteristic of Protestant theology generally.[27] Of the nineteenth-century writers in English, only Cunningham used the concept of "dictation," and at that in a metaphorical and carefully qualified sense.[28] The basic inspirational idea was modified by the term "plenary" in the writings of Lee and Orr, while Strong sought to clarify the meaning of inspiration by the use of the expression "dynamical inspiration."[29] Where other orthodox theological writers entertained the doctrine of verbal inspiration, they did so in a manner that disclaimed completely any mechanical delineation of the method of inspiration, and allowed proper scope for the spontaneous expression of the individual personality in the process of writing.[30] What

[23] J. I. Packer, *NBD*, p. 564.

[24] Cf. E. Brunner, *Revelation and Reason*, pp. 127f.; G. Hebert, *Fundamentalism and the Church of God* (1957), p. 56; A. Richardson, *Chamber's Encyclopaedia* (1959 ed.), p. 114; J. Huxtable, *The Bible Says* (1962), pp. 64ff.

[25] Cf. *De Consensu Evang.* II, 12; R. Preus, *The Inspiration of Scripture* (1955), pp. 53ff.

[26] Cf. H. Heidegger, *Corp. Theol.* II, 34; W. Bucan, *Inst. Theol.* I, 4, 2.

[27] J. I. Packer, *Fundamentalism and the Word of God: Some Evangelical Princ'ples* (1958), p. 79.

[28] W. Cunningham, *Theological Lectures* (1878), pp. 349ff.

[29] W. Lee, *The Inspiration of the Holy Scriptures* (1857), pp. 21ff.; J. Orr, *Revelation and Inspiration*, p. 211; A. H. Strong, *Systematic Theology* (1949 ed.), pp. 208ff.

[30] This attitude was represented by such scholars as C. Wordsworth, *The Inspiration of the Bible* (1861), p. 5; C. Hodge, *Systematic Theology* (1873), I, pp. 156f.; W. B. Pope, *Compendium of Christian Theology* (1879 ed.), I, 171, 183; C. H. Waller, *Authoritative Inspiration* (1887), pp. 200f.; H. C. G. Moule, *Veni Creator* (1890), pp. 53f.; B. B. Warfield, *The Inspiration and Authority of the Bible* (1951 ed.), pp. 153ff., 173n. J. M. Gray specifically rejected the mechanical view of inspiration as a tenet of American conservative belief, *The Fundamentals* (1917 ed.), II, 16; British scholars in the evangelical area never adhered to it at any time, and even repudiated it, as Hebert conceded, *Fundamentalism and the Church of God*, p. 56.

470

both British and American conservative writers were concerned to safeguard was the fact of inspiration, and not any particular theory as to the method by which it was achieved.

In any consideration of the nature and fact of inspiration it would seem the course of wisdom to refrain from going beyond what the Bible itself has to say concerning this extremely important doctrine. It appears evident from the reference in Second Timothy that inspiration did not terminate with the individuals responsible for the composition of the Scriptural writings, as maintained by many liberal thinkers,[31] but in the written end-product of their inspiration. For the prophets of the Old Testament period, divine revelation was basically verbal, but was accompanied on occasions by certain visionary concomitants which, as Köhler has recognized, also constitute verbal revelation.[32]

Great caution should be urged at this point, however, against reading into the Biblical concept of inspiration ideas derived from the Latin term *inspiratio*. While there is no explicit denial that a divine accentuation or heightening of the native human abilities of the individual prophet took place in certain instances, the Old Testament as a whole does not teach that such was a general preliminary to prophetic pronouncements. In ways that obviously differed according to the personality of the individual involved, the authors of the various Scriptural writings were used by God to produce the message that He desired to communicate through them to mankind.[33] Until more is known about the psychology of the Hebrew prophetic consciousness, it appears unwise to add to the statement that the kind of inspiration under which the Biblical authors produced their writings did not detract from the exercise of the human personality, but instead brought the creative faculties of the individual composers into particular focus for their task. Their sense of responsibility extended to the factual accuracy of their material, and in this connection it should be noted that many of the alleged errors in Scripture are nothing more than misinterpretations of the oriental scene by the western mind, or are the product of sheer ignorance of facets of ancient Near Eastern life on the part of modern scholars.

In the view of the present writer, the usage of terms such as "verbal" and "plenary," although they are meant to safeguard the fact of inspiration, tends to obscure the issue in the minds of many thinkers, and in some instances these words introduce actual confusion into the concept.

---

[31] Cf. S. Mowinckel, *The OT as Word of God*, pp. 25f.

[32] L. Köhler, *OT Theology* (1957), p. 103.

[33] Cf. G. H. W. Lampe, *IDB*, II, p. 714. For a Roman Catholic treatment of the doctrine of Biblical inspiration see J. Levie, *La Bible, Parole Humaine et Message de Dieu* (1958), E. tr. S. H. Treman, *The Bible, Word of God in Words of Men* (1962); J. L. McKenzie, *Myths and Realities: Studies in Biblical Theology* (1963), pp. 37ff.

Perhaps the safest course would be to speak simply of the inspiration of Scripture, without introducing any other kind of qualification that could be taken as pointing to some opinion as to the mode of inspiration which the situation clearly does not warrant.

Brunner was correct in assuming that the closest analogy to verbal inspiration is in the prophetic experience of revelation.[34] This does in fact characterize inspiration proper as the process by which God stirred His chosen servants to communicate His salvation, and to preserve it for posterity in written form. Scripture thus constitutes written revelation in precisely the same way as the prophetic oracles consisted of spoken revelation. Again it should be observed that the Old Testament narratives relating to divine self-disclosure in "redemptive history" are not merely human testimony to divine revelation, but actually constitute the essence of the revelation itself. Just as the prophetic experience of the divine afflatus validated and certified the truth of that aspect of the divine mind and will that the servants of God were concerned to communicate, so the concept of inspiration may be taken in general terms as a guarantee of an essential harmony, whether involving meaning or fact, between the mind of God and the words of men as contained in the Biblical narratives.

Neo-orthodox writers have generally taken pains to clarify their conviction that the "Word of the Lord" cannot be identified with the totality of the Scriptural corpus. Consequently they have stressed that while Scripture contains the divine Word, it ought not to be regarded as consisting of the Word of God *in toto*. That this is rather an artificial approach to the question of Biblical inspiration was pointed out by Griffith Thomas, who wrote:

> It is sometimes said that the Bible *is* the Word of God, while at other times it is said that the Bible *contains* the Word of God. These are both true, if held together, though either alone is liable to misapprehension. If we only say the Bible *is* the Word of God, we are in danger of forgetting that it contains the words of men also, many of which are not true in themselves, though the record that they were spoken is true and reliable. If, on the other hand, we limit our belief to the phrase, the Bible *contains* the Word of God, there is the opposite danger of not knowing which is God's Word and which is man's, an entirely impossible position. The Bible *is* the Word of God in the sense that it conveys to us an accurate record of everything God intended man to know and learn in connection with his will. The Bible *contains* the Word of God in the sense that in it is enshrined the Word of God which is revealed to us for our redemption.[35]

While it is true that the setting of the divine proclamations in past ages was a deliberate element in the self-revelation of God, it is important to note, as Ellison has pointed out, that the Scripture as a record is not in

[34] E. Brunner, *Revelation and Reason*, p. 122 n. 9.
[35] W. H. Griffith Thomas, *The Principles of Theology* (1930), p. 119.

472

itself life-giving.[36] From this standpoint it cannot be regarded as the agent of revelation *per se,* for the simple reason that it is never more than an instrument to be used by the Holy Spirit of God in order to make the revelation contained in Scripture personal to the believer.

C. INFALLIBILITY AND INERRANCY

The concepts of inerrancy[37] and infallibility have frequently been applied by conservative writers to the Scriptural narratives in order to indicate the completeness of inspiration and authority. Some would argue strongly, however, that to set up inerrancy as the basis of a doctrine of inspiration is in their view open to the serious objection that the demonstration of inaccuracies, errors, or inconsistencies, whether actual or alleged, immediately involves the rejection of the idea of inspiration as well as that of inerrancy. Such an objection was the basis of Dewey Beegle's attempt to relate inspiration to an errant Scripture on the premise of a subjective definition of revelation.[38] As a prime indication of error in the original text of the Old Testament he adduced the reign of Pekah of Israel, who according to 2 Kings 15:27 ruled for twenty years, but whose actual reign, based on Assyrian sources, lasted probably not more than eight years.[39]

While at first sight there appears to be a serious discrepancy in the Biblical text at this point by comparison with extra-Biblical sources, a number of considerations have to be borne in mind. First, any computation of regnal years must be made according to the practices current in the appropriate period of ancient Near Eastern life. Second, not all of the factors that led the chronologist to assign a twenty-year rule to Pekah may be evident from a reading of the Biblical narrative. Third, the temptation to identify Pekah with his precursor Pekahiah must be resisted in the interests of an honest attempt to ascertain and do justice to the facts of the case. From the Assyrian Eponym Chronicle it is clear that the reign of Pekah terminated in 732/31 B.C., and that on the basis of the death of Pekahiah in 740/39 B.C., the rule of Pekah over Israel did in fact last not more than eight years.

On the other hand, 2 Kings 16:1 states explicitly that Ahaz began to reign in the seventeenth year of Pekah. This need present no problem, however, when it is remembered that Ahaz was co-regent with Jotham his father from 744/43 B.C. until 732/31 B.C., the year in which Pekah died, becoming the senior partner in this alliance in 735 B.C., the event to which the Kings reference most probably alludes. What is significant

---

[36] H. L. Ellison, *EQ*, XXVI (1954), pp. 213f.

[37] This is not a "modern doctrine" as some liberals, e.g. A. G. Hebert, *The Authority of the Old Testament* (1947), p. 98, have supposed, being in fact orthodox Church teaching until the seventeenth century.

[38] D. M. Beegle, *The Inspiration of Scripture* (1963).

[39] *ARAB,* I, sect. 816; cf. *MNHK,* pp. 119ff.

for the computation of the Pekah regime is the fact that the king reckoned his years from 752 B.C., that is to say, the year following the death of Jeroboam II. Since Pekah was an adjutant in the army of Pekahiah, king of Israel, 742/41-740/39 B.C., and quite possibly of Gileadite stock,[40] it may well have happened that in the period of unrest following the death of Jeroboam II he seized power in Gilead and established firm control over that part of Transjordan. If this was actually the case, it would go far towards explaining the insecurity of Menahem and the intervention of Tiglathpileser III, to whom Pekah fell victim. While the Old Testament narratives make no specific mention of Pekah as the head of a Gileadite monarchy from 752 B.C., the tradition by which he reckoned his dates from the year after the death of Jeroboam II is of considerable significance in this regard. As Curtis has pointed out, such a Gileadite regime would, when computed with the accession of Pekah to the throne of Israel in 740/39 B.C., enable him to lay claim to a total reign of twenty years, as recorded in Kings.[41] Probably the best explanation of the situation is that the period of his reign consisted of partly usurped years. That such a practice was not unknown in the Near East is indicated by the fact that in the Raameside records of Egypt, Haremhab, *ca.* 1300 B.C., usurped the regnal years of Akhenaton and certain of his successors.

To regard the Old Testament statement as a factual error, in the manner of Beegle, constitutes a vast oversimplification of the problem, which is certainly amenable to a very different solution. As has been observed previously, so many of the alleged errors in the Biblical record are the product of occidental ignorance of ancient Near Eastern life and customs, rather than the work of the original authors. This is one reason why conservative scholars deprecate the confident pronouncements concerning errors which are sometimes made. As Thiele has so clearly shown, there is no adequate reason to doubt that the chronologists of the Old Testament were honest individuals who were as much concerned for the accuracy of their facts as for the characteristics of the various rulers whose reigns were duly recorded. Again it needs to be observed that, in the realm of historical phenomena in particular, archaeological discoveries have shown beyond reasonable doubt the amazing accuracy of the Old Testament material as compared with other historical sources in antiquity.

To the present writer, two basic issues are involved in the question of infallibility. The first is whether in fact the concept of infallibility is really a concomitant of inspiration or not. Some have pointed out that the term itself is not Biblical in nature, and was not especially prominent in the theology of the Reformers. It can be applied most properly only

---

[40] H. B. MacLean, *IDB*, III, p. 709; cf. S. J. De Vries, *IDB*, I, p. 593.

[41] J. B. Curtis, *JBL*, LXXX (1961), pp. 362f.; similarly J. Gray, *I and II Kings: A Commentary* (1963), pp. 63f.

to the prophetic and apostolic writings as the authoritative revelation of God which culminated in the work of Jesus Christ and as authentic records of that revelation. In the last resort, however, infallibility is the characteristic of the Divine Author of Scripture and then, by derivation, of the writings of which Scripture is composed.

The second issue concerns the true meaning of infallibility. This will need careful examination if it is not to go beyond what the Bible actually claims for itself in this regard. Here Scripture makes it explicit that its testimony to the saving revelation and redemption of God in Christ is reliable, and that it furnishes an authoritative norm of faith and conduct for the believer. It shows that the Word of God achieves its intended objective, and at the same time serves as a medium through which the Holy Spirit, by whom it has been given, can speak to mankind. In an inspired Scripture, therefore, it would seem logical to expect infallibility as here defined to be a normal constituent element.

IV. PROBLEMS IN OLD TESTAMENT THEOLOGY

A. The Covenant

The attempt by Eichrodt to demonstrate the essential unity of Israelite faith by relating it to the central concept of the Covenant brought a welcome emphasis to bear upon what is surely one of the most characteristic facets of Hebrew religious life. The idea of a covenant as a bond linking two parties by agreement has been demonstrated archaeologically from the second millennium B.C. in the ancient Near East.[1] The Hebrew בְּרִית probably goes back to the Akkadian word *birîtu*, signifying a bond or fetter, while the Hebrew expression כָּרַת בְּרִית, meaning literally "to cut a covenant," has been found in two instances on the Qatna texts, which probably date from the fifteenth century B.C. One tablet containing this expression consisted of an agreement in which a number of men contracted to enter into the service of one another and discharge certain obligations. The other instance occurred on a tablet that listed the rations of food to be received by the men who had thus contracted for service.[2] These contracts were doubtless inspired by the agreements made between cities and states during the Mari Age,[3] which in turn depended upon earlier Sumerian originals.

Second-millennium B.C. covenants among the Hittites have been shown to consist of suzerainty and parity agreements.[4] In the former only the inferior party was bound by an oath, whereas in the latter both sides were under an obligation to abide by the oath which sealed the agreement. In the suzerainty treaty, which, according to Mendenhall, was the principal form, the vassal did not only have to take an oath, but had also to profess his faith in the integrity and magnanimity of the overlord. Such legal undertakings between a great king and a vassal normally commenced with a preamble in which the instigator of the covenant was

[1] Cf. D. J. McCarthy, *Treaty and Covenant, A Study in Form in the Ancient Oriental Documents and in the OT* (1963).

[2] W. F. Albright, *BASOR*, No. 121 (1951), pp. 21f.

[3] Cf. G. E. Mendenhall, *BA*, XI, No. 1 (1948), p. 18.

[4] G. E. Mendenhall, *BA*, XVII, No. 3 (1954), pp. 50ff.; reprinted as *Law and Covenant in Israel and the Ancient Near East* (1955); cf. Mendenhall in *IDB*, I, pp. 714ff.

identified and his credentials established.[5] This was followed by an outline of the historical relations between the parties entering into the agreement (cf. Exod. 20:2; Josh. 24:2f.), with proper stress upon the integrity of the overlord and his graciousness towards his vassal (Deut. 7:7).[6] Then followed the description of the obligations to be imposed upon and accepted by the vassal, and this normally included a prohibition against the latter's engaging in foreign alliances (cf. Exod. 20:3; 34:14; Josh. 24:14). A further provision stipulated that the document should remain in the deposit of the vassal and be read publicly at intervals, in order to remind him of the nature of the obligations undertaken (cf. Exod. 25:16, 21; Deut. 31:9ff.; Josh. 24:26; 1 Kgs. 8:9). A concluding portion normally listed the deities as witnesses and enumerated the blessings or curses that would occur according as the covenant was kept or violated (cf. Exod. 23:20ff.; Lev. 26:3ff.; Deut. 27:12ff.). In Joshua 24:22 the Israelites replaced the heathen deities as witnesses; cf. Isaiah 1:2; Hosea 2:21f.; and Micah 6:2. The remarkable parallels to the Covenant relationship between God and Israel set the Sinai agreement firmly and authentically against a second-millennium B.C. milieu, and do not require a date for the Covenant outside the Heroic Age.

The significance of the Hebrew Covenant, however, can only be understood most fully against the background of the Old Testament itself, for while the idea of an agreement between two responsible contracting parties is implicit in the Sinai Covenant, the contract itself clearly involves a dispensation of grace and promise for the future.[7] The first reference to a covenant in the Old Testament is the agreement with Noah before the Flood (Gen. 6:18ff.). The nature of an Old Testament covenant is shown clearly by the post-diluvian pact with him. In this instance, as in others, the approach was initiated by God but the benefits were universal and unconditional. The Abrahamic Covenant contained the same concept of divine dispensation, but interpreted it more narrowly to include the promises connected with the inheritance of Canaan, the multiplying of the offspring of Abraham, and the general assurance of divine support for the people. In the latter regard, however, the Covenant exhibited certain particularistic features, such as the exclusion of Ishmael (Gen. 17:18ff.) and the restriction of the blessing as issuing through the offspring of Abraham rather than being given to all mankind. Yet as in the Hittite suzerainty treaties, the overlordship and supremacy of God were made quite evident at the commencement, and the responsibility for keeping the provisions of the agreement was placed squarely upon Abraham and his offspring. In these circumstances it

[5] Cf. Exod. 20:1f., Josh. 24:2; M. G. Kline, *Treaty of the Great King* (1963), pp. 10ff.

[6] Cf. *ANET*, p. 204.

[7] Cf. J. Murray, *The Covenant of Grace* (1953), p. 31.

should be noted that the unilateral bestowal of divine grace and the human obligation to observe the conditions set out in the Covenant are complementary rather than mutually exclusive factors. There is a pronounced spiritual element underlying the entire contractual procedure, which if entertained seriously would demand a high degree of consecration and single-mindedness from the human participants. Certain other concomitant features indicate the great antiquity of the Abrahamic Covenant, as Mendenhall has shown, which serve to place it firmly within the pre-Mosaic era.[8]

As a result of activities of the Wellhausen school, the Mosaic Covenant was regarded as a form of tribal religious relationship in which the deity was little more than the symbol of the tribe itself. On this basis it was affirmed that it was only with the eighth-century prophets that a sense of awareness of the ethical content of this relationship developed, and this was followed in the immediate pre-exilic period with the enunciation of the Covenant concept proper in the thought of the prophet Jeremiah. As the result of modern archaeological discoveries, however, it is now possible to place the Mosaic Covenant confidently against the background of the Late Bronze Age. It is important to notice further in this connection that there was an avowed social and political aspect to the Covenant relationship as well as a purely religious one. The concept of the Sinai agreement would be virtually meaningless were it not for the fact that the religious and ethical norms that it contained were designed to produce a reciprocal action in strictly social terms. Not merely were the adherents bound together in loyalty to the Deity, but they were linked by the Covenant relationship as the *people* of God. It was at this juncture that they received a unique identity. They became the specific medium of divine revelation in "saving history," and at the same time they received a missionary vocation as the divine witnesses to the surrounding pagan nations.[9] Quite aside from its religious implications, the Covenant furnished a distinctive form and structure for the social life of the Israelite community. Yet in all this it must never be forgotten that it was the religious nature of the Covenant that furnished its characteristic uniqueness.

Basic to the continuance of the relationship was the demand that divine holiness should be the governing factor in Israelite life (cf. Lev. 19:2; Deut. 6:4). This holiness would be made apparent in the continuing obedience of the religious community to the commands of God, and would constitute the means by which the Covenant agreement would continue to function for the blessing and prosperity of Israel (Lev.

---

[8] *IDB*, I, p. 718.

[9] For H. H. Rowley, *Israel's Mission to the World* (1939), pp. 2ff., this "wider vision" was to be interpreted predominantly in terms of post-exilic religious developments.

26:3ff.). Disobedience, whether in the form of passive negligence or active rebellion, constituted an act of sin that could speedily undermine the entire Covenant relationship if it assumed communal proportions. In this sense von Rad was correct in asserting that the individual was so closely identified with the group that when he committed an act of sin it had repercussions throughout the entire community.[10] However, it should be observed that sin belongs properly to the category of the sacred rather than the social, and that it constitutes an affront to and an assault upon the holiness of God. The weakness of the presentation by von Rad in this area of Old Testament theology is his deficient view of sin, characterized by his reluctance to consider man as a fallen creature. This attitude was shared by many contemporary German scholars, who were influenced by the philosophical speculations of Nietzsche.

Although the theological concepts of the Old Testament do not lend themselves with particular readiness to attempts at systematization, as Eichrodt conceded, there can be little doubt that the Covenant idea must be given an important place in any formulation of the unity of Scripture. The New Testament clearly envisaged a continuation of the Covenant tradition of the Old Testament, and the supreme expression of this tendency is found in the Last Supper (Matt. 26:28; Mark 14:24; Lk. 22:20; 1 Cor. 11:25), where the New Covenant was thought of in terms of the atonement for human sin by Jesus Christ on Calvary. Not merely is Christ therefore the mediator and surety of the New Covenant; there is a very real sense in which He Himself constitutes the New Covenant. However, it must again be emphasized that in any study of the Old Testament concept of the Covenant it is of prime importance to envisage the idea in its own terms. Where continuity with the New Testament is at issue, the interpreter should avoid strenuously any explanation that depends upon a Greek or western background of thought or practice. This unfortunately was not seen clearly by J. B. Payne, who in a comprehensive and unusual study of the Covenant from a conservative standpoint preferred to employ the term "testament" in the Graeco-Roman sense of a last will and testament as the structure for his work.[11] He restricted the idea of a covenant to the relationship that existed between man and God prior to the fall, and he maintained that such a situation was more marked by a synergistic quality than subsequent dispositions of divine grace. Despite the erudition and painstaking work of the author, it is fallacious to assume that the word $\delta\iota\alpha\theta\eta\kappa\eta$ in Hebrews 9:15ff. was being employed exclusively in the western sense of a last will and testament, for as such it is inappropriate as a general description of divine dealings with men.

[10] G. von Rad, *Theologie des AT, I*, pp. 216ff.
[11] *The Theology of the Older Testament* (1962).

B. THE MESSIAH

No survey of Old Testament theology would be complete without some attention being devoted to the concepts of the Messiah and the Servant of the Lord. The idea of an "anointed one" occurred frequently in the writings of the Old Testament, and was not by any means restricted to the ruler of the last days. Frequently it pointed to the ruler over Israel or Judah during the monarchy; in the Pentateuch it was occasionally applied to the High Priest in the exercise of certain of his ritual functions (Lev. 4:3ff.; 6:15 *et al.*). The title "the Lord's Anointed" was applied to Saul (e.g. 1 Sam. 24:6), David (2 Sam. 19:22), Zedekiah (Lam. 4:20), and to the Davidic king (e.g. 1 Sam. 2:35; Hab. 3:13), as well as to a non-Israelite figure, Cyrus of Persia (Isa. 45:1). The central figure of Jewish apocalyptic expectation was specifically associated with the term in Daniel 9:25f. As F. F. Bruce has indicated, the reference to Cyrus is helpful in adducing some of the more prominent elements of the Old Testament messianic concept.[12] Cyrus was described as a man chosen by God (Isa. 44:28) to accomplish a purpose of redemption for the chosen people (Isa. 45:11f.) and to bring judgment upon the enemies of God (Isa. 45:1ff.), over whom he was to be given the dominion. In all this he was not acting on a basis of individual responsibility, but as the agent of God Himself. While functioning in a secular sense, as indeed some of the anointed kings of Israel did (e.g. Jehu, 1 Kgs. 19:16), he was at the same time a distinct soteriological figure, which is characteristic of the most developed concepts of the Messiah.

The antiquity and nature of the messianic expectation have been a matter of considerable debate among scholars, influenced not a little by the views of the participants concerning facets of Old Testament literary criticism. By way of observation it should be noted that the messianic concept of the Hebrews, like certain other Old Testament eschatological emphases, has no proper counterpart in ancient Near Eastern culture. The messianic expectation was linked normatively with the house of David, which consummated the promises contained in the final blessing of Jacob (Gen. 49:9f.).[13] The prophecy of Nathan (2 Sam. 7:12ff.; cf. Ps. 89:3ff.) furnished religious sanction for the permanence of the Davidic dynasty, and employed it as an additional assurance of redemption within the framework of the Covenant, consistent with its provisions. Although the Hebrew kingship did not carry any of the significance for religious life that was so commonly found in contemporary Near Eastern thought, the ideas of king and Messiah were associated on occasions to the point where the royal Psalms could speak of the ruler as the adopted

---

[12] *NBD*, pp. 811f.
[13] On Shiloh see E. Jenni, *IDB*, III, p. 362; N. K. Gottwald, *IDB*, IV, p. 330.

son of God (Ps. 2:7), as the one who insured law and justice in Israel (Ps. 72:1ff.) and brought divine blessing to the people (Ps. 72:6ff.), and as the victor over all his enemies (Ps. 21:9ff.), who ruled over the whole earth for ever (Pss. 21:5; 72:5ff.). Although phraseology of this kind did not actually deify the ruler, there can be little disagreement that it was distinctly reminiscent of similar Babylonian utterances. Thus there was a firm basis in the monarchy for the expectation of an eschatological figure to whom the characteristics glowingly attributed to the earthly David could easily be transferred (cf. Ezek. 34:23).

According to Mowinckel, the figure of the Messiah was originally political, commencing with the adoption by Israel of the Canaanite model of kingship, suitably modified and transformed to align itself readily to the Hebrew covenant ideal.[14] The Israelite king was held to be superhuman and divine, reflecting Canaanite patterns of kingship,[15] and as the anointed of God he received special gifts of wisdom. Since, in the opinion of Mowinckel, the true ideal of kingship never became an actuality in Israel, there emerged the expectation that an anointed one of God would ultimately arise. In this sense the Messiah is an eschatological figure who belongs properly to the "last days." Since all the indisputable messianic passages in the Old Testament writings regard the collapse of the Davidic monarchy as historical fact, the Messiah must be a creation of the post-exilic period, and cannot logically be posited in pre-exilic documents that might otherwise be regarded as predicting his emergence. Those passages of the Old Testament belonging to the monarchy that appear to be messianic must be regarded as addressed to the reigning monarch of the day, and therefore devoid of proper eschatological significance.

This rather circular and certainly highly subjective form of reasoning has been challenged in part by Knight, who questioned whether the rulers mentioned in Kings could ever have been thought of as addressed in the kind of language employed in the royal Psalms.[16] Careful study shows that, in point of fact, a messianic pattern similar to that accorded to Cyrus emerges from the royal Psalms. Thus the king meets with world opposition (Pss. 2:1ff.; 110:1), but is victorious through the power of God (Pss. 45:3ff.; 89:22f.; 2:6ff.; 18:46ff.; 110:1f.) and establishes a universal domain (Pss. 2:8ff.; 18:43ff.; 72:8ff.; 110:5f.) characterized by peace (Ps. 72:7) and prosperity (Ps. 72:16). This king is the enemy of the oppressor and the protector of the poor (Ps. 72:2f.) and righteous (Ps. 72:7). His rule is everlasting (Pss. 21:4; 45:6; 72:5), as are his name (Ps. 72:17) and his memory (Ps. 45:17); and he is the recipient of perpetual blessing from God (Ps. 45:2). More specifically he is heir to the

[14] *He That Cometh*, pp. 4ff.
[15] *Ibid.*, p. 59.
[16] *A Christian Theology of the OT*, pp. 300f.

481

covenant of David (Ps. 89:28ff.) and the priesthood of Melchizedek (Ps. 110:4), as well as being the son of God (Pss. 2:7; 89:27), seated at the right hand of the Father (Ps. 110:1), and divine in nature (Ps. 45:6). Even the most exalted flight of poetic fancy could scarcely have envisaged the monarchs of Israel and Judah in such terms, particularly since Kings and Chronicles were apt to evaluate the behavior of certain of those notable figures in a distinctly critical manner from time to time.

It would appear, therefore, that some lofty spiritual ideal was being expressed by such sentiments as those found in the royal Psalms. Furthermore, it should be noted that the messianic concept in Israel contained other motifs that cannot be traced back directly to the royal ideal. Aside from the rather obscure promise of a ruler for Judah in the blessing of Jacob, there is the mystic connotation of a paradise situation in which the redemption of fallen man was promised through the activity of a soteriological figure of ancient origin (cf. Gen. 3:15, RSV; Job 15:7ff.; Ezek. 28:2; Mic. 5:2). More particularly the ideas of the mysterious birth of the Messiah (Isa. 7:14; Mic. 5:2f.) and the peace of paradise (Isa. 11:6ff.) have nothing whatever to do with the association of the king and the Messiah. Therefore it would seem imprudent to follow Mowinckel in rejecting all those messianic passages that do not define the Messiah in the most rigid eschatological sense; and it is instead legitimate, with Vriezen, to regard as messianic all those prophecies of the Old Testament that placed an individual in a position of prominence as a savior and deliverer.[17] On this basis it would be possible to regard Messiah as the antitype of the "first Adam" and also of Moses (cf. Deut. 18:15ff.).

The annunciation formula in Isaiah 7:14 concerning the birth of a Messiah has been illumined to some extent by a wider understanding of its ancient Near Eastern setting. It has been described by Engnell as a "divine-royal formula," which in pagan mythology was commonly associated with the announcement of the birth of a child to the gods.[18] A declaration of birth similar to that in Isaiah is also found in connection with Hagar (Gen. 16:11) and Sarah (Gen. 17:19). At Ras Shamra an annunciation to the goddess Nikkal was phrased:

tld btl [t   "A virgin will give birth . . .
hl ǵlmt tld b[n   A damsel will bear a son . . ."[19]

As Hammershaimb pointed out, *ǵlmt*, the equivalent of the Hebrew עלמה, was a designation for the mother-goddess, or, better still, the queen who subsequently gives birth to the royal heir.[20] What is impor-

[17] *An Outline of OT Theology*, pp. 350ff.
[18] *Studies in Divine Kingship in the Ancient Near East* (1943), p. 133.
[19] C. H. Gordon, *Ugaritic Handbook*, text 77, line 7.
[20] *Studia Theologica*, III (1951), p. 128; cf. C. H. Gordon, *Journal of Bible and Religion*, XXI (1953), p. 106; E. R. Lacheman, *ibid.*, XXII (1954), p. 43.

tant to notice, however, is that this term refers to Nikkal before her marriage took place, not after it. Thus, it would appear that in Canaanite usage *btlt* and *ǵlmt* were virtually synonymous;[21] and the former constituted the standard designation in the mythological texts for Anat as a virgin (*btlt 'nt*).[22] Although *ǵlmt* was not a technical designation denoting a *virgo intacta*, for which (as Gordon has pointed out)[23] no term existed in the ancient Near East, it is of some significance to observe that it never occurred in the cuneiform Canaanite texts as a description of a married woman. This fact is important in view of the appeal by Mowinckel to the *Legend of Keret*, in which he understood the *ǵlmt* to be the wife of Keret, thus making the עלמה of Isaiah other than a virgin.[24] A careful reading of the text, however, shows that the wife of Keret is consistently described after her marriage as "lady Hry" (*m't ḥry*) and "your wife" (*a'tk*), but never as *ǵlmt*. Clearly the Ras Shamra texts lend no support to those who claim that the Hebrew עלמה can be used of a married woman.[25] Against those who maintain that the Hebrew language has a completely unmistakable word for "virgin," namely בתולה and that if "virgin" had been meant in Isaiah's annunciation formula this word would have occurred there, it merely needs to be remarked that among the seven occurrences of עלמה in the Old Testament, there is not one instance where the word was clearly used of a woman who was not a *virgo intacta*, whereas in Joel 1:18, a בתולה is said to be weeping for the *husband* of her youth.

Messianic figures in the Old Testament include the Branch (Jer. 23:5; 33:15), the Seed of the Woman (Gen. 3:15), and the Son of Man (Dan. 7:1ff.), but by far the most prominent was the Servant of the Lord in Isaiah. Not only was this Servant charged with responsibility towards a covenant people in bondage (Isa. 42:18ff.), but he was also given a mission to the Gentiles (Isa. 42:1ff.). While Cyrus would constitute the instrument of deliverance who would liberate and restore the faithful remnant, it was the Servant who would bring that remnant back to God (Isa. 49:1ff.). The Servant was designated by the name Israel (Isa. 49:3) simply because the nation as a whole had foregone any right to the use of that exalted title. The distinction between the Servant and the nation was then made clear (Isa. 49:14ff.), and the faithful Israelites were

[21] E. J. Young, *Studies in Isaiah* (1955), p. 167; cf. Mowinckel, *He That Cometh*, p. 114.

[22] C. H. Gordon, *Ugaritic Handbook*, Texts 6:19; 49:II:14; III:22f.; IV:45; 128:II:27.

[23] *Ugaritic Manual* (1955), I, p. 249b.

[24] S. Mowinckel, *He That Cometh*, pp. 113f.

[25] As maintained by Kimchi (cf. L. Finkelstein, *The Commentary of David Kimhi on Isaiah* [1926], p. 49); K. Marti, *Das Buch Jesaja* (1900), p. 76; B. Duhm, *Das Buch Jesaia*, p. 75, and many subsequent commentators. Cf. R. D. Wilson, *PTR*, XXIV (1926), p. 316.

urged to adopt his piety and dedication as their model for living. The act of salvation—national and universal—which the Servant was to achieve (Isa. 51:1ff.), involved his life in society and his substitutionary death (Isa. 53:1ff.), followed by his exaltation. On the basis of this accomplishment Israel would be called to enter the New Covenant (Isa. 54:1ff.), and the salvation wrought by the work of the Servant would be made available to all those in need (Isa. 55:1ff.).

Few topics in Old Testament theology have been discussed more widely than the question of the identity of the Divine Servant, and few have been less amenable to a consensus of scholarly opinion.[26] Prior to the nineteenth century the Christian Church interpreted Isaiah 53 as a messianic prophecy. For the first three hundred years of the Christian era the Church commonly identified the Servant with the righteous—whether on an individual or collective basis—before the standard messianic interpretation became general.[27] When European scholars such as Semler, Koppe, and Eichhorn denied Isaiah's authorship of chapters forty and following, they gradually forsook the concept of a Davidic Messiah in favor of interpreting the Servant as the entire nation of Israel.[28] This tendency was not uniform, however, for J. C. R. Eckermann regarded the Servant as the ideal Israel, on the ground that there was a clear difference between the state and its citizens.[29] This view was subsequently adopted by Vatke and Ewald, being expounded to foster the expectation that the spiritual Israel would be instrumental in the restoration of the moribund mortal Israel.[30] Samuel Davidson followed Ewald in abandoning the traditional messianic interpretation and identifying the Servant with the ideal Israel.[31] In this he was supported by Cheyne, A. B. Davidson, and S. R. Driver.[32] The principal difficulty attached to this view was that it was completely unable to explain how an ideal Israel could die for the sins of an actual Israel as part of a redemptive scheme.

The theory that the Servant constituted the faithful minority within the large nation was first suggested by Paulus, and given considerable

---

[26] Cf. A. Causse, *Israël et la vision de l'humanité* (1924), p. 54; *RSL*, p. 3.

[27] Cf. C. R. North, *The Suffering Servant in Deutero-Isaiah* (1948), pp. 9ff.

[28] J. S. Semler, *Abhandlung von freier Untersuchung des Canons* (1771-75); J. B. Koppe, *D. Robert Louth's Jesaias neu übersetzt nebst einer Einleitung und critischen philologischen und erlaüternden Anmerkungen mit Zusätzen und Anmerkungen* (1779-81); J. G. Eichhorn, *Allgemeine Bibliothek der biblischen Litteratur* (1794). Cf. J. L. McKenzie, *Second Isaiah* (1968), pp. xliiiff.

[29] *Theologische Beyträge* (1790).

[30] W. Vatke, *Die Religion des AT, I* (1835). H. Ewald, *Die Propheten des Alten Bundes* (1840).

[31] *An Introduction to the OT* (1863), III, pp. 62ff.

[32] T. K. Cheyne, *Isaiah Chronologically Arranged* (1870), pp. 176, 181; A. B. Davidson, *OT Prophecy* (1903), pp. 437ff.; S. R. Driver, *Isaiah: His Life and Times* (1888), p 179.

prominence by Knobel and Kuenen.[33] On this view the task and glory of the Messiah were to be transferred during the exile to a section of the Israelite community, which would atone for the sins of the nation and thereby achieve its redemption. Unfortunately this interpretation also failed to show how a portion of the people could die in exile in order to atone for the iniquities of Israel as a whole and effect justification for the people of God. Other attempts to account for the identity of the Divine Servant associated him with the prophetic order in some manner, or with a particular historical individual such as Hezekiah, Isaiah himself, Jeremiah, or some unknown personage.[34]

[33] H. E. G. Paulus, *Philologischer Clavis über das AT für Schulen und Akademien. Jesaias* (1793); A. Knobel, *Der Prophet Jesaia* (1843); A. Kuenen, *The Prophets and Prophecy in Israel. An Historical and Critical Enquiry* (1877).

[34] For the prophetic order, see W. Gesenius, *Der Prophet Jesaja* (1821); G. M. L. De Wette, *Opuscula theologica: Commentatio de morte Jesu Christi expiatoria* (1830); J. C. K. Hofmann, *Weissagung und Erfüllung im A und NT* (1841). For Hezekiah, see K. F. Bahrdt, *Die Kleine Bibel, I* (1780). For Isaiah, C. F. Staüdlin, *Neue Beiträge zur Erläuterung der biblischen Propheten* (1791). For Jeremiah, B. Duhm, *Die Theologie der Propheten* (1875). For an unknown personage, H. Ewald, *Die Propheten des Alten Bundes* (1840). Delitzsch' celebrated "pyramid theory," *Biblical Commentary on the Prophecies of Isaiah* (1890 ed.), p. 236, saw the concept of the Servant as having its lowest level rooted in the entire nation of Israel. In a more developed sense it envisaged a spiritual rather than an actual Israel; and at its highest point it represented the person of the Redeemer-Messiah. Cheyne, *The Prophecies of Isaiah* (1880), and G. A. Smith, *The Book of Isaiah* (1890), approved this idea; however, it was resisted by a number of European scholars, who still sought to identify the Servant with some historical personage. Duhm abandoned his association of the Servant with Jeremiah, *Die Theologie der Propheten*, pp. 287ff., for one regarding the Servant as an unknown Teacher of the Law who died of leprosy, *Das Buch Jesaja übersetzt und erklärt* (1892), pp. 278ff. Bertholet, in maintaining a diverse authorship of the four Servant oracles, thought that the Servant was the martyred scribe Eleazar, who met death at the hands of Antiochus Epiphanes; *Zu Jesaja 53: Ein Erklärungsversuch* (1899); cf. 2 Macc. 6:18ff. Ernst Sellin proposed no less than four theories of the personage of the Servant, successively identifying him with Zerubbabel, *Serubbabel: Ein Beitrag zur Geschichte der messianischen Erwartung und der Entstehung des Judentums* (1898); Jehoiachin, *Studien zur Entstehungsgeschichte der jüdischen Gemeinde nach dem babylonischen Exil. I. Der Knecht Gottes bei Deuterojesaja* (1901); Moses, *Mose und seine Bedeutung für die israelitisch-jüdische Religionsgeschichte* (1922); and Deutero-Isaiah, *Neue Kirchliche Zeitschrift*, XLI (1930), pp. 73ff., 145ff.; cf. *ZAW*, LV (1937), pp. 177ff. This last identification was supported by H. M. Orlinsky, *The So-Called "Suffering Servant" in Isaiah 53* (1964), pp. 8ff. Rudolf Kittel associated the Servant with an anonymous contemporary of Deutero-Isaiah, *Der Prophet Jesaja erklärt von Dr. August Dillmann* (1898), *Zur Theologie des AT. II. Jesaja 53 und der leidende Messias im AT* (1899), *Gestalten und Gedanken in Israel* (1925). Weir held to an identification with Cyrus, *Westminster Review*, CLXIX (1908), pp. 309ff. Still in favor of a collective interpretation of messianic functions, however, were Budde, *Die sogenannten Ebed-Jahwe Lieder und die Bedeutung des Knechtes Jahwes in Jes. 40-55; Ein Minoritätsvotum* (1900); Giesebrecht, *Beiträge zur Jesajakritik* (1890), pp. 146ff.; and A. S. Peake, *The Problem of Suffering in the OT* (1904) and *The Servant of Yahweh* (1931).

The most serious treatment of the view that the Servant was in fact Deutero-Isaiah was undertaken by Mowinckel, who denied the collective interpretation and maintained that there was a sharp distinction between the Servant as represented in the four oracles on the one hand, and in surrounding material on the other.[35] In the latter the Servant was in fact the nation of Israel, whereas in the oracles the active missionary vocation of the Servant pointed, among other indications, to his essential individuality. This "autobiographical" theory encountered considerable difficulty with the fourth Servant oracle (Isa. 52:13-53:12).[36] Other difficulties Mowinckel disposed of by resorting to the favorite critical device—textual emendation. The view that the author propounded appeared to make the prophetic figure describe his own sufferings and death in anticipation of these events, a feature that failed to win the approval of some scholars who followed Mowinckel in other aspects of the theory. For them it was more preferable to suppose that the fourth oracle had been composed by a disciple of the prophet shortly after his death.[37] Even Mowinckel was compelled to modify his original view, for in 1931 he advanced the opinion that the oracles composed by Deutero-Isaiah had been assembled by his disciples who themselves were the authors of the material assigned by critical scholars to Trito-Isaiah. Furthermore, the Servant oracles were neither written by Deutero-Isaiah nor originally included in the first edition of his oracles.[38] According to Mowinckel the Servant had already met his death before the songs were completed, and while he did not formally deny the possibility that the Servant was Deutero-Isaiah, he came to recognize that he might well be a purely futuristic personage.[39] Concerning such a view it needs only to be remarked that such a tentative and internally inconsistent theory will hardly carry lasting conviction, and not least because it requires a forced and artificial interpretation of the Hebrew text if it is to be the least valid.

In a broadly messianic interpretation of the Servant, Nyberg, a member of the Scandinavian school, thought of him as a supra-individual figure belonging alike to the past, present, and future.[40] For him the Servant concept contained religious elements from Ras Shamra, the Tammuz liturgy, and the history of Israel, and reflected both individual

[35] S. Mowinckel, *Der Knecht Jahwäs* (1921).

[36] For scholarly opinion as to the scope of the oracles see *RSL*, p. 6 n. 1.

[37] E.g. P. Volz, *Jesaia II übersetzt und erklärt* (1932), pp. 149ff.

[38] Cf. S. Mowinckel, ZAW, XLIX (1931), pp. 87ff., 242ff., *Acta Orientalia*, XVI (1938), pp. 1ff., 40ff.

[39] Cf. *He That Cometh*, pp. 228f.; C. R. North, *Scottish Journal of Theology*, III (1950), pp. 363ff.

[40] H. S. Nyberg, *Svensk Exegetisk Årsbok*, VII (1942), pp. 5ff.

and collective characteristics.[41] A similar position was reached by another Scandinavian scholar, Ivan Engnell, who while stressing the presence of mythological elements in the Servant oracles, pointed out their regal background and claimed that the term "Servant" was actually a royal title.[42] He agreed with Mowinckel in recognizing that insofar as the Servant was an individual, he was essentially a figure of the future. Although the Servant was not a direct prediction of Jesus Christ, he was nevertheless basically a messianic figure.

Any attempt to derive the Servant concept from pagan Canaanite or Babylonian religious sources is open to the serious objection that the Servant of the Lord as envisaged in Isaiah was a strictly Israelite development for which there are no proper points of connection with the cult of a dying and rising deity. This is all the more certain since the larger context inveighed consistently against pagan idolatry, which was uniformly treated with contempt and scorn.[43] Furthermore, as Young has shown, the theological ideas underlying the concept of the Servant are radically different from any analogous material at Ras Shamra.[44]

Modern supporters of the traditional messianic interpretation of the Servant have relied to some extent upon the masterly expositions of Fischer.[45] Roman Catholic scholars who have adhered to this position included Feldmann, Condamin, and Van Hoonacker.[46] In the Dutch Reformed Church the messianic concept of the Servant was urged by Schelhaas and Edelkoort among others.[47] In a penetrating survey of the vast literature connected with the discussion of the identity of the Servant in Isaiah, C. R. North concluded that the idea moved from the nation of Israel to an individual and pointed forward to Jesus Christ, in whom the expectation was subsequently realized,[48] a position which had elements in common with that of J. van der Ploeg.[49] H. H. Rowley discerned a greater degree of oscillation in the Servant concept than North was prepared to allow, making the idea of a corporate personality a

---

[41] Cf. W. A. Irwin, *The Prophets and Their Times* (1941), pp. 234f.; J. P. Hyatt, *JNES*, III (1943), pp. 79ff.

[42] I. Engnell, *Svensk Exegetisk Årsbok*, X (1945), pp. 31ff.; *BJRL* (1948), pp. 54ff.; cf. G. Oestborn, *Tōrā in the Old Testament*, pp. 56ff.; S. Mowinckel, *Studia Theologica*, II (1949), pp. 71ff.; A. R. Johnson in S. H. Hooke (ed.), *The Labyrinth* (1935), pp. 99f.

[43] *RSL*, p. 43.

[44] E. J. Young, *Westminster Theological Journal*, XIII (1950-51), pp. 19ff.

[45] J. Fischer, *Isaias 40-55 und die Perikopen vom Gottesknecht* (1916), *Das Buch Isaias übersetzt und erklärt, II. Teil: Kapitel 40-66* (1939).

[46] F. Feldmann, *Der Knecht Gottes in Isaias Kap. 40-55* (1907), *Das Buch Isaias übersetzt und erklärt* (1926); A. Condamin, *Le Livre d'Isaïe: Traduction critique avec notes et commentaires* (1905); A. van Hoonacker, *Het Boek Isaias* (1932).

[47] J. Schelhaas, *De lijdende Knecht des Heeren* (1933); A. H. Edelkoort, *De Christusverwachting in het Oude Testament* (1941).

[48] C. R. North, *The Suffering Servant in Deutero-Isaiah* (1948).

[49] J. van der Ploeg, *Les Chants du Serviteur de Jahvé* (1936).

preferable interpretation.[50] For him the idea of the Servant developed from the thought of Israel as the Servant of God to the concept of an individual Servant of a supreme spiritual quality without at the same time sacrificing the basic theme of Israel as the Servant. His conclusions, however, were to a large extent those of the traditional messianic interpreters.

Mention should be made of the mythological view of the Servant advocated early in the twentieth century by Gressmann and Gunkel.[51] According to this theory the fourth Servant song was to be understood in terms of the Adonis-Tammuz cult, being based on one of the ritual songs of the dying and rising deity. For Gressmann the Servant was neither the nation of Israel nor any historical individual, while Gunkel showed that the Servant as described in Isaiah far surpassed any of the notable figures in previous Israelite history. However, despite their appeals to the Tammuz liturgies, neither Gressmann nor Gunkel was able to establish a connection between the nature-myths and the Biblical sources.[52] This is scarcely surprising, since the monotheism of Isaiah would never have countenanced such origins or affiliations, nor admitted to any consonance between the atoning death of the Servant and the periodic ritual demise of the Babylonian Tammuz deity, which bore no atoning significance. Although a few scholars subsequently professed to see elements of the Adonis-Tammuz cult in the Servant oracles, the mythological view of the Servant attracted few advocates after the time of Gressmann.[53]

Some justification for the vast and complex literature dealing with the Servant of the Lord is immediately apparent upon even a casual reading of the Servant oracles. In the first of these (Isa. 42:1-4) the Servant was recognized as the one who had been divinely chosen and empowered by the Spirit to bring true religion to the nations of the world, a task in which he would persist until it was accomplished. The second oracle (Isa. 49:1-6) portrayed the Servant as recognizing his divine call from birth and his consequent preparation for his exalted task. He constituted the Israel in whom God would be glorified, and his work was that of illuminating the Gentiles so as to make the divine salvation universal. In the third oracle (Isa. 50:4-9 or 50:1-11) the speaker, who was presumed to be the Servant, described his daily contact with God and proclaimed his confidence in divine vindication, despite the fact that his immediate task presented certain difficulties. The final oracle (Isa. 52:13–53:12)

---

[50] RSL, pp. 23, 54ff.; C. R. North, op. cit., p. 216.

[51] H. Gressmann, Der Ursprung der israelitisch-jüdischen Eschatologie (1905), Der Messias (1929); H. Gunkel, Die Religion in Geschichte und Gegenwart (1912), III, cols. 1540ff.

[52] Cf. W. W. Graf Baudissin, Adonis und Esmun (1911), p. 424.

[53] E.g. F. M. Th. Böhl, De "Knecht des Heeren" in Jezaja 53 (1923), pp. 24ff.; G. H. Dix, JTS, XXVI (1925), pp. 241ff.; S. Mowinckel, ZAW, XLIX (1931), pp. 256f.

488

described the promised exaltation of the Servant, which, however, would be preceded by violence culminating in the death of the Servant and his burial with the wicked.

In such a composite picture it is possible to see individual, collective, actual, and ideal elements at one and the same time, which makes for no small difficulty in interpretation. A fully collective theory of the Servant must face the objection that the character of the Servant depicted in Isaiah is radically different from that of Israel as found elsewhere in the Old Testament. Purely individual interpretations of the Servant, whether as an historical personage such as Jehoiachin, Uzziah, or Cyrus, or as an unknown contemporary of the prophet are also inadequate on the ground that the description of the Servant was most probably not intended as the portrait of any one individual.[54] The Servant was represented as an anonymous yet ideal figure, and was clearly not meant to be identified with the nation of Israel, which was admittedly imperfect (Isa. 53:6). While the theory of a corporate personality, as advanced by Eissfeldt and Wheeler Robinson, attempted to take a comprehensive view of the functions ascribed to the Servant by assuming that the concept could pass readily from nation to individual and *vice versa*, it failed to give adequate precision to the character of the Servant as an emergent and ultimately established individual by being unable to distinguish clearly between Israel and the Servant.[55]

One variation of the traditional messianic interpretation has envisaged the Servant as the future Messiah depicted in the role of the pre-exilic king, who was thought to have suffered certain ritual chastisements as part of an annual enthronement liturgy. In this sense the king was the representative and perhaps even the embodiment of the people over whom he ruled, and through his ritual "sufferings" the people were "redeemed" on an annual basis.[56] Such a theory fails to take account of the fact that the Hebrew kings were never considered to be the embodiment of their subjects, and does not recognize the consistent religious tradition of Israel in the matter of redemption and atonement, whose ritual performances were entirely a matter for the priests, not the king. National forgiveness was amply provided for under the law in the Day of Atonement ceremonies, and nowhere is there any suggestion that this annual "redemption" was connected with the position or function of the ruler. An even more serious objection to such an approach is that at

---

[54] E.g. R. Kittel, *Geschichte des Volkes Israel*, III, pp. 222ff.; W. O. E. Oesterley and T. H. Robinson, *Hebrew Religion: Its Origin and Development*, pp. 303ff.

[55] O. Eissfeldt, *Der Gottesknecht bei Deuterojesaja* (1933); H. Wheeler Robinson, *The Cross of the Servant* (1926).

[56] Cf. H. Zimmern in E. Schrader (ed.), *Die Keilinschriften und das AT* (1903), pp. 384ff.; L. Dürr, *Ursprung und Ausbau der israelitisch-jüdischen Heilandserwartung. Ein Beitrag zur Theologie des AT* (1925), pp. 134ff.

present nothing that can be considered as real evidence has been adduced in support of an annual enthronement festival in Israel.

There appears to be no adequate reason for maintaining that the traditional messianic interpretation is wedded to an excessively mechanical doctrine of inspiration, as North and others have implied.[57] In the first instance the picture of the Servant is sufficiently indistinct to admit of differences between the Servant and Jesus Christ the Messiah. Secondly, the Servant is not the only messianic figure in Isaiah, the problem here being compounded by a wholly arbitrary division of the prophecy into numerous segments of greatly diverse chronology, and for which there is no textual warrant or evidence whatever.

Furthermore, there are no grounds for supposing that the prophet was completely unaware of the significance of the Servant oracles, although it seems equally clear that their deepest implications escaped both the immediate writer and the Israelite nation as a whole. Even when the oracles were illumined by the life and work of Jesus Christ, there were still many who professed an inability to perceive the meaning of these passages in relationship to Christ as Messiah. Whatever may be the nature of the interpretation that is ultimately assigned to these enigmatic sections in Isaiah, the fact remains that the mission of the Servant received its fullest and most distinctive expression in the atonement of Christ on Calvary. Or as North has remarked, "On all hands it is agreed that whoever was the original of the Servant, none except Christ was its fulfilment."[58]

In a study of the way in which messianic prophecy came to its fruition, F. F. Bruce held that the words of Isaiah 55:3 as quoted in Acts 13:34 marked the link between the Davidic line and the person of the Servant.[59] This latter was originally Israel after the flesh, but in becoming an individual realized in his own self the ideal Israel. In the person and work of Jesus Christ the Davidic Messiah and the Servant became one. This view rests to some extent upon the observations of Delitzsch, and has the advantage of preserving the organic continuity between the Old and New Testaments. It also serves to show that, despite differences that inevitably arise over the interpretation of the Servant in the prophecy of Isaiah, the Christian can do no better than follow the example of one of the earliest evangelists of the primitive Church, and in taking the Servant oracles, begin to preach Jesus from them.[60]

Despite the limitations of the foregoing survey of Old Testament theological studies, enough has been said to indicate the interest of

[57] C. R. North, *The Suffering Servant in Deutero-Isaiah*, p. 207.
[58] C. R. North, *IDB*, IV, p. 294.
[59] F. F. Bruce, *The Sure Mercies of David* (1954); cf. H. L. Ellison, *The Servant of Jehovah* (1953).
[60] R. S. Cripps in L. W. Grensted (ed.), *The Atonement in History and in Life* (1929), p. 93; cf. the criticism in E. J. Young, *Studies in Isaiah* (1955), p. 103.

scholars in developing the field as an area of investigation in its own right. The problems presented by such an undertaking are as numerous as they are fascinating, and if the mind of the ancient Hebrew writers is to be interpreted correctly it is of the utmost importance that scholars should approach their task against a background of sound ancient Near Eastern methodology, and not that of occidental speculative philosophy. As H. H. Rowley has remarked, writers who discover in the text what they themselves bring to it, instead of first finding what the text was intended to mean and then perceiving what it has come to mean, are a peril to themselves and to their readers alike.[61] A properly accredited theology of the Old Testament must be based firmly upon the revealed Word of God, and not merely constitute some kind of commentary upon the faith or knowledge of a particular author. When scholars are prepared to submit to the authority of the Old Testament Scriptures and study them on their own terms, the spiritual message of these ancient writings will emerge in all its clarity and grandeur to furnish an all-important corrective for the distorted outlook of mortal man.

[61] *RSL*, p. ix.

Part Eight

THE PENTATEUCH

I. THE STUDY OF THE PENTATEUCH

The first major division of the Hebrew canon consisted of the five books with which the English Bible commences. It had long been associated in the ancient Jewish mind with the legislative activities of Moses, and in post-exilic times the corpus was known as the "Torah" or Law. This proper noun was derived from the Hebrew root ירה, one of whose meanings is "to teach." The Torah was a manual of direction or guidance, and this usage was in full accord with the emphasis that tradition had placed upon the legal element dominant in this body of writings. It did not minimize the importance of the historical or narrative sections of the Torah, however, for it was recognized that such material constituted the essential temporal setting for the legislation itself.

The fundamentally legal character of the Torah can be appreciated from the many references in the Bible to the "law of God" (Neh. 10:28f.), the "book of Moses" (Ez. 6:18; Neh. 13:1; Mk. 12:26), the "Law" (Josh. 8:34; Ez. 10:3; 2 Chron. 14:4; Lk. 10:26), the "book of the law of Moses" (Josh. 8:31; 23:6; 2 Kgs. 14:6; Neh. 8:1),[1] and other analogous expressions. The Torah was first described as "Pentateuch" in the commentary by Origen on the Fourth Gospel,[2] although it is possible that this designation, from the Greek words πέντε ("five") and τεῦχος ("scroll"),[3] may have been employed by the Hellenistic Jews of Alexandria as early as the first Christian century to correspond to the Talmudic description of the Torah as חמשה חומשי תורה ("the five fifths of the Law"; cf. *Sanhed.* 28a). In Latin Tertullian employed "Pentateuch" as a proper name in his disputes with the Marcionites.[4]

The Hebrew title of each of the five books is simply the initial word of that work; the English title is derived from the Greek (by way of the Latin), and indicates the initial subject of each book. Apart from Numbers, the Greek titles were used by Philo, who attests to the division of the Pentateuch into five sections, as does Josephus. Such a partitioning was familiar to those who made the LXX translation of the Torah about 250 B.C., and this in itself reflects a tradition of considerable antiquity.

---

[1] Cf. *YIOT*, p. 39.

[2] *PG*, XIV, col. 444.

[3] Τεῦχος originally meant "implement," but was subsequently used of a case for carrying papyrus rolls, and later for the roll itself.

[4] *PL*, II, col. 282.

The division of the Torah into five parts was doubtless prompted as much by the nature of the subject matter as by the fact that the leather scrolls that were available in earlier times would each probably only accommodate about one-fifth of the whole Pentateuch.

As Pfeiffer has pointed out, it should be noted that the Pentateuch is a single work in five volumes, not a collection of five different books.[5] There is a further sense in which it can be regarded as the first stage of a nine-volume work, that is to say, Genesis to Kings, that described Hebrew history and religious institutions from the creation to the events immediately consequent upon the fall of Jerusalem in 587 B.C. Thus, as Weiser has shown, after placing the creation of the earth in a universal setting, the Pentateuch describes the manner in which Israel came into existence as a people, and presents the fundamental traditions of the Hebrews up to a point prior to their entrance into the Promised Land.[6] According to this pattern the individual books can be summarized roughly as follows:

I. Primeval History with a Mesopotamian Background, Gen. 1—11
II. History of the Patriarchs, Gen. 12—50
III. The Oppression of Israel and Preparations for the Exodus, Exod. 1—9
IV. The Exodus, Passover, and the Arrival at Sinai, Exod. 10—19
V. The Decalogue and the Covenant at Sinai, Exod. 20—24
VI. Legislation Relating to the Tabernacle and Aaronic Priesthood, Exod. 25—31
VII. The Idolatrous Violation of the Covenant, Exod. 32—34
VIII. The Implementation of Regulations Concerning the Tabernacle, Exod. 35—40
IX. The Law of Offerings, Lev. 1—7
X. The Consecration of the Priests and Initial Offerings, Lev. 8—10
XI. The Laws of Cleanliness, Lev. 11—15
XII. The Day of Atonement, Lev. 16
XIII. Laws Concerning Morality and Cleanliness, Lev. 17—26
XIV. Vows and Tithes, Lev. 27
XV. Numberings and Laws, Num. 1—9
XVI. The Journey from Sinai to Kadesh, Num. 10—20
XVII. Wanderings to Moab, Num. 21—36
XVIII. Historical Retrospect to the Wilderness Period, Deut. 1—4
XIX. Second Speech, with an Hortatory Introduction, Deut. 5—11
XX. Collected Statutes and Rights, Deut. 12—26
XXI. Cursing and Blessing, Deut. 27—30
XXII. The Accession of Joshua and Death of Moses, Deut. 31—34

[5] *PIOT*, p. 129.
[6] *OTFD*, pp. 70f.; cf. *PIOT*, pp. 130ff.

Aside from the books of Genesis and Deuteronomy, which present certain special problems, the division of the Hebrew text into the present five books hardly accords with the structure of the material itself. Were the latter to be divided at Exodus 19 and Numbers 10 respectively, the contents would fall into three convenient categories consisting of the history of Israel up to the Sinai period, the revelation at Sinai itself, and the departure from the peninsula towards the plains of Moab.

A. Antecedents of the Developmental Hypothesis

There is no reason to doubt that by the time of Ezra the Pentateuch was considered to be the authoritative revelation of God to Moses, and the norm for faith and morals. Since that time it has been traditional for Judaism, Islam, and Christianity to accept Moses not merely as the mediator of the divinely revealed laws (Exod. 18:13ff.; 31:18; 34:28, *et al.*), but also as the author of the entire Pentateuch. Such ancient writers as the compiler of Ecclesiasticus (24:23), Philo, Josephus, and the Mishnaic and Talmudic authorities accepted without question the Mosaic authorship of the Torah.[7] The only question that arose was in connection with the passage relating to the death of Moses (Deut. 34:5f.), and in this connection Philo and Josephus affirmed that Moses described his own death, whereas the Talmud credited Joshua with having composed eight verses of the Torah, presumably the closing section of Deuteronomy.

So rigid did tradition become concerning Mosaic authorship of the Pentateuch that to deny it was, for some Jews at least, tantamount to excluding oneself from Paradise.[8] This attitude was attacked in the early Christian era by sectarians of different religious standpoints.[9] Second Esdras 14:1-48 describes a story telling how the lost Torah, along with other books, were dictated by Ezra under divine inspiration to five secretaries during a forty-day period.[10] Views of this kind influenced some orthodox Christian theologians to the point that Jerome, for example, seems to have vacillated between Moses and Ezra as the author of the Pentateuch.[11] The Nazarenes denied the Mosaicity of the work, as did Celsus and Ptolemy, who also questioned its literary unity, while the *Clementine Homilies* held to the radical view that the Pentateuch consisted of a corrupt and deviate transcript of the oral pronouncements of Moses.

The existence in the text of certain scribal glosses indicating an interval of time between the period of the writer and that of Moses (e.g.

---

[7] Philo, *Vita Mosis*, III, 39; Josephus, *AJ*, IV, 8, 48; Mishnah, *Pirqe Ab.* I, 1; Talmud, *Bab. Bath.* 14b.

[8] Cf. A. Westphal, *Les sources du Pentateuque* (1888), I, p. 25.

[9] Cf. H. Holzinger, *Einleitung in den Hexateuch* (1893), pp. 11f., 25ff.

[10] Cf. *APOT*, II, pp. 542ff., 620ff.

[11] Cf. *PL*, XXIII, col. 227; XXV, col. 17.

Gen. 12:6; 13:7; 32:33; Deut. 3:14; 34:6 *et al.*) led certain medieval Jewish scholars to question the Mosaic authorship of the Pentateuch as a whole. On such a basis Ibn Ezra (1088-1167) recorded that a certain Rabbi Isaac (perhaps Isaac of Toledo, 982-1057) had dated Genesis 36:31 in the reign of Jehoshaphat, a view that he himself denounced. The medieval Roman Catholic commentator A. Du Maes, in a work entitled *Josuae Imperatoris Historia,* published in 1574, maintained that the Pentateuch had been compiled by Ezra the scribe from ancient written sources, basing his views mostly upon the incidence of later scribal names for such ancient sites as Laish and Kiriath-arba (Gen. 14:14; Deut. 34:1; Gen. 13:18; 23:2, *et al.*).

The possibility that subsequent scribal additions had been made to the Mosaic Pentateuch was recognized by the Spanish Jesuit commentator B. Pereira in his work on Genesis (1594-1600); and similar views were held by J. Bonfrère a quarter of a century later. The philosopher Thomas Hobbes in his *Leviathan* (1651) adopted the position of Du Maes, although he credited Moses with all that the Pentateuch claimed for him. The apparent discrepancies and anachronisms that had perplexed certain medieval Jewish exegetes also troubled the philosopher Benedictus de Spinoza, who in his *Tractatus Theologico-Politicus* (1670) concluded that Ezra had compiled the history of his nation, utilizing a mass of ancient written material including some by Moses, and that he himself had interpolated Deuteronomy, which according to Spinoza comprised the legal code promulgated by Ezra.

The speculations of Spinoza may be said in some senses to have ushered in the period of critical study of the Pentateuch, which commenced in earnest with the divisive theories of authorship proposed by the Roman Catholic author Richard Simon in 1678 and the Arminian Jean Le Clerc in 1685, an era when much of Old Testament scholarship was confined to critical study of the Pentateuch. A comprehensive survey of the various trends of thought in this area has been provided in part one of the present work; hence, it will be sufficient at this point to recapitulate the development of literary criticism in brief outline.

The first attempt at a documentary theory of Pentateuchal origins came in 1753, when the French physician Jean Astruc published his speculations anonymously in a work that maintained that Moses had compiled Genesis from two principal ancient *"mémoires"* and a number of shorter documents.[12] He identified the two main sources from the non-interchangeable use of the divine names יהוה (Jehovah), and אלהים (deity); and, according to the developed form of his theory, the sections that employed the latter belonged to an A source and those in which the

---

[12] *Conjectures sur les mémoires originaux dont il parait que Moyse s'est servi pour composer le Livre de la Genèse. Avec des Remarques, qui appuient ou qui éclaircissent ces Conjectures.*

former occurred came from a B source. This formulation was sufficient, in Astruc's view, to account for the repetitions and alleged discrepancies that some earlier critics had observed, but it is important to note that Astruc did not deny the Mosaic authorship of Genesis, and actually went to some lengths to defend it. He also recognized something that the majority of his critical successors failed to acknowledge, namely, that the divine names could not be utilized successfully as criteria for the purpose of analyzing the entire Torah.

Astruc's work with the A and B sources convinced him that the divine names were inadequate for dividing Genesis into supposed "*mémoires,*" and he was not slow to point out that certain passages, such as Genesis 14, did not fit in any sense into a documentary analysis. In order to complete his work he found it necessary to invoke the presence of remnants of ten sources of Midianite or Arabian origin in addition to his A and B material, and when even these insertions proved to be insufficient to meet his critical needs he was compelled to discover the existence of certain textual "interpolations."[13]

The abiding merit of this approach is that in asserting that Moses may have utilized written memoirs for the purpose of compiling Genesis, Astruc doubtless correctly assessed the facts of the case. His fundamental error lay in his subjective estimate of the nature and extent of the underlying source material and his ignorance of the principles by which documents and books were compiled in the ancient Near East. He may well have been aware of the latter to some extent, however, for he was careful to insist that his basic criteria, the divine names, were unsuitable for purposes of analyzing the book of Genesis into documents.

One would think that the difficulties of Astruc's approach to the problems associated with the compilation of Genesis would have made it sufficiently clear to any possible successors in the field that critical reconsideration of Astruc's methods was needed. But this was not the case, and nothing daunted, a German scholar named J. G. Eichhorn published a three-volume *Einleitung* (1780-83), in which he expanded the views of Astruc into an early form of the classic documentary theory. Although he claimed independence of Astruc, Eichhorn's fundamental approach was essentially the same as that which had been adopted by the French physician. He finally abandoned his earlier views as to the Mosaic authorship of the Pentateuch, divided Genesis and Exodus 1-2 into sources designated J(ehovistic) and E(lohistic), and held that they had been edited by an unknown redactor.

Following the trend made popular by Eichhorn, the Scottish Roman Catholic priest Geddes investigated the "*mémoires*" identified by Astruc and between 1792 and 1800 developed the fragmentary hypoth-

[13] Cf. H. Osgood, *The Presbyterian and Reformed Review*, III (1892), pp. 83ff.; A. Lods, *Jean Astruc et la critique biblique au XVIIIe siècle* (1924).

esis of Pentateuchal origins. The theory maintained that the Torah had been compiled by an unknown redactor from numerous fragments that had originated in different circles, one Elohistic and the other Jehovistic, and that it had probably attained its final form in Jerusalem during the reign of Solomon. In this hypothesis Geddes was followed by J. S. Vater, who endeavored to trace the growth of the Pentateuch from over thirty fragments, and to a lesser extent by W. M. L. De Wette, who maintained that much of the legal material was comparatively late in nature, not earlier than the time of David.[14] De Wette also followed Jerome in identifying Deuteronomy with the legal code recovered from the Temple during the reign of King Josiah.

The emphasis by De Wette upon one basic document supplemented by numerous fragments was developed in 1831 by H. Ewald, who, in a review of J. J. Stähelin's *Kritische Untersuchungen über die Genesis* (1830), maintained that the chief Pentateuchal document was the Elohistic source, which carried the narrative from the creation up to the beginning of the settlement under Joshua, and that this was supplemented by the Jehovistic narrative, whose compiler was also the final redactor of the material as a whole. At a later period Ewald abandoned this "supplementary theory," and asserted that the Pentateuch contained fragments that did not go back either to J, E, or Deuteronomy.

B. THE MODERN THEORY OF PENTATEUCHAL ORIGINS

The modern form of the theory of Pentateuchal origins in terms of underlying documentary sources came with the work of Hupfeld, who sought to remedy the difficulties of the "supplementary hypothesis" by introducing even more supplements. In his *Die Quellen der Genesis und die Art ihrer Zusammensetzung von neuen untersucht* (1853), he maintained that the J passages constituted a continuous document rather than supplements to an earlier E source and that the Elohistic material was itself composite and consisted of the original Elohist (E^1) and the later Elohist (E^2). The three documents were assembled in their present form, according to Hupfeld, by a redactor whose individualistic approach to his task itself occasioned many of the "difficulties" in the Pentateuch. A year later, when E. Riehm published his *Die Gesetzgebung Mosis im Lande Moab* (1854), a work that sought to demonstrate the independent character of Deuteronomy, the four principal documents of the liberal school had been isolated and dated in the order E^1, E^2, J, and D.

The developmental hypothesis took a step forward with the work of K. H. Graf, who adopted the suggestion of E. G. Reuss, J. F. L. George, and W. Vatke that the Levitical legislation was later than the date as-

---

[14] J. S. Vater, *Commentar über den Pentateuch* (1802-1805). W. M. L. De Wette, *Beiträge zur Einleitung in das AT* (1807).

signed to Deuteronomy, and that it could not have arisen any earlier than the exilic period. Consequently he affirmed that the source designated E^1 and known as P(riestly Code) by modern liberal scholars, was the latest rather than the earliest of the documents that underlay the Pentateuch. This conclusion involved a change in the earlier order E^1 E^2 J D, and set the stage for a debate as to whether the correct chronological sequence was EJDP (E^2JDE^1) or JEDP. When Abraham Kuenen, who had (in part at least) worked independently of Graf, published his *De Godsdienst van Israel* (1869-70), he assured the success of the Graf JEDP sequence, which also found support in the work entitled *Das Vorexilische Buch der Urgeschichte Israels*, published in 1874 by August Kayser.

It was left to Julius Wellhausen in his *Die Composition des Hexateuchs* (1876-77) to bring this hypothesis to its highest point of development. In this work and subsequent publications he held that the earliest parts of the Pentateuch came from two originally independent documents, the Jehovist and the Elohist. The former was dated about 850 B.C. and came from religious circles in the southern kingdom; the latter supposedly emanated from the northern kingdom about 750 B.C. The two were combined by an unknown redactor or editor (R^{JE}) about 650 B.C. Wellhausen regarded Deuteronomy as a product of the period of Josiah, about 621 B.C., and maintained that it was added to the existing corpus by yet another editor (R^D) about 550 B.C., to make a group of Pentateuchal material equivalent to JED. The Priestly Code, which was supposed by the literary theorists to have been compiled between 500 and 450 B.C. by priestly authors, was then presumably added by another anonymous redactor (R^P) to the already existing material to produce JEDP by about 400 B.C.; and the Pentateuch in its extant form emerged about 200 B.C.

Most of the larger critical introductions to the Old Testament will furnish the student with an overwhelming mass of data relating to the contents of these supposed documents. While it is not the intention of the present author to reproduce this kind of material, it may well be useful at this juncture to present a brief outline of what these alleged sources have generally been held to contain.

The Jehovistic narrative (J), postulated as dating from the ninth century B.C., is thought to have had its rise in Judah, partly because of references to territorial expansion in Genesis (Gen. 15:18; 27:40) and partly because of the general ascendancy of Judah as depicted in the source material isolated (cf. Gen. 49:8ff.). In this alleged document can be found narratives dealing with events which occurred between the time of the creation and the entry of Israel into Canaan. The literary style is deemed to constitute an outstanding example of epic composition, worthy of the tradition of Homer. Like that of other proposed Pentateuchal source documents, the extent of J has always been a matter of some dispute, and this factor has precluded a firm determination of its date. The J source is held by its proponents to be intensely nationalistic in outlook, and shows particular interest in recording the activities of the Hebrew patriarchs. From a theological standpoint it is alleged to be notable for its anthropomorphic representation of the deity, who frequently assumed quasi-human form and communed with men.

The Elohistic source (E) is generally dated a century later than J by advocates of the Graf-Wellhausen theory, and its Ephraimite origin has been postulated on the basis of the omission of the stories of Abraham and Lot, which had to do with Hebron and the cities of the valley, and also because of the special emphasis thought to be given to Bethel and Shechem (Gen. 28:17, 31:13, 33:19f.). A further reason for postulating a northern origin for this material lies in the prominence given to the activities of Joseph, the ancestor of the northern tribes of Ephraim and Manasseh. This alleged document is supposed to contain less continuous narrative than J, and in any event it is thought to be more fragmentary. Theologically it is held to be of interest on account of its religious and moralistic emphases, an outstanding example of this being the command to sacrifice Isaac (Gen. 22:1ff.) as a means of teaching the patriarch Abraham that true sacrificial offering is an inward, motivated affair, and not a matter of external ritual.

The alleged Deuteronomic document (D) corresponds in large measure to the canonical book of Deuteronomy. Fundamental to the approach of the Graf-Wellhausen school was the view that the law-book discovered in the time of Josiah (2 Kgs. 22:3ff.) comprised at least part, if not actually the whole, of Deuteronomy. Attention was drawn to the correspondence between D and the trend of the religious reformation promulgated under Josiah, particularly with regard to the centralization (2 Kgs. 23:4ff.; Deut. 12:1ff.) and purification (2 Kgs. 23:4ff.; Deut. 16:21f.; 17:3; 18:10f.) of the cultus. D embodied a religious philosophy of history that formulated the terms of divine blessing and judgment and demonstrated the necessity for a pronounced sense of social justice under the provisions of the Covenant relationship. For the critical school, D comprised a collection of exhortations and legal enactments compiled during the apostasies of Manasseh and combined editorially with J and E after the time of Josiah.

The Priestly Code (P) was regarded as a compilation of legal and ceremonial material derived from various periods of Israelite history, and codified in such a manner as to organize the legal structure of the post-exilic Jewish theocracy. While P was held to contain certain narrative sections, it was thought to be more concerned with the mechanics of genealogies and the origins of ritualistic or legalistic practices and concepts than with the direct recording of events. The highly detailed nature of much of its contents, as with the description of the Tabernacle (Exod. 25:1-27:21), along with the complex ritual and legal material which it preserved, has been taken as an indication of the fact that the source had its origins in the post-exilic period. The theological outlook of the P document envisaged God as utilizing the legislation for a means of grace, in that the concepts of holiness and ceremonial purity would serve as a vehicle for conveying divine blessing to Israel.

The evolutionary approach of the Graf-Wellhausen school proved extremely attractive to the naturalistic tendencies of the contemporary theological mind. Largely through the writings of W. Robertson Smith and S. R. Driver, the Graf-Wellhausen scheme of documentary analysis gained widespread acceptance in the English-speaking world. For many years it was venerated as axiomatic for scholarly faith and practice in the Old Testament field, and any individual who was sufficiently imprudent either to criticize it or attempt to reject it ran the risk of being scorned by his fellows and consigned to academic oblivion. It is only within recent times that archaeological and other discoveries have forced upon scholars the necessity for adopting a much more critical approach to the general Wellhausenian position, and have made radical assessments of it an increasingly frequent outcome.

Documentary analysis of the materials in the earlier portions of the Hebrew canon of Scripture did not stop with the work of Wellhausen, however. Following a suggestion made in 1883 by Karl Budde, an attempt was made by Rudolf Smend to formulate a different kind of documentary hypothesis.[15] He maintained the existence of two Jehovists, J^1 and J^2, regarding them as two parallel authors whose literary activity was in evidence throughout the Hexateuch. While he believed that D and P were marked by numerous additions or supplements, he insisted upon the unity of the Elohistic source. The material that Smend had described as J^1 was identified by Otto Eissfeldt as a "Lay Source" (L) or *Laienquelle*, because it stood in marked contrast to the Priestly document and emphasized the nomadic ideal in opposition to the Canaanite way of life.[16]

Morgenstern purported to discover a Kenite document (K), which supposedly dealt with certain biographical details in the life of Moses and described the relations between Israel and the Kenites.[17] Following the same general trend, R. H. Pfeiffer thought that he detected the existence of a non-Israelite source in Genesis, which he designated S (South or Seir).[18] He maintained that it differed materially from the "Lay Source" identified by Eissfeldt, and also from J^1, being restricted to Genesis and being characterized by its own special concerns. The division of the Priestly material by von Rad into two principal segments, P^A

---

[15] *Die Erzählung des Hexateuchs auf ihre Quellen untersucht* (1912).
[16] O. Eissfeldt, *Hexateuch-Synopse* (1922), p. 5 *passim; ETOT*, pp. 191ff.
[17] J. Morgenstern, *HUCA*, IV (1926-27), pp. 1ff.
[18] *PIOT*, pp. 141, 159ff.; *ZAW*, XLVIII (1930), pp. 66ff.

and P^B,[19] was an offshoot of the atomizing tendencies that were given expression in the writings of B. Baentsch, who in his commentary on Leviticus in the Nowack *Handkommentar* series (1903) professed to find no fewer than seven main sources of P, and the activity of at least two redactors.

Although the minute dissections of the literary-analytical school had fallen into disfavor to a large extent by the 1920's, C. A. Simpson flouted current trends in England by continuing to pursue conjectural documentary sources through the Hexateuch with all the fervor of a bygone era of stylistic analysis.[20] In defiance of the fundamental criticisms levelled against his methods by Rowley[21] and others, Simpson published his *Composition of the Book of Judges* (1957), in which he continued to employ his subjective techniques.

But perhaps the credulity of the faithful was most heavily taxed in 1958 by the continued insistence of Eissfeldt upon the presence of the L document in Genesis.[22] For him, even the most complete documentary hypothesis should leave room for isolated fragments, and on this basis it was clearly his duty to gather up these solitary elements and combine them, willy-nilly, into another document related to the J source. It apparently did not occur to Eissfeldt that the very fact of their isolation— assuming for the moment that these fragments are as genuine as the literary analysts would have their readers believe—militated against their ever having either constituted a documentary unity or having manifested such a character. In order to suit the purposes of a doctrinaire analysis, these fragments were dragooned with characteristic Teutonic precision into yet another "document," and presented for the approval of Old Testament scholarship as a whole. The comparative lack of enthusiasm with which this latest source has been received is a sufficient judgment upon its validity.

Part one of the present work has described the manner in which conservative scholars attacked the various divisive hypotheses of Pentateuchal origins. In 1847, F. W. Hengstenberg published an English version of his masterly work on the Pentateuch under the title *Dissertations on the Genuineness of the Pentateuch,* and he was followed in some of his conclusions by Drechsler.[23] H. Ch. Havernick, C. F. Keil, H. M. Wiener, E. Naville, W. Möller, J. Orr, and many others championed the Mosaic authorship of the Pentateuch in one way or another, while

---

[19] G. von Rad, *Die Priesterschrift im Hexateuch* (1934).

[20] C. A. Simpson, *The Early Traditions of Israel: A Critical Analysis of the Pre-Deuteronomic Narrative of the Hexateuch* (1948).

[21] H. H. Rowley, *The Society for Old Testament Study Book List* (1949), p. 34.

[22] O. Eissfeldt, *Die Genesis der Genesis. Vom Werdegang des ersten Buches der Bibel* (1958), an expanded form of his article on Genesis in *IDB*, II, pp. 366ff.; *ETOT*, pp. 191ff.

[23] M. Drechsler, *Die Einheit und Echtheit der Genesis* (1838).

among liberal scholars, some of the conclusions of the analytical school, particularly with respect to the dating of the Priestly Code, were hotly contested by A. Dillmann, H. L. Strack, W. W. Graf Baudissin, and E. König, as well as in the earlier writings of R. Kittel.

More recently the methodology of the nineteenth-century liberal Protestants of Germany has come under attack by R. D. Wilson, O. T. Allis, G. Ch. Aalders, E. J. Young, G. T. Manley, C. H. Gordon, and numerous others.[24] In a rather different way the classic documentary theory of Pentateuchal composition has been the object of sustained criticism by a group of Scandinavian scholars including Pedersen, Engnell, Haldar, Nyberg, Bentzen, and others. By drawing heavily upon comparative studies they have managed to make considerably more room than was the case previously for a recognition of the fact of oral transmission alongside that of documentary sources, and in general they have stressed the great reliability of material passed along by word of mouth.

The "traditio-historical" approach of the Swedish school has proved unacceptable to many liberal writers because in their view it over-emphasizes the role of oral tradition and places too little stress upon literary analysis.[25] Accordingly, scholars such as Widengren[26] and Mowinckel[27] have sought in their teachings to modify the importance that Nyberg, Birkeland, and others had attributed to the place of oral tradition, an undertaking in which they were only partially successful. Important criticisms of the Wellhausenian methodology were also made by Hermann Gunkel and Hugo Gressmann, who were primarily responsible for the development in the field of literary criticism of the form-critical method or *Gattungsforschung*. Their objections to the positions adopted by the Wellhausen school included accusations of lack of vision and disregard of the archaeological and psychological discoveries that alone augured for historical reality.[28]

C. GENERAL PRESUPPOSITIONS OF THE GRAF-WELLHAUSEN HYPOTHESIS

Because the Graf-Wellhausen theory of Pentateuchal origins has exerted a profound influence for a prolonged period over the minds of Old Testament scholars, however, a fairly close look should be taken at its fundamental postulates and energizing factors. At the outset it must be recognized that far more was involved in the Wellhausenian presentation

---

[24] R. D. Wilson, *A Scientific Investigation of the OT* (1926), reprinted, with annotations by E. J. Young (1959); O. T. Allis, *The Five Books of Moses* (1943); G. Ch. Aalders, *A Short Introduction to the Pentateuch* (1949); E. J. Young, *Introduction to the Old Testament* (1949, rev. 1958, 1960); G. T. Manley, *The Book of the Law* (1957); C. H. Gordon, *Christianity Today*, IV, No. 4 (1959), pp. 131ff.

[25] Cf. G. W. Anderson, *Harvard Theological Review*, XLIII (1950), pp. 239ff.

[26] *Literary and Psychological Aspects of the Hebrew Prophets* (1948).

[27] *Prophecy and Tradition* (1946).

[28] Cf. J. Coppens, *The OT and the Critics* (1942), p. 71.

than mere considerations of documentary analysis. The Graf-Wellhausen school based its critical studies upon a philosophical evolutionary theory that had a great deal in common with the speculations of Hegel. Against such an evolutionary *Zeitgeist* the advocates of critical theories of Pentateuchal analysis developed a monolinear view of Hebrew history that followed a pattern similar to that formulated by Darwin with respect to biology. Commencing with humble beginnings in animism and primitive culture, Hebrew history as they saw it progressed little by little to its climax in the post-exilic period. The religion of Israel was thought to have advanced in a similar fashion from the simple sacrifices on family altars in the settlement period to the vastly more complex liturgical celebrations of the Priestly Code, the latter being assigned by the members of the Graf-Wellhausen school generally to some point in the later post-exilic era.

Behind this disarmingly simple view of progress was a powerful emotional force grounded upon two suppositions. The first comprised that peculiar facet of the western outlook that assumes that it is both possible and desirable to resolve the complexities of a given situation by reducing the "many to the one," as Socrates endeavored to do with the Greek gods of his own day. As a result one should attempt to posit a single interpretative principle for some branch of study or for the whole of phenomena represented by contingent existence. The second premise was that, as a consequence of the material and intellectual advances of the late eighteenth and early nineteenth centuries, it was possible to conceive of humanity as progressing steadily and relentlessly towards advanced goals of social, cultural, and ultimately spiritual development.

In the light of subsequent events, both presuppositions have been proved to be completely erroneous. The "glimpses of ultimate reality" that fall within the purview of any given individual are invariably fragmentary, occasional, and of extremely short duration. Neither in biology nor in any other field, whether within the descriptive sciences or out of them, is it even remotely possible to fasten upon a single potentially interpretative concept and make it the definite standard by which everything else is to be judged. Those who have followed Darwin in the biological field in endeavoring to make "evolution" such an interpretative principle for organic life have received unexpected setbacks as the general area of scientific knowledge has widened. Thus it is now recognized from geological studies that progress occurs by spasms or leaps, and not by the slow, scarcely perceptible procedures of improvement or differentiation postulated by Darwin and his followers. As regards the optimistic views current at the end of the nineteenth century concerning the inevitable material, intellectual, and moral progress of the species *homo sapiens,* numerous sociological, theological, and other studies have made it abundantly apparent that technological development and social uplifting have not been accompanied by a corresponding degree of maturity in the human spirit, and that ultimately the outlook for the human race is best expressed in negative and deteriorative, rather than in positive and progressive terms.

All of this, of course, was not apparent to the nineteenth-century pundits of evolutionary philosophy. So absolutely assured were they of their opinions that even their methodology was subordinated to doctrinaire considerations, a procedure that has proved in other circumstances to be as disastrous in its results as it is ill-advised in theory. As far as the Graf-Wellhausen school of literary criticism was concerned, the methods it adopted were for the most part in complete accord with the spirit of the age. What they did not perceive, unfortunately, was that their procedures were founded less upon scientific discipline than upon the emotional upsurge of contemporary rationalism.

In particular, the methodology of the European critical scholars exhibited many of the flaws and weaknesses of the German national character, tendencies that are seen most clearly in the approach of Wellhausen himself. This gifted scholar was clearly obsessed by a resolute desire to prove his thesis—once he found a clue in the work of previous thinkers—by every possible means, including the maximum exercise of native ingenuity and imagination, and the assembling and forcing into service of anything that might pass for evidence or function as some kind of proof of his contentions. If Wellhausen was at all aware of the dangers inherent in this kind of methodology he certainly made no attempt to rectify them, and he may even have consoled himself with the *ad verecundiam* argument that other great minds had utilized exactly the same approach.

In company with others, Wellhausen exhibited that remarkable characteristic of the German mind which consists in the ability to arrive at definitive conclusions on the basis of only part of the total evidence, accompanied by a distinct reluctance to introduce anything more than the slightest theoretical modifications even when much more complete evidence—the nature of which requires substantial changes in the theory as a whole—is available. More remarkable still is the ability of the German mind to utilize the resultant hypothesis and its earlier supporting evidence as a means of refuting—to its own satisfaction at least—both the later evidence and the modifications of the original formulation that it demands. Thus the theoretical position that has been adopted initially becomes virtually sacrosanct, however flimsy its foundations may subsequently be discovered to be. After all this it is a matter of personal honor to engage in its defense and to esteem it as the only possible and legitimate explanation of the phenomena under consideration.

To this gross error of dogmatic statement of conclusions on an extremely inadequate basis of factual evidence, Wellhausen and his followers added the contemporary rationalistic prejudices against the supernatural. Historically, as has been observed previously, the Graf-Wellhausen school adopted a rather skeptical and positivistic approach consistent with the spirit of Hegelian philosophy. On the basis of such an *a priori* evolutionism all facts were made to conform to the theory of literary analysis, in an exaggerated emphasis upon the concept of unilinear development.[29] All social, religious, and institutional phenomena were made to fit into a given mold, and this frequently involved an unabashed emendation or excision of portions of the Hebrew text when particular passages proved hostile to the general theory, or a thoroughgoing reconstruction of historical processes, based upon nothing more substantial than the most subjective of considerations.

Like so many other positivists, Wellhausen and his followers assumed that analogies between mechanistic materialism and aspects of the descriptive sciences were in fact the same thing as scientific method. This tendency, along with a remarkable facility for committing the gross logical fallacy of begging the question, made for further grave weaknesses in the methodological system of the Graf-Wellhausen school. In fairness to the historical development of this situation, however, it should be observed that within recent years most liberal writers have spared their readers the embarrassment attached to the claim that their literary-critical method is scientific. Whether this has resulted from a genuine insight into the theoretical position adopted, or merely from the assured belief that there can no longer be any serious question as to the scientific nature of their procedures, is difficult to ascertain. What can be remarked, however, is that in properly accredited scientific research the investigator is first confronted by a mass of facts that he is required to study carefully and subsequently to classify and categorize in accordance with the best traditions of his discipline. This process in itself involves many revisions, particularly as new knowledge becomes available while the work is proceeding.

By adopting canons of inductive reasoning, which involves arguing from what is known to what is unknown, the research worker gradually builds up in his mind some kind of theoretical explanation of the known facts. The hypothesis thus resulting may well be highly tentative and imperfect at the best, and should it happen that it requires substantial modification somewhat later as the result of the impact of what T. H. Huxley once called "one ugly little fact," the truly scientific investigator will make whatever changes are demanded by the situation, even if he is compelled to begin his research *de novo* to all intents and purposes. To commence the task of investigation with an *a priori* theoretical position; to organize the available material into conformity with this approach; and to manipulate or transform any obdurate facts to the point where, at worst, they will not entirely overthrow the basic postulates, is the very

---

[29] Cf. *FSAC*, p. 84; Albright, *History, Archaeology and Christian Humanism* (1964), pp. 136f.

antithesis of scientific method. Thus for the Wellhausenian and other analogous schools of literary criticism that depend upon the *a priori* deductive approach to pretend to those who are not nourished upon the humanities that their methodology is scientific is to invite nothing less than derision and ridicule for their pains. Equally serious was the manner in which the school of Wellhausen could accept previously expressed opinions in a completely uncritical fashion. Thus Wellhausen was able to write: "I learned through Ritschl that Karl Heinrich Graf placed the law later than the prophets; and, almost without knowing his reasons for the hypothesis, I was prepared to accept it."[30]

The ability that German scholars generally exhibited in rationalizing their way out of awkward situations was only matched by their utter self-confidence and peremptoriness. Despite the significantly wide divergence of opinion in critical circles, Wellhausen could write in the most categorical manner about anything upon which he chose to make a pronouncement. With supreme arrogance the critical savants designated their findings as constituting "the most assured results of Biblical scholarship," as "showing incontrovertibly" or as "demonstrating conclusively." The fact that such findings were based upon the flimsiest of what could be styled as evidence did not disturb the confident investigators for one moment.

Whatever else may be adduced in criticism of Wellhausen and his school, it is quite evident that his theory of Pentateuchal origins would have been vastly different (if, indeed, it had been formulated at all) had Wellhausen chosen to take account of the archaeological material available for study in his day, and had he subordinated his philosophical and theoretical considerations to a sober and rational assessment of the factual evidence as a whole. While he and his followers drew to some extent upon the philological discoveries of the day and manifested a degree of interest in the origins of late Arabic culture in relation to Semitic precursors, they depended almost exclusively upon their own view of the culture and religious history of the Hebrews for purposes of Biblical interpretation.

Wellhausen took almost no note whatever of progress in the field of oriental scholarship, and once having arrived at his conclusions, he never troubled to revise his opinion in the light of subsequent research in the general field. He ignored completely such vastly important discoveries as the Tell el-Amarna tablets, even though Hugo Winckler had made the texts readily available in a critical edition. Even as late as 1893 the faithful followers of Wellhausen were still propounding his dictum that, since writing was only utilized about the time of David, Moses could not possibly have written the Pentateuch even if he had wanted to.[31]

---

[30] *Prolegomena to the History of Israel* (1885), p. 3.
[31] So H. Schultz, *OT Theology* (1893), I, p. 25.

That this bizarre postulate could even have been suggested seriously, let alone accorded axiomatic status by Wellhausen and his disciples, can only be accounted for by assuming an irresponsible and wanton neglect of a body of archaeological evidence that was already enormous while Wellhausen was formulating his critical theories. The process of agglomeration began with the copying in 1765 of some trilingual inscriptions from Persepolis by the Danish scholar Carsten Niebuhr,[32] and continued with the labors of H. C. Rawlinson from 1835 on. The decipherment of Akkadian resulted from the activities of French scholars under Botta at Khorsabad from 1842 and at Nineveh and Nimrud under Layard from 1845 on. Sumerian inscriptions on bricks and tablets from sites such as Nippur, Erech, and Larsa were described by Rawlinson from 1855 on, and the language was deciphered as the result of pioneer studies by Hincks and Oppert.

This linguistic material was supplemented by such actual sources as the Rosetta Stone, discovered in 1789, the Behistun Inscription, transcribed in 1835 by Rawlinson, the Kuyunjik tablets unearthed at Nineveh from 1845 on, the Black Obelisk of Shalmaneser III, found in 1846, and the Monolith Inscription issuing from the same period, the excavations at Susa from 1852 and 1864, the discovery of the Moabite Stone in 1868, and other material, the nature of which attested invariably to its great antiquity. This corpus comprised part of the evidence that Wellhausen ought to have taken into account when he was formulating his hypothesis. Unfortunately, however, his preoccupation with the subjective literary analysis of the Pentateuch and his disregard for anything that might interfere in any way with the development of his thesis precluded an objective examination of this sort of evidence. As a result, his theory was unbalanced and prejudiced heavily in favor of purely arbitrary and subjective considerations from the very beginning.

Subsequent adherents of the Graf-Wellhausen theory of Pentateuchal origins stood firmly in the tradition established by the great master. For them the Old Testament narratives were replete with confused repetition of events, characterized by gross historical, topographical, and other errors in the text, and overlaid with a tissue of pagan mythology of such a sort as to require the attention of highly skilled analytical minds before the real trend of events could be outlined at all satisfactorily. Later research, however, has revealed that a great many of these objections were more artificial than real, and depended for their veracity upon the basic assumptions of the liberal school, which, as has been mentioned above, were gravely deficient from the very outset.

For example, one of the many objections raised against the historical reliability and integrity of the Pentateuch dealt with an alleged conflict of tradition in regard to the place where Aaron died. According to one of

---

[32] Cf. S. N. Kramer, *Sumerian Mythology* (1961), pp. 3ff.; *FSAC*, pp. 32ff.

the sources that scholars purported to identify, he died on Mount Hor (Num. 20:22; 21:4; 33:33; Deut. 32:50), but according to a "different" tradition he died at Moserah (Deut. 10:6). A careful reading of the text shows that in point of fact there is absolutely no conflict in the tradition concerning the death of Aaron at all. The word מוסרה in Deuteronomy 10:6 means "chastisement," and as such designates the event of the death of Aaron, not the place. This allusion makes it clear that his decease on Mount Hor constituted a reproof for the trespass at Meribah (Num. 20:24; Deut. 32:51), and that, like Moses, he was excluded from the Promised Land because of his rebellion against God. The two supposedly conflicting traditions are thus in complete harmony, and preserve the facts that Aaron died on Mount Hor while the people encamped below in mourning. In order to mark this sad occasion, which, with his own exclusion from the Promised Land, lay heavily upon the mind of Moses (Deut. 1:37; 3:23ff.), the incident and the camp-site were designated Moseroth (Num. 33:31; Deut. 10:6).

In an attempt to elucidate the route taken by the wandering Israelites as they approached Edomite and Amorite territory in preparation for their assault upon Canaan (Num. 21:10ff.), E. G. Kraeling was "quite surprised" to find himself further to the south at the River Arnon,[33] primarily because he assumed, quite without warrant, that the Hebrew term הפסגה was actually the name of a mountain, following the fashion in critical circles. He was thus reduced to the normal expedient of identifying and separating "early" and "late" narrators, and of attempting to reconcile and harmonize their testimonies so as to present a constructive interpretation of the situation. In point of fact there is no reason whatever for assuming that there was ever just one single place named "Mount Pisgah." On each occasion when the term *Pisgah* occurs in the Hebrew text it is accompanied by the definite article, showing that it was not a single identifiable location but rather a common noun. Derived from a root which in later Hebrew meant "to cleave," and represented as such in the LXX, the term described a ridge crowning a hill or mountain which, when viewed from beneath, presented an uneven outline. It thus meant "the elevated ridge," and as such was applied to various sites in Palestine, and not to one specific mountain. It can be noted here that the documentary analysis of Pentateuchal written sources is particularly weak in its attempts to interpret the Wilderness wanderings of the Israelites, a matter that will be considered subsequently.

Quite aside from being beguiled and misled by a faulty methodology, liberal scholars have contrived to make their own difficulties in process of supporting the Graf-Wellhausen critical position. Thus H. H. Rowley, in his attempt to present an authoritative basis for what he held to be the Maccabean dating of the book of Daniel, employed inferior secondary

[33] *Rand McNally Bible Atlas* (1956), p. 122.

sources comprising translations of the Nabonidus Chronicle[34] as a means of building up a composite image of a "Gobryas."[35] Rowley then employed his "Gobryas" to demolish theories suggesting the identification of Darius the Mede with Gobryas, and by direct implication rejected the historicity of Darius the Mede. This example rested, as Whitcomb has pointed out,[36] upon the assumption that "Gobryas" was not only a combination of the persons named Gubaru and Ugbaru in the cuneiform sources, but also the "Gobryas" of Herodotus and Xenophon and the "Gaubaruva, son of Mardonius a Persian" in the Behistun Inscription. Had Rowley based his studies upon more reliable translations, and especially upon the cuneiform of the Nabonidus Chronicle, he would have become aware of the fact that Gubaru and Ugbaru, who were mentioned in connection with the fall of Babylon in 539 B.C., were regarded as two distinct individuals in the Chronicle. This simple distinction, properly pursued, would have led to an entirely different formulation of his views regarding the identity of Darius the Mede, a task which, in the event, was left for J. C. Whitcomb to accomplish. Unfortunately for the speculations of Rowley on this particular question, his methodological error was as elementary as it was egregious.

Although the foregoing may well have been an honest mistake, the same cannot be said for certain ambivalent tendencies which have marred liberal criticism over the years. Thus it is curious, to say the least, that many scholars are perfectly content to allow the validity of evidence from Josephus concerning the fact that Jaddua was High Priest during the time of Alexander the Great,[37] and hence assign a date between 350 and 250 B.C. for the work of the Chronicler, but are completely unwilling to recognize from the same source the correctness of the testimony to the fact that the book of Daniel was in its completed form by 330 B.C.[38]

While many of the European adherents of the Graf-Wellhausen hypothesis have modified their views to the extent of recognizing that the results of literary criticism in its apogee were rather arid and sterile, there is little evidence at the time of writing that they are willing to part serious company with the documentary theory of Pentateuchal origins in its present form. Thus, in a recent compendium of material dealing with Old Testament interpretation, C. Westermann's *Essays on Old Testa-*

[34] I.e., other than the translation of Sidney Smith, *Babylonian Historical Texts Relating to the Downfall of Babylon* (1924).

[35] H. H. Rowley, *Darius the Mede and the Four World Empires in the Book of Daniel* (1935), pp. 20ff.

[36] J. C. Whitcomb, *Darius the Mede: A Study in Historical Identification* (1959), p. 26; cf. D. J. Wiseman, *NBD*, pp. 293f., *Notes on Some Problems in the Book of Daniel* (1965), pp. 9ff.

[37] *AJ*, VI, 7, 2; XI, 8, 5.

[38] *AJ*, XI, 8, 5.

ment Hermeneutics (1963), Zimmerli could recognize only the barest elements of originality in the patriarchal narratives, which for him had been heavily reinforced by material dating from the pre-conquest period, and had been largely rewritten by the "Yahwist" to stress the emergent element of promise.[39] But another contributor to the volume, Hesse, could hardly go as far as that, for he asserted that while the Old Testament envisaged Abraham as the bearer of the promise and the tried and true man of faith, "we cannot accept this witness from the Old Testament without further ado, because we know that this Abraham never existed in this way."[40] In harmony with traditional German critical authoritarianism, Hesse never troubled to inform his readers as to the nature and content of his special fount of knowledge concerning Abraham.

In the same work Walter Eichrodt continued to perpetuate the old attitude of radical criticism in his statement that the historical material of the Old Testament is highly stylized and cannot be accepted at face value, since for him and his fellow-critics, "Old Testament history has received in essential points a quite different aspect from that which it could have had for a generation untouched by the historical work of the last two centuries."[41] Here again Eichrodt is only prepared to consider the witness of the Old Testament to itself after the text has been thoroughly reworked according to the canons of classical literary criticism, and appears unwilling to recognize the substantial gains made towards the rehabilitation of the traditional text of the Old Testament historical material as the result of modern archaeological, linguistic, historical, and other research.

Much of the credit for a return to the view that the Old Testament is an authentic document of religious history must go to the archaeologically oriented school of W. F. Albright. Through rigorous emphases upon linguistics and archaeology, this renowned scholar has contributed more to the accumulating fund of knowledge concerning Old Testament life and times than any other individual in the field. To some extent Albright has broken with the traditions of Wellhausen, particularly since 1940, in his insistence on the primacy of archaeology in the broad sense as a method of control, as well as upon the substantial historicity of the patriarchal tradition and the precedence of oral tradition over written literature.[42] Yet while he has claimed a greater sympathy towards the Mosaic traditions now than previously, he has asserted that the oldest document in the Old Testament that has survived in approximately its

[39] Pp. 90ff.
[40] P. 298.
[41] P. 232.
[42] *FSAC*, p. 2.

original form is the Song of Deborah,[43] a pronouncement that has a curious Wellhausenian ring about it. Such a statement is certainly remarkable, to say the least, in view of the known antiquity of writing in Near Eastern cultures, as well as the fact that the processes of writing *per se* are referred to nearly forty times in the Pentateuch alone.

That Albright actually holds to the documentary analysis of the Pentateuch, albeit modified to some extent by the emphasis upon oral tradition as found in the form-critical school, is apparent from his attempts at dating the "Pentateuchal documents."[44] He has maintained in this connection that J and E were transmitted separately, being written down not later than 750 B.C.; that Deuteronomy was written in the time of Josiah, not as a pious fraud (contrary to the views of some Wellhausenians) but as an earnest attempt to recapture and express the Mosaic tradition, and that the Priestly Code is almost certainly not pre-exilic. Like many other liberal scholars he handicaps himself when dealing with the question of Mosaic monotheism by the quite gratuitous assumption that "all our literary sources are relatively late. . .and that we must depend on a tradition which was long transmitted orally."[45]

In spite of his professed objectivity, it is difficult to believe that Albright is, by and large, following the direction to which the facts point. With one breath he can adhere in broad principle to the Graf-Wellhausen theory, and with another he can state quite confidently that the foundations of literary criticism have been seriously undermined by the manuscript discoveries from 4Q.[46] While still supporting a somewhat modified Graf-Wellhausen position he can abandon the "developmental character" of Old Testament history in favor of the unity of tradition implied by the records. Unfortunately, however, in postulating the existence of "divergences from basic historical fact,"[47] Albright commits precisely the same error as that characteristic of the nineteenth-century critical writers, who interpreted the traditional data in accordance with their own peculiar philosophy of history. While it is important to realize, as Burrows has pointed out,[48] that the accuracy of the history and the truth of the interpretation must not be confused, it is equally necessary to emphasize the accredited historical character of much of the material that, in critical circles, has hitherto been explained away in terms of myth, legend, folk-lore, and empirico-logical thought.

Although Albright has been in advance of many liberal thinkers in recognizing that most prophecies are actually anthologies of oracles or

---

[43] *Recent Discoveries in Bible Lands* (1956), p. 90.
[44] *FSAC*, pp. 250f.
[45] *FSAC*, p. 257.
[46] *Samuel and the Beginnings of the Prophetic Movement* (1961), p. 11.
[47] *Archaeology and the Religion of Israel* (1955), p. 176.
[48] *WMTS*, p. 5.

sermons,[49] he has insisted upon placing the prophecy of Isaiah in a special category, in that for him it contains extraneous material. This view is an obvious concession to the critical speculations of the Graf-Wellhausen school, and is absolutely incapable of being substantiated either by internal or external evidence. By contrast, the situation is quite different in the case of the book of Jeremiah, in which there seem to be distinct traces of extraneous matter (e.g. Jer. 52:1ff.).

The followers of Albright naturally share his ambivalence in matters of historical and theological interpretation. Thus it is possible for F. M. Cross and J. Bright to assign an early date to the Tabernacle, a position that is eminently justified in the light of the archaeological evidence;[50] but at the same time they expound a somewhat modified Graf-Wellhausen critical position. This is a curious anomaly, to say the least, for according to classical literary criticism the Tabernacle emerged from priestly sources and was widely regarded as a completely idealistic reverse projection of the later Temple into the remote past. Yet neither Cross nor Bright appears to recognize that the views which they hold regarding the date of the Wilderness Tabernacle constitute such a fundamental criticism of the Graf-Wellhausen position as to amount to its rejection in one cardinal area of its development.

Pursuing the lead afforded by these facts, it would appear possible that if the theory is vulnerable in this vital area, it may well be deficient in other important respects also. Unfortunately, Albright and his followers, while doubtless recognizing the compelling force of this kind of logic, are apparently unwilling to jettison the traditions of Graf and Wellhausen and strike out independently along a new line of investigation, following the direction in which the facts point. Judging once more from their writings, the members of the Albright school would seem to have as little real sympathy for supernaturalism in the Old Testament as did Alt and his followers.[51]

Of all the criticisms levelled against the Graf-Wellhausen hypothesis in recent years, by far the most significant was that published by C. H. Gordon in 1959.[52] This renowned archaeologist and Near Eastern scholar rejected what he described as "the badge of interconfessional academic respectability" largely on the ground of archaeological evidence. His conclusions were stimulated by a comparison of the eleventh tablet of the Gilgamesh Epic with the Genesis account of the construction of the ark. He became impressed with the absurdity of assigning the Genesis description to the Priestly Code and to the era of the Second Temple, as

[49] FSAC, p. 275.
[50] F. M. Cross, BA, X, No. 3 (1947), pp. 55ff.; Bright in BHI, pp. 146f.
[51] O. T. Allis, Christianity Today, III, No. 17 (1959), p. 9.
[52] C. H. Gordon, Christianity Today, IV, No. 4 (1959), pp. 131ff.

the Graf-Wellhausen school did, without doing precisely the same for the remarkably similar Gilgamesh Epic account of the ark.

Consequently he was able to argue that the pre-Abrahamic traditions of the book of Genesis, such as that involving the Deluge, were not in fact late Priestly Code material at all. Instead, he concluded that they were pre-Mosaic, and that it was extremely difficult to single out any detail that was attestably late. This had been clear for some time from the evidence presented by Sumerian and Akkadian cuneiform sources, and was made certain by the texts recovered from Ras Shamra (Ugarit), where whole literary themes, as well as specific phrases, occurred in tablets of pre-Mosaic date. Such a position represented a crystallizing of earlier tendencies in the thought and writings of Gordon,[53] and led him to separate the real literary sources of the Pentateuch from the spurious ones advanced by the Graf-Wellhausen school.

From his studies of Ugaritic material Gordon became aware of the high degree of culture in Canaan prior to the emergence of the Hebrews as a sedentary people, and as a result he was able to reject quite readily the notion advanced by earlier literary critics that the formative stages of Israelite religion and society were essentially primitive. Gordon suggested as a conclusion to his article that subsequent Old Testament studies could only be based most satisfactorily upon an exacting and accredited scientific methodology in which the spurious and imaginary would be rejected in favor of the genuine and factual, and the *a priori* deductive system of classical liberalism replaced by an inductive approach that would pursue with resolution any specific direction indicated by the facts of the situation.

Enough has been said in relationship to the general criticism of the Graf-Wellhausen methodology and its doctrinaire exercise by generations of scholars to demonstrate the fundamental weaknesses of such an approach. It can only be a matter for the deepest regret that the methods of literary criticism were formulated without any but the most casual reference to the actual characteristics of contemporary Near Eastern literature insofar as it was available to scholars, since in a great many areas it exhibits remarkable similarities to the writings of the ancient Hebrews. What is quite certain is that, in any new methodology that may be adopted by scholars in the future, the compositions of ancient Near Eastern nations must be utilized as an external control over subjective theories of literary origins of Biblical material.

D. Criteria of the Graf-Wellhausen Hypothesis

1. YHWH and Elohim. Against the background of the foregoing discussion it is now possible to take a more detailed look at the criteria that were held to validate the Graf-Wellhausen theory in the minds of its

[53] Cf. *UL*, pp. 6f.

adherents. As has been observed in preceding pages, the earliest criterion to be employed in isolating the alleged underlying documentary sources of the Pentateuch was the variant usage of the divine name, with *YHWH* (יהוה, Eng. Jehovah) used exclusively in one document and *Elohim* (אלהים) in the other. In refuting the validity of this procedure it can be said at once that no other religious document from any of the ancient Near Eastern cultures can be shown to have been compiled in this manner. The Gilgamesh Epic, for example, incorporates older material, particularly in the Deluge story, but it is neither desirable nor possible to attempt to analyze the Epic into underlying "documentary" sources on the basis of a variation in the usage of the divine names. Were one to undertake this procedure there would emerge as many theoretical documents as the number of deities mentioned in this ancient cuneiform composition.

The inadequacy of using the divine names *YHWH* and *Elohim* as criteria for distinguishing supposed documents in the Pentateuchal corpus can be further demonstrated by using as a control another characteristically Semitic body of material, the Koran. While this is many centuries removed historically from the composition of the Pentateuch, there can be little serious doubt that, as Albright has pointed out, the transmission of the Hebrew Torah must have resembled that of the Tradition (*ḥadîth*) in Islam.[54] Many years ago, in his study of the divine names in the Koran, R. D. Wilson showed that certain *suras* of the Koran preferred the designation of God as *Allah* (e.g. IV, IX, XXIV, XXXIII), whereas others employed *Rab* (e.g. XVIII, XXIII, XXV); in precisely the same way that portions of Genesis favored *YHWH* (e.g. 7:1ff.; 11:1ff.; 18:1–19:28), whereas others used *Elohim* (e.g. Gen. 1:1–2:3; 6:9ff.; 17:2ff.) as the divine name.[55] Yet in spite of the existence in the Koran of exactly the same kind of criterion as that employed by the European literary critics for the formulation of their theory of Pentateuchal origins, there is absolutely no support whatever among Islamic scholars for a documentary approach to studies of the Koran on the basis of difference in usage between *Allah* and *Rab*.

In any question of the relative occurrences of *YHWH* and *Elohim* as criteria for determining the presence of underlying documentary sources, the evidence of textual criticism both from the Pentateuch of the LXX version and from the Qumran manuscript fragments has to be taken into consideration. The LXX version of the Torah exhibits a greater variation in the use of the divine names than that apparent in the MT. This situation would suggest, among other things, that if the translators of the LXX Pentateuch knew about the existence of the

---

[54] *FSAC*, p. 258. For the origin and authenticity of the Islamic Tradition see J. Fueck, *ZDMG*, XCIII (1939), pp. 1ff.

[55] R. D. Wilson, *PTR*, XVII (1919), pp. 644ff.

alleged documents underlying the finished structure of the Law, they were not influenced to any significant extent by those considerations that, according to the Graf-Wellhausen theory, had determined the activities of the anonymous redactors of the various manuscript sources. On the contrary, they had evidently prepared the LXX version of the Law against a background of obvious freedom of choice from whatever families of manuscripts were available for the task of translation.

That there were at least three distinct families of Hebrew manuscripts in existence in the pre-Massoretic period has been demonstrated convincingly as a result of the manuscript discoveries at Qumran, and in particular from the fragments recovered from 4Q, thereby confirming the opinion that there was considerably more variety in the text of early Pentateuchal manuscripts than was the case with the MT itself. Since the latter has traditionally been used as the basis of documentary analysis in view of the fact that it was regarded as the "fixed" text, it is interesting to speculate as to what might have happened to the entire Graf-Wellhausen theory had one or more pre-Massoretic texts been available for the use of nineteenth-century literary critics. The answer has in fact been supplied to a large extent by Albright, who, as mentioned above, has stated that the fragmentary manuscripts recovered from 4Q have already seriously undermined the foundations of detailed literary criticism.

It will be recalled from earlier discussion that the use of the divine names as a criterion for literary analysis had been attacked in a number of quarters at the end of the nineteenth century. Notable in this connection were Dahse and Wiener, both of whom called attention to variations in the LXX text, and argued from this to the fact that it is impossible to be certain of the usage of the names *YHWH* and *Elohim* in the original Hebrew text. According to their view, the incidence of the divine names in the MT and the LXX ought to be uniform if the premises upon which the documentary theory was based were to be considered valid, and as such the names occurring in the LXX ought to be just as reliable a criterion for documentary analysis as those found in the MT. Skinner attempted to meet this argument by endeavoring to show on grounds of textual criticism that the MT was more reliable than the LXX in this matter, and it must be observed that, while his efforts met with some success, he failed to come to grips with the fundamental issues raised by Dahse and Wiener.[56] What is even more unfortunate is the fact that his arguments have been gravely weakened by the textual evidence from Qumran, which shows that it was eminently possible for the translators of the LXX version to have had several manuscript families of the Pentateuch at their disposal, whose nature and contents

---

[56] J. Skinner, *The Divine Names in the Book of Genesis* (1914).

were by no means identical in all respects with those of the Massoretic tradition.

The difficulties encountered by critics in employing the single names for deity are multiplied greatly when the use of a compound such as YHWH-Elohim (Gen. 2:4–3:24) is considered. According to the Graf-Wellhausen theory, a conflation of J and E sources into JE was held to account for this phenomenon. This in itself posed a difficult problem for the critical scholars who propounded this explanation, since it involved a combining of the divine names that in theory were supposed to furnish the vital clues to the existence of separate documents. This embarrassing situation was made more acute by the realization that, with characteristic independence of the strict Massoretic tradition, the LXX version contained many more instances of this combination than are apparent in the Hebrew (e.g. Gen. 4:6, 9; 5:29; 6:3, 5). Turning from the Scriptures to "control" material, it is now known that there is ample evidence for the use of compound names for deities in Ugaritic, Egyptian, and Greek literature. Thus, as Gordon has shown, it was a commonplace at Ugarit for deities to have compound names allotted to them.[57] One god was known as Qadish-Amrar, another Ibb-Nikkal, another Koshar-Hasis, and so on. Quite obviously the multiplicity of divine names in the Pentateuch must be evaluated against such a background, particularly in view of the close literary relationship that has been shown to exist between Ugaritic and Biblical Hebrew. On the basis of such comparisons it is apparent that, by themselves, YHWH and Elohim need not imply dual authorship in any given chapter of the Pentateuch any more than the incidence of Baal and Haddu would in a Ugaritic myth.

Probably the most familiar example of this tendency in antiquity can be seen in the combined name Amon-Re, the god who became the great universal deity as a result of Egyptian conquests during the Eighteenth Dynasty.[58] Amon, it will be recalled, was the ramheaded deity of the capital city Thebes; and Re was revered as the old universal sun-god. The fusion of the religious universalism associated with Re and the political leadership in the Thebes of Amon underlies the fact of the compound name "Amon-Re" as a single entity. The *stele* of Ikhernofret (*ca.* 1800 B.C.) goes considerably further than a great many other Egyptian sources in the matter of multiple divine names, for it offers no fewer than four different names and epithets of the god Osiris, both singly and in combination, in harmony with contemporary practices in this matter.

As Gordon has pointed out, scholars can do much to account for the combination of the elements in YHWH-Elohim by suggesting, for example, that the multiple form can be explained in terms of the equation

[57] *GBB*, p. 160; *UL*, p. 6.
[58] J. Černý, *Ancient Egyptian Religion* (1952), pp. 38, 61f.

519

"*YHWH* equals *Elohim*."[59] But when the view is seriously propounded that *YHWH-Elohim* is the result of documentary conflation, it becomes as impossible to accept this contention as it is to argue that Amon-Re emerged as a designation because certain scribes combined an "A" document with an "R" document. Even a cursory examination of Egyptian religion shows just how widespread was the custom of describing deities in terms of compound names. To give one more example only, in some localities of ancient Egypt the sun-deity Re was also known as Sobek-Re, the crocodile-god, while at Elephantine he was identified with Khnum, who appeared as a ram, and was known as Khnum-Re.[60]

As far as Greek culture is concerned, classical scholars have long been familiar with the reference in Herodotus to Themistocles' attempt to extort money from the Andrians by informing them that he came with two persuasive deities named "Persuasion-and-Necessity."[61] The Andrians refused to pay, however, on the ground that they were saddled with certain impecunious deities whose names were "Poverty-and-Impotence." The parallel with the religious traditions of Ras Shamra can be seen when it is observed that the names of the Ugaritic deities are able to be written with the conjunction "and," as with "Qadish-and-Amrar," "Koshar-and-Hasis," and so on. Exactly the same phenomenon occurred in the Greek combinations "Kratos-Bia-te" and "Kratos kai Dike," the personified forms of strength and might, in the writings of Aeschylus.[62]

The phenomenon of coupled or compound names is thus well attested in Near Eastern antiquity. Precisely what the combination *YHWH-Elohim* was intended to signify, however, is open to some question. Whereas *Elohim* designated the idea of deity in a general sense, *YHWH* constituted a specific divine name, and if the former was used as a universal name for God, it is possible that *YHWH* was meant to indicate the more restricted Deity of the Covenant. It may also be that the close association and interchange of the two designations in the Pentateuch points to an attempt on the part of the author or authors to emphasize the ideas associated with each name.[63] Certainly these and similar problems pertaining to the incidence of the divine names in the Torah have shown their inadequacy as criteria for the whole process of documentary analysis.[64] If this actually constituted the cornerstone of the Graf-Wellhausen hypothesis, as the writings of liberal critics indicate, it is clearly a most fragile structure upon which to build.

2. *Multiple names*. Other criteria employed in attempts to outline or recover the underlying documents or "hands" in the Pentateuch have

[59] C. H. Gordon, *Christianity Today*, IV, No. 4 (1959), p. 133.
[60] Cf. H. Frankfort, *Ancient Egyptian Religion* (1961), p. 20.
[61] *Hist.*, VIII, 111.
[62] *Prom. Solut.*, 12; *Choeph.*, 244.
[63] Cf. I. Engnell, *Gamla Testamentet* (1945), I, pp. 194ff.
[64] Cf. *YIOT*, pp. 140ff.

included double names for individuals, racial groups and places, as well as multiple divine names.[65] Thus the incidence of Reuel as an alternative designation of Jethro was held to point to the presence of different documentary sources, as was the use of Canaanites as a variant form of Amorites, or Horeb as an alternative description of the location of Sinai. The falsity of multiple names as a criterion for the differentiation of underlying documentary sources may be attested from even the most casual perusal of the "control" material emanating from the ancient Near East. There are literally hundreds of examples from Egypt of variant personal names, as with the military commander designated Sebekkhu, who was also known as Djaa. With reference to such usages involving groups, Kitchen has called attention to the Manchester Museum *stele* from the time of Sesostris III (*ca.* 1800 B.C.), in which Djaa described his single Palestinian enemy by no fewer than three terms: *Mntyw-Sst* (Asiatic bedouin), *Rtnw* (Syrians), and *'Amw* (Asiatics).[66]

In early Old Testament narratives the terms "Amorite" and "Canaanite" were frequently used either interchangeably, or else in the form of double designations or "pairs." In a wide sense the word "Canaanite" could describe the hinterland of the Syro-Palestinian coast, and in consequence it could be used of Syria-Palestine in general. The dispersed families of the Canaanites (Gen. 10:15ff.) also included the Hittites, Jebusites, Amorites, Hivites, and Girgashites, who lived in an area extending from Sidon to Gaza, then inland to the southern Dead Sea region, and thence northwards to Lasha, a site of uncertain location. This broad designation also appeared in the fourteenth-century B.C. Amarna tablets, in which the kings of Babylon and elsewhere occasionally employed "Canaan" to describe the Syro-Palestinian territories under the military control of Egypt. In the narrow sense, "Canaanite" was regarded as the equivalent of "merchant" (Job 41:6; Isa. 23:8; Ezek. 17:4; Zeph. 1:11), a usage reflected on a *stele* from the time of Amenophis II (*ca.* 1440 B.C.).[67] The term "Amorite" was also employed in both a wide and a restricted sense in antiquity, the former being the virtual equivalent of "Canaanite" (Gen. 10:15f.; Num. 13:17ff.; Josh. 24:15, 18), while the latter was used to describe the Amorites more specifically as part of the population of the hill-country of Palestine (Num. 13:29; Josh. 5:1; 11:3). On the basis of such evidence it is clearly incorrect to regard these and other double designations as indications of diverse authorship, for the use of the terms in this way is entirely out of harmony with the external records, which themselves are not characterized by underlying "hands," and do not admit of any such literary analysis.

---

[65] E.g. *DILOT*, p. 119; O. Eissfeldt, *Einleitung in das AT* (1956 ed.), p. 217; *ETOT*, pp. 182ff.
[66] K. A. Kitchen, *NBD*, p. 349; *Ancient Orient and Old Testament* (1966), p. 123.
[67] Cf. *ANET*, p. 246; B. Maisler, *BASOR*, No. 102 (1946), p. 9.

As regards place names of a dual character, the triumphal paean found on the celebrated Israel *stele* of Meneptah (*ca.* 1224-1216 B.C.), described Egypt variously as *Kmt* and *T'-imri'*,[68] while Memphis was designated by three terms, *Mn-nfr*, *'Inb-ḥd* and *'Inb*.[69] It is important to realize that these and many similar examples that could be cited from monuments and other texts are from sources which have absolutely no literary pre-history extending beyond the immediate period of their composition, so that the possibility of "hands" and underlying documentary sources is completely precluded.

A study of Near Eastern writings shows that the considerations that apply to the literary prehistory of *stelae* and similar inscriptional sources are also valid for compositions on papyrus or ostraca, which have had a prolonged history of transmission. Since none of this "control" material was compiled according to the methods elaborated by the Graf-Wellhausen school, it seems only proper to conclude that the composition of the Pentateuch followed contemporary scribal and compilatory patterns, and was not the result of redactional manipulation of artificial documentary sources.

3. *Gattungsforschung*. While form-criticism of the *Gattungsforschung* variety may theoretically be a valid means of isolating laws, poems, and the like,[70] any explorative technique of this kind must always be subordinated to sound knowledge concerning ancient literary phenomena as a whole, otherwise the exponents will simply fall into precisely the same methodological error as that committed by the Graf-Wellhausen school. In point of fact, such a contention appears to have constituted the basic criticism brought against the form-critical school of Gunkel and Gressmann by Sidney Smith, who rightly protested against the arbitrary demolition of prophetical writings into tiny portions to conform to rigidly classified types of literature.[71]

The fact that scholars now possess first-hand, datable, contemporary, and comparative material with which to exercise objective control over the forms of Old Testament literature as well as over the different varieties of literary criticism, has made possible a closer inspection of the recording and transmissional methods employed by the scribes of Near Eastern antiquity. In both Mesopotamia and Egypt scribes were educated to a high degree of literary proficiency, and were renowned for their consistent accuracy in recording and copying.[72] An Egyptian religious papyrus from about 1400 B.C. carried a certification to the effect that the scribes regarded the book in its extant written form as complete

---

[68] *ANET*, pp. 376ff.
[69] K. A. Kitchen, *Ancient Orient and Old Testament*, p. 124.
[70] So *BHI*, pp. 63f.
[71] S. Smith, *Isaiah XL-LV* (1944), pp. 6ff.
[72] Cf. *FSAC*, pp. 78f.

from beginning to end, having been copied, revised, compared, and verified sign by sign.[73] If this was the case in Mesopotamia and Egypt, there is no warrant for the assumption that the Hebrews were any less careful or accurate in the matter of their own sacred writings.

Equally well attested is the fact that ancient Near Eastern scribes occasionally revised the grammar and spelling of the ancient texts with which they were dealing, with the intent of making the meaning of specific passages as clear as possible to the reader. Such an unexceptionable practice is of great antiquity, and has been followed faithfully, if sometimes unobtrusively, down to the present time in revisions of sacred literature. Whereas modern changes are apt to be slight, alterations were both minor and thoroughgoing in antiquity. Thus, as Kitchen has shown, the celebrated "Instruction" of Ptah-hotep, originally compiled in terse Old Egyptian about 2400 B.C., was supplied some five hundred years later with extensive grammatical revisions in Middle Egyptian.[74] Despite this activity it is still possible to distinguish clearly between the "received text," which is Middle Egyptian in linguistic character, and the textual form of the original work which emerged from the Old Kingdom period. In the *Tale of Sinuhe*, which unquestionably dates from the Twelfth Dynasty and for which there are numerous manuscripts dating from *ca.* 1800 B.C. to *ca.* 1000 B.C., a thirteenth-century copy substituted a Late Egyptian negative, *bw*, for the Middle Egyptian *n* in one passage, and a Late Egyptian loan-word *ym* (sea) for the Middle Egyptian term *nwy* (waterflood) in another. Such "late" words merely serve to date the particular manuscript of the *Tale of Sinuhe*, and have no bearing upon determining the period of its original composition.

This pattern of scribal revision is very important for the study of those Old Testament passages that contain allegedly "late" words, since it shows that only the text of the particular manuscript is comparatively late. As such the incidence of a "late" word is irrelevant as an argument against an earlier date of composition of the section under consideration. Along with revisions of spelling and the inclusion of glosses on the text, the scribes of antiquity frequently replaced an earlier proper name by its later form. This latter phenomenon may well account for such apparent anachronisms as the mention in the Pentateuch of the "way of the land of the Philistines" (Exod. 13:17), at a time when the Philistines had yet to occupy the Palestinian coastal region in any strength.

Egyptian scribes also allowed certain terms to appear sporadically in ancient sources, such as the Pyramid Texts of ca. 2400 B.C., then permitted the usage of such words to lapse for some centuries, and ultimately revived them at a very late date, sometimes two millennia after the original usage of the terms. In ignorance of this now well-

---

[73] J. Černý, *Paper and Books in Ancient Egypt* (1952), p. 25 n. 131.
[74] K. A. Kitchen, *NBD*, p. 350.

attested custom, nineteenth-century literary critics assumed that words that were rare or of supposedly late date could be employed as criteria for establishing the comparative lateness of the passage or material in which they occurred. However, using the same criteria, the Sixth Dynasty pyramids of Egypt (*ca.* 2400 B.C.) would have to be post-dated by two millennia, simply because words found in their inscriptions do not recur until the Graeco-Roman period. What the critics failed to realize is that the Old Testament passages containing "demonstrably late" words could also be interpreted as actually enshrining evidence attesting to the earliest use of these terms. As Kitchen has remarked, where such critical methods are so obviously inapplicable to texts of the Biblical period emerging from the closest neighbors of Israel, the most serious misgivings about the validity of a vast amount of current Old Testament literary criticism must be raised; and these are raised on purely literary grounds well attested by tangible objective data without any recourse to theological predispositions or considerations.[75]

A common contention of the critical school to the effect that short passages must necessarily be early and *vice versa* has been disproved by reference to ancient Near Eastern literary sources. The Egyptian *Admonitions of Ipuwer*, dating as early as 2000 B.C., contained lengthy tirades against the inequities of contemporary society and the shortcomings of the central administration, showing that long pronouncements were by no means unknown in the pre-patriarchal period.[76] Similarly, Sidney Smith cited lengthy sequences from Babylonian oracles that stood in the same general literary tradition, thereby making it evident that the length of a passage has no necessary bearing upon its date.[77]

As remarked above, many of the supposed anachronisms of the Pentateuch can be explained on the basis of successive scribal revisions that had the effect of bringing the text up to date in certain areas. In Genesis 40:15, the reference to Canaan as the land of the Hebrews is clearly the result of this kind of activity, which is seen again, for example, in the use of the name Dan (Gen. 14:14; Deut. 34:1), the reference to the Israelite monarchy (Gen. 36:31), the description of Moses as a prophet of Israel (Deut. 34:10), and the use of the phrase "unto this day" (Gen. 32:32; Deut. 3:14; 34:6), as well as the various scribal glosses that furnished the later forms of earlier place names (Gen. 14:8, 15, 17; 16:14; 23:2; 35:6). There is, however, nothing inherently anachronistic about the mention of a "king" in Deuteronomy 17:14, as Weiser alleges,[78] since the passage in question is a foretelling of events still to take place, and not a record of past occurrences.

---

75 *Ibid.*
76 *ANET*, pp. 441ff.
77 S. Smith, *Isaiah XL-LV*, p. 8 n. 47.
78 *OTFD*, p. 72.

One of the commonest critical grounds for positing differences of authorship subsisted in the doublets or repetitions, with their variant forms, that are to be found on occasions in the Old Testament text. But as C. H. Gordon has pointed out, such repetitions were typical of ancient Near Eastern literature, as illustrated profusely from Babylonian, Ugaritic, and even Greek compositions.[79] In the Koran, which is of considerably later date, although strictly Semitic in tradition, there are scores of examples of repetition dealing, among other things, with the teaching of Mohammed on the unity of God and the condemnation of unbelievers. Every *sura* of the Koran commences with the words "In the name of the merciful and gracious God," and the degree of duplication and repetition in the work can be gauged from the fact that, out of one hundred and fourteen *suras*, seventy-seven condemn the unbelievers directly by name, while many of the remainder do so by implication. As far as the Biblical world is concerned, the tastes of the times called for duplication, as illustrated by the way in which both Joseph and Pharaoh had prophetic dreams in duplicate, while in a later period the dismay of the prophet Jonah was described in two separate stages, each accompanied by a question from God (Jon. 4:4, 9). The consonance of this kind of material is such that it would be petulant to go so far as to suggest that it arose from several different sources.

One particular type of duplicate is of especial interest because of the extra-Biblical collateral material now available. Judges 4 furnishes the prose account of the victory of Deborah; the poetic form occurs in the following chapter. Because the two accounts contain variations in matters of detail, it has long been argued by critical scholars that the poetic version was older than the prose account, on the ground that verse-form is supposedly "much better adapted for oral transmission than is any kind of prose."[80] However, to presume to pronounce in favor of a disparity in age or provenance between two such accounts on the basis of the nature or style of the literary vehicle is entirely specious. Study of "control" material makes it clear that in ancient Egypt, historic events were sometimes recorded simultaneously in prose and poetic versions, and that not only was provision made for the major differences appropriate to the two literary media, but also that, on occasions, a third version of a pictorial nature was made in order to celebrate the event. In approaching such questions as those relating to the authorship and date of the two accounts in Judges 4 and 5, therefore, it is of far greater importance for the student to be aware of scribal usages in ancient Near Eastern society than to be beguiled by the subjective speculations of the

---

[79] C. H. Gordon, *Christianity Today*, IV, No. 4 (1959), p. 132; cf. J. Pedersen, *Israel I-II* (1926), p. 123; J. Muilenburg, *VT suppl. III* (1953), pp. 97ff.; W. H. Brownlee, *The Meaning of the Qumrân Scrolls for the Bible* (1964), pp. 258f.

[80] *FSAC*, p. 66.

occidental scholarly mind, which have issued in a logical but totally unrealistic system of interpretation. It might also be opportune to observe at this juncture that for millennia it has been a common practice for Semitic orientals to memorize long genealogical tables as a means of establishing their ancestry and marking the passing of the various generations. Although this material does not appear in poetic form in the Old Testament, the Semitic mind had experienced little difficulty in mastering it and transmitting it over many generations, thus throwing some doubt on the common belief that poetry is a more suitable vehicle than prose for such a purpose.

4. Stylistic variations. As contrasted with more recent trends, the early critical analyses of the Pentateuch made much of differences in literary style, which, it was alleged, could be recognized readily from the text and could be taken as indicating the existence of underlying "hands" or documents. In the minds of some scholars considerations of style became so completely subjective as to be virtually worthless, and even the more responsible exponents of the art of literary analysis exhibited considerable confidence in their use of style as a means of determining the existence of source material, even though some of them, such as Driver,[81] confused literary "characteristics" with analytical "criteria." When, however, this methodological approach is subjected to examination by comparison with extra-Biblical "control" material from the Near East, it becomes apparent that the critical procedures of the nineteenth-century scholars are completely absurd, since it is now known that a great many oriental writings of antiquity exhibit precisely the same literary phenomena.

Thus Kitchen has shown that the biography of the Egyptian general Uni, dated in the Sixth Dynasty about 2300 B.C., contains flowing narrative (the J and E of the critical school) in those sections where his various state activities and his campaigns are described, while at intervals he employed two stereotyped refrains to indicate the recognition by the pharaoh of his successive accomplishments (corresponding roughly to P_1 and P_2). In addition, his biography included the victory-paean that he and his army chanted during their return from the Palestinian campaign (a special H, or hymnal, source). This work was carved in stone at the specific request of Uni, and there is absolutely no possibility that the final form was developed through or during any literary prehistory by means of a number of documents.[82] This is clear from the fact that the events the biography contains fell within the adult career of one specific individual, and that the work itself was commissioned, composed, written, and executed in stone within a period of a few months at the most. Equally clearly there cannot possibly be any "hands" underlying its

[81] *The Book of Genesis* (1920 ed.), pp. vii ff.
[82] K. A. Kitchen, *NBD*, p. 349.

style, which merely varies with the nature of the subjects under immediate consideration, and in any event is made to conform to canons of literary suitability. This is but one example from dozens of available Egyptian and other texts, occurring from the last three millennia B.C., a corpus of material that is invaluable for the light it throws upon the compositional techniques of Near Eastern scribes in particular.[83]

5. *The Tabernacle.* A few other difficulties confronting adherents of the Graf-Wellhausen theory may be mentioned briefly at this juncture. The Tabernacle, which was confidently assigned to a post-exilic date and held to have been based upon late Temple practice, can hardly have been later than the monarchy, since it lacked such important features of pre- and post-exilic worship as singers, a point that Wellhausen apparently failed to notice. The geography of the Wilderness wanderings, with its wealth of detail, contrasts strangely with the rather general character of the references to the geography and topography of Canaan, which would be quite remarkable had the narratives of the wanderings been composed in the manner in which critical scholars have suggested. In particular, the fact that there are no specific references or allusions to Jerusalem in the Pentateuch would be unthinkable in any alleged source emanating from the southern kingdom in the ninth century B.C.

This in turn leads to the question whether Jerusalem was ever intended to play a dominant role in the centralization of cult-worship, and raises issues concerning the real reason for the composition of Deuteronomy, which according to critical theories of an earlier generation was supposed to have been written in order to promote the centralization of worship. Again, the fact that certain passages in Deuteronomy presuppose a knowledge of portions of the so-called Priestly Code[84] compiled, in the view of the theorists, at a much later date than Deuteronomy, presents awkward problems for the exponents of the classical documentary theory to which they have yet to address themselves satisfactorily.

6. *The Samaritans.* One of the more disconcerting pieces of evidence with which the critical school has had to deal in attempting to formulate late dates for certain sources has been that presented by the Samaritan Pentateuch. Most commonly the nineteenth-century liberal writers either ignored the existence of this document,[85] or else, where they tried to come to grips with the problem, they furnished at best a poor and unsatisfactory explanation of the situation.[86] Occasionally a very garbled

---

[83] Cf. C. H. Gordon, *HUCA*, XXVI (1954-55), p. 67; *UL*, p. 6.

[84] Compare Deut. 22:9-11 and Lev. 19:19; Deut. 24:14 and Lev. 19:13; Deut. 25:13-16 and Lev. 19:35; Deut. 28 and Lev. 26; Deut. 12 and Lev. 17, *et al.* Lev. 11 is also earlier than Deut. 14:3-21.

[85] E.g. F. H. Woods, *HDB*, II, pp. 363ff. It was described by E. König in *HDB Extra Volume* (1904), pp. 68ff.

[86] E.g. E. Nestle, *The New Schaff-Herzog Encyclopedia of Religious Knowledge* (1908), II, p. 130.

story by Josephus[87] was quoted to the effect that Sanballat, who was regarded as a contemporary of Alexander the Great, had sent his son-in-law, Manasseh, to Samaria to function as High Priest. The scholars who mentioned this story assumed that Manasseh had taken the Torah with him, and that this subsequently came to constitute the Samaritan Scriptures. However, according to Josephus, this Manasseh was also the grandson of Eliashib, the High Priest in the time of Ezra and Nehemiah, and may perhaps have been alluded to in Nehemiah 13:28. Aside from other considerations, however, Josephus said nothing about a lawbook's having been taken by Manasseh to Samaria; and in any event, this Manasseh lived a century later than Nehemiah, when the division between the Jews and Samaritans had become consolidated.

While the origins of the Samaritans have traditionally been connected with events somewhat subsequent to the fall of Samaria (2 Kgs. 17:24ff.), it must be remembered that this is based on a Judaean account, which as Macdonald has pointed out constitutes something quite different from what the Samaritans themselves believed about their origins and the existence and nature of the "First Kingdom" in the time of Joshua.[88] In their *Chronicles* the followers of Uzzi, the Samaritan High Priest in the early monarchy period, were said to have been taken into captivity at the time when Samaria fell, and to have come back to Mount Gerizim in the First Return under their High Priest Seraiah some years later. The precise date is unknown, and while the Samaritan *Chronicles* tend to confuse it with the Second Return, roughly contemporary with that of the Judaean exiles under Zerubbabel, it was most probably the situation described in 2 Kings 17:24ff.

According to Samaritan tradition, there was a famine in Canaan after the fall of Samaria in 722 B.C., and the hardships of this experience, combined with the incidence of a plague of lions, prompted the remaining inhabitants to ask the king of Assyria to send back to Palestine those who had previously cultivated the land in the northern kingdom. The Assyrian ruler, who was not mentioned by name, requested the Samaritans, who at that time were living in Harran, to return to Canaan. For their part, according to the tradition, they insisted that they could only insure divine favor if the true worship of God was restored to Mount Gerizim. The king agreed to assist them in this matter, with the result that they returned to Canaan, apparently with other pagan colonists, rebuilt the ruined sanctuary on Mount Gerizim that had been given its traditional site by Joshua, and never thereafter departed from the Prom-

---

[87] *AJ*, XI, 8, 2; cf. R. Brinker, *The Influence of Sanctuaries in Early Israel* (1946), pp. 217f.

[88] J. Macdonald, *The Theology of the Samaritans*, pp. 14ff.; cf. H. H. Rowley in B. W. Anderson and W. Harrelson (eds.), *Israel's Prophetic Heritage* (1962), pp. 208ff.

ised Land, as the existence of a few Samaritan families at the present day near Nablus indicates.

On this view the breach between Samaritans and Judaeans occurred, not in the time of Ezra, but in the days of Eli, who took it upon himself to establish an apostate sanctuary of God at Shiloh, despite the clear prescription of the Law that true worship was to be carried on at Mount Gerizim.[89] The Judaean account in Kings denied the antecedent history claimed by the Samaritan tradition, and regarded them as descendants of the colonists whom Shalmaneser of Assyria is said to have brought from Cutha, Babylon, Hamath, and elsewhere in Mesopotamia to repopulate the land after the fall of Samaria in 722 B.C. From a study of the *Annals* of Sargon and from a reference in Chronicles to a "remnant of Israel" (2 Chron. 34:9) it would appear that after 722 B.C. the local population of Samaria comprised the remainder of the native Israelites in addition to the foreign colonists from Mesopotamia. Evidently other Judaean sources, particularly the prophets (cf. Isa. 11:12f.; Jer. 23:5f.; 31:17ff.; Ezek. 37:16f.), either did not know of, or else ignored, the tradition that Samaria was an impure admixture of pagan Mesopotamians and surviving northern Israelites.[90]

What is known, however, is that in the time of Ezra the Samaritans stated that they had been using the method of sacrifice to God as prescribed in the Torah as far back as the days of Esarhaddon of Assyria (Ez. 4:2). Whether stated deliberately in this manner or not, the Samaritan claim would seem to support the Judaistic tradition that the Samaritans were worshippers of the God of the Hebrews by the seventh century B.C. Samaritan faith and practice was based upon the Torah alone, and this fact, along with other elements in their tradition, would suggest that their Pentateuch, whose canon is identical with that of the Hebrew Torah,[91] was in its extant form by that time at the very latest. This naturally raises questions as to the date of the Samaritan Pentateuch and also brings up the problem of the relationship between it and the MT and similar texts. As has been observed in an earlier chapter, most scholars followed Gesenius with regard to the latter in his conclusion that the Samaritan Pentateuch was a secondary version of the MT.[92] Among those who did not hold to this opinion was Pfeiffer, who suggested that the Samaritan Pentateuch may in fact represent a version as

[89] T. H. Gaster, *IDB*, IV, p. 191.
[90] M. Gaster, *The Samaritans: Their History, Doctrines and Literature* (1925), pp. 12ff.
[91] For differences of text see Ch. Heller, *The Samaritan Pentateuch: An Adaptation of the Massoretic Text* (1923); J. Montgomery, *The Samaritans: The Earliest Jewish Sect* (1907), p. 286.
[92] Cf. M. Gaster, *The Samaritans: Their History, Doctrines and Literature*, pp. 102, 133.

old as the MT.[93] Paul Kahle also placed an increased emphasis upon the nature of the Samaritan Pentateuch in his study of their Scriptures.[94]

More recently the Samaritan Qumran manuscript 4QEx[a] has demonstrated the antiquity of the text and the degree of constancy with which it was transmitted without, however, pronouncing upon the priority of its text over that of the Massoretic tradition.[95] In addition, the great antiquity of the Samaritan recension has been increasingly emphasized as the result of photographic examination of the Abisha' scroll at Nablus.[96] It is difficult to see precisely how the Samaritan text can constitute a relatively late branch of tradition separating from the main Jewish line and going back at its earliest to Hasmonaean times, as Cross has maintained.[97] Such an argument, which rests upon precarious palaeographic grounds,[98] has been rightly criticized by Rowley.[99]

There are certain clear indications within the text of the Samaritan Pentateuch itself that it is of pre-exilic origin. It is written in the angular script, rather than the Jewish "square" or Aramaic character, and it exhibits some confusion between the letters "d" and "r," which are also quite similar in form in the later Aramaic script, and between "m" and "n." This confusion could hardly have originated in the post-exilic scripts, and obviously goes back to the early angular Phoenician prototype or to such inscriptions as that on the *stele* of Mesha or that of the Siloam tunnel. An interesting feature of the Samaritan tongue was that none of its gutturals was pronounced at all in the Pentateuch, which would indicate that their enunciation dated from the time of Ahab and his successors, when the non-guttural Phoenician dialect was popular in Israel.

Jewish tradition has preserved the important fact that the Pentateuch was originally written in the angular script, and that Ezra was the instigator of a change into the square variety of character so as to make it differ from the Samaritan form of script.[100] As Gaster has pointed out, the only reason for so drastic a step could have been to break completely with tradition and to eliminate the Samaritan text from circulation among the Jews.[101] Such a change could not have occurred later than the time of Ezra, and may even have happened at an earlier period, as adduced from many instances in the LXX translation that are clearly due to the use of a manuscript written in square characters.

[93] *PIOT*, pp. 101ff.

[94] P. E. Kahle, *The Abisha' Scroll of the Samaritans* (1953).

[95] Cf. P. W. Skehan, *JBL*, LXXIV (1955), pp. 182ff.

[96] Cf. P. Castro, *Sefared* (1953), pp. 119ff.; R. E. Moody, *Boston University Graduate Journal*, X (1957), pp. 158ff.

[97] F. M. Cross, *The Ancient Library of Qumran* (1961), p. 172.

[98] *FSAC*, p. 336.

[99] H. H. Rowley, *Men of God* (1963), p. 272.

[100] *Sanhed.* 21b. Cf. R. Brinker, *The Influence of Sanctuaries in Early Israel*, pp. 221f.

[101] M. Gaster, *The Samaritans: Their History, Doctrines and Literature*, p. 28.

Evidence of this kind would argue strongly against the supposition that the Samaritans acquired their text from Ezra, since it is clear from the separation of the scripts that the Samaritan Pentateuch was already in existence in his day, and had been for some considerable time previously. If these considerations are disregarded it becomes increasingly impossible to explain precisely why the Jews should have received the Pentateuch from Ezra in a comparatively late script, while the Samaritans, who are alleged to be only borrowers and imitators, preserved the older and more original script. On the basis of this and other evidence[102] it is impossible to accept the hypothesis that the Samaritans acquired their Pentateuch from Manasseh after his expulsion from Jerusalem by Ezra, the alleged compiler of the document. There can be no doubt that the Pentateuch had been in the possession of the Samaritans for a great many generations prior to the visit of Ezra to Jerusalem. Since it would not have been possible at any time during the period of religious schism and political division between the northern and southern kingdoms to promulgate any body of legislation of a kind that both parties could have adopted without any recriminations, it can only be concluded that the Pentateuch must have been in existence in written form prior to the political rift between the northern and southern tribes.

If this reflects what actually transpired, the very latest date that could be assumed for the compilation of the Torah in its present form would be some period prior to the death of Solomon. In the view of the present writer the Pentateuch was in fact in substantially its extant form by the time the prophet Samuel died, but whether this is the case or not, the evidence for an early dating of the Law as furnished by the Samaritan Pentateuch militates decisively against the Graf-Wellhausen documentary hypothesis of Pentateuchal origins, since according to the latter neither D nor P had yet been written when the Samaritan Pentateuch was already in its final canonical form.

E. A PROPER METHODOLOGICAL APPROACH TO PENTATEUCHAL STUDIES

It is only fair to recognize in a study such as the present one that the Graf-Wellhausen theory has come under increasingly vigorous assault within recent years, even in critical circles, and that more and more liberal scholars are expressing serious doubts about its validity at many important points. Some of these are able to see that such alleged sources as J, E, D, and P can no longer be regarded as points on the dateline, but ought to be interpreted preferably as streams of tradition, in the flow of which there is both old and new material.[103] There can therefore be said to be a real sense in which current liberal attempts to grapple with

---

[102] Cf. R. Brinker, *The Influence of Sanctuaries in Early Israel*, p. 222.
[103] So G. H. Davies, *IDB*, IV, p. 503.

the problems of the Old Testament have diverged to a considerable extent from the confident criticism of former years.

That this is only true in a very limited respect, however, is borne out by the fact that there has yet to be a large-scale abandonment of the Graf-Wellhausen methodology and its faulty presuppositions. Many scholars undoubtedly cling to this hypothesis, inadequate as it has been shown to be, simply because they lack a suitable, ready-made replacement. Indeed, H. H. Rowley has, on more than one occasion, stated his own willingness to abandon it, provided that a more satisfactory hypothesis is adduced to replace it.[104] The present writer can only speak for himself in expressing the earnest hope that the scholarly world will not have to endure yet another supposedly "scientific" hypothesis that purports to explain the origins of Old Testament literature. What is required is a thoroughgoing attempt to replace any and all developmental hypotheses by a correct methodology grounded firmly upon an assured foundation of knowledge concerning the manifold facets of ancient Near Eastern life, which, in setting the Biblical writings in proper historical and cultural perspective, will furnish authoritative information as to scribal customs and usages in the realm of ancient literary activity.

Instead of approaching the Old Testament literature with the *a priori* supposition that it is replete with error, internal contradictions, unhistorical material, and gross textual corruptions, the application of a proper methodology will require a careful examination of the Hebrew text in the light of what is now known about the divergent streams of life in the ancient Near East from at least the third millennium B.C. That this trend is already being reflected in the work of some scholars has been indicated by Orlinsky, who wrote: "More and more the older view that the Biblical data were suspect and even likely to be false, unless corroborated by extra-biblical facts, is giving way to one which holds that, by and large, the Biblical accounts are more likely to be true than false, unless clear-cut evidence from sources outside the Bible demonstrates the reverse."[105]

The enormous amount of available comparative material from Near Eastern sources has made it very evident that in the field of Old Testament studies very little can be taken as absolutely settled, and least of all the much-touted "assured results of Biblical criticism" that emerged from the last century. Indeed, it is now apparent that much of what passed for "scientific research" in the Victorian and subsequent eras will have to be re-investigated entirely, this time from a properly based

[104] E.g. in his review of F. V. Winnett, *The Mosaic Tradition* (1949) in *JTS*, I (1950), p. 195; *Theology Today*, V (1948), p. 124; *The Growth of the OT* (1950), p. 46.

[105] H. M. Orlinsky, *Ancient Israel* (1954), p. 8.

methodological approach, rather than from an emotional or ideological standpoint.[106]

Whatever the numerous and grave faults of their methodology, the classical contributors to the development of the Graf-Wellhausen hypothesis were undoubtedly masters of their craft. Although their approach was dominated to a disproportionate extent by Hegelian presuppositions, they generally managed to express their findings in language that, if not infrequently authoritarian in tone, was nonetheless direct and unequivocal in its intention. Even in translation the writings of most nineteenth-century German scholars are characterized by a degree of clarity and even elegance that has long departed from the scene of Old Testament studies, having been replaced to a large extent by a technical jargon that includes such dubious and frequently misunderstood terms as "sacral kingship," "amphictyony," and the like.

In view of the grave shortcomings of the Graf-Wellhausen approach to the problems of the Pentateuch, and to the Old Testament in general, any new study will need to be based firmly upon an accredited methodology that will utilize the vast quantities of control material now available to scholars throughout the world, and will argue inductively from the known to the unknown instead of making pronouncements from a purely theoretical standpoint that bears only a slight relation to some of the known facts. For those who regard the Scriptural narratives as self-authenticating, such a procedure will be scarcely necessary or desirable. In this connection, however, it should be noted that the application of a proper methodology is not, *per se*, inimical to any doctrine of the inspiration and authority of Scripture. Rather, it constitutes an attempt to replace an incorrect and faulty method of approach by one that is based upon a thorough knowledge of the cultural *milieux* from which the various parts of Scripture emerged, or to which they can be related, as a

---

[106] As has been noted, the inadequacies of the analytical-literary method when applied to the writings of Classical Greek authors such as Homer have long since been recognized by scholars in the field (cf. J. A. Scott, *The Unity of Homer*, 1921; GBB, pp. 218f.), who have shown that the procedure was based upon inconsequent reasoning and false statistics (cf. W. J. Martin, *Stylistic Criteria and the Analysis of the Pentateuch*, 1955, pp. 6ff.).

Precisely the same result has occurred regarding the work of Omar Khayyam. Sixty years of meticulous research by literary experts resulted in the verdict that Omar had actually written very little poetry indeed, and that the quatrains of later poets had been foisted upon this semi-legendary character. One distinguished German scholar actually went so far as to state that the name of Omar Khayyam ought to be eradicated from the history of literature. Manuscript discoveries just prior to 1950, however, brought a radical change to this situation, for one manuscript, dated 1207, some 75 years after the death of the poet, was found to contain 252 quatrains, and this appears to constitute only a selection from a larger corpus, pointing unquestionably to the fact that Omar Khayyam was actually a poet of considerable stature (A. J. Arberry, *The Listener*, September 21, 1950, pp. 382ff.).

means of understanding as fully as possible the meaning and significance of the divine revelation.

It is equally important that such an approach not be construed as a means of solving the problems associated with the origins, nature, and development of the cultural and religious traditions of Israel merely by relating them to, and perhaps attempting to derive them from, the ethnic religions of the ancient Near East in a manner that would appear to emphasize superficial similarities and minimize or ignore entirely the fundamental and essential divergences. It is an axiom of the descriptive sciences that, in all questions of comparison, differences are more significant than similarities, and this principle will also be borrowed by any correctly grounded methodology of Old Testament study.

Such an attitude will recognize that the Old Testament does, in fact, contain "error" in the sense that numerous examples of accredited scribal mistakes of different kinds can be discerned from an examination of the Hebrew.[107] These and other similar errors are the property of every age, and one function of textual criticism is to call attention to their existence so that due notice can be taken of them in translation or in attempts to recover a genuine pre-Christian text of the Old Testament.

An accredited methodology will avoid the atomizing or fragmentizing of Biblical narratives, and in rejecting such "sources" as J, E, D, P, H, and L as spurious will instead concentrate upon the nature and provenance of the genuine sources that underlie certain of the Old Testament writings. The early chapters of Genesis, rather than being dismissed as legendary or mythical, will actually be seen to be Mesopotamian in character, and will be examined accordingly against their appropriate literary and cultural background. The real source material of the Pentateuch and other writings will be seen in such cited material as the "Book of the Generations of Adam" (Gen. 5:1), the "Book of the Wars of YHWH" (Num. 21:14), the "Book of Jashar" (Josh. 10:13; 2 Sam. 1:18), the "Book of the Covenant" (Exod. 24:7; 2 Kgs. 23:2 et al.), the many documentary sources underlying the books of Kings and Chronicles, and so on. In particular it will also be recognized that a creative individual such as Moses could, like Homer, work with the matrix of the tradition to select his subject matter from earlier and contemporary sources, reshape it, and fashion it into a masterpiece of enduring literary and spiritual value.

---

[107] To cite but one of several such examples, there is an obvious case of scribal confusion between the letters ו and ד in 2 Samuel 8:13, where ארם should be emended to אדם. A clear transcriptional error is apparent in 2 Kings 7:6, where the original text evidently read "Musurites," which has been preserved as "Egyptians" (מצרים). Another mistake is the mention of Jehoiakim in Jeremiah 27:1, instead of Zedekiah, who is obviously indicated by the general context. For further examples of scribal errors in transmission see part four, section III-C above.

Taking the Old Testament on its own terms against a background of collateral material from the ancient Near East also requires a recognition of the fact that written and oral material are both early phenomena. The oral never appears consistently before the written in the ancient Near East, and the evidence furnished by secular sources shows that both forms frequently co-existed for lengthy periods of time. While some sections of the Old Testament probably circulated in oral form before being committed to writing, the high literacy of the ancient Near East points, as Gordon has shown, to a maximum of written sources lying behind the Scriptural narratives.[108]

The specific usage of ספר (book) in this connection is to be understood strictly in terms of a written document, since the word was never employed in relationship to oral material. Again, the very concept of law (tôrāh) needs to be interpreted against an oriental background rather than that of ancient Rome, as was common in early critical circles. Even in Mesopotamia, where codified law was an early and familiar concept, the law-courts did not cite the codes in handing down decisions, but instead functioned in accordance with custom, precedent, and accepted tradition, a point that has still not been grasped by some occidental scholars. As Gordon has indicated,[109] the kind of law reflected in the Homeric writings is designated *themistes* (*Odyssey*, XVI, 403), and indicates the sum total of oracles by which the gods regulated society. This has much in common with the Hebrew idea of Torah, since even a casual reading of the Pentateuch shows that there is comparatively little which can be called law in the strictest sense of that term. The spirit of Torah actually subsists in the oracles which God delivered to Moses, and as such is in full accord with the traditions of the Heroic Age.

While even the most restrained variety of modern literary criticism tends to fragment the material under investigation, a correct methodological approach will never lose sight of the fundamental unity of such classic compositions as the Pentateuch. As Gordon has remarked, this document, for all its diversity, was considered to be an integral whole by both Jews and Samaritans for many centuries.[110] If it is broken down into its component parts typologically, it appears to be a patchwork quilt of badly stitched sources, telling as it does about the cosmos, litigation, war, social institutions, sacrifice, agriculture, and a variety of other topics.

In this connection, however, it is important to notice that such subjects were also worked into the composition of the celebrated Shield of Achilles,[111] a fact that again mirrors accurately the literary and cultural

[108] *GBB*, p. 283.
[109] *GBB*, pp. 248f.
[110] *GBB*, pp. 281f.
[111] The cosmos, *Iliad*, XVIII, 483ff.; social institutions, XVIII, 490ff.; sacrifices, XVIII, 558ff.

traditions of the period extending from the fifteenth to the tenth century B.C. Since the Torah was the supreme guide of conduct and life for the ancient Hebrews, it was necessary for this work to cover all those aspects of existence that they would encounter, and the totality of this experience must accordingly be matched by a holistic view of the Pentateuch.

An examination of the narrative material from such a standpoint shows not merely that the various parts have been arranged in chronological order as a single work in five volumes, but that the Pentateuch is actually a part of a tightly organized group of literary material that extends from Genesis to 2 Kings. In this *schema* the Torah exercises a fundamentally important role as the epic of nationhood, whose two constituent parts were the patriarchal and Exodus sequences. In the former the land of Canaan was promised to the forefathers of Israel and was actually acquired by them to some limited extent. In the latter, the way was opened for their descendants, the true inheritors of the Promised Land, to return and take formal possession of it.

While it is inappropriate methodologically to compare the Pentateuch with the Iliad as literature, since they are, of course, entirely different types of compositions, it is important at the same time to observe that both works served much the same purpose for their readers. For the Greeks, the Homeric writings constituted Scripture *par excellence*, and were venerated as the divinely inspired guide for life. In precisely the same fashion the ancient Hebrews looked for advice and help to the divine revelation given to the people through Moses, a situation that once again reflects the general ethos of the Heroic Age.

Enough has been said to make it clear that a proper methodology will regard the whole as something more than the sum of its parts, and that it will eschew the fragmenting of the material under study in favor of what might be called an "inductive holism." Fundamental to this methodology, as has been observed previously, is the setting of the literature under scrutiny against its proper historical, religious, and cultural background in Near Eastern antiquity, the isolation of major and minor parallels, and the singling out of special details within the fabric of the whole for specific study.

To the task of elucidation will be brought all the available resources of philology, archaeology, and other related disciplines in a resolute determination to go where the ascertained facts lead, regardless of whether particular theories, in part or in whole, stand or fall in the process. Such observations as are made will need to be checked continually against existing and newly discovered facts alike, and if necessary revised in the light of the evidence at hand. Only when these safeguards have been exercised will the work of the scholar remain unimpeded by imposing but faulty hypothetical systems, and his results be grounded firmly on a factual basis.

The following estimate of the Pentateuch is an attempt to envisage the work holistically as an organic body of material subject to processes of growth, codification, and editing within the Mosaic period. It takes cognizance both of the fact of post-Mosaic additions and also the tradition that accorded early veneration to the Torah as the normative guide for the life of the nation. It must be emphasized that, contrary to the views of some scholars, the Mosaic Torah is not the codification of the priestly cult, for the admixture of historical narrative, Levitical rules, and specifically moral and ethical principles furnishes convincing evidence of more than a purely cultic concern. The true spirit of the Torah is to be found not so much in the strict concept of law as in the oracles that God spoke to Moses.[112] It is this factor that transcends the purely local and historic interpretation of the enactments at Sinai, and by removing the faith of Israel from a strictly tribal context has given the divine revelation through Moses a universal applicability.

In view of certain scholarly trends to relegate Moses to a minor position in the development of the characteristic Hebrew faith and assign instead the beginnings of the true Israelite ethos to some sort of amphictyonic situation in the settlement period, it should be pointed out that ancient Hebrew tradition unanimously credits Moses with a substantial place in the mediation of the Law and is wholly opposed to any concept that would place the beginnings of national historic, moral, and spiritual tradition at some point during or subsequent to the occupation of Canaan under Joshua. However, Hebrew tradition itself must be assessed critically, particularly in view of the fact that among the rabbis the figure of Moses had achieved the eminence accorded to a superman, and that in character he was quite unlike the harassed, frequently frustrated, yet consistently energetic man of God depicted in the Pentateuchal writings. Any estimate of the person and work of Moses must be entertained within the strict limits of the Pentateuchal data and related to the contemporary ancient Near Eastern life-situation. In particular it is of fundamental importance to avoid the emotional overtones that have become attached to the words "Moses" and "Mosaic" since the advent of literary criticism, and which have resulted in such extreme positions as the denial of the very existence of Moses on the one hand, or the attributing to him of every word and syllable of the Pentateuch on the other.

The present study will have made it clear that, aside from any other considerations, Moses played a highly original role in the revelation of the divine nature and will to nascent Israel, as well as in the task of sifting and correlating earlier northwest Semitic and specifically Israelite legalistic concepts and behavioral practices. From the very beginning of the tradition Moses was specifically credited with such portions of the

[112] *GBB*, pp. 248f.

text as the judgment against Amalek (Exod. 17:14), the Book of the Covenant (Exod. 20:22–23:33, along with the Decalogue), the restoration of the Covenant (Exod. 34:27, referring to Exod. 34:10-26), an itinerary (Num. 33:1ff., referring to the source underlying Num. 33:3-40), the bulk of Deuteronomy referring to the renewal of the Covenant and the reinforcement of its laws, and the two poetic sections that concluded Deuteronomy.

The concentration in one man of the ability to write historical narrative, to compose poetry, and to collate legal material is by no means as unique as earlier critical writers were wont to assume. As Kitchen has pointed out, an illustration of this kind of ability from ancient Egypt at a period some seven centuries prior to the time of Moses has been furnished in all probability by Khety (or Akhtoy), son of Duauf, a writer who lived in the time of the pharaoh Amenemhat I (ca. 1991-1962 B.C.).[113] This versatile individual apparently combined the functions of educator, poet, and political propagandist, and wrote the *Satire of the Trades* as a text for use by students in the scribal schools. He was probably commissioned to give literary form to the *Teaching of Amenemhat I*, which was a political pamphlet popular in the Eighteenth to Twentieth Dynasties as an exercise to be copied by schoolboys.[114] In addition, he may have been the author of a popular *Hymn to the Nile*,[115] which with the foregoing works was also frequently copied out by scribes.[116] Quite clearly, then, it is by no means inherently impossible for a talented individual to have engaged during the Amarna period in the kind of literary activity traditionally ascribed to Moses.

Of course it must always remain a matter of conjecture as to precisely how many laws were original with Moses, and how many, particularly as reflected in the book of Deuteronomy, must be considered against four centuries of sedentary Israelite life in the Goshen region and against the period of occupation of Transjordan by two-and-a-half tribes prior to the death of Moses. Equally uncertain is the actual extent to which Moses recorded personally the written material credited to him. It may well be that the presence of third person pronouns in various sections of the Mosaic enactments indicate that these sections were dictated. Quite possibly many of the small or isolated sections in the Hebrew text were committed initially to the priests for safekeeping, and only at a later period were the manuscript pieces assembled into some sort of mosaic and joined together into a roll.

[113] K. A. Kitchen, *NBD*, p. 849.
[114] *ANET*, pp. 418f.
[115] *ANET*, pp. 372f.
[116] Cf. A. Gardiner, *Hieratic Papyri in the British Museum, Third Series* (1935), I, pp. 40ff.; G. Posener, *Littérature et Politique dans L'Égypte de la XIIe Dynastie* (1956), pp. 4ff., 19 n. 7, 72f.

While in the view of the present writer leather would be the preferred material for preserving the enactments, it should be noted that good papyrus, when available, made for quite sturdy and durable documents. Thus a sheet from the criminal register of the prison at Thebes was used at different times over a period of seventy years, and in the end still served adequately to record a bequest to servants.[117]

It is now abundantly evident from the many comparative sources available to scholars that detailed codes such as those found in the Pentateuchal writings are by no means anachronistic, as was commonly imagined by an earlier generation of literary critics. Nor is it any longer either necessary or desirable to assign the origin of many of the Mosaic enactments to the eighth or seventh centuries B.C.[118] Instead, Pentateuchal legislation must now be examined against a background of a common intellectual and cultural heritage,[119] from which an understandable similarity of antecedents naturally emerges. The uniqueness of the Hebrew enactments then becomes apparent in the realization that striking differences point to an absence of direct borrowing on the part of the Hebrews.[120]

If the vitality of the divine revelation to man is to be appreciated properly, it is important to avoid the temptation to regard the Mosaic legislation as an essentially static corpus, and instead see it as an organic collection of material subject to certain controlled processes of growth and modification. Thus it is quite possible that in the post-Mosaic period some of the enactments were altered somewhat to suit changing circumstances, a process that is perfectly legitimate in any culture, and which does not in any sense vitiate the provenance of the original legislation. No doubt some of the duplications and inconsistencies in Pentateuchal law of which Hahn speaks[121] were due, not to the rise of separate though parallel cultic regulations, as he and many other liberal writers suppose, but to the deliberate attempt on the part of the responsible authorities, whether priestly or other, to adapt the traditional legislation to the point where new conditions of life would be properly accommodated. This doubtless underlies the situation whereby the provisions of Numbers 26:52-56 relating to inheritance were modified by the circumstances detailed in Numbers 27:1-11 and Numbers 36:1-9, or where the regulations for an offering to cover sins of ignorance or inadvertence (Lev. 4:2-21) were changed by the provisions of Numbers 15:22-29. Again, it is of importance to note the witness of the text to the fact that

---

[117] K. A. Kitchen, *The Tyndale House Bulletin*, No. 2 (1957), pp. 1ff., Nos. 5-6 (1960), p. 18.

[118] Cf. J. Bright, *BANE*, pp. 22f.

[119] Cf. T. J. Meek, *Hebrew Origins*, pp. 49ff.

[120] *Ibid.*, p. 69.

[121] *OT in Modern Research*, p. 32 n. 58.

some later additions were made to the Book of the Covenant in the time of Joshua (Josh. 24:26).

When compilation of this living legal corpus was being contemplated, a unitary objective was achieved by reference to the general chronological order of events, a natural and useful device under the circumstances. However, as will be observed later, the compiler, whether Moses or someone else, frequently took the opportunity of inserting other relevant material when two rolls needed to be joined together. Some such insertion would almost certainly have been made while the smaller units were in process of being assembled, as appears to be the case in the section of enactments of Exodus 19:1–23:33, where the skillful blend of legal and historical material nullifies critical attempts to break down the material into such entirely imaginary sources as J and E. Even when a particular book was in substantially its final form long after the time of Moses, there would still be occasion for alterations or additions. This again is in full accord with the general literary traditions of the ancient Near East, where the scribes regularly revised ancient literary and other documents by removing obvious archaic grammatical and orthographical forms and making such additions as the immediate situation required.[122]

The use of the term "code" with reference to the Mosaic enactments should not be interpreted as meaning that Moses was the promulgator of some kind of civil legislation for Israel. From the outset the nation was intended to be a holy people, and, as will be pointed out below, the relationship in form and structure of a document such as Deuteronomy to the Near Eastern treaties of the second and first millennium B.C. demonstrates that Israel was bound in a spiritual vassal-union with God, the great King. Because God was an essentially moral and ethical Being, the essence of the Covenant relationship was to be manifested at that exalted spiritual level. The treaty obligations were specifically intended to be normative for all areas of the national life, since they were formulated on the basis that the very fact of day-to-day living under the provisions of the Covenant itself constituted a profound religious experience. For this reason, if for no other, it is not too much to suggest that the Pentateuchal ideal derives, not so much from the *Sitz im Leben des Volkes* of the settlement period, but from the mediatorial office and specific *doctrina* of Moses as the recipient of revelation.

The emphasis in the present work that the Pentateuchal material was in written form at an earlier rather than a later period has been entertained deliberately, partly as a safeguard against the views of the "oral-traditionists," who so frequently misinterpret the evidence from the ancient Near East, and partly because the witness of contemporary life in the ancient Near East fully substantiates such a possibility. As Kitchen

[122] *FSAC*, p. 79.

has pointed out, the uniform testimony of oriental literary practice demanded that matters that were considered important or were required to be recorded for posterity should be written or inscribed in permanent form, and not left to the care of bards and campfire romancers.[123]

In the view of the present writer, almost the entire body of Pentateuchal material could have been easily extant in practically its present form by the late Joshua period. No doubt the passing of time brought certain editorial activities to bear upon the Hebrew text in the form of explanatory glosses, insertions, and revisions of language and spelling, consistent with the practices of Babylonian, Egyptian, and other Near Eastern scribes. Even when cognizance has been taken of this situation, there appears to be no substantial ground for denying that the Pentateuch in virtually its extant form was in existence by the time of Samuel.

The Pentateuch is a homogeneous composition in five volumes, and not an agglomeration of separate and perhaps only rather casually related works. It described, against an accredited historical background, the manner in which God revealed Himself to men and chose the Israelites for special service and witness in the world and in the course of human history. The role of Moses in the formulation of this literary corpus appears pre-eminent, and it is not without good reason that he should be accorded a place of high honor in the growth of the epic of Israelite nationhood, and be venerated by Jews and Christians alike as the great mediator of the ancient Law.

[123] *NBD*, p. 850.

II. THE BOOK OF GENESIS

A. NAME AND OUTLINE

While Genesis is an anonymous work, as are the other four books of the Pentateuch, its attributive author is Moses. However, to what extent he wrote any of its contents, with the possible exception of all or part of the Joseph narratives, is unknown. In attributing Mosaic authorship to the Pentateuch as a whole, conservative scholars have pointed out that the Torah in its entirety must not necessarily be assumed to have been the work of his own hands, any more than any of the *stelae* of antiquity were the product of direct activity on the part of their attributive authors. Some writers, such as Young,[1] have not precluded the possibility that the writer drew on earlier written sources, but in general the ascription of Mosaicity to the Pentateuch implies its historicity and its formulation by Moses under divine inspiration, with the supposition that later editors may have revised the contents somewhat in accord with the traditions of the ancient Near Eastern scribes.[2]

The Jews designated Genesis according to its initial word, בראשית which is almost always incorrectly translated in English by the phrase "In the beginning."[3] In Talmudic times the work was known as the "Book of the Creation of the World," while the English title "Genesis" was actually derived from the LXX rendering of Genesis 2:4a, "This is the book of the γενέσεως of heaven and earth," and from the subsequent headings (Gen. 5:1; 6:9; 10:1; 11:10; 11:27; 25:12; 25:19; 36:1; 36:9; and 37:2), the nature of which will be dealt with shortly.

On the basis of the extant Hebrew text the book can be analyzed as follows:

I. Prehistory: the Creation Record, 1:1–2:3
II. The Story of Man, 2:4–11:26

[1] *YIOT*, pp. 42ff.

[2] R. D. Wilson, *A Scientific Investigation of the OT* (1959 ed.), pp. 48ff. For a refutation of the theory that the arrangement of the Pentateuch arose by adaptation to a triennial synagogue lectionary cycle, see J. R. Porter in *Promise and Fulfillment* (ed. F. F. Bruce, 1963), pp. 163ff.

[3] E. A. Speiser, *Genesis* (1964), p. 3, has "When God set about. . . ." A more accurate rendering would be "By way of beginning. . . ."

III. The Choice of Abraham, 11:27—23:20
IV. The Choice of Isaac, 24:1—26:35
 V. The Choice of Jacob, 27:1—36:43
VI. The Choice of Judah; the Joseph Narratives, 37:1—50:26

B. תולדת AND THE ORIGINS OF GENESIS

According to the Graf-Wellhausen documentary hypothesis of Pentateuchal origins, Genesis assumed its present form through various editorial processes that saw a combination of elements of J, E, and P sources into a continuous document. In the view of those who advocate the "traditio-historical" approach to the problem of Pentateuchal compilation, Genesis arose through the preservation of "cycles of tradition" that grew up in various areas in oral form. These "traditions" developed around focal events such as the Passover and other similar occurrences significant for the religious life of the nation and found expression in the rituals and liturgies of the Israelites. In the more moderate forms of both these views there is no necessary attempt to deny historicity to the material involved, even though most of the scholars who support these approaches would prefer to attribute general rather than specific historicity to the subject matter.

The present writer does not support either of these positions, and prefers to examine the problem of the compilation of Genesis against a background of ancient Near Eastern literary activity. It should be observed as a general principle that there may well be quite a number of sources designated in the Old Testament writings which have not actually been recognized as such by most modern scholars. Genesis appears to be a case in point, with the clue to the underlying sources being provided, not by the incidence of the divine names or the presence of supposed duplicate narratives, but by the phrase translated "these are the generations of," an expression that has perplexed a great many scholars, and regarded by the exponents of the classic documentary theory as a characteristic of the Priestly Code.

In order to appreciate the significance of the Hebrew term תולדת, it will be necessary to examine briefly the nature and format of cuneiform communications in the ancient world. Clay was the preferred material upon which the wedge-shaped symbols were impressed, and the resultant tablets, which could contain a wide range of literary material, varied in size and shape from a tiny square to a large cylinder. The general style of a tablet furnished some indication as to its contents; and as far as single tablets were concerned the material communicated usually consisted of letters, contracts, invoices, business correspondence, genealogical tables, and the like. Generally speaking individual tablets were not made too large, partly because of the sheer weight of the clay and more particularly because a large tablet would be more likely to break than a smaller one.

543

It was the normal practice in Near Eastern antiquity for single communications of this kind to commence with some sort of title, followed by the body of the text, and then a colophon, which would sometimes contain, among other things, a hint as to the identity of the scribe or owner of the tablet and the date when the tablet was written. The imprint of a button or cylinder seal upon the clay tablet helped to identify the owner of the communication. If a more lengthy communication required more than one tablet, the proper sequence of the series was preserved by a system of titles, catch-lines, and numbering. The title was normally taken from the opening words of the tablet, and these were frequently repeated at the end of each subsequent tablet, being followed by the serial number of that particular tablet. The catch-line attempted to insure the continuity of the narrative by repeating the first few words of the following tablet at the end of the previous tablet, so that, if a series of tablets became disarranged, there could be no doubt as to which word or words were to be read immediately after the conclusion of a tablet. This practice is still followed in some modern legal documents, and occurs also in the Hebrew Bible, where on the bottom left-hand margin the first word or two of the following page is to be found.

The colophon, which concluded the individual tablet or the series, normally contained the name of the scribe or the owner of the tablet, as has been remarked above, and frequently it also included some attempt at dating. In addition, it often embodied the title given to the narrative, and if the tablet was part of a series it furnished the serial number and a statement as to whether the tablet did or did not conclude the series.

That the expression "these are the generations of" is a distinguishing phrase of Genesis has long been recognized by adherents of the Graf-Wellhausen theory, as well as by more conservative scholars. S. R. Driver affirms that

> . . .the narrative of Genesis is cast into a framework, or scheme, marked by the recurring formula *"these are the generations* (lit. begettings) *of"* . . .the entire narrative as we now possess it is accommodated to it.[4]

While Ryle could state that the phrase bore a close relation to the structure of the Priestly Code in Genesis, he rejected the subdivision of the book on the basis of this formula, although on entirely subjective grounds.[5] Other commentators of widely varying schools of thought, however, divided Genesis up into sections that commenced with the phrase.[6]

[4] S. R. Driver, *The Book of Genesis* (1904), p. ii; *DILOT*, pp. 6f.

[5] H. E. Ryle, *The Book of Genesis* (1914), pp. xi-xii.

[6] So Spurrell, Lenormant, Skinner, Carpenter, Bullinger, Lange, Keil, Wright, and others.

But while scholars were agreed as to the importance of the expression, they appear to have misunderstood entirely both its usage and its significance for the literary origins of Genesis. The reason for this is quite simple, for as Wiseman has pointed out, many of the sections in Genesis commence, as is frequently the case in ancient documents, with a genealogy.[7] This practice led scholars to associate the phrase "these are the generations of" with the genealogical list in those cases where such a register of individuals followed; hence they assumed, quite without warrant, that the phrase was being employed as a preface or introduction. Thus Driver could consider it as belonging properly to a genealogical system, implying that the person to whose name it was prefixed was of sufficient importance as to make a break in the genealogical series. For Driver it also indicated that the person named, along with his descendants, would form the subject of discussion in the ensuing section until another name was reached that could be considered prominent enough to form the commencement of a new passage.

This assertion, however, is completely contrary to the facts, for an examination of the evidence in relation to the latter part of the statement would indicate that Abraham, the most prominent person in Genesis, ought certainly to have been named in connection with the phrase under discussion. Yet curiously enough, while other lesser individuals were mentioned in the various records in this manner, there is not one instance where the phrase "these are the generations of Abraham" occurs in the Hebrew text. Furthermore, the phrase does not by any means always belong to a genealogical list, since in certain cases there is no addendum of such tabular material.

What is evident, however, is that the principal facts concerning the individual involved have been recorded *before* the incidence of the phrase in question, and that they are not recorded after its occurrence. Thus when the expression "These are the generations of Adam" (Gen. 5:1) occurs, nothing more is stated about Adam apart from a mention of his age at death. Again, the record that follows the sentence "These are the generations of Isaac" (Gen. 25:19) is not so much a history of Isaac, son of Abraham, as a chronicle of events that occurred in the lives of Jacob and Esau. Still further, after the phrase "These are the generations of Jacob" (Gen. 37:2), the narrative deals with the story of Joseph, and mentions Jacob only in a rather incidental manner as the unfolding of the events warranted. This peculiarity has been a source of perplexity and embarrassment to the vast majority of commentators schooled in the critical methods of Graf, Kuenen, and Wellhausen, and in view of the fact that the phrase quite clearly does not constitute an introduction or preface to the history of a person, as is commonly imagined, it is of some importance to determine its precise meaning.

[7] *New Discoveries in Babylonia About Genesis* (1958), p. 46.

The Hebrew for "generations" in the expression under discussion is תולדת, and not the ordinary Hebrew word דור, which is translated "generations" over one hundred and twenty times in the older English versions. דור corresponds to the word "generations" as implied by common English usage, and can refer to a past (Isa. 51:9) or future (Exod. 3:15) period, a class of people (Deut. 32:5), or to the heirs of a covenant (Gen. 17:7, 9). תולדת occurs ten times in Genesis in such a manner as to lend itself to the division of the material associated with it into eleven sections, each being styled "the generations of . . . ." It also occurs in isolation from a stereotyped phrase in Genesis 10:32; 25:13; 36:9 and elsewhere in the Old Testament.

The word originated in the Hebrew root ילד, "to bear," "to beget," which doubtless accounts for the English rendering "generation." But from the time of the Hebrew lexicographer Gesenius it has been apparent from Old Testament usages of the word that it means a "history," "narrative," or "genealogical record" of a family or some other such social unit. As has been observed above, the LXX has rendered the term by γενέσεως, and it is of some interest to the Christian student to note that the expression βίβλος γενέσεως Ἰησοῦ Χριστοῦ, "the book of the genealogy of Jesus Christ" in Matthew 1:1 reflects closely the Hebrew phrase ספר תולדת אדם, "book of the genealogy of Adam" in Genesis 5:1. The Hebrew word was used regularly for the collection of Jewish traditions concerning the life of Jesus, and in modern times it has formed part of the title of Yehezkel Kaufmann's eight-volume history of Israelite religion.

Thus the term תולדת is used to describe history, and more particularly in Genesis, at all events, of family history in its origins. Quite clearly, therefore, the phrase "these are the generations of" points back to the beginnings of the family history, and not forward to its later development through a line of descendants. In this connection it is of some interest to note that the phrase that occurs in Genesis 2:4 obviously points back to the narrative of the creation of the cosmos contained in the preceding chapter. It could not refer to the narrative that follows, since that section contains no reference whatever to the creation of the heavens. As Wiseman has commented, the phrase is only appropriate as a concluding sentence, so that most commentators, notwithstanding their usual interpretation of the phrase, made the story of creation terminate with it.[8] Had they but perceived that all such sections of Genesis conclude with this formula, they would have possessed the key to the composition of the book. As it was, the majority of scholars found themselves in serious methodological difficulties in their assumption that the expression "these are the generations of" was employed in all the remaining instances as an initial, rather than a terminal phrase.

[8] *Ibid.*, p. 48.

On only two occasions in Genesis does a genealogical list follow the expression in the absence of intervening words, and yet here both lists are quite complete even without its use. While the formula is not necessarily connected with a genealogical table, in almost every instance a list of immediate descendants is given before the phrase occurs in the Hebrew text. It is therefore obvious that the formula did not constitute a preamble to a genealogical table, but that it was in fact an ending of such a list. Notice should also be taken of the mention of סַפֶּר, translated "book," in Genesis 5:1, where the reference can only be to a written "record" on a clay tablet, and also of the LXX version of Genesis 2:4, which reads, "This is the book of the origins of the heavens and the earth."

A final point in connection with the significance of תּוֹלְדֹת is that in at least some cases the person mentioned in connection with the phrase might well have been the owner, or possibly the writer, of the tablet in question, if Mesopotamian scribal practices are actually in evidence in the manner suggested. Thus in Genesis 6:9, the phrase "These are the generations of Noah" does not necessarily mean "This is the history involving Noah," since it is primarily the succeeding section that describes the activities of this individual. Instead, the expression could well be interpreted as meaning "This is the history written (or possessed) by Noah," which once more would be in full accord with ancient Near Eastern literary practices. Again, in Genesis 10:1, the mention of the sons of Noah implies that the preceding record of family history was in their possession, a practice that can be documented extensively from family archives recovered from Nuzu, Mari, and elsewhere in ancient Mesopotamia.

In Genesis 11:27, the reference to the "generations of Terah" contains little information about that individual except that he was the son of Nahor. Quite evidently it was intended to indicate that Terah either wrote, or else had compiled for him, the list of his ancestors found in verses 10 to 27. The excavations at Mari have shown the extent to which genealogical tables were treasured in antiquity as a means of establishing pedigree and for other social purposes, so that there is nothing inherently impossible in the action of Terah in this regard.

C. The Sources of the Book

The foregoing discussion can be summarized, therefore, by stating that the term תּוֹלְדֹת can be held to indicate the presence of a colophon in the text, and to constitute part of the concluding sentence of each section, thereby pointing back to a narrative already recorded. Accordingly it is eminently possible to regard its incidence as indicating the presence of a genuine Biblical source in the text.[9] It is not by any means accidental

[9] Cf. C. H. Gordon, *Christianity Today*, IV, No. 4 (1959), p. 133.

that much of the material in which the phrase under consideration occurs was either of Mesopotamian provenance or was written under the influence of Mesopotamian culture. Accordingly the present writer feels justified in following Wiseman in the assertion that Genesis contains in the first thirty-six chapters a series of tablets whose contents were linked together to form a roughly chronological account of primeval and patriarchal life written from the standpoint of a Mesopotamian cultural milieu.[10]

1. The Eleven Tablets. Such a view is based upon the conviction that this approach alone does the fullest justice to the literary phenomena of much of Genesis, particularly in the light of what is now known regarding the antiquity of writing, the diverse nature of literary communications in the Near East during the second millennium B.C., and the special characteristics of contemporary scribal techniques. The tablets that may be isolated will be seen to have a title, a residuum of textual matter, and a colophon, along with certain additional features to be noted subsequently. The sources can be described briefly as follows:

Tablet 1: Gen. 1:1—2:4. The origins of the cosmos
Tablet 2: Gen. 2:5—5:2. The origins of mankind
Tablet 3: Gen. 5:3—6:9a. The histories of Noah
Tablet 4: Gen. 6:9b—10:1. The histories of the sons of Noah
Tablet 5: Gen. 10:2—11:10a. The histories of Shem
Tablet 6: Gen. 11:10b—11:27a. The histories of Terah
Tablet 7: Gen. 11:27b—25:12. The histories of Ishmael
Tablet 8: Gen. 25:13—25:19a. The histories of Isaac
Tablet 9: Gen. 25:19b—36:1. The histories of Esau
Tablet 10: Gen. 36:2—36:9. The histories of Esau
Tablet 11: Gen. 36:10—37:2. The histories of Jacob

Apart from Tablets one and two, which deal with the origins of the cosmos and mankind respectively, and do not contain proper names in their colophons, there appears to be no event recorded in which the person or persons named could not have written either from personal knowledge or from other reliable sources. Furthermore, where individuals are mentioned by name in the colophons, the history recorded in the various sections isolated above and identified with suggested tablets ceases in all instances prior to the death of the person named at the conclusion of the tablet. The present writer is of the opinion that the foregoing classification of material represents the genuine literary sources underlying the first thirty-six chapters of Genesis.

[10] Wiseman, *op. cit.,* pp. 53ff.; cf. his *Creation Revealed in Six Days* (1958), pp. 46f.

On closer examination the first postulated tablet (Gen. 1:1–2:4) bears the title "God created the cosmos," interpreting the phrase "the heavens and the earth" as a *merismus* form, and this title is repeated in the colophon (Gen. 2:4). There is no series number associated with the latter; the colophon contains no personal or other names, and there is no catch-line linking it with the second suggested tablet (Gen. 2:5–5:2), which deals with the origins of mankind. The abruptness of the transition from Genesis 2:4 to the following verse might indicate that the original title of the second proposed tablet had either been lost in antiquity, or else had been deliberately removed in process of editing. Be that as it may, the colophon of this source contained no proper name and no evidence of ownership. It is just possible that the scribe who wrote the tablet attempted to convey the antiquity of his material by using the phrase, "in the day that God created mankind" (Gen. 5:1), a circumstance that may also be true for the expression "when they were created" in Genesis 2:4. In the light of the critical theories common in an earlier generation, which repeatedly asserted the influence of Mesopotamian traditions over those of the Hebrews, it is significant to note that more recent appraisals now limit this as far as the material covered by the first two tablets is concerned to a possible three points, including the initial waters and the divine respite after the creation of man.

Tablet three, as isolated above (Gen. 5:3–6:9a), bears the title "And man," narrates his descent, and mentions Noah, who is named in the colophon (Gen. 6:9a), perhaps in his capacity as owner of the source. The title of Tablet four (Gen. 6:9b–10:1) is "Shem, Ham and Japheth," and the text deals with the Flood and its aftermath. This material is terminated by the colophon in Genesis 10:1, where the allusion to the period "after the Flood" may perhaps constitute a scribal attempt at dating. The title of the tablet, it will be noted, is repeated in the colophon. Tablet five (Gen. 10:2–11:10a), is apparently entitled "The sons of Japheth," and deals with the Table of Nations and the Babel incident. It is concluded by the colophon, "These are the generations of Shem."

Tablet six (Gen. 11:10b–11:27a) is comparatively brief, and is entitled simply "Shem." It contains the genealogical list of Terah, and mentions his death, along with the fact that Nahor lived on until Abram was seventy-five years old. If the reference in Genesis 11:26, which recorded the age of Terah, was actually a scribal attempt at dating, then according to the Samaritan Pentateuch it was written just one year after the last chronological event mentioned in it, namely the death of Nahor. The repetition of "Abram, Nahor, and Haran" before and after the colophon formula indicates that the phrase constitutes a catch-line, and conforms to the usual scribal procedure of repeating the first words of the subsequent tablet after the last line of its precursor.

Tablets six and seven are thus linked in series, with the latter (Gen. 11:27b–25:12) forming a lengthy account of the life of Abraham and concluding with his death. The title of the tablet is apparently "Abram, Nahor, and Haran," and the text can presumably be dated by the reference to Isaac dwelling at Beer-lahai-roi (Gen. 25:11). These family histories were evidently in the possession of Ishmael, brother of Isaac, and seem to be closely linked with the brief contents of Tablet eight (Gen. 25:13–25:19a), as indicated by the colophon. The events recorded in Tablets seven and eight ceased just prior to the death of Isaac, who was mentioned either as the possible writer or else as the owner of the tablets. He survived Ishmael by some fifty-seven years, according to the text, and presumably came into possession of the family records on the death of his brother.

The title of Tablet nine (Gen. 25:19b–36:1) is apparently "Abraham begat Isaac," and the narrative content deals at length with the relationship between Jacob and Esau, and with subsequent events in the life of Jacob up to the death of Isaac. Possibly the reference to his interment constitutes a scribal attempt at dating, but whether this was actually the case or not, the histories were clearly of Edomite origin, as the explanatory gloss in Genesis 36:1 would indicate. Tablet nine was followed closely by Tablet ten (Gen. 36:2–36:9), a fragmentary record also from Edomite sources and dealing with the descent of Esau. There is little doubt that Pfeiffer was correct in postulating the existence of a "South" or "Seir" source in Genesis,[11] but owing to his improper methodological approach to the literary problems of Genesis he was only able to isolate a few relevant fragments, and he included in his S^1 and S^2 much that had no connection whatever with Mount Seir.

Quite evidently Tablets nine and ten belonged to such a "source," as did the final text, Tablet eleven (Gen. 36:10–37:2), part of which Pfeiffer attributed to S^1. Genesis 36:31, placed at the commencement of a list of Edomite kings, is obviously a post-Mosaic editorial or scribal comment. It could only have been written at a time when Israel had a king, since it is not a theoretical anticipation of the possibility of kingship, as in Deuteronomy 17:14ff., but evidently originates in the reality of an Israelite kingdom. As such it may well represent editorial activity on the part of the prophet Samuel. Immediately before the colophon in Genesis 37:2 is the statement that Jacob was living in the land of Canaan, and this can be taken as evidence for the time and place of the composition of Tablet eleven. Within a few years Jacob had moved into the land of Egypt, but this reference points to his place of abode when his historical record was closed. Jacob had obviously returned to the south country and taken up his residence in Hebron, where his father Isaac was living.

11 *PIOT*, pp. 159ff.

It can hardly be mere coincidence that the material discussed so far has been preserved in so characteristically an ancient Near Eastern fashion. As with all similar ancient literature, these tablets constituted highly valuable sources for the delineation of patriarchal origins, and it is a testimony to their antiquity and to the esteem in which they were held that they have survived in the Hebrew text in something which in all probability approximates to their original form, a circumstance that makes it possible for them to be recovered by means of the application of an accredited methodology. Precisely who was responsible for editing this material is, of course, unknown, but since another such tablet can be recovered from the text of Numbers (perhaps Num. 1:1–3:1), it seems legitimate to suppose that the redactional activity was by and large the work of Moses.

In view of the overwhelming support given by Near Eastern literary traditions for the recovery of such clearly indicated underlying sources, it can only be a matter of considerable regret that some eminent oriental-ists have refused to follow the course indicated by the facts in their translations of Genesis. Thus T. J. Meek rendered תולדת in Genesis 2:4 by the expression, "the following are the origins of the heavens," thus completely misunderstanding the significance of the original.[12] In the same manner E. A. Speiser treated the colophon of Genesis 5:1 as though it were a heading.[13] While this may have been due in part in his translation to sheer considerations of format, it still remains the case that the reader would have no inkling whatever of the real character of the constituent source, being invited instead to relate the composition of Genesis to the outworn traditions of the literary-critical school. Like other thoroughgoing advocates of the Wellhausenian position, Speiser could hardly be expected to adopt a format that would belie his convic-tions with regard to the origin and nature of the Pentateuchal writings. Meek, however, was in an entirely different category, since he consis-tently professed independence of any given literary-analytical scheme.[14] It can only be concluded, therefore, that he was either unaware of the significance of the evidence, or else that he, like many other scholars, refused to go where the facts of the matter led.

2. *The Joseph narratives.* The remainder of Genesis deals with the Joseph narratives (Gen. 37:2b–50:26), the Egyptian background of which has been so well attested by scholars as to make further comment

---

[12] *Genesis* in *The Complete Bible: An American Translation* (ed. J. M. Powis Smith and E. J. Goodspeed, 1939), p. 2.

[13] *Genesis,* p. 39 and elsewhere; but cf. p. 280, where תולדת is specifically related to what precedes.

[14] T. J. Meek, *Hebrew Origins* (1960 ed.), p. xi.

unnecessary.[15] Most probably this material was still in oral form when Moses was alive, and it may be that it was he who reduced it to writing in magnificent literary Hebrew. Quite possibly Moses was responsible for substituting leather for the Amarna Age tablet-form vehicle of communication.[16] In this general connection it should be noted that whereas in certain instances in the Pentateuch Moses was directed to inscribe the divine revelation upon durable material such as stone (Exod. 34:28), it is probable that the more durable leather came to be employed at this period by the Hebrews as writing material in general preference to papyrus, used extensively in all periods of Egyptian history.[17] Quite aside from the Jewish tradition that the Torah should always be written upon leather, since this was apparently the original material vehicle of its transmission, the passage in Numbers 5:23f. only makes the fullest sense if leather was the material which the people were using at that time.

If it is correct to assume that the major part of Genesis was transmitted by means of cuneiform tablets, it is comparatively easy to imagine the process by which it was ultimately compiled, given the existence of a Joseph story comparable to the *Tale of Sinuhe,* whether it was a written Egyptian document or an oral Hebrew tradition.[18] A person such as Moses would have been eminently suited to the task of assembling ancient records and transcribing them in edited form as a continuous record on a leather or papyrus roll. Given this basic·document, it would be well within the realm of possibility to envisage the activity of scribes of later generations in matters of textual revision, the incorporating of marginal comments, or the bringing up to date of certain chronological material (e.g. Gen. 36). For while it is important to affirm the general literary fixity of the material as a whole, it is also necessary to allow sufficient freedom for accredited scribal activity to operate in a customary manner at later stages, in consonance with the traditions evident in ancient Near Eastern literary sources.

There can be no real question as to the immense antiquity of the source material that is to be found in Genesis. Evidence for this includes the large number of Babylonian words that occur in the earlier part of the book, the topographical references, such as those relating to Sodom and Gomorrah (Gen. 10:19),[19] and the number of glosses required to bring ancient names up to date (e.g. Gen. 14:2, 3, 7, 8, 15, 17; 16:14;

[15] Cf. K. A. Kitchen, *The Tyndale House Bulletin,* Nos. 5-6 (1960), pp. 4ff., *NBD,* pp. 344ff., 656ff.; C. H. Gordon, *The World of the OT* (1958), p. 139; P. Montet, *L'Égypte et la Bible* (1959); J. Vergote, *Joseph en Égypte* (1959).

[16] On the use of leather in Egypt see A. Shorter, *JEA,* XX (1934), p. 34; cf. A. Scott, *JEA,* XIII (1927), p. 239.

[17] Cf. J. S. Wright, *EQ,* XXV (1953), p. 7.

[18] Cf. J. S. Wright, *How Moses Compiled Genesis. A Suggestion* (1946).

[19] Cf. J. P. Harland, *IDB,* IV, pp. 395ff.

23:2; 35:19). Primitive geographical expressions such as the "south country" (Gen. 20:1; 24:62) and the "east country" (Gen. 25:6), which were used in the days of Abraham, never recurred in the Old Testament narratives as a description of the countries adjoining the south and east of Palestine, since these regions subsequently acquired familiar and well-defined designations. Archaeological discoveries at Mari, Nuzu, Boghazköy, and elsewhere have been of particular value in furnishing abundant literary materials for an understanding of the narratives concerning the Hebrew patriarchs and the conditions of life that existed in Palestine and Egypt during the Amarna Age and the Hyksos periods.[20]

D. THE MATERIAL OF GENESIS

By definition Genesis is the Book of Origins, the great introduction to the drama of human redemption. The prologue is cast in universal terms suitable to the subject-matter, and depicts the creative activity of God in fashioning the cosmos and placing man upon the earth. The universality of sin is depicted, along with the fact that, as rebellion against God, it must always stand under divine judgment, a situation exemplified by the account of the Deluge. The rise of Abraham, the first of the two major emphases of the Pentateuchal writings, is associated with covenantal relationships, and the stage is thus set for the occurrence of the second great concern of the Torah, namely the deliverance of Israel from Egypt in the dramatic event of the Exodus.

1. Creation and fall. Considerations of space preclude anything more than the briefest of comments upon the fascinating material contained in the early chapters of Genesis. (The relationship of the concept of "myth" to this corpus has already been discussed in part seven.) A very common obstacle to the understanding of Genesis 1 is the notion that the chapter is "at variance with the scientific account of the beginning of the world."[21] In point of fact, however, there are surprising consonances with scientific discoveries and theories,[22] a situation that is all the more amazing since Genesis 1 was never meant to constitute a scientific document in the accepted occidental sense.

The general pattern of creative progress can be easily illustrated by reference to geological discoveries, which, of course, are infinitely more detailed in their descriptions of phenomena. Although Genesis only deals with the major divisions of geological time, there is still in evidence a remarkable degree of parallelism with the findings of geology, a fact that cannot be ignored in any assessment of the material at hand. Earlier generations of Biblical scholars were accustomed to point out,

[20] Cf. H. H. Rowley, *BJRL*, XXXII (1950), pp. 44ff., reprinted in *RSL*, pp. 269ff.
[21] D. W. Cleverley Ford, *A Key to Genesis* (1951), p. 1.
[22] A. R. Short, *Modern Discovery and the Bible* (1949), pp. 89ff.; B. Ramm, *The Christian View of Science and Scripture* (1954), pp. 221ff.

frequently with great restraint,[23] that the unscientific nature of the cosmology in Genesis 1 was evident in such matters as the mention of "grass" immediately after the emergence of land from the primeval oceans and prior to the creation of the heavenly bodies. In explaining this phenomenon it must first be noted that the standpoint of the first chapter of Genesis is an ideal geocentric one, as though the writer were actually upon the earth at that time and in a position to record the developing phases of created life as he experienced them. From such a standpoint the heavenly bodies would only become visible when the dense cloud-covering of the earth had dispersed to a large extent, subsequent to the formation of an atmosphere (רָקִיעַ). Secondly, the importance of the position assigned to the emergence of vegetation has been greatly increased by the discovery that animal life could not have been sustained until there was an adequate amount of vegetation to supply the requisite atmospheric oxygen through the process of photosynthesis. The mechanisms of photosynthesis are still imperfectly understood, but in general it involves the replacement of carbon dioxide in the air as one result of the interaction of sunlight on the green pigment chlorophyll present in leaves, grass, trees, and other vegetable matter.

Since the first chapter of Genesis is clearly not intended to comprise a scientific document—if only because of its sheer untechnical language—it is obviously undesirable to posit concordist theories of the relationship between the creation narratives and the findings of modern descriptive science. Having said this, however, it is necessary to remind the reader that the phases of development recorded in Genesis 1 are by no means as unaligned with the findings of modern science as was supposed by earlier writers on the subject. What is of primary importance for the Biblical student as well as for the scientist is to realize that the Genesis narrative must be interpreted from the standpoint of its anonymous author before pontifications are made as to when it is and is not "scientific."

The reference to the irrigation-canals of Pishon and Gihon (Gen. 2:11) makes it clear that the activity of earliest man was contemplated against a background of Mesopotamian irrigation culture, a fact which places the beginnings of the race considerably nearer to historic time than many writers have imagined hitherto. The two stories of creation (Gen. 1:1–2:4a; Gen. 2:4b-25) are typical of ancient scribal practices, as has been observed previously, but in this connection it should be noted that they are not duplicates, as many scholars have imagined. In point of fact they are not even strict repetitions of one another, for the first presents a general description of the creative situation as a whole while the second discusses one specific aspect of it, namely man in his physical

[23] Cf. H. E. Ryle, *The Book of Genesis* (1914), p. 12; S. R. Driver, *The Book of Genesis*, pp. 21f.

environment, and relates it to particular geographical considerations. If two separate tablets are involved here, as has been suggested above, the phenomenon of repetition would point to the preservation of two traditions relating to human origins, one dealing in cosmological generalities and describing the earth in relation to the universe, while the other focused more direct attention upon *homo sapiens* in his geographical surroundings, and involved the use of what the author prefers to style "religious drama" in recounting the mystery of the creation of woman. Despite related elements, the two passages in question can hardly be held to be either duplicate narratives or even genuine parallels in the commonly accepted sense, for the first account speaks in completely general terms, while the second deals from a rather different standpoint with a single locality and a specific pair of individuals.

From the time when George Smith first introduced the Gilgamesh Epic to English readers, it was commonly assumed that the original material underlying Genesis 1 as a whole was the Babylonian Creation Epic known as *Enuma elish*,[24] even though Wellhausen himself could discover no mythological ingredients in Genesis 1 save for chaos,[25] a view that his followers either repudiated or ignored. A more careful study of similarities and differences, however, has made it evident that resemblances between the Babylonian and Israelite cosmogonies are not as close as had been imagined previously.[26] So distinct has been the reaction that some scholars have even gone so far as to declare the probability that the Babylonian epic has no connection of any kind or at any point with the corresponding material in Genesis, and that each is *sui generis*.[27] Although it seems hardly possible to make such positive claims at the present, Heidel's conclusion that the relationship between the two sources is once again an open question is certainly quite proper.[28]

The Genesis narrative dealing with the creation of woman has invariably been misrepresented in such versions as those which translate the Hebrew word צלע as "rib." The word carries a number of meanings, and in Genesis 2:21f., the situation is somewhat obscured by the form of the "religious drama" in which the creative act is cast. Here צלע evidently means "an aspect of the personality," and not a skeletal rib, as commonly imagined. Even though the statement "bone of my bone and flesh of my flesh" might appear to imply such a rendering, a literal bone is not

[24] G. Smith, *The Chaldean Account of Genesis* (1876); cf. his piece in *Transactions of the Society of Biblical Archaeology*, II (1873), pp. 213ff. For other versions of Babylonian creation myths see A. Heidel, *The Babylonian Genesis* (1951), pp. 61ff.

[25] J. Wellhausen, *Prolegomena to the History of Israel*, p. 298.

[26] Cf. H. E. Ryle, *The Book of Genesis*, p. xxxii; G. von Rad, *Genesis*, p. 48.

[27] J. V. Kinnier Wilson in *DOTT*, p. 14; cf. D. F. Payne, *Genesis One Reconsidered* (1964), pp. 10ff.

[28] A. Heidel, *The Babylonian Genesis*, p. 139.

intended to be understood, since the removal of the עֵלָע from man was not accompanied by a corresponding extraction of flesh. Instead, the phrase is simply meant to demonstrate the organic and spiritual unity of the subdivided species, which is further reflected in the play on words involving "man" (אִישׁ) and "woman" (אִשָּׁה). The dramatic form of the narrative thus conceals the spiritual equation "Man = male + female," teaching that the personality of an individual of the species *homo sapiens* can only be most fully expressed when it is complemented in proper and compatible marital unity by that of another individual of the opposite sex. The comment in Genesis 2:24 exemplifies the Biblical ideal of monogamic marriage, and may well be an editorial comment added by Moses and designed to inculcate the uniqueness of a relationship which binds a man even more closely to his wife than to his parents. This ancient passage is thus as important for the doctrine of man as it is for the Biblical teaching concerning marriage.

It can be noted in general that there is no close extant mythological parallel to the material to be found in Genesis 2, even though certain of the details are not unique to the Biblical narrative. For example, the Sumerian story of Enki and Ninhursag seems to have had some sort of paradise background, and there is a minor reference to a "rib," but aside from these possible features there are very few other resemblances.[29] By way of conclusion it can be remarked with Engnell that neither Genesis 1 nor 2 stands alone, for while the two chapters have their individual teaching, they are integral to the book as a whole and, indeed, to the entire Pentateuch.[30]

The "religious drama" that describes the pristine rebellion of man against God (Gen. 3:1-24) contains certain resemblances to Babylonian sources such as the Adapa myth, which deals with a squandered opportunity for gaining immortality, but despite this fact it does not contain such extremely important *motifs* as the serpent.[31] This Genesis narrative manifests examples of *merismus* (Gen. 3:5, 22; cf. Gen. 2:9) which, as mentioned earlier in the present work, are of very great importance in any attempt to understand the meaning and spiritual significance of the drama. Thus the "tree of the knowledge of good and evil" is actually the symbol for the entire range of moral knowledge or experience. The subtlety of the temptation that confronted Eve lay in the opportunity presented to her of being able, without apparent effort, to intuit all experience in the manner in which God would seem to do. By any standards of comparison this latter is no mean feat, and when related through processes of flattery and deception to the alleged intuitive

---

[29] Cf. S. N. Kramer, *History Begins at Sumer* (1958), pp. 193ff.

[30] I. Engnell in M. Noth and D. W. Thomas (eds.), *Wisdom in Israel and in the Ancient Near East* (1955), p. 109.

[31] Cf. *ANET*, pp. 101ff.; S. G. F. Brandon, *Creation Legends of the Ancient Near East* (1963), pp. 126ff.

capacities of a woman it presented an overwhelming temptation for the female not merely to dominate the male, contrary to the intention of the Creator, but also to emulate divine activity in terms of the apperception of experience.

The passage that mentions the Nephilim (Gen. 6:1-4) has, by common consent of the literary-critical school, been dismissed as myth and has been subjected to such implausible explanatory crudities as the suggestion that the Nephilim were actually "fallen angels."[32] To relegate such an ancient section to the realm of myth or legend as popularly understood by liberal scholars is to preclude immediately the possibility of any rational interpretation of the text, and to miss entirely the invaluable anthropological insights into the interrelation of *homo sapiens* and pre-Adamic species which the passage contains, and which are amenable to those scholars who are equipped to pursue them.

2. *The Flood, Babel, and the nations.* A number of versions of a deluge story have been discovered among the cuneiform documents excavated at various Near Eastern sites. A Sumerian tablet from Nippur, dated about 2000 B.C., told of a pious king-priest named Ziusudra who was warned about an approaching deluge from heaven, which he was able to avoid by building a boat.[33] This story evidently had literary antecedents in earlier centuries, and occurred in Akkadian versions from both Babylonia and Assyria in more than one form. The best known of these is contained in the eleventh tablet of the Gilgamesh Epic, and this demonstrates certain affinities with its Sumerian precursor, including a dependence upon Sumerian liturgical sources.[34] In the Gilgamesh Epic the survivor, Utnapishtim, informed Gilgamesh, the legendary king of Uruk, of the way in which the powerful water-deity Ea had warned him of the coming inundation, and how he had constructed a boat in the contemporary fashion in order to preserve himself, his family and his possessions, as well as certain local fauna. The flood lasted for seven days, and the boat finally came to rest upon Mount Nisir in northwestern Persia. These cuneiform accounts exhibit points of contact with the Biblical narrative, and these may be explained either by common reference to an actual original or historical event, or by the fact that a standard method of escaping from the worst effects of the devastating flash-floods of Mesopotamia was being described in mythological or epic fashion. Attempts on the part of literary-critical scholars to discern in the Hebrew text the presence of what they regard as duplicate accounts of the Flood encounter serious difficulties,[35] and can hardly be taken with

[32] J. Skinner, *A Critical and Exegetical Commentary on the Book of Genesis* (1910), pp. 139ff., for the theories and literature.
[33] Cf. A. Heidel, *The Gilgamesh Epic and OT Parallels* (1949 ed.), pp. 103f.; S. N. Kramer, *Sumerian Mythology* (1944), pp. 97f.
[34] *The Gilgamesh Epic and OT Parallels*, pp. 85f.
[35] E.g. *IBOT*, p. 27.

much seriousness, as Aalders has pointed out.[36] The literary style, the standpoint of the writer, and the internal consistency of the narrative all indicate the fundamental unity of the Deluge narrative, and stand united in the face of attempts to disprove the integrity of the material. All endeavors to relate the Flood to some specific archaeological period have proved inconclusive at the time of writing, and can be illustrated by reference to the various levels of water-laid clay as excavated at Ur, Kish, Uruk, Farah, and elsewhere.[37] Most of the alluvial strata uncovered at these sites were evidently occasioned by river-flooding of unusual severity, and if the Genesis Deluge was actually one of these serious local floods it would have occurred after 4000 B.C., the general date assigned to the earliest of the alluvial levels found at Ur.

If, as seems probable, the Biblical Deluge was a comparatively local affair, the natural concern of Noah and his family would be for the preservation of only the most immediate fauna of the neighborhood in the ark, thus precluding some of the fanciful interpretations of the situation as furnished by artists and others. No certain geological evidence of the Flood is known, and consequently there is no ground for the belief that the Genesis Deluge covered the entire world. Much of the evidence cited in support of the latter theory can be explained either in terms of the history of the structure of mountains or else as the vestiges of glacial activity in the so-called Quaternary Ice Age and its associated geological changes. There is, however, no definite evidence of this at hand, and any attempt to relegate the events described in Genesis to a flood in an actual historical period must be regarded, for the present at least, as tentative.

In the light of the geographical knowledge that is now known to have existed in the second millennium B.C., it is no longer necessary to assume a date of composition for the Table of Nations (Gen. 10:2-32) either as early as the monarchy (for the so-called J source) or as late as the post-exilic period (for the Priestly Code). In point of fact, the absence of Persia from this Table would be extremely difficult to explain if the list had been largely compiled and edited to its extant form by priests who owed their return from exile and their presence in Judaea to the religious policy of the Persian regime. The scope of the Table of Nations depends to some extent upon the interpretation of "earth" in Genesis 10:32, which can either be "the whole world" in a comprehensive sense, the "known world" in a more restricted manner, or else some specific "country." While most expositors prefer to think of ארץ in verse 32 as implying "the known world," the fact that many of the names in the Table are as yet unidentified would indicate that a wider estimate of

---

[36] G. Ch. Aalders, *A Short Introduction to the Pentateuch*, pp. 45ff.

[37] Cf. A. Parrot, *The Flood and Noah's Ark* (1950), pp. 50ff.; R. K. Harrison, *Archaeology of the OT* (1962), pp. 9f.

the situation than that available to modern scholars fell within the purview of the ancient scribes.

Identifications in the list dealing with the descendants of Japheth that have received general, though not exclusive, scholarly assent include Gomer (*Cimmerians*), Ashkenaz (*Scythians*), Madai (*Medes*), Javan (*Ionians*), and Dodanim (*Rhodes*). Similar identifications from the list of Ham include Cush (*Ethiopia*), Sheba (*Saba*), Mizraim (*Egypt*), Caphtorim (*Cretans*), Heth (*Hittites*), and Hivites (*Hurrians*). A few accepted identifications from the list of Shem include Elam, Asshur (*Assyria*), Sheba, and Aram (*Aramaeans*).

The Table of Nations is unquestionably of ancient origin, partly because of its literary form but principally on account of its contents. It is quite possible, however, that the latter were subjected to slight scribal revision from the time of Moses onwards, since such peoples as the Cimmerians, Scythians, Philistines, and Medes do not appear in written documents until after the end of the second millennium B.C. On the other hand, these peoples obviously existed as tribes or racial groups long before they appeared in extant records, as for example with the peoples of southern Arabia, who only occur in written documents in the first millennium B.C., but who are known to have existed prior to that time. Certainly the Philistines were familiar as one group that lived in Palestine during the patriarchal period, even though they were augmented significantly by waves of immigrants at a considerably later time.

The narrative dealing with the construction of a city and a high tower at a site later known as Babel (Gen. 11:1-9) has an obviously Babylonian background, and this, combined with the fact of its early date, probably accounts for the incident being mentioned nowhere else in the Old Testament. Interpreters have generally assumed that the city, like the tower (Gen. 11:8), was incomplete at the dispersion of the population, and that the tower (מגדל) was intended to be a staged structure such as the *ziggurats* of Babylonia, which were first developed in the early third millennium B.C. While there is no archaeological evidence to date that would confirm the existence of a city at Babylon prior to the First Dynasty (*ca.* 1800 B.C.), Babylonian tradition, along with a text of Sharkalisharri, king of Agade about 2250 B.C., which mentioned his restoration of the *ziggurat* at Babylon, would seem to point clearly to the existence of an earlier sacred city on the site.[38] The name "Babel" was explained by popular etymology in terms of a similar Hebrew root בלל to imply "confusion" or "mixing." Babel thus constituted a synonym for the confusion provoked by the linguistic differences that were part of the divine punishment for the attitude of human pride displayed in the construction of the city and the tower.

[38] D. J. Wiseman, *NBD*, p. 116.

Attempts to locate the site of the tower of Babel have been made for many centuries, but with indifferent success. Some scholars have identified it with the *ziggurat* at Babylon that had been given the Sumerian name Etemenanki ("The Building of the Foundation-platform of Heaven and Earth"), and whose present site is a pit, Es-Saḥu, as deep as the original *ziggurat* was high. Other authorities have identified Babel with the ruins of a staged tower still in evidence at Borsippa (Birs Nimrud), some seven miles south-southwest of Babylon. This view is improbable for the reason that the structure involved is almost certainly from the Neo-Babylonian period. Yet another identification places the tower of Babel at Dūr-Kurigalzu (Aqar Quf), west of Baghdad, but this again is unlikely since the city was only constructed there about 1400 B.C. All that can be said on the matter with certainty is that the Biblical narrative bears all the marks of a reliable historical account of the construction of buildings that have not yet been traced.

Occidental interpreters of this narrative have not infrequently thought of the building of the *ziggurat* in terms of medieval European attempts to glorify God by the construction of a massive cathedral. Such a view rests upon a fundamental misunderstanding of what the ancient Mesopotamians had in mind when they were building their *ziggurats*. Excavations have shown that such a structure constituted the logical development of the small central shrine around which the other houses in the primitive village-settlements of the Chalcolithic period were grouped. It was intended to be the equivalent of a mountain, that is to say, an eminence of the earth with its characteristic concentration of life-giving forces. As such the *ziggurat* furnished a suitable setting for divine life and power to be manifested by creating precisely those conditions under which proper communion with God would be possible. This, however, did not entail the veneration of a transcendent deity, as in Christianity, but rather a sense of community with an essentially immanent god.

3. The Mesopotamian coalition of Genesis 14. To the present, archaeological discoveries have been unable to furnish conclusive information regarding the members of the Mesopotamian coalition that fought against the kings in the cities of the plain (Gen. 14:1ff.). Certain difficulties exist in connection with the identification both of Amraphel and the territory over which he ruled. The MT, the Samaritan Pentateuch (Gen. 14:1), the LXX, and the Syriac versions all designate him clearly as "king of Shinar," but the Samaritan Pentateuch (Gen. 14:9), the targums and the Qumran *Genesis Apocryphon* specifically record that he was king of Babel. Shinar was the country in which the great Babylonian cities of Erech and Akkad were located (Gen. 10:10), and was situated in a plain in which early migrants had settled and had founded the city and *ziggurat* of Babel (Gen. 11:2). The LXX interpreted "Shinar" (Heb. שִׁנְעָר) to mean "Babylonia" or "the land of Babylon," following the traditions of Genesis 10:10.

On philological and other grounds it is improbable that "Shinar" can be equated with "Sumer" or southern Babylonia, as some scholars have proposed. It is also interesting to note that, although the Syriac term Sen'ar designates the environs of Baghdad, no earlier name for Babylon which might correspond with "Shinar" has yet come to light. Albright suggested that the land over which Amraphel ruled might have been the west-Semitic Sangār in Syria, known to the Egyptians of the Amarna period by that name and appearing in the Tell el-Amarna tablets in the Akkadian form Shankhar.[39] However, a Syrian location for the kingdom seems unlikely, since the narrative of Genesis 14 appears to envisage Mesopotamia as the general area from which Amraphel came. Perhaps the reference is to the district of Singhar in Upper Mesopotamia, although this cannot now be known for certain.

The discovery at Susa in 1901 of the famous Code of Hammurabi led many contemporary scholars to identify Amraphel with that renowned Akkadian ruler. However, they were confronted almost immediately with some pressing philological problems which proved difficult to resolve. The "l" at the end of Amraphel was a particular matter of contention, with some scholars maintaining that it was in fact the Akkadian determinative particle "ilu" or "god." This view is improbable since in cuneiform the determinative symbol invariably precedes the name with which it is associated. If the "l" is linked with the following Hebrew word מֶלֶךְ ("king") as other scholars suggested, it destroys the sense of the phrase, which is clearly a standardized literary expression.

Other indecisive approaches to the problem included the theory that the Hebrew form 'amrāphel was actually a scribal error for 'mrphi (Ammurapi; Ḥammurabi), or that it was a compressed transcription of the Akkadian title Ammurapi-ili ("Hammurabi is my god"). Such arguments tend to posit corruptions of the text for which there is no factual evidence, and at the best they are philologically unconvincing. There would therefore appear to be no sound reason for maintaining the identification of Amraphel and Hammurabi, particularly as it remains unsubstantiated by Mesopotamian history as such.

Chedorlaomer, an ancient Elamite king who led the Mesopotamian coalition against the resurgent kings of Sodom, Gomorrah, and the other cities of the valley, is equally obscure as an historical person in extra-Biblical sources. The *Genesis Apocryphon* agreed with the pseudepigraphical *Book of Jubilees* (XIII:22) in naming Chedorlaomer as the leader of the invading Mesopotamian confederacy, but this opinion may well be dependent upon purely Biblical sources. Despite extensive investigation into the early phases of Elamite history, the names of a number of the founders of Elamite dynastic power are still unknown.

[39] Cf. *ANET*, pp. 243, 247.

The LXX form of the name is *Chadollogomor,* which implies a vocalization which is rather different from that of the Massoretes, and points to the assimilation of "r" with "l" and the pronunciation of "o" as "gho," making *Codorlaghomer.* Written in cuneiform, the Elamitic version would most probably have comprised a combination of *Kutir* (or *Kudur*), meaning "servant," and the term *Lagamar,* which appears in several Elamite texts as a divine name. The element *Kutir* (or *Kudur*) was a common Elamite word, and occurred regularly in Elamite proper names, as for example in *Kutir-Naḫḫunte. Kutir* (or *Kudur*)-*Lagamar* would thus comprise a genuine Elamitic construction meaning "servant of (the god) Lagamar," a title which could be borne quite legitimately by a ruler.

To the present, however, no individual bearing the specific name Kutir (or Kudur)-Lagamar has been recognized from extra-Biblical records of any kind. Cuneiform tablets have yielded the name of an Elamite monarch, Kudur-KU.MAL, which is now read as Kutir-nahuti (the Sumerian KU.MAL being the equivalent of the Babylonian *nāḫu*), and have spoken of him as the conqueror of Babylon. Perhaps he is to be equated with Kutir-Naḫḫunti I of Elam, who ruled about 1625 B.C., and some scholars, including Albright, have identified him with the Chedorlaomer of Genesis 14.[40]

This view, however, involves both philological and historical difficulties. It is possible to argue philologically that the form Naḫundi is the equivalent of the west-Semitic word *La'mr* (*La'nd*), but the latter with its alternative suggests the probability of confusion between the final ר and ד in the ancient Hebrew script. Quite aside from this, however, the absence of proper controls from Elamite cuneiform sources makes such an approach somewhat precarious. Historically the above identification requires a late date for Abraham, which is contrary to the evidence provided by the fate of the cities of the valley.[41]

The approximate date of the catastrophe which overtook Sodom, Gomorrah, and neighboring sites may be conjectured from the evidence supplied by pottery remains discovered at Bab edh-Dhra'. This festival site appears to have been frequented from about 2300 B.C. to about 1900 B.C., and the cessation of such visits may have coincided with the destruction of Sodom and the other cities of the valley, from which the worshippers apparently came on pilgrimages to the site. The evidence of Genesis 14 thus furnishes the important corollary that Abraham was living about 1900 B.C., or near the end of the twentieth century B.C., since he was in the vicinity when the cities perished.

[40] Albright, *BASOR,* No. 88 (1942), pp. 33ff.
[41] Cf. W. F. Albright, *BASOR,* No. 14 (1924), pp. 5ff., *AASOR,* VI (1924-25), pp. 58ff.; J. P. Harland, *BA,* V, No. 2 (1942), pp. 17ff., VI, No. 3 (1943), pp. 41ff., and in *IDB,* IV, pp. 395ff.

Suggestions by earlier Assyriologists to the effect that Chedorlaomer could well be identified with a person named Kudur-lah(gu)mal, who was mentioned in several late Babylonian legends, were based in part on the assumption that the Tudhul(a) named in one of the sources was in fact "Tidal king of nations" (Gen. 14:1). While the name Tid'al can almost certainly be identified with the Hittite name Tudhalia, it is as impossible to be sure that the "nations" over which Tidal ruled were Hittite, or even Hurrian, peoples as it is to identify Tidal himself with any degree of assurance or to place him firmly within a given chronological situation. Of the four or five Hittite kings who bore the name Tudhalia, all except the first one date from between 1400 and 1200 B.C., and therefore lived long after the date entertained for Abraham in the present work. Tudhalia I lived about 1740 B.C., which is still too late for the time of Abraham on the evidence furnished by the destruction of Sodom and Gomorrah. It is known, however, that in the early second millennium B.C., Asia Minor and northern Syria were not political unities, but were divided up among various small states and groups. Quite possibly, therefore, Tidal may have been an early Tudhalia who governed a federation of Hittite and Hurrian groups on the borders of southeast Asia Minor and northern Syria, perhaps about the nineteenth century B.C.[42]

4. *The patriarchal narratives.* The extent to which the patriarchal narratives have been illumined by the recovery of second-millennium B.C. cultural remains from Mari, Nuzu,[43] and Alalakh has been dealt with elsewhere in the present work. Accordingly it merely remains to observe that the avowed reluctance of contemporary German scholars such as Noth and von Rad to credit these narratives with a firm background of historicity is due entirely to their disinclination to face up to the implications of the archaeological evidence. No serious methodological approach to the patriarchal era can possibly afford to dispense with or neglect the evidence for the nature and vitality of second-millennium B.C. society in northern Babylon and Syria. There can be no doubt that the archaeological evidence recovered to date has brought an inestimable wealth of detail to bear upon the patriarchal narratives, and has set the traditions relating to Abraham, Isaac, and Jacob against a properly accredited background of second-millennium B.C. social life. As Albright has remarked, in no case are these patriarchal stories mere reflections of the life of Israel in the divided monarchy, as used to be maintained by most

[42] Cf. D. J. Wiseman, *NBD*, p. 1276.
[43] For Nuzu see C. H. Gordon, *The Living Past* (1941), pp. 156ff.; *IOTT*, pp. 100ff.; H. H. Rowley, *BJRL*, XXXII (1950), pp. 76f.; *BHI*, pp. 60ff. For Alalakh see D. J. Wiseman, *The Alalakh Tablets* (1953).

of the literary critics.[44] Instead, they actually go back almost a thousand years to the Middle Bronze Age.

One of the more serious misinterpretations of the Hebrew text in favor of advancing evidence for the presence of a supposed "duplicate" account can be seen in connection with the story of Joseph. Critical scholars generally have long argued for the presence of two different sources underlying the text, one of which (Gen. 37:25, 28b) recorded that Joseph was sold by his brothers to an Ishmaelite caravan which took him to Egypt, while the other (Gen. 37:28a, 36) narrated that the Midianites took Joseph from the dry cistern in which he had been placed on the advice of Reuben, and subsequently sold him to Potiphar.[45] However, the apparent contradictions can be cleared up quite readily by a proper understanding of the circumstances involved. In Egypt, the Midianites, or, more properly, Medanites (as in the Hebrew of Gen. 37:36), sold Joseph to Potiphar, who was said to have obtained him from the Ishmaelites (Gen. 39:1). While the caravan from Gilead was predominantly Ishmaelite, it also included Midianites. The latter were found in parts of Transjordan from Moab to Edom, and were linked to Abraham through Midian, son of the concubine Keturah (cf. Gen. 25:1ff.). They were desert-dwellers who were associated with both the Ishmaelites and the Medanites. It is important to notice that there is a certain degree of overlapping in the use of the terms "Medanites" and "Midianites," as also in the case of "Midianite" and "Ishmaelite." The latter is made explicit in Judges 8:24, which identified Midianites and Ishmaelites; and with regard to the former it should be observed that both Medan and Midian were spoken of as being the sons of Abraham by Keturah (Gen. 25:2; cf. 1 Chron. 1:32).

As Kitchen has pointed out,[46] the use of multiple terms in narratives is not indicative of disparate documents, but is characteristic of ancient Near Eastern stylistic usage. Evidence for an analogous occurrence of three terms within a few lines of narrative can be adduced from the *stele* of the Egyptian Sebekkhu (*ca.* 1850 B.C.), who referred to the one general enemy which he confronted on his Palestinian campaign as *Mntyw-Sst* ("Asiatic bedouin"), *Rntw ḥst* ("vile Syrians") and *'mw* ("Asiatics"). Since this source was commissioned by one man and executed as a unit, a matter that has been observed previously, there can be absolutely no question as to the possibility of underlying separate documents. In the narrative of Genesis 37:28, the word "they" refers, not to the Midianites, but to the brothers of Joseph, who were taxed with the

---

[44] Albright, *Religion in Life*, XXI, No. 4 (1952), p. 542.

[45] Cf. *DILOT*, pp. 17f.; H. E. Ryle, *The Book of Genesis*, p. 356; T. H. Robinson in *The People and the Book* (ed. A. S. Peake, 1925), pp. 153ff.; *IBOT*, p. 29; G. von Rad, *Genesis*, p. 348; A. S. Herbert, *Genesis 12-50* (1962), p. 124; E. A. Speiser, *Genesis*, p. 291.

[46] K. A. Kitchen, *NBD*, p. 657; *Ancient Orient and Old Testament*, p. 123.

deed (Gen. 45:5) when Joseph ultimately revealed his true identity to them.[47]

    ✿   ✿   ✿   ✿   ✿

Genesis, the book of beginnings, introduces the readers to the great drama of redemption. The first eleven chapters of the book may be regarded as the prologue, which is cast in universal terms. The drama proper commences with the rise of Abraham, whose position in relationship to the subsequent Israelite nation constitutes one of two principal themes upon which the Pentateuch is built. In the prologue the reader is furnished with an account of the creation of the world and of man, the incidence of sin as a universal concept, and the corollary that by definition it must always stand under divine judgment. The character of the Deity as holy and righteous is complemented by evidence of grace and mercy, one result of which is that a remnant of sinful humanity survived the drastic punishment meted out to the wicked in the Flood.

The divine answer to the iniquity of man appears in the personage of Abraham, who exemplified the moral and spiritual ideals demanded by the Creator from those who would aspire to fellowship with Him. In the drama of salvation the descendants of Abraham had a vital role to play, for they would ultimately constitute an elect and covenanted group whose responsibility it would be to witness to their pagan neighbors concerning divine mercy, grace, and power. The process by which the offspring of Abraham attained to the status of election, which comprised the second major theme of the Pentateuch, is the concern of Exodus.

On the whole the text of Genesis has been preserved in good condition, a fact that may be attributed to the degree of veneration in which the Torah was held, and the resultant care taken in the transmission of the text. In a document such as Genesis, which draws on extremely ancient sources, there are naturally some problems of interpretation and construction, such as those presented by Genesis 4:7; 14:14; 41:8; and others. Versions such as the Samaritan Pentateuch and the LXX occasionally preserve what appears to be a better reading than that found in the MT, as in Genesis 4:8; 29:34; 38:3; 47:21; 50:26; and a few others.

Supplementary Literature

Alt, A. *Der Gott der Väter.* 1929.
Böhl, F. M. Th. *Das Zeitalter Abrahams.* 1930.
Chaine, J. *Le Livre de la Genèse.* 1948.
Eichrodt, W. *Die Quellen der Genesis.* 1916.
Finn, A. H. *The Creation, Fall, and Deluge.* No date.
Kidner, D. *Genesis.* 1967.
Robast, K. *Die Genesis.* 1951.

---

[47] Cf. B. Jacob, *Das erste Buch der Tora, Genesis* (1934), pp. 706f.; G. Ch. Aalders, *A Short Introduction to the Pentateuch*, pp. 48f.; J. H. Hertz, *The Pentateuch and Haftorahs: Genesis* (1929), p. 316.

III. THE BOOK OF EXODUS

The second book of the Torah was given its name from the opening
words ואלה שמות ("and these are the names"), which were sometimes
shortened by the Jews to שמות ("names"). It was the LXX that designated the work according to its principal theme, Ἔξοδος (Exod. 19:1),
and this was followed by the Vulgate (*Exodus*) and the English versions.

Exodus serves as a connecting link between the narratives of Genesis
and the subsequent legislative material of the Pentateuch. It deals with
the fortunes of the Hebrews after the propitious times of Joseph, and its
principal concern is with the events leading up to, and immediately
following, the Exodus from Egypt. Although the narratives appear to be
set against the background of the Avaris era, the chronological picture is
outlined in only the most general terms, consistent with the Hebrew
treatment of history as a sequence of events and not a series of dates.[1]

The book can be analyzed as follows:

I. The Hebrews in Bondage and Preparation for Their Deliverance,
   ch. 1-12
   A. Preliminary genealogy, 1:1-6
   B. The bondage in Egypt, 1:7-22
   C. The childhood of Moses, 2:1-10
   D. Biography of Moses, 2:11–4:26
   E. The afflicting of the Israelites, 4:27–6:13
   F. Genealogical table, 6:14-27
   G. Moses and Aaron before Pharaoh, 6:28–7:25
   H. The plagues of Egypt, 8:1–11:10
II. The Exodus and the Journey to Mount Sinai, ch. 13–19
   A. Institution of the Passover, 12:1-28, 43-50
   B. Final plague and withdrawal from Egypt, 12:29-42, 51
   C. Ordinances concerning firstlings and unleavened bread, 13:1-16
   D. Preliminaries to departure from Egypt, 13:17-22

---

[1] W. J. Martin, *NBD*, p. 404.

B. COMPILATION AND AUTHORSHIP

According to the tenets held by the members of the critical school, the authorship of Exodus was to be conceived of in terms of the hypothetical documents J, E, and P,[2] to which Eissfeldt added his "Lay" source,[3] as has been remarked above. Although Pfeiffer could doubtless have adduced some evidence for the presence of his "S" or "Southern" source in Exodus, he did not pursue it beyond Genesis. All critical reconstructions, of course, imply oral transmission of the material—a position that is quite remarkable in view of the repeated references to writings and records—and go on to postulate a prolonged interval of time between the occurrence of the events and the writing, despite the evidence of the ancient world to the contrary. An equally common critical presupposition involved the view that the customs and rites

[2] So A. H. McNeile, *The Book of Exodus* (1937), p. ii; *DILOT*, pp. 22ff.; *OTFD*, pp. 99ff.

[3] *Einleitung in das AT* (1956 ed.), pp. 230ff.; cf. *IDB*, II, p. 370, *ETOT*, pp. 194ff.

contained in Exodus were antedated and represented as having already been propounded and put into operation in the Mosaic age.[4]

To support a view of the essentially fraudulent nature of such a composition it was also a commonplace procedure in critical circles to remark that the narrators enriched the narrative material from their own imagination, with the result that the traditions acquired a miraculous element in the centuries that intervened between the original events and the times in which the composers of the various sources lived.[5] The unlikely event of Moses' being an historical figure in any acceptable sense of that term was coupled with assertions as to his complete lack of ability to write down a series of moral precepts such as that which is found in the Decalogue. Particular criticisms were also directed at the Tabernacle, whose historicity was uncompromisingly rejected by all followers of Wellhausen.

Those who supported the Mosaicity of Exodus were generally ready to admit that it was not by any means written as a continuous narrative; that there may well be indications of editorial activity, some perhaps emerging from the post-Mosaic era, and that quite probably the earliest portion of the book to be committed to writing after the Decalogue and the Covenant Code was the Song of Moses and Miriam (Exod. 15:1-21). It is also well within the bounds of possibility that there were later insertions in the Covenant Code (a matter which will be considered subsequently) and apparent dislocations of the text. Conservative scholars also recognized that archaeological discoveries have furnished evidence for the antiquity of the Tabernacle concept, in direct contradiction to the Wellhausenian view, and that the narratives of the Wilderness wanderings present some perplexing problems of fact and interpretation for the members of the critical school.

Furthermore the critical hypothesis, which unfortunately does not rest upon quite as substantial a basis of argument as Eissfeldt[6] and others have supposed, contains some curiously self-contradictory elements in relationship to Exodus. As Martin has pointed out, it is strange that P, which according to literary-critical theory was written from a priestly standpoint, does so little in the book to enhance the status of the priesthood.[7] Instead it is Moses, the political leader, who remains the great hero, while the one who allows the people to lapse into idolatry is Aaron, the priest, whom Moses rebukes for his infidelity and whom he subsequently reinstates. This, as the narratives of Exodus make clear, was not the only lapse on the part of the leader of the priestly cult. Furthermore, if the whole corpus of material was arranged in such a

---

[4] E.g. S. R. Driver, *The Book of Exodus* (1918), p. lxv.

[5] McNeile, *The Book of Exodus*, p. cxii.

[6] *Einleitung in das AT*, p. 288.

[7] W. J. Martin, *NBD*, p. 405.

manner as to furnish an ideal picture of the theocracy as it was supposed to have existed in the Mosaic age,[8] it can only be observed that, in the light of the stubbornness and intractability of the people, the entire project miscarried to an alarming degree.

The view that Moses was the substantial author of Exodus is based partly upon the fact that making a direct recording of happenings is alleged to have been the regular custom of Moses, and this tradition is in complete harmony with what is now known about the transmission of events by scribes in Near Eastern antiquity. Thus it would appear from Exodus 17:14 that Moses recorded the battle with Amalek immediately after the event. The "book" thus produced would correspond to the "annals" of Egypt and other ancient Near Eastern nations, in which, by ancient custom, all events worthy of note were recorded. The most accessible, and doubtless the preferred, material available in the Wilderness for making such records would be leather. In Exodus 24:4 Moses is said to have written "all the words of the Lord" in a manner suggesting that he transcribed the contents of the Decalogue and the so-called Covenant Code as he remembered them onto some kind of durable material. In addition, in Exodus 34:27, Moses was given a similar, though rather different, set of regulations, and on that occasion he was instructed to commit them to writing, presumably while he was still in the Sinai region.

The actual process by which the extant book of Exodus was compiled is, of course, entirely unknown, but in the light of ancient Near Eastern scribal practices it may have taken somewhat of the following form. The compiler, whether Moses himself or some such individual as Joshua or Eleazar who undertook the task either while Moses was still alive or immediately after his death, would have as a basic source-residuum the Decalogue and the Book of the Covenant, the latter perhaps being somewhat shorter than its extant form; the Song of Moses and Miriam, the various ordinances concerning sabbath observance, and the sources dealing with the specifications for the Tabernacle, the detailed contents of which would seem to indicate that they were already in written form at a very early period. Whatever elements of this corpus were still in oral form would be written down at that time, and the sources assembled into some kind of order with the aim of covering the general sequence of events rather than conforming to a precise chronological order or pattern.

The dominant theme of the document was, of course, the deliverance from Egypt in the supreme event of the Exodus, but in order to preserve the pattern of internal coherence the compiler or compilers evidently thought it necessary to introduce material that would constitute a brief prelude to the account of the Exodus itself. This section, which com-

[8] Driver, *The Book of Exodus*, p. xii.

prises Exodus 1:1-17, served to establish the identity of the enslaved Israelites, thereby sequentially linking the Joseph narratives in Genesis with the bondage in Egypt and introducing the personage of Moses the deliverer. Quite possibly one section of the scroll that contained Exodus ended at this point, and before another one began with the narrative of events in Egypt, a list dealing principally with the family tree of Moses and Aaron was inserted so as to ground these two important individuals in the history of the Hebrew people.[9]

In some respects it might have been better from a sheer narrative standpoint if the section containing the names in Exodus 6:14-27 had been inserted after Exodus 4:26, although even in its present position the continuity of the narrative as a whole is far from being seriously disturbed. Quite possibly Exodus 6:10-13 and 6:28—7:7 point to the place where one roll ended and another began. This may be adduced from the similarities between them, which would make it possible for the second roll to be read intelligibly yet independently of its immediate precursor. A somewhat similar situation may be said to exist in the relationship of 2 Chronicles 36:22f. to Ezra 1:1-3a, where the former is utilized as an elaborate "catch-line" in the accredited Mesopotamian manner so as to insure the continuity of the narrative.

What appears to have been a new section of scroll carried on the story of Exodus 12:28, where there is a possible dislocation of the text. Exodus 12:43-50 may well have come immediately after Exodus 12:28, so as to preserve the general order of events relating to the institution of the Passover. This would then be followed chronologically by the final plague and the departure from Egypt, as recorded in Exodus 12:29-42, 51. It is possible that Exodus 12:42 is an editorial comment added by a later hand during processes of revision, and may perhaps date from the time of Samuel. Exodus 13:1-16, which deals with ordinances concerning firstlings and unleavened bread, also seems to be out of place in relation to the strict order of events, but while the passage in question may not have been communicated to Moses at the precise moment that its insertion into the extant composition might suggest, it was clearly important priestly material, and as such was associated intimately with the text of the Passover enactment. As Stafford Wright has commented, the historian has to decide continually whether to arrange his history by subjects or in a strict chronological order, and frequently he is forced to compromise between the two in his finished narrative.[10] So in this instance, a number of Passover regulations of early date were inserted into a gap in the story.

Perhaps another roll of the history commenced with Exodus 13:17-22, which narrated the preliminary movement of the Israelites away from

[9] J. S. Wright, *EQ*, XXV (1953), p. 12.
[10] *Ibid.*, p. 13.

Egyptian territory. As with the previous proposed roll, it commenced with an introductory section covering much of the same ground as Exodus 12:37-41 in order to preserve the general sequence of events. The narrative then continued to the giving of the Decalogue at Sinai (Exod. 20:1-17), but to what extent it is possible to say that this passage marked the conclusion of another section of leather scroll is unknown. What can be asserted, however, is that the contents of Exodus 20:22—23:33 once existed as a separate document, the so-called Covenant Code, or else were extant in conjunction with the Decalogue, since in Exodus 24:4 Moses wrote down "all the words of the Lord," presumably in order to formulate the record of the Covenant that had been instituted at that time.[11]

There seems little doubt that, in view of the fundamental importance for Hebrew faith and destiny of the events at Sinai, Moses intertwined history and laws in his narratives from the very beginning. Nor can it be reasonably objected that this procedure was entirely accidental, since it was of obvious importance for the revelation of God to be firmly grounded in temporal events, and for the faith of Israel to be regulated in terms of moral and social legislative concepts. The most that can be said concerning the length of this proposed section of the Exodus is that it may have concluded either about Exodus 19:25 or Exodus 20:18-21. It is not outside the bounds of possibility, however, that the latter was the introduction to a new section of the scroll. The narrative of chapter 24:1-8 concerning the ratification of the Covenant is closely associated with the Decalogue and the Book of the Covenant for obvious reasons, but whether Exodus 24:9-11 also belongs to this period or is a somewhat later insertion is open to some question.

The historical sequence was continued in Exodus 24:12 with the account of Moses' return to Sinai, and it may be that still another section of the Exodus scroll commenced with Exodus 25:1, when a complete roll of regulations concerning the Tabernacle was inserted. Apparently Moses received this material in oral form only at Mount Sinai, but such was its importance for the religious life of the nation that the details were preserved with meticulous care and inserted at the most appropriate point in the large narrative, which probably terminated with Exodus 31:11, 18. The brief section comprising Exodus 31:12-17, which dealt with certain sabbath enactments, may constitute a dislocation, and perhaps belonged originally in some manner to the fragment represented by Exodus 35:1-3.

A resumption of the historical sequences was undertaken with the narratives dealing with the golden calf (Exod. 32:1), and included the sequel to this act of apostasy, along with a further group of regulations

[11] For theories concerning the relation of Moses to the Decalogue see H. H. Rowley, *BJRL*, XXXIV (1952), pp. 81ff., reprinted in his *Men of God*, pp. 1ff.

given at Sinai. It would appear from the evidence presented by Exodus 34:27 that these enactments also existed in independent form at one period, and this document may have constituted the source upon which Moses drew in compiling this particular section of the Exodus scroll. If an additional break is made after Exodus 34:28, the rest of the book can be taken as a record of how the details prescribed on Mount Sinai were carried out. The entire roll concluded with a colophon dealing with the completed Tabernacle and the narrative of the guiding cloud (Exod. 40:36-38), a theme that was picked up again in Numbers 9:15-23.

Any conjecture as to how Exodus arrived at approximately its extant form ought to consider that post-Mosaic and non-Mosaic additions may be present in the text. This is not a matter of very great concern, however, since it is now well known that ancient Near Eastern scribes regularly revised ancient material in certain matters of style and content when making fresh copies, and saw no incompatibility between such activity and the attribution of pristine authorship to the material under revision. Post-Mosaic elements in Exodus have generally been thought to include Exodus 6:26f.; 16:33ff.; and 16:36. In connection with the first of these references, it has commonly been said that one would only write of individuals in such a manner if they were already dead, but as Young has pointed out, these two verses follow a genealogy, and in effect they comprise a colophon to the list, with the meaning of "this is the genealogy of Moses and Aaron to whom God spoke."[12] Thus when verse 26 is compared with verse 14 of the same chapter, it carries exactly the same force as verse 27 when it is compared with verse 13, thus raising some doubt as to whether or not it is actually post-Mosaic.

In Exodus 16:33-35, it is the phrase "before the testimony" that occasions the difficulty, as well as the reference to the Israelites eating manna for a forty-year period. The "testimony" comprised the Covenant tablets, which, according to the strict sequence of the narratives, had not yet been given to the nation. However, there is nothing in the reference that would necessarily preclude its insertion into the Exodus scroll within the lifetime of Moses. But if it is a genuine post-Mosaic scribal addition, it may be that Exodus 16:34-36 constituted an editorial comment designed to explain the significance of manna for the benefit of future generations of Israelites. The passage merely states that the pot of manna[13] was preserved near the tablets of the Covenant, and that manna had been the intermittent food of the Israelites throughout the generation of wandering in the Wilderness. Neither of these facts requires a particularly late date.

In Exodus 16:36, the gloss explaining the value of an omer has been thought to indicate a time of composition when such information was no

---

[12] *YIOT*, pp. 72f.
[13] On manna see K. A. Kitchen, *NBD*, p. 780.

longer current. Against this contention it merely needs to be observed that the word עמר is used throughout the chapter (vv. 16, 18, 22, 32, 33, 36) in a manner which would make its significance immediately evident to anyone who was at all acquainted with the phenomena of the wanderings. The word does not appear elsewhere in the Old Testament. The term was employed in a twofold sense of the measure itself (Exod. 16:18, 32f.) and the amount measured (Exod. 16:16, 22, 36) in such a way that, even if Exodus 16:36 is a part or the whole of an editorial gloss, the homogeneity of the narrative is preserved without apparent difficulty. In this as in other sections of Exodus it is important for the greatest caution to be exercised before pronouncements are made as to the post-Mosaic nature of specific passages, since given literary phenomena are not necessarily amenable to explanation in terms of one situation only.

With regard to the possibility of non-Mosaic interpolations, it is apparent that Exodus 11:3, which recorded that Moses was a person of high esteem in the land of Egypt, can hardly be ascribed to the great legislator without implications of pride and self-esteem, at least for the occidental mind. But here again there is very little difficulty in supposing that this is a characteristic redactional gloss, originating perhaps as a marginal comment and being subsequently incorporated into the text during the normal processes of scribal revision.

It is impossible to overestimate the importance of the first half of Exodus for the faith and history of the Hebrew nation. One weakness of the Graf-Wellhausen theory of Pentateuchal literary origins was that it contrived to diminish the majesty of the events which occurred at Yam Suph and Mount Sinai in favor of an emphasis upon alleged documentary sources whose nature and content were a matter of considerable dispute in those very critical circles from which they had emerged. In a reaction against the purely documentary approach, Pedersen declared his independence of the Wellhausenian theory by suggesting that Exodus 1—15 comprised the central core of the Pentateuch, and that it was derived ultimately from cultic ceremony.[14] For him the material comprised a cult-legend constituting a separate entity, and was not the result of a mechanical combination of independent parallel expositions. Inequalities in the text could not be explained satisfactorily simply by the assumption of separate "sources," for the narrative was not so much a straightforward history as a celebration of the divine victory by the worshipping people in the Passover festival. For Pedersen the story of the Exodus was intended primarily to describe those exploits in which God was glorified and a nation was made great.

While this view went far towards correcting the gross imbalance of the Wellhausen school, it raised certain important issues of its own. One of

[14] J. Pedersen, *Israel, Its Life and Culture*, III-IV (1940), pp. 726ff.

these was the question as to whether the cultus actually originated the Exodus material, or whether it simply used it in a variety of ways. Since liturgical forms in general tend to draw upon already existing material, the question of origins once again comes very much to the fore. Since Exodus speaks specifically of certain written sources, it is quite difficult to see precisely how the "legend" can have originated with the cultus as such. While liturgical movements and oral-traditionist circles may perhaps play a useful part in perpetuating certain historic events of profound spiritual significance, it is a very different matter to say they are responsible for creating either the tradition or the material underlying it. The principal point that Pedersen appears to be making over against the classical analytical theory is that since the material is, on his understanding, of a liturgical character, it is incorrect to assume that literary criticism can solve the basic problem regarding its form. Given this premise he is undoubtedly correct in his conclusion.

Much the same questions arise in connection with the liturgical interpretation of Exodus 20–24 as favored by von Rad.[15] For him the entire Sinai episode was a cultic legend, whose life-situation comprised a cultic festival embracing the themes of exhortation, recitation of the Decalogue and Covenant Code, the promise of blessing, and the conclusion of the Covenant. However valid this interpretation may be, it is, as Wright has pointed out, impossible to assume without question that the tradition, even in all of its written form, was created by the cultic ceremonies and their officiants.[16]

A nihilistic view of the origin of Hebrew tradition, based upon a fairly orthodox form of liberal criticism, was espoused by M. Noth, who has appropriated some of the results of the Uppsala school of Engnell to his own theories without, however, abandoning the documentary approach to Pentateuchal problems.[17] Noth maintained that the traditions of the Pentateuch were only to be understood against the background of a supposed amphictyonic society in Palestine during the Judges period. While the five major themes of the Exodus, the entrance into the Promised Land, the assurance to the patriarchs, the Wilderness wanderings, and the Sinai revelation can be isolated from the corpus of tradition, the whole sequence was held to be independent of the figure of Moses, who for Noth was only a minor tribal sheik.[18] Aside from his dependence upon a totally inadequate methodology (whose erroneous nature is by no means offset by the recognition that the alleged sources J and E both go back to a common original source or *Grundlage*),[19] Noth's

[15] G. von Rad, *Das formgeschichtliche Problem des Hexateuchs* (1938), reprinted in *Gesammelte Studien zum AT* (1958), pp. 9ff.

[16] G. E. Wright, *IDB*, II, p. 195.

[17] Noth, *Überlieferungsgeschichte des Pentateuch* (1948).

[18] *Ibid.*, pp. 190f.

[19] *Ibid.*, pp. 40ff.; cf. his *Exodus* (1962), p. 10 *passim*.

application of the *Überlieferungsgeschichtliche* method defeats its own purpose in making it clear that, for him, the *Überlieferung* has actually no real *Geschichte* at all.

C. THE MATERIAL OF EXODUS

1. Moses. The vagueness that characterized the attitude of the early critical scholars towards the personage of Moses still persists, unfortunately, in a good many quarters. No doubt these writers were eminently justified in protesting against the rabbinic concept of the great lawgiver as a quasi-divine being, an image that is in no way either encouraged or fostered in the Pentateuch itself. But in rejecting it they also contrived to dispense with the personality of the man who towered over all other Israelites in the second millennium B.C. His name, מֹשֶׁה, which is a play on the root *mšh*, "to draw out," was probably given to him by his mother, since the pun is Semitic in form.[20] The name does not appear to be the Amarna Age Egyptian word *ms(w)*, or "child," nor does it seem to correspond at all to the related grammatical form in a compound name such as *Har-mose*. It is possible that it constitutes an ellipsis for a longer form, or it may have been a strictly Semitic designation that was assimilated in some manner to the common word *ms(w)* by the Egyptian adoptive mother of Moses.

The vast increase within recent years of knowledge concerning the conditions of life in ancient Egypt has furnished an enriched background for an examination of the early life of Moses. In the New Kingdom period there were numerous royal residences and *harîms* in various parts of Egypt including the eastern Delta region, where ladies of noble blood resided along with royal concubines and other personnel.[21] The "daughter of pharaoh" who rescued the infant from the river would be the adolescent offspring of one of the pharaohs by a concubine or some lesser paramour, and not one of the chief princesses of full royal blood. Children of the *harîm*, especially male princes, were frequently educated under the supervision of the *harîm* overseer, and at a rather later stage the princes were placed in the care of tutors, who saw to it that their charges were educated by the priestly caste in reading and writing, the transcription of classical texts, civil administration, and in certain physical accomplishments.[22] On completing their course of instruction the royal princes could serve in a variety of capacities, either with the armed forces, the civil service, or in one of the numerous provincial strongholds of Egyptian religion.

---

[20] K. A. Kitchen, *NBD*, p. 843; on the problem of the name see A. H. Gardiner, *JAOS*, LVI (1936), pp. 192ff.; J. G. Griffiths, *JNES*, XII (1953), pp. 225ff.

[21] Cf. R. A. Caminos, *Literary Fragments in the Hieratic Script* (1956), pp. 19ff.

[22] Cf. F. L. Griffiths and P. E. Newberry, *El Bersheh* (1894), II, p. 40.

In the matter of writing ability, which earlier generations of liberal scholars refused to consider in relation to Moses, it has now been made abundantly clear by archaeological discoveries that a number of scripts were available for use by a literate person in the New Kingdom period. As a Semite, Moses would have experienced no difficulty whatever in using the simple linear proto-Canaanite alphabet for purposes of communication. The fact that such a script was freely utilized in Egyptian territory some two centuries before the time of Moses has been illustrated by the discovery of early fifteenth-century B.C. informal notations and dedications by Semitic captives from the Egyptian east Delta region who were being employed to work the Sinai turquoise mines.[23]

Even more eloquent testimony to the use of the "proto-Sinaitic" linear script by Semites in Egypt was furnished by an ostracon recovered from the Valley of the Queens at Thebes, some 350 miles south of Palestine and the eastern Delta region.[24] As Kitchen has stated, if mere workmen or their foremen at Theban tomb-sites and Sinai mines had no inhibitions about employing this script for mundane lists and religious memorials, it is both unwarranted and unrealistic to ascribe precisely those inhibitions to the eventual leader of an embryo nation, especially one conditioned in Egyptian attitudes to the written word, in favor of a theoretical oral tradition which is patently at variance with the usage of the ancient Near East.[25] In the light of the foregoing evidence, the suggestions of Nielsen that such a script ought to be considered as limited to specialist usage is particularly ludicrous.[26]

With regard to the topography of the early chapters of Exodus, it can be said that there was nothing especially unusual about the escape route that Moses chose when fleeing from Egypt (Exod. 2:15). In taking an easterly direction across the border he was following the time-honored route of Sinuhe, who himself also had left Egypt hurriedly some 600 years earlier,[27] and one which was commonly used by runaway slaves later on in the thirteenth century B.C.[28] If the reference in Exodus 1:11 to the building, or reconstruction, of Pithom and Rameses by Hebrew forced labor is to the period of rebuilding under Rameses II (ca. 1290-1224 B.C.), it alludes to one of the most active and brilliant eras in the whole spectrum of Egyptian history. During this time Rameses II moved his capital from Thebes to Avaris, and entered upon

---

[23] Albright, BASOR, No. 110 (1948), pp. 12f., 22.
[24] Cf. J. Leibovitch, Annales du Service des Antiquités de L'Égypte, XL (1940), p. 119, fig. 26, and pls. xvi, xix:50; Albright, BASOR, No. 110 (1948), p. 12 n. 33.
[25] K. A. Kitchen, NBD, p. 844.
[26] E. Nielsen, Oral Tradition (1954), pp. 24ff.
[27] ANET, p. 19.
[28] ANET, p. 259.

a program of reconstruction and expansion, the nature of which has become evident as a result of excavations at the site.[29]

That Moses should be able to gain ready access to the pharaoh, particularly since Tanis-Avaris was located in the northeast Delta region, is not at all surprising in view of the way in which people were able to present petitions freely to Rameses II, as recorded in Papyrus Anastasi III.[30] Work-journals belonging to the New Kingdom period have furnished, among other reasons for absenteeism, the offering of sacrifices by workmen to their gods,[31] and in view of the widespread nature of animal cult-worship in the eastern Delta region it is not in the least unrealistic to suppose that the Hebrews could request, and expect to receive (Exod. 8:26f.; 10:9, 25f.), a three-day absence from work in order to celebrate their own religious feast in the Wilderness without at the same time provoking Egyptian religious antagonism.[32]

2. *The ten plagues.* The early exponents of the literary-critical analysis of the Pentateuch professed to find evidence of duplicate accounts in the narratives dealing with the plagues of Egypt. According to Driver[33] this comprised the terms of the command addressed to Moses, the request made of Pharaoh, the description of the plague, and the formula that expressed the obstinacy of Pharaoh, all of which were supposed to agree frequently with corresponding differences in the sections of Exodus 3:1 –7:13, which the members of the critical school had assigned "on independent grounds" to P and JE. A careful examination of the text, however, shows that the close sequences of the narrative indicate the very opposite of underlying multiple sources. Thus, while the command in Exodus 7:15 was given to Moses, it was executed by Aaron (Exod. 7: 19f.) in strict accordance with the agreement in Exodus 7:1f., where God appointed Aaron as the spokesman-prophet for Moses. The theoretical basis of the chapter is thus a unity, a fact borne out by the development of the narrative. Although there are slight variations of phraseology in evidence, they are obviously merely stylistic considerations, and any attempt to employ them as indications of underlying duplicate material constitutes an improper use of the textual evidence.

Against the contention that in one record the description of the plagues is given at some length, whereas in the other it is very brief, it only needs to be remarked that here again there is stylistic variation evident without any essential difference in the narrative content. In the case of six of the first nine plagues, a formal demand was made of Pharaoh for the release of the people. In the account of the sixth and

---

[29] Cf. P. Montet, *Les nouvelles fouilles de Tanis* (1929-1933).

[30] P. Montet, *L'Égypte et la Bible*, p. 71; ANET, p. 471.

[31] A. Erman, *Life in Ancient Egypt* (1894), pp. 124f.

[32] P. Montet, *L'Égypte et la Bible*, pp. 99ff.

[33] *DILOT*, p. 25.

ninth plagues, the record of the preceding affliction terminated with the statement that Pharaoh refused to let the captive Israelites go free. Consistent with this pattern is the fact that the first six plagues were announced beforehand, and that in four instances they took effect as Moses stretched out his hand with his rod. This also occurred in connection with the third plague, which was not spoken of to Pharaoh. In the two remaining descriptions where the plague was not announced beforehand, mention was made either of the hands of Moses stretched towards the sky (the ninth plague), or of handfuls of ashes sprinkled skywards (the sixth plague). Stylistic diversity can certainly be granted in these descriptions, but there is clearly nothing to support the theory of an interwoven duplicate account of the plagues.[34]

A similar explanation can be given for the use of two different verbs, "to make heavy" (כבד) (Exod. 7:14; 8:15, 32; 9:7, 34; 10:1) and "to make strong" (חזק) (Exod. 7:22; 8:19; 9:12; 11:10), to describe the "hardening" of the will of Pharaoh. Quite obviously a process is involved in which a man whose will was slow to be affected gradually became first stubborn and then outrightly defiant, as a study of the incidence of these terms in the Hebrew text clearly indicates.

In conclusion it can be said that the critical presuppositions themselves are inconsistent, for the alleged distinguishing traits as related to the foregoing material do not always correspond with the theory. For example, the Hebrew of Exodus 8:5, which is supposed to restrict the divine command to Moses alone, actually mentions the name of Aaron explicitly as well, a fact which is also true for the Hebrew of Exodus 8:8, 12; 9:27; and 10:3, 8, 16. To eliminate the troublesome words "and Aaron" by the simple expedient of attributing them to a later editor, as was commonly undertaken by critical scholars in order to bolster the theory, is as unwarranted as it is unnecessary on a straightforward interpretation of the textual evidence. Such tiny literary fragments of the plague-accounts as would constitute a part of the hypothetical documentary sources and the schematic uniformity of features postulated for them correspond to no known ancient Near Eastern scribal or literary phenomena, making the unitary view of the plague narratives the only one that can be related logically and factually to observable physical and literary occurrences.

3. The revelation of the Divine Name. A great deal of discussion has surrounded the revelation of the Divine Name in Exodus 3:14 and 6:3.[35] The latter passage furnished the first "clue" to the distinguishing of the

---

[34] For the plague phenomena see G. Hort, ZAW, LXIX (1957), pp. 84ff., LXX (1958), pp. 48ff.

[35] For the literature see P. van Imschoot, *Théologie de l'Ancien Testament* (1954), p. 7; Th. C. Vriezen, *Theologie des AT in Grundzügen* (1956), pp. 164ff.

various alleged Pentateuchal documents.[36] In view of the common assumption that there are "different" names for God in the Pentateuch it should be noted that the Torah in particular and the Old Testament in general confine themselves to one *name* only, *YHWH*, and utilize all the others as titles or descriptions of deity. Ignoring this rather elementary fact, the members of the liberal school developed their theoretical approach on the basis that, while Exodus 6:3 stated that the name *YHWH* had not been known to the patriarchs, it appeared freely in the narratives concerning their lives. The inherent contradiction thus entertained was crystallized by Rowley as follows:

> Obviously it cannot be true that God was not known to Abraham by the name Yahweh [Exod. 6:3] and that He was known to him by that name [Gen. 15:2, 7]. To this extent there is a flat contradiction that cannot be resolved by any shift.[37]

Part of the problem lies in the fact that most English-speaking authors have taken the verses at their face value as they stand in the English versions of the Bible, and as far as Exodus 6:3 is concerned, this is an unfortunate situation, as will be shown presently.

With respect to the tetragrammaton *YHWH*, where considerations of sanctity demanded the substitution of Adonai in articulation, its pronunciation in the form "Yahweh" was arrived at from transliterations of the name into Greek in early Christian writings. Thus Clement of Alexandria preserved the form *iaoue*,[38] while Theodoret favored the rendering *iabe*.[39] There can be no question that the name is connected etymologically with the Hebrew word היה, "to be," or more preferably with an earlier variant form of the root הוה. However, it can no longer be regarded as an imperfect causative form of the root הוה, but must be considered instead as a regular substantive in which the root הוה is preceded by the preformative י.[40] As a proper noun it constitutes the name of a Person, in contrast with titles such as Elyon, El Elyon, and Elohim. The name emphasizes the being or existence of God in personal terms, and thus brings Him into relationship with other, human, personalities.

It may be noted in passing that the form "Jehovah" resulted from the transcribed vowels of Adonai being combined with the consonants of the

[36] Cf. J. Skinner, *The Divine Names in the Book of Genesis*, p. 171; A. H. McNeile, *The Book of Exodus*, pp. cxiii, 34.

[37] H. H. Rowley, *The Biblical Doctrine of Election* (1950), p. 25; cf. his *The Rediscovery of the OT* (1945), p. 60, *The Growth of the OT* (1950), pp. 20f., *The Unity of the Bible* (1953), p. 25, *The Faith of Israel* (1956), pp. 41f.

[38] *Stromat.*, V, 6, 34; cf. A. Deissmann, *Bibelstudien* (1895), p. 11; W. W. von Baudissin, *Kyrios*, II (1929), p. 216.

[39] *Quaestiones in Exodum*, I, p. 133.

[40] L. Köhler and W. Baumgartner, *Lexicon in Veteris Testamenti Libros* (1953), I, pp. 368f.; cf. L. Köhler, *Vom Hebräischen Lexikon* (1950), pp. 17f.

tetragrammaton *YHWH*, a form that is first attested from about A.D. 1100. Since the original pronunciation of *YHWH* is unknown, any modern vocalization must be regarded as tentative at the best.[41] While most contemporary scholars dislike the form "Jehovah," and prefer to use "Yahweh" or some similar transcription, it should be observed that the former is at least a genuine hybrid, and its long tradition of usage in English ought to insure it at least some place in modern literature dealing with the Old Testament.

The statement in Exodus 6:3 that God was the *Elohim* of the antecedents of Moses immediately suggests that the latter would be acquainted with the name of the family deity. The question of Moses in Exodus 3:13 should be interpreted as an attempt to investigate the character or meaning of the name, since it is introduced by means of the interrogative particle *māh*, "What?", and not by the particle *mî*, "Who?" which is the normal manner of inquiring as to the name of someone.[42] The following verse raises three possibilities of interpretation: first that the name of God is *Ehyeh*, secondly that it is *Ehyeh asher Ehyeh*, and finally that it is *YHWH*. Earlier generations of critical scholars supposed that there had been a conflation of several sources at this point, but there is absolutely no textual evidence that can be adduced to support this view. An alternative approach is to think of the three expressions as correlative, and intended by the original author to explain each other.

In a comprehensive survey of the problems presented by this verse, Reisel accepted the traditional answer that *Ehyeh* is the clue to the entire situation, and held that it posits a relationship between itself and the recurring phrase, "I am the God of your father(s) . . . ," thus placing the Name directly in the context of the Covenant.[43] The root *hyh* has generally been understood in the static sense of existence, as in the Latin phrase *Ego sum qui sum*, but a more dynamic interpretation sees the expression as an example of *paronomasia*, where two verbs of related origin are used to emphasize the unity of action inherent in the basic verb-concept. On such an interpretation God would be actively engaged in revealing Himself as the God of creation and the Covenant.

Reisel favored a compromise between the static and dynamic approaches in order to relate satisfactorily the concepts of divine existence and readiness.[44] However, his suggestion as to "readiness" seems to interpret the play on words in Exodus 3:14 inadequately, since the emphasis appears to be on the fact that God was already at work on behalf of His people. Buber is nearer the true meaning in his translation,

---

[41] On this see M. Reisel, *The Mysterious Name of Y.H.W.H.* (1957), pp. 56ff.

[42] M. Buber, *Moses* (1946), p. 48; cf. J. A. Motyer, *The Revelation of the Divine Name* (1959), pp. 17ff.

[43] M. Reisel, *op. cit.*, pp. 6ff.

[44] *Ibid.*, pp. 18ff.

"I will be as I will be," and in his suggestion that the expression contains the assurance of continuing divine power and enduring presence with the Israelites in the process of their deliverance.[45]

The sequel in Exodus 6:2f. has been misconstrued by adherents of the documentary theory to the point where it has been regarded as a duplicate version of the account in chapter 3. Even a brief comparison will show that such is far from being the case, for there is no reference to a burning bush, no desert scene, and no parting from Jethro. The locale is Egypt, there is no reluctance expressed by Moses, and his partner in the enterprise is his brother Aaron, making the narrative a continuation of that found in chapter three, and not a "duplicate" of it. This passage contains the crux of the problem relating to the revelation of the Divine Name. As observed earlier, it not merely furnished the "clue" to the distinguishing of the imagined underlying documents, but also led to the commonly accepted critical opinion that the patriarchs did not know the name *YHWH*. A break with the latter tradition was made by Reisel, who based his arguments in part upon the assertion that *yādhaʿ* means "to acknowledge" as well as "to know," and that *nōdhaʿtî*, which he retained in preference to the general critical emendation of *hôdhaʿtî*, does not mean "I have made known," but "I have manifested."[46] On such a textual foundation Reisel interpreted the verse in the sense that the promises made to the patriarchs were now being realized.

Clearly the problems presented by Exodus 6:3 are not as simple as the straightforward rendering of most English versions would appear to suggest. In the light of general Semitic usage it is possible to interpret the word "name" as expressive of "honor" or "character," so that when God revealed Himself as El Shaddai, it was with the intention of furnishing the patriarchs with the insight into the divine character which was appropriate to that title. A rather different approach has been suggested by Martin, who interpreted the text in terms of the presence of an elliptical interrogative, and rendered it, "for did I not let my name *YHWH* be known to them?"[47] If C. H. Gordon is correct in his belief that the Hebrew word *loʾ* frequently approximates its English literal equivalent, the verse might well be rendered, "but by my name *YHWH*, behold, I was known to them."

In the light of the foregoing discussion the present writer would tend to follow Motyer, in rendering Exodus 6:3 as follows, "And God spoke to Moses, saying unto him: I am YHWH. And I manifested myself to Abraham, to Isaac and to Jacob in the character of El Shaddai, but in the character expressed by my name YHWH I did not make myself

---

[45] M. Buber, *Moses*, pp. 39ff.
[46] M. Reisel, *op. cit.*, pp. 27ff.
[47] W. J. Martin, *Stylistic Criteria and the Analysis of the Pentateuch*, pp. 17f., and in *NBD*, p. 405.

known to them,"[48] with the reservation that the elliptical interrogative rendering suggested by Martin may well be probable as an alternative. Such an approach does not deny to the patriarchs the knowledge of the name *YHWH*, though it may well preclude knowledge of the significance of that name in such circles.[49] It is in accordance with proper Near Eastern methodology, and it makes possible a theological synthesis of Genesis and Exodus that is in harmony with a truly Biblical form of progressive revelation. If Reisel is correct in his emphasis upon a background of covenantal theology, the revelation to Moses is not just that of a name *per se*, but of a Covenant-keeping Deity manifesting His character as one who is already fulfilling the promises given to the patriarchs. Thus the name *YHWH*, familiar from the pre-Mosaic period, would appear as the central idea inherent in the text, namely, that of the Covenant loyalty of the God of Israel, already revealed as one who keeps His promises.[50]

Such a revelation is, of course, of pre-eminent importance in the light of the mighty act of God in the deliverance achieved at the Exodus, and in the provision that was made for a more comprehensive Covenant relationship at Sinai. This interpretation also lends proper balance to the twofold principal themes of the Torah, and shows the importance of their interrelationship for the future history of the nation.

4. The Book of the Covenant. The Covenant association between God and Israel has been examined in the light of second-millennium B.C. international treaties[51] elsewhere in the present work, and will not be recapitulated at this particular point. Suffice it to say that of equal importance with the provision by the Covenant of a nucleus about which Israelite historical tradition and spiritual life could be fostered was the fact that the Hebrews were unique in the ancient world for their attempts to interpret the whole of national existence in terms of a solemn covenantal agreement with a single deity.

The Book of the Covenant, which was read by Moses at the ratification of the divine agreement with Israel at Sinai, was most probably in the first instance the record of the Decalogue (Exod. 20:2-17). However, it has become customary in scholarly circles to refer to Exodus 20:22–23:33 as the "Book of the Covenant," which in any case is the oldest extant codification of Hebrew law. It is an amalgam of civil and criminal

---

[48] J. A. Motyer, *The Revelation of the Divine Name,* p. 12. Cf. O. T. Allis, *The Five Books of Moses* (1943), p. 28.

[49] Cf. A. B. Davidson, *The Theology of the OT* (1904), p. 68.

[50] M. Reisel, *op. cit.,* pp. 28f.

[51] G. E. Mendenhall, *BA,* XVII, No. 3 (1954), pp. 50ff., reprinted as *Law and Covenant in Israel and the Ancient Near East* (1955), *IBD,* I, pp. 714ff.; cf. M. G. Kline, *Treaty of the Great King* (1963); J. A. Thompson, *The Ancient Near Eastern Treaties and the OT* (1964).

legislation, ritual rules, and humanitarian prescriptions, and the corpus is of such a nature that it could have been revised or supplemented to a limited extent in the immediate post-Mosaic age without any violence to its substantial Mosaicity. Thus Exodus 22:18, 19, 31; and 23:1 may be later additions, perhaps dating from the Judges period. But whether this was actually the case or not, it is incorrect to suppose, with Alt, that the origins of this code must be sought outside the nation of Israel,[52] or with Pfeiffer, that the Book of the Covenant resulted from successive enlarged editions whose final form was not much earlier than the post-exilic date assigned by the critical school to the ultimate edition of the Pentateuch.[53]

The Book of the Covenant includes "precedents" and "statutes," the former appearing as case-laws and the latter as categorical law, normally in the form of prohibitions. The casuistic or case-law type is the dominant form of law known from the ancient Near East, as observed previously, and in the Covenant Code it is expressed in conditional terms: "If a man does...he shall pay...." The "statutes" have been described as categorical or "apodictic" in nature, and comprise definite prohibitions that do not specify precisely how they are to be implemented. Yet another form of law that is quite similar to the apodictic variety commences in Hebrew with an active participle and closes with the strongly worded expression, "he shall surely be put to death." This type not infrequently replaced the casuistic class where the death penalty was prescribed.

In the light of the suggestion by critical scholars that the agricultural and community legislation presupposes a date for the Covenant Code not earlier than the time of Samuel, it should be remembered that the Israelites were originally intended to journey from Sinai directly to the Promised Land, within the space of a few years at the most. Due, however, to the events which occurred near Kadesh (Num. 13:1ff.), the situation was changed in order to punish the rebels by insuring that they died in the Wilderness. Furthermore, it is important to realize that the enactments concerning agricultural and other activities had as much bearing upon the past life of the Israelites in the Goshen region as upon the conditions of their future existence.

Too often it is forgotten that the Israelites at Sinai were in fact the heirs of four centuries of agricultural and pastoral experience in a rich and fertile region of the Nile delta, and that neither they nor their forefathers had ever been true desert nomads in the modern Bedouin sense.[54] It is quite possible that some of the legislative elements of the

---

[52] A. Alt, *Die Ursprünge des israelitischen Rechts* (1934), p. 24.

[53] R. H. Pfeiffer, *Harvard Theological Review*, XXIII (1931), pp. 99ff.; *PIOT*, p. 211.

[54] Cf. K. A. Kitchen, *The Tyndale House Bulletin*, Nos. 5-6 (1960), pp. 13f.

Covenant Code had been formulated during the period when the Hebrews were living in the land of Goshen, while others may have emerged from the sojourn at Kadesh and even in Transjordan to represent the nucleus of material relating to social behavior that was thoroughly Mosaic in character and origin. What is clear is the fact that there was certainly no need for the Israelites to be settled in Canaan before such laws and regulations could be promulgated.

The contents of the Covenant Code in its extant form can be analyzed as follows:

I. The General Form of Israelite Worship, 20:22-26

II. Civil Legislation, 21:1–23:13
    A. The rights of slaves, 21:2-6, 7-11
    B. The principle of *lex talionis*, 21:12-32
    C. Laws concerning property, 21:33-36
    D. Laws concerning theft, 22:1-4
    E. Laws concerning property damage, 22:5-6
    F. Laws concerning dishonesty, 22:7-15
    G. Laws concerning seduction, 22:16-17
    H. Laws involving social and religious obligations, 22:18-31
    I. Protection of rights, 23:1-13

III. Ceremonial Legislation Dealing with the Three Principal Feasts, 23:14-19

IV. The Relation of the Covenant God to His People, 23:20-33

The principle upon which the laws in the Book of the Covenant were arranged is not immediately apparent. The case-laws present affinities with the codes of Ur-Nammu, Lipit-Ishtar, Hammurabi, and Eshunna, as well as with certain aspects of Hittite legislation, although they also reflect consistently a simpler way of life. It has been suggested also that the Covenant Code can be divided up into sections, each of which falls within the scope of one of the ten commandments to comprise a "running Midrash to the Decalogue,"[55] though to what extent this was the intention of the compiler is uncertain at present.

5. Sinai and the Wilderness wanderings. Brief mention ought to be made in passing of the problems associated with the location of Mount Sinai, which have been a matter of considerable debate since the mountain itself has not been identified with absolute accuracy. Suggested peaks have included Jebel Mūsa ("mount of Moses"), the neighboring Ras eṣ-Ṣafṣafeh, Jebel Serbāl, or a volcanic mountain near al-Hrob. The latter two are improbable on topographical grounds, while the tradition associated with Jebel Mūsa only goes back to the pilgrimage of Silvia

---

[55] E. Robertson, *The OT Problem* (1950), p. 95. Cf. A. E. Guilding, *JTS*, XLIX (1948), pp. 43ff.; H. Cazelles, *Études sur le Code de l'Alliance* (1946).

(*ca.* A.D. 388) and the time of Justinian (A.D. 527-565). The peaks of
the mountain itself are somewhat smaller than those of neighboring ones
to the west, south, and east. Against the claim of Ras eṣ-Ṣafṣafeh is the
lack of tradition specifying it as a holy place, despite the presence at its
foot of a large plain which could have accommodated the Israelite
tribes. While Sinai was also called Horeb ("wilderness") in the Old
Testament, this usage unfortunately throws no light upon the topographical problem. Many modern scholars follow ancient tradition in identifying Mount Sinai with Jebel Mūsa, which has its own small though
elevated plain, and thus could have witnessed the events connected with
the lawgiving.

The exact route followed by the Israelites in their journey from the
Reed Sea to the edge of Moabite territory is still largely a matter for
speculation, because few if any Israelite names of sites as recorded in
the Pentateuchal narratives have survived in the late Arabic nomenclature of the Sinai peninsula. Despite this drawback, however, the traditional route is certainly feasible in entertaining the idea of a journey
from the Yam Suph along the western coastal strip of the Sinai peninsula
to Marah, generally identified with 'Ain Hawrah, and Elim, identified
with the Wadi Gharandel.

That the subsequent camp was still in the area south of the Yam Suph
(Num. 33:10) indicates clearly that the Israelites had not followed the
northern or "Philistine" route, as earlier scholars suggested. Dophkah,
situated outside the Wilderness of Sin, has been regarded as a "smelt-
ery,"[56] and identified with Serabit el-Khadem, but in actual fact it
could well be any copper-mining area of the metalliferous sandstone belt
that extends across south-central Sinai, and which also favors a southerly
route for the Exodus. There appears to be little doubt that Kadesh is to
be identified with 'Ain Qudeirat, which is preferable on topographical
grounds to the common association of Kadesh with 'Ain Qudeis, lying
some five miles to the southeast. However, it is highly probable that
during the thirty-eight-year stay of the Israelites at Kadesh, the facilities
for water and vegetation afforded by 'Ain Qudeis and other oases in the
region were utilized to the full.

While there are numerous problems of identification connected with
the narratives of the Wilderness wanderings as preserved in Numbers
20:22ff. and 33:38ff.,[57] some of the incidents during that period furnish
an accurate reflection of the natural phenomena of the region. Clearly
the Israelites were familiar with the water-retaining capacities of Sinai
limestone (Exod. 17:1ff.; Num. 20:2ff.), and the digging of wells indicates an awareness of the presence of water immediately below the

[56] *WBA*, p. 64; *WHAB*, p. 39.
[57] Cf. J. D. Davis and H. S. Gehman, *Westminster Dictionary of the Bible* (1944),
pp. 638f.

surface of the ground in various areas of Sinai, the Negeb, and southern Transjordan (Num. 21:16ff.). The incidence of quail (Exod. 16:13; Num. 11:31ff.) furnishes some topographical hints as to the route of the Exodus, for since the birds were caught in the spring and during the evening, it is evident that they were returning in their normal migratory pattern to Europe across the upper limits of the Gulfs of Aqabah and Suez. This again supports, rather incidentally, a southerly direction for the Exodus.[58]

6. The Tabernacle. An important section of Exodus (chapters 25–31) deals with the instructions for the making and equipping of a portable shrine known as the Tabernacle, the place where the congregation of Israel could meet for worship and divine guidance. It contained, among other sacred objects, the richly ornamented acacia-wood Ark of the Covenant.[59] The evidence from Egypt for ancient prefabricated structures employed in cultic and other connections has been examined earlier in this book. All that need be said at this juncture is that such evidence antedates the very late and inexact parallels afforded by the pre-Islamic *qubbāh,* a miniature red leather tent with a dome-shaped top, which was utilized for carrying the idols and cultic objects of the tribe.[60] It also refutes decisively the charges of late fantasy or unrealism commonly held by the Wellhausen school, which are still entertained by some scholars.[61] The demonstrable antiquity of such prefabricated shrines is, in fact, a fundamental criticism of the Wellhausenian position, and in the light of the available evidence it is captious to refuse the Tabernacle and the Ark of the Covenant a Mosaic date, particularly since, as Albright has remarked,[62] they were completely foreign to sedentary Canaanite practice, and in any event are known to have persisted for some time after the conquest of Palestine.

The instructions for the manufacture of the Tabernacle were in the nature of being general records rather than constituting a detailed plan, and this makes for a certain lack of precision in the overall description. Thus the information furnished in Exodus makes it difficult to decide whether the Tabernacle proper had a flat, somewhat sagging drapery roof, or one which was tentlike in shape with a ridge-pole and a sloping roof.[63] Again, in the light of the general nature of the specifications,

[58] Contrary to C. S. Jarvis, *Yesterday and Today in Sinai* (1931), pp. 169f.; J. Gray, *VT,* IV (1954), pp. 148ff.; *WBA,* p. 65; *BHI,* p. 114.

[59] Cf. A. R. S. Kennedy, *HDB,* IV, pp. 653ff.; F. M. Cross, *BA,* IX, No. 3 (1947), pp. 55, 60; D. W. Gooding, *The Account of the Tabernacle* (1959); K. A. Kitchen, *The Tyndale House Bulletin,* Nos. 5-6 (1960), pp. 7ff., *NBD,* pp. 1231ff.

[60] Cf. J. Morgenstern, *HUCA,* XVII (1942), pp. 153ff., XVIII (1943-44), pp. 1ff.

[61] E.g. A. Bentzen, *Introduction to the OT,* II, p. 34.

[62] *FSAC,* p. 266.

[63] R. K. Harrison in the *Zondervan Pictorial Bible Dictionary* (1963), p. 822.

there is no valid ground for assuming that the text relating to the altar of incense and the laver (Exod. 30:1-10, 17-21) is dislocated, as some scholars of an earlier generation maintained. Instead, there is every reason to suppose that the present order is both original and deliberate.[64]

Some of the archaic technical terms associated with the Tabernacle merit a degree of consideration at this juncture. The designation אֹהֶל מוֹעֵד (Exod. 33:7) or "tent of meeting" was first applied to a structure that antedated the Tabernacle proper. It was pitched outside the camp, and Joshua was its sole attendant (Exod. 33:11) in the absence of a recognized and regularized priestly order. Apparently its function was that of a place of revelation, where the people met with God. The word מוֹעֵד has been discovered in an Egyptian document dated about 1100 B.C., referring to an assembly of the citizens of Byblos, and the term occurs again in Isaiah 14:13, where the reference is to the assembly of the gods in the remote northern regions, a popular theme in Canaanite pagan writings.

There seems no doubt, therefore, that the "tent of meeting" or the "tabernacle of the congregation" referred to in Exodus 33 was an interim structure, based upon the pattern of a simple desert shrine, and combining political and social functions with the religious revelation given by God to His covenanted assembly. The critical view that alleged that there was a discrepancy between the primitive "tent of meeting" of the older E source and the elaborate, unhistorical structure of the later P material was based upon the interpretation rather than the factual content of the Hebrew text, and in the light of the evidence for the Tabernacle as an historical structure it must be dismissed as pure fantasy.

The word מִשְׁכָּן, commonly used to designate the Tabernacle, is related to the ordinary Canaanite term for "dwelling-place" (mšknt), and meant originally "a tent," thus reflecting the nomadic background of the Tabernacle-worship generally. A related verb, שָׁכֵן (A.V. "dwell") was employed to describe God as "tabernacled" with men (Exod. 25:8; 29:45),[65] a usage found in a number of ancient Semitic writings, which means "to encamp." The sense was that of God revealing Himself on earth in the midst of His chosen people, and as such was clearly distinguished from the use of the verb יָשַׁב, "to dwell," "inhabit," which was only employed in the Old Testament of God dwelling in heaven.

Exodus is a remarkable testimony to the saving acts of a God who has revealed Himself as the supreme Lord of nature and history alike. The central theme of this fundamentally important section of the Torah is the

[64] A. H. Finn, JTS, XVI (1915), pp. 449ff.; cf. his The Unity of the Pentateuch (1928 ed.), pp. 444f., 467.

[65] Cf. John 1:14, ἐσκήνωσεν ἐν ἡμῖν.

demonstration of power inherent in the divine deliverance of Israel from bondage in Egypt. However, the Exodus itself was no isolated act, for in conjunction with the Covenant relationship it furnished the emotional and spiritual basis for the conviction that the new nation was in fact the Chosen People of God.

The Hebrew text of Exodus is surprisingly free from transcriptional errors, although there has apparently been some confusion between similar letters in the ancient script, as in Exodus 23:25 and 34:19. The text of Exodus 1:16 is obscure, primarily because the meaning of the phrase וראיתן על־האבנים was lost at an early period, and there is also some uncertainty as to how Exodus 32:29 is to be translated in view of the divergences between the MT and some of the ancient versions.

Supplementary Literature

Allis, O. T. *God Spake by Moses*. 1951.
Finegan, Jack. *Let My People Go: A Journey Through Exodus*. 1963.
Gressmann, H. *Mose und seine Zeit*. 1913.
Jepsen, A. *Untersuchungen zum Bundesbuch*. 1927.
Kyle, M. G. *Moses and the Monuments*. 1920.
Lucas, A. *The Route of the Exodus of the Israelites from Egypt*. 1938.
Mowinckel, Sigmund. *Le Decalogue*. 1927.
Noth, M. *Die Gesetze im Pentateuch*. 1940.
von Rad, G. *Moses*. 1960.
Volter, D. *Mose und die aegyptische Mythologie*. 1912.
de Wit, C. *The Date and Route of the Exodus*. 1960.

IV. THE BOOK OF LEVITICUS

A. Name and Outline

The third book of the Torah is referred to in Jewish usage as ויקרא, "and he called," the word with which it begins. In the Mishnah its contents were described by such terms as "priests' law," "priests' book," and "law of the offerings." In the LXX it bore the title *Leuitikon* or *Leueitikon,* an adjective qualifying the word *Biblion* ("book"), that is, the Levitical Book. This was rendered as *Leviticus* in the Vulgate; from this the English title is taken. The book itself is a collection of enactments intended to constitute the legal basis for the organized civil and religious life of the Chosen People. These laws were largely ritual, since it was naturally of considerable importance for the Israelites to be acquainted with the regulations concerning worship at the Tabernacle. At the same time it must be noted that the place Leviticus occupies in the Pentateuchal corpus exhibits the clear intention of the compiler to continue the narrative of the experiences at Sinai and to relate the legislation to the role of Israel as a witness to the power of God in human affairs. The name indicates that the legal corpus was the general responsibility of the cultus, and that the contents were the particular concern of the Levitical priesthood.

Leviticus can be subdivided into sections and analyzed as follows:

I. The Law of Sacrifice, ch. 1–7
  A. The burnt offering, 1:1-17
  B. The meal or cereal offering, 2:1-16
  C. The peace offering, 3:1-17
  D. The sin offering, 4:1–5:13
  E. The guilt offering, 5:14-19
  F. Conditions necessitating atonement, 6:1-7
  G. Burnt offerings, 6:8-13
  H. Cereal offerings, 6:14-23

I. Sin offerings, 6:24-30

J. Regulations concerning guilt offering, 7:1-10

K. Regulations for peace offering, 7:11-21

L. Prohibition of fat and blood, 7:22-27

M. Further regulations concerning peace offering, 7:28-38

II. The Consecration of Priests, ch. 8—10

    A. Preparation for anointing, 8:1-5

    B. The anointing ceremony, 8:6-13

    C. The consecration sacrifice, 8:14-36

    D. Instructions concerning sin offering, 9:1-7

    E. Entering of the Aaronides upon their office, 9:8-24

    F. The fate of Nadab and Abiram, 10:1-7

    G. Prohibitions concerning drunkenness of priests, 10:8-11

    H. Rules concerning the eating of consecrated food, 10:12-20

III. The Clean and Unclean, ch. 11—15

    A. Clean and unclean species, 11:1-47

    B. Purification after childbirth, 12:1-8

    C. Laws concerning leprosy, 13:1—14:57

    D. Purification after secretions, 15:1-33

IV. The Day of Atonement, ch. 16

V. Ritual Laws, ch. 17—25

    A. The blood of sacrifice, 17:1-16

    B. Religious and ethical laws and punishments, 18:1—20:27

    C. Canons of priestly holiness, 21:1—22:33

    D. Consecration of seasons, 23:1—24:23

    E. Sabbatical and jubilee years, 25:1-55

VI. Promises, Warning, and Appendix, ch. 26—27

As is apparent from the foregoing analysis, the contents of Leviticus fall within the purview of ritual law. This corpus, however, is a remarkably self-contained unit comprising two basic themes whose focal point is the chapter dealing with the Day of Atonement (Lev. 16). The first major emphasis occupies Leviticus 1—15, and can be said to be concerned with the removal of the defilement that separates men from God. The second broad consideration, taken up in the final eleven chapters of the book, is that of the means by which the disrupted fellowship between man and God can be restored. This general structure is not wholly dissimilar to the bifid nature of Isaiah and Daniel, for example, and it ought to be recognized as mechanical in the sense that the priestly material in Leviticus was arranged to conform to this kind of pattern.

Leviticus is composed of technical cultic material that was the prerogative of the priesthood, in contrast to Deuteronomy, which is a popular exposition of the more esoteric priestly writings and is related more specifically to the idea of the Covenant obligations. Furthermore, Leviticus contains certain unique prescriptions involving, for example, such widely different aspects of life as the Day of Atonement and the regulations concerning leprosy, which do not occur in any other ancient Near Eastern religious corpus.

B. DATE AND AUTHORSHIP

The priestly nature of the material in Leviticus affords important evidence for its probable date. In antiquity, all forms of education were under the supervision of the priesthood, a tradition that was established by the Sumerians.[1] Various branches of the priesthood were responsible for the different specialized areas of professional training, whether in the fields of law, the cultus, medicine, civil administration, the diplomatic service, and so on. In these major areas the procedural canons upon which the profession depended were generally committed to writing at a very early period, and following the conservatism of Sumeria they invariably remained almost completely unchanged. Of course, they were enriched over the centuries by means of additions to the basic corpus, and new material, faithfully modeled upon the old, appeared from time to time. However, the weight of Sumerian tradition was such that it formed alike the religious and secular basis for the whole of Mesopotamia and some of the lands beyond, so that, for example, the literary and liturgical forms of Akkad leaned heavily upon their Sumerian precursors, while the various types of law in the Near East reflected closely the traditions of the Sumerians. One of the principal reasons why the literature of that virile people has survived at all is that the pupils in the scribal schools copied out assiduously earlier literary sources instead of occupying themselves by and large with what would now be known as "creative writing."

Much the same can be said for ancient Egypt, where a great deal of the literature basic to the various professions came from a very early date. The so-called "Pyramid Texts" actually go back to the third millennium B.C., as does the Memphite theology, which magnified the deity Ptah as the First Cause. Early dating of professional sources and texts is also evident in Egyptian medicine, which attained to a definitely higher level than that of the Babylonians, particularly in the early days of the Old Kingdom period. While the four principal medical papyri are assigned roughly to the middle of the second millennium B.C.,[2] this only represents the date established on philological and other grounds for the particular papyrus manuscript under consideration, and does not refer to

---

[1] Cf. J. Kaster, *IDB*, II, pp. 27ff.

[2] The Edwin Smith surgical papyrus (*ca.* 1600 B.C.), the Ebers papyrus (*ca.* 1500), the Hearst papyrus (*ca.* 1500), and the Berlin papyrus 3038 (*ca.* 1290 B.C.).

the contents of the various documents in terms of provenance, which long antedated their written form. There seems little doubt that a good deal of traditional Egyptian medicine reaches back to the third millennium B.C., and that it was given stature by Imhotep (*ca.* 2650 B.C.), the chief minister, architect, and physician of Djoser, from whom a great many medical and other traditions descended.

The scribal practices of the ancient Near East point to a custom of preserving at an early stage those sources of information or procedure that were of importance to the particular profession. As regards cultic functionaries, the liturgies and rituals that they utilized were committed to writing and treasured in one form or another for many succeeding centuries. They were not transmitted down the ages in an oral form before emerging in their written state, as the modern oral-traditionists imagine. The primary purpose of oral usage was to afford the material in question widespread contemporary dissemination, and any other interpretation of the situation places a wrong emphasis upon the oral element in ancient Near Eastern usage. This contention is supported, as observed above, by the religious rituals and incantations from the third-millennium B.C. texts in the pyramids of Unis, Teti, and Pepi I (Fifth to Sixth Dynasties) at Saqqarah as well as by the third-millennium B.C. Sumerian religious texts, divine hymns, and mythological compositions from Ur, Nippur, and elsewhere. Equally important, whereas the Egyptian material, which was written on papyrus, was revised from time to time by various generations of scribes, the Sumerian literature has been handed down as it was actually written by the ancient copyists, unmodified and uncodified by later compilers and commentators.

Where specifically priestly traditions of an esoteric nature are concerned, and especially where they related to the cultus rather than to some other sphere of priestly activity such as government service or administration, the founding traditions of Mesopotamia and Egypt alike point to an early written recording of this kind of material. The fact that it may have been of a rather restricted character meant that it was generally only accessible to responsible persons who might or might not revise it, add to it, or compare with it other enactments, rituals, or similar prescriptions for particular usage. In general, however, it remains true that whereas Egyptian scribes undertook the revision of many ancient documents at specific times, their Mesopotamian counterparts preferred to transmit the material at hand much as they themselves had received it.

In the light of the available evidence it is therefore clear that one of the most egregious errors ever committed by the members of the Graf-Wellhausen school was to assign the Priestly Code, and particularly that portion of it which comprised Leviticus, to the post-exilic period, despite the assertions of Kuenen and a few other scholars that there might possibly be earlier material in the code as a whole. If the Graf-

Wellhausen school had been less obsessed with its determination to introduce law and order into the Pentateuchal compositional situation, whatever the cost, and had been prepared to be influenced by facts even as they were then known and available, the result would almost certainly have been to date the P material early rather than late, a conclusion that has finally been arrived at by one or two of the more perceptive liberal scholars.[3]

With regard to the questions relating to the authorship and compilation of Leviticus, the author is nowhere named in the composition as being responsible for a part or the whole of the work. This is quite different from the situation obtaining in Exodus, where Moses was named specifically as the author of certain sections of the work (cf. Exod. 17:14; 24:4; 34:27). Leviticus includes material from the revelation at Sinai (Lev. 7:37f.; 26:46; 27:34), but this, of course, does not answer the question of authorship. While it is possible that an editor or writer of a later generation arranged the Mosaic traditions in the order in which they are extant in Leviticus, there is also an equal possibility that the contents of the book were organized into something like their present order during the lifetime of Moses. If the priestly traditions of the ancient Near East mean anything at all, this would certainly have been the case for the prescriptions relating to the various offerings, the consecration of the priesthood, and the ceremonies involving the Day of Atonement, as well as for the unique specifications concerning hygiene.

The theories of the Graf-Wellhausen school concerning ancient Hebrew sacrifice were crystallized by Wellhausen, who laid down the principle that the sense of sin in Israelite sacrifice was a decidedly late development.[4] This view, modified somewhat as it was by later followers of Wellhausen, was effectively disproved by R. J. Thompson.[5] One of the most fundamental postulates in the Wellhausenian reconstruction of Israelite religion was swept away in this manner, and with it the necessity for ascribing the so-called P material to the post-exilic period. If it is legitimate to assume that the prescriptions concerning the sacrificial ritual and the ordering of the priesthood are as ancient as the traditions of the Hebrews would suggest, it is also permissible to think in analogous terms of other distinctive sections of Leviticus such as the laws governing hygiene. The distinction between clean and unclean animals (Lev. 11:1-47) has no parallel whatever in ancient life, particularly since the legislation in question is founded upon dietary principles unknown elsewhere in the Near East. If these precepts had emerged from the post-exilic period, as critical scholarship has long maintained, there would be

[3] E.g. Y. Kaufmann, ZAW, XLVIII (1930), pp. 22ff., VT, IV (1954), pp. 307ff., *The Religion of Israel* (tr. Greenberg, 1960), pp. 175ff. Cf. GBB, p. 293 n. 1.
[4] *Prolegomena to the History of Israel*, p. 81.
[5] *Penitence and Sacrifice in Early Israel Outside the Levitical Law* (1963).

clear indications in the text of the kind of situation that obtained in contemporary Babylonian medicine, where the empiricism of the code of Hammurabi had long succumbed to the influence of the magical practices inherent for many centuries in Mesopotamian therapeutics.

As it is, the dietary prescriptions are firmly grounded in attested procedures (Lev. 11:3f., 9f.), and it is to these, rather than to considerations of magic and sorcery, or the place that the proscribed species occupied in pagan religious practices, that the contents of the hygienic code must be related. Since highly organized medical material of various kinds was known both in Babylonia and Egypt from at least the second millenniun B.C. onwards, there is no *a priori* reason why the hygienic code of Leviticus cannot be confidently credited to its attributive author Moses. In view of the tenacity with which this code was held in subsequent ages it is difficult to see how it could have emerged from a period subsequent to that of Moses without being recognized and dismissed as patently spurious and fraudulent. Nor is there valid ground for drawing a significant distinction in point of time between the antiquity of the tradition itself and the written form in which it has been preserved, for there is no specific element in the prescriptions that requires a date later than the end of the Amarna period.

The same may be said about the section containing the laws governing leprosy (Lev. 13:1–14:57), which are recorded in considerable detail. The passage is an obvious unity, and deals in a manner unprecedented in antiquity with one of the most urgent medical problems of the Near East. Precisely where leprosy originated is unknown, but it was certainly a familiar affliction in Mesopotamia and the countries of the Orient generally as far back as the third millennium B.C. Evidence for the existence of the ailment in Egypt is very scanty, and in any event needs critical appraisal before any conclusions can be drawn from it.

As with all medical functions in antiquity, it was the task of one particular branch of the priesthood to discharge the diagnostic and therapeutic procedures. The organization of the material in the section under discussion is similar to that of comparable ancient medical sources from the Near East, except that there is no hint whatever of the influence or authority of magic. The techniques are empirical in the best sense of that term: the symptoms are considered with a view to the possibility of differential diagnosis and the therapy enjoined is based upon the principle of prevention rather than attempts at radical cure, doubtful herbal therapy, or other similar procedures. Again, had the contents of this section originated in the post-exilic period, or even been edited at that time from ancient traditions, it is not easy to see how the material could possibly have escaped all traces of the demonism that had come to constitute the frame of reference alike for contemporary pathology and therapeutics. Yet this section, like other unique enactments in the book of Leviticus, reflects with complete fidelity the Sinai

594

ideal of the one, supreme, all-powerful deity who repudiated the existence of pagan gods, denied the validity and authority of magical practices, and expressly prohibited their usage in any area of Hebrew life.

It is difficult to see how the regulations concerning leprosy could have arisen from any other than the Mosaic period without arousing the gravest of suspicions on the part of the priesthood, whose duty it was to safeguard and administer them. Since the section under discussion is a manifest unity, there seems to be no adequate reason for supposing that it did not represent for the ancient Hebrews what the early medical enactments of Egypt and Mesopotamia did for their particular cultures; and there is no cause to deny that it is genuine, original, and untroubled by subsequent scribal revision, since none would be necessary in the nature of the case.

Whereas the passages concerning dietary regulations and the diagnosis of leprosy could be related equally well to a semi-nomadic or an urban milieu, the narratives involving the Day of Atonement (Lev. 16:1-34) can only be envisaged against an original desert scene. The Tabernacle, with its furnishings and priesthood, dominated the religious situation; the people were described in terms of an encampment, and when the live goat had been made the recipient of national sins of inadvertence by symbolic imposition of hands, it was driven out into the wilderness. The origin of this event is too securely guarded by Hebrew tradition to be assigned to any other period than that of Moses, and the narrative description in which it is couched exhibits a freshness and vitality that could hardly be the work of one who composed it many centuries after its initial occurrence.

These observations should not be taken as contending that Leviticus was necessarily written on one occasion or within a very short interval of time, any more than might be the case with many other important pieces of legislation in antiquity. While the final unity of the composition makes it difficult to assess the manner of compilation, it may be possible as a result of close inspection to discern some of the stages by which the book reached its extant form. In the first instance it might well be that the introductory formula, "And the Lord spoke unto Moses (and Aaron) saying. . ." is a stereotyped way of introducing a fresh element in the revelation, which might have been recorded on a separate section of leather and joined with other similar sections after having been sorted and classified.[6]

[6] Cf. J. S. Wright, *EQ*, XXV (1953), p. 14. This would imply that some of the component sections of the book included Lev. 1:1–3:17; 4:1–5:13; 5:14-19; 5:20-26 (Heb.); 6:1-11 (Heb.); 6:12-16 (Heb.); 6:17–7:21 (Heb.); 7:22-38; 8:1–10:20; 11:1-47; 12:1-8; 13:1-59; 14:1-32; 14:33-57; 15:1-33; 16:1-34; 17:1-16; 18:1-30; 19:1-37; 20:1-27; 21:1-24; 22:1-16; 22:17-25; 22:26-33; 23:1-8; 23:9-22; 23:23-25; 23:26-32; 23:33-44; 24:1-23; 25:1–26:46; and 27:1-34. Such sections might have

Another example of the homogeneity of the work occurs in connection with the prohibitions concerning the eating of blood. This particular ban was first imposed in Leviticus 3:17, along with the prohibition of fat, and was renewed in Leviticus 7:26, where blood alone, whether that of animals or fowls, was specifically forbidden to be consumed. But in Leviticus 17:11 the rationale of the procedure previously enjoined without particular explanation was made plain in the stated relationship between the living flesh and its nutrient stream.

It is in the light of this pronouncement that the rituals associated with the shedding and sprinkling of sacrificial blood as contained in the first seven chapters of Leviticus have to be assessed theologically, thus making for a unity of thought in these sections. Once again, this is not to say that they were necessarily written on one and the same occasion, for it is probable that some interval of time elapsed before the various pronouncements were transcribed and assembled. On the other hand, it is important to recognize the originality and antiquity of the pronouncements, formulating as they did the basic attitudes of the ancient Hebrews towards sacrifice.

In precisely the same manner there are two links in the first seven chapters of Leviticus with the regulations concerning impurity, dealt with in some detail in chapters eleven to fifteen. In Leviticus 5:2 and 7:21, there is a pronouncement that deals with the ceremonial condition of impurity, acquired as the result of contact with an unclean thing or a prohibited rite, and with the status of the offender as a consequence. This situation was clarified in Leviticus 11:26f., a passage that contains the principles underlying the concepts of uncleanness and explains the extent to which the defilement is pervasive. This situation constitutes no mere literary accident, but it is rather a deliberate attempt to introduce homogeneity into the interpretation of the book as a whole.

---

comprised certain portions of the divine revelation given to Moses at various times during the period of Wilderness wanderings, and subsequently assembled according to suitability of topic, perhaps with some editorial changes in the interests of continuity. There is no guarantee that the foregoing suggested analysis into what appear to be component parts represents the actual facts of the compilatory situation, and it is only postulated on the assumption, which may be entirely gratuitous, that the introductory phrase in each case is a technical heading carried by the various units that were assembled to comprise the whole. Nor is there any means of knowing whether or not certain of these units were joined together in a subsection of the extant work and permitted to enjoy independent local circulation for some time. It may well be that the regulations concerning offerings (1:1–7:38) had once been in existence in priestly circles as a separate unit to constitute a manual of procedure. This appears to be indicated by the fact that Lev. 7:35-38 constitutes some kind of colophon which includes the titles of the various conjoined sections, attestation of ownership, and the date and place of the enactments. Yet whether this is actually the case or not, the section has been accommodated remarkably well to the overall pattern of the book of Leviticus.

From the standpoint of purely historical continuity, it might appear that chapters 11–15 constitute a block of material inserted haphazardly into a place where one portion of leather roll may have followed another, since Leviticus 10:20 concludes the incidents consequent upon the death of the sons of Aaron, and Leviticus 16:1 picks up the thread of the historical narrative once more at that precise point. However, it has already been noticed that the chronicler or historian has always to decide whether he is to follow the time-sequence dictated by the events themselves, to arrange his history in terms of topics or subjects, or to compromise between the two methods of approach. The latter procedure appears to have been adopted here, for while chapters 11–15 evidently constitute an insertion, they are by no means inimical to the organizational unity of Leviticus, being firmly integrated into the pattern of the whole by means of the antecedent references in Leviticus 5:2 and 7:21. This contention is further reinforced by the fact that the prescription in Leviticus 10:10 can be interpreted in the light of the detailed differentiation between clean and unclean species as contained in chapter 11. On such a basis there can be no serious doubt as to the suitability of chapters 11–15 for inclusion in the text of Leviticus in their present position, for when viewed in the light of the work as a whole the regulations dealing with purity and impurity demonstrate how necessary it was for the Israelites to impose a barrier between themselves and sin.

In a pattern of reversed parallelism that is not entirely unknown in bifid literary compositions,[7] there is a reference in Leviticus 20:25 to the regulations of chapter 11 which deal in detail with clean and unclean species. This verse thus serves to integrate the commandments of chapters 18 to 20 with those found in chapters 11 to 15, thus further preserving the coherence of the book. This principle of integration casts considerable doubt upon the supposedly separate existence of chapters 17 to 26, the so-called "Law of Holiness," as maintained by the members of the critical school. The designation of "Holiness Code" (H) was first applied to this material by A. Klostermann in 1877,[8] and it was subsequently taken over by Wellhausen[9] and his followers. Some of the latter detected instances of agreement with Ezekiel, another bifid composition, and promptly assigned the "Code" to a post-exilic date, evidently ignoring the possibility that Ezekiel was reflecting statements from the Torah in his utterances.

Be that as it may, there are clear traces of deliberate attempts to integrate chapters 17 to 26 into the narrative of Leviticus as a whole.

---

[7] Compare the tentative parallelisms of Isaiah as listed by W. H. Brownlee in *The Meaning of the Qumrân Scrolls for the Bible*, pp. 247ff.

[8] Cf. his later work, *Der Pentateuch: Beiträge zu seinem Verständnis und seiner Entstehungsgeschichte* (1893), pp. 368ff.

[9] *Die Composition des Hexateuchs* (1889), pp. 151ff.

Thus in Leviticus 21:1–22:16, expressions like those which occur in Leviticus 11:44f., 19:2 and 20:7 are repeated with reference to the ceremonial condition of the priests. Even if this section originally enjoyed independent existence for a time—a view that is by no means as assured as critical scholars have imagined in the past—it is rather doubtful if chapter 25 was ever part of such a combination of literary prescriptions. The reference in Leviticus 25:1 indicates that the following material relating to the sabbath of the land and the jubilee was revealed to Moses by God on Mount Sinai, just as was the case with the colophon in Leviticus 7:35ff., making it difficult to see how either of these two enactments could have been a post-exilic priestly invention, as was suggested by an earlier generation of critical scholarship. It seems well within the bounds of probability, therefore, that chapter 25 may have constituted an insertion into material which in other respects was concerned with canons of holiness, and as such it may not have comprised part of any original "Holiness Code" at all. This is not to imply, of course, that the prescriptions concerning the jubilee belong necessarily to any other period than that of Moses, a matter which in any event is scarcely an issue, since many modern liberal scholars, along with a few of their earlier counterparts, have conceded the ancient nature of the jubilee enactments.

A literary mosaic such as Leviticus is seldom easy to disentangle, particularly in view of the fact that the extant work has been compiled with consummate editorial skill into a literary and theological unity. Equally difficult is the task of resolving supposedly component elements into some sort of chronological sequence, even on the assumption that this would be necessary or desirable in an oriental composition. Whatever shades of critical opinion most writers espouse, all are agreed that Leviticus is essentially a priestly document. In the light of the evidence afforded by Near Eastern literary sources generally, it would seem prudent to assign the composition of the work to an earlier rather than a later date, and, if the Mosaic ascriptions and historical allusions found in the text are as genuine as they purport to be, to envisage the recording of the material, subject to possible minor revisions, within an interval of no more than a few years from the time when it was first promulgated in oral form.

C. THE MATERIAL OF LEVITICUS

1. The sacrificial system. From a great many standpoints Leviticus is fundamental to any understanding of the Biblical revelation to man. Not the least significant of these is the meaning of the work for the religious institutions of Israel in general, and for the sacrificial system in particular. While regulations governing sacrifice can be found scattered throughout the Pentateuch (e.g. Exod. 20:24ff.; 34:25ff.; Num. 15:1ff.; Deut. 12:6ff.), the sacrificial Torah as such comprises Leviticus 1–7. As observed above, the material offerings were required to conform to certain canons of cleanness, and were restricted to particular species of animals and birds.

The general principle undergirding the concept of an offering appears to have been that of property (2 Sam. 24:24), so that whereas it was legitimate to sacrifice domesticated animals and birds, which were in a sense the property of man through his own enterprise, it was not deemed permissible for wild animals to be sacrificed, since they were regarded as already belonging to God (cf. Ps. 50:10). The basic theme of property was even more evident in the case of vegetable and cereal offerings, which had been produced as a result of human labor. An extension of this principle related to property that had been acquired unlawfully; this also was unacceptable as a sacrifice to God (Deut. 23:18).

In accordance with the belief that only the very best of the species could constitute a legitimate offering, the male was generally preferred to the female; in any case matters of physical perfection and maturity were consistently emphasized. The economic state of individuals or families was considered sympathetically in the tariffs to the point where the poor were permitted to substitute a cheaper offering for a more expensive one. The earliest attestable public sacrifices were the feast of unleavened bread, with which the Passover had been linked by the time of the settlement period (Josh. 5:10ff.), the feast of weeks or firstfruits (Pentecost), and the feast of tabernacles (Exod. 23:14ff.; 34:18ff.; Deut. 16:1ff.). With the last of these there may have been associated certain rites connected with the renewal of the Covenant (cf. Deut. 31:10ff.; Josh. 24:1ff.). Additional public and private festal observances were also provided for in the Torah (cf. Num. 28:1ff.; 29:1ff.).

The major altar offerings described in Leviticus 1–5 followed a stereotyped ritual pattern of six acts, of which the worshipper executed three and the priest performed three.[10] In the individual rite the worshipper brought his sacrificial offering to the Tabernacle forecourt, laid his hand upon it in a manner implying that it represented the offerer himself, and then slaughtered the animal. On the occasion of a public communal sacrifice the animal was killed by a priest, the sacrificial blood was collected in a basin by the officiant and spattered against the four sides of the altar. In the case of small offerings such as birds, the diminished quantity of available blood was drained out beside the altar. Some portion of the sacrifice, including specified areas of fat, was then burned, and this procedure was even applied to cereal offerings. When a burnt offering was sacrificed, however, the entire animal was consumed by fire except for the hide, which became a priestly perquisite (Lev. 7:8). The remaining portions of the sacrifice were then eaten as a meal, either by

[10] R. J. Thompson, *NBD*, p. 117.

the priests and worshippers together as with the peace offering, by the priests and their families, or by the priestly caste alone.

The different kinds of offerings can be described briefly as follows:

(a) burnt offering (עלה), apparently the typical Hebrew sacrifice, which became a regular sacrifice at an early period (1 Kgs. 9:25) and remained dominant throughout Old Testament history. The כליל (Deut. 33:10; 1 Sam. 7:9; Ps. 51:19) was basically the same as the עלה, but exhibited some variations.

(b) cereal or meal offering (מנחה), found in the Old Testament either as a present (e.g. Judg. 3:15), as a general reference to sacrifice (e.g. 1 Sam. 2:29; Mal. 2:13), or more specifically to the Levitical cereal offering. The term מנחה carried a propitiatory sense, and was not understood in the rituals generally as a mere "gift." It was frequently, though not invariably, an accompaniment to burnt and peace offerings.

(c) peace offering, generally described in Leviticus by the term זבח שלמים or זבחי שלמים, although זבח and שלמים were sometimes used interchangeably. By itself the שלמים may have constituted an expiatory offering, and when associated with זבח may have formed a rite of propitiation and reconciliation.

(d) guilt or trespass offering (אשם), usually involving ceremonial defilement and associated with such ceremonies as the cleansing of a leper (Lev. 14:1ff.) or the purification of a woman after childbirth (Lev. 12:1ff.).

(e) sin offering (חטאת), similar to the guilt offering in that it involved ceremonial defilement, but as exemplified in the Law it applied to deception or misappropriation (Lev. 6:1ff.) and seduction (Lev. 19:20ff.). The relationship between the two offerings is obscure, but the חטאת seems to have referred more to offenses against God and the אשם to violations of a general social nature.[11]

Since the pagan neighbors of Israel also indulged in sacrificial rites, it is natural to expect certain points of contact in ritual and intent. Excavations at Lachish (Tell ed-Duweir) uncovered the remains of three Canaanite shrines, built between the fifteenth and thirteenth centuries B.C., near to which large quantities of animal bones were found in a pile of debris. On examination most of them were found to have come from the right foreleg of the animal, which corresponds to the prescriptions for Hebrew sacrifice in Leviticus 7:32 and attests to the antiquity of that passage.

11 On Hebrew sacrifice generally see W. P. Paterson, *HDB*, IV, pp. 329ff.; R. A. S. Macalister, *ERE*, XI, pp. 31ff.; J. J. Reeve, *ISBE*, IV, pp. 2638ff.; S. G. Gayford, *Sacrifice and Priesthood* (1924); W. O. E. Oesterley, *Sacrifices in Ancient Israel* (1937); H. H. Rowley, *The Meaning of Sacrifice* (1950); F. D. Kidner, *Sacrifice in the OT* (1952); R. de Vaux, *Studies in OT Sacrifice* (1964).

An offering analogous to the מנחה was mentioned in a sacrificial tariff from Ugarit;[12] a propitiatory peace offering appears to have been known there also.[13] Votive and tributary offerings were familiar to all the peoples of the ancient Near East,[14] as were schedules of sacrifices, especially in Babylonia.[15] Offerings of firstfruits have been attested from Mesopotamian, Hittite, south Arabic, and Aegean sources.[16] The same is true for the sacrifice of male children in honor of Hadad—recorded in north-Mesopotamian texts from the tenth to the seventh century B.C.— the offerings of children to Molech—described in texts from the Third Dynasty of Ur and in the eighteenth-century B.C. tablets from Mari— and the Aegean custom of passing children through flames in order to augment their strength. Human sacrifice was expressly prohibited among the Hebrews (Lev. 18:21; 2 Kgs. 23:10; Jer. 32:35), but whether the denunciation of the Ammonite deity Molech (Moloch) was a repudiation of genuine human sacrifice or a rejection of Aegean customs of invigoration or of attempting to acquire immortality has been a matter of some debate among scholars.[17]

While pagan and Hebrew sacrificial systems had certain common interests and objectives such as the desire for fellowship with the deity, the provision of atonement for ceremonial defilement, and the assurance of continued divine blessing, the Hebrew enactments were distinctive as the outcome of a unique covenantal relationship. The bond of union between God and Israel, which was forged at Sinai in order to give the nation its distinctive moral and spiritual undergirding and to furnish it with a sense of missionary destiny, was quite unlike anything else of a contractual nature in the ancient Near East.

The concept of divine holiness constituted the essence of the Sinai Covenant, and this factor was emphasized throughout the Pentateuchal legislation as a stated requirement in Israelite life. But whereas the demand that the Hebrews should be a holy nation was based upon the elevated moral and ethical content of the term "holy" (קדש) as exhibited by the divine nature, the pagan neighbors of Israel in their own dealings with local or national deities knew nothing of such advanced religious concepts, and their use of the term generally had refer-

[12] *Corpus Inscriptionum Semiticarum*, I, 145.
[13] D. M. L. Urie, *EQ*, LXXXI (1949), pp. 75ff.
[14] Cf. T. H. Gaster, *IDB*, IV, pp. 148ff.
[15] *ANET*, pp. 343ff.
[16] *ARAB*, I, sect. 616f.; *Corpus Inscriptionum Semiticarum*, I, 166.3; *Keilschrifturkunden aus Boghazköi*, XII, 4, iv, 3f.; Isoc. *Panegyr.* 6ff.
[17] E.g. O. Eissfeldt, *Molk als Opferbegriff im Punischen und Hebräischen und das Ende des Gottes Moloch* (1935), opposed by W. Kornfeld, *Wiener Zeitschrift für die Kunde des Morgenlandes* (1952), pp. 287ff., and H. Dronkert, *De Molochdienst in het Oude Testament* (1953).

ence to a person dedicated to the service of a particular deity, as, for example, a cultic prostitute.

In connection with the implementing of covenantal provisions, the ceremonies associated with the annual Day of Atonement (Lev. 16:1-34) were of fundamental importance in Hebrew national life. On the tenth day of the seventh month (September-October) the Israelites observed their most solemn day of obligation. All work was forbidden, and the people were required to observe a strict fast. The High Priest, garbed in simple attire for the occasion, offered sacrifice for the entire priesthood and entered the Most Holy Place in an incense-burning ceremony. Subsequently a male goat was offered as a sacrifice for the people, and some of the blood was taken into the Most Holy Place, where it was sprinkled ceremonially about the Ark.

After purifying the Holy Place (Lev. 16:18f.), the High Priest took a second goat and confessed over it the sins of inadvertence committed by the nation as a whole. This animal was then driven into the desert, where it symbolically carried away the sins of the Israelites. Additional sacrificial rites concluded the ceremonies of the day, which had the effect of reminding Israel that the various sacrifices made at the altar of burnt offering were not of themselves sufficient to atone for sin. Alone of all other sacrificial occasions, the blood was brought into the Most Holy Place by the High Priest as the representative of the people on the solemn Day of Atonement.

The purpose of the sacrificial enactments, as defined in Leviticus, was to effect an "atonement" on behalf of the person offering the sacrifice. The Hebrew verb כפר, "to atone," has been related to the comparatively late Arabic word *kafara*, "to cover"; to the Akkadian term *kuppuru*, "to wipe away," and to the Hebrew noun *kōphēr*, "ransom." The latter best suits the specific purpose of Israelite sacrificial theory as elaborated in Leviticus 17:11, which identified the life with the blood and laid down the principle that the blood "makes atonement by reason of the life" (RSV). The animal victim thus constituted a substitute for the human sinner, and the offering up of its life in sacrifice effected a vicarious atonement for sin. The emphasis of this verse, which is crucial for the interpretation of Hebrew sacrifice, is opposed both to the theory that the death of the victim was only meant to release the life inherent in its blood so that the latter might constitute the atonement and to the view that the death of the animal was a quantitative penal satisfaction. The Hebrew sacrificial system must always be envisaged against a background of the Covenant principle of divine grace, and in this context the emphasis upon the categories of personal relationship is most properly expressed in the theory of substitution, where the chosen victim dies in the place of the human sinner.

It is far from easy to decide from the text if the sacrificial offering was meant to be a propitiation of divine anger as well as an expiation for human sin, for while there are undoubtedly some instances where the verb signifies "propitiation" (Exod. 32:30; Num. 16:41ff.), there are others where it simply means "to cleanse," as with the furnishings of the Tabernacle (Exod. 29:37; Ezek. 43:20). What is clear, however, is that man as a sinner incurs divine wrath, that God has provided the sacrificial system in order that human transgressors might return in penitence to fellowship with Him, and that God graciously permitted the death of a sacrificial victim as a substitute for the death of the sinner.

It should be noted in any study of the Hebrew sacrificial system that it was not by any means a complete and final scheme whereby all forms of sin could be removed. Much of the atonement procedure was concerned with sins of accident, inadvertence, or omission which individuals had committed, and there was no forgiveness for sins of sheer human obduracy (Num. 15:30), which by definition placed a man outside the range of Covenant mercies. Idolatry and apostasy also fell within this general area of self-exclusion from Covenant grace, and in the main it can be stated that for breaches of the Covenant agreement no form of sacrifice was of any avail. It is in the light of this latter consideration that the cultic denunciations of the prophets and their rejection of sacrifice need to be interpreted.

2. *Cleanliness and uncleanliness.* The classification of animal species into clean and unclean categories (Lev. 11:1-47) is significant because, being part of the Pentateuchal medical code, it constituted the basis of dietary regulations that are still adhered to by orthodox Jews and by those Gentiles who are concerned with maintaining good physical health. This categorizing is also important in view of the fact that it is unique in the annals of Near Eastern literature because its emphasis is not so much upon the avoidance of magical practices associated with certain animal species as upon the positive delineation of dietary principles intended to insure the physical well-being of the individual and the nation alike through a consistent prophylactic approach.

It is to be noted, of course, that the provisions of the Sinai revelation repudiated the very idea of magic as an influence in human life, and in this regard the Israelites were once again unique in the ancient world. As an additional safeguard against the taint of this all-pervasive factor in Near Eastern life, the practice of magic in any of its manifold forms was expressly prohibited by the Torah at all levels of Hebrew life. The system of therapeutics and preventive medicine enunciated in the Pentateuch, particularly in Leviticus, was grounded upon an empirical basis, in marked contrast to the approach of contemporary peoples, who were dominated by *a priori* magical considerations and as a result tended invariably to spiritualize pathological phenomena in terms of the activity of demons. The closeness of the relationship between the principles underlying the medical sections of Leviticus and those of the Covenant of Sinai, along with the fact that written medical traditions in the Near East tend invariably to be early rather than late, give strong support for crediting this material to Moses and the Wilderness period of Israelite history.

The Pentateuchal medical code recognized that healthy individual existence involved certain fundamental principles of hygiene that by nature required acceptance at both an intellectual and an emotional level. What was particularly distinctive about this situation was that the differentiation between clean and unclean, permissible and prohibited, was grounded in ethical considerations. The Mosaic law was a decided advance upon pagan concepts of cleanness and uncleanness, in that both these categories were made relative to the idea of holiness as associated with the God of Sinai. However, in the light of both the ceremonial and the therapeutic regulations it is important not to overestimate the nature of cleanness. In itself it could never be considered as the equivalent of holiness, but at best as a rather negative state whose existence implied that a positive holiness was attainable.

The medical code elaborated the principles of hygienic living in terms of seven basic enactments, five of which were contained in Leviticus and the remaining two elsewhere in the Torah. These were the sabbath for individuals (Lev. 23:3, et al.) and the land (Lev. 25:2ff.), dietary rules (Lev. 11:2ff.), circumcision (Gen. 17:11; Deut. 10:16), regulations concerning sexual relationships (Lev. 18:6ff.), provision for individual sexual hygiene (Lev. 15:2ff.), purification rituals (Lev. 1:9ff.; 14:2ff.; 15:2, et al.), and sanitary procedures (Deut. 23:12ff.; Num. 31:19ff.).

In view of the ethical concept of health that these regulations reflect, it should be remarked that they were not intended to exemplify some mysterious connection between morality and health so much as to emphasize that the observance of the precepts enshrined in the corpus of legislation would of itself insure a great measure of freedom from the diseases and scourges which afflicted neighboring peoples. Consequently, insofar as the Israelites followed the prescribed rules for sanitation, isolation, hygiene, and sexual behavior they were assured of the kind of immunity to disease that magic could never afford.

As regards the dietary regulations, the division of species into clean and unclean (Lev. 11:1ff.) is to be regarded not so much as a reaction against Egyptian totemism or the protest of a superior religion against contemporary pagan customs as the positive delineation of beneficial and noxious foods respectively. The specific concern of Leviticus 11:2 was with the kind of animal whose flesh could be ingested without any resultant harm to individual or communal health. Quadrupeds that were clovenfooted, parted the hoof, and chewed the cud were alone permitted for food. Such a designation of the ruminants proper excluded carnivorous and predatory species, and the list of possible animals was further restricted by the prohibition of swine, camels, hares, and coneys, which did not fulfill all the conditions necessary for "cleanness." It will be observed that the "clean" animals were exclusively vegetarian, and as such would be less likely to transmit infection than would the carnivorae, which fed on flesh that invariably decayed rapidly under conditions of a warm climate.[18]

The prohibition concerning the flesh of swine is interesting partly on hygienic grounds, and partly because of the place that the animal occupied in Egyptian cult-worship. According to Herodotus,[19] the pig was originally sacred to Osiris, and the cultic celebration of that deity involved the slaughter of a pig outside the houses of the participants. The violation of tabus regarding the pigs was remedied by means of a close and immediate contact with Osiris in the form of the Nile River. It does not seem likely, however, that the question of cult-worship was quite as important a consideration in the prohibition of swine for food as were purely dietary and hygienic reasons. Even under the most carefully supervised modern conditions of slaughtering and processing, the flesh of the pig is far more potentially dangerous as a source of infection than that of any of the other quadrupeds normally eaten for food. The pig is the intermediate host for several parasitic organisms producing afflictions of varying severity, and under warm climatic conditions the optimum opportunity is afforded for these organisms to develop when ingested.[20]

[18] The wild animals specified as suitable for food were the fallow-deer (probably *Dama vulgaris*), the gazelle (*Gazella dorcas, Gazella Leptoceras*), the roebuck (perhaps *Bubalis bucephalus*), the ibex (*Capra nubiana*), the addax (*Antilope addax*), the antelope (*Oryx beatrix*), and the mouflon (*Ovis tragelaphus*), Deut. 4:14; cf. F. S. Bodenheimer, *Animals and Man in Bible Lands* (1960), p. 41 *passim*. Of the prohibited quadrupeds the camel was already valuable as a source of milk in patriarchal times (Gen. 32:15), although great care had to be taken lest the milk sour before being ingested. The hare, which was also forbidden for food, existed in numerous varieties in Palestine, the most common being the *Lepus capensis aegyptius, Lepus europaeus connori,* and *Lepus europaeus syriacus.* The coney (*Procavia syriaca*) or rock-badger was also common: in general appearance it resembled a rabbit.

[19] *Hist.,* II, 47.

[20] One of the characteristic infections, trichiniasis, results from the parasitic *Trichinella spiralis* found in raw or partially cooked pork or pork products, and in the developing stages the invasion and migration of the organism are typified by symptoms of malaise, febrile states, vomiting, edema of the face and legs, muscular pains, and urticarial rash. Botulism and other food poisoning result from infection due to contaminated pork products, and in severe cases respiratory failure is a complication. At other times the ingestion of pork products issues in an allergic condition accompanied by malaise, some fever, and a rash. A more common infection is that of the *Taenia solium,* where the pig is the intermediate host and man the definitive host. The developed worm is about ten feet long with approximately one thousand segments, and is derived from the *Cysticercus cellulosae* parasite sometimes present in raw or improperly cooked pork. A rare degeneration of this condition is seen in somatic taeniasis, when nodules form in the muscles and the brain to produce

The medical code appears to have regarded as one class all the creatures that inhabited the waters, and in consequence merely divided them into clean and unclean categories, the latter embracing all those species without fins and scales. This distinction was also observed elsewhere in the ancient Near East, notably in Egypt. The exclusion from the Israelite diet of all edible crustaceae, many of which live on sewage and putrefying matter, would forestall the ravages of enteric or the paratyphoid fevers, or even of spirochaetal jaundice infection from the *Leptospira icterohaemorrhagiae*.

A similar principle applied to the legislation concerning the clean and unclean fowls. Leviticus 11:13 enumerated those which were unsafe for human consumption, but did not furnish any specific list of clean species. The rapacious, aquatic, and predatory kinds of birds were excluded, since their flesh, if eaten, might transmit infection from carrion. The pigeon, turtle-dove, goose, quail, domestic fowl, and partridge were numbered among the clean birds used by the Israelites. Four varieties of locusts were permitted for food (Lev. 11:21f.), a situation that reflected accurately the life of the desert nomad, who regularly included small insects such as grasshoppers or locusts in his diet. The species allowed were the locust (*Aedipoda migratoria*), the bald locust (*Acrydum peregrinum*), the cricket (*Aedipoda cristata*), and the grasshopper, probably the smallest of the locust tribe. These insects were eaten at all stages of their growth, and regarded from early antiquity as a palatable food. The Levitical code (Lev. 11:23) prohibited the eating of "all winged creeping things that have four feet," an expression that apparently

---

symptoms like epilepsy, or else become palpable subcutaneously. Yet another disease that can be contracted from ingesting improperly prepared pork has come to the notice of medical research in recent years. It is called "toxoplasmosis," and in its symptomatic form resembles pneumonia. While the method of its transmission still is imperfectly understood, it is widespread among animals, particularly pigs and rodents. The toxoplasma organism in pork is unaffected by the periods of pork storage prescribed by occidental food laws, and seems to be able to survive the usual cooking temperatures. It occurs in a cyst-like mass called a "pseudo-cyst," the structure of which is resistant to freezing or the action of gastric juices, but it tends to be broken down when subjected to prolonged cooking at above average temperatures. It should be observed in passing that the ruminants proper are not wholly free from parasites themselves, for the flesh of the ox is occasionally the intermediate host for the parasite *Taenia saginata*, and man, the definitive host, acquires the infection through eating improperly cooked flesh containing the organism *Cysticercus bovis*. The resultant tapeworm is about twenty feet long and has approximately two thousand segments. The parasitic organism known as *Diphyllobothrium latum* is a worm of about thirty feet with some three thousand segments. Man is the definitive host and fish the intermediate host, with infection occurring when caviar or imperfectly cooked fish are ingested. A pathological condition known as *tularemia*, marked by malaise, rigor, febrile states, and glandular swellings can also result in certain parts of the world, including North America, from eating poorly prepared fish or rabbits.

designated all swarming creatures of marine or terrestrial habitats, which in Leviticus 11:29 included vermin and reptiles. The latter were universally detested as loathsome and unclean, generally being associated with demonism.

Closely allied with the designation of suitable and unsuitable foods was the concern for protecting food and water from possible contamination by unclean objects. Levitical law (Lev. 11:31ff.) gave specific directions concerning vessels and foodstuffs that had been allowed to come into contact with any unclean thing. The principles underlying modern systematized public health are particularly prominent here, for the protection of foodstuffs would obviate the ravages of afflictions such as food-borne polioencephalitis, food-poisoning, the enteric fevers, and parasitic worms. Pollution of water was also avoided rigorously, for it too was recognized as a likely source of infection, disease, and death. An earthen vessel containing water defiled by anything unclean was itself deemed unsafe for use and had to be destroyed. But if an unclean animal or insect contaminated an article made of wood, or a garment of skin, or a sack (Lev. 11:32, RSV), it was considered sufficient to immerse it in water until the evening in order to cleanse it satisfactorily. Fountains, large pools, and streams were considered safe and clean. There is no doubt, once again, that the insistence upon maintaining a clean water supply was the means of preventing diseases and afflictions. Quite clearly a preventive approach to the problems of diet and hygiene was the only really satisfactory one, considering the necessary improvisations of nomadic existence in a desert milieu and the certainly primitive culinary standards of the time of the Wilderness wanderings and even later.

3. *Leprosy.* Another important aspect of the preventive approach to pathological problems involved the diagnosis and treatment of leprosy.[21] The Hebrew צרעת is a generic term derived from a root containing the idea of affliction with an eruptive cutaneous ailment. The Greek term *lepra* indicated a skin condition characterized by the appearance of rough, scaly patches, and was most probably a description of psoriasis. However, the term appears to have been rather indefinite, so that the LXX rendering could well have included leucodermia, favus infection, and psoriasis as well as true leprosy. For a skin disease that was much closer to the latter, the Greeks employed the term elephantiasis, which the Vulgate rendered as *lepra*, thereby adding to the terminological confusion. While leprosy was known in Mesopotamia as far back as the third millennium B.C., only one instance of true leprosy has been discovered to date in Egyptian mummies, giving some substance to the belief

[21] Cf. R. K. Harrison, *IDB*, III, pp. 111ff.; H. M. Spinka, *Journal of the American Scientific Affiliation*, XI (1959), pp. 17ff.; R. G. Cochrane, *Biblical Leprosy: A Suggested Interpretation* (1961), pp. 3ff.

that the individual concerned may have been an immigrant from Syria or Mesopotamia.

The organism causing leprosy was discovered by Hansen in 1871, who showed that the disease resulted from infection by the minute schizomycetous fungus *Mycobacterium leprae*. There are three commonly described varieties of clinical leprosy at present. The nodular type results in the formation of facial lumps and generalized thickening of the tissue. In addition, degenerative changes take place in the mucous membranes of the nose and throat. The second variety, the anesthetic, is less severe and is distributed in association with the cutaneous nerves. The thickening of the nerves causes discoloration and loss of feeling in certain areas of the skin, and after some time blisters form on these anesthetic patches. Perforating ulcers frequently occur on the feet, and portions of the upper extremities often become afflicted with necrosis and fall off, leaving a healed stump (*lepra mutilans*). This form of leprosy is chronic, sometimes lasting thirty years. A third or mixed variety exhibits a combination of all of the foregoing symptoms in varying degrees. Diagnosis of leprosy (or "Hansen's disease," as modern medical practitioners prefer to designate it) is established by demonstrating the presence of the bacillus *leprae* in the nodules or blisters.

The description of diagnostic techniques and quarantine regulations makes it quite evident that among other cutaneous conditions true clinical leprosy was being envisaged in the Levitical prescriptions. The Hebrew of chapter 13 is technical, suited to a professional textbook for the priest-physician. The language is like that of the Egyptian medical texts, and it is as obscure to the modern Biblical student as most advanced texts are to beginners in other fields of knowledge. For the average Bible reader the situation is further complicated by the obsolete English terminology occasionally used to translate the Hebrew. Such unfortunate renderings include "scall" (RSV "itch") and "tetter," the latter being virtually meaningless, but still perpetuated by the RSV (Lev. 13:39).

The affliction described could have occurred spontaneously (Lev. 13: 2-17); it could have been consequent upon a furuncle (Lev. 13:18-23) or a burn on the skin (Lev. 13:24-28), or it might have arisen on the head or beard (Lev. 13:29-44). The first clinical indications included the presence of a swelling or subcutaneous nodule, a cuticular crust, and a whitish-red spot. If on examination these symptoms indicated subcuticular penetration resulting in depigmentation of the small hairs occurring in that area of the skin, the patient was tentatively pronounced unclean. If only one of these symptoms was present, he was quarantined for seven days and then re-examined. If no further degeneration was evident he was isolated for another week, after which he could be declared clean.

A chronic form of the disease was indicated by the presence of white hairs and red granular or ulcerated tissue in an elevated area of depigmented skin. Any person who exhibited these symptoms was pronounced unclean by the priests. If a patient manifested a white cutaneous condition covering his entire body he was considered clean (Lev. 13:13), and would probably have been the victim of what modern medicine would describe as acquired leucodermia (*vitiligo*). But if, on subsequent examination, he was found to be ulcerated, he was to be declared unclean (Lev. 13:14), although this drastic pronouncement could be revoked if the ulceration merely constituted the mild pustulation common to most cutaneous diseases.

Fundamental to the diagnosis of clinical leprosy was the extent to which cutaneous penetration had occurred. If the disease had affected the epidermis and had not produced morbid changes in the local hair, the affliction was not regarded as especially serious in nature. As such it might have been eczema, leucodermia, impetigo, psoriasis or some allied cutaneous disease. But if the condition under examination had infiltrated the dermis (*corium*), and had caused the local hairs to split or break off and lose their color, then leprosy was to be suspected.

In the matter of differential diagnosis, the presence of a white or inflamed spot on the site of an old boil or burn (Lev. 13:18-28) was of importance to the priest-physicians of Israel. If the dermis had not been penetrated, a seven-day quarantine period was imposed, after which the patient was again examined. If the swelling or pustule remained localized, the diagnosis of leprosy was excluded. The actual condition involved is obscure, and may have been a keloid or connective-tissue growth of the skin which usually arises in the scar of some previous injury or disease. The most probable diagnosis is that of diffuse symmetrical scleroderma (*sclerema adultorum*), in which uniform patches of the skin become hardened and thickened.

The foregoing diagnostic procedures were applied to the incidence of diseases affecting the scalp also (Lev. 13:29-37), and if quarantine showed that the disease was not progressing, one of several differential diagnoses was entertained. Where the presence of leprosy was definitely established, the afflicted person was banished from society, ordered to dress distinctively, and announce his uncleanness. Appropriate ritual ceremonies were prescribed for those occasions on which spontaneous healing occurred, and the leper was then declared clean (Lev. 14:1-32). Quite obviously the priest-physicians of the Mosaic and subsequent ages in Israel were able to distinguish between what modern physicians would describe as acute and chronic varieties of a number of skin diseases. That the term צרעת is not the same as modern clinical leprosy is immediately apparent from the fact that it was also used to describe, among other conditions, a "leprosy" of houses and clothing, neither of which is affected by the bacillus *leprae*. On the other hand, against the background of information provided in Leviticus, the Hebrew priest would be able to diagnose the genuine incidence of Hansen's disease without undue difficulty, even though he was approaching the clinical situation from an ancient oriental, rather than a modern occidental, diagnostic standpoint. This is substantiated by the manner in which present-day textbooks on leprosy refer to the remarkable passages relating to the diagnosis and prevention of leprosy in Leviticus.[22] This material is all the more significant because its technical nature attests to its antiquity, and also because it comprises the first formulation of the principles of quarantine and preventive medicine as applied to leprosy to be recovered from the culture of the ancient Near East.

The deteriorated condition of garments (Lev. 13:47-59) probably resulted from the incidence of dampness, mold, or fungus. Its occurrence was taken seriously, and the material thus affected was burned if the deterioration showed signs of spreading; otherwise washing was deemed sufficient to render the article clean. If discoloration of the walls of a house occurred (Lev. 14:34-47), the usual principle of quarantine was again applied. Affected masonry or woodwork had to be removed and replaced by new material, and it seems evident that the regulations enjoined in this connection were directed at halting the spread of dry rot in the woodwork and discouraging the growth of lichens, fungi, and mineral precipitates on the masonry of houses. Sterilization by washing was also prescribed for the incidence of various bodily secretions, whether of a benign nature such as a seminal emission (Lev. 15:16-18) and menstruation (Lev. 15:19-24), or of a more malignant character (Lev. 15:2), the latter perhaps including leukorrhea and gonorrhea.

4. Marital relations. That a strict attitude towards the marital union of those near of kin was typical of the Mosaic legal code is indicated by the enactments of Leviticus 18:1-30. These prohibitions have a distinct bearing upon the marital customs of the day and age. They contrast sharply with the customs among the Egyptians—who never had any specific formulation of marriage laws and where questions of consanguinity were ignored in favor of the dictates of the matriarchate—among the Canaanites—where fornication, adultery, bestiality, and incest were accredited functions of the sexual life as depicted in the Ras Shamra tablets[23]—and among the Hittites—where certain forms of bestiality were permitted (perhaps as the vestigial remains of an ancient animal cult), although incestuous relationships were prohibited.[24]

[22] R. P. Strong (ed.), *Stitt's Diagnosis, Prevention and Treatment of Tropical Diseases* (1944), I, p. 814.

[23] A. van Selms, *Marriage and Family Life in Ugaritic Literature* (1954), pp. 74ff.

[24] E. Neufeld, *The Hittite Laws* (1951), pp. 188ff.

The intention of the Levitical legislation was to represent sexual intimacy with those near of kin as a shameful act, and the list of prohibited degrees included a considerable number of relationships of affinity as well as consanguinity. While it would be unreasonable to expect in this delineation an exhaustive treatment of the problem, the resultant statements relating to consanguinity and affinity are remarkably comprehensive. The general principle was enunciated in Leviticus 18:6 in the form of a preamble, and successive verses illustrated the forbidden degrees of kinship in greater detail. These, however, constituted representative cases, and should not be thought of as indicating an exhaustive catalog or statement of possible incestuous combinations.

The prohibitions appear to reflect three fundamental concepts: first, that nearness of relationship in blood constitutes an impediment to union, and involves all ascendants and descendants but only the nearer cases of collaterals; secondly, that near relationship of affinity, or connection by marriage, is to be interpreted in the light of the contention that a man and his wife are "one flesh," that is, kin or blood relations; and finally, that relationship through the woman is exactly analogous to relationship through the man on the basis of the "one flesh."

Of the prohibited degrees, six were relationships of consanguinity and eight were of affinity. The enactment concerning the sister of a wife (Lev. 18:18), which is one of the closest relationships of affinity, has been a matter of dispute among scholars for many years. The prohibition was evidently designed in order to prevent a man from marrying the sister of a living wife, thus precluding further unions of the kind entered into by Jacob, who married Leah and Rachel (Gen. 29:23ff.).[25] At the same time it should be recognized that the marriage of a man with the sister of his deceased wife was not prohibited by the enactment, either expressly or by implication.

In any assessment of the rationale of these laws, it must be observed that the moral and social aspects appear to have predominated over any supposed biological or genetic considerations. Anthropologists have long been familiar with the dangers inherent in primitive and nomadic endogamous community life, where consistent patterns of marriage between close relatives would quickly result in an effective centralizing of influence, property, and wealth in the hands of a very few families. Such a restricted concept of social organization would thwart the development of an adequate social consciousness, and would be entirely out of harmony with the humanitarian concerns of the Covenant Code and other Pentateuchal legislation of a like order. It is perhaps not without significance that the occasions on which the Levitical prescriptions for marriage were flouted were set against a background of advanced social degeneration (Am. 2:7).

[25] Cf. D. R. Mace, *Hebrew Marriage* (1953), pp. 152f.

The legislation does not appear to be either aware of, or amenable to, the concept that consanguineous union results in such conditions as familial idiocy or degeneration of the stock. It is now well known that, in the absence of clearly defined hereditary predispositions towards degeneration or disease in the stock itself, the consanguineous union of certain types of animals can be perpetrated over successive generations without any observable deterioration in mental or physical functions, provided always that bad recessive qualities are eliminated in the breeding process along with the more obvious dominant ones which may emerge. Much the same can be said also for human consanguineous unions, which are not as deleterious as some writers have imagined, despite the danger of a substantial increase in genes of the same origin. There does not appear to be any accredited physiological basis for the prohibitions concerning consanguineous union, as seems evident when the sequences are historically demonstrable. Thus Ruffer, in a study of Egyptian royalty from the Eighteenth Dynasty onwards, concluded that the issue was not obviously impaired by the marriage of those of near kinship, and showed that such pathological conditions as were demonstrable were hereditary in nature, with gout and obesity being the most notable.[26] These observations are all the more interesting in the light of the "control" that can be exercised over the study by the fact that the physical and mental attributes of the royalty of Egypt from the Eighteenth Dynasty onwards are attestable historically.

The average age of the Ptolemaic kings was sixty-four years, and according to extant records they were not subject to epilepsy, deaf-mutism, idiocy, infertility, insanity, or general deterioration of the familial stock, thus making it evident that a prolonged tradition of marriage within the prohibited degrees of marriage as enumerated in Leviticus had no discernibly detrimental effect upon them. It would appear, therefore, that other than purely biological or medical considerations were being contemplated when the laws concerning consanguinity were promulgated.

❋ ❋ ❋ ❋ ❋

Limitations of space preclude further discussion of the contents of Leviticus, important as it is for the entire fabric of Hebrew social, moral, and religious life. It should be observed, however, that the book is of great importance for the Christian student since it provides the necessary background for a theological understanding of the sacrifice and priesthood of Jesus Christ, both of which are expounded at some length in the Epistle to the Hebrews. Leviticus is rightly prized by the Jews as constituting the book which contains binding regulations with regard to sin and atonement, sanctification and physical health. The Christian

[26] M. A. Ruffer in *Studies in the Palaeopathology of Egypt* (ed. R. L. Moodie, 1921), pp. 325ff.

Church has traditionally based its table of prohibited degrees of marital relationship upon that found in Leviticus, and had it followed more rigorously the hygienic and dietary principles enshrined in that ancient legislation, it would have gained many more of the benefits contemplated in the Hebrew ideal for the health and well-being of the individual and the community alike.

The Hebrew text of Leviticus has been remarkably well preserved, which is hardly surprising in view of its priestly character. One or two slight improvements can be made upon the MT tradition by reference to such ancient versions as the Samaritan Pentateuch, the LXX, and the Peshitta, as in Leviticus 7:21; 25:47 and 26:39, but these are very minor. Fragments of Leviticus recovered from Qumran give support to the MT tradition, as do two fragments of the book found by Yigael Yadin at Masada during the 1964-65 season of excavating.

Supplementary Literature

Bonar, A. A. *Commentary on Leviticus*. 1861.
Cazelles, H. *Le Lévitique*. 1958.
Chapman, A. T. and A. W. Streane. *The Book of Leviticus*. 1914.
Dussaud, R. *Les origines cananéennes du sacrifice israélite*. 1921.
Gispen, W. H. *Het Boek Leviticus*. 1950.
Heinisch, P. *Das Buch Leviticus*. 1935.
Hicks, F. C. N. *The Fulness of Sacrifice*. 1946.
Hooke, S. H. *The Origins of Early Semitic Ritual*. 1938.
James, E. O. *The Origins of Sacrifice*. 1933.
Kornfeld, W. *Studien zum Heiligkeitsgesetz*. 1952.
Noth, M. *Leviticus*. 1964.

V. THE BOOK OF NUMBERS

A. NAME AND OUTLINE

The Jewish Synagogue named this book either וידבר ("and he spoke") or ־במדבר ("in the desert of"), after its first word or after one of the early words in the initial verse. An older name in Jewish circles was "The Fifth of the Musterings," a designation meant to indicate that particular portion of the five Mosaic writings describing the numberings of the Israelites.[1] The LXX translators gave the title Ἀριθμοί (Numbers) to the work, and this was followed by the Vulgate (*Numeri*) and English versions.

By contrast with Leviticus, which is almost entirely legislative, Numbers, like Exodus, combines history with legal enactments. The bulk of the work is concerned with the vicissitudes of the Israelites in their Wilderness wanderings subsequent to the Exodus until the time when, some thirty-eight years later, they were on the point of entering the Promised Land. The book can be analyzed in its extant form as follows:

I. Preparations for Leaving Sinai, ch. 1:1–10:10
   A. The census and marshalling of the tribes, 1:1–4:49
   B. Sundry legislation, 5:1–6:27
   C. Offerings at the dedication of the altar, 7:1-89
   D. The candlestick, the consecration of Levites, and rules concerning their service, 8:1-26
   E. The second passover, the cloud, and the use of silver trumpets 9:1–10:10

II. From Sinai to the Plains of Moab, ch. 10:11–21:35
   A. Preliminary movement from Sinai, 10:11-36
   B. Unrest among the tribes, 11:1-15
   C. The provision of quails, 11:16-35
   D. Miriam's leprosy, 12:1-16
   E. The twelve spies, 13:1–14:45
   F. Miscellaneous commands, 15:1-41

---

[1] J. H. Hertz, *The Pentateuch and Haftorahs*, p. 567.

G. Korah, Dathan, and Abiram, 16:1–17:13
H. The service of the priests and Levites, 18:1-32
I. The law of purification, 19:1-22
J. Miriam's death; events at Meribah, 20:1-13
K. Edom's refusal to let Israel pass; Aaron's death, 20:14-29
L. The journey to the plains of Moab, 21:1-35

III. Events in the Moabite Plains, ch. 22–36
A. Balaam, 22:1–24:25
B. Baal-peor, 25:1-18
C. The second census, 26:1-65
D. Inheritance rights of daughters; the successor of Moses, 27:1-23
E. Regulations concerning offerings; vows of the women, 28:1–30:16
F. War against Midian, 31:1-54
G. Inheritance in Transjordan, 32:1-42
H. Israelite encampments, 33:1-49
I. Allotment of territory west of Jordan; appointment of Levitical and refugee cities; marriage of heiresses, 33:50–36:13

B. COMPILATION OF NUMBERS

The composition of Numbers presents problems similar to those encountered in connection with Exodus and Leviticus. It can be assumed quite legitimately that the phrase "And the Lord spoke to Moses, saying . . ." represents the beginning of a new section of material, and that the introductory formula, when restricted to that specific expression, can be held to preface an agglomeration of material of a revelatory, instructional, didactic, legislative, or other character. When, however, this prefatory phrase is related to a particular locality, as for example in Numbers 1:1, where the Lord is said to have communed with Moses in the Wilderness of Sinai at a specific time, the implication is that the subsequent material must be regarded as historical and Mosaic in origin. This is not to say, of course, that certain modifications or revisions of material prefaced by the formula were not entertained at a later period, for as has been observed previously, such a procedure was an accredited scribal practice in parts of the ancient Near East. What it does imply, however, is that the component sections of Numbers must be contemplated against a desert milieu, and must be assessed consistently on such a basis. To regard certain possible scribal additions or recensions undertaken at a later period as evidence that the entire work was in fact of a comparatively late order, and needs to be projected back to an earlier age if it is to be credited to Moses in any sense at all, is an incorrect procedure methodologically and an improper use of the available evidence. Many modern scholars have now diverged from the Wellhausenian position in this regard to the extent that they acknowledge that the book contains material from very early times,[2] which may in fact be Mosaic in character and origin.

While there is an overall chronological pattern to Numbers, certain of the sections appear only loosely related to the particular period of the Wilderness wanderings with which they have been associated in process of compilation. Thus the promulgations made in connection with vows (Num. 30:1ff.) and the miscellaneous items relating to cultic and other observances (Num. 15:1ff.) could have emerged from any one of the years of sojourn in the Wilderness, and in consequence need not reflect any specific topographical or chronological situation. Numbers appears to be more fragmentary than its precursors in the Torah, and this is particularly evident in chapters 20 and 21, where the original form was probably in the nature of short topographical notes such as could be found in a travel diary.

This general difference in tone from that evident in Exodus and Leviticus has led many scholars to reject the Mosaic authorship of Numbers, and on the basis of an occidental scheme of documentary analysis to assign it to such avowedly hypothetical literary sources as J, E, P, and L. It is true, of course, that the scribal activity of Moses was mentioned only in Numbers 23 (cf. 5:23; 11:26), and that some sections of the book (e.g. 12:3; 15:22f.; 32:34) appear to have been composed by someone other than the great Hebrew legislator, or even abstracted from some such source as the "Book of the Wars of the Lord" (Num. 21:14).

In the light of what is known about processes of scribal revision in Egypt and certain other areas of the ancient Near East, there appears to be no difficulty whatever in assuming that the reference in Numbers 12:3 concerning the modesty of Moses constitutes an addition by a later hand, quite possibly either that of Joshua or Samuel. The objections raised in critical circles to the supposed non-Mosaic nature of Numbers 15:22 are much less assured, however, since the purpose of the reference was to stress the revealed origin of the sacrificial offering and its mediation to Israel through Moses. In such a case the allusion to Moses in terms of the third person would be entirely proper, although nonetheless emphatic.

A more accredited post-Mosaic insertion is evident in the reference in Numbers 21:14f., where there is a brief citation from a source designated "The Book of the Wars of the Lord." This is a genuine Pentateuchal source, unlike the hypothetical documents favored by the members of the Graf-Wellhausen school, albeit quoted in the briefest of forms. It was evidently a record of the mighty acts of God on behalf of Israel, and was most probably in its earlier stages of writing during the late Wilderness

---

[2] E.g. F. M. Cross, *BA*, X, No. 3 (1947), pp. 52ff.; J. Marsh, *IB*, II, p. 138; G. H. Davies, *IDB*, IV, p. 503.

period. Information concerning this matter is both scarce and uncertain, since the book has only survived in the fragment mentioned above. The events referred to in Numbers 21:15 can only have been written down subsequent to the time of Moses, but were quite probably in extant written, and certainly in oral, form by the time of Joshua when the ancient Book of Jashar, a national epic that commemorated the heroic course of Israelite history under God, was also taking substantial shape. Thus there are no reasonable grounds for supposing that the insertion, which probably commenced with the gloss in Numbers 21:13b, is any later than the time of Samuel, and it may well have arisen in the settlement period.

Similar considerations apply to the content of Numbers 32:33ff., which comprises an enumeration of Transjordanian cities built by the offspring of Gad, Reuben, and Machir, son of Manasseh. Quite clearly such constructional activity was only possible after the fulfilment of the promise made by those tribes to attend to their military responsibilities (Num. 32:17). Once again there appears little difficulty in regarding this section as a later scribal or editorial insertion to describe the outcome of the promises made earlier in the chapter to Moses. As such it completed the narrative in the form of a commentary upon subsequent events, and may even have been drawn up in this manner to redress any implied neglect of the Transjordanian Hebrews in the light of the prominence given to the Israelite victories during the conquest period. In connection with the constructional activities of these Transjordanian Hebrews, it should be noted that they were engaged in the hasty repair, rather than the actual founding, of such settlements as Aroer and Ataroth (cf. Num. 32:26f.), since Gilead was already long inhabited. It seems quite probable that Numbers 32:34-42 was a product of the settlement period, and may well have been introduced into the text of Numbers by the time of Samuel at the very latest. This is apparent from the fact that the names of certain of the sites were ancient Canaanite strongholds whose designation was to be altered, as noted in the gloss in Numbers 32:38, a situation that accords well with the late conquest period. Aside from these few possibilities of post-Mosaic addition, the internal evidence of Numbers consistently affirms that the regulations and laws it contains were revealed to Israel through the mediatorial offices of Moses and occasionally Aaron. Furthermore, it supports without equivocation the impression that these laws were promulgated against a desert milieu, and that they were implemented during the time spent in the Wilderness wanderings. Thus, apart from the foregoing passages that might conceivably constitute somewhat later additions, there is no single factor in the entire contents of Numbers that is in any respect incompatible with the conditions which are stated to have obtained during the period of desert sojourn.

617

Certain problems arise in any attempt to speculate as to the mechanics of compilation of Numbers, however. The first four chapters appear curiously situated, to say the least, since they do not particularly serve to integrate the book with the historical narrative as it terminated in Exodus. If the presence of the stereotyped formula in Numbers 1:1 and 2:1 indicates that these chapters were originally separate records that were placed side by side in the scroll, it then becomes difficult to account for the presence of what appears to be a genuine colophon in Numbers 3:1. If the latter as such refers to either or both preceding chapters, it is far from easy to see how they could have been Mosaic or Aaronic in any sense different from that of analogous material ascribed to Moses and Aaron.

But if Numbers 3:1 does not constitute the colophon of some preceding historical narrative, it becomes difficult to assess precisely what place the verse has in the early chapters of Numbers. The reference in Numbers 1:1, which speaks of the Wilderness of Sinai, can hardly be the title of a tablet whose colophon refers to a revelation upon Mount Sinai itself, so that if Numbers 3:1 is genuinely colophonic in form, it may be that only a fragment of the preceding material has been preserved, which in total amount may have exceeded the contents of the first two chapters or, on the other hand, may only have survived partially and without title in chapter two. Whatever the nature of their origin, the first four chapters of Numbers are a manifest unit in their final form, dealing as they do with the census and the regulations for the departure from the Sinai region.

The records of chapters 5 and 6 contain material relating to the rules governing the Nazirite order, uncleanness, and the jealousy ordeal, indicating that a group of specifically cultic promulgations was attached to the priestly records of the census and the regulations for the marshalling of the tribes. The general standpoint of the first four chapters reappears in chapter seven, which dealt with the offerings of the princes for the consecration of the Tabernacle. The same theme was continued in Numbers 8:1-4, and described the lamps in the Tabernacle, but it was interrupted in Numbers 8:5 by what may well have been the beginning of a fresh leather scroll or a new section of such material.

It is possible that Numbers 8:5-26, dealing with the separation of the Levites, was dislocated in the process of assembling the book, since as far as its contents are concerned it could easily have followed Numbers 4:49. An accredited historical section is represented by Numbers 9:1-14, which depicts events occurring prior to the first census and somewhat before the Tabernacle was erected, which again appears to be dislocated from the standpoint of a purely historical sequence. Quite possibly at least some of the priestly material in chapters five to eight antedated the first census-list, and if this is so the latter would have been added as prefatory material once the priestly enactments had been assembled, and not *vice versa*.

While the material arrangement of the early chapters in Numbers appears somewhat strange to the western mind, it is noteworthy that the finished form of the material sets the priestly enactments firmly against the records of the Sinai period of the Wilderness wanderings so as to authenticate them and demonstrate their originality in respect to the cultus. While the sections could possibly be interpreted as having been assembled rather haphazardly in contrast to occidental methods and standards, it remains true that they were collected in a fashion that was neither accidental nor inconvenient as far as the original compiler was concerned. This fact alone should serve as a warning against an injudicious approach to the problems of compilation of the book, and a reminder that the needs of an oriental people were the primary consideration of the editor or editors responsible for the finished product.

The gradually unfolding introduction of Numbers 9:15 seems to indicate quite clearly the commencement of another roll in the narrative, which carries the history of the Wilderness wanderings to the sojourn at Hazeroth without any discernible break (Num. 11:35). This was followed by the complaint of Miriam and Aaron against Moses (Num. 12:1ff.), which resulted in Miriam's being afflicted with a skin disease. From Hazeroth the Israelites moved to Paran, and the narrative described the succession of events which culminated in failure to enter the Promised Land (Num. 15:41).

The enactment relating to sacrifice (Num. 15:1-32) was probably inserted into the narrative at this juncture so as to provide legislative backing for the ritual procedures to be followed immediately upon entering Canaan. If this law was as mandatory and comprehensive in scope as the text appears to indicate, it obviously antedated the more elaborate sacrificial prescriptions of Leviticus, and evidently belonged to an early period of the sojourn to constitute an interim injunction for the remainder of the desert era.

Were this actually to be the case, it would indicate, as Wright has pointed out,[3] that Amos was correct in suggesting that the people as a whole did not offer animal sacrifices in the Wilderness (Am. 5:25). The sections dealing with sabbath violation (Num. 15:32-36) and the making of fringes for clothing (Num. 15:37-41) are obvious insertions of literary fragments of priestly interest that have a desert situation for their background, but which need not be in strict chronological order.

Much the same considerations apply to the contents of chapters 16, 18, and 19, where priestly concerns are obviously at the forefront. Chapter 17, dealing with the budding rod of Aaron, is obviously of Wilderness origin, although it is difficult to do more than assign it broadly to the

[3] J. S. Wright, *EQ*, XXV (1953), p. 15.

period prior to the encampment in the plains of Moab. Chapters 20 and 21 narrate incidents that took place in the same general phase of the wanderings, and depict with considerable fidelity the tensions of Israelite life at that time. The records are brief almost to the point of being fragmentary, so that important occasions, such as the situation attending the death of Aaron, were dealt with in a rather perfunctory manner. It is within the bounds of possibility that these chapters constituted part of an abbreviated travel diary, and that they were assembled by an editor somewhat after the death of Moses and supplemented by an itinerary of that particular phase of the wanderings and a triumphal paean (Num. 21:27-30), perhaps in fragmentary form, as well as by a snatch of a popular work-song (Num. 21:17b-18b).

The narratives describing the prophetic activities of Balaam (Num. 22:1–24:26) are of interest partly because they illustrate the role of the Mesopotamian seer in military affairs, and partly because of the problems associated with their composition and integrity. The name "Balaam" (בלעם) has been variously understood to mean "the clan brings forth," "glutton," or, as suggested by Albright, "the (divine) uncle brings forth," the last being based upon a comparison of בלעם with the thirteenth-century B.C. Amorite proper name *Yabil-'ammu*.[4]

Balaam was unusual in the Old Testament as a foreigner who was subject to the command of God, and whose career exhibited the tremendous potency attributed in the Old Testament and elsewhere in the ancient Near East to the spoken word.[5] He lived in Pethor on the River Euphrates, south of Carchemish, probably the *Pitru* of the Assyrian texts,[6] described as situated on the River Sagur near its junction with the Euphrates. Precisely how the narratives relating to his oracles came to be in written form is unknown. It seems difficult to imagine that they could have been recorded by an Israelite scribe, since no Hebrews were present when the incidents described took place. It may be that a disciple of the Mesopotamian seer was responsible for the survival of the narratives, although this cannot be regarded as being any more than purely conjectural. What is evident, however, is that the traditions concerning Balaam were well known in oral form by the time of Joshua (Josh. 13:22), and if the written narratives were not already extant by then, they could hardly have been delayed much beyond the period of the Judges.

In the view of the present writer they were in written form not later than the twelfth century B.C., and were inserted during the settlement phase into the historical sequence of Numbers. In any event they ought not to be regarded in any sense as dating in their extant form from a period later than the time of Samuel. Chapter 25:1-18 can be construed as

---

[4] W. F. Albright, *JBL*, LXIII (1944), p. 232.
[5] R. F. Johnson, *IDB*, I, p. 341.
[6] *ANET*, p. 278; cf. W. F. Albright, *BASOR*, No. 118 (1950), p. 15 n. 13.

620

forming an appendix to the Balaam oracles, and it is instructive in the light of the fact that the Mesopotamian seer subsequently associated himself with the Midianites and counselled them to entice Israel into the licentious cult-worship of Baal-peor (Num. 31:16). The chapter is thus placed into proper religious and historical context, and forms a fitting conclusion to material that is thoroughly Mesopotamian in character, as exemplified by discoveries at Mari and elsewhere that have demonstrated the role occupied by diviners in relationship to military affairs.

Numbers 26:1 apparently represents the commencement of another roll of priestly material that contained data relating to the second census, the record of the appointment of Joshua as the successor of Moses, and certain other details of interest to cultic and administrative circles in Israel. The insertion of such material at that particular juncture in the narrative raises some question as to the rationale of the arrangement, especially where the regulations concerning the feasts are involved. In contemplating the situation against a desert background it seems quite probable that the insertion actually reflected a chronological reminder to the Israelites to the effect that the rather casual practices with regard to celebrations and other cultic requirements (cf. Josh. 5:5) obtaining in the Wilderness were shortly to be replaced on entrance into the Promised Land by the more rigorous stipulations as set forth generally in the priestly enactments of Leviticus. On the other hand, as Wright has suggested, Numbers 28 and 29 may have existed as "festival offerings" independently of the somewhat more general regulations for the people as found in Leviticus 23, and may have been promulgated in their extant form as an act of cultic discipline.[7]

Presumably a further section of the assembled scroll of Numbers commenced with chapter 31, which dealt with the revenge taken upon the Midianites. This material comprised Numbers 31:1–32:32, and included a statement concerning the allotment of land on the east side of the Jordan to certain of the tribes. The remaining chapters of the book comprise a miscellany of material that included a general catalog of the places visited by the Israelites between the time of the Exodus and the entrance into Canaan, as well as regulations concerning the division of the land once it had been acquired, and various laws that envisaged a sedentary state in Canaan.

If the foregoing analysis corresponds in any respect to the manner in which Numbers was actually assembled from written sources, it will be seen that it was compiled by means of a far less elegant literary process than that underlying either Genesis, Exodus, or Leviticus. Quite possibly this very fact could be used as an argument for the early date of the composition, on the assumption that the combination of historical, cultic, and other material against a desert life-situation would tend to result in

---

[7] J. S. Wright, *EQ*, XXV (1953), p. 16.

a more haphazard literary arrangement than that obtaining for purely cultic regulations, as in Leviticus, for narratives of a primarily historical nature, as in Exodus, or for pre-existing literary, and perhaps oral material, as in Genesis.

The relationship between the various sections of Numbers is by no means clear to modern observers, and becomes even more obscure when contemplated against a background of classical European documentary analysis. Most probably the framework was of a chronological order, marked by specific links with the general narration of events, and amplified by means of various regulations and statistical data, especially where these had a bearing upon the desert life-situation of the Wilderness wanderings. It should be remembered that ancient scribes generally did not distinguish between cultic, judicial, social, and moral enactments as carefully as their modern counterparts, which probably goes far towards accounting for the fact that the connection between apparently unrelated sections of a book such as Numbers was more obvious to the people for whom the work was intended than for readers in a different day and age.

What may reasonably be assumed to be post-Mosaic segments of Numbers, along with the brief narrative form of portions such as chapters 20 and 21, might suggest that a good deal of responsibility for the final form of the scroll was exercised some time after the death of Moses by a compiler or editor, perhaps even Joshua, who drew upon Mosaic and other material so as to produce Numbers in something that approximated closely to its extant form. In the view of the present writer there is no single section of the work that requires a date later than the time of Samuel, and the bulk of the work is regarded as issuing from the Mosaic era itself.

C. THE MATERIAL OF NUMBERS

1. The encampment. The history narrated in Numbers covered a period of some thirty-eight years, and embraced the time between the second and fortieth years of the Exodus era (cf. Num. 1:1; 7:1; 9:1, 15; 10:11; 33:38; Exod. 40:2; Deut. 1:3). At Sinai a census was taken of the people one month after the erection of the Tabernacle (Exod. 40:17), and included those who could serve in a military capacity to arrive at a total of 603,550 individuals (Num. 1:46). The census in chapter 2 gave the tribes in their camps in the order in which they were related to the tent of meeting, and presupposes a condition in which the Israelites were not settled in the Promised Land.

The arrangement of the tribes by their standards in the form of a hollow rectangle around the Tabernacle (Num. 2:2ff.), long held by liberal critics to constitute an indication of the late date of the priestly material in the Pentateuch, is now known to have been a common deployment of encamped forces in the Amarna period. As Kitchen has remarked, it is significant in this connection to note that precisely the same strategic layout was utilized by Rameses II, the contemporary of Moses, in his Syrian campaign, when the large portable war-tent of the divine king was pitched in the center of a rectangular encampment of the army divisions.[8] It is especially noteworthy that this important Egyptian comparison should have emerged from the very century in which Moses lived, for later on, in the first millennium B.C., such military encampments changed their shape, as indicated by the round form of deployment on Assyrian reliefs.[9] Therefore it appears eminently probable that the arrangement depicted in Numbers indicates that Moses was utilizing earlier Egyptian training in the military arts for the welfare of the infant Israelite nation.

Another matter which has a decided bearing upon the antiquity of the sources in Numbers relates to the use of long silver trumpets for convening a civil assembly as well as for religious and military purposes (Num. 10:1ff.). Such trumpets were in common use in Egypt during the Amarna Age,[10] and some particularly elegant specimens that were interred with the pharaoh Tutankhamen (ca. 1350 B.C.) were recovered by Howard Carter in the twentieth century.

Equally ancient is the use of six wagons drawn by oxen for the service of the Tabernacle (Num. 7:3ff.). As Kuentz has shown,[11] ox-drawn wagons were employed regularly on campaigns in Syria by the pharaohs from the time of Tuthmosis III (ca. 1470 B.C.) onwards for several centuries.[12] It only remains to be observed that the wagons of Moses and the Israelites in Sinai,[13] which were drawn generally by two yoked oxen, compare favorably with the ten wagons (עגלה)[14] drawn by six spans of oxen that transported supplies for 8,000 quarrymen of Rameses IV (ca. 1160 B.C.) from the Nile valley into the desert areas of the Wadi Hammamat, between the Nile and the Red Sea, under conditions very similar to those obtaining in the Sinai peninsula.[15] In these, as in so many other respects, a proper use of the available evidence serves to dispose of uninformed subjective criticisms of the genuineness of the narratives.

2. Legal enactments. The rite which has become known to scholars as the "jealousy ordeal" (Num. 5:11-31), is of some interest because it was

---

[8] K. A. Kitchen, *The Tyndale House Bulletin*, Nos. 5-6 (1960), p. 11, *NBD*, p. 847; cf. Ch. Kuentz, *La Bataille de Qadech* (1928-34), pls. 34, 39, 42.

[9] Cf. G. Contenau, *Everyday Life in Babylonia and Assyria* (1954), pl. 17.

[10] Cf. H. Hickmann, *La Trompette dans l'Égypte Ancienne* (1946), p. 46.

[11] Ch. Kuentz, *La Bataille de Qadech*, pl. 39.

[12] Cf. *ANET*, p. 240.

[13] K. A. Kitchen, *NBD*, p. 847.

[14] Num. 7:3, 6f. The Egyptian word '*grt*, "wagon," was derived from the Hebrew.

[15] *ARE*, IV, sect. 467.

not entirely unknown among other peoples of antiquity.[16] In this enactment Numbers supplemented the prescriptions of Leviticus, for whereas
the latter had pronounced the death penalty upon both participants in
an adulterous act, the former outlined the procedure to be followed
when a man suspected his wife of adultery that he was actually unable
to prove. The dramatic ritual that the woman was required to undergo,
all the more significant for its advanced degree of psychological suggesti-
bility, is distinctly reminiscent of the forms of treatment prescribed by
the Babylonian priest-physicians of the second millennium B.C.[17] From
the standpoint of the history of therapeutic procedures in Israel, it is of
some interest to note that the narrative under discussion is the only one
in the entire Old Testament to mention the oral administration of
potions or medicines.

Numbers 6 furnishes the regulations that governed an institution
familiar to the Hebrews throughout their entire history. The charismatic
body known as the Nazirites (AV "Nazarite") exemplified the concepts
of consecration and holiness inherent in the Mosaic Torah, although the
origin of certain Nazirite practices is obscure and most probably
antedates Moses. Historically the Nazirite was a sacred person, who in
the earlier stages of the institution became charismatic as a result of a
divine endowment, which may or may not have been initiated from the
human standpoint by a specific maternal vow.[18]

At a later stage of Israelite history the Nazirite acquired his special
spiritual status as the result of a vow which he undertook of his own
accord. In all periods, however, this particular concept of sanctity and
consecration to God was marked outwardly by abstinence from wine and
strong drink (the latter generally approximating to intoxicating liquor)
and by permitting the hair of the head to remain uncut through the
period covered by the vow of self-dedication. The pre-Mosaic origin of
the latter appears in the fact that many primitive peoples, along with
some Semites, frequently left the hair uncut during certain undertakings
that necessitated more than purely human help, and subsequently consecrated the hair to the service of their particular deity (cf. Judg. 5:2).
Echoes of this general procedure are not unknown at the present day
among Semitic peoples, as Lods has shown with reference to modern
Bedouin Arab tribes.[19]

The enactments in Numbers 6 fall conveniently into three groups, of
which the first consisted of prohibitions.[20] One of the most important of
these required the Nazirite to abstain from any form of alcoholic bever-

---

[16] Compare Code of Hammurabi, sect. 132 in *ANET*, p. 171; G. B. Gray, *A Critical and Exegetical Commentary on Numbers* (1903), p. 44.

[17] R. K. Harrison, *IDB*, III, p. 332.

[18] J. C. Rylaarsdam, *IDB*, III, p. 526.

[19] A. Lods, *Israel* (1932), p. 305.

[20] J. D. Douglas, *NBD*, pp. 871f.

age or from any of the ingredients from which such a drink might be made. This regulation may perhaps have been designed as a warning to individuals and society as a whole against the dangers inherent in alcoholism, a condition that was widely prevalent in ancient Near Eastern society and was not entirely unknown among the Hebrew priesthood (cf. Lev. 10:9). Abstinence from any form of alcohol would thus insure that the Nazirite was firmly in control of his faculties at all times in his special relationship of sanctity towards God and witness to the nation of Israel. This view seems preferable to the explanation offered by Kittel, who conjectured that abstinence in this area constituted a protest against Canaanite culture and pointed to the superiority of the nomadic ideal.[21] A second prohibition concerned the hair of the head, which was to be left in its natural condition during the entire period of consecration to God, perhaps in the belief that the hair was in some manner the seat of life and virility.[22] Finally, the Nazirite was not permitted to approach a dead body, even that of a relative, lest his state of ceremonial purity should be contaminated by contact with that which was deemed unclean.

The second section in the Nazirite enactments (Num. 6:7-12) concerned violation of the vow, whether through inadvertence or otherwise. Under such conditions the Nazirite was required to submit to detailed purificatory procedures, and to commence his period of dedication anew if he so desired. A final section of the regulations (Num. 6:13-21) was concerned with the sacrificial acts required of the Nazirite at the termination of his vow, which included the cutting and burning of the hair.

Despite the rather serious restrictions imposed upon an individual by the law of the Nazirites, it was not entirely impossible for normal domestic or social duties to be carried out, and there was nothing in the enactments which required a votary to live under something approaching a monastic regime. The distinctive feature of the status attached to the Nazirites was that of complete individual consecration alike of body and personality to the divine service. It extended to the ordinary members of Israelite society a form of holiness normally associated only with the priesthood, and afforded an individual the kind of status enjoyed by groups such as the Rechabites (Jer. 35:5).

Early Nazirites were lifelong devotees, as in the case of Samuel, who was not specifically named a Nazirite in the MT (1 Sam. 1:11), but who was described as such in a fragment of the book of Samuel recovered from 4Q, which terminated 1 Samuel 1:22 with the words, "he shall become a Nazirite for ever,"[23] thus confirming a Mishnaic tradition. Samson was evidently another permanent Nazirite, and although doubts

---

[21] R. Kittel, *Geschichte des Volkes Israel* (1925), II, p. 250.
[22] Cf. G. B. Gray, *JTS*, I (1900), p. 206.
[23] F. M. Cross, *BASOR*, No. 132 (1953), pp. 15ff.

have been expressed as to his status,[24] he was certainly a charismatic figure in the normal sense of that term. It is difficult to tell from the stories concerning Samson whether he actually abstained from wine or not. However, the affinities between Samson and the Nazirites were sufficiently self-evident to allow him to have been thought of as a Nazirite, even though he may not have fulfilled all the technical prescriptions of Numbers 6.

In the time of Amos, the perversity of Israel was such that individuals deliberately attempted to undermine the institution by encouraging the Nazirites to adopt patterns of behavior that were completely at variance with their principles (Am. 2:11f.). From the exilic period onwards the Nazirites became increasingly related to a fixed interval of consecration, as opposed to the lifelong dedication of the individual evident in earlier days. Motives other than sanctification, obedience, and penitence were entertained,[25] and in the immediate pre-Christian period casuistry began to appear in connection with the enactments.[26]

3. The Wilderness wanderings. The narrative of Numbers 10:11 shows that, in the second year of their departure from Egypt, the Israelites left the Sinai region and journeyed to Kadesh-barnea, in the vicinity of the Promised Land. Kadesh was located on the borders of the Wilderness of Zin and the Wilderness of Paran (Num. 12:16; 13:26), and has frequently been identified with the spring of 'Ain Qudeis, some sixty-six miles southwest of the southern end of the Dead Sea. Modern explorers, however, have shown that the water supply at 'Ain Qudeis is very limited,[27] and that 'Ain Qudeirat, approximately five miles northwest of 'Ain Qudeis, is a much more suitable location for Kadesh.[28] However, there can be little doubt that the entire group of springs in that area was utilized at one time or another during the thirty-eight-year sojourn of the Israelites, with 'Ain Qudeirat being the principal source of water.

Not long after the second occurrence of the quail (Num. 11:31ff.), Moses was criticized by Aaron and Miriam for marrying a woman described as "Cushite." Presumably his first wife Zipporah had died subsequent to being returned by Jethro to Moses (Exod. 18:2), although this fact is nowhere stated in the text. The term "Cushite" is usually taken as the equivalent of "Ethiopian," and as such the woman concerned may have left Egypt among the Israelites and their followers. If, however, "Cushite" is to be derived from *Kushu* and the Hebrew "Cushan," associated with Midian (Hab. 3:7), the woman could con-

[24] Cf. G. B. Gray, *A Critical and Exegetical Commentary on Numbers*, p. 60.
[25] Cf. *BJ*, II, 15, 1.
[26] Cf. the Mishnaic *Tract Nazir.*, V, 5ff.
[27] C. L. Woolley and T. E. Lawrence, *PEF Annual*, III (1914-15), pp. 53ff. and pls. 10ff.; D. Baly, *Geography of the Bible* (1957), p. 266.
[28] Y. Aharoni, *The Holy Land: Antiquity and Survival* (1957), II, 2-3, pp. 295f. and figs. 1-3.

ceivably have come from a family stock related to that of Jethro and Zipporah. The cutaneous affliction that struck Miriam (Num. 12:10ff.) by way of punishment, and which was described in the text by the generic Hebrew term translated "leprosy," was evidently not equivalent to Hansen's disease. Precisely what its exact nature was is difficult to determine, and the most that can be said from the untechnical description of the phenomenon is that it may have constituted some such transient form of skin eruption as psoriasis.

The incident involving the dispatch of scouts to Canaan occupies a strategic position in the history of the Wilderness wanderings. The land of Canaan was fertile and pleasant, as the spies soon discovered, but its inhabitants were powerful and militant (Num. 13:17ff.). On hearing this report the perfidious Israelites rebelled against Moses and Aaron, and would have stoned them and returned to Egypt, had it not been for divine intervention at the peak of the crisis. Despite the magnanimity exhibited by Moses, the Israelites were sentenced to sojourn in the Wilderness areas until the rebellious generation had died out (Num. 14:20ff.). In connection with this episode it is important to remember that Israel was intended to have crossed from Egypt directly into the Promised Land via Sinai within the space of a very few years at the most, and that the enforced stay in Sinai was not part of the original plan for the infant nation.

As has been stated previously, this situation needs to be noted carefully in connection with the legislation contained in Exodus 22 and 23, which relates to a settled agricultural situation and looks back to a long tradition of Hebrew sedentary activity in this regard (cf. Deut. 11:10). There is absolutely no evidence to suggest that the ancient Hebrews were ever nomads in the sense of the modern desert Bedouin Arab. Studies in ancient Mesopotamian life have shown that a community such as Ur of the Chaldees, for example, was typically urban in nature, and based, as was the case with similar settlements in early Mesopotamia, upon a thoroughly agricultural and pastoral economy.[29] The patriarchal migration to Canaan was set against a similar background (Gen. 26:12, *et al.*), and the 430-year period of Israelite settlement in the eastern Delta region of the Nile was of a specifically sedentary and agricultural character. During their sojourn in Goshen, the Hebrews inhabited a region that was renowned for its lush pastures and cultivated crops and for its marshes teeming with game-birds, fish, and other forms of wild life.[30] Under such conditions it is simply unthinkable for anyone to suppose that the inhabitants of the Goshen region could not have augmented and sustained the agricultural and pastoral experience of their less sedentary precursors during a period of four centuries. Quite aside from the nature

[29] Cf. H. A. Frankfort, *The Birth of Civilization in the Near East* (1951), pp. 49ff.
[30] *ANET,* pp. 470f.

627

of the political and other conditions in Egyptian territory during the Hyksos period, there was ample opportunity for the dwellers in the east Delta region to become acquainted with the current situation in neighboring Canaan, since there was a constant crossing of the frontier by both Egyptians and Semites.[31]

Thus there is absolutely no reason why Moses, or anyone else in an analogous position, should not have been able to draw upon a prolonged tradition of agricultural and pastoral activity among the Hebrews in attempting to plan for a pattern of sedentary life in Canaan. Certainly there was absolutely no necessity whatever for the Israelites to occupy the territory before the appropriate legislation could be given, as was commonly imagined by an earlier generation of critical scholars. In fact, far from envisaging a purely future situation, a great many of the enactments in Exodus 22 and 23 actually look back to the four centuries of sedentary activity in the land of Goshen. It is well within the limits of possibility that some of the legislative material in these two chapters had its origin within that period of time, and that the lessons learned in connection with organized social life were subsequently incorporated, perhaps in a revised form to some extent, into the corpus of civil enactments promulgated under the direction of Moses, and that as such they could therefore be regarded as Mosaic in the best sense of the term.

It should be noted in passing that there were several distinct desolate areas located in the peninsula of Sinai, through which the Israelites passed in their journeyings. These included the *Wilderness of Shur* in the northwest part of the peninsula east of Goshen, the *Wilderness of Etham*, a zone controlled by Egyptian military forces situated between Lake Timsah and the Bitter Lakes, the *Wilderness of Sin*, located near Elim in the western part of Sinai and within striking distance of the oasis of Dophkah, the *Wilderness of Paran*, a desolate area in the east-central region of the Sinai peninsula bordering the Arabah and the Gulf of Aqabah, and the *Wilderness of Zin*, a rather ill-defined tract of territory including the extensive area between the Hebrew camp-site at Kadeshbarnea and the *"Scorpion Pass"* marking the later border of Judah (Josh. 15:3).

4. The rebellion of Korah, Dathan, and Abiram. Rebellion appears to have been a periodic feature of Israelite life during the Wilderness wanderings, of which the revolt of Korah, Dathan, and Abiram is illustrative. Critical scholars have long been accustomed to discern the presence of at least two, and possibly three, different narrative sources underlying the extant account. Thus it has been alleged that the rebellion of Dathan and Abiram (Num. 16:12ff.) was that of laymen against the

---

[31] *ANET*, pp. 258f.; K. A. Kitchen, *The Tyndale House Bulletin*, Nos. 5-6 (1960), p. 14.

civil authority of Moses, while that of Korah, against Moses and Aaron, was concerned primarily with religious matters. Traces of a third account have been supposed to subsist in the opposition of the tribe of Levi to the rights claimed by the Aaronites. In addition, it has also been maintained that the fate of the two different parties varied, with the first being swallowed by the earth and the second being devoured by means of heavenly fire.[32]

In view of these criticisms it should be noted initially that the narratives do not deal with two separate revolts, but with a joint or twin rebellion in which Korah protested against the ecclesiastical role of Moses and Aaron (Num. 16:3), while Dathan, Abiram, and On challenged the civil authority of the two Israelite leaders. The data of the text will not permit a legitimate division of the narrative into supposed underlying documents, for the true nature of the revolt is only seen most properly when the passage in question is regarded as unitary. On such a basis it will be evident that three grounds of discontent were being raised: the first was that Moses and Aaron had set themselves above the remainder of the people (Num. 16:3, 13); the second that Moses had failed to bring Israel to the Promised Land (Num. 16:14); and the third that Moses and Aaron had monopolized the functions of the priesthood (Num. 16:7-11).

To unite various grievances in a joint act of protest was as familiar a procedure in antiquity as it is at the present day. While the incident is depicted as a bifurcated attack upon authority, it is also manifested as united in nature, since Numbers 16:1-3 makes it explicit that Korah, Dathan, Abiram, and On, along with the two hundred and fifty princes, acted as a corporate unit. As regards the fate of the conspirators, the text does not say specifically that Dathan and Abiram were consumed by the earth, but only mentions Korah in this respect, although if he were regarded as the leader of the rebellion, his followers would naturally be subsumed under his designation, as Numbers 16:32f. indicates. However, the mention of Korah alone in this respect is not without significance for the critical analysis, since it was only the latter that posited such a fate for Dathan and Abiram. When fire is mentioned it should be noted that Korah was not included among those who were burned, since that fate was reserved for the two hundred and fifty princes (Num. 16:35). The incident is only amenable to a proper interpretation when the narrative is read as a unitary account, a situation made clear by a careful examination of the text.

Of the various explanations offered for the phenomenon of the earth's swallowing up the rebels, an attractive one has been proposed by Hort, who located the incident in the Arabah between the Dead Sea and the

[32] *DILOT*, pp. 63ff.

Gulf of Aqabah.[33] In several parts of this region are to be found mud flats in various stages of development, the upper layers of which are formed of mud, clay, and salt. When dry such a structure can be crossed readily, but when wet it will not bear weight to any significant extent. Hort has supposed that the Israelites withdrew from the tents of the rebels just before a storm approached. The latter weakened the crust of the ground to the point where it collapsed, and during the storm the two hundred and fifty princes were struck by lightning. While in the nature of the case it is impossible to say precisely what happened on that occasion, the physical conditions that obtain in specific areas of the Sinai peninsula need not be regarded in any sense as incompatible with the tenor of the narrative.

5. *Balaam*. Archaeological discoveries in Mesopotamia have thrown a good deal of light upon the activities of such individuals as Balaam, as was observed previously. Texts recovered from Mari on the middle Euphrates have demonstrated the existence of different varieties of prognosticating priests who included the diviner (*bārûm*), the oracle-priest (*āpilum*), and the ecstatic seer (*maḫḫûm*), all of whom were well recognized in the eighteenth century B.C. and whose traditions were perpetuated in other areas of the ancient Near East to a large extent, including Ugarit. This latter fact is of interest in that the Balaam oracles (Num. 22–24) are full of Ugaritic parallels, and like the Song of Miriam (Exod. 15:1ff.) go back in their written form to between the thirteenth and twelfth centuries B.C.

An interesting seal bearing the legend "Manum, the *bārû*, the servant of Ea" was recovered from a thirteenth-century B.C. stratum at Bethshan, and was assigned to the early second millennium B.C., indicating the long tradition of Mesopotamian divinatory influence in Canaan. It would thus appear, as Daiches pointed out long ago, that Balaam was a typical Mesopotamian diviner (cf. Josh. 13:22), hired in accordance with the customs of the day for a specific purpose.[34] He was not primarily a prophet, even though, when subject to the will of God, he behaved in a manner very similar to that of the later Hebrew prophets. While the way in which the Balaam oracles came to be included in Numbers is unknown, as observed above, it is clear that the traditions concerning the Babylonian diviner were well established in the time of Joshua (Josh. 13:22), and it is quite possible that they may have come originally from Moabite sources. Linguistic and other considerations would suggest that the oracles were in written form by the twelfth century B.C., and that they were probably inserted into the text of Numbers in order to complement the history at some point either in the settlement period or even earlier, and in any event not later than the time of Samuel.

---

[33] G. Hort, *Australian Biblical Review*, VII (1959), pp. 19ff.

[34] S. Daiches, *Hilprecht Anniversary Volume* (1909), pp. 60ff.

In connection with the Balaam material it used to be asserted by an earlier generation of critics that Numbers 25 contained two underlying narratives.[35] The first of these was supposed to describe the way in which the Israelites were led into idolatry through immoral relations with Moabite women, while the second dealt with the suggestion of Balaam, who was then living in Midian, that the women should seduce the Israelites into idolatry and insure their destruction as the result of divine anger. This sort of speculation was typical of the conjectural atomizing of the Hebrew text undertaken by an earlier generation of literary critics, for even a casual reading of the material makes it clear that the counsel of Balaam was never mentioned in the text of chapter 25. The view that maintained that one account described the seduction of Israel into idolatry whereas the other merely referred to intermarriage is refuted by the fact that the *qubbāh* referred to in Numbers 25:8 was the sacred tent, before whose door the penitent Hebrews were weeping, and as such it has no connection whatever with a place reserved for prostitution, as the Vulgate rendering of *lupanar* or "brothel" would seem to indicate.

However, it remains true that fornication at the "door of the tabernacle of the congregation" was not unknown among both priests and laity in Israel during times of moral laxity, and was inevitably an occasion for the punishment of the nation (cf. 1 Sam. 2:22ff.). The conflict between Moabites and Midianites in the narrative is more apparent than real, for as was pointed out in connection with the Joseph narratives, there was a considerable amount of overlapping of Midianites, Ishmaelites, Medanites, and Moabites from the late patriarchal period onwards (cf. Gen. 25:2; 37:36; Judg. 8:24; 1 Chron. 1:32). There are thus no adequate textual or historical grounds for regarding the narrative as anything other than the unity which it purports to be.

6. *The census-lists.* The census-lists preserved in chapters 1 and 26 have occasioned considerable debate on the part of scholars generally. In certain particulars the problem here is that of other large numbers preserved in different parts of the Old Testament, especially in the earlier records of Hebrew history. As has been observed in a previous chapter, the situation is made appreciably more difficult by the presence of variant figures in the different texts and versions. In any event, numbers in antiquity were peculiarly liable to corruption in transmission, and there are several instances in the Old Testament narratives where a good deal of uncertainty exists regarding the correctness of the MT.

As far as the census in the first chapter of Numbers is concerned, some conservative scholars have accepted the text at face value, and have argued from Numbers 1:46 to the conclusion that the total of Israelite

---

[35] G. B. Gray, *A Critical and Exegetical Commentary on Numbers,* pp. 381ff.; *DILOT,* p. 67, *et al.*

warriors who attained their majority, along with other elements of the populace, amounted in all to a total of between two and three million Israelites in the Wilderness.[36] Despite protests that God would have been able to supply food for the needs of so great a multitude, a literal estimate of this kind raises a number of pressing problems, as critical scholars have pointed out.[37] An understanding of the contemporary situation with reference to the population of Canaan is instructive in this respect, for it is evident from sources such as the Tell el-Amarna tablets, as well as from the excavation of Canaanite cities of the thirteenth century B.C., that the overall population of the Promised Land was itself well below three million people.[38] If inferences from Exodus 23:29 and Deuteronomy 7:7, 17, 22 that the Israelites were fewer in number than the Canaanites are correct, it is clearly erroneous to take the census numbers at their face value.

Various expedients have been resorted to in an attempt to make the numbers conform to modern occidental concepts of "reality." One of these consists in the suggestion that the Hebrew word אֶלֶף, rendered as "thousands" in translations of the two census-lists, should actually be interpreted as "family" or "tent-group," as in Judges 6:15,[39] and this would give totals of between five and six thousand warriors. Substantially the same argument, presented against a background of more recent archaeological knowledge, was advanced by Mendenhall,[40] and followed, among others, by Bright.[41] The former argued that אֶלֶף should be taken as indicating a tribal sub-unit instead of being translated as "thousand," so as to bring the final computation to a more "realistic" level of population.

A similar attempt to reduce the large numbers found in Old Testament narratives generally, including those of Numbers, was made by Clark,[42] who suggested that the consonants of 'eleph should be revocalized so as to produce the word 'allûph, which with its Ugaritic cognate means "chief," "leader," or "captain." Thus in the census recorded in Numbers 1, it could have been possible for the word 'allûph to have been replaced by 'eleph during processes of transmission, which on a purely oral basis would be readily understandable. For Clark, then, the

---

[36] E.g. A. A. MacRae in F. Davidson, A. M. Stibbs, and E. F. Kevan (eds.), *The New Bible Commentary* (1953), p. 165; *YIOT*, p. 55.

[37] E.g. G. B. Gray, *A Critical and Exegetical Commentary on Numbers*, pp. 11ff.

[38] Cf. J. Garstang, *Joshua-Judges* (1931), pp. 120f.

[39] A. H. McNeile, *The Book of Numbers* (1911), p. 7; W. M. F. Petrie and C. T. Currelly, *Researches in Sinai* (1906), pp. 207ff.; W. M. F. Petrie, *Egypt and Israel* (1911), pp. 42ff.; J. Garstang, *Joshua-Judges*, p. 120.

[40] G. E. Mendenhall, *JBL*, LXXVII (1958), pp. 52ff.

[41] *BHI*, p. 144; cf. J. M. Wenham, *Tyndale Bulletin* (1967), No. 18, pp. 1ff.

[42] R. E. D. Clark, *Journal of the Transactions of the Victoria Institute*, LXXXVII (1955), pp. 82ff.

62,700 persons recorded for the tribe of Dan might well have read originally 60 captains and 2700 warriors.

None of these attempts to scale down the Old Testament numbers is able to account satisfactorily for all the data involved, and hence the suggestions made cannot be taken as uniformly valid for purposes of interpretation. If other evidence from Near Eastern sources concerning numbers generally is of any value in this connection, it would imply that the Old Testament numerical computations rest upon some basis of reality which was quite familiar to the ancients, but which is unknown to modern scholars. In the view of the author, the numbers in the census-lists and in such narratives as the Exodus from Egypt are used as symbols of relative power, triumph, importance, and the like, and are not meant to be understood either strictly literally or as extant in a corrupt textual form. By any standards the majesty and the miracle of the deliverance of Israel at the Yam Suph could only be expressed numerically in terms of enormous quantities, which taken on a purely literal basis are far in excess of what åctually obtained at the time. Similarly, in the census-lists, the important and influential groups tended to be written up in terms of large numbers, while the more insignificant tribes were accorded much less prominence.

The long list of names which has preserved various stations in the Wilderness (Num. 33:19-35) along with the description of the route taken past Edom (Num. 20:22ff.; 21:4ff.; 33:38-44) presents numerous problems of identification. Most of the station-names fall within the thirty-eight-year period of sojourn at Kadesh-barnea, and cannot be located readily at the present. That the list is genuine seems apparent from the fact that the incidents associated with this period reflect accurately the natural phenomena of the area in which the stations are supposed to have been located. Thus the producing of water by means of a blow upon rock shows acquaintance with the water-retaining properties of Sinai limestone.[43] Similarly the excavating of shallow wells, as in Numbers 21:16ff., indicates the known incidence of sub-surface water in various parts of the Sinai peninsula and southern Transjordan.[44] G. E. Wright has suggested that the reason why the detailed list of stations between Mount Sinai and Kadesh as recorded in Numbers 33:16-36 was preserved so carefully was that pilgrimages of the kind undertaken at a subsequent period by Elijah (1 Kgs. 19:4ff.) may have been a frequent occurrence during the early days of Israelite national history.[45] While this may well be true, it is surely just as valid to argue that the pilgrimages could never have been carried out at all successfully had the list of stations not been preserved in some detail in the first place. The

[43] C. S. Jarvis, *Yesterday and Today in Sinai*, pp. 174f.
[44] N. Glueck, *Rivers in the Desert* (1959), p. 22.
[45] G. E. Wright, *IDB*, IV, p. 376.

form of the material under discussion suggests that it was in writing from a very early period, since it is simply an itinerary of the most compact and summary fashion, and unsuitable for serious transmission over subsequent generations in oral form in the manner so commonly suggested by liberal scholars.

✿   ✿   ✿   ✿   ✿

Numbers must never be regarded as merely comprising a catalog of the outstanding incidents which marked the Israelite sojourn in the Wilderness. Not only did the book record such events, but it interpreted them so as to demonstrate the Covenant love of God for His people in every emergency of distress and danger, as well as the stern and severe judgments of God against apostasy and rebellion. This revelation is uniformly evident throughout the book, and furnishes a theological emphasis that serves to integrate the literary selections into one harmonious corpus. The theme of divine holiness, so apparent in Leviticus, is also central to the theology of Numbers. While God dwells in the midst of His people, His innate sanctity demands that any who approach Him do so through carefully prescribed rules.

Because of the reciprocal nature of the Covenant agreement, it was of fundamental importance that Israel should reflect the holiness of her God in her subsequent dealings with the inhabitants of the Promised Land. This obligation was reinforced by the message of the Biblical narratives, which showed that God could engage a heathen diviner to serve His own purposes, a theme that was to be repeated with some variation in a later age of prophecy. Similarly, the fact that Israel was in Covenant relationship with the God of Sinai did not mean that any breach of that sacred agreement on her part would be tolerated by an indulgent deity. The consistency and justice of God as revealed to Israel were marked by a note of sternness, implying that any transgression of the Covenant would meet with an appropriate punishment. It was thus not without significance that Israel should experience the severity of God just prior to entering the Promised Land to fulfil her destiny.

The text of Numbers has not been as well preserved as that of Leviticus, although there is comparatively little in the way of actual corruption. In Numbers 21:14 something appears to have dropped out of the Hebrew, while in Numbers 21:18 Mattanah is probably not a place name, as in the RSV, but rather a noun derived from the root *nāthan*, and meaning "gift." Some difficulties of translation also exist in connection with Numbers 21:30 and 23:10.

Supplementary Literature

Binns, L. E. *The Book of Numbers.* 1927.
Eissfeldt, O. *Hexateuch-Synopse.* 1922.
Fish, S. *The Book of Numbers.* 1950.
Kennedy, A. R. S. *Leviticus and Numbers.* No date.

VI. THE BOOK OF DEUTERONOMY

A. NAME AND OUTLINE

The fifth book of the Torah was known in Jewish circles by the name אלה הדברים ("these are the words"), or simply דברים ("words"). It was also familiar to the Jews as משנה התורה, or sometimes merely משנה, from the words of Deuteronomy 17:18. Another title by which Deuteronomy was known in Jewish circles was *sēpher tôkhāhôth* or the "book of admonitions." The English designation was derived from the LXX τὸ δευτερονόμιον τοῦτο in Deuteronomy 17:18 (rendered by the Vulgate as *Deuteronomium*), which reflects an incorrect understanding of the words "copy of this law."

Deuteronomy comprises a collection of the last addresses given by Moses to the Israelites in the plains of Moab, and can be analyzed as follows:

I. The Acts of God, ch. 1:1—4:43
   A. Introduction; review of divine guidance, 1:1-46
   B. Events from Kadesh to the victories over Sihon, Og, 2:1—3:29
   C. Exhortation to obey the law, 4:1-43

II. The Law of God, ch. 4:44—26:19
   A. Introduction, 4:44-49
   B. Exposition of the Decalogue, 5:1—11:32
   C. Exposition of the principal laws of Israel, 12:1—26:19
      1. Centralization of worship, 12:1-32
      2. Punishment of idolatry, 13:1-18
      3. Dietary rules, 14:1-29
      4. The slaves and the poor, 15:1-23
      5. Three annual feasts, 16:1-17
      6. Appointment of judges, 16:18-20
      7. Prohibition of sacred trees and pillars, 16:21-22
      8. Punishment of idolatry, 17:1-7
      9. Court of appeal, 17:8-13
      10. Choosing a king, 17:14-20
      11. Priests, Levites, and prophets, 18:1-22
      12. Criminal laws, 19:1-21

Deuteronomy perpetuates the tradition of Exodus that direct recording of events, statutes, and other material was the usual practice of Moses. Whereas nothing was said in this regard concerning the transcription of Leviticus and Numbers, Deuteronomy makes it clear that its contents were substantially the work of Moses (Deut. 31:9ff., 24ff.). Such a reference to "this law" is presumably to one section of Deuteronomy, and not to the Pentateuch as a whole. It is important to note that the work is actually what it purports to be, namely a collection of laws rather than a legal treatise drawn up for the ordering of the common life according to certain predetermined principles.[1]

While it is true that the spirituality implicit in the book is in essential harmony with that of other legalistic works in the Pentateuch, the contents of Deuteronomy comprise an assemblage of material issuing from various periods of the Wilderness wanderings, and should not be regarded technically as a "second law," as the English title might seem to imply. The work contains the essentials of Leviticus rewritten in such a manner as to make the more priestly and esoteric material amenable to the populace, and in this sense Deuteronomy can be said to comprise a popular version of the Levitical law, thereby approximating to something

---

[1] L. Köhler, *Hebrew Man* (1956), p. 141.

like an "Everyman's Torah." On the other hand, the relationship of Deuteronomy to the Book of the Covenant must not be forgotten, since for at least some of the Old Testament writers the Book of the Covenant appears to have been synonymous with Deuteronomy (2 Kgs. 23:2, 21; 2 Chron. 34:30).

B. AUTHORSHIP, COMPILATION, AND DATE OF DEUTERONOMY

Of the apparently post-Mosaic additions to Deuteronomy, the geographical descriptions in Deuteronomy 1:1f. are of particular interest. The book is rich in such data, which invariably view the land of Canaan from the outside.[2] In Deuteronomy 1:1 the expression "beyond the Jordan" (עבר הירדן) has been taken to imply the standpoint of one who was in Palestine,[3] and so to point to a post-Mosaic age for the verse in question. The phrase is found elsewhere in the Pentateuch (Gen. 50:10f.; Num. 22:1; 32:32; 35:14; Deut. 4:46), and although it is possible to assume that its incidence is non-Mosaic, since Moses never crossed the Jordan,[4] it is equally correct to assert that Moses could have known the geography of the situation without actually having visited the locations involved. The River Jordan figured prominently in Deuteronomy, being mentioned no fewer than twenty-six times. Of the occurrences, fifteen referred to the crossing of the river, one defined the boundaries of the territory of Reuben, and other occurrences were mentioned in the form of the expression "beyond the Jordan." That this phrase was rather indefinite is apparent from the fact that on twenty-four occasions it was accompanied by some modifying clause such as "towards the sea" or "towards the sunrising."[5] Indeed, the Hebrew phrase could well be rendered by an expression analogous to "by the banks of" or "at the ford of" the Jordan, or, if Gemser is correct, "in the region of the Jordan."[6] The necessity for clarity in the use of the phrase is apparent from Numbers 32:19, where it was employed to indicate both sides of the river by the children of Reuben and Gad. In each case an additional qualifying word was deemed necessary in order to make completely clear which side of the Jordan was intended to be signified. The words were used on six occasions in Deuteronomy (1:1, 5; 4:41, 46, 47, 49) of the eastern side—always in conjunction with some qualifying clause—and three times in speeches by Moses with reference to the western side (Deut. 3:20, 25; 11:30). In Deuteronomy 11:30 it was used of the western area with a defining clause, but in Deuteronomy 3:8, again with proper qualification, of the eastern side. The reference in Joshua 9:1,

---

[2] Cf. G. T. Manley, *EQ*, XXI (1949), pp. 81ff.
[3] *DILOT*, pp. 84f.
[4] So G. Ch. Aalders, *A Short Introduction to the Pentateuch*, p. 107.
[5] G. T. Manley, *The Book of the Law* (1957), p. 49.
[6] *VT*, II (1953), pp. 349ff.

however, was to the western bank, which presumably was the home of the narrator. The expression "beyond the Jordan," therefore, would appear to be as lacking in specific definition as the modern term "Transjordan," and the fact that the latter name can be employed intelligibly without requiring residence in the Near East would suggest that the use of the phrase cannot by itself indicate or determine the location of the writer.

While many of the places mentioned in Deuteronomy 1:1 were familiar to the narrator, and as such were recorded without explanation, they have proved difficult to identify in modern times. However, the explanatory gloss in Deuteronomy 1:2 is of some interest in the light of the customary identification of Mount Sinai with Jebel Mūsa. The tradition of an eleven-day period for the journey from Horeb via Mount Seir to Kadesh has been vindicated by Aharoni, who traced the route from the starting-point of Jebel Mūsa to Dahab on the east coast of Sinai, and continued northward and across the peninsula to 'Ain Qudeirat (Kadesh).[7] This identification would imply that the places mentioned in Deuteronomy 1:1 had a similar basis in fact, and it is possible that, if they are not actually Mosaic, they may have been preserved by one or more of the Levitical priests mentioned in Deuteronomy 31:9.

Perhaps a rather more assured post-Mosaic addition may be seen in Deuteronomy 3:14-17, which dealt with the assigning of lands, situated apparently on both sides of the Jordan, to the tribes of Israel. Whereas the delineation of Transjordanian territory is comparatively detailed, and suggests close acquaintance with the contemporary situation, the description of the allocation of supposedly Canaanite territory (Deut. 3:17) is of a very general nature. This latter would indeed be surprising had the passage in question emerged from a period even as late as that of the Judges, when the division of the land was known in detail. If the ערבה of Deuteronomy 3:17 refers to some area other than the familiar Arabah, a term applied in a general sense to the rift valley running from the Sea of Galilee to the Gulf of Aqabah, the standpoint of the author could well be that of one living in Transjordan.

The word ערבה really describes conditions of the soil, and has been transferred from such a restricted usage to the wider function of designating whole areas of "steppe" land. Although such regions were rather arid they afforded a certain amount of pasture, and Deuteronomy entertained the concept of steppe-land in connection with Moreh (Deut. 11:30) and the "plains of Moab" (Deut. 34:1, 8). Both these areas stood well above the Jordan valley, and made for excellent natural camp-sites. By contrast, the "way of the Arabah from Elath" (Deut. 2:7) described the low-lying terrain south of the Dead Sea, and in this it was in agreement with the modern description of the Arabah, which begins

---

[7] Y. Aharoni, *The Holy Land: Antiquity and Survival,* II, 2-3, pp. 289f., 293, fig. 7.

properly to the south of the Scorpion cliffs and terminates in the Gulf of Aqabah. In the light of the foregoing considerations it is far from certain that the section under examination is genuinely non-Mosaic. If it is, however, it can hardly be assigned to a period much later than the time of Joshua.

Another brief passage that has occasioned considerable discussion in relation to Mosaic authorship was the one which mentioned the death of Aaron at Moserah, and the subsequent journey of the Israelites from that place to Jotbath by way of Gudgod (Deut. 10:6f.). This has presented difficulty in view of the stated fact that the death of Aaron occurred long after the Sinai sojourn, and at Mount Hor (Num. 20:22ff.), making it difficult to see precisely why the incident was introduced at that point in the narrative. Furthermore, the order of the stations on the route was listed in Numbers 33:31ff. as Moseroth, Bene-jaakan, Hor-haggidgad and Jotbath, which is different from that of Deuteronomy 10:6f.

In this connection it should be noted that the various references to the death of Aaron (Num. 20:22ff.; 33:38f.; Deut. 10:6; 32:50f.) are supplementary rather than contradictory. While they are rather different in nature, they are by no means inconsistent in their presentation of fact. Although in the strictest sense Mount Hor was the physical scene of the death of Aaron, the name "Moserah" or "Moseroth" described the character of that event as "chastisement."[8] That this word was used as a common noun is indicated by the plural form in Numbers 33:30f. Like Massah, Meribah, and Taberah it denoted the nature of the event as well as the place where the incident occurred. Any analysis that ascribes Numbers 33 to a post-exilic source and then attempts to make Deuteronomy 32:48-52 conform to this pattern can be dismissed immediately, since the itinerary in Numbers is undoubtedly very ancient.

The geographical interest of the compiler is evident in the preservation of names such as those under immediate discussion. Bene-jaakan was prefixed in Deuteronomy 10:6 by the word "Beeroth" or "wells," indicating a concern for water. The site was obviously an oasis, and while it cannot be located with absolute certainty at present it was evidently in the vicinity of Ezion-geber. Jotbath is perhaps the modern 'Ain Tabah, about twenty-two miles north of Ezion-geber. The description in Deuteronomy 10:7 would imply that it was situated in a swampy depression that could rapidly become a shallow lake in the wintertime. Gudgod, another of the four places spoken of as having been visited on the way to Kadesh-barnea, was described in Numbers 33:33 as Hor-haggidgad or "the cave (?) of Gidgad." That there may perhaps have been some early textual confusion at this point seems apparent from the LXX version, which read *har* for *ḥōr*, and rendered it "the mountain of Gadgad." A location near the modern Wadi Ḥadaḥid may possibly be

---

[8] G. T. Manley, *EQ*, XXVII (1955), pp. 201ff.

implied by the reference, but this is uncertain at best. Other considerations apart, Deuteronomy 10:6f. bears the marks of being a textual
insertion, perhaps from a Levitical priestly source interested in perpetuating the traditions concerning Aaron and the tribe of Levi, recording the
fact that Eleazar succeeded to priestly office. This latter is in harmony
with subsequent statements regarding Phinehas as the officiating priest
in Israel during the early Judges period (cf. Josh. 24:33; Judg. 20:28).

The view that Deuteronomy was substantially Mosaic in origin was,
with a few exceptions, held by both Jews and Christians until the
nineteenth century. With the rise of liberal criticism the Mosaic authorship of the book was denied, and it was assigned tentatively to the
period of Josiah. Wellhausen gave classic expression to a view of the
authorship and date of Deuteronomy which soon gained widespread
scholarly acceptance by maintaining that the author of the composition,
which for him comprised chapters 12 to 26, was a prophet, who compiled the material about 622 B.C. The ostensible intention of this individual was to reform current religious practices and to abolish the pagan
"high places" in favor of centralizing worship in Jerusalem. To further
this laudable plan the author, Wellhausen alleged, concealed his work
in the Temple and permitted it to be "discovered" by Hilkiah the High
Priest during renovations to the fabric of the building. When its contents
were perused, they were found to be so relevant to the contemporary social and religious situation that the reforms described in 2 Kings 22 and
23 were the result.[9] This novel theory was an integral part of the evolutionary reconstruction of Hebrew religion which Wellhausen promulgated upon a basis of Hegelian philosophy. At first it was regarded as
heresy, but so pervasive was the influence doctrinaire Wellhausenism had
on the contemporary mind that it was soon accepted by a majority of
scholars, thereby becoming one of the more important tenets of the classical liberal criticism of the Pentateuch. The closely established relationship between the work of the "Deuteronomist" and the religious reforms
of King Josiah has always been integral to the orthodox Wellhausenian
theory of Israelite religious development. As H. H. Rowley, an adherent
of the Graf-Wellhausen approach to Old Testament studies, has commented, "the Code of Deuteronomy is . . . of vital importance in Pentateuchal criticism, since it is primarily by relation to it that the other
documents are dated."[10]

Although as early as 1805 De Wette had proposed a seventh-century
B.C. date for Deuteronomy in the belief that it was actually the law-book
used by Josiah in his religious reforms, other scholars accepted a quite
different view of the matter. Assuming that the legal code recovered

---

[9] J. Wellhausen, *Die Composition des Hexateuchs* (1889), p. 76 *passim, Prolegomena to the History of Israel* (1885), p. 9 *passim*.
[10] H. H. Rowley, *The Growth of the OT*, p. 29.

from the Temple was the "Holiness Code" (Lev. 17–26), Berry suggested that Deuteronomy was definitely of post-exilic origin,[11] while Kennett proposed a date in the time of Haggai and Zechariah, that is to say, about 520 B.C.[12] Hölscher adopted a similar view in placing the book at least one hundred years after the time of Josiah,[13] while Pedersen and other members of the Uppsala school supposed that the work reached its final form about 400 B.C., though recognizing that parts of it existed in writing at a much earlier period.[14]

Not all scholars agreed that Deuteronomy should be assigned to a later rather than an earlier date, however. Ewald placed the composition of the work in the time of Manasseh;[15] Westphal related it to the earlier period of the reign of Hezekiah.[16] Von Rad held that Deuteronomy may have arisen in circles of "country Levites," and have been in its completed form shortly after 701 B.C.[17] The pre-monarchic origin of the work was asserted by Robertson, who maintained that it may have been largely the work of Samuel.[18]

A similar position was adopted by Brinker, who in process of refuting the arguments for a Josianic date of Deuteronomy regarded the legislation as basically Mosaic, with supplements made by priests and judges from decisions given at different sanctuaries.[19] For Brinker the guiding principle of Deuteronomy was not that of the centralization of worship in Jerusalem, as maintained by the critical school, but the protection of the people from the threat of Canaanite idolatry.[20] W. F. Albright, although adhering to the broad pattern of liberal criticism, assigned the Song of Moses (Deut. 32:1-43) to the time of Samuel, following Eissfeldt,[21] and demonstrated its archaic nature in the light of the manuscript scraps recovered from 4Q.[22] It will be clear from the foregoing selection of scholarly views that there has been considerable doubt as to the actual date of the book even in liberal circles, and while most adherents of the Wellhausenian position would posit a seventh-century B.C. date for the origin of Deuteronomy, an increasing number

---

[11] *JTS*, XXVI (1925), p. 156.
[12] *Deuteronomy and the Decalogue* (1920), pp. 6ff.
[13] ZAW, XL (1922), pp. 161ff.
[14] *Israel*, III-IV, p. 96.
[15] *History of Israel* (1876), I, p. 127.
[16] *The Law and the Prophets* (1910), p. 304.
[17] *Studies in Deuteronomy* (1953), p. 66.
[18] *The OT Problem*, p. 42.
[19] *The Influence of Sanctuaries in Early Israel*, pp. 189ff.
[20] Cf. A. C. Welch, *The Code of Deuteronomy* (1924), p. 195.
[21] *BPAE*, p. 45.
[22] W. F. Albright, *VT*, IX (1959), pp. 339ff.; cf. P. W. Skehan, *BASOR*, No. 136 (1954), pp. 12ff., *JBL*, LXXVIII (1959), p. 22.

of scholars have finally become aware of the need for a more flexible position on the whole matter than was once the case.[23]

One of the important points at issue in the discussion of the provenance and date of Deuteronomy has been the question of the centralization of worship, which for many has been held to be the principal theme of the composition. Deuteronomy 12 prescribed that all sacrifices and offerings would be brought in the Promised Land ". . . unto the place which the LORD your God will choose" (Deut. 12:5, 11, 14, 18, 21, 26). This matter was interpreted along Hegelian lines by Wellhausen and his followers to the point where it was assumed, quite without proof, that Jerusalem was the place where the cult was intended to be centralized.[24]

Not all critical scholars were convinced by this sort of reasoning, however, for as Skinner pointed out, the book itself laid no stress whatever upon the peculiar claim of Jerusalem to be the sole place of worship.[25] Rowley also observed correctly that there was nothing in Deuteronomy to the effect that the central and solitary legitimate sanctuary was to be located in Jerusalem.[26] A. C. Welch maintained that apart from Deuteronomy 12:1-5, which he regarded as a later insertion, there was no prescription that stipulated that sacrifices could only be offered upon one altar.[27]

The regulations concerning sacrifice in Deuteronomy 12 represent an expansion of the provision recorded in Exodus 20:24, where the scene was set in Horeb.[28] But when the religious situation that would be encountered in Canaan once the tribes began to occupy the terrain was contemplated, the different conditions required a somewhat diverse approach from that of a desert milieu. Accordingly it is important to notice that Deuteronomy 12:14, which speaks of the place that the Lord will choose in the jurisdiction of one of the tribes, does not necessarily imply that there will be one, and only one, tribal territory where God may be worshipped.[29]

The real force of the contrast in Deuteronomy 12 is not between many altars of God and one, but between those of the Canaanites dedicated to alien deities and the place where the name of God is to be revered. As Manley has put it, the thing which is in question is not their

---

[23] Cf. C. R. North, *OTMS*, p. 82. For the literature on the date and composition of Deuteronomy see H. H. Rowley, *Studies in OT Prophecy Presented to T. H. Robinson* (1950), pp. 157f.

[24] *Prolegomena to the History of Israel*, p. 368.

[25] J. Skinner, *Prophecy and Religion: Studies in the Life of Jeremiah* (1922), p. 167.

[26] H. H. Rowley, *Studies in OT Prophecy Presented to T. H. Robinson*, p. 166.

[27] A. C. Welch, *The Code of Deuteronomy*, p. 31.

[28] *Ibid.*, p. 30.

[29] Cf. R. Brinker, *The Influence of Sanctuaries in Early Israel*, p. 199.

number but their character.[30] Whether the words be interpreted to mean one or more centers, however, it still remains true that they do not of themselves exclude the possibility that there were other duly authorized altars for Israelite worship. Although the building of one official altar on Mount Ebal was commanded in Deuteronomy 27:1ff., the rule enshrined in Deuteronomy 16:21f. entertained the existence of several such places in Canaan.

The assumption that Jerusalem was the place intended by Deuteronomy where the cultus was to be centralized is entirely subjective in nature, and has no textual warrant for it whatever. This theory has been criticized by von Rad as in fact resting upon a very slender basis.[31] In the German original of his *Studies in Deuteronomy* he maintained that the command in Deuteronomy 27:1-8 to build an altar upon Mount Ebal and to inscribe the Law upon stones raised a "barricade" against the centralization theory.[32] His observation is mild to say the least; in point of fact the command relating to Mount Ebal is absolutely fatal to the position of Wellhausen and his followers. It specifically prescribes that which the Law is supposed to prohibit, and even utilizes the words of Exodus 20:24, which, according to the critical viewpoint, the Deuteronomic law was intended to revoke. Furthermore, it was confirmed by the account in Joshua 8:30-35, which described the building of the altar by Joshua. A comparison of Deuteronomy 27:1-8 and Joshua 8:30-35 shows that while both passages are related, they are quite independent of each other in matters of detail. The Deuteronomic passage commands first of all the setting up of stones, which are then to be covered with a cement coating, after which an altar is to be erected. The account in Joshua commences with the altar of unhewn stones and then proceeds to the matter of the inscription, making no mention of the cement coating. In Deuteronomy nothing is said about judges and officers, or of the reading of the Law, while the account in Joshua contains no reference to the dividing of the tribes, and in any event cannot be considered at all "Deuteronomic" in terms of literary style.

That both passages appear to have a firm basis alike in Hebrew religious tradition and history appears evident from the fact that Shechem, situated in the uplands of Ephraim in the vicinity of Mount Gerizim, was one of the sites from which fragments of primitive writing belonging to the conquest period were recovered.[33] Since Deuteronomy 27:1-8 cannot

[30] G. T. Manley, *The Book of the Law*, p. 132.
[31] G. von Rad, *Studies in Deuteronomy*, p. 68.
[32] G. von Rad, *Deuteronomium Studien* (1947), p. 47.
[33] Cf. E. Nielsen, *Shechem, A Traditio-Historical Investigation* (1955), pp. 3ff.; G. E. Wright, *BASOR*, No. 144 (1956), pp. 9ff., *BA*, XX, No. 1 (1957), pp. 19ff., *BASOR*, No. 148 (1957), pp. 11ff.; B. W. Anderson, *BA*, XX, No. 1 (1957), pp. 10ff.; W. Harrelson, *BA*, XX, No. 1 (1957), pp. 2ff.; H. C. Kee and L. E. Toombs, *BA*, XX, No. 4 (1957), pp. 82ff.

be dismissed as a later insertion,[34] it clearly confirms the ordinary meaning of Deuteronomy 12 in that it forbids any association with Canaanite worship and looks forward to a national cultic center, but allows for the worship of God at any duly authorized altar elsewhere. Thus the centralization theory of Wellhausen—described frequently as the keystone in his system of chronology[35]—is evidently far from being firmly fixed. As with so many other postulates of classical liberalism, it can only be supported by a misreading of the history, and by contrived and artificial interpretations of the Hebrew text.

What seems to have transpired during the early conquest and settlement periods was that the tribes gathered at intervals around the Tabernacle, following the traditions and practices familiar from the Wilderness wanderings. Altars were erected and sacrifices offered at such places as Shechem, Ophrah, and Ramah, but Mount Gerizim was firmly fixed as the place appointed by Moses for whatever central observations of the cultus were deemed necessary. A relapse into Canaanite idolatry was followed by a religious revival when the Temple in Jerusalem was constructed, but further syncretism and religious degeneration ensued until the southern kingdom was taken into captivity in the sixth century B.C. by the Babylonians.

The Deuteronomic law fits admirably against such a background of history and cultic practice if it is placed at the close of the Mosaic period. The Canaanites were then in sole occupation of the Promised Land, apart from the area where the Philistine cities were located, and one prominent feature of the subsequent Israelite conquest of the territory was to be the destruction of pagan shrines so as to remove all temptation from the midst of Israel. The gifts and sacrifices of the Chosen People were to be brought only to an authorized altar, accompanied by the proper ritual safeguards. The altar of God was not to be defiled by the pagan fertility symbols common at that period (Deut. 16:21f.), nor was there to be any taint of admixture with Canaanite religious practices (Deut. 12:29ff.). After the Jordan had been crossed the Israelites were to erect an altar upon Mount Ebal and inscribe the Law of Moses on prepared stones (Deut. 27:1ff.). The primitive character of the enactment in Deuteronomy 27:1-8 is evident from the absence of such words as *ba'al* and *bāmôth*, and by the indefiniteness of the allusions to the "place" where God would allow His Name to be revered.

Of all possible claimants to this high honor, Jerusalem is clearly the least likely. In the time of Joshua it was a Jebusite fortress that had been bypassed during the second stage of the conquest. It was only brought within the orbit of Israelite life during the time of David, and at that

---

[34] S. R. Driver, *A Critical and Exegetical Commentary on Deuteronomy* (1895), p. 294.

[35] E.g. by G. W. Anderson, *OTMS*, p. 283.

from a standpoint of purely political expediency, since it was situated in neutral territory and therefore could claim the loyalty of northern and southern tribes alike without prejudice to either. Furthermore, it is important to notice that Jerusalem as a proper name does not occur in the Pentateuch, although it was spoken of in the fourteenth-century B.C. Tell el-Amarna tablets. It has been assumed that the designation "Salem" in Genesis 14:18 and Psalm 76:3 is a shortened form of "Jerusalem," but this view, which owed a great deal to Josephus, has never gone unquestioned in Christian circles since the time of Jerome and Eusebius. There seems little doubt that the name "Salem" cannot be considered to be either another name for Jerusalem or an abbreviated form of the designation of the city, the pre-Israelite origin of which is assured, but rather that in Genesis it referred to some quite distinct locality, and that in the Psalter it constituted a poetic and religious appellation. If it is correct to assume, with Eusebius in his *Onomasticon,* that the Salem of Genesis referred to a village of the Jordan valley south of Scythopolis, it might be possible to identify the site with the Salim of John 3:23, tentatively localized at Umm el-ʿAmdan. If the AV rendering of Genesis 33:18, "Shalem, a city of Shechem," which is based upon Greek, Latin, and Syriac textual traditions, is correct, Salem could well be identified with the village of Salim, some four or five miles east of Balaṭa-Shechem.

What is made clear in this general connection by the book of Deuteronomy is that Moses appointed a central place in Canaan, namely Mount Ebal, the more northerly of the two mountains that overshadow the modern town of Nablus, two miles northwest of ancient Shechem, as the locale for major cultic celebrations. There is no evidence that the prescription of Deuteronomy 27:1-8 commanded a centralizing of the cultus as such in the Ebal-Gerizim area; instead the site was to be regarded as focal to Israelite national and spiritual aspirations. It is not without significance, therefore, that the Samaritans have venerated Mount Gerizim as the place where God chose to put His Name (Deut. 12:5).[36] As C. H. Gordon has pointed out in this connection, the Samaritans are right in their claim that the text has been tampered with in order to suppress the priority of their Gerizim shrine and convey the impression, fostered in orthodox Judaeo-Christian circles, that Moses had Jerusalem in mind as the center of subsequent Hebrew national worship.[37] The Samaritans, who insist that the "place" of Deuteronomy 12:5 is Gerizim and not Jerusalem, have a better argument in that the altar erected "near" Gerizim was the only one built in accordance with the specific orders of Moses. Several Hebrew manuscripts and ancient versions show that the text has been altered at this point, since the altar was actually "on" Mount Gerizim. The Samaritan view

---

[36] Cf. E. Robertson, *The OT Problem,* pp. 157ff.
[37] *IOTT,* pp. 132f. Cf. J. Macdonald, *The Theology of the Samaritans,* p. 16.

is obviously correct, but the trend of history has been such as to make heretics of them and bestow orthodoxy upon Judaism.

If it was not the aim of the author of Deuteronomy to institute a centralization of worship in Jerusalem, what is to be said about the claim that his object was to reform current practices in religion and to abolish the במת or "high places"? That the latter consideration was not paramount in any attempted centralization of the cultus appears clear from the fact that the במת were not mentioned at all in Deuteronomy 12. Furthermore, the aim of the author was, as Pedersen has pointed out, to protect the Israelite community against Canaanite influence, and insure that the Chosen People would obey the divinely revealed laws of the Covenant relationship.[38] At the time contemplated by Deuteronomy, Israelite worship had not become sufficiently depraved to require the kind of thoroughgoing reformation characteristic of later periods in the history of the southern kingdom.

Part of the difficulty involved in this situation has resulted from the doctrinaire pronouncement of Wellhausen to the effect that the book was to be dated about 622 B.C., and ought to be credited with serving as the stimulus for the reforms of Josiah. To set the matter in correct perspective it needs only to be observed that the reformation of Josiah resulted in an abolition of idolatry, and not in the establishing of a centralized sanctuary, the latter having obtained since the days of Solomon. If the book was composed about 680 B.C. by a follower of Isaiah, as Rowley proposed in a modification of the views of Driver, it is significant that no mention occurred either of the במת or of Jerusalem in the centralization issue.[39] Furthermore, there are no traces in the extant work of the influence of the prophet Isaiah, whether of a literary or a doctrinal nature. Deuteronomy is written in flowing Hebrew prose of great elegance and beauty, and is essentially oratorical and hortatory, in accordance with its general purpose. By contrast, Isaiah was a poetic genius whose wealth of imagination and vividness of expression combined with a chaste and dignified literary style to perpetuate the majesty and dimension of his communion with God.

In Deuteronomy there is no doctrine of a "remnant," no occurrence of the prophetic formula "thus saith the Lord," and no use of the title "the Holy One of Israel." Finally, it is extremely difficult to conceive of the book of Deuteronomy as constituting anything approaching a program of religious reform purporting to come from a disciple of Isaiah in the early days of the reign of Manasseh. While the reforms of both Hezekiah and Josiah may have drawn in part for their inspiration upon the contents of Deuteronomy, the correspondence of the legal material in

[38] J. Pedersen, *Israel, I-II*, p. 27.
[39] H. H. Rowley, *The Growth of the OT*, p. 31. S. R. Driver, *A Critical and Exegetical Commentary on Deuteronomy*, p. lv.

the work with what transpired in the reigns of Hezekiah and Josiah is not sufficiently close to make evident an immediate dependence upon the provisions of Deuteronomy.

The nature and extent of the law-book discovered by Hilkiah in the Temple has been a matter of considerable discussion among scholars for many decades. From the time of De Wette it was considered axiomatic that it comprised the bulk of Deuteronomy, but this view has been contested increasingly by modern scholars.[40] The fact is that it is simply impossible to determine from the text (2 Kgs. 22:3ff.) either the length or the contents of the "book of the Torah." It may have included part of Deuteronomy, but it could equally have comprised the Book of the Covenant, either in its original or in an augmented form.

A much more serious problem has been presented by the view of De Wette and his followers that Deuteronomy was a "pious fraud." That such an assertion is entirely out of harmony with what is now known of literary practices among ancient Near Eastern scribes has been made plain by Albright, who has stated that it cannot be emphasized too strongly that there is hardly any evidence at all in the ancient Near East for documentary or literary fabrications.[41] A few such are known from Egypt, including the Bentresh *stele* and the decree of Djoser on a cliff near Elephantine, both of which purport to reach back to very ancient times. It is now known, however, that both these inscriptions belong properly to the Ptolemaic era, and emerge from a time when the ethos of the ancient Orient had already vanished.

Arguments that suggest the possibility of "pious fraud" are therefore based upon analogies from the Graeco-Roman period, and as such have no bearing upon the literary practices of the ancient Near East, where such fabrications simply did not occur. As C. H. Gordon has shown, the fact that neither Josiah nor his immediate precursors knew anything of the Law does not prove that the ספר recovered by Hilkiah was necessarily a forgery.[42] Throughout the ancient Near East law codes generally, whether they claimed divine origin, as did the Code of Hammurabi, or not, were regularly disregarded in actual life. Mesopotamian judges consistently omitted any reference to law codes in their court decisions, preferring instead to be guided by tradition, public feeling, and their own estimate of the situation confronting them. Processes of codification naturally took cognizance of custom and previous experience in the matter of legal precedents, but once they had been formulated such codes were only studied by research scholars, and in general had very

---

[40] For the literature on the subject see O. Eissfeldt, *Einleitung in das AT*, pp. 186ff. De Wette was anticipated in his conclusions by Athanasius, *PG*, XXVII, col. 44; Chrysostom, *PG*, LVII, col. 181, LXI, col. 58; Jerome, *PL*, XXIII, col. 227, XXV, col. 71; and Procopius, *PG*, LXXXVII, i, col. 915f.

[41] *FSAC*, p. 78.

[42] *IOTT*, p. 239.

little bearing upon current legal and social practice. Thus the rediscovery of lost Sumerian legal codes some centuries after their promulgation would have constituted as complete a surprise to the contemporary Babylonians generally as the finding of the "book of the Torah" did to Josiah. The significance of the latter event is that the trend of religious and social affairs in the kingdom of Judah was confronted anew by the prescriptions of a forgotten law-book whose inspiration guaranteed it success as an instrument of religious revival where other legal codes in the Near East had failed in their laudable aim of raising the moral, social, and religious tone of national life.

In view of the peculiar difficulties attaching to the liberal view of the authorship and date of Deuteronomy, it seems important to emphasize at this juncture that there is nothing in the work that can be proved conclusively to be incompatible with substantial Mosaic authorship. The legal content is primitive and authoritarian in nature, and is thoroughly permeated with the moral, ethical, and humanitarian concepts inherent in the Covenant relationship. Brinker, following Robertson, appears to be incorrect in his view that Deuteronomy was an expansion of the Mosaic "Book of the Covenant," and formulated by a council of priests under the supervision of Samuel.[43] The two books of Samuel do not contain the word "tôrāh" or "law," nor do they suggest the existence of a conclave of priests and scribes. Furthermore, the leader of Israel appointed by Samuel was a charismatic נגיד or "military commander," and not the מלך or "king" envisaged by Moses (Deut. 17:14ff.). The simplest and most probable account of the authorship and date of Deuteronomy is that Moses "wrote" the legislation himself, that is to say, chapters 12 to 26, and that the discourses and the concluding poems were added at a somewhat later time.

The structural unity and integrity of Deuteronomy have been emphasized by Kline, in the light of the rediscovery of treatises of major kings of Near Eastern antiquity.[44] While there is nothing either new or particularly unusual in a comparison of Hittite suzerainty treaties with the form of the Covenant agreement at Sinai, the application of this concept to Deuteronomy as a whole is an unusual departure in the field of literary criticism. Kline has shown that when Deuteronomy is viewed holistically or as an integer, it exhibits on a large scale the complete covenantal formulation of the ancient Near East; and he has made it clear that this phenomenon points to its fundamental structural unity.

[43] R. Brinker, *The Influence of Sanctuaries in Early Israel*, p. 223; E. Robertson, *The OT Problem*, pp. 60ff.

[44] M. G. Kline, *Treaty of the Great King* (1963), pp. 13ff.; cf. G. E. Mendenhall, *BA*, XVII, No. 3 (1954), pp. 50ff., republished as *Law and Covenant in Israel and the Ancient Near East* (1955), *IDB*, I, pp. 714ff.; K. Bultzer, *Das Bundesformular. Seine Ursprung und seine Verwendung im AT* (1960); D. J. Wiseman, *The Vassal-Treaties of Esarhaddon* (1958).

As such it can no longer be considered the product of a series of redactions of the document that produced the Josianic reformation. The so-called "two introductions" to the book (Deut. 1–4 and 5–11) need not be regarded now as the product of two editorial hands, since in the suzerainty treaties of the ancient Near East an historical prologue regularly follows the preamble and precedes the stipulations of the agreement. In the light of this situation Deuteronomy 1:5–4:49 qualifies admirably as just such an historical prologue.[45] Deuteronomy 5–11 must now be recognized as expounding the Covenant way of life in precisely the same manner as chapters 12 to 26, which together declare the demands of the suzerain. The differences between Deuteronomy 5 to 11 and 12 to 26 only represent for Kline variant treatments of this one theme, namely the stipulations of the suzerain in relation to his subjects. In the same manner it is possible to relate the appendix material (Deut. 31–34) to the treaty pattern discerned in earlier sections of the book, and to see in it a concern for succession rights which, according to Near Eastern parallels, were an important part of the legal deposition to which allegiance was required.

Kline is further interested in the date of Deuteronomy, since his marshalling of Covenant parallels down to the time of Esarhaddon (681-669 B.C) does not in itself require a Mosaic date for the book. Arguing from a difference in form between second- and first-millennium B.C. treaties, he has maintained that there is an "early" and a "late" structure for ancient Near Eastern covenants generally. For him, the most remarkable difference is that the historical prologue, the distinctive second section of the second-millennium B.C. treaties, is no longer found in the later texts.[46] Without any doubt, therefore, Deuteronomy belongs to the classic stage in this process of documentary evolution, and furnishes significant confirmation of the *prima facie* case for the Mosaic origin of the Deuteronomic treaty of the Great King.

While it is still uncertain at the time of writing as to precisely how far the language of covenant in the Old Testament has been shaped by wider concepts, this consideration has little bearing upon the important problems of literary criticism with regard to Deuteronomy. There can be no question that the study undertaken by Kline is of the greatest significance for any future discussion of the questions relating to the authorship and date of the composition, and that his work has the undeniable merit of being properly based upon an accredited Near Eastern methodology. As Kline himself has remarked:

> . . . Now that the form critical data compel the recognition of the antiquity not merely of this or that element within Deuteronomy but of the Deuteronomic treaty in its integrity, any persistent insistence on a final edition of the book

[45] Kline, *op. cit.*, p. 31; cf. J. A. Thompson, *The Ancient Near Eastern Treaties and the OT* (1964), pp. 13f.

[46] Kline, *op. cit.*, pp. 42f.

around the seventh century B.C. can be nothing more than a vestigial hypothesis, no longer performing a significant function in Old Testament criticism.[47]

Of the institutions included in Deuteronomy, that which has become known as the "levirate law" (Deut. 25:5ff.) is of interest in that it constitutes an expansion of the Levitical marriage promulgations, and affords regularized status to a custom found among people other than the Hebrews. The term "levirate" is derived from the Latin *levir* or "husband's brother," and the legislation thus characterized required that when a married man died without leaving children, his brother was to take his widow in marriage and raise a family on behalf of the deceased man. The purpose of the legislation was to prevent the marriage of an Israelite woman to an outsider; to provide for the purely material and emotional needs of the bereaved woman, and to continue the name of the dead man within the nation of Israel. The custom thus reinforced the importance for many Semitic peoples of endogamous marriage, and the production of offspring from such unions.

One form of this tradition was made evident in the story of Judah and Tamar (Gen. 38:8ff.), where Onan took the wife of his deceased brother Er, but refused to impregnate her at copulation on the ground that his own children would not have the primary inheritance. However, this instance is hardly typical of levirate marriage as such, and in any event it furnishes no ground for any concept of birth control in antiquity, as some scholars have maintained. The book of Ruth indicates that the custom occasionally extended beyond the brother of a husband, but again the general situation is rather different from that contemplated in Deuteronomy.[48] As in ancient Hittite law, the act of Boaz extended the levirate custom to other male relatives of the deceased in the event that no brothers survived.

The levirate law did not apply if daughters had been born, and regulations for the inheritance of such individuals constituted an early concern of codified Hebrew law (Num. 27:1ff.). Even though the provisions of Numbers 27:9-11 might appear to ignore or even contravene the general provisions of the levirate law, it seems evident that these regulations would be operative where there were daughters only; when a childless wife had died before her husband did, when the brother of the late husband refused to take the childless widow, or when the wife remained childless after being married to the brother.

Levitical law (Lev. 18:16; 20:21) prohibited a man from marrying his brother's wife, as has already been observed. Thus, if the document in which such legislation is as late and priestly as adherents of the Graf-Wellhausen theory have popularly supposed, it is curious that such an

---

[47] *Ibid.*, p. 44.
[48] O. J. Baab, *IDB*, III, p. 282.

authoritative pronouncement would ignore entirely, if not directly repudiate, the long-established Hebrew custom of the levirate and its variations. However, it would appear that the emphasis in Leviticus was upon sexual relations rather than marriage as such. The provision in Leviticus 20:21 is analogous to that in the preceding verse, and in neither case is it possible to decide from the text whether the uncle or the brother is already dead. At all events, the institution was designed to preserve the homogeneity of the family group, to perpetuate the name of its male members in Israel, and to provide in a characteristically humanitarian fashion for the welfare of the widow.

The influence of Deuteronomy upon the historical and prophetic writings is a matter of some concern in the light of the arguments adduced in the present work for its antiquity and substantial Mosaicity. It can be stated immediately as a general principle that Deuteronomy deals in a distinctive prophetic manner with the lessons to be learned from the trend of past events, having regard, of course, to the central fact of the Covenant relationship. In an historical composition such as 1 and 2 Kings, the compiler is also looking back to the Covenant ideal, and like the author of Deuteronomy expounds events against a theological background. The two books of Kings are directly concerned with the implications of the Covenant for the life of Israel, and judgment is pronounced both upon individuals and the nation as a whole in accordance with the degree to which they are thought to have strayed from the Covenant ideal.

The familiarity of the prophets with the Law generally is apparent from the books of Joshua and Kings (cf. Josh. 1:8; 8:34; 1 Kgs. 2:3f.); and the Deuteronomic law in the sense of "statutes and judgments" was by no means unknown to David (Ps. 18:22). The latter phrase occurred again in the pronouncement of the prophet Ahijah to Jeroboam (1 Kgs. 11:33f.), when he charged the people with forsaking the precepts that David himself had kept. In 2 Kings 14:6, the authority of the "book of the law of Moses" was appealed to, the reference being to Deuteronomy 24:16. Again, the "Book of the Covenant" mentioned in 2 Kings 23:2 was evidently intended to be synonymous with a part of Deuteronomy. Thus it appears that for some time before the historical books were written, the Israelites believed that a book of the law of Moses existed that had regulated the conduct and aspirations of such notable individuals as Joshua, David, and Amaziah.

In much the same manner the eighth-century B. C. prophets knew of the existence of a *tôrāh*, for the word was used by Hosea (4:6; 8:1, 12), Amos (2:4), Micah (4:2), Isaiah (1:10; 2:3; 5:24; 8:16, 20), and Zephaniah (3:4). While the term can refer to a body of "teaching," including the oracles of the prophets themselves, it is also apparent from the context that in certain definite instances it indicates the existence of a body of divine law that the priests had to teach (Hos. 4:6; Zeph. 3:4) and the people had to observe (Isa. 5:23f.; Hos. 4:6; 8:1, 12). Besides these explicit references to a *tôrāh* there are indications that particular enactments contained in Deuteronomy were well known in Israel. These included the law of the landmark (Hos. 5:10 and Deut. 19:14), the need for a standard measure (Am. 8:5; Mic. 6:10f. and Deut. 25:13ff.), the triennial payment of the tithe (Am. 4:4 and Deut. 14:28), and the authority of the priest (Hos. 4:4ff.; Zeph. 3:4 and Deut. 17:12; 24:6).

All this does not prove, of course, that the eighth-century B.C. prophets were acquainted with Deuteronomy either in its developing or extant form, nor, for that matter, that they had the least knowledge of J or E. What it does indicate, however, is that the religious traditions enshrined in the Pentateuch had been perpetuated over successive generations, albeit, perhaps, in limited circles. This is entirely consistent with the general situation in the ancient Near East, where individuals and communities alike pursued their lives in happy and untroubled indifference to extant written legal codes.

Regarding the influence of Deuteronomy upon the work of Jeremiah, critical scholars have varied considerably in their estimates of the situation. Driver discerned traces of Deuteronomy on nearly every page of Jeremiah; [49] but J. N. Schofield, who assigned a comparatively late date to Deuteronomy, denied that Jeremiah ever knew the work, and regarded any similarities as being due to the influence of the prophet upon the compilers of Deuteronomy.[50] For the present it will be sufficient to note that indications of the influence of Deuteronomy that can be discerned in Jeremiah are similar to those found in earlier prophets. In some instances, however, there is a greater degree of precision (e.g. Jer. 11:1-5), which may possibly owe something to the discovery of the law-book in the Temple. If Jeremiah was at all familiar with the contents of the latter, he manifests no awareness that its supposed intent was to restrict the offering of sacrifices to Jerusalem. Indeed, the opposite is true to some degree in that Jeremiah preserved the tradition that there was once a legitimate altar of the God of Israel at Shiloh. For Jeremiah the moral law was predominant, as in the Pentateuchal legislation generally, and while he did not entirely reject the cultic ritual he insisted upon its purity and the superiority of the moral law.

In the prophetic writings from Amos to Jeremiah, there are certain observable trends corresponding to the national development as depicted in the historical books. But whereas in these works there is a gradual change as the religious fortunes of Israel decline, the outlook of

---

[49] S. R. Driver, *A Critical and Exegetical Commentary on Deuteronomy*, p. xlvii.

[50] J. N. Schofield in *Studies in History and Religion Presented to H. W. Robinson* (ed. E. A. Payne, 1942), pp. 44ff.; a reply by H. H. Rowley is found in *Studies in OT Prophecy Presented to T. H. Robinson*, pp. 157ff.

Deuteronomy is consistently more optimistic and elevated, viewing the destiny of the individual and the nation in the light of a Covenant relationship that was vital and full of meaning for Israel. The virility of the Deuteronomic proclamation of salvation as a present reality, as contrasted with the forbidding eschatology of the eighth- and seventh-century B.C. prophets, speaks of an earlier age of religious fervor in which enthusiasm for the ideals of the Covenant was still running high. For von Rad this situation is problematical and paradoxical, deriving as it does from the setting of Horeb but addressed, as he supposes, to the Israel of the later regal period.[51] Accordingly it should be noted that there is neither problem nor paradox if the work is taken at its proper face value and assigned to the Mosaic period, instead of being distorted and manipulated so as to fit into some purely fictional scheme of supposed literary and historical development. What von Rad and so many other liberal writers have failed to take into proper consideration is the fact that the prophets derived their fundamental theological concepts from the Law, and that in their exposition of the various facets of the Covenant relationship and its implications for the life of the nation they adduced no single theological element that was not already present in some form in the Mosaic legislation.

C. The Material of Deuteronomy

The time and circumstances of the book can be held unquestionably to be that of the last days of Moses, and into this framework there has been inserted the collection of legal material that emerged for the most part from an earlier period of the Wilderness wanderings. The book commences with a lengthy discourse relating the nature of divine guidance from the Horeb period to the sojourn at Kadesh-barnea (Deut. 1:5–3:29). This served as an adequate introduction to one of the principal themes of the work, namely an exhortation to the Israelites to obey the revealed Law of God (Deut. 4:1-43). Such an arrangement appears to be normal and original, and there are no evident dislocations of the text, although there may perhaps be a few later additions present in the narrative.

The second address of Moses (Deut. 4:44–26:19) deals in a comprehensive sense with the Law of God, and commences with the foundation-principle of the theocracy, namely the Decalogue, in an extended form. This all-important canon of spirituality was rooted firmly in the history of the Wilderness period by means of a reminder of the phenomena that accompanied the initial revelation of the Law, so that no one could doubt either its supernatural origin or its fundamental historicity. The ethical and moral implications of the Covenant relationship (Deut.

---

[51] G. von Rad, *Studies in Deuteronomy*, pp. 72f.

6:4ff.) prefaced a series of enactments relating to situations envisaged as occurring once the Promised Land had been occupied.

Of great importance among other matters was the question of idolatry, which constituted an ever-present threat to the integrity of the Covenant relationship between Israel and her God. Since idolatry was inextricably intermingled with other alien threads in the pattern of Canaanite religious and social life, it was clear that the Israelites had no other choice than to exterminate the Canaanite inhabitants of the land. This section of material (Deut. 7:1-26) again follows in natural sequence, but it is interrupted by Deuteronomy 8:1-20, which comprises a reminder of the divine dealings with Israel in the past so that the nation would not forget God in the future. Although the section is rather independent, it is not out of harmony with the following important portion of the speech (Deut. 9:1–10:11), in which the past sins of Israel were recounted as a means of warning the nation against self-righteousness. The ethical precepts of the Covenant (Deut. 10:12-22) are again evident in the following section (Deut. 11:1-32), in which the ultimate choice of blessing or affliction was set deliberately before the people.

The first two Mosaic discourses are homogeneous, and relate the general ethical concepts underlying the Sinai revelation to the nationalistic aspirations, social responsibilities, and spiritual obligations of the Israelites in the Promised Land. As such they constitute the religious preamble to an exposition of the main regulations that would govern Israelite life. Deuteronomy 12:1–26:19 is the section concerned with this material, and consists of statutes and ordinances that repeat in part the legislation of Mount Sinai, but which also consider certain circumstances not covered by that stage of revelation. As observed above, the general intent of the legislation was to regulate the entire life of the nation as the holy people of God prior to the entrance into Canaan, and while the arrangement of the enactments was comprehensive, it was not specifically related to chronological sequences, and so was somewhat discursive in nature. This situation befits a collection of laws and statutes that have arisen during an interval of time, or which tend to envisage future situations on the basis of past experience. Deuteronomy 12:17-19 appears to have existed as a separate fragment, and its insertion into the text of chapter 12 tends to disrupt the pattern of the narrative. More properly it belongs to the section dealing with the tithes (Deut. 14:22-29), and could well have been placed after Deuteronomy 14:29.

The preceding chapter is evidently a unity, dealing as it does with diviners and idolatry. The essence of the Levitical laws concerning uncleanness and cleanness is recapitulated in Deuteronomy 14:3-21, as is the material relating to the sabbath of the land in Deuteronomy 15. Much the same is true of the enactments involving the Passover (cf. Exod. 12:1ff.), which follow the traditions concerning the three annual feasts (cf. Exod. 23:16; 34:22; Lev. 23:15ff.; Num. 28:26ff.; 29:12ff.).

The term "passover" apparently included all the sacrifices offered during the seven days of *mazzôth* as well as the paschal lamb itself (Deut. 16:2). An administrative fragment has evidently survived in Deuteronomy 16:18-20, while Deuteronomy 16:21–17:1 seems to comprise another independent section relating to idolatrous practices. Closely associated with the latter, however, is Deuteronomy 17:2-13, which deals with judicial procedures and questions of appeal. In this passage the tradition of Numbers 15:30 is continued in the verdict rendered against the man who behaves in an obdurate and self-willed fashion (Deut. 17:12).

A section of quite a different character (Deut. 17:14-20), which like certain others appears to have been inserted rather haphazardly into the framework of the book, has to do with the principles governing the choice of a king. The standpoint of the narrative is undeniably futuristic, and the life-situation is clearly that of the Wilderness rather than the settled conditions of a much later age that had been projected back into the earlier history of the nation so as to furnish some justification in the Torah for the existence of the Davidic monarchy. This passage is of interest also for the light it sheds upon the activity of Moses as a chronicler of events and enactments relating to the infant nation.

As Wright has remarked in this connection, a verse such as Deuteronomy 17:18, which commands the future king to "write for himself in a book a copy of this law, from that which is in charge of the Levitical priests" presupposes either that the people knew that Moses was recording the speeches day by day, or that he actually had the script in front of him as he was speaking.[52] The reference to "a copy of this law" is to the particular enactment concerning the king, and not to Deuteronomy as a whole. It was because this phrase was incorrectly understood by the LXX translators as referring to the whole of the fifth book of Moses that the name "Deuteronomy" or "second law" arose in the first place.

Another isolated fragment dealing with the rights of the priests and Levites (Deut. 18:1-8) follows the enactment concerning the appointment of a king. In connection with this and similar passages in Deuteronomy it has frequently been maintained by liberal scholars that the book knows of no distinction between the priests and the Levites. A careful examination of the Hebrew text, however, shows that this view is untenable, for the Levitical priests (Deut. 18:1) were distinguished from the Levites who were thought of as scattered throughout Israel (Deut. 18:6f.).

Furthermore, the fact that different portions were ascribed to priests in Deuteronomy 18:3ff. and to Levites in Deuteronomy 18:6ff. would

[52] J. S. Wright, *EQ*, XXV (1953), p. 6.

suggest that the distinction was maintained without difficulty.[53] Whereas Numbers characteristically described the priests as the "sons of Aaron," Deuteronomy frequently employed the expression "the priests the Levites," rendered "the Levitical priests" in the RSV. This appears to be quite legitimate, since in a book such as Numbers, which was intimately concerned with the consecration of the Levites (Num. 8:5ff.), it would be entirely proper for the priests to be designated as the sons of Aaron. By contrast, in Deuteronomy, which is a work of a more general and prophetic character, a generic form of description is appropriate. The phrase "the priests the Levites" (Deut. 17:9, 18; 18:1; 24:8; 27:9; cf. Josh. 3:3; 8:33) appears to mean "the priests of the tribe of Levi," to whom the Deuteronomic code assigned a variety of duties (cf. Deut. 17:8f., 18; 24:8; 27:9).

An independent fragment warning against participation in pagan magical rites can be seen in Deuteronomy 18:9-14, which is followed by another isolated section relating to the rise of a prophetic figure. The juxtaposition of these two passages was presumably intended to depict the relative natures of false and true prophecy. Once Israel had entered the Promised Land there would arise the necessity for further divine revelation that would be based upon, and be of a character with, the moral, ethical, and legislative enactments of Sinai. To meet this need the prophetical institution would be established, and would be quite distinct in nature from all contemporary pagan forms of prophetism. The prophet would be an Israelite, and, like Moses, would function as a mediator between God and the Chosen People (Deut. 18:14f.).

Certain laws governing criminal behavior were the concern of chapter 19, with the first three verses dealing with the cities for refugees, and like Numbers 35:9-34 constituting an elaboration of the law first given in Exodus 21:12ff. The content of Deuteronomy 19:14 seems to imply that the boundaries that earlier individuals had established should not be removed by later settlers, since such activity was equivalent to theft. A small independent section (Deut. 19:15-21) dealt with the laws involving witnesses, and established the legal principle of *lex talionis* or retribution in kind. The procedures to be adopted in the case of future wars reflected the humanitarian concerns of the Sinai legislation in that an attack upon an enemy town ought only to be made after an offer of peace had been spurned. Even when a siege was in progress, the fruit trees in the vicinity were to be spared.

A group of laws of diverse character can be found in chapters 21 to 25. Of some interest is the procedure for the expiation of a murder committed by an unknown person (Deut. 21:1-9), which reflected ancient Mesopotamian practices in this regard.[54] The legislation concern-

[53] D. A. Hubbard, *NBD*, p. 1029.
[54] Cf. *ANET*, p. 167.

ing marriage with a woman captured in war (Deut. 21:10-14), which inculcated thoughtfulness and forbearance on the part of victorious Hebrew males, stood in its humanitarian concerns in entire contradistinction to the brutal and callous attitudes of contemporary pagan nations in this regard. The same general emphasis is continued in Deuteronomy 22:1-12, which treated of correct social attitudes under particular circumstances, and also engendered respect for the animal species. Sexual relationships were the subject of the legislation in Deuteronomy 22:13-29.

The rights of citizenship in the congregation (Deut. 23:1-25) dealt with those who were to be excluded (Deut. 23:1-9), the purity of the camp in time of war (Deut. 23:10-15), the prohibition of religious prostitution (Deut. 23:17), and other rights of citizenship (Deut. 23:16, 18-25). The enactments concerning divorce were set out in summary form (Deut. 24:1-4), and a specific provision exempted the newly married man from service in war for an entire year (Deut. 24:5). Among other prohibitions assembled in chapter 24 were warnings against the oppression of the poor (Deut. 24:10-15), against injustice (Deut. 24:14-17), and a lack of charity towards underprivileged members of society.

A section that furnished additional evidence of the profoundly humanitarian concern of the Torah related, among other matters, to corporal punishment. Extreme severity in this matter was prohibited (Deut. 25:1-3), in contrast with some of the procedures followed in contemporary cultures, and the spirit of humanitarianism and toleration was extended quite naturally to the animal creation (Deut. 25:4). A brief section that seems to have no immediate logical connection with what precedes or follows dealt with the procedures attending levirate marriage (Deut. 25:5-10), which has already been discussed above.

The conclusion of this important body of legislation was marked by various enactments concerning equitable business dealings (Deut. 25:11-16), an order for the extermination of the Amalekites (Deut. 25:17-19), and the ritual for the thanksgivings at the presentation of the firstfruits and tithes. It is not without significance that the closing sections of the Book of the Covenant (Exod. 20:22–23:33) also contained the law of the firstfruits (Exod. 23:19), which would suggest that the Deuteronomic legislation drew for its inspiration upon much that the Covenant Code contained.

The legislative corpus of Deuteronomy 12:1–26:19 can be classified into three principal groups according to the specific terms employed in the text. The first of these classes is "judgments" (מִשְׁפָּתִים), which describes a rule established by authority or formulated by ancient custom, and serving either as a precedent or as a guide to a judge under certain specified conditions. Typical of this sort of enactment is the content of Exodus 21. In this connection it is interesting that many of the judgments occurring in that chapter can be paralleled by the case-law represented in the Code of Hammurabi and in other Semitic collections of laws from the pre-Mosaic period. There is no reason to doubt that the Israelites were acquainted with at least some of this secular legislative material during the Goshen period, and if the Mosaic enactments contain laws that had their origin among the Israelites at that time, as has been suggested already in the present work, it is quite probable that non-Israelite legislation applicable to the sedentary situation in Goshen would also be incorporated into the legal structure as having, in some sense at least, an accredited background in Hebrew tradition.

The second term, "statutes" (חק), was derived from a root meaning "to engrave," "to inscribe," and as such designated a permanent rule of conduct. It differed from the "judgment" in that whereas in the latter the appeal was to the judge, in the former it was to conscience and to God.[55] The distinction was made clear in the case of Solomon (1 Kgs. 6:12), who was instructed to "walk" in the statutes of God, and to "execute" His judgments. The statutes were generally in the nature of moral precepts, and as such constituted a divine rule of life. They do not occur in this form in other Semitic legal codes, for fairly obvious reasons. While some dealt with religious institutions such as different kinds of offerings, others were concerned with the laws of justice, purity, clemency and the like.

The third category, or "commandments" (מצות), was more generally applicable. In Deuteronomy the word referred predominantly to commands that were not to be considered as binding or permanent obligations but could be fulfilled in one operative act. Such commandments included the destruction of pagan shrines, the appointment of officers and judges, and the establishing of cities for refugees.

Notice should again be taken of the fact that the foregoing body of legal material is essentially a collection of laws rather than a law-book in the strictest sense of that term. The difference between these concepts, as Köhler has pointed out, is that a collection of laws lacks the unified and thoroughgoing spirit that results when a lawgiver sets out his individual precepts with the specific intention of laying down the law.[56] This had already been done in essence in the Decalogue, the Covenant Code, and other supplementary legislation; and all that Deuteronomy did was to rewrite the relevant material in such a manner that the laws governing national life would be as available to the people as they were to the priesthood. Deuteronomy, of course, was not meant to preserve the technicalities of the Law in the same manner as Leviticus, but, like the Code of Hammurabi, was intended to be accessible to all who had as their concern the spiritual and ceremonial requirements of the Law. This

---

[55] G. T. Manley, *NBD*, p. 309.
[56] L. Köhler, *Hebrew Man*, p. 171 n. 1.

consideration is important in view of the fact that, whatever the specific oral or written promulgations of the law, ancient Near Eastern peoples generally tended to live either according to inclination or in deference to the traditions and customs of their forbears, secure in the knowledge that the law-books were stored in temple archives, should it ever become necessary for some priest-scholar to consult them for research purposes. Because of the essential nature of Deuteronomy as a collection of laws, it is as impossible to divide the work up into strata through the use of supposed literary criteria as it is to attempt to assign a specific date to any particular legislative item.

The renewal of the Covenant with God (Deut. 27:1–30:20) involved the ratification of the Law and the engraving of its precepts upon stones to be set in position upon Mount Ebal. Here also an altar was to be erected for the offering of burnt and slain sacrifices. The standpoint of the narrative is clearly futuristic, with the occupation of the land of Palestine represented as yet to occur (Deut. 27:2ff.). The method of engraving the Law upon cement-surfaced rocks was well known in antiquity. Apparently a stylus was to be used upon an already prepared surface, as was the custom in Egypt. The engraving of the law of the land upon stone monuments that were readily accessible to the public was also known to the peoples of the ancient Near East, as can be illustrated by reference to the celebrated Code of Hammurabi.

Verses nine and ten of chapter 27 furnish an important connecting link in the narrative, in that they unite its two sections by means of a divine injunction to Israel to obey the Law. Blessings were to be expressed at the top of Mount Gerizim, and curses from the twin peak of Mount Ebal (Deut. 27:12f.), the general theme being continued in chapter 28, in which the first fourteen verses set out the blessings consequent upon obedience, while the remainder of the chapter delineated the courses which would accompany disobedience. Deuteronomy 29:1–30:20 can be regarded as a renewed declaration of the Covenant established at Sinai, and as concluding the Covenant section proper.

The group of appendices (Deut. 31:1–34:12) contained among other items the appointment and commission of Joshua (Deut. 31:1-8, 14-23), and the specific reference to the activity of Moses as a compiler of the Law. There can be no question that the reference to a "book" is to anything other than a written source, since the term ספר was never employed in the ancient Near East of orally transmitted material. The obvious concern of Moses was that the essentials of the legislation which was to be the guide of the nation in its future pilgrimage should be readily available to the priesthood at the least (Deut. 31:26) before his own death, an attitude that was amply justified in the light of subsequent events. The reference in Deuteronomy 31:22 might be taken as implying that Moses wrote down the song that followed before he actually recited it to the people. There is no warrant on the basis of either internal or external evidence for the assumption that the Song of Moses (Deut. 32:1-43) is to be dated as late as the fifth century B.C.[57] or even in the time of Jeremiah or Ezekiel.[58]

The poem, like some other sections of Deuteronomy, comprises a prophetic anticipation of the future: the Exodus had occurred within the recent past, and ahead stretched the occupation of the land of Canaan. The general setting of the poem is rooted in the events of the patriarchal age, and the theology is that of uncovenanted grace. There is no single element of the poem incompatible with Mosaic authorship, nor are there any evident editorial glosses or insertions in the material. The concepts and vocabulary are compatible with the late Amarna period. Certain rare words occur only in the Pentateuchal writings, and other expressions have been found in the texts from Ras Shamra. Among the words found only in the Pentateuch are יֶשֻׁרוּן (Deut. 33:5, 26) and גֹדֶל (Deut. 3:24; 11:2; Num. 14:19).

Whereas the Song of Moses was possibly in written form before it was actually delivered to the Israelites orally, the blessing of Moses (Deut. 33:1-29) was originally extant orally. From Deuteronomy 33:1 it would appear that the one who recorded the blessing is to be distinguished from Moses himself, and this is in full accord with normal Mesopotamian practice. From the many examples of benedictions that have survived from Nuzu society,[59] it is evident that a pronouncement of this sort uttered by a man who was dying had an irrevocable and legally binding status accorded to it. Thus the Mosaic benediction stands firmly within the tradition of the patriarchs as recorded in Genesis (Gen. 27:27ff.; 49:3ff.) and can be viewed with complete confidence as being both genuine and original.

The fact that Simeon was not mentioned in the blessing need not be taken as an indication that the material reached its extant form long after Simeon had been absorbed into Judah, as earlier liberal scholars were wont to maintain, since the utterance, being prophetic, envisaged the situation mentioned in Genesis 49:7, where the identity of Simeon as a tribe was prophesied to disappear (cf. Josh. 19:2ff.). However, there seems no valid reason for denying that the Simeonites were included in the general blessing bestowed upon Israel (Deut. 33:29), even though they were not mentioned specifically by name. There is thus no warrant whatever for assigning the blessing to some date within the period of the divided monarchy, as Riehm, Stade, and other earlier critics did.[60]

---

[57] *PIOT*, p. 280.

[58] *DILOT*, pp. 96f.

[59] R. K. Harrison, *Archaeology of the OT*, pp. 28f.

[60] D. E. Riehm, *Einleitung in das AT* (1889), I, p. 313; B. Stade, *Geschichte des Volkes Israel* (1887), I, pp. 150ff.

The final chapter, which described the death and burial of Moses, is of some interest because of the attitude adopted in antiquity towards its composition. Josephus, among other Jewish authorities, believed that Moses wrote the account of his own death,[61] a view that was modified somewhat in rabbinic circles, where the words were assigned to Joshua.[62] *Baba Bathra* stated that Moses wrote his own book and the section concerning Balaam and Job. Joshua wrote his own book and eight verses of the Law (i.e. Deut. 34:5-12). Among later Jewish exegetes, Ibn Ezra taught that chapter 34 had been compiled by Joshua.[63]

Some early liberal critics set great store by the fact that, since Moses could not possibly have written the account of his own death, he could not be regarded in any serious sense as the attributive author of the Pentateuch, an opinion that is as illogical as it is fatuous. From the evidence presented by the text it would appear that once the "book of the law" had been placed near the Ark of the Covenant as a witness to Israel (Deut. 31:24ff.), the literary activity of Moses came to an end. Whatever the nature of the book that he compiled, it did not contain chapters 32 to 34 at the very least. However, the Mosaicity of this latter is not open to serious doubt in terms of general provenance, and there is every reason for thinking that it was added to Deuteronomy in order to complete the narrative content of the work not long after Moses died. Jewish tradition may well be correct in assuming that Joshua was the author of at least part of the final chapter of Deuteronomy, although the actual facts of the situation are, of course, unknown.

As a whole, then, the book of Deuteronomy may be regarded quite legitimately as a popular promulgation of the spiritual and moral issues inherent in the Covenant revelation at Sinai. While many of the enactments are compressed in an obviously artificial manner into a framework of discourse that is related chronologically to the last month of the forty years of Wilderness wanderings, there can be no denial of their validity for the continued moral health and material prosperity of the nation. The regulations are in strict accord with the more technical prescriptions of Leviticus, making the entire work, in the words of Keil, "a hortatory description, explanation, and enforcement of the most essential contents of the Covenant revelation and the Covenant laws, with emphatic prominence given to the spiritual principle of the law and its fulfilment, and with a further development of the ecclesiastical, judicial, political and civil organization which was intended as a permanent foundation for the life and well-being of the people in the land of Canaan."[64]

[61] *AJ*, IV, 8, 48.
[62] *Bab. Bath.*, 14b.
[63] J. H. Hertz, *The Pentateuch and Haftorahs*, p. 916.
[64] C. F. Keil and F. Delitzsch, *Biblical Commentary on the OT* (1949 ed.), III, p. 270.

The theology of Deuteronomy is comparatively simple and unsophisticated, and is in complete harmony with other aspects of religious thought attributed to overall Mosaic origin. Characteristic of the book is its monotheistic outlook, whether such be regarded as incipient[65] or genuine.[66] The concept of the Covenant relationship is predominant, and the future destiny of the nation as the People of God, obedient to the provision of the Sinai agreement, is consistently at the forefront of the theological outlook of the work. The power that underlay the mighty acts of God at the time of the Exodus from Egypt can constitute a continuing experience if the Covenant is honored, and this theme is emphasized repeatedly in Deuteronomy. For His part God will be with His people in prosperity and adversity alike, and will fight for them in battle wherever they are engaged by the enemy, just as He did when they were at the mercy of the Egyptians. The positive, futuristic outlook of the book can well be illustrated by references to the two most frequently occurring phrases in Deuteronomy: "go in and possess," which is found 35 times, and "the land which the LORD thy God giveth thee," which occurs 34 times. Optimism, faith, and divine power are the hallmarks of the prophetic outlook of the author.

While the Hebrew text of Deuteronomy has been well preserved, there are certain difficulties evident in translation that appear to have arisen in part through processes of transmission. Thus in Deuteronomy 4:33, which is parallel to Deuteronomy 5:26, the adjective "living" is omitted from the MT but occurs in two Hebrew manuscripts, as well as in the LXX. In Deuteronomy 11:24, the preposition "to" has evidently dropped out of the text immediately before the word "Lebanon." In Deuteronomy 20:19 the end of the verse is only intelligible if read as an interrogative sentence. Some doubt as to the proper vocalization of the MT exists in Deuteronomy 4:48; 5:10; 20:8; 28:22; 31:7; 33:26.

Supplementary Literature

Bertholet, A. *Deuteronomium*. 1899.
Horts, F. *Das Privilegrecht Jahves*. 1930.
McNeile, A. H. *Deuteronomy, Its Place in Revelation*. 1912.
Siebens, A. R. *L'Origine du code deutéronomique*, 1929.
Welch, A. C. *Deuteronomy: The Framework to the Code*. 1932.

[65] So H. H. Rowley, *The Rediscovery of the OT*, p. 88, *ET*, LXI (1949-50), pp. 333ff.
[66] Cf. *FSAC*, pp. 2, 257ff., Albright, *Samuel and the Beginnings of the Prophetic Movement*, p. 4; *KRI*, pp. 212ff.

Printed in the United States
15559LVS00003B/4